Intellectual Property:
The Law of Trademarks, Copyrights, Patents, and Trade Secrets

Intellectual Property: The Law of Trademarks, Copyrights, Patents, and Trade Secrets

Deborah E. Bouchoux

WEST LEGAL STUDIES
Thomson Learning™

Africa • Australia • Canada • Denmark • Japan • Mexico • New Zealand • Philippines
Puerto Rico • Singapore • Spain • United Kingdom • United States

NOTICE TO THE READER

West Legal Studies Staff:

Business Unit Director: Susan Simpfenderfer
Executive Editor: Marlene McHugh Pratt
Acquisitions Editor: Joan Gill
Editorial Assistant: Lisa Flatley
Executive Marketing Manager: Donna Lewis
Executive Production Manager: Wendy Troeger
Production Editor: Betty L. Dickson
Cover Design: Connie McKinley
Cover Art: Artville

Library of Congress Cataloging-in-Publication Data

Bouchoux, Deborah E., 1950–
    Intellectual property: law of trademarks, copyrights, patents, and trade secrets /
Deborah E. Bouchoux.
    p. cm.
    Includes index.
    ISBN 0-7668-1355-X
    1. Intellectual property—United States. 2. Trademarks—Law and legislation—United
States. 3. Patent laws and legislation—United States. 4. Copyright—United States. 5.
Trade secrets—United States. 6. Legal assistants—United States—Handbooks, manuals,
etc. I. Title.

KF1570.B68 1999
346.7304'8—dc21   99-048957

For my mother
Mabel K. Eckmann

TABLE OF CONTENTS

Preface / xv
Acknowledgments / xvii
List of Figures / xviii

Part I   Introduction to Intellectual Property / 1

Chapter 1   Introduction to Intellectual Property Law / 3
Chapter Overview / 3
Intellectual Property Law Basics / 3
Types of Intellectual Property / 4
Agencies Responsible for Intellectual Property Registration / 8
International Organizations, Agencies, and Treaties / 10
The Increasing Importance of Intellectual Property Rights / 11
Role of Intellectual Property Professional / 12
Chapter Summary / 13
Discussion Questions / 14

Part II   The Law of Trademarks / 15

Chapter 2   Foundations of Trademark Law / 17
Chapter Overview / 17
Introduction to Trademarks and Service Marks / 17
Purpose and Function of Trademarks / 17
Types of Marks: Trademarks, Service Marks, Certification Marks, and Collective Marks / 18
Acquisition of Trademark Rights / 20
Common Law Rights, Federal Registration Under the Lanham Act, and State Trademark Rights / 21
Categories of Marks / 23
Trade Names and Business Names / 25
Protectable Matter / 25
Exclusions from Trademark Protection / 28
United States Patent and Trademark Office / 30
Role of Intellectual Property Professional / 32
Chapter Summary / 32
Discussion Questions / 33

Chapter 3   Trademark Selection and Searching / 35
Chapter Overview / 35
Selecting and Evaluating a Mark / 35
The Trademark Search / 36
Role of Intellectual Property Professional / 42
Chapter Summary / 42
Discussion Questions / 43

Chapter 4   The Trademark Registration Process / 45
Chapter Overview / 45
Preparing the Application / 45

Filing the Application, Docketing Critical Dates, and Initial Role of the United States Patent and Trademark Office / 56

The Examination Process / 58

Postexamination Procedure / 63

Registration / 66

The United States Patent and Trademark Office's TRAM Line / 68

Role of Intellectual Property Professional / 68

Chapter Summary / 69

Discussion Questions / 70

Chapter 5 **Postregistration Procedures, Trademark Maintenance, and Transfer of Rights to Marks / 71**

Chapter Overview / 71

The Affidavit of Use / 72

The Affidavit of Incontestability / 73

Renewal of Registrations / 74

Docketing Requirements / 74

Loss of Trademark Rights / 75

Trademark Use and Compliance Policies / 76

Trademark Policing and Maintenance / 78

Use of Marks Owned by Third Parties / 79

Transfer of Ownership of Rights in Trademarks / 79

Role of Intellectual Property Professional / 88

Chapter Summary / 88

Discussion Questions / 89

Chapter 6 **Inter Partes Proceedings, Infringement, and Dilution / 91**

Chapter Overview / 91

Inter Partes Proceedings / 91

Infringement of Trademarks / 96

Dilution of Trademarks / 103

Related Trademark Claims / 105

Role of Intellectual Property Professional / 106

Chapter Summary / 107

Discussion Questions / 108

Chapter 7 **New Developments in Trademark Law / 109**

Chapter Overview / 109

The Internet / 109

Hyperlinking and the First Amendment / 113

Other Cyberspace Trademark Issues / 114

Role of Intellectual Property Professional / 116

Chapter Summary / 116

Discussion Questions / 117

Chapter 8 **International Developments in Trademark Law / 119**

Chapter Overview / 119

Applications in the United States Based on Foreign Applications and Registrations / 120

Securing Trademark Protection in Foreign Countries / 123

Effects of New International Agreements (NAFTA and GATT) / 128

International Associations / 128

Role of Intellectual Property Professional   /   129
Chapter Summary   /   130
Discussion Questions   /   130

Part III   The Law of Copyrights   /   131

Chapter 9   Foundations of Copyright Law   /   133
Chapter Overview   /   133
Introduction to Copyrights   /   133
Common Law Rights and Rights Under the 1976 Copyright Act   /   134
The United States Copyright Office   /   136
Role of Intellectual Property Professional   /   137
Chapter Summary   /   137
Discussion Questions   /   138

Chapter 10   The Subject Matter of Copyright   /   139
Chapter Overview   /   139
Introduction to Copyrightability   /   139
Originality of Material   /   139
Fixation of Material   /   140
Works of Authorship   /   141
Exclusions from Copyright Protection   /   145
Compilations, Collections, and Derivative Works   /   149
Role of Intellectual Property Professional   /   152
Chapter Summary   /   152
Discussion Questions   /   153

Chapter 11   The Rights Afforded by Copyright Law   /   155
Chapter Overview   /   155
Introduction   /   155
Rights of Reproduction   /   156
Rights to Prepare Derivative Works   /   156
Rights of Distribution and the First Sale Doctrine   /   157
Rights to Perform the Work Publicly   /   159
Rights to Display the Work Publicly   /   162
Rights to Perform Copyrighted Sound Recordings   /   163
Other Limitations on Exclusive Rights   /   163
Moral Rights   /   164
Compulsory Licenses   /   166
Role of Intellectual Property Professional   /   166
Chapter Summary   /   167
Discussion Questions   /   167

Chapter 12   Copyright Ownership, Transfers, and Duration   /   169
Chapter Overview   /   169
Copyright Ownership Issues   /   170
Joint Works   /   170
Ownership in Derivative or Collective Works   /   171
Works Made for Hire   /   172
Transfers of Copyright   /   175
Termination of Transfers of Copyright   /   176

Duration of Copyright / 179
Role of Intellectual Property Professional / 182
Chapter Summary / 183
Discussion Questions / 184

Chapter 13 Copyright Registration, Searching Copyright Office Records, and Notice of Copyright / 185
Chapter Overview / 185
Introduction / 185
The Application for Copyright Registration / 186
Deposit Materials / 191
The Application Process and Registration of Copyright / 195
Searching Copyright Office Records / 198
Obtaining Copyright Office Records and Deposit Materials / 199
Copyright Notice / 200
Role of Intellectual Property Professional / 204
Chapter Summary / 204
Discussion Questions / 205

Chapter 14 Copyright Infringement / 207
Chapter Overview / 207
Introduction to Copyright Infringement / 207
Elements of Infringement / 208
Contributory Infringement and Vicarious Infringement / 211
Defenses to Infringement / 212
Infringement Actions / 218
Remedies for Infringement / 219
Role of Intellectual Property Professional / 221
Chapter Summary / 221
Discussion Questions / 222

Chapter 15 New Developments in Copyright Law and the Semiconductor Chip Protection Act / 223
Chapter Overview / 223
Introduction / 224
Copyright Protection for Computer Programs / 224
Copyright Protection for Automated Databases / 230
Copyright in the Electronic Age / 231
Recent Developments in Copyright Law / 235
Terms of the Trade / 238
Semiconductor Chip Protection / 239
Role of Intellectual Property Professional / 241
Chapter Summary / 242
Discussion Questions / 243

Chapter 16 International Developments in Copyright Law / 245
Chapter Overview / 245
Introduction / 245
The Berne Convention / 246
Treaties Supplementing the Berne Convention / 247
The Uruguay Round Agreements Act / 248
The Universal Copyright Convention / 249

Gray Market Goods   /   250
Summary of United States Relations with Foreign Nations   /   250
Role of Intellectual Property Professional   /   251
Chapter Summary   /   251
Discussion Questions   /   252

Part IV   The Law of Patents   /   253

Chapter 17   Foundations of Patent Law   /   255
Chapter Overview   /   255
Introduction to Patents   /   255
Rights Under Federal Law   /   256
United States Patent and Trademark Office   /   257
Patentability   /   259
Design Patents   /   266
Plant Patents   /   267
Double Patenting   /   269
The Orphan Drug Act   /   270
Role of Intellectual Property Professional   /   270
Chapter Summary   /   270
Discussion Questions   /   271

Chapter 18   Patent Searches and Applications   /   273
Chapter Overview   /   273
Patent Searching   /   273
The Patent Application Process   /   275
Prosecuting the Application   /   285
Postissuance Actions   /   292
Term and Maintenance of Patents   /   299
Role of Intellectual Property Professional   /   300
Chapter Summary   /   300
Discussion Questions   /   301

Chapter 19   Patent Ownership and Transfer   /   303
Chapter Overview   /   303
Ownership Rights   /   303
Sole and Joint Inventors   /   304
Disputes over Inventorship   /   304
Inventions Made by Employees and Independent Contractors   /   305
Assignment of Patent Rights   /   306
Licensing of Patent Rights   /   308
Invention Developers and Promoters   /   308
Role of Intellectual Property Professional   /   309
Chapter Summary   /   309
Discussion Questions   /   310

Chapter 20   Patent Infringement   /   311
Chapter Overview   /   311
Direct Infringement, Inducement to Infringe, and Contributory
    Infringement   /   311
The First Sale Doctrine   /   313

Claims Interpretation / 313
Defenses to Infringement / 315
Remedies for Infringement / 316
Resolving an Infringement Dispute / 318
Patent Infringement Litigation / 319
Role of Intellectual Property Professional / 321
Chapter Summary / 321
Discussion Questions / 322

Chapter 21 New Developments and International Developments in Patent Law / 323
Chapter Overview / 323
New Developments in Patent Law / 324
Introduction to International Patent Protection / 325
The Paris Convention / 326
The Patent Cooperation Treaty / 328
The European Patent Organization / 331
Foreign Filing Licenses / 332
Agreement on Trade-Related Aspects of Intellectual Property Rights / 333
Applications for United States Patents by Foreign Applicants / 333
Role of Intellectual Property Professional / 334
Chapter Summary / 334
Discussion Questions / 335

Part V The Law of Trade Secrets and Unfair Competition / 337

Chapter 22 Trade Secrets Law / 339
Chapter Overview / 339
Introduction to Trade Secrets Law / 339
Determination of Trade Secret Status / 342
Liability for Misappropriation of Trade Secrets / 343
Employer-Employee Relationships / 345
Protection for Submissions / 348
Defense to Trade Secret Misappropriation / 349
Remedies for Misappropriation / 350
Trade Secret Litigation / 351
Trade Secret Protection Programs / 352
New and International Developments in Trade Secrets Law / 354
Role of Intellectual Property Professional / 355
Chapter Summary / 356
Discussion Questions / 357

Chapter 23 Unfair Competition / 359
Chapter Overview / 359
Introduction to Unfair Competition / 359
Passing Off / 361
Misappropriation / 362
Right of Publicity / 362
False Advertising / 367
Product Disparagement / 369
Dilution / 370

Infringement of Trade Dress   /   371
International Protection Against Unfair Competition   /   372
Role of Intellectual Property Professional   /   373
Chapter Summary   /   373
Discussion Questions   /   374

Chapter 24   Intellectual Property Audits and Due Diligence Reviews   /   375
Chapter Overview   /   375
Introduction to Intellectual Property Audits and Due Diligence Reviews   /   375
Practical Aspects of Intellectual Property Audits   /   376
Conducting the Audit   /   377
Postaudit Activity   /   380
Role of Intellectual Property Professional   /   381
Chapter Summary   /   382
Discussion Questions   /   382

Appendix A   Table of Treaties   /   385

Appendix B   State Trademark Registration Provisions   /   391

Appendix C   Resources   /   397

Appendix D   Forms Appendix   /   403
Form 1   Trademark Application   /   404
Form 2   Statement of Use   /   406
Form 3   Request for Extension of Time to File Statement of Use   /   407
Form 4   Combined Affidavit Under Sections 8 and 15 of the
          Lanham Act   /   408
Form 5   Application for Renewal of Trademark   /   409
Form 6   Request for Extension of Time to File Notice of Opposition   /   411
Form 7   Opposition to Registration of Trademark   /   412
Form 8   Consent to Use and Register Agreement   /   413
Form 9   Petition to Cancel Trademark Registration   /   415
Form 10   Complaint for Trademark Infringement   /   417
Form 11   Trademark Settlement Agreement   /   420
Form 12   Work for Hire Provisions   /   422
Form 13   Employee Nondisclosure and Noncompetition Agreement   /   423
Form 14   Evaluation Agreement   /   426
Form 15   Confidentiality Agreement   /   427

Appendix E   Selected Statutes   /   429

Glossary   /   465

Index   /   481

PREFACE

The Congress shall have power to promote the progress of science and useful arts, by securing for limited times to authors and inventors the exclusive right to their respective writings and discoveries.

U.S. Const. art. 1, § 8, cl. 8

The field of intellectual property (sometimes referred to as IP) is one that is rapidly growing. Just a few years ago, individuals who identified themselves as practitioners in the field of intellectual property were met with blank stares. Now IP professionals are in constant demand, and it is a rare issue of any legal periodical that does not include advertisements for IP practitioners. Many experts believe this rapid growth can be attributed to the spread of computer and communications technologies throughout the world. Reflecting this, more technology-related legislation was introduced in the 105th Congress than in any previous Congress. Trademark and patent applications filed at the U.S. Patent and Trademark Office have doubled in just the past five years. Similarly, there is increased emphasis on the need to enhance protection of written materials, including computer software, through copyright registration.

Today's competitive businesses recognize that nearly 80 percent of their value can lie in their intellectual property. With increased technology and global communication come greater challenges to protect intellectual property. Misappropriation or infringement of valuable proprietary information is a keystroke away. Thus, companies and law firms value the expertise of IP professionals who can assist in adopting strategies to ensure IP assets are fully protected.

The recent increased interest in intellectual property coupled with nearly daily changes in intellectual property law has caused a relative scarcity in texts that provide both sound foundational concepts together with the practical advice needed to ensure success for IP professionals.

This text provides a comprehensive guide to each field within the umbrella of intellectual property, namely, trademarks, copyrights, patents, trade secrets, and unfair competition. The methods by which each is created, procedures to register or protect each, duration of rights, protection from infringement, and new and international developments will be addressed for each of these fields of intellectual property.

Each chapter begins with an introduction to the topics covered therein and concludes with a brief overview of the material presented. Information is arranged in a building-block approach so the reader is presented with comprehensive coverage of each topic. Discussions of each field of intellectual property conclude with a section on the new and emerging issues in that field and then an overview of international implications, such as the methods by which intellectual property can be protected in other countries.

The substantive overview of each topic is complemented by the use of forms, sample agreements, checklists, and other practical guides. References to useful resources and web sites are provided so readers can gather additional information. The specific tasks in which IP professionals are involved are fully addressed. Finally, discussion questions are provided to ensure thorough understanding of each topic. A glossary highlights critical terms and selected trademark, copyright, and patent statutes are provided.

The field of intellectual property is one of the most dynamic and challenging of all legal specialties. Many of the issues are cutting edge: How can a domain name be protected? How can a company ensure its trade secrets are not misappropriated by an employee? What is the best way to protect a computer program that may be obsolete in three years? How can a business be sure its web site does not infringe that of a third party? How can intellectual property be protected in a global economy?

Providing assistance to intellectual property owners thus provides unique opportunities for learning and growth. Moreover, the field of intellectual property is inherently interesting. All of us see and recognize trademarks each day. All of us read books, watch movies, and use inventions. Thus, readers bring a wealth of practical and firsthand knowledge to the study of intellectual property law. This text allows readers to link their experience as consumers with the substantive information presented to ensure intellectual property owners are provided a full range of strategies and methods to protect their valuable assets.

ACKNOWLEDGMENTS

No text is the product solely of its author. Many individuals contributed significantly to the development of this text. As always, my first thoughts go to Susan M. Sullivan, Program Director of the Lawyer's Assistant Program at the University of San Diego. Sue gave me my first opportunity to teach and has always provided support and encouragement. She is a respected colleague and valued friend.

My current Program Director, Gloria Silvers of the Legal Assistant Program at Georgetown University in Washington, D.C. continues to display enthusiasm and passion for education. She has been of invaluable assistance and a tremendous source of encouragement.

Special thanks to the reviewers who evaluated the manuscript on behalf of the publisher and provided clear and concise analysis. Their comments and suggestions were of great assistance.

William C. Milks, III Esq.
Sonoma State University

Ric Schaffran
UCLA Extension

Darlene Klinksieck
Arter & Hadden

Dennis Morris
Cal Poly/San Luis Obispo

Carol Desmond
Mercy College

Finally, my most sincere appreciation to the following individuals at Delmar Publishers who provided guidance and support throughout the development of this text: Joan Gill, Developmental Editor, Lisa Flatley, Editorial Assistant, and Betty Dickson, Production Editor. Additionally, Linda Ireland provided excellent suggestions and comments as she edited the entire text. Thanks also to Scott Rohr and Gustafson Graphics of St. Paul, Minnesota, for their typesetting and production of the text, as well as their input for graphical displays within the text.

Last, but of course, not least, deepest thanks and love to my husband Don and our children, Meaghan, Elizabeth, Patrick, and Robert, for their amazing patience and understanding while I worked on this text.

I would also like to acknowledge the following companies and publishers who permitted me to reproduce trademarks or copyrighted material for this text:

The American Red Cross granted permission to use its AMERICAN RED CROSS DESIGN® mark.

Black and Decker Corporation granted permission to use its BLACK & DECKER® mark.

Dayton-Hudson Brands, Inc. granted permission to use the TARGET (& BULLSEYE DESIGN)® mark.

Dell Computer Corporation granted permission to use the DELL (STYLIZED)® mark.

Federal Express Corporation granted permission to use its FEDEX Logo. FedEx® is a registered service mark of Federal Express Corporation.

General Mills, Inc. granted permission to use its CHEERIOS® and BETTY CROCKER (& SPOON DESIGN)® marks.

Hallmark Cards, Inc. granted permission to use its HALLMARK (& CROWN DESIGN)® mark.

Kellogg Company granted permission to use its KELLOGG'S CORN FLAKES AND EGGO marks. KELLOGG'S CORN FLAKES® and KELLOGG'S® and KELLOGG'S® EGGO® are registered trademarks of Kellogg Company. All rights reserved. Used with permission.

Nabisco, Inc. granted permission to use the MR. PEANUT DESIGN®, OREO®, and RITZ® marks

Starbucks Corporation granted permission to use the STARBUCKS (& DESIGN)® mark.

Texaco Inc. granted permission to use the TEXACO (& STAR DESIGN)® mark. Courtesy of Texaco Inc.

LIST OF FIGURES

Figure 2–1	Types of Marks
Figure 2–2	Categories of Marks
Figure 2–3	Protectable Matter
Figure 2–4	Matter Excluded from Protection
Figure 2–5	Frequently Called PTO Telephone Numbers
Figure 3–1	Trademark Data Sheet (U.S. Applicant)
Figure 4–1	Power of Attorney
Figure 4–2	List of International Classes
Figure 4–3	Schedule of PTO Filing Fees (Trademark Matters)
Figure 4–4	Comparison of Marks
Figure 4–5	*Official Gazette*
Figure 4–6	Trademark Prosecution Flowchart
Figure 5–1	Assignment of Trademark
Figure 5–2	PTO Recordation Cover Sheet
Figure 5–3	Trademark License Agreement
Figure 6–1	Cease and Desist Letter
Figure 7–1	Designation of Domestic Representative
Figure 7–2	Letter to Client
Figure 12–1	Assignment of Copyright
Figure 12–2	Copyright Duration
Figure 13–1	Copyright Questionnaire
Figure 13–2	Completed Copyright Application
Figure 17–1	List of Famous U.S. Patents
Figure 18–1	Claims for Utility Patent
Figure 18–2	Small Entity Statement
Figure 18–3	Schedule of Patent Fees
Figure 18–4	Information Disclosure Statement
Figure 18–5	Patent Prosecution Flowchart
Figure 18–6	Issued Patent
Figure 19–1	Patent Assignment
Figure 24–1	Intellectual Property Audit Questionnaire

Introduction to Intellectual Property

Introduction to Intellectual Property Law

Intellectual property law protects the results of human creative endeavor. Intellectual property is generally thought to comprise four separate fields of law: trademarks, copyrights, patents, and trade secrets. A *trademark* is a word, name, symbol, or device used to indicate the origin, quality, and ownership of a product or service. Rights in trademarks are created by use of a mark; registration with the U.S. Patent and Trademark Office is not required, although it offers certain advantages. *Copyright* protects original works of authorship, including literary, musical, dramatic, artistic, and other works. Just as trademarks are protected from the moment of their first public use, copyright exists from the moment of creation of a work; registration of a copyright with the U.S. Copyright Office, while affording certain benefits, is not required. A *patent* is a grant from the U.S. government that permits its owner to exclude others from making, selling, or using an invention. Patents exist only upon issuance by the U.S. Patent and Trademark Office. A *trade secret* consists of any valuable commercial information that, if known by a competitor, would provide some benefit or advantage to the competitor. No registration or other formalities are required to create a trade secret, and trade secrets endure as long as reasonable efforts are made to protect their secrecy.

INTELLECTUAL PROPERTY LAW BASICS

Intellectual Property Defined

There are three distinct types of property that individuals and companies can own: *real property* refers to land or real estate; *personal property* refers to specific items and things that can be identified, such as jewelry, cars, and stock; and *intellectual property* refers to the fruits or product of human creativity, including literature, advertising slogans, songs, or new inventions. Thus, property that is the result of thought, namely, intellectual activity, is called **intellectual property.** In some foreign countries, intellectual property is referred to as **industrial property.**

Many of the rights of ownership common to real and personal property are also common to intellectual property. Intellectual property can be bought, sold, and licensed. Similarly, it can be protected against theft or infringement by others. Nevertheless, there are some restrictions on use. For example, if you were to purchase the latest bestseller by John Grisham, you would be entitled to read the book, sell it to another, or give it away. You would not, however, be entitled to make photocopies of the book and then distribute and sell those copies to others. Those rights are retained by the author of the work and are protected by copyright law.

The Rationale for Protection of Intellectual Property

Intellectual property is a field of law that aims at protecting the knowledge created through human effort in order to stimulate and promote further creativity. Authors who write books and musicians who compose songs would be unlikely to engage in further creative effort unless they could realize profit from their endeavors. If their work could be misappropriated and sold by others, they would have no incentive to create further works. Pharmaceutical companies would not invest millions of dollars into research and development of new drugs unless they could be assured that their inventions would enable them to recover these costs and develop additional drugs. Thus, not only the creators of intellectual property but the public as well benefit from protecting intellectual property.

On the other hand, if the owner of intellectual property is given complete and perpetual rights to his or her invention or work, the owner would have a monopoly and be able to charge excessive prices for the invention or work, which would harm the public. Intellectual property law attempts to resolve these conflicting goals so that owners' rights to reap the rewards of their efforts are balanced against the public need for a competitive marketplace. Thus, for example, under federal law, a patent for a useful invention will last for only twenty years from the date an application for the patent is filed with the U.S. Patent and Trademark Office (PTO). After that period of time, the patent expires and anyone is free to produce and sell the product.

Types of Intellectual Property

The term *intellectual property* is usually thought of as comprising four separate, but often overlapping, legal fields: trademarks, copyrights, patents, and trade secrets. Although each of these areas will be discussed in detail in the chapters that follow, a brief introduction to each discipline is helpful. (See chart on inside front and back covers of text comparing and contrasting the various types of intellectual property.)

Trademarks and Service Marks

What Is Protectable   A trademark or service mark is a word, name, symbol, or device used to indicate the origin, quality, and ownership of a product or service. A **trademark** is used in the marketing of a product (such as REEBOK® for shoes), while a **service mark** typically identifies a service

---

intellectual property: The result or product of human creativity, including trademarks, copyrights, and inventions; generally *intellectual property* comprises the field of trademarks, copyrights, patents, and trade secrets

industrial property: The term used in some foreign countries to refer to intellectual property

trademark: A word, logo, phrase, or device used to indicate the origin, quality, and ownership of a product or service; technically, *trademark* refers to a mark that identifies a product, while *service mark* refers to a mark that identifies services

service mark: A word, name, symbol, or device used to indicate the origin, quality, and ownership of a service

(such as STARBUCKSⁿ for restaurant services). A trademark or service mark identifies and distinguishes the products or services of one person from those of another.

In addition to words, trademarks can also consist of slogans (such as THE KING OF BEERSⁿ for Budweiser beer), designs (such as the familiar swoosh that identifies Nike products), or sounds (such as the distinctive laugh of Woody the Woodpecker).

Trademarks provide guarantees of quality and consistency of the product or service they identify. Thus, upon encountering the golden arches that identify a McDonald s restaurant, consumers understand the Big Mac they purchase in Chicago will be the same quality as one purchased in Seattle.

Companies expend a great deal of time, effort, and money in establishing consumer recognition of and confidence in their marks. Yet not all words, phrases, or symbols are entitled to protection as trademarks. A chain of stores that sells electronic goods could not obtain a registered trademark for Electronic Goods inasmuch as the name is generic, yet CIRCUIT CITYⁿ is a nationally recognized mark for the retail sale of electronic goods, equipment, and appliances. Marks may not be protectable if they are generic in nature or merely descriptive of the type of products or services they identify. Generally, marks that are protectable are those that are coined (such as KODAKⁿ), arbitrary (such as SHELLⁿ for gasoline), or suggestive (such as STAPLESⁿ for office supplies).

Federal Registration of Trademarks   Interstate use of trademarks is governed by federal law, namely, the United States Trademark Act (also called the Lanham Act), found at 15 U.S.C. § 1051 *et seq*. See Appendix E. Additionally, trademarks are provided for in all fifty states so that marks that cannot be federally registered with the U.S. Patent and Trademark Office (PTO) because they are not used in interstate commerce can be registered in the state in which they are used.

In the United States, trademarks are protected from their date of first public use. Registration of a mark is not required to secure protection for a mark, although it offers numerous advantages, such as allowing the registrant to bring an action in federal court for infringement of the mark. Applications for federal registration of trademarks are made with the PTO. Registration is a fairly lengthy process, generally taking anywhere from twelve to twenty-four months or even longer. The filing fee is $325 per mark per class of goods or services covered by the mark.

A trademark registration is valid for ten years but may be renewed for additional ten-year periods thereafter as long as the mark is in use in interstate commerce. Additionally, registrants are required to file an affidavit with the PTO between the fifth and sixth years after registration and every ten years to verify the mark is in continued use. Marks not in use are then available to others.

Trademarks are among the most visible items of intellectual property, and it has been estimated that the average resident of the United States encounters approximately fifteen hundred different trademarks each day. A properly selected, registered, and protected mark can be of great value to a company or individual desiring to establish and expand market share. There is perhaps no better way to maintain a strong position in the marketplace than to build

TEXACO

goodwill and consumer recognition in the identity selected for products and services and then to protect that identity under federal trademark law.

Copyrights

What Is Protectable   **Copyright** is a form of protection governed exclusively by federal law (17 U.S.C. § 101 *et seq.*) granted to the authors of original works of authorship, including literary, dramatic, musical, artistic, and certain other works. See Appendix E. Thus, books, songs, plays, jewelry, movies, sculptures, paintings, and choreographic works are all protectable. Computer software is also protectable by copyright.

Copyright protection is available for more than merely serious works of fiction or art. Marketing materials, advertising copy, and cartoons are also protectable. Copyright is available for original works; no judgment is made about their literary or artistic quality. Nevertheless, certain works are not protectable by copyright, such as titles, names, short phrases, or lists of ingredients. Similarly, ideas, methods, and processes are not protectable by copyright, although the expression of those ideas is.

Copyright protection exists automatically from the time a work is created in fixed form. Thus, similar to trademark law, securing a registration for a work (with the U.S. Copyright Office) is not required for a work to be protected, although registration does provide significant advantages, such as establishing a public record of the copyright claim and providing a basis upon which an infringement suit may be brought in federal court and in which statutory damages and attorneys' fees may be recovered.

The owner of a copyright has the right to reproduce the work, prepare derivative works based on the original work (such as a sequel to the original), distribute copies of the work, and to perform and display the work. Generally, violations of such rights are protectable by infringement actions. Nevertheless, some uses of copyrighted works are considered "fair use" and do not constitute infringement, such as use of an insignificant portion of a work for noncommercial purposes or parody of a copyrighted work.

Federal Registration of Copyrights   Neither publication nor registration of a work is required for copyright protection, inasmuch as works are protected under federal copyright law from the time of their creation in a fixed form. Registration, however, is inexpensive, requiring only a $30 filing fee, and the process is expeditious. In most cases, the Copyright Office processes applications within four to five months.

Copyrighted works are automatically protected from the moment of their creation for a term generally enduring for the author's life plus an additional seventy years after the author's death. After that time, the work will fall into the public domain and may be reproduced, distributed, or performed by anyone. The policy underlying the long period of copyright protection is that it may take several years for a painting, book, or opera to achieve its true value, and, thus, authors should receive a length of protection that will enable the work to appreciate to its greatest extent.

Patents

What Is Protectable   A **patent** is a grant from the U.S. government that permits its owner to prevent others from making, using, or selling an invention.

copyright: Right protecting original works of authorship, including literary, musical, dramatic, artistic, and other works, from unauthorized reproduction, sale, performance, distribution, or display

patent: A grant from the U.S. government permitting its owner to exclude others from making, selling, or using an invention for a limited period of time

There are three types of patents: utility patents, which are the most common patents and which cover useful inventions and discoveries (such as the typewriter, the automobile, and genetically altered mice); design patents, which cover new, original, and ornamental designs for articles (such as furniture); and plant patents, which cover new and distinct plant varieties (such as hybrid flowers or trees).

Patent protection is available only for useful, novel, and nonobvious inventions. Generally, patent law prohibits the patenting of an invention that is merely an insignificant addition to or alteration of something already known. Moreover, some items cannot be protected by patent, such as scientific principles.

Federal Registration of Patents   Patents are governed exclusively by federal law (35 U.S.C. § 100 *et seq.*). See Appendix E. To obtain a patent, an inventor must file an application with the PTO (the same agency that issues trademark registrations) that fully describes the invention. Patent prosecution is expensive, time-consuming, and complex. Costs can run into the thousands of dollars, and it generally takes nearly two years for the PTO to issue a patent.

Patent protection exists for twenty years from the date of filing of an application for utility and plant patents and fourteen years from the date of grant for design patents. After this period of time, the invention falls into the public domain and may be used by any person without permission.

Patents promote the public good in that patent protection incentivizes inventors. In return for fully describing the invention in the patent application, the inventor is granted an exclusive but limited period of time within which to exploit the invention. After the patent expires, any member of the public is free to use, manufacture, or sell the invention. Thus, patent law strikes a balance between the need to protect inventors and the need to allow public access to important discoveries.

Trade Secrets

What Is Protectable   A **trade secret** consists of any valuable business information that, if known by a competitor, would afford the competitor some benefit or advantage. There is no limit to the type of information that can be protected as trade secrets; recipes, marketing plans, financial projections, and methods of conducting business can all constitute trade secrets. There is no requirement that a trade secret be unique or complex; thus, even something as simple and nontechnical as a list of customers can qualify as a trade secret as long as it affords its owner a competitive advantage and is not common knowledge.

If trade secrets were not protectable, companies would have no incentive to invest time, money, and effort in research and development that ultimately benefits the public. Trade secret law thus promotes the development of new methods and processes of doing business in the marketplace.

Protection of Trade Secrets   Although trademarks, copyrights, and patents are all subject to extensive statutory schemes for their protection, application, and registration, there is no federal law relating to trade secrets and no formalities are required to obtain rights to trade secrets. Trade secrets are protectable under various state statutes and cases and by contractual agreements between parties. For example, employers often require employees to sign confidentiality

trade secret: Any valuable commercial information that, if known by a competitor, would provide some benefit or advantage to the competitor

agreements in which employees agree not to disclose proprietary information owned by the employer.

If properly protected, trade secrets may last forever. On the other hand, if companies fail to take reasonable measures to maintain the secrecy of the information, trade secret protection may be lost. Thus, disclosure of the information should be limited to those with a "need to know" it so as to perform their duties, confidential information should be kept in secure or restricted areas, and employees with access to proprietary information should sign **nondisclosure agreements.** If such measures are taken, a trade secret can be protected in perpetuity.

Other means by which companies protect valuable information is by requiring employees to sign agreements promising not to compete with the employer after leaving the job. Such covenants are strictly scrutinized by courts, but generally, if they are reasonable in regard to time, scope, and subject matter, they are enforceable.

Other Intellectual Property Rights

Although the most common types of intellectual property are trademarks, copyrights, patents, and trade secrets, other intellectual property rights exist and will be discussed in the chapters that follow. Some of these rights include semiconductor chip protection, plant variety protection, the right of publicity, and rights relating to unfair competition, including passing off, misappropriation, and false advertising.

Additionally, intellectual property rights often intersect and overlap. Thus, the formula for Coca-Cola is a trade secret, while the distinctive script in which the words COCA-COLA® are displayed is a trademark. Generally, computer programs are protectable under copyright law, patent law, and as trade secrets, while the name for a computer program, such as WINDOWS®, qualifies for trademark protection. Jewelry may be protected both under copyright and design patent law. Legal practitioners in the field of intellectual property law must fully understand how the various types of intellectual property intersect so that clients can achieve the widest possible scope of protection. For example, although an item of jewelry can be protected as a design patent, securing a patent is complex and expensive. Moreover, a design patent lasts only fourteen years from the date of grant of the patent. In contrast, securing copyright protection for the same article of jewelry is easy and inexpensive. More importantly, copyright protection endures during the life of the work's creator and for seventy years thereafter. Trade secrets that are properly protected can endure perpetually. Thus, intellectual property owners need to consider the complementary relationships among trademark, copyright, patent, and trade secrets law so as to obtain the broadest possible protection for their assets.

AGENCIES RESPONSIBLE FOR INTELLECTUAL PROPERTY REGISTRATION

United States Patent and Trademark Office

The agency charged with granting patents and registering trademarks is the **United States Patent and Trademark Office (PTO),** one of fourteen

nondisclosure agreement:
An agreement requiring a party to maintain information in confidence; also called *confidentiality agreement*

United States Patent and Trademark Office (PTO):
The agency within the Department of Commerce charged with registering trademarks and granting patents

agencies within the U.S. Department of Commerce. The PTO, founded more than two hundred years ago, employs more than five thousand employees and is located in sixteen buildings in Arlington, Virginia. Its official mailing address is Commissioner of Patents and Trademarks, Washington, DC 20231. The PTO is physically located at 2900 Crystal Drive in Arlington, Virginia. Its web site is http://www.uspto.gov. The PTO web site offers a wealth of information, including basic information about trademarks and patents, fee schedules, forms, and the ability to search for trademarks and patents. Since 1991, under the Omnibus Budget Reconciliation Act, the PTO has operated in much the same way as a private business, providing valued products and services to customers in exchange for fees that are used to fully fund PTO operations. It uses no taxpayer funds.

The PTO is one of the busiest of all government agencies, and as individuals and companies begin to understand the value of intellectual property, greater demands are being made on the PTO. For example, over the past five years the PTO has seen a 50 percent increase in the number of trademark and patent applications. In 1997, the PTO issued 122,977 patents and registered 112,509 trademarks.

Legislation introduced in the 105th Congress (S. 421) would establish the PTO as a performance-based organization that would be managed by professionals, which would result in the creation of a new political position, deputy secretary of commerce for intellectual property. Changing the PTO from an agency within the Department of Commerce to a governmental corporation would make the PTO equivalent to other similar organizations, such as the Tennessee Valley Authority and the Federal Deposit Insurance Corporation. The PTO is presently transitioning to paperless processing of trademark applications, a process it expects to complete in 2000. Additionally, the PTO has published the full text and images of two million patents (all patents since 1976) and the text and images of one million trademarks on the Internet, allowing users to view, download, and print the images they want.

Citations to many cases in this text will be to "U.S.P.Q.," a reference to *United States Patent Quarterly,* a reporter of cases decided by the **Trademark Trial and Appeal Board (TTAB)** as well as patent and copyright cases.

Library of Congress

The **Library of Congress,** sometimes referred to as "Jefferson's Legacy," was established in 1800 as a legislative library. It is America's oldest national cultural institution and is the largest repository of recorded knowledge in the world. Thomas Jefferson is considered the founder of the Library of Congress, and his personal library is at the heart of the Library inasmuch as in 1814 the Library's three thousand volumes were burned by the British, and Jefferson sold his personal library collection of 6,487 volumes to the Library of Congress for $23,940 the next year.

The Library of Congress is the copyright agency for the United States and is in charge of examining the more than 600,000 copyright applications filed each year, issuing registrations, and maintaining copyright deposits in its vast collection.

The Library of Congress is located at 101 Independence Avenue SE, Washington, DC 20559-6000, and its web site is http://lcweb.gov. Basic

Trademark Trial and Appeal Board (TTAB): Department of the PTO that resolves inter partes proceedings and other matters affecting trademarks

Library of Congress: The agency charged with examining copyright applications, issuing registrations, and maintaining copyright deposits

information about copyrights, forms, and other valuable information can be obtained for free and downloaded from the Internet.

INTERNATIONAL ORGANIZATIONS, AGENCIES, AND TREATIES

There are a number of international organizations and agencies that promote the use and protection of intellectual property. Although these organizations are discussed in more detail in the chapters to follow, a brief introduction may be helpful:

- **International Trademark Association (INTA)** is a not-for-profit international association composed chiefly of trademark owners and practitioners. More than 3,400 companies and law firms in more than 115 countries belong to INTA, together with others interested in promoting trademarks. INTA offers a wide variety of educational seminars and publications, including many worthwhile materials available at no cost on the Internet (see INTA's home page at http://www.inta.org). INTA is located at 1133 Avenue of the Americas, New York, NY 10036-6710 (212/768-9887).
- **World Intellectual Property Organization (WIPO)** was founded in 1883 and is a specialized agency of the United Nations whose purposes are to promote intellectual property throughout the world and to administer twenty-one treaties dealing with intellectual property, including the Paris Convention, Madrid Protocol, the Trademark Law Treaty, and the Berne Convention. More than 160 nations are members of WIPO. WIPO is headquartered in Geneva, Switzerland, and its home page is http://www.wipo.int/eng/index/htm.

There are also a number of international agreements and treaties that affect intellectual property. Among them are the following:

- **Berne Convention for the Protection of Literary and Artistic Works (the Berne Convention).** The Berne Convention was created in 1886 under the leadership of Victor Hugo to protect literary and artistic works. It has more than 135 member nations. The United States became a party to the Berne Convention in 1989. The Berne Convention is administered by WIPO and is based on the precept that each member nation must treat nationals of other member countries like its own nationals for purposes of copyright (the principle of "national treatment").
- **Madrid Protocol.** The Madrid Protocol came into existence in 1996 and allows trademark protection for nearly thirty countries and all fifteen countries of the European Union by means of a centralized trademark filing procedure. Legislation has been introduced that would make the United States a party to the Madrid Protocol. This treaty, when fully implemented, will facilitate a one-stop, low-cost, efficient system for the international registration of trademarks by permitting a U.S. trademark owner to file for registration in any number of member countries by filing a single standardized application form with the PTO, in English, with a single set of fees.

International Trademark Association (INTA): A not-for-profit international association devoted to promoting trademarks

World Intellectual Property Organization (WIPO): A specialized agency of the United Nations with more than **one hundred and sixty** member nations that promotes intellectual property throughout the world and administers various multilateral treaties dealing with intellectual property, including the Berne Convention

Berne Convention: An international convention adhered to by more than one hundred and thirty-five nations that requires its members to treat nationals of other countries as their own nationals for purposes of copyright

Madrid Protocol: An agreement adhered to by nearly thirty countries and the E.U. (but not the United States) that provides an "international trademark registration" that would be valid in all member nations

- **Paris Convention.** One of the first treaties or "conventions" designed to address trademark protection in foreign countries was the Paris Convention of 1883, adopted to facilitate international patent and trademark protection. The Paris Convention is based on the principle of reciprocity so that foreign trademark and patent owners may obtain in a member country the same legal protection for their marks and patents as can citizens of those member countries. Perhaps the most significant benefit provided by the Paris Convention is that of priority. An applicant for a trademark has six months after filing an application in any of the more than 135 member nations to file a corresponding application in any of the other member countries of the Paris Convention and obtain the benefits of the first filing date. Similar priority is afforded for utility patent applications, although the priority period is one year rather than six months. The Paris Convention is administered by WIPO.

- **North American Free Trade Agreement (NAFTA).** The NAFTA came into effect on January 1, 1994, and is adhered to by the United States, Canada, and Mexico. The NAFTA resulted in some changes to U.S. trademark law, primarily with regard to marks that include geographical terms.

- **General Agreement on Tariffs and Trade (GATT).** GATT was concluded in 1994 and is adhered to by most of the major industrialized nations in the world. The most significant changes to U.S. intellectual property law from GATT are that nonuse of a trademark for three years creates a presumption the mark has been abandoned and that the duration of a utility patent is now twenty years from the filing date of the application (rather than seventeen years from the date the patent issued, as was previously the case).

(See Appendix A, Table of Treaties.)

THE INCREASING IMPORTANCE OF INTELLECTUAL PROPERTY RIGHTS

While people have always realized the importance of protecting intellectual property rights, the rapidly developing pace of technology has led to increased awareness of the importance of intellectual property assets. Some individuals and companies offer only knowledge. Thus, computer consultants, advertising agencies, and software implementers sell only brainpower. Similarly, some forms of intellectual property, such as domain names and moving images shown on a company's web page, did not even exist until relatively recently. Internet domain names such as www.ibm.com are valuable assets that must be protected against infringement.

Moreover, the rapidity with which information can be communicated through the Internet has led to increasing challenges in the field of intellectual property. The day after the movie *Titanic* swept the Oscars, more than fifty web sites offered illegal or pirated copies of the film. Books, movies, and songs can now be copied, infringed, and sold illegally with the touch of a keystroke.

The Office of the United States Trade Representative has estimated that U.S. industries lose between $41 and $61 billion annually from piracy, counterfeiting of goods, and other intellectual property infringements.

Paris Convention : An agreement adhered to by more than one hundred and thirty-five member nations providing that foreign trademark and patent owners may obtain in a member country the same protection for their trademarks and patents as can citizens of the member country

North American Free Trade Agreement (NAFTA): A trade agreement entered into in 1991 by the United States, Canada, and Mexico

General Agreement on Tariffs and Trade (GATT): Agreement adhered to by most industrialized nations aimed at increasing international trade and that resulted in some changes to U.S. trademark and patent law, notably relating to the duration of patent protection

ROLE OF INTELLECTUAL PROPERTY PROFESSIONAL

Because of the increasing array of intellectual property (IP) that can be created in our high-tech society and the increasing ease with which it can be infringed, intellectual property law is a growing practice area. Ten years ago, few law firms had intellectual property law departments and intellectual property matters were handled by small firms that specialized in the field. Today, nearly every large law firm has a department devoted exclusively to intellectual property, and IP professionals are courted and valued. In September 1998, the *National Law Journal* reported that attorneys in the field of intellectual property law were the highest paid of all legal specialties. Every legal newspaper and journal contains advertisements for IP professionals, and in many cases, specialists in the field of intellectual property law are paid more than their counterparts in other fields. For example, in September 1998, the *National Law Journal* reported that compensation for intermediate attorneys in intellectual property was the highest of all practice fields, outstripping some areas by nearly $30,000 annually.

Among the tasks commonly performed by IP professionals are the following:

- assisting in trademark searching to clear marks for use and preparing, filing, and monitoring trademark registration applications, maintenance, and renewal documents;
- preparing, filing, and monitoring copyright registration applications;
- assisting in patent searching and preparing, filing, and monitoring patent applications;
- drafting license agreements for licensing of trademarks, copyrights, and patents;
- preparing employment agreements and noncompetition agreements;
- assisting in intellectual property audits to determine the extent and value of a client's intellectual property; and
- assisting in protection of trade secrets by developing and implementing policies for protection of trade secrets.

Many of the issues presented in intellectual property law are cutting edge issues: protection of Internet domain names; copyright piracy on the Internet; importation of counterfeited or "knockoff" goods; and development and patenting of wonder drugs. Thus, the field is exciting and presents unique opportunities for learning and growth. Additionally, there is a great deal of client contact, and playing a part in a client's selection of a new name or mark for a product, bringing a new product to market, and protecting that property from infringement or misappropriation by others is interesting and exciting.

Along with these unique opportunities for learning and growth come concomitant duties of ethics and confidentiality. In many instances, clients disclose highly confidential information to attorneys and paralegals. Plans for marketing, newly discovered inventions, new product names, new songs, methods of doing business, and plans to sue another company for infringement may be disclosed by clients so that the legal team can help obtain protection for the client. Although it may be tempting to share such interesting information with others, attorneys and paralegals are under strict ethical duties to maintain the confidentiality of client work. They must not take files home from the office without permission, discuss confidential client matters in social settings or even in office building elevators, or leave files where they are accessible by others. When in doubt, they should avoid disclosure.

In sum, intellectual property is a growing, exciting, and dynamic area, offering unique opportunities and challenging work. The field changes on nearly a daily basis, the issues are interesting, and IP professionals are valued members of a legal team devoted to ensuring that clients receive the broadest possible scope of protection for their creative assets.

In many cases, the most valuable assets a company owns are its intellectual property assets. For example, the value of the trademarks and service marks owned by the Coca-Cola Company has been estimated at $24 billion. Thus, companies must act aggressively to protect these valuable assets from infringement or misuse by others. The field of intellectual property law aims to protect the value of such investments.

CHAPTER SUMMARY

The term *intellectual property* is generally thought of as comprising four overlapping fields of law: trademarks (protecting names, logos, symbols, and other devices indicating the origin and source of products and services); copyrights (protecting original works of authorship); patents (grants by the federal government allowing their owners to exclude others from making, using, or selling the owner's invention); and trade secrets (any commercial information that, if known by a competitor, would afford the competitor an advantage in the marketplace). Patents must be issued by the federal government, while rights in trademarks are created by use of marks and rights in copyright exist from the time a work is created in fixed form. Nevertheless, registration of trademarks and copyrights offers certain advantages and benefits. Trade secrets are governed by various state laws, and registration is not required for existence and ownership of a trade secret. Trademarks and trade secrets can endure perpetually as long as they are protected, while copyrights and patents will fall into the public domain and be available for use by anyone after their terms expire.

As our world becomes increasingly reliant on technological advances, greater demands and challenges are made on IP practitioners. The field is an exciting and challenging one and offers significant opportunities for hands-on involvement by IP professionals.

DISCUSSION QUESTIONS

1. Indicate whether the following items would be protectable as trademarks, copyrights, patents, or trade secrets:

   a mascara brush

   the design of cupped hands used by Allstate Insurance Company

   a videocassette recorder

   the theme music from the Tonight Show

   a ballpoint pen

   the slogan "We bring good things to life"

   the recipe for Mrs. Fields' Chocolate Macadamia Nut Cookies

2. The author Henry James (1843–1916) wrote the novel *Daisy Miller*. If a movie studio wished to make a movie of the novel, would it be required to obtain copyright permission from James's heirs? Discuss.

3. Assume that Eli Lilly Company develops a new drug for the treatment of diabetes. A patent application for the drug is filed in 1998. When will the patent expire and the drug enter into the public domain?

4. DreamWorks SKG studio uses a distinctive logo of a child sitting on the tip of a quarter moon. How long may DreamWorks SKG use this logo?

5. Describe how the Internet can pose a threat to a copyrighted book, play, song, or movie.

PART

II

The Law of Trademarks

Foundations of Trademark Law

CHAPTER
OVERVIEW

Trademarks surround us every day and help us make valuable and informed decisions about the products and services we purchase. There are four types of marks: *trademarks* are used for goods; *service marks* are used for services; *certification marks* are used to certify some quality of a product or service; and *collective marks* indicate membership in an organization. Some marks, namely those that are coined or "made up," like EXXON®, are stronger than others, namely those that describe or suggest something about a good or service. Not all matter is protectable: marks that disparage a person or that are scandalous cannot be protected. On the other hand, even some unusual devices can be protected, such as sounds and fragrances. Trademarks come into existence through use; they need not be registered with the U.S. Patent and Trademark Office to be protected, although federal registration affords several advantages to a trademark owner.

INTRODUCTION TO TRADEMARKS AND SERVICE MARKS

Although there was some use of trademarks or symbols in the Middle East and Far East several centuries ago, contemporary trademark law can be traced back to use of trademarks during the medieval period in Europe by merchants who sought to distinguish the goods they sold from those sold by others by applying a mark or symbol to their goods. By viewing the mark, purchasers would immediately be able to identify the craftsperson who made the goods and make an informed decision about the quality of the materials. The use of symbols by medieval craftspeople to distinguish and identify their goods is the direct antecedent for the modern use of trademarks such as COCA-COLA®, MICROSOFT®, and CREST®.

PURPOSE AND FUNCTION OF TRADEMARKS

Trademarks perform two critical functions in the marketplace: they provide assurance that goods are of a certain quality and consistency, and they assist

consumers in making decisions about the purchase of goods. If a trademark such as NIKE® could be counterfeited and used by another on inferior merchandise, there would be no incentive for the owners of the NIKE mark to produce high-quality shoes and to expend money establishing consumer recognition of the products offered under the NIKE marks. Thus, protection of trademarks results in increased competition in the marketplace, with both the producer of goods and services and the consumer as the ultimate beneficiaries. Businesses benefit because they can reap the rewards of their investment in developing and marketing a product without fearing another business will deceive consumers by using the same or a confusingly similar mark for like goods, and consumers benefit because they are able to identify and purchase desired goods.

The value inherent in achieving consumer loyalty to a particular product or service through the maintenance of consistent quality of the products or services offered under a mark is called **goodwill.** The goodwill associated with a trademark continues to increase over time as additional sales are made of the product offered under a mark and consumers associate the mark with its owner. There is no doubt that the goodwill inherent in a trademark can be among a company's most valuable assets. As discussed in Chapter 1, the COCA-COLA marks have been valued at $24 billion, and the COCA-COLA mark is the most recognized mark in the world.

Trademarks thus provide the following functions:

- they identify one maker's goods or services and distinguish them from those offered by others;
- they indicate that all goods or services offered under the mark come from a single producer, manufacturer, or "source";
- they indicate that all goods or services offered under the mark are of consistent quality; and
- they serve as an advertising device so that consumers link a product or service being offered with a mark (for example, when many consumers see or hear the phrase JUST DO IT®, they immediately think of Nike products).

Thus, a consumer who purchases GAP® khaki pants in Dallas is assured that the fit and style is the same as a pair that would be purchased in Philadelphia, and that the item is the product of a single source, namely, Gap Inc.

Trademark law is a part of the broader law of unfair competition or unfair trade practices. Infringement of another's trademark is a species of unfair competition. Other acts of unfair competition include false advertising and infringement of copyrights, patents, or trade names. The law of unfair competition is meant to protect consumers and eliminate unfair business practices. Trademark law is a vital part of the broad protection afforded by the law of unfair competition.

goodwill: The value inherent in achieving consumer loyalty to a particular product or service through maintenance of consistent quality of the products or services offered under a mark

TYPES OF MARKS: TRADEMARKS, SERVICE MARKS, CERTIFICATION MARKS, AND COLLECTIVE MARKS

There are four different types of marks: trademarks, service marks, certification marks, and collective marks.

The modern definition of *trademark* is that it is a word, name, symbol, or device, or a combination thereof, used by a person (including a business entity), or which a person has a bona fide intention to use, to identify that person's goods and distinguish them from those manufactured by others. 15 U.S.C. § 1127. A *service mark* is a word, name, symbol, or device, or a combination thereof, used by a person, or which a person has a bona fide intention to use, to identify and distinguish the services of one person from those of others and to indicate the source of those services. Thus, a trademark is used to identify *goods,* such as CHEERIOS® for cereal, LEXUS® for cars, or JIM BEAM® for whiskey. A service mark is used to identify *services,* such as H & R BLOCK® for accounting services, T.G.I. FRIDAY'S® for restaurant services, and FEDEX® for transportation services.

Federal Express

While the term *trademark* thus refers to some physical and tangible good, and *service mark* refers to an intangible service, in common usage the term *trademark* is often used to refer to marks for both goods and services. Throughout this text, discussions related to "trademarks" will also apply to service marks unless otherwise noted. Similarly, the term **mark** will be used as a synonym for both trademarks and service marks. The federal statute governing trademark law, the U.S. Trademark Act (the Lanham Act, found at 15 U.S.C. § 1051 *et seq.*) itself states that the term *mark* includes any trademark, service mark, collective mark, or certification mark. See Appendix E. 15 U.S.C. § 1127.

A **certification mark** is a word, name, symbol, device, or combination thereof, used by one person to certify that the goods or services of others have certain features in regard to quality, material, mode of manufacture, or some other characteristic. Examples of certification marks are the GOOD HOUSE-KEEPING® and Underwriters Laboratory seals of approval. Certification marks are, by their very nature, unlike any other types of marks. They do not indicate the origin or source of the goods or services, and they are not used by the actual owner of the goods or services. Rather, the mark is placed on the goods or used in connection with the services of another to certify something about the goods or services. Thus, a toaster that carries the GOOD HOUSE-KEEPING® seal of approval signifies to consumers that the toaster has been reviewed, tested, and found to meet certain standards in regard to quality, safety, price, or some other characteristic. The toaster is not made by the Good Housekeeping people. They merely certify that the goods or services offered under their mark meet certain objective and preestablished standards. The owner of a certified mark may lose rights to the mark if it arbitrarily refuses to allow use of a mark by one whose products or services meet its stated certification standards.

A **collective mark** is one used by a collective membership organization, such as a labor union, fraternity, or professional society, to identify that the person displaying the mark is a member of the organization. Thus, the FUTURE FARMERS OF AMERICA® mark indicates membership in a certain organization.

(See Figure 2–1 for further examples of the four types of marks.)

A company may use several marks. An examination of a can of Coca-Cola reveals multiple marks: the words COCA-COLA®, the stylized WAVE DESIGN®, and the slogan THINGS GO BETTER WITH COKE®. All of these marks are used on one product and all are protected by the Coca-Cola Company.

mark: A trademark or service mark

certification mark: A word, name, symbol, or device used by one person to certify that the goods or services of others have certain features in regard to quality, material, or some other characteristics

collective mark: A mark used by a collective membership organization (such as a union or fraternity) to identify that the person displaying the mark is a member of the organization

FIGURE 2–1
Types of Marks

Type of Mark	Example
Trademark	COMET® (for cleanser)
Service Mark	HYATT® (for lodging services)
Certification Mark	UNION MADE® (for clothing)
Collective Mark	MORTGAGE BANKERS ASSOCIATION® (for membership in an organization)

ACQUISITION OF TRADEMARK RIGHTS

In most foreign countries, trademark rights arise from registering the mark with a governmental entity. The law in the United States is quite different: trademark rights arise from adoption and *use* of a mark, not from registration. Thus, a person using a mark may have valid and enforceable rights in a mark even though the mark is not registered with the PTO. Such an owner will have priority even over a subsequent user who has secured a federal registration for a mark with the PTO.

The "use" required to establish trademark rights is more than token use; it must be public use. While actual sales of products or services are not required, a certain level of presale activity is required. For example, sales within a company or to personal friends are insufficient to show use, while soliciting and accepting orders is usually sufficient to show commercial use.

Establishing a date of first use is critical for a trademark owner because priority of trademark rights is measured from this date. If one party first used a mark on September 15, 1998, and another first used a mark on October 15, 1998, the prior user will be able to preclude the junior user from using a confusingly similar mark.

Although the general rule is that acquisition of trademark rights stem from use, there is one exception to this rule: the **intent-to-use application.** Until 1989, the United States was one of only two countries in the world that required that a mark be in actual use before an owner could file an application to register it. After an applicant had begun using the mark and then filed an application, the PTO might refuse registration of the mark on the basis it was confusingly similar to a prior mark or was subject to some other defect. The applicant would then have invested substantial money and time in developing the mark, in using it in commerce, marketing, and advertising, and in applying for registration, only to be told the mark was unregistrable. To remedy this situation, the Trademark Law Revision Act of 1988 allowed persons to file applications for marks based on a bona fide intent to use the mark in commerce in the future. If the PTO determines the mark is unregistrable, the applicant will not have expended any sums other than the PTO filing fee and can readily file another application for a new mark. If the PTO determines the mark is registrable, the applicant must then commence use of the mark in **interstate commerce** and provide a statement verifying such use to the PTO before the mark can proceed to registration. Interestingly enough, however, once the mark proceeds to registration, priority is measured from the date the intent-to-use application was *filed,* even though that filing date may precede actual use in commerce by more than three years.

Intent-to-Use Application:
A trademark application for which no actual use of a mark has been made but rather alleging the applicant's bona fide intent to use the mark in the future

interstate commerce:
Commerce between or among states

Minimal or token use cannot serve as the basis for securing or maintaining a registration, ensuring that an owner does not reserve or "warehouse" a mark by making only sporadic use of it with the intent to block others from using it rather than having a true commercial intent to exploit the mark for sales. Moreover, the PTO desires to clear its records of unused marks, or "deadwood," so that such unused marks may be available by others.

The use required is "bona fide use of a mark in the ordinary course of trade and not made merely to reserve a right in a mark." 15 U.S.C. § 1127. Thus, an owner must make use of a mark as would be typical in the industry or trade. If a product is extremely expensive, such that only a few units are sold each year, this may be sufficient use if such meager sales are the norm in the relevant industry.

Just as use is required to acquire rights in a mark, continued use is required to maintain rights in a mark. Failure to use a mark for three years creates a presumption the mark has been abandoned.

COMMON LAW RIGHTS, FEDERAL REGISTRATION UNDER THE LANHAM ACT, AND STATE TRADEMARK RIGHTS

Common Law Rights

As discussed, in the United States, trademark rights arise from use of a mark. It is not necessary to secure permission or registration from any governmental entity to acquire trademark rights. A party who is using a mark without any such governmental registration is said to have a **common law trademark.** This common law trademark can be enforced in any geographical area in which the mark is used. Thus, if an owner uses the mark CAKERY CRAVINGS in connection with a pastry shop in Portland, Oregon, the owner will be able to preclude later users from using a confusingly similar mark in connection with similar goods or services in Portland and in a reasonable area of expansion beyond Portland.

Federal Registration

Although there is no requirement that a trademark owner apply for or secure federal registration of a mark with the PTO, registration on the PTO's Principal Register does offer several advantages:

- nationwide constructive use effective from the filing date of the application;
- nationwide notice to the public of an owner's claim to a mark, thereby precluding a later user from claiming it used a mark in good faith in a remote territory and should be able to continue use;
- the ability to bar importation of goods bearing infringing trademarks (assuming the registration is deposited with the U.S. Customs Service);
- the right under the Paris Convention to obtain a registration in various foreign countries based upon the U.S. registration;
- the right to bring an action in federal court for trademark infringement and recover lost profits, damages, costs, and possibly triple damages and attorneys' fees;

common law trademark: A mark used by a party without any governmental registration

- incontestable status of the registration after five years of continuous use subsequent to the registration;
- the right to use the registration symbol ® with the mark;
- a possible basis to claim priority to an Internet domain name; and
- *prima facie* (literally, "on its face") evidence of the validity of the registration, the registrant's ownership of the mark, and the registrant's exclusive right to use the mark in connection with the identified goods and services.

Additionally, because individuals should search the PTO records before adopting a new mark, a mark that is registered or applied for with the PTO may deter a party from seeking a registration for a similar mark, thus avoiding expensive litigation.

In sum, while federal registration is not required to secure trademark rights, registration provides several advantages and enhances the level of protection an owner has for a mark.

The federal statute governing trademark rights is the **Lanham Act** (also called the Trademark Act) enacted in 1946 and named for Congressman Fritz Garland Lanham (D. Texas), the then-chair of the House Patent Committee (which also proposed legislation relating to trademarks) who introduced the legislation. The Lanham Act has been amended numerous times. Perhaps the most significant amendment was the Trademark Law Revision Act of 1988 that allowed for intent-to-use applications and reduced the life of a registration from twenty years to ten years in order to clear the PTO files of deadwood.

In 1993 legislation was enacted to implement commitments made by the United States in the North American Free Trade Agreement (NAFTA), affecting registration of geographically misdescriptive terms and precluding registration of marks that are primarily geographically deceptively misdescriptive.

The **Uruguay Round Agreements Act** was enacted in 1994 to implement the General Agreements on Tariffs and Trade (GATT) in the United States. GATT is a multilateral treaty among one hundred nations aimed at reducing barriers to trade and expanding trading on a worldwide basis. A portion of GATT entitled **Trade-Related Aspects of Intellectual Property Rights (TRIPS)** bars registration of a mark for wine or liquor if the mark identifies a place other than the origin of the goods and was first used after 1996. Thus, a new wine cannot use the mark "Napa" unless the product originates in that region of California. GATT also increased the period of time of nonuse of a mark that would result in abandonment from two years to three years.

State Registration

It is possible that a mark may not qualify for federal registration, generally because it is not used in interstate commerce but is used only within the confines of one state, namely, in **intrastate commerce.** Thus, the owner of the CAKERY CRAVINGS mark used solely in Portland might seek to register the mark in Oregon. Each one of the fifty states has its own trademark act. Generally, obtaining a state registration is a fairly expeditious and inexpensive process. Forms are available from each state's secretary of state, located in the state capital. The state registration confers benefits only within the boundaries of the state. Thus, the owner of CAKERY CRAVINGS could not preclude another from using the same or a similar mark in Seattle, Washington. Armed

Lanham Act: The federal statute found at 15 U.S.C. § 1051 *et seq.* governing the law of trademarks; also called the *United States Trademark Act*

Uruguay Round Agreements Act: A 1994 act that implemented GATT and amended U.S. copyright law to provide remedies for pirated sound recordings of live performances and to provide automatic restoration of copyright in certain foreign works

Trade-Related Aspects of Intellectual Property Rights (TRIPS): Agreement promulgated in accordance with the 1994 General Agreement on Tariffs and Trade providing intellectual property protection for GATT members

intrastate commerce: Commerce conducted within the borders of one state

with a *federal* registration, however, the owner could preclude the later Seattle user. There is no procedural or substantive advantage of securing state registrations in addition to a federal registration. The federal registration is nationwide in scope and should be sought whenever a mark qualifies for federal registration. (See Appendix B for a summary of state trademark registration provisions.)

CATEGORIES OF MARKS

Although marks can consist of words, symbols, designs, slogans, or a combination thereof, not every term is protectable. Even among marks that are protectable, some marks are stronger than others. In determining strength of marks, courts recognize several categories of marks. In ascending order of strength and protectability, the five categories are generic, descriptive, suggestive, arbitrary, and fanciful or coined marks.

- A **generic mark** is not truly a mark at all but is merely a common name of a product, such as *soap* or *beverage*. Such generic terms are not protectable and cannot be exclusively appropriated by one party inasmuch as they are needed by competitors to describe their goods. The Ninth Circuit Court of Appeals recently held that a colorful grape-leaf design placed on a wine bottle label was a generic emblem for wine and could not be appropriated by a winery. *Kendall-Jackson Winery, Ltd. v. E & J Gallo Winery,* 150 F.3d 1042 (9th Cir. 1998). In some cases, marks that were once valid have become generic through misuse. Examples of marks that were once trademarks but are now generic terms are *aspirin, cellophane, escalator,* and *thermos*. Thus, owners of many well-known marks take great pains to ensure their marks do not become generic. The familiar refrains "SCOTCH® brand adhesive tape" and "Q-TIP® brand cotton swabs" encountered in advertising are meant to protect marks and to ensure that consumers do not use the term *Scotch tape* to describe all adhesive tape or the term *Q-tip* to refer to any cotton swab, thereby "genericizing" a once-valued trademark. Xerox's ad campaign "when you use 'Xerox' the way you use 'aspirin,' we get a headache" is similarly aimed to preserve the distinctiveness of the XEROX® mark.

- A **descriptive mark** tells something about the product or service offered under a mark by describing some characteristic, quality, ingredient, function, component, or other property of the product or service. For example, in *In re Bed & Breakfast Registry,* 791 F.2d 157 (Fed. Cir. 1986), BED & BREAKFAST REGISTRY was held merely descriptive of lodging registration services, and in *Hunter Publishing Co. v. Caulfield Publishing Ltd.,* 1 U.S.P.Q.2d 1996 (T.T.A.B. 1986), SYSTEMS USER was held merely descriptive of a trade journal directed at users of data processing systems. Because descriptive terms merely describe the goods or services, rather than identify the source of a product, they are not registrable with the PTO until the consumer links the mark with a single source. That learned association is called **secondary meaning** or *acquired distinctiveness*. Descriptive marks cannot be registered until secondary meaning is shown. Typically, secondary meaning is shown by demonstrating a significant level of advertising, sales, and consumer

generic mark: An unprotectable common name for a product or service

descriptive mark: A mark that describes some characteristic of the goods or services offered under it and is unregistrable unless secondary meaning is shown

secondary meaning: An association by a consumer who has learned to link a mark with its source; also called *acquired distinctiveness*

survey evidence, to prove that when consumers encounter a mark such as SYSTEMS USER they immediately identify it with its offeror. Laudatory terms such as *best, extra,* and *super* are also considered merely descriptive and are not registrable without proof of secondary meaning.

- A **suggestive mark** suggests something about the goods or services offered under the mark but does not immediately describe them. A suggestive mark requires some imagination or thought to reach a conclusion about the goods or services offered under the mark. For example, ORANGE CRUSH® was held suggestive of an orange-flavored beverage, *see Orange Crush Co. v. California Crushed Fruit Co.,* 297 F. 892 (D.C. Cir. 1924), and GREYHOUND BUS® was held suggestive of transportation services. A suggestive mark is registrable without proof of secondary meaning or distinctiveness.

- An **arbitrary mark** is a commonly known word that is applied to an unfamiliar product. Some of the best-known arbitrary marks are CAMEL® for cigarettes and APPLE® for computers. While the terms are found in a dictionary, they have no relevance when applied to the goods in question and are thus arbitrary. Arbitrary marks are registrable without proof of secondary meaning.

- **Fanciful,** or *coined,* **marks** are those that are invented and have no dictionary meaning. Marks such as KODAK®, PEPSI®, and XEROX® are examples of fanciful or coined marks. Such marks are entitled to the greatest level of protectability because it will be difficult for others to claim they innocently created a highly similar mark for similar goods or services.

You can readily see that companies creating names face a commercial dilemma. The company likely wants the name to identify something about the product or service itself so that consumers encountering the new name or mark can determine what product or service is being offered. However, if the mark communicates something about the product, it is merely descriptive and cannot be registered without proof of secondary meaning. If a coined mark, such as XEROX, is selected, it tells the consumer nothing about the product or service offered, and the company will need to expend substantial sums in advertising to teach consumers to link the mark with the goods.

suggestive mark: A mark that suggests something about the goods or services offered under it; a suggestive mark is registrable without proof of secondary meaning

arbitrary mark: A mark using a common dictionary word for an unrelated product, such as APPLE for computers

fanciful mark: A wholly invented mark; also called *coined mark*

FIGURE 2–2
Categories of Marks

Type of Mark	Example	Registrability
Generic	PEANUTS (for peanuts)	Not registrable
Descriptive	SNO-RAKE (for rake for removing snow)	Not registrable without proof of secondary meaning
Suggestive	GOLDEN NUGGETS (for cookies)	Registrable
Arbitrary	POPCORN (for feathers)	Registrable
Fanciful or coined	TRALEE (for cellular phones)	Registrable

TRADE NAMES AND BUSINESS NAMES

A **trade name** or *commercial name* is one used to identify a business or company and its goodwill, while trademarks and service marks identify goods and services. A symbol or name used only as a business name cannot be registered as a trademark or service mark. If the business name, however, also serves to identify and distinguish goods and services, it may be registrable under the Lanham Act. For example, when Hallmark places its business name on its letterhead and business cards, such use is as an unregistrable trade name or business name. When the HALLMARK (& CROWN)® mark appears on greeting cards, however, it is being used as a trademark and may be registered as such.

Some business owners believe that when they incorporate in a state or file partnership papers with a state agency, such filing serves to protect their names because the state agency will check to ensure that no similar name is already being used within the state. Approval by a state to use a name in connection with a business is merely that—the company is entitled to use the name in connection with the business itself within that state. Using the name on goods themselves or in connection with services, namely, as a trademark or service mark, is far different. Once the mark is so used in commerce, the company acquires trademark or service mark rights.

PROTECTABLE MATTER

Introduction

The definition of a trademark or service mark is that it is a word, name, symbol, device, or any combination thereof, used to identify products or services. Clearly, words such as B. DALTON BOOKSELLER® and designs such as Mercedes Benz's segmented circle or the Mr. Peanut design can function as trademarks. There are, however, a host of other items that can be protected as marks, generally because of the flexibility in the language of the Lanham Act allowing for registration of a "symbol" or "device." A symbol or device might include anything capable of conveying meaning to a person, such as sounds, smells, and shapes. Legislation introduced in the 106th Congress (H.R. 1125), entitled "The Truth in Rock Act," would protect the names and images of performing groups under the Lanham Act so they could stop copycat groups from performing under their names.

Slogans, Letters, and Numbers

A slogan can constitute a trademark if it is distinctive. Thus, the slogan HAVE IT YOUR WAY® is protectable. Alphanumeric symbols (letters and numbers) may be protectable as long as they are not merely descriptive. Thus, broadcast station call letters such as NBC are registrable. Similarly, numbers can function as marks. If the numbers or letters describe something about the product or service offered under the mark, however, they will not be registrable unless proof of secondary meaning is shown. Thus, the mark "VT220" for computer hardware peripherals was held merely descriptive and unregistrable because "VT" stood for "video terminal" and "220" was a mere model number.

trade name: A name used to identify a business or company

Foreign Terms

Foreign terms are registrable as long as they comply with the requirements of the Lanham Act. Foreign wording will be translated into English and then examined by the PTO for descriptiveness. Thus, the mark VINO would not be allowed for wine inasmuch as its immediate translation is "wine," the very product offered under the mark. Similarly, the word OPTIQUE, a French word meaning "optic," was refused registration for eyeglasses because it was merely descriptive. *In re Optica Int'l,* 196 U.S.P.Q. 775 (T.T.A.B. 1977).

Shapes

Shapes or configurations can function as trademarks if they are distinctive rather than functional. Thus, the famous Coca-Cola bottle shape is registered with the PTO, and a competitor who adopts a confusingly similar shape container for its product will likely be enjoined from use.

Trade Dress

The total image of a product, such as size, shape, color, texture, and graphics, may be protected. This total image is called **trade dress.** In the famous case *Two Pesos, Inc. v. Taco Cabana, Inc.,* 505 U.S. 763 (1992), the U.S. Supreme Court protected the overall image or trade dress of a Mexican restaurant chain from infringement by a competitor who used similar colors, seating configurations, and décor. Although the trade dress itself (the overall image) cannot yet be registered as a mark, it is protected under the laws of unfair competition. (See Chapter 23 for discussion of trade dress.)

Color

Until relatively recently, a single color was not protectable as a trademark. This general rule was based on the color depletion theory: there are only a limited number of colors in the world; if businesses could appropriate a color and exclude others from using it, competition would be impaired. The present rule is that a trademark may consist of color as long as the color is not functional. Thus, Owens-Corning was allowed a registration to protect the pink color of its insulation. *In re Owens-Corning Fiberglas Corp.,* 774 F.2d 1116 (Fed. Cir. 1985). Pink has no functional or utilitarian purpose when applied to the goods and does not deprive competitors from using other colors. Similarly, in 1995, Qualitex Company was allowed to protect its green-gold ironing board pads on the basis that there was no competitive need in the industry for the green-gold color, inasmuch as numerous other colors are equally usable for similar goods. *Qualitex Co. v. Jacobson Products Co.,* 514 U.S. 159 (1995). However, the makers of the pink PEPTO-BISMOL® stomach medicine were unable to protect its pink color. The court held that the color pink was functional when used in connection with the medicine because the pink color had a pleasing appearance to one with an upset stomach. *Norwich Pharmacal Co. v. Sterling Drug, Inc.,* 271 F.2d 569 (2d Cir. 1959). In sum, protecting color is still a complex and evolving legal field.

trade dress: The overall image of a product or service

Fragrances, Sounds, and Moving Images

A fragrance can function as a trademark if it is distinctive and not functional. For example, in *In re Clarke,* 17 U.S.P.Q.2d 1238 (T.T.A.B. 1990), a floral fragrance was allowed as a trademark for sewing thread and embroidery yarn and was not functional when used in connection with those goods. A fragrance used in connection with products known for such features, such as perfumes or air fresheners, however, would likely be held functional and not registrable. Similarly, sounds can function as trademarks. The famous three-note chime used by NBC was the first registered sound trademark. The roar of the MGM lion and Woody Woodpecker's distinctive laugh are also registered. A recently filed trademark application by Harley-Davidson, Inc., seeks registration for the sound of its motorcycles. The trademark application identifies the mark as follows: "The mark consists of the exhaust sound of a Harley-Davidson motorcycle." Finally, the Internet has given rise to applications for marks that consist of moving images, such as Microsoft Company's spinning EXPLORER globe.

Designs

A design can function as a trademark as long as it is distinctive rather than merely functional or ornamental. Some designs are protected on their own, such as Nike's famous "swoosh" design, the alligator that appears on shirts, and McDonald's arches. If the design is merely background material, however, and does not create a separate commercial impression, or if it consists solely of some simple geometric shape, such as an oval or square, it cannot be protected without proof of secondary meaning.

Serialized Literary Titles

The title of a single book or movie title is generally not protectable. The title of a serialized work, such as THE BRADY BUNCH® or NEWSWEEK®, however, can be protected as a trademark or service mark.

(See Figure 2–3 for further examples of protectable matter.)

Protectable Matter	Example
Words	REAL TIME (for wearing apparel)
Letters	WROC (for radio broadcasting services)
Numbers	1054 (for cleaning products)
Foreign terms	CHAT ROUGE (for computer programs)
Shapes	Distinctive shape for coffee filters (as long as not functional)
Trade dress	Overall commercial impression of packaging, label, text, and graphics (for a can of chili)
Color	Blue (for container for wine, so long as not functional)
Fragrance	Floral fragrance for bookmarks
Design	CHECKERBOARD DESIGN (for food products)
Literary title	PARENT'S PARADE (for serialized magazine)

FIGURE 2–3
Protectable Matter

EXCLUSIONS FROM TRADEMARK PROTECTION

Not every word, design, or slogan can function as a trademark. It has already been noted that generic matter cannot be registered and that merely descriptive marks cannot be registered unless secondary meaning is shown. There are several additional bars to registration found in the Lanham Act.

Disparaging or Falsely Suggestive Marks

The Lanham Act (15 U.S.C. § 1052 (a)) forbids registration of a mark that disparages or falsely suggests an association with persons, institutions, beliefs, or national symbols. Thus, WESTPOINT for guns was held to falsely suggest a connection with the U.S. Military Academy and was refused registration. *In re Cotter & Co.*, 228 U.S.P.Q. 202 (T.T.A.B. 1985). In April 1999, the TTAB canceled seven trademark registrations owned by the NFL football team the Washington Redskins on the basis the marks disparage Native Americans. The ruling does not prevent the team from using the marks, but it could jeopardize the revenue generated by licensing the marks because the team can no longer sue for infringement of the marks under the Lanham Act, thus severely limiting its ability to preclude knockoff or counterfeited items bearing the team's logos. The team plans to appeal the ruling.

Insignia

Flags, coats of arms, and other insignia of the United States or any foreign nation cannot be registered.

Immoral or Scandalous Matter

Immoral or scandalous matter cannot be registered. For example, a graphic depiction of a dog defecating that was used on clothing was refused registration as scandalous. The mark was also found to disparage Greyhound Corporation because the dog was reminiscent of the Greyhound dog used by the company in connection with its transportation services. *Greyhound Corp. v. Both Worlds, Inc.*, 6 U.S.P.Q.2d 1635 (T.T.A.B. 1988).

Names and Portraits of Living Persons

A mark comprising a name, portrait, or signature of a particular living person cannot be used without his or her consent, and a name, signature, or portrait of a deceased U.S. president cannot be used without his widow's consent. Thus, the portrait of the actor Paul Newman that appears on various food products must be with his consent.

Deceptive Matter

Marks comprising deceptive matter cannot be registered. Thus, SILKEASE was held deceptive when applied to clothing not made of silk in *In re Shapely, Inc.*, 231 U.S.P.Q. 72 (T.T.A.B. 1986), and CEDAR RIDGE was held deceptive for hardboard siding not made of cedar. *Evans Products Co. v. Boise Cascade Corp.*, 218 U.S.P.Q. 160 (T.T.A.B. 1983).

Mere Surnames

A mark that is primarily merely a surname cannot be registered without proof of secondary meaning. Thus, names such as "Smith" or "Higgins" cannot be registered, while a name such as "King" would be registrable inasmuch as it has a significance or meaning other than as a surname. A review of PTO records discloses that McDonald's Corporation's numerous registrations for its MCDONALD'S® marks routinely claim that the mark has acquired distinctiveness through its continuous and exclusive use. The PTO will examine telephone books to determine if a mark is primarily merely a surname. If the surname is combined with additional matter, such as other words or a design, it may be registrable. Thus, HUTCHINSON TECHNOLOGY® was registrable. *In re Hutchinson Technology, Inc.*, 852 F.2d 552 (Fed. Cir. 1988).

Geographical Terms

Marks including geographic terms, such as references to countries, states, towns, streets, and rivers, present special problems. When a geographic term is used to describe the place goods or services come from, it is considered descriptive and unregistrable. Thus, THE NASHVILLE NETWORK was held primarily geographically descriptive of various entertainment services where the applicant was located in Nashville and many of the programs it distributed were produced in Nashville. *In re Opryland USA, Inc.*, 1 U.S.P.Q.2d 1409 (T.T.A.B. 1986). Such marks cannot be registered without proof of secondary meaning. On the other hand, NANTUCKET® for shirts was allowed because the shirts offered under the mark did not come from Nantucket and consumers would not immediately associate Nantucket with shirts. *In re Nantucket, Inc.*, 677 F.2d 95 (C.C.P.A. 1982). Similarly, use of DUTCHBOY® for paint was held acceptable because of its arbitrariness: there is no known connection between paint and Holland. *National Lead Co. v. Wolfe*, 223 F.2d 195 (9th Cir. 1955).

As a result of NAFTA, the Lanham Act now prohibits registration of a geographically deceptively misdescriptive mark even if the mark has secondary meaning. Thus, a mark such as PERRY NEW YORK for clothing not originating in New York would not be registrable because consumers, upon encountering the mark, would be deceived into reacting favorably to it due to the renown of New York in the clothing and fashion industry.

Additionally, under GATT, the Lanham Act was amended to bar registration of any geographic mark for wines and spirits not originating from the place identified in the mark. Thus, the word *Bordeaux* can only be used in connection with goods from the Bordeaux region of France. Finally, some geographic terms have become generic and can never be registered, for example, *French fries*, *Swiss cheese*, and *Bermuda shorts*.

Descriptive and Confusingly Similar Marks

Marks that are merely descriptive or are confusingly similar to those used by a senior user are not registrable. Refusals by the PTO to register descriptive or confusingly similar marks will be discussed in detail in Chapter 4.

American Red Cross

FIGURE 2-4
Matter Excluded from Protection

Nonprotectable Matter	Basis for PTO Refusal
Design of international "slash" symbol placed over a portrait of President Lincoln (for place mats)	Mark would disparage or bring a person into contempt or disrepute
FLAG OF ITALY (for pasta)	Insignia of a foreign nation
Graphic pictures of nude figures (for wearing apparel)	Immoral or scandalous matter
Photograph of Brad Pitt (for salad dressing) (unconsented)	Unconsented use of living person's portrait
PETERSON (for hiking boots)	Primarily merely a surname
LEATHERETTE (for gloves made of vinyl)	Deceptive
PARISIAN EROS (for perfume not from Paris)	Geographically deceptively misdescriptive
BREADSPREAD (for margarine) (without proof of secondary meaning)	Merely descriptive
NIKEE (for athletic gear)	Confusingly similar to a registered mark
SPIROS' OLYMPIC RESTAURANT (& DESIGN OF FIVE RINGS)	Statutorily protected matter
SHAPE OF PIANO (needed for acoustical reasons)	Functional

Functional Devices

A mark or device that is as a whole functional cannot be registered as a trademark because it would deprive others of the right to share a needed device. Thus, protection might be refused for the shape of a matchbook cover when the shape functions to make the product useful. Because competitors would need to use the same shape of cover for their products to be effective, one party cannot exclusively appropriate it.

Statutorily Protected Marks

Finally, certain marks are protected by federal statute from use or confusingly similar use by another, such as the Red Cross logo and the Olympic rings and associated wording.

(See Figure 2-4 for a table of matter that is excluded from trademark protection.)

UNITED STATES PATENT AND TRADEMARK OFFICE

The government agency responsible for reviewing trademark applications and issuing registrations is the U.S. Patent and Trademark Office (PTO). The official address for many communications sent to the PTO is Commissioner of Patents and Trademarks, Washington, DC 20231. The physical location of the trademark section of the PTO, however, is not in Washington, DC but is 2900 Crystal Drive, Arlington, Virginia 22202. The PTO is currently scattered

Assignment Office	(703) 308-9723
Certified Copies	(703) 308-9726
Director's Office	(703) 308-9000
Fees	(703) 308-HELP
File by Fax	(703) 308-9096, 9097, or 9098
Finance Office	(703) 308-9810
Forms	(703) 308-9000
Intent-to-Use Branch	(703) 308-9550
Office of Assistant Commissioner of PTO	(703) 308-9100
Oppositions	(703) 308-9300
Postregistration Information	(703) 308-9550
Search Library	(703) 308-9800
Trademark Assistance Center	(703) 308-9000
Trademark Manual of Examining Procedure	(703) 308-9000
Trademark Trial and Appeal Board	(703) 308-9300
TRAM (Trademark Reporting and Monitoring) Status Line	(703) 305-8747

FIGURE 2–5
Frequently Called PTO
Telephone Numbers
(Trademark Matters)

throughout sixteen buildings spread over one mile. The PTO maintains an excellent web site at http://www.uspto.gov, offering general information, updates on new issues, forms for downloading, a database of more than one million registered and pending trademarks, statistics, lists of PTO fees, and a wide variety of other valuable information. (See Figure 2–5 for a list of frequently called PTO telephone numbers.)

The trademark section of the PTO is divided into a variety of different departments, such as one handling assignments, one dealing with postregistration matters, and one dealing with intent-to-use applications. Due to the spread of computer and communications technology throughout the world, the workload of the PTO continues to increase. For example, the number of U.S. trademark applications in 1994 grew by 13 percent over the 1993 figures. In 1997 alone, the PTO registered 112,509 trademarks. Additionally, reflecting the globalization of brand names and the world economy, the number of non-U.S. applicants continues to increase.

ROLE OF INTELLECTUAL PROPERTY PROFESSIONAL

The role of IP professionals prior to searching and application for registration is generally limited to research, particularly research regarding whether the mark satisfies the requirements of the Lanham Act for registrability. Each element of the mark should be examined to determine whether it is descriptive, disparaging, comprises merely a surname, includes a living person's surname without consent, and so forth. Design elements of marks should also be considered to ensure the design feature is a separate and distinct portion of the mark, rather than mere background. Additionally, some preliminary discussions should take place with the mark's owner to determine whether federal registration is permissible or whether the owner will be limited to state trademark registration because the mark is not (and will not be) used in interstate commerce.

CHAPTER SUMMARY

Trademarks play a valuable role in our economy. They serve to distinguish one merchant's goods or services from those of another and provide assurances of quality and consistency to consumers. There are four different types of marks: trademarks (used for goods); service marks (used for services); certification marks (used to certify a quality of a good or service); and collective marks (used to show membership in an association). Rights to marks are acquired through use. There is no need to file an application for federal registration of a mark with the PTO to acquire or maintain rights to a mark, although registration does offer significant advantages to a trademark owner.

Not all words, letters, and symbols are protectable. Generic words cannot be trademarked, and descriptive marks can be trademarked only upon proof of secondary meaning. Suggestive, arbitrary, and coined marks are all registrable without proof of secondary meaning. Certain types of marks are excluded from federal protection, such as scandalous marks, deceptive marks, and geographically deceptively misdescriptive marks.

DISCUSSION QUESTIONS

1. Classify the following marks as trademarks or service marks: TACO BELL®, MR. CLEAN®, SPAGHETTIO-Os®, and SYLVAN LEARNING CENTER®.
2. Robert Talbott, the owner of "Talbott's Clothiers," a small shop in San Jose, California, would like to protect his business name. Discuss the appropriate methods he may use.
3. Jane Hollis, the proprietor of a catering business located in Reno, Nevada, wishes to secure federal registration for her catering services. She mails a flyer advertising her catering services to a friend in Utah. Is this use sufficient to support an application for federal registration?
4. Assume Jane Hollis's business has grown from its Nevada inception and she now has a branch office in Lake Tahoe, California. Should Hollis file a state registration or a federal registration to protect her mark? Discuss.
5. Assume Hollis first used her mark in Reno in 1995, but did not file an application for federal registration. A third party files a trademark application with the PTO for a similar mark, alleging a date of first use in interstate commerce of 1996. Discuss the rights of each party.
6. Discuss whether a person could likely obtain a trademark registration for the following marks for the goods or services indicated, and discuss the objections, if any, that the PTO would make.

Mark	Goods or Services
CHOCO-CHIPS	Chocolate morsels or chips
PASSIONATE NIGHTS	Perfume
POLLO	Chicken
PRIMUS	Banking services
HD-400	A luxury car
CRACKERZ	Crackers
ECONOMY AIR LINES	Air transportation
HOT SPOT	Magazine

7. Could the design of a lampshade be trademarked if the design is the best and most effective way of dispersing light? Discuss.
8. Discuss whether the mark UNITED STATES CREDIT SERVICES could be registered.
9. Could the mark JIMMY CARTER PEANUTS be registered? Discuss.

Trademark Selection and Searching

CHAPTER OVERVIEW

As discussed in Chapter 2, not every word, slogan, or design can be protected as a trademark or service mark. Therefore, great care must be given to selecting a mark to identify one's goods or services. Once a mark is selected, a trademark availability search should be conducted to determine if the mark is available for registration. Searches are conducted of the PTO records, state trademark records, business directories, journals, telephone books, and Internet uses to determine whether a proposed mark may conflict with a mark already in use. Although no search can guarantee that a mark will be accepted by the PTO for registration, a search allows a trademark owner to anticipate problems that may arise in the registration process and provides a snapshot of other marks in the marketplace.

SELECTING AND EVALUATING A MARK

Selecting a Mark

Selection of a mark occurs in a variety of ways. Some companies hold contests and encourage employees to create a mark for a new product line or service. Other companies engage sophisticated research firms that will conduct surveys and create a mark and a **logo** or design for the company. There are name creation software programs that help individuals and companies create marks. Once the mark is selected, it must be screened and evaluated for use and registrability. Failure to exercise this due diligence might result in the expenditure of time and money in advertising, using, and applying for a mark that is rejected for registration by the PTO or, in the worst case scenario, might subject the owner to damages for trademark infringement.

Reviewing a Proposed Mark

Once a mark is selected, it should be carefully scrutinized to ensure that it will not be excluded from protection under the Lanham Act. Considerations

logo: A design used as a trademark

include whether the mark contains scandalous material, whether consent from a living person will be required, whether the mark is generic, and whether the mark is descriptive of some feature of the goods and services offered under the mark. If the mark includes foreign terms, these should be translated to ensure they are not scandalous or merely descriptive. Many law firms specializing in trademark work use a questionnaire form or data sheet to gather basic information from clients about their marks and to aid in determining registrability (see Figure 3–1 for an example).

THE TRADEMARK SEARCH

Once a proposed mark has been selected, a trademark search should be conducted to ensure that the proposed mark is not confusingly similar to a mark that is the subject of a registration or pending application at the PTO or that is in use on a common law basis.

In addition to disclosing potential conflicting marks, a search will provide some indication of the relative weakness or strength of the mark. If there are numerous marks including words similar to the proposed mark for the same or related goods, the field is said to be "crowded," and the mark, while it may achieve registration, may be weak and entitled to a narrower scope of protection than a strong, unique, and distinctive mark. A review of other marks also enables the IP team to anticipate some of the problems that may arise during the registration process and possible objections the PTO may have to the application.

Although there is no statutory requirement to conduct a search to determine whether a mark is available for use and registration, two recent cases have discussed whether trademark users have a duty to conduct searches and have suggested that conducting only a limited search may result in a finding of bad faith or willful infringement in certain circumstances, particularly when the trademark user has been counseled to conduct a comprehensive search. *See International Star Class Yacht Racing Ass'n v. Tommy Hilfiger U.S.A., Inc.,* 146 F.3d 66 (2d Cir. 1997), and *Securacomm Consulting Inc. v. Securacom Inc.,* No. 95-cv-05393 (D.N.J. Jan. 20, 1999).

Scope of Search

There are a variety of sources that can be reviewed to locate potentially conflicting marks. Because there are literally hundreds of thousands of marks registered or applied for at the PTO, and thousands of journals, trade magazines, directories, telephone books, Internet sources, state records, and state trademark registrations that might contain other marks or business names, a computer-assisted or online search is the most effective method of searching. Moreover, an online search can be constructed to search only for similar marks used in connection with similar goods and services. Thus, if the client wishes to use MARTIPPE for fountain pens, there is little to be gained from looking for similar marks used in connection with orange juice inasmuch as consumers would not likely be confused by the coexistence of two similar marks for such dissimilar products.

Both LEXIS® and WESTLAW®, the computer-assisted legal research systems, offer access to numerous databases that may point out conflicts. One of

FIGURE 3–1
Trademark Data Sheet
(U.S. Applicant)

Please provide the following information to enable us to prepare and file an application for registration of your mark with the United States Patent and Trademark Office (PTO).

1. Describe the mark.
   a. Words: _____

   b. Logo: _____ [describe and attach sample logo] _____

   c. Are the words "stylized" (for example, should they be displayed in any particular manner, script, or typeface or is standard printing acceptable)?
   _____

2. Describe the Applicant.
   a. Full name: _____

   b. Full address: _____

   c. Type of legal entity (corporation, partnership, etc.) _____

   d. Organized under the laws of the state of _____

   e. Name of authorized person who will sign the application and other documents and his/her title: _____

3. Describe with particularity all of the goods and/or services that are or will be offered under the mark or for which protection is being sought.
   _____

4. Consult your records and state, with respect to use of the mark by you (or any predecessor) on or in connection with any of the above-described goods or services:
   a. Has the mark been used in intrastate sales or advertising? If so, give date of first use anywhere.
   _____

   b. Has the mark been used in interstate commerce within the United States? For example, has there been a transaction with an out-of-state customer or has media advertising the goods or services offered under the mark been conducted across state lines? If so, give the date the mark was first used in interstate commerce in the United States (or in foreign commerce between a foreign country and the United States). Note that use of the mark in advertising preparatory to opening a business is not sufficient.
   _____

   c. Is there a bona fide intent to use the mark in the United States if it has not yet been used in the United States? _____

5. Provide information as to how the mark is actually used (if it is in use).
   a. Newspaper or other media advertising: ____ Yes ____ No

   b. Signs or store displays: ____ Yes ____ No

   c. Direct mail, such as brochures: ____ Yes ____ No

   d. Labels, tags, packaging: ____ Yes ____ No

   e. Other (describe): _____

6. If the mark is in use, please provide at least five original specimens showing the mark as it is actually used in connection with the sale or advertising of the goods or services. If the mark is used in connection with goods, then labels, tags, boxes, or other packaging are acceptable *as long as they show the mark.* If the mark is used in connection with services, then brochures and other advertising materials are likely acceptable *as long as they show the mark.* If the specimens are bulky, you may provide photographs of the specimens as long as the mark is clear and legible in the photos.

the best known databases is TRADEMARKSCAN®, a product of Thomson & Thomson. TRADEMARKSCAN (federal) contains information on active registered trademarks and service marks as well as applications filed at the PTO (for active marks since 1884 and inactive marks since 1984), while TRADEMARKSCAN (state) provides similar information on marks registered with the secretaries of state of all fifty states, the District of Columbia, and Puerto Rico. Other online databases include journals, magazines, and periodicals. Most of the databases are also offered on CD-ROM format, allowing IP practitioners to purchase discs and conduct their own searches. The discs are then periodically replaced and updated.

Using the purchased CD-ROM discs, many practitioners conduct an in-house preliminary search of the records of the PTO to determine if there is a potentially conflicting mark that is the subject of a federal registration or application. If the results of this preliminary search show the mark may be available, a full or comprehensive search is then conducted to review the various journals, press releases, Internet domain name directories, state records, and telephone books for other names and marks. The preliminary search is often called a **knockout search** because its primary purpose is to eliminate or knockout identical or nearly identical marks. Often paralegals conduct the knockout search and provide an initial review of the marks revealed. The results are communicated to the client along with recommendations for the next step to take. If a mark is intended to be used only for a short time, perhaps during a limited promotional campaign, a knockout search may be sufficient by itself.

Alternatively, for those located near Washington, DC, the PTO maintains a Trademark Search Room in Arlington, Virginia, that contains a copy of every registered United States trademark. The Search Room is open to the public every weekday. For information, call (703) 308-9800. Additionally, more than eighty libraries throughout the United States (mostly in major cities) are designated as **Patent and Trademark Depository Libraries.** These libraries receive a wealth of information from the PTO, and trademark searching can be done at these libraries. See the PTO web site at http://www.uspto.gov for a list of the Patent and Trademark Depository Libraries.

Since August 1998, the PTO has offered a trademark database at its web site that includes the text of more than one million trademarks. Follow the instructions presented to access the "USPTO Web Trademark Database." Marks can be searched by name, registration or application number, or by Boolean searches. Although a search of this newly created database can provide a quick answer to very basic questions about availability of marks (much the same way a knockout search does), it is no substitute for a thorough search of other possible uses of marks, such as those used as Internet domain names, unregistered marks, and those registered with individual states. Moreover, trademark applications are not entered into the database until one to two months after filing, resulting in incomplete data.

The most complete analysis of potentially conflicting marks is provided by professional trademark search firms. These companies review the records of the PTO for existing registrations, pending applications, and state trademark registrations, and they perform a "common law" search of various journals, directories, press releases, and Internet references to locate unregistered names and marks. Such a search is called a **comprehensive** or *full* **search.** Because

knockout search: A preliminary search of PTO records designed to disclose identical or nearly identical marks; often followed by a *comprehensive search*

Patent and Trademark Depository Libraries: Public libraries throughout the United States that maintain selected trademark and patent records

comprehensive search: A search of trademarks registered or applied for at the PTO, state trademark registrations, and common law sources such as periodicals, directories, and the Internet there are literally thousands of journals, directories, telephone books, and other publications in which names and marks may appear, these professional search firms can save considerable time and money and, more importantly, provide a more thorough search than that which an individual can conduct on his or her own. Some of these companies advertise that their databases include more than one million marks that can be checked against the client's mark for potential conflicts. These companies will check for identical and phonetically equivalent marks for similar goods and services and will also check for foreign equivalents. Thus, a search for KARCOAT will disclose marks such as CARCOAT and CARKOAT. Marks with design elements also must be searched; these searches are usually a bit more expensive than searches for marks comprising solely words due to the time-consuming task of comparing other design marks to the proposed mark.

Costs for full availability searches can run from $350 for results available in five business days to approximately $700 for same-day searches. These costs do not reflect an attorney's time in evaluating the results and providing a report to a client, but rather reflect only the costs of obtaining a report that discloses potentially conflicting marks. Some companies will send the report by express mail or other overnight service or may send it via facsimile (although due to the voluminous nature of many reports, this is not a common practice). Another more recent alternative is that the report may be sent to an office via electronic transmission or e-mail. The search company will post the report to a bulletin board server, and the law firm then retrieves the search. The report is typically divided into three sections: results gained from reviewing PTO registrations and applications; results gained from reviewing state trademark records; and the common law results (references to marks in magazines, telephone directories, Internet domain names, and so forth).

Most of the professional searching firms will tailor the search to specific requirements, so that they will conduct only common law searches, or only an Internet domain name search, an international search, and so forth. Intellectual property practitioners who engage the professional searchers on a routine basis often obtain volume discounts.

A client interested in protecting his or her mark in foreign countries should conduct a search of the records of each country in which an application will be filed. Although the U.S. search firms can conduct such searches, interpreting the results and predicting how a foreign trademark office would view the application is very difficult for U.S. practitioners who typically are not experts in foreign trademark law. Therefore, most law firms that do trademark work have established relationships with their counterparts in foreign countries and rely upon these **associates** to conduct a search and report the results. The foreign associate then files the trademark application and prosecutes it, while the U.S. attorney generally supervises the process and communicates the progress of the application to the client.

Among the better known professional search companies are the following:

Corsearch, Inc.
16 W. 22nd Street, 8th Floor
New York, NY 10010
(800) 732-7241
http://www.corsearch.com

Thomson & Thomson
500 Victory Road
North Quincy, MA 02171
(800) 692-8833

associates: Attorneys in foreign law firms who work with attorneys in U.S. firms regarding intellectual property matters

CCH Trademark Research
Corporation
300 Park Avenue S.
New York, NY 10010
(800) 872-6275

Government Liaison Services, Inc.
3030 Clarendon Boulevard
Arlington, VA 22201
(800) 642-6564

Evaluating Trademark Search Reports

Once the results of the search have been obtained, they must be evaluated so that the fundamental question whether the mark is available for use and registration can be answered. The evaluation begins with an analysis of each mark or name provided in the report and a comparison of it to the proposed mark to determine whether they are confusingly similar. This analysis requires one to take into account the overall commercial impressions presented by the marks; their similarity in regard to sight, sound, and meaning; the relative strength or weakness of the marks based on their descriptiveness or suggestiveness; and the goods or services offered under each mark.

A typical search entry will appear as follows:

Mark	DURATIP
Reg. No.	1,718,980
Reg. Date	Nov. 30, 1997
Filing Date	Aug. 1, 1996
Date of first use	July 15, 1996
Goods	Stationery and paper
I.C.	16
Owner	Murphy & Grady, Inc.
	1010 Second Avenue
	San Diego, CA 92010

If a client wishes to use the mark MARTIPPE in connection with fountain pens, the existence of DURATIP for stationery and paper may present a conflict. The DURATIP mark is similar in appearance to MARTIPPE (with only a few letters being different), and paper and stationery may be viewed as related to fountain pens. Consumers who encounter MARTIPPE may believe it is somehow connected with the DURATIP mark or that the goods offered under MARTIPPE are sponsored by the makers of the goods offered under the DURATIP mark. On the other hand, if there are numerous other marks including *dura, mar, tip,* and other similar prefixes and suffixes for related goods, this may be a sign that the marks are weak and thus they have been allowed to coexist. If numerous similar marks for similar goods or services coexist, it is less likely that a mark will be refused or attacked.

In many instances, paralegals provide the initial review of the search report and flag potential problems or "hits" for an attorney's later evaluation. Paralegals also play a key role in investigating some of the sources revealed in the report. By contacting the owner of a mark, it may be discovered the mark is no longer in use or that the company has ceased doing business. Marketing materials can be reviewed to determine the actual manner in which the DURATIP mark is used. The file for a conflicting mark can be obtained from the PTO to determine what objections were made to the application by the PTO and how the owner overcame them.

Reporting the Results to the Client

A formal written report will then be prepared for the client. The letter, often called an "availability" or "clearance" report, typically includes the following elements:

- a description of the mark that was the subject of the search;
- a description of the method of the search, the databases that were checked, and the dates applicable to the search parameters;
- a section describing limitations on the search report, such as a disclaimer or statement that the results of the search cannot be guaranteed and that, due to errors in cataloging records and files, some marks might not be disclosed in the search;
- a discussion of potentially conflicting marks;
- the opinion in regard to availability of the mark for use and registration; and
- recommendations for further action or investigation, if needed.

The heart of the report is the attorney's opinion in regard to whether the mark is available. Because this is the portion of the report in which the client is most interested, the opinion should be stated clearly and should outline any risks in using the mark. The attorney may state, "We believe the MARTIPPE mark is distinguishable from the references disclosed in the report and may be available for use and registration in connection with fountain pens," or, conversely, may state, "Based on our review of the results, we do not recommend that you use or apply for registration of MARTIPPE." The attorney may even go so far as to inform the client that use of MARTIPPE could subject the client to risk of an infringement action.

Providing the opinion is often a difficult and time-consuming task. Clients are often in a rush to launch a new product or service and are eager to adopt a mark. They may have already begun an advertising campaign. There may be significant pressure from the client to obtain a favorable response. All of these factors, coupled with the uncertainty inherent in subjective comparisons of marks, makes trademark opinion work difficult and stressful.

Investigating and Resolving Conflicts

The report of the trademark search results may disclose several potential conflicts, and the IP team may seek the client's permission to investigate these conflicts further. Alternatively, some investigation may be done before the report is provided to the client. If the client is wedded to a mark that may be barred by another mark, several options can be explored.

- Further investigation can be conducted using other databases, such as Dun & Bradstreet, to determine the amount of business conducted by the potential opposer. Private trademark investigators may be hired to go to the place of business and see how the mark is being used, by obtaining actual paper and stationery displaying the DURATIP mark. A search can be conducted of records at the PTO or through *Shepard's Citations* to determine if the owner of DURATIP has aggressively protected its mark through litigation.
- The owner of DURATIP can be contacted to obtain consent to use and register the client's mark. The client may pay some money for this

ROLE OF INTELLECTUAL PROPERTY PROFESSIONAL

Intellectual property professionals play a significant role in the clearance and prosecution stage of a trademark application. Although legal advice can be given only by attorneys, there are numerous activities in which other IP professionals will be involved:

- obtaining information about the client's proposed mark;
- conducting a preliminary in-house knockout search to eliminate bars to registration;
- ordering and reviewing a comprehensive search;
- consulting with the IP team regarding potentially conflicting marks disclosed in searches; and
- conducting investigations of potentially conflicting marks.

consent or may agree to display the mark only in connection with specified goods or in a certain typeface and format.
- The client might seek to obtain a license to use a mark from another or might seek to acquire the other mark through an assignment for a certain sum of money.

If none of these alternatives are fruitful, the client might revise its mark, in which case a new search must be conducted for the new mark.

CHAPTER SUMMARY

Once a client has selected a mark, the mark should be subjected to a search to ensure that no other party has secured rights to the mark or to a confusingly similar mark or name. Failure to conduct a search or failure to conduct an adequate search may be characterized by a court as carelessness and weigh in favor of a party who alleges infringement. Reviewing search results and reporting results to clients is difficult and time-consuming. Often follow-up investigation is needed to determine whether potentially conflicting marks remain in use or are in use with related goods or services. Conducting a search, however, will result in a snapshot of the marketplace, providing information about competitors, conflicting marks, and how the PTO has handled applications for similar marks.

If the search "clears" the mark, an application should be filed with the PTO for registration of the mark if the mark has been used in interstate commerce or the client has a bona fide intent to use the mark in interstate commerce.

DISCUSSION QUESTIONS

1. Give some advantages of conducting a comprehensive search.
2. What is a knockout search?
3. If a client intends to launch a nationwide campaign for GLOBALTRAX (& GLOBE DESIGN) for its accounting services, what type of search should be conducted?
4. Assume the client intends to use GLOBALTRAX (& GLOBE DESIGN) for a one-month special promotional campaign. What type of search should be conducted?
5. If the search for GLOBALTRAX (& GLOBE DESIGN) discloses GLOBALTRUCKS for undisclosed goods or services, what should be done?

The Trademark Registration Process

From the discussion in Chapter 2, it is clear that federal registration of a mark offers a trademark owner distinct advantages over mere reliance on common law or state trademark rights. There are two primary paths to registration: a use-based application (alleging use in interstate commerce) and an intent-to-use application (alleging a bona fide intent to so use the mark in the future). Both types of applications share many common features and progress through the registration process in a fairly similar fashion. The process for federal registration of a mark can be expensive and can take as long as twelve to eighteen months, even if there are no significant problems or delays.

PREPARING THE APPLICATION

Introduction

Once a mark has been selected and evaluated for use and registrability, an application for federal registration of the mark should be prepared and filed. The written application comprises a request for registration, the name of the applicant, the citizenship of the applicant, the address of the applicant, an identification of the goods and/or services offered under the mark, a drawing of the mark, a verification signed by the applicant or agent or attorney, and, usually, the basis for filing the application, namely, whether the application is based on actual use of the mark or the owner's intent to use the mark. The process of moving an application through the PTO is called **prosecution.**

The application must be in English. Forms for applications are provided by the PTO (see Appendix D, Form 1, Trademark Application). If the form provided by the PTO is not used, the application should be on lettersize (namely 8½ inches by 11 inches) paper, typewritten, double-spaced, with margins of at least 1½ inches at the left and top of the pages. The application should be written on only one side of the paper.

prosecution: The process of moving a trademark or patent application through the PTO

The PTO prefers but does not generally require that the documents submitted be originals. Photocopies may be submitted (except for foreign registrations and certain other special documents for which certified copies are required). Thus, if a client signs an application and returns it to your office by facsimile (fax), you may photocopy the signature page, attach it to the application, and file it with the PTO, as long as the signature is legible.

Under a pilot program, the PTO permits the filing by fax of certain papers and documents; however, trademark applications are not acceptable by fax. They must be hand-delivered to the PTO, filed by mail, or submitted electronically. Under the PTO's new Trademark Electronic Application System (TEAS), one can fill out a trademark application form electronically and submit it directly to the PTO over the Internet, paying by credit card or PTO deposit account. The online application forms are located at http://www.uspto.gov/teas/e-teas/index.html.

All of the requirements relating to the filing and prosecution of trademark applications are governed by the ***Trademark Manual of Examining Procedure*** (TMEP), an excellent source of materials with numerous examples and case citations. Most trademark practitioners keep the TMEP handy at all times. The TMEP is also available on the PTO web site.

The Applicant

An application to register a mark can be made only by the owner of the mark or, in the case of an intent-to-use application, by a person who has a bona fide intent to use the mark in commerce. Applicants may be natural persons or business entities such as corporations, partnerships, associations, unions, or other organizations. Government entities such as nations, states, municipalities, and other governmental bodies also can apply to register marks that they own. For example, the U.S. Army Recruiting Department is the owner of the registered mark BE ALL YOU CAN BE.®

The applicant's name must be in correct legal form. Thus, a corporation that owns a mark should be identified in the application by the name set forth in its articles of incorporation. Clients often abbreviate their corporate names or make mistakes in the punctuation of their corporate names. Because the certificate of registration will issue in the name of the applicant as set forth in the application, errors in an owner's name will result in errors in the certificate of registration. Therefore, the secretary of state in the state in which the corporation was incorporated may need to be contacted to verify the precise spelling and punctuation of the corporate name.

If the application is a person or business that conducts business under a fictitious business name, for example, "Sam Smith, doing business as 'Sam's Cheesecake Factory,'" the application should include the assumed name.

If the applicant is a partnership, for example, "Balboa Gardens Partners," the application should be made by the partnership itself and should identify the state in which the partnership was organized.

Identifying an applicant as a "company" will result in rejection of an application because the term *company* does not have a specific meaning; the applicant must be expressly identified as a corporation, a partnership, a joint venture, a limited liability company, and so forth.

A trademark or service mark application is usually filed in the name of one party. Historically, the PTO has been reluctant to accept applications by joint

Trademark Manual of Examining Procedure: A PTO publication containing rules and regulations related to the prosecution and registration of trademarks

> Applicant hereby appoints B. Parker Livingston, Jr., Sam N. Ibrahim, Holly M. Ford, and the firm of Livingston, Gregory, & Hartson, all members of the Bar of the District of Columbia, and all having an address at Suite 801, 655 15th Street NW, Washington, DC 20006, to prosecute this application to register and transact all business in the U.S. Patent and Trademark Office in connection therewith, to receive the Certificate of Registration, and to represent it in all proceedings affecting the mark that may arise in the U.S. Patent and Trademark Office after the registration has been granted.

FIGURE 4–1
Power of Attorney

applicants because ownership by more than one party seems to be contrary to the function of a trademark to identify a single commercial source. Although an application by joint applicants is acceptable in some instances, for example, by a husband and wife who share joint ownership of a mark, an examining attorney at the PTO will carefully scrutinize applications by joint applicants to ensure that both parties own the mark in common. A joint venture or a partnership cannot be joint applicants. A joint venture or a partnership is a single business applicant that owns a mark.

The application must specify the applicant's citizenship. For an individual, it is sufficient to state that the applicant is a citizen of the United States, France, or some other country. For a corporation or other business entity, the state or country of organization must be identified. Thus, a statement that the applicant is "ABC Inc., a corporation organized under the laws of the State of California" is acceptable.

The written application must provide the address of the applicant, including the zip code number. An individual may identify a residence or business address. Corporations and other business entities should set forth their business addresses.

Representation by Attorney

An owner of a trademark may file and prosecute his or her own application for registration of the mark or may be represented by an attorney or other individual licensed to practice before the PTO. Typically, an application is filed by an attorney familiar with trademark practice and usually includes a power of attorney (see Figure 4–1), designating a named attorney to represent the applicant regarding all matters related to the mark. In such a case, the PTO will communicate only with the designated representative.

Identification of Goods or Services

The application must identify the goods and/or services offered or to be offered under the mark that is the subject of the application. Careful consideration must be given to drafting this part of the application. Goods and services are categorized by the PTO into forty-two separate classes, called **International Classes** because many other nations use this same classification system established by WIPO. Until 1973, the PTO used a different classification scheme, called the United States Classification Scheme. Each class requires a filing fee of $245. Thus, an application for the mark RALPH LAUREN® to be used in connection with paint in International Class (I.C.) 1,

International Classes: The categorization of goods and services into 42 separate topics for trademark purposes; class(es) of goods or services must be identified in a trademark application

cosmetics in I.C. 3, stationery in I.C. 16, beverage glasses in I.C. 21, and clothing in I.C. 25, for a total of five classes, would require a filing fee of $1,225. A registered mark only receives protection for those classes in which it is registered. Thus, if in an effort to save $245, the application for the RALPH LAUREN mark does not include drinking glasses in I.C. 21, there will be no registration for the mark for those goods. Preparing the application requires careful analysis of all of the goods/services for which the mark will be used to ensure that the mark receives all the protection it needs. A detailed listing of the international classes with numerous examples is found in chapter 1400 of TMEP, available on the PTO's web site. (See Figure 4–2 for a list of the international classes and explanation of the goods/services in each class.)

FIGURE 4–2
List of International Classes

International Class	Goods/Services	Explanatory Note
1	Chemicals	Includes chemicals used in industry, science, photography, manures, adhesives used in industry
2	Paints	Includes paints, varnishes, lacquers, raw natural resins
3	Cosmetics and cleaning preparations	Includes bleaching preparations and other substances for laundry use, soaps, cleaning preparations, perfumery, cosmetics, hair lotions
4	Lubricants and fuels	Includes industrial oils and greases, lubricants, candles, and wicks
5	Pharmaceuticals	Includes pharmaceuticals and other preparations for medical use, disinfectants, materials for dressings, food for babies
6	Metal goods	Common metals and their alloys, metal building materials, pipes and tubes made of metal, safes
7	Machinery	Machines and machine tools, motors and engines (except for land vehicles), agricultural implements
8	Hand tools	Hand tools, cutlery, sidearms, razors
9	Electrical and scientific apparatus	Scientific , nautical, surveying, electrical, photographic, optical apparatus and instruments, cash registers, apparatus for recording, transmission,

FIGURE 4–2
List of International
Classes (continued)

International Class	Goods/Services	Explanatory Note
		or reproduction of sound or images, magnetic data carriers, recording discs, calculating machines, data processing equipment and computers, computer games; computer software
10	Medical apparatus	Surgical, medical, dental, and veterinary apparatus and instruments, suture materials
11	Environmental control apparatus	Apparatus for lighting, heating, steam generating, cooking, drying, refrigerating, water supply, and sanitary purposes
12	Vehicles	Vehicles, apparatus for locomotion by land, air, or water, engines for land vehicles
13	Firearms	Firearms, ammunition and projectiles, explosives, fireworks
14	Jewelry	Precious metals and goods in precious metals, jewelry, precious stones, clocks, watches, chronometric instruments
15	Musical instruments	Includes mechanical pianos, musical boxes, electrical and electronic music instruments
16	Paper goods and printed matter	Paper, cardboard, printed matter, photographs, stationery, artists' materials, typewriters and office requisites (except furniture), instructional and teaching material, playing cards, magazines, books
17	Rubber goods	Rubber, gum, plastics in extruded form, packing material, flexible pipes (not of metal)
18	Leather goods	Leather and imitations of leather, trunks, traveling cases, umbrellas, whips, saddlery
19	Nonmetallic building materials	Building materials (nonmetallic), asphalt, pitch,

FIGURE 4–2
List of International
Classes (continued)

International Class	Goods/Services	Explanatory Note
		nonmetallic rigid pipes for building
20	Furniture and articles not otherwise classified	Furniture, mirrors, picture frames, goods of wood, cork, wicker, bone, cane, amber, and substitutes for all these materials
21	Housewares and glass	Household or kitchen utensils and containers (not of precious metal), combs and sponges, brushes, articles for cleaning purposes, glassware, porcelain, earthenware
22	Cordage and fibers	Ropes, string, nets, tents, awnings, tarpaulins, sails, sacks
23	Yarns and threads	Yarns and threads, for textile use
24	Fabrics	Textile goods not in other classes, bed and table covers
25	Clothing	Clothing, footwear, headgear
26	Fancy goods	Lace and embroidery, ribbons, braid, buttons, pins, needles, artificial flowers
27	Floor coverings	Carpets, rugs, mats, linoleum, wall hangings (nontextile)
28	Toys and sporting goods	Games and playthings, sporting goods, decorations for Christmas trees
29	Meats and processed foods	Meat, fish, poultry, game, preserved and cooked fruits and vegetables, jams and jellies, eggs, milk and milk products, edible oils and fats
30	Staple foods	Coffee, tea, sugar, rice, flour and preparations made from cereals, bread, pastry and confectionery, honey, mustard, salt, yeast
31	Natural agricultural products	Agricultural, horticultural, forestry products, and grains not in other classes, living animals, fresh fruits and

International Class	Goods/Services	Explanatory Note
		vegetables, seeds, natural plants and flowers
32	Light beverages	Beers, mineral and aerated waters, and other nonalcoholic drinks, fruit drinks and juices, syrups
33	Wine and spirits	Alcoholic beverages (except beers)
34	Smokers' articles	Tobacco, smokers' articles, matches
35	Advertising and business	Advertising, business management, business administration, office functions, retail store services
36	Insurance and financial	Insurance, financial affairs, monetary affairs, real estate affairs
37	Building construction and repair	Building construction, repair, installation services
38	Telecommunications	Includes services allowing at least one person to communicate with another by sensory means
39	Transportation	Transport, packaging, and storage of goods, travel arrangement
40	Treatment of materials	Includes mainly services rendered by the mechanical or chemical processing or transformation of objects or substances, for example, dyeing a garment or destruction of trash
41	Education and entertainment	Education, providing of training, entertainment, sporting, and cultural activities
42	Miscellaneous	Providing of food and drink, temporary accommodation, medical care, beauty care, veterinary services, legal services, scientific research, computer programming, providing services by Internet, services not in other classes

FIGURE 4–2
List of International Classes (continued)

If a mark is used for more than one class of goods or services, the applicant may either file a combined application, listing all of the goods and services in the same application, or file entirely separate applications for each class of goods/services. The filing fees will be identical. Some attorneys prefer to file separate applications, believing that a defect in regard to one class of goods or services in a combined application will hold up registration for the mark in all classes. For example, if three separate applications are filed for goods in I.C. 3, 21, and 25, and there is a delay with regard to the goods in I.C. 25, the other applications may proceed to registration, thereby allowing the applicant to secure a registration for the mark at least in regard to some goods. The final decision on whether to file a combined application or separate application is one of tactics and strategy.

The PTO requires that the identification of goods or services be as clear, accurate, and concise as possible. The accuracy of identification language is of particular importance because, while an identification may be limited or clarified, no addition to, or expansion of, an identification is permitted after an application is filed. Thus, if an application is filed on January 1 for women's clothing in I.C. 25 and the applicant later wishes to add perfume (in I.C. 3) to the application, such an amendment would not be allowed. The applicant would be required to file an additional application that would then have a later filing date than the first application filed January 1. The applicant may, however, amend the original application to clarify that the clothing to be offered consists of blouses, skirts, and pants. An applicant cannot attempt a blanket filing for "all the goods in I.C. 9." Such an application would be refused by the PTO. If an applicant incorrectly classifies clothing in I.C. 26 rather than in I.C. 25, the PTO will allow correction of this error.

Typically, the PTO requires that the applicant use terms such as *namely* and *consisting of* when identifying goods. Thus, an identification of "cosmetics, *namely* lipstick and deodorant" is acceptable, while an identification of "cosmetics, *including* lipstick and deodorant" will be refused as indefinite and overbroad inasmuch as a reader cannot tell the exact goods that will be offered under the mark from reading the identification.

Finally, due to the increased volume of applications for computer-related goods in I.C. 9, the PTO expressly requires that identifications of goods for computer software or comparable goods must specify the purpose or function of the program. For example, the following descriptions would be acceptable to the PTO: "computer software for word processing" or "computer software for preparation of federal income tax returns." A broad description such as "computer programs in the field of medicine" is not acceptable.

Basis for Filing Application and Method of Use

The application submitted to the PTO usually specifies one of the following bases for the application (and usually states the manner in which the mark is used):

- actual use of the mark in commerce, specifying a date of first use in commerce and specifying the method of use, such as stating that the mark is affixed to the goods offered under the mark (15 U.S.C. § 1051(a));
- a bona fide intent to use the mark in commerce and specifying the mode or manner in which the mark is intended to be used, such as stating the

mark will be used in advertising offering the services (15 U.S.C. § 1051(b));

- a bona fide intent to use the mark in commerce and a claim that the mark is the subject of a prior foreign application (15 U.S.C. § 1126(d)); or
- a bona fide intent to use the mark in commerce and a claim that the mark is the subject of a prior foreign registration (15 U.S.C. § 1126(e)). Applications based on foreign applications and registrations are discussed in Chapter 8.

If the basis for filing the application and method of use are not set forth in the application, they can be supplied during examination of the application.

Drawing of Mark

One of the most critical parts of the application is the **drawing** or the display of the mark. Because the drawing is used when the mark is ultimately published in the PTO publication *Official Gazette* and is reproduced in the actual certificate of registration, the drawing must conform with specific PTO requirements.

There are two types of drawings: typed form drawings and special form drawings. A *typed form drawing* is simply a typewritten display of the mark. For example, the word KRAFT® constitutes a typed drawing. In reality, the display is not a "drawing" at all. A typed form drawing is used when the mark consists solely of words or numbers with no pictorial or graphical element. If the application uses any special characteristics such as bolding or italicizing of the mark, the mark will be registered in such fashion. Such a mark (or one displaying letters in script or some other unique font or display) is referred to as "stylized." A *special form drawing* presents a mark that consists solely of a pictorial or design element or words and numbers together with a pictorial or design element. For example, the well-known display of Paul Newman on various food products is an example of a special form or design mark. As long as the special form will reproduce satisfactorily, it may be photocopied for the PTO. If the mark will not reproduce satisfactorily, an artist or draftsperson may have to be hired to produce a pen and ink drawing.

The drawing must be set forth on the drawing page, a single sheet of letter-size paper. The drawing itself cannot be larger than 4 inches high and 4 inches wide. Thus, there may be a need to photocopy the mark several times to reduce it to the appropriate size for the PTO.

The precise and exacting requirements for the drawing page correlate to the method for searching conducted in the PTO Trademark Search Library. If individuals could display marks in any format they desired, searching the PTO records to determine if a confusingly similar mark exists would be nearly impossible. Moreover, the PTO ultimately publishes the marks in its publication, the *Official Gazette*. Conformity in display of marks allows for ready review of the published marks.

Because applications filed under the 15 U.S.C. § 1051(b) are based on an intent to use the mark in the future, an applicant may not have made a final determination on the exact appearance of a mark at the time an application is filed. For intent-to-use applications, the PTO will allow some minor variation between the drawing submitted at the time the application is filed and the mark as actually used. Nevertheless, the drawing must be a substantially exact representation of the mark as it will eventually be used.

drawing: The display of the mark applied for in a trademark application; may be a *typed form* (typewritten display) or *special form* (a design mark or a design mark with words)

Official Gazette: The weekly publication of the PTO that publishes trademarks for purposes of opposition and publishes information about issued patents and patents available for sale or license

If an applicant wishes to claim color as a feature of the mark, the application must so specify. For example, the applicant will be required to state "the mark is shown in the color blue." If color is not claimed, the mark may be displayed in any color. Generally, therefore, color is claimed only when such a feature is critical to recognition of the mark, such as the golden color of McDonald's "golden arches" mark.

Specimens

If the application is made under 15 U.S.C. § 1051(a) and alleges that the mark has been used in commerce, the PTO will require that the applicant submit proof of such use by providing a "**specimen**" of the mark showing exactly how the mark is seen by the public. One specimen must be filed for each class of goods named in the application. Thus, if the application is for HELENA (& SWAN DESIGN) for soap in I.C. 3 and sweaters in I.C. 25, two specimens must be submitted.

Actual tags, bags, labels, and other similar items are highly preferred over photocopies. For example, the best specimen for the soap just described would be a wrapper for the soap, clearly showing the mark HELENA (& SWAN DESIGN). An appropriate specimen for the sweaters would be an actual tag that is sewn into the back of the garments. If the mark appears on a bulky item, such as a refrigerator or park bench, it would be ludicrous to send in the refrigerator or bench itself. Even its packaging would be cumbersome. In such cases, the PTO will accept a photograph as long as the mark can be readily seen as being affixed to the item.

Advertising material is not acceptable as a specimen for *goods*. Thus, merely including a brochure or ad about products such as soap or clothing is insufficient. Similarly, letterhead displaying the mark and other similar materials such as invoices and business cards are not acceptable. The PTO wishes to ensure that the mark is in actual use on the goods in question. Thus, mere promotional materials do not show use of goods.

Such advertising materials may, however, be sufficient to show use of a mark in connection with *services*. Thus, if the mark CHUCKY'S FUN TIME is used for restaurant services, an advertisement, coupon, brochure, direct-mail leaflet, and menu would be acceptable specimens inasmuch as there will be no actual product or good displaying the CHUCKY'S FUN TIME mark.

A specimen need not be submitted at the time of filing an application. An appropriate specimen must be submitted, however, during the examination process for an application based on actual use of mark and after the PTO approves the application and when a statement alleging use is submitted by an applicant whose application is based on an intent to use the mark. Until October 30, 1999, the PTO required three specimens for each class to be submitted at the time of filing of a use-based application. At present, one specimen per class is required and although applicants may submit specimens during examination, the PTO expects most applicants will continue to submit the specimen with their use-based applications.

Declaration and Signature

The application must be signed by and include a declaration or verification by the applicant or its agent or attorney. The **declaration** is a statement

specimens: Samples of tags, labels, packaging, or advertising materials showing how a trademark or service mark is used in commerce

declaration: A statement by an applicant for a trademark registration acknowledging that statements in the application are true

placed at the end of the application whereby the signatory acknowledges that the statements in the application are true and that the signatory understands that willful false statements are punishable by fine or imprisonment and may jeopardize the validity of the application or any registration resulting from the application. The declaration is intended to impress upon the signatory the seriousness of the trademark application procedure to ensure that applicants do not claim earlier use dates than those to which they are entitled and do not attempt to "lock up" marks for the purpose of reselling them to others. The applicant or its agent or attorney must then sign the application. If the application is one made by an individual, this individual will sign the document. If the applicant is a corporation or partnership, the application is usually signed by an officer of the corporation or a general partner, respectively. Joint applicants should each sign the application. Applicants not domiciled in the United States must appoint a "domestic representative" in the United States, namely, a party, typically a law firm, who will receive documents and notices affecting the mark.

The Principal and Supplemental Registers

The application should designate whether the application seeks registration on the Principal Register or the Supplemental Register. Registration on the **Principal Register** is preferred because it offers a wider scope of protection for a mark. A mark not eligible for registration on the Principal Register, for example, a descriptive mark that has not yet acquired secondary meaning, will be registered on the **Supplemental Register.** Registration on the Supplemental Register is an indication that a mark does not yet distinguish, but ultimately is capable of distinguishing, the applicant's goods or services from those of another. Once the mark has acquired distinctiveness, a new application can be filed seeking registration on the Principal Register. In fact, after five years of substantially continuous and exclusive use of a mark, there is a presumption that it has acquired the necessary distinctiveness to allow for registration on the Principal Register.

The distinctions between registrations on the Principal Register and Supplemental Register are as follows:

- While a registration on the Principal Register is *prima facie* evidence of the registrant's exclusive right to use of the mark, registration on the Supplemental Register has no such evidentiary effect.
- A registration on the Principal Register is constructive notice of a claim of ownership so as to eliminate a defense of good faith in an infringement suit, but a Supplemental Registration has no such effect.
- While a registration on the Principal Register may become incontestable after five years of registration, a Supplemental Registration may never achieve that status.
- Registration on the Supplemental Register cannot be used to stop importations of infringing goods into the United States.

On the other hand, registration on the Supplemental Register does afford some protections:

- An action for infringement of the mark can be brought in federal court.
- The registration will be on file with the PTO and can be cited by the PTO against another's subsequent application to register a confusingly similar mark.

Principal Register: The most preferred roll or register for registration of trademarks conferring wide protection for a mark and indicating that the mark distinguishes the registrant's goods and services from those of others

Supplemental Register: The roll or register for marks not qualifying for registration on the PTO Principal Register; registration on the Supplemental Register is an indication that the mark does not yet distinguish the registrant's goods or services from those of others

- The registration will be located through standard searches of PTO records, thus possibly deterring others from using or applying for a similar mark.
- The registrant is entitled to use the registration symbol ®.

FILING THE APPLICATION, DOCKETING CRITICAL DATES, AND INITIAL ROLE OF THE UNITED STATES PATENT AND TRADEMARK OFFICE

Filing the Application

The application must be filed with the PTO within a reasonable time after it has been signed by the applicant, generally less than six months after signature. The application must be accompanied by a filing fee in the amount of $245 for each class of goods and/or services. As an alternative to including a check for the filing fee, some applicants establish **deposit accounts** with the PTO and deposit a certain amount of money into an account against which fees can be drawn. Trademark fees are set forth at the PTO web site at http://www.uspto.gov. (see Figure 4–3 for a schedule of PTO filing fees.)

The application can be filed in person at the PTO or can be mailed using either first-class or express mail of the U.S. Postal Service. The official address for many communications sent to the PTO is Commissioner of Patents and Trademarks, Washington, DC 20231, but the actual physical location of the offices of the trademark section of the PTO is 2900 Crystal Drive, Arlington, VA 22202-3513, and this address should be used on most mail sent to the PTO, including applications. Documents mailed to the PTO should include a certificate of mailing, verifying the date the correspondence was placed in the U.S. mail. When the PTO receives the application, it will perform a cursory review to ensure that the minimum required elements of the application (and the filing fee) are present. The mailroom will then stamp the application with a serial or filing number that will accompany the application throughout the entire application process. The serial number is critical because the PTO responds to inquiries only if a serial number is known. At present, all applications begin with the two-digit number "75-."

Most applicants include either a duplicate copy of the application with a self-addressed stamped envelope or a "come-back card," requesting that the PTO stamp the duplicate application or the postcard with the date of filing and application filing number so the applicant can verify filing. Otherwise, the PTO may take several weeks to send the applicant the official filing receipt verifying filing of the application.

The filing date of the application is critical because it initiates various time limits. For example, applicants have a duty to inquire about the status of an application if they do not hear from the PTO within one year of any filing. Thus, the filing date should be calendared or docketed so that you can ensure the PTO has provided you with the official filing receipt within one year of the filing date. Similarly, if the application is filed based on an applicant's intent to use the mark in the future, the filing date constitutes **constructive use** of the mark. For example, if an intent-to-use application is filed on June 1, 1998, and the mark is ultimately registered, the date for determining priority between

deposit account: Prepaid accounts established with the PTO, against which application and other fees are drawn by applicants

constructive use: Use of trademark other than actual use; for intent-to-use trademark applications, the application filing date constitutes constructive use of the mark (assuming the mark achieves registration)

FIGURE 4 3
Schedule of PTO Filing
Fees (Trademark Matters)

Application for registration, per class	$325
Filing an amendment to allege use, per class	$100
Filing a statement of use, per class	$100
Filing a request for extension of time to file a statement of use, per class	$150
Application for renewal, per class	$400
Additional fee for late renewal or late section 8 affidavit, per class	$100
Issuing a new certificate of registration	$100
Filing an amendment or correction to registration certificate	$100
Filing section 8 affidavit of use of mark, per class	$100
Filing declaration to achieve incontestability, per class	$200
Petition for cancellation, per class	$300
Notice of opposition, per class	$300
Dividing an application, per each new application (file wrapper) created	$100
Certified copy of registered mark	$15
Copy of trademark file wrapper	$50
Recording a trademark assignment (for first mark)	$40
For subsequent marks in the same document	$25 each

conflicting parties is June 1, 1998, even though the mark may not have been actually used until December 1, 1998, and may not have achieved registration until July 1, 1999. Finally, if an applicant wishes to file an application for the mark in a foreign country, it has six months from the filing date within which to do so and thereby claim the date of the filing in the United States.

Docketing Critical Dates

Many law firms and offices that do a significant amount of trademark work have sophisticated computer programs that automatically docket critical dates. Such systems will automatically flag a file and provide notification that no action has been taken on an application in nearly twelve months so the applicant may investigate the problem. Nevertheless, most firms (and some malpractice carriers) also require that trademark practitioners maintain their own dockets, whether by means of an independent computerized system or a simple tickler file composed of index cards and divided into monthly categories, to serve as reminders of needed action in the coming months. The very nature of trademark work is deadline-sensitive. Failure to take certain actions on a timely basis may result in abandonment of a mark or application unless the delay was unintentional. Therefore, the utmost care must be taken to protect a client s interests. Develop a docketing system that works effectively and maintain it diligently. Failure to do so may be malpractice.

Initial Role of the United States Patent and Trademark Office: The File Wrapper and the Official Filing Receipt

When the PTO receives an application, it creates a threefold legal-size file, called a **file wrapper,** to hold the papers related to the application. The file

file wrapper: The official PTO file containing all papers relating to a trademark or patent application

wrapper is the official PTO file, and it contains the drawing, specimen, and all communications with the PTO.

Within four to eight weeks after an application is filed, the PTO will mail the applicant a document called the **Official Filing Receipt.** The official filing receipt will confirm the filing date of the application, provide a serial number, and confirm all details of the application, including dates of first use, basis for filing, applicant's name and address, the goods or services offered under the mark, and the international class. Because the official filing receipt reflects what the PTO believes to be the pertinent details of the application, it should be carefully scrutinized for correctness. If there are any errors, even minor spelling mistakes, the applicant should immediately inform the PTO in writing. Failure to notify the PTO of some discrepancy may result in the certificate of registration including the erroneous information. Once the official filing receipt is received, the docketing system should be updated to ensure that additional action is taken on the application within six months thereafter.

THE EXAMINATION PROCESS

Examination Procedure

After the PTO issues the official filing receipt, the application is assigned for review to an examining attorney, typically new attorneys employed by the PTO. Many move into private practice after a few years with the PTO. Examining attorneys are assigned to "law offices" within the PTO, each of which has responsibility for certain types of applications. For example, all applications relating to computer programs may be assigned to Law Office 6, while all applications dealing with business services may be assigned to Law Office 14. Concentrating similar applications in a given law office allows examining attorneys to become expert with certain types of applications, thereby facilitating the registration process. It is the function of an examining attorney to review the application, search the PTO files to determine if the mark applied for is confusingly similar to another, make a determination on whether the mark is registrable, and ultimately either refuse registration of the mark or approve it for publication. Examination is the least predictable stage of the prosecution process. Applications by the same party for identical or similar marks, called **companion applications,** will be handled by the same examining attorney. Likewise, applications by different parties for conflicting marks, called **conflicting applications,** will be handled by the same examining attorney so that related issues can be acted upon consistently and expeditiously.

Office Actions and Refusals to Register Marks

Approximately six months after the application is filed, the examining attorney assigned to the application will issue a "first action" or **Office Action** regarding the application if there are any defects in the application. If there are no defects, the PTO will approve the application for publication in the *Official Gazette,* the weekly publication of the PTO. The office action is a written communication sent by the examining attorney to the applicant (or, more likely, to the applicant's attorney) that states that the mark has been refused registration

Official Filing Receipt: A document issued by the PTO confirming the filing of a trademark application

companion application: Related trademark applications by the same applicant

conflicting application: Trademark applications filed by different parties for conflicting or confusingly similar marks

Office Action: Written communication from the PTO refusing registration of a trademark or patent and specifying reasons for the refusal

and explains why registration has been refused. All office actions must be responded to within six months. To monitor pending applications, call the PTO status line or **TRAM line** (703/305-8747), a recorded information system that provides updates on the progress and status of applications and registrations, or check the new Trademark Applications and Registration Retrieval System on the PTO's web site.

Curing Informalities and Technical Defects in the Application In many instances, the application may contain deficiencies that must be corrected before the application may be approved. For example, the applicant's name may be identified as "Lee Inc.," in the application itself and yet be signed by an officer on behalf of "Lee Co." The drawing may be too large and may need to be reduced. The specimen may not show use and a new specimen may be required. The identification of goods or services may lack specificity and the examining attorney may require clarification to the identification. In many instances, the office action suggests that the applicant telephone the examining attorney to resolve the issue (within the six-month period for response) and often suggests a remedy for the defect. The applicant and the examining attorney are often able to resolve the issue in such a telephone communication. Thereafter, the examining attorney will issue an **Examiner's Amendment** setting forth the agreed-upon correction or clarification, thereby eliminating the need for the applicant to file a formal written response to the office action. The application will proceed to publication after the examiner's amendment has corrected any technical informality in the application. The PTO encourages such telephonic communications because they expedite the application process.

Substantive Refusals In many instances, the refusal to register is not due to some minor or technical error in the application that can be readily corrected, but is due to a more significant or substantive defect. In these cases, the examining attorney will set forth the reason the mark has been refused registration. The applicant will then have six months to respond in writing to the office action and present arguments supporting registration. Some of the more common substantive refusals to register are as follows:

- the mark is immoral or scandalous;
- the mark is deceptive;
- the mark disparages a person or a national institution or displays the flag or insignia of a nation;
- the mark displays a portrait of a living person without his or her consent;
- the mark is primarily merely a surname;
- the mark is geographically deceptively misdescriptive;
- the mark is merely descriptive; or
- the mark is confusingly similar to another registered or applied-for mark at the PTO.

Applicants who receive an office action refusing registration on one of the these grounds generally submit written arguments to persuade the examining attorney to allow the mark for registration. Case law and other evidence may be cited. For example, if the mark is refused on the basis it is primarily merely a surname, the applicant may submit telephone book evidence to show the name

TRAM line: The Trademark Reporting and Monitoring system maintained by the PTO allowing individuals to check the status of a trademark application or registration (703/305-8747)

Examiner's Amendment: A written communication from the PTO setting forth an agreed-upon clarification or correction to a trademark application is so rare that consumers who encounter the mark would not perceive it to be a surname. If a person's consent is needed, the applicant should secure it.

Refusals on the Basis of Descriptiveness   One of the most serious refusals occurs when the examining attorney refuses registration on the basis the mark is merely descriptive and is thus barred under 15 U.S.C. § 1052(e)(1). The applicant will then submit a response to the office action arguing that the mark is not descriptive. Common arguments asserted by the applicant are as follows:

- The applicant may argue that the mark is not descriptive but is rather suggestive and therefore entitled to registration. To support such an assertion, the applicant may cite marks in case law that have been found to be suggestive and analogize them to the mark at issue. The applicant may also conduct a search of PTO records to locate other similar marks that were allowed to proceed to registration. The PTO, however, is not bound by its past actions and may characterize the earlier allowed marks as mistakes that it need not repeat.
- The applicant may argue that the cases cited by the examining attorney in support of the refusal to register are inapplicable and attempt to distinguish the present situation from that presented in the case law relied upon by the examining attorney.
- If the mark has been in commerce for five years, there is a presumption that it has acquired distinctiveness. In such a case, the PTO will allow the applicant to claim distinctiveness under 15 U.S.C. § 1052(f). The wording for a claim of acquired distinctiveness is as follows:

  > The mark has become distinctive of Applicant's goods [or services] through the Applicant's substantially exclusive and continuous use in commerce for at least the five years immediately before the date of this statement.

- If the mark has not acquired distinctiveness through continuous use for five years, the applicant may attempt to show the mark has acquired distinctiveness or secondary meaning through its significant use, sales, and advertising such that consumers associate the mark with applicant. The applicant typically submits evidence consisting of sales and advertising data and declarations from customers and consumers who confirm they are familiar with the mark and recognize the applicant as the source of the goods offered under the mark.

disclaimer: In trademark law, an acknowledgment by an applicant that exclusive rights in certain wording in a mark, usually descriptive or generic wording, are not claimed; a notice placed on trademarked goods that the owner of the goods is not affiliated with another; in patent law, the cancellation of invalid claims in an issued patent

If none of these arguments are successful, the applicant may be allowed to amend the application to seek registration on the Supplemental Register *if* use of the mark has begun. Applications based solely on intent to use cannot be transferred to the Supplemental Register until after the applicant has shown actual use of the mark.

If only a portion of the mark is descriptive or generic, that portion may be *disclaimed*. The purpose of a **disclaimer** is to allow registration of a mark that includes nonregistrable matter. For example, in the mark BOLERO TASTY COFFEE (used in connection with coffee), the words *tasty coffee* would likely have to be disclaimed because they merely describe something about the goods offered under the mark. A disclaimer is an acknowledgment by an applicant that he or she does not claim exclusive rights in the matter disclaimed (in this case, the wording *tasty coffee*), apart from the mark as a whole. Disclaimers preserve the rights of other businesses to use needed terms such as *tasty* and *coffee*. Some marks, called **composite marks,** consist of both wording and design elements. If the wording in a composite mark is descriptive or generic, the applicant may have to disclaim exclusive rights to all of the wording, leaving the applicant with exclusive rights only to the design component. An applicant may not disclaim an entire mark.

A disclaimer does not affect one's common law rights; neither does it mean that the mark as a whole is not protectable. In the hypothetical, use by another company of VOLERO TASTY COFFEE could likely be enjoined on the basis of confusing similarity; however, a mark such as SUNRISE TASTY COFFEE would likely be allowable, inasmuch as the marks can be distinguished on the basis of their nondescriptive components.

The proper wording for a disclaimer is as follows:

No claim is made to the exclusive right to use "tasty coffee" apart from the mark as shown.

Refusals on the Basis of Confusing Similarity   In addition to refusing to register a mark on the basis that it is merely descriptive, another substantive ground for refusal to register is that the mark applied for so resembles a mark registered or applied for with the PTO that, when used in connection with the goods or services of the applicant, it would be likely to cause confusion, mistake, or to deceive consumers. 15 U.S.C. § 1052(d).

In determining whether a mark applied for is confusingly similar to a prior registered or applied-for mark, a variety of factors, identified in *In re E. I. DuPont DeNemours & Co.,* 476 F.2d 1357 (C.C.P.A. 1973), are considered:

- the similarity of the marks in their entireties in regard to appearance, sound, connotation, and commercial impression;
- the similarity and nature of the goods or services offered under the respective marks;
- the similarity of the channels of trade in which the goods or services are offered, for example, whether the goods or services offered under the mark are offered through retail or wholesale channels of trade;
- the buyers to whom sales are made, and the conditions of such sales, for example, whether purchases are made on impulse or after due care and deliberation;
- the fame of the prior mark (sales, advertising, length of use, and so forth);
- the number and nature of similar marks in use on similar goods or services; and
- the nature and extent of actual confusion.

The goods or services need not be identical for confusion to be found, as long as they are related in some manner. Thus, MARTIN's for bread was held likely to be confused with MARTIN's for cheese on the basis the marks were used in connection with related food products. *In re Martin's Pastry Shoppe, Inc.,* 748 F.2d 1565 (Fed. Cir. 1984). If the item is purchased by consumers on

composite mark: A mark consisting of words and a design element

"impulse," such as an inexpensive beverage, confusion will be more likely than if the item is expensive, is purchased by sophisticated consumers, and is purchased only after great thought and care. The PTO does not use a mechanical approach in determining whether confusion is likely to occur; rather, an examination is made of all the factors. If there is any doubt about whether there is a likelihood of confusion, doubt will be resolved against the newcomer. Additional information relating to likelihood of confusion analysis is found in Chapter 6 in the discussion of trademark infringement. (See Figure 4–4 for a comparison of some marks alleged to be confusingly similar.)

An applicant whose mark is rejected on the basis of confusing similarity will attempt to overcome the refusal to register by citing case law and analogizing cases in which confusion was not found, submitting evidence showing that the goods are not in the same channels of trade and that they are offered to different or sophisticated purchasers, and by submitting copies of other registered marks that have been allowed to coexist.

Alternatively, the applicant may contact the owner of the cited mark and seek a license to use the mark or seek its consent to coexistence and registration. The applicant may need to pay the prior user some amount of money to secure the consent. Although the PTO is not bound to accept such a coexistence agreement, generally the PTO does so, believing that the owners of marks are in the best position to evaluate whether conflicts might exist and that if they believe no confusion would result from coexistence of the marks, the PTO should affirm their decision. See Chapter 6 for further discussion of consent agreements.

Responses to Office Actions   An applicant has six months to respond to an office action. Failure to respond within the appropriate time period will result in abandonment of the application unless the delay was unintentional.

As soon as an office action is received, its response date should be docketed. The client should then be informed in writing of the basis for the PTO's refusal to register the mark. The law firm typically recommends a course of action and provides an estimate of the costs and fees the client can expect to incur in responding to the office action along with some assessment of the likelihood of success. The IP professional should continue to monitor the matter to ensure the client provides appropriate and timely instructions so the law firm can respond to the office action.

In some instances, a second office action may be issued after the applicant's response to the initial office action. Ultimately, the application will either proceed to the next step (publication) or will be subject to a "Final Refusal." Once a final refusal has been issued, the applicant's only recourse is to comply with the examining attorney's requirements, request reconsideration by bringing new matter before the examining attorney, or appeal the refusal to the Trademark Trial and Appeal Board (TTAB). Alternatively, the applicant can initiate an action in federal district court where the issues will be determined *de novo* (literally, "anew"). Adverse decisions of the TTAB are reviewable by the U.S. Court of Appeals for the Federal Circuit and then by the U.S. Supreme Court if it decides to take the case. The Federal Circuit can set aside PTO findings only when the findings are arbitrary, capricious, an abuse of discretion, or unsupported by substantial evidence. *Dickinson v. Zurko,* No. 98-377 (U.S. June 10, 1999).

FIGURE 4–4
Comparison of Marks
Alleged to Be Confusingly
Similar and Action Taken
by PTO and Courts

Mark # 1	Mark #2	Result
CONFIRM (for medical-related goods)	CONFIRMCELLS (for blood reagents)	Confusingly similar
LAREDO (for land vehicles)	LAREDO (for pneumatic tires)	Confusingly similar
LITTLE PLUMBER (for liquid drain opener)	LITTLE PLUMBER (for advertising services)	Not confusingly similar
BIGGS (for grocery and general merchandise store)	BIGGS (& DESIGN) (for furniture)	Confusingly similar
GOLDEN GRIDDLE PANCAKE HOUSE (with "Golden Griddle" disclaimed) for restaurant services	GOLDEN GRIDDLE (for table syrup)	Confusingly similar
CAREER IMAGE (STYLIZED) (for women's clothing and store services)	CREST CAREER IMAGE (for uniforms)	Confusingly similar
TMM (for computer software)	TMS (for computer software)	Confusingly similar
COBBLER's OUTLET (for shoes)	CALIFORNIA COBBLERS (STYLIZED) (for shoes)	Not confusingly similar
BEST JEWELRY (& DESIGN) (for jewelry store services)	JEWELERS' BEST (for jewelry)	Not confusingly similar

POSTEXAMINATION PROCEDURE

Publication in the *Official Gazette*

Assuming the applicant responds satisfactorily to the office action, the examining attorney will approve the mark for publication in the *Official Gazette* (sometimes called the OG; see Figure 4–5), a weekly subscription publication of the PTO. The mark as applied for (wording, design, or some combination thereof) will be reproduced as the applicant set it forth in the drawing page together with an identification of the owner, the filing date, the goods or services offered under the mark, and the filing date and serial number of the application. The purpose of publication is to afford interested parties the opportunity to review the mark and oppose its registration, generally on the basis that the mark is confusingly similar to another mark. Opposition actions are discussed in Chapter 6.

An opposition (or request for extension of time to oppose) must be filed within thirty days of publication of the mark in the OG. By law, extensions of up to one hundred and twenty days from the date of publication may be granted; however, if both parties agree, additional extensions are usually granted by the PTO in order to allow the parties to work out their difficulties. Once again, docketing of dates is critical. A law firm not only should docket the date of its

FIGURE 4–5
Official Gazette

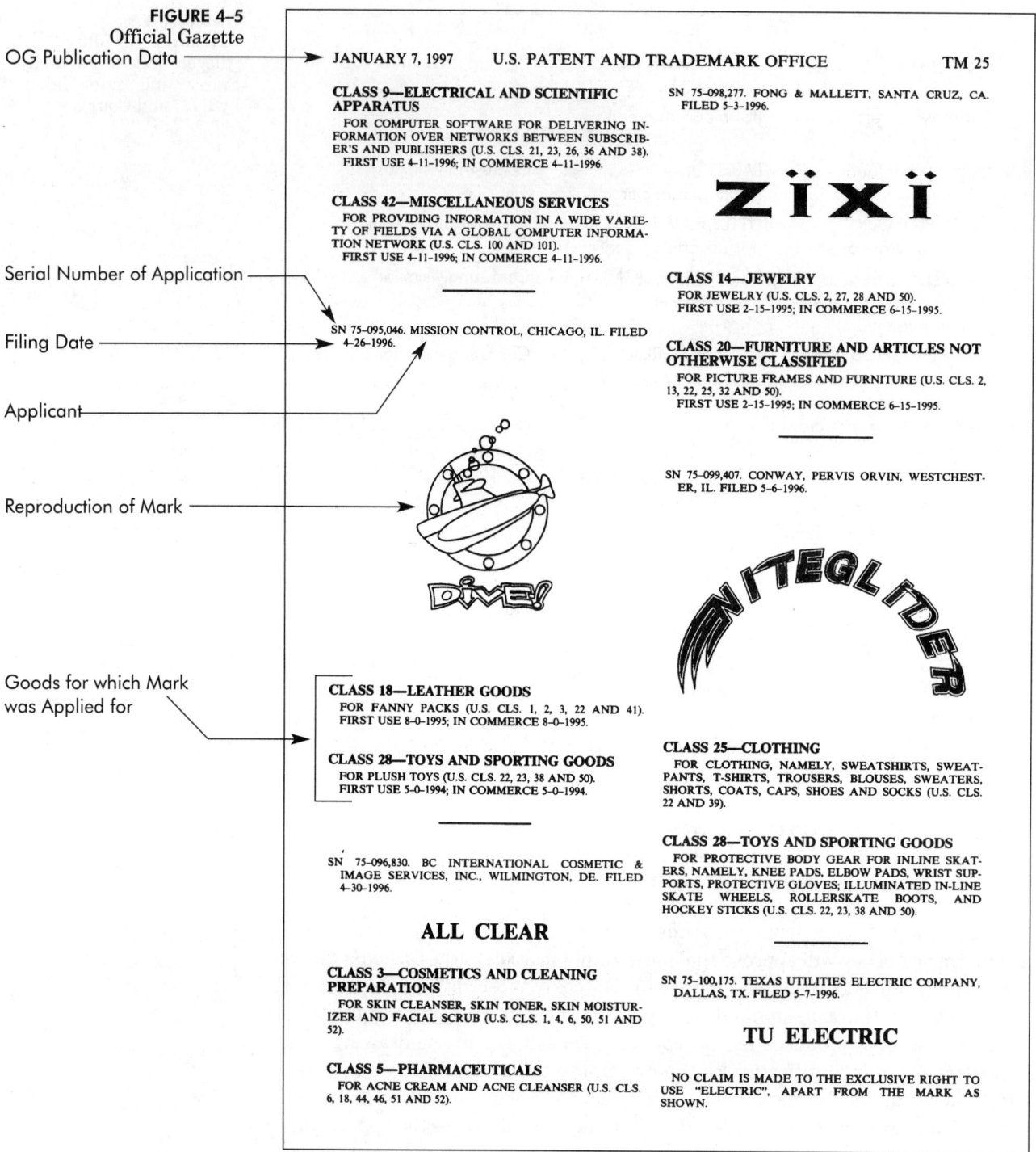

OG Publication Data

Serial Number of Application

Filing Date

Applicant

Reproduction of Mark

Goods for which Mark was Applied for

own clients' applications (so it can confirm that no one has opposed the clients' marks and, thus, the marks will proceed to registration), but also should review the OG to search for marks that may conflict with clients' marks and then notify the clients so they can have the opportunity to oppose other applications.

Because thousands of marks are published in the *Official Gazette* each week, it is virtually impossible for a firm with an active trademark practice to devote the effort needed to reading each week's *Official Gazette.* Most law firms suggest their clients authorize one of the professional search firms to conduct a **watch service** to review the *Official Gazette* and notify the firm of potential conflicts on a timely basis so the law firm can then inform the client that a conflicting mark may need to be opposed. Watch services can also monitor all applications filed at the PTO after a client s application so immediate action can be taken against a conflicting mark. The cost of the watch services is approximately $300 per year per mark, although costs can be higher if several international classes need to be watched or if the mark includes unique design features.

Intent-to-Use Applications and Statements of Use

If the application was based upon the applicant s actual use of the mark in commerce, the **actual use application** will proceed to registration after the publication period. If the application was based on the applicant s intent to use the mark in commerce in the future, the mark cannot proceed to registration until actual use has been shown.

Thus, for intent-to-use (ITU) applications, after publication (and no opposition), the PTO will issue a **Notice of Allowance,** notifying the applicant that the ITU application has been allowed, and granting the applicant six months (which may be extended for five additional six-month periods, up to a total of three years) within which to commence use of the mark and submit a statement and specimen verifying such use and the dates of first use. For example, if an ITU application has been published for opposition (with no one filing an opposition), and a notice of allowance is issued on June 1, 1999, the applicant will have until December 1, 1999, to file its **Statement of Use** (together with a specimen). If use is not commenced by December 1, 1999, the applicant may request an additional six-month period by alleging that it continues to have a bona fide intent to use the mark. Additional six-month extensions may be granted if the applicant alleges its continued good faith intent to use the mark and shows good cause for the extension, such as stating the additional time is needed to conduct market research and promotional activities.

Note that the first request for extension of time is granted automatically; subsequent extensions must show good cause why the extension should be granted. If no statement of use is submitted by June 1, 2002, the application will be deemed abandoned (unless the delay was unintentional). Filing fees of $100 are required for a statement of use and $150 for each request for extension of time to file a statement of use for each class of goods/services covered by the application. (See Appendix D, Form 2, Statement of Use, and Form 3, Request for Extension of Time to File Statement of Use.)

The statement of use verifies that the mark is in use in commerce, specifies the date of first use, and is accompanied by a specimen (label, packaging, and so forth for goods or promotional material for services) showing actual use of the mark. If the application was a combined application (for example, for pens in I.C. 16 and clothing in I.C. 25), and the applicant can only show use in regard to goods in one class, the application can be divided, with one class proceeding to registration and one lagging behind.

If use of a mark was actually commenced during the application process of an ITU application, the applicant may file an amendment to its original application (called an **Amendment to Allege Use**) alleging that use has occurred and providing a specimen showing such use. The only significant difference

watch service: Service provided by a private company, usually a trademark search firm, to review the *Official Gazette* and PTO records for potentially conflicting marks

actual use application: A trademark application based on an applicant s use in interstate commerce of a trademark

Notice of Allowance: Document issued by the PTO informing a trademark applicant that an intent-to-use application has been allowed and granting the applicant a specified time period within which to begin use of the mark in order to secure registration for it; document issued by the PTO informing a patent applicant that a patent application has been allowed and granting the applicant a specified time period within which to pay an issue fee so a patent will be issued

Statement of Use: Document filed by an intent-to-use trademark applicant verifying that the mark is in actual use in interstate commerce; required to receive a trademark registration

Amendment to Allege Use: Document filed during prosecution of an intent-to-use trademark application, alleging that use of the mark has begun

between an amendment to allege use and a statement of use is the time of filing. The amendment to allege use may be filed during the initial examination phase, while the statement of use is not filed until after the PTO issues a notice of allowance. An amendment to allege use filed after the examining attorney approves the application for publication will be rejected. The period within which the amendment to allege use cannot be filed is called the **blackout period.**

Once a mark that is the subject of an intent-to-use application achieves registration, the filing date of the application is deemed to be the date upon which the owner first used the mark. This "constructive use" date is important to the trademark owner because it will allow the owner to defeat an intervening user who may have actually used the mark before the intent-to-use owner but after the intent-to-use owner's application filing date. For example, assume the following dates:

- Intent to use application filed by Jones Inc. for WESTOVER on February 1, 1998.
- Actual use by Smith Co. for EASTOVER for related goods on June 1, 1998.
- Use-based application filed by Smith Co. for EASTOVER on July 1, 1998.
- Notice of allowance issued for WESTOVER on February 1, 1999.
- Statement of use filed for WESTOVER on May 1, 1999, alleging actual use occurred on April 15, 1999.
- Registration issued for WESTOVER on August 1, 1999.

Given these dates, WESTOVER has priority over EASTOVER because once WESTOVER achieved registration, it was as if its owner had actually used the mark on the date it filed its application, namely, February 1, 1998, a date prior to June 1, 1998, the date of first use of EASTOVER.

REGISTRATION

For a use-based application, registration will occur after publication in the *Official Gazette* if no opposition is filed to the application. For an intent-to-use application, registration will occur after publication in the *Official Gazette,* notice of allowance of mark, and submission of the statement of use and requisite specimen. The application process for use-based applications can take twelve to eighteen months or longer, and the process for intent-to-use applications can take from eighteen to forty-two months, or longer.

Eventually, however, the PTO will issue a **Certificate of Registration** for the mark. The term of the registration is presently ten years from the date the mark is registered (until November 16, 1989, the term was twenty years). The certificate will include all of the pertinent information about the mark and the owner and will set forth a registration number and a registration date. The mark as applied for will be reproduced. The law firm should carefully review the certificate and request a correction of any errors. Once the mark is registered, the owner (now called the **registrant**) can use any of the following registration notices in connection with the mark (assume the mark is MARTIPPE):

blackout period: The period after approval of an application for publication in the *Official Gazette* within which an amendment to allege use of a mark cannot be filed

Certificate of Registration: Document issued by the PTO confirming registration of a trademark

registrant: The owner of a trademark registration issued by the PTO

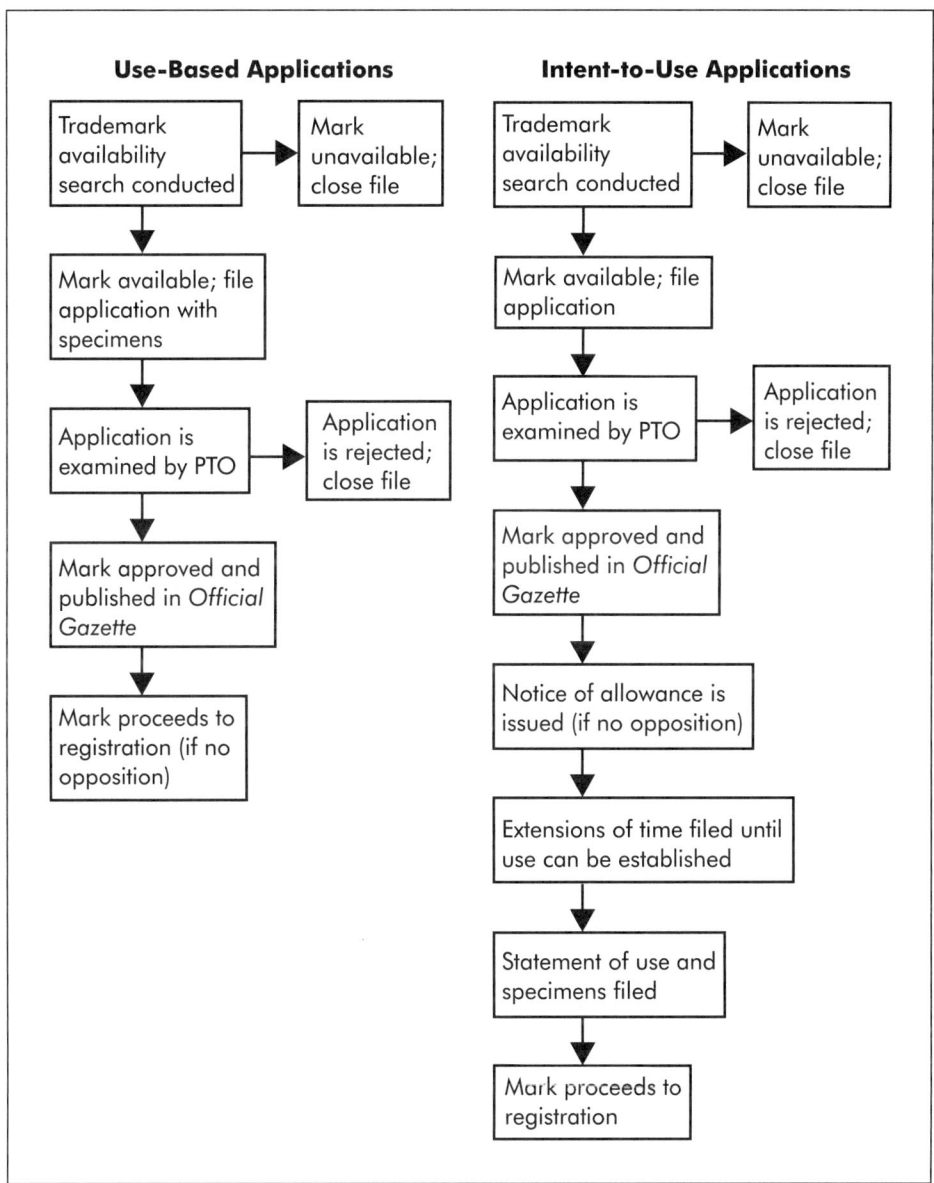

FIGURE 4–6
Trademark Prosecution
Flowchart

- MARTIPPE Registered in U.S. Patent and Trademark Office;
- MARTIPPE Reg. U.S. Pat. & Tm. Off.; or
- MARTIPPE® (this is the most common notice).

The federal registration symbol or language cannot be used with a mark unless it has been registered with the PTO. Until that time, trademark owners and applicants often use the designation "TM" (for trademark) or "SM" (for service mark) placed alongside the mark to notify others the owner claims rights in the mark. Once the law firm receives the certificate of registration, it will forward the certificate to the client along with pertinent information about monitoring the mark, using the registration notice, and pertinent dates to maintain the mark. Once again, the law firm must be certain to docket the critical dates to avoid abandonment of the registration. For example, between the fifth and sixth years after registration, the registrant must file a continued use affidavit with the PTO verifying the mark is still in use or the registration will be canceled (to clear the PTO files of **deadwood** and allow unused marks to be used by others). Additionally, the registration must be renewed before its ten-year period of duration expires.

(See Figure 4–6 for a trademark prosecution flowchart that shows each step of the prosecution process.)

THE UNITED STATES PATENT AND TRADEMARK OFFICE'S TRAM LINE

The PTO maintains an automated system called the TRAM (Trademark Reporting and Monitoring) System that allows applicants and interested persons to check the status of an application or registration. After the welcoming message, you will be instructed to enter an application number or registration number. You will be given recorded status updates and information relating to the application or registration. Five requests may be entered per call. The TRAM line or status line is an invaluable tool, allowing parties to track applications and to receive information and critical dates. Many IP practitioners routinely call the TRAM line and take notes on the progress of an application so they will be ready to respond if a client has questions about an application. The TRAM line number is (703) 305-8747. Alternatively, the PTO web site offers a

deadwood: Unused marks that the PTO desires to clear from its records

ROLE OF INTELLECTUAL PROPERTY PROFESSIONAL

Intellectual property professionals typically have significant responsibility in the prosecution stage of a trademark application. In many law offices, primary responsibility may be assigned to paralegals, with attorney involvement limited to supervising and advising the paralegal and providing advice to the client on suggested strategies to overcome refusals to register. Among the many tasks IP professionals assume responsibility for are the following:

- gathering information from clients to assist in preparing applications;
- preparing the trademark application;
- reviewing specimens that support use of a mark for consistency and proper display of mark;
- filing the application and confirming same to client;
- reviewing the official filing receipt;
- reviewing office actions and reporting same to client;
- performing research for responses to office actions;
- assisting in preparing responses to office actions;
- reviewing the *Official Gazette* to ensure client's mark is accurately reproduced;
- reviewing notice of allowance for intent-to-use applications;
- preparing statement of use and gathering specimens for intent-to-use applications;
- reviewing certificate of registration for accuracy;
- assisting in reporting registration to client;
- docketing all critical dates throughout the prosecution process; and
- monitoring the progress of the application.

new method of monitoring the status of applications and registrations. This new system, called Trademark Applications and Retrieval ("TARR") allows checking of an unlimited number of applications and registrations.

CHAPTER SUMMARY

After searching and clearance of a mark for availability, an application should be filed with the PTO for registration of the mark. If the mark has actually been used in interstate commerce, the application should be accompanied by a specimen showing how the mark is actually used.

The application will be carefully reviewed by an examining attorney to determine if it meets the statutory requirements and whether any marks similar to the proposed mark have been registered or applied for in the same or related industries. The examining attorney's objections are enumerated in an "office action." An applicant has six months to respond to an office action. The process continues until either the application is finally refused or it is allowed for publication in the *Official Gazette,* a weekly government publication. Individuals who believe they may be injured by the proposed registration have a statutory period within which to oppose registration of the mark. If no opposition is filed, the mark will proceed to registration.

If the applicant has not yet engaged in actual use of the mark, the procedure is essentially the same. The application will be reviewed by an examining attorney, who will approve it, publish it for opposition in the *Official Gazette,* and issue a notice of allowance. The applicant will then have six months to begin use of the mark in commerce and file a statement of use verifying such use with an actual specimen attached. Extensions of time may be granted. After review of the statement of use and specimen, the mark will be registered. Registration is a complex and lengthy process even if there are only minimal problems.

DISCUSSION QUESTIONS

1. Would an identification of "computer goods" be acceptable in a trademark application?
2. Identify an appropriate specimen that would support use of the following marks:

   FRANKLIN VID-A-RAMA   for rental of videos
   SHELBY HATCH   for designer scarves
   HUDSON CHIN-CHIN   for restaurant services
   INTERVAL   for computer consulting services

3. If an application was filed on January 10 and you had not received any correspondence from the PTO by December 10, what should you do?
4. If an application for VACOT SMART BANKING (for banking and financial services) is refused on the basis of descriptiveness, how should the applicant respond?
5. Assume the applicant for an intent-to-use application is issued a notice of allowance for the mark on February 16, 1999. Discuss the deadlines applicable to the application.
6. Assume the owner of the registered mark TRACOR COMPUTER SYSTEMS (for computer software) has disclaimed "computer systems." A later applicant files for GRAY-COR COMPUTER SYSTEMS for computer hardware. Discuss whether the marks are confusingly similar.
7. If the mark THE WINE SELLER (for retail store services offering wine) is refused on the Principal Register, would an amendment to the Supplemental Register be acceptable?

CHAPTER
5
Postregistration Procedures, Trademark Maintenance, and Transfer of Rights to Marks

The Lanham Act imposes various requirements on registrants after registration of marks to ensure that only marks in use remain on the registers. Thus, registrants must file an affidavit between years five and six after registration and in the year before the end of each successive ten year period after registration to allege continued use of the mark and file an application for renewal within one year before the end of the registration term and every ten years thereafter. Failure to file the appropriate documents will result in cancellation of the registration for a mark.

Rights to marks can be lost by other means as well, primarily when the mark becomes generic or when the mark is abandoned by nonuse. Trademark owners often institute trademark use and compliance policies to ensure marks are not lost through genericide or abandonment.

Because a trademark is a form of property, it can be transferred or assigned to another if the goodwill symbolized the mark is assigned with it. Similarly, a mark may be licensed to another party to use, as long as the trademark owner controls the nature and quality of the goods or services offered by the licensee.

THE AFFIDAVIT OF USE

Background

Although a registration is valid for ten years, between years five and six after a registration is issued, and in the year before the end of each ten year period after registration, the registrant is required to file an **Affidavit** (or *Declaration*) **of Use** with the PTO, verifying that the mark is still in use in commerce in connection with the goods or services identified in the registration. Failure to submit the affidavit of use, called a "section 8 affidavit," within the appropriate deadline (or within a six-month grace period) will lead to cancellation of the registration. Requiring registrants to notify the PTO that marks are still in use allows the PTO to clear its files of deadwood, making unused marks available for others. Nevertheless, the mark may still be used by its owner who will continue to have common law rights to the mark even though the registration for the mark has been canceled.

If the registration covers goods or services in several classes, the registrant must verify that the mark is in use in connection with all of the goods or services. If the mark is in use with regard to some items, but not for others, the registrant must indicate such. The registration will be canceled as to any goods for which the mark is not in use. The PTO filing fee is $100 per class of goods or services. Filing during the grace period results in additional fees.

Changes in Ownership of the Mark

The section 8 affidavit must be filed by the owner of the registration. Often, marks are transferred or assigned to other new owners who fail to notify the PTO of the change in ownership. Although the section 8 affidavit is filed by the new owner, PTO records may continue to reflect the original registrant. In such cases, the section 8 affidavit is refused until the appropriate changes are made to the PTO records showing proper continuity of title, called the **chain of title,** to the party now filing the section 8 affidavit. Even a change in the state of incorporation is a change of legal entity. Thus, if a Virginia corporation dissolves its status in Virginia so it can become a Delaware corporation, unless the PTO has received formal notification of such change, as well as documentary evidence, such as certified copies of the Delaware incorporation documents, a section 8 affidavit will not be accepted.

Changes in the Mark

When filing the affidavit, the owner must attach a specimen showing the mark as it is presently used for each class of goods or services identified in the registration. Thus, if the mark is used in connection with coffee creamer in I.C. 29 and coffee in I.C. 30, a specimen (generally labels, tags, packaging materials, or containers) for each class must be provided. If the mark as presently used differs from the mark as registered, the PTO must determine whether the change is material. If the change is determined to be a material alteration, the section 8 affidavit will be refused.

Because trademarks evolve over time (for example, consider the periodic updating of the BETTY CROCKER® portrait mark), alterations in marks are common. The PTO will review the original specimen and compare it with the

Affidavit of Use: Document filed by a trademark registrant between fifth and sixth years and every ten years after registration verifying the mark is still in use; also called *Declaration of Use* or *Section 8 Affidavit*

chain of title: Documentation of continuity of ownership or title to a trademark, copyright, patent, or other property right

current specimen; if they are substantially the same, the affidavit will be accepted. A material alteration will result in a refusal on the basis that the mark currently in use is a new mark and that the registered mark is no longer in use. Generally, a mere pluralization in wording or a slight change in nonessential background design may be acceptable. Thus, if wording in a mark appears in a different typeface or script, it will likely be accepted. The addition of wording or design elements, however, will likely result in a refusal, requiring the registrant to file a new application and begin the registration process anew.

If the PTO agrees that a change is not material and accepts the section 8 affidavit, the registrant will usually be encouraged to amend the registration so it conforms to the mark as presently used.

If the registered mark is not in use in commerce, the owner may provide facts to the PTO showing that nonuse is excusable due to special circumstances rather than any intent to abandon the mark and must state the date use of the mark stopped and when it is expected to resume. Merely stating that the applicant does not intend to abandon the mark is not sufficient. Additionally, reduced demand for the product or service does not excuse nonuse; ordinary economic or social conditions that result in nonuse of the mark cannot be excused, because these are exactly the types of marks the PTO wants to eliminate. On the other hand, if there is some governmental regulation that precludes the owner from using the mark (for example, some prohibition against the sale of insecticides or certain chemicals), nonuse would be acceptable. Similarly, if the mark is not being used because of plant retooling (and production is scheduled to resume at some point), fire, illness, or other catastrophe, the nonuse might be excused. As soon as the external cause passes, the owner must resume use within a reasonable amount of time.

THE AFFIDAVIT OF INCONTESTABILITY

Section 15 of the Trademark Act permits owners of registrations on the Principal Register to file affidavits whereby the right to use the registered marks for the goods or services set forth in the affidavit becomes **incontestable.** A section 15 affidavit, also called an **Affidavit of Incontestability,** may not be filed until the mark has been in continuous use for at least five consecutive years. Thus, the section 15 affidavit is often combined with the first section 8 affidavit in one submission to the PTO. The filing fee for the section 15 affidavit is $200 per class of goods or services identified in the registration.

The benefit to filing a section 15 affidavit is that it significantly reduces the challenges that may be made to a mark. Generally, a mark that is incontestable cannot be attacked unless it has become generic, has been abandoned, or was procured by fraud. Thus, incontestability precludes challenges to a mark on the basis that it is descriptive or that it is confusingly similar to a mark owned by a prior user.

In addition to verifying that the mark has been in continuous use, the section 15 affidavit must state that there has been no decision adverse to the registrant s claim of ownership of the mark, or to the registrant s right to register the mark, or to keep the mark on the Principal Register. The affidavit must also state that there is no proceeding involving these rights pending in the PTO or any court.

incontestable: A trademark registered on the Principal Register that is protected from certain challenges after its registrant files a section 15 affidavit alleging continuous use for five years

Affidavit of Incontestability: Document filed by the owner of a mark registered on the Principal Register after five years of continuous use that reduces the challenges that may be made to a mark; also called *Section 15 Affidavit*

No registrant is required to file a section 15 affidavit; however, for obvious reasons, if the mark has been in continuous use and satisfies the other conditions, a registrant should be strongly encouraged to do so to immunize the mark from various challenges. Only marks registered on the Principal Register (not the Supplemental Register) may become incontestable under section 15. (See Appendix D, Form 4, for a combined affidavit under sections 8 and 15.)

RENEWAL OF REGISTRATIONS

Any trademark registration issued after the Trademark Law Revision Act (namely, November 16, 1989) has a duration of ten years. Before that date, registrations were valid for twenty years. Within one year before expiration of each pertinent period, the registrant must renew the registration or it will be automatically canceled (although common law rights to the mark may still exist if the mark is in use). The new **renewal** period for all marks is ten years. Although the application for renewal must be filed within a one-year period before each expiration date, there is a grace period of six months following the expiration of a registration during which an application for renewal may be filed. The filing fee for an application for renewal is $400 per class of goods or services. Filing during the grace period results in additional fees of $100 per class. The Section B affidavit required every ten years can be combined with the renewal application in a single document filed every ten years.

The requirements previously discussed for section 8 affidavits (filed between years five and six after registration and every ten years after registration) and applications for renewal are the same:

> the document must be filed by the owner of the mark. If the owner identified for the application for renewal is different from the one identified in the registration itself, the PTO will require that a chain of title be established;
> a specimen for each class affected must be presented;
> if the mark is no longer used for certain goods or services, the mark cannot be renewed for such (unless the owner can show special circumstances excusing nonuse); and
> if the mark shown in the specimen supporting renewal is materially different from the mark shown in the registration certificate, the renewal application will be refused.

(See Appendix D, Form 5, Application for Renewal of Trademark Registration.)

DOCKETING REQUIREMENTS

renewal: Document filed with the PTO or Library of Congress to maintain a trademark or copyright registration for an additional term

As discussed, certain actions must be taken to maintain a trademark or service mark registration. Failure to take the appropriate action in a timely fashion will result in cancellation of a registration. Although an owner can petition the commissioner to review refusals of section 8 affidavits and applications for renewal, such refusals are seldom reversed, and the decision of the commissioner is final (unless the registrant appeals to the appropriate court within sixty days). The registration will then be canceled.

Because cancellation is such an extreme result, the utmost care must be given to docketing critical dates. While many IP professionals maintain their own docketing systems, others use the services of one of the professional search firms (identified in Chapter 3) to docket these critical dates. Because ownership of companies is in flux, marks evolve, and contact between the law firm and the registrant may have been intermittent in the years following registration, trademark maintenance (namely, handling affidavits of use under section 8, affidavits of incontestability under section 15, and applications for renewal under section 9) can be difficult and time-consuming.

LOSS OF TRADEMARK RIGHTS

While registrations can be canceled due to failure to file appropriate documents with the PTO, as discussed earlier, rights to marks can also be forfeited due to **abandonment** of marks, failure to protect marks, or improper assignment or licensing of the mark.

The Lanham Act (15 U.S.C. § 1127) provides that a mark will be deemed to be abandoned when either of the following occurs:

- the mark has become a generic name; or
- use of the mark has been discontinued with intent not to resume use. Nonuse for three consecutive years is *prima facie* evidence of abandonment.

Genericide

As discussed in Chapter 2, a mark can become generic (referred to as **genericide**) when consumers begin to call the product or service offered under the mark by the mark. Examples of once-valid marks that have become generic terms are *aspirin, yo-yo,* and *escalator.* XEROX Corporation has always been worried that its famous mark would become generic due to consumers' misuse of the mark in saying, "I'm going to make a xerox of this document." XEROX Corporation has therefore expended substantial amounts of money in attempting to ensure consumers use the mark correctly by consistently saying in advertising copy "XEROX® brand copiers are . . ." Similarly, Kimberly-Clark's promotional materials always refer to "KLEENEX® brand tissues" to ensure the mark does not become generic through consumers saying, "I need a kleenex."

Abandonment by Nonuse

The more common means by which a mark becomes abandoned is through nonuse. Mere cessation of use is insufficient; the nonuse must be coupled with an intent not to resume use for abandonment to occur. There is a presumption that a mark has been abandoned if it has not been used for three years. Once a party can demonstrate such nonuse for three years, the trademark owner has the burden of rebutting the presumption of abandonment by proving that mark has not been abandoned.

In determining whether abandonment due to nonuse has occurred, courts have concluded that "intent to resume use" means an intent to resume use within the reasonably foreseeable future. In one famous case, CBS stopped

abandonment: Loss of trademark rights through nonuse coupled with an intent not to resume use; loss of patent rights through express intention to relinquish rights

genericide: Loss of rights in a trademark occurring when consumers begin calling a product or service offered under a mark by the mark itself

using the AMOS AND ANDY mark due to civil rights objections. When a third party began using the mark twenty years later, CBS sued for infringement, arguing that it intended to resume use of the mark when social policies permitted. The court held the mark had been abandoned because CBS did not have an intent to use the mark in the reasonably foreseeable future. *Silverman v. CBS Inc.,* 870 F.2d 40 (2d Cir. 1989).

The trademark owner need not use the mark everywhere in the United States; use anywhere is usually sufficient. However, trademark owners cannot make sporadic and token sales merely for the purpose of reserving rights in a mark. Press releases and other similar announcements by a company that it is discontinuing a product line associated with a mark likely shows an intent not to resume use from which abandonment will be inferred.

A trademark owner challenged with an allegation that his or her mark has been abandoned through nonuse may attempt to show special circumstances that would justify nonuse. These special circumstances are similar to those that excuse nonuse when a registrant files a section 8 affidavit or an application for renewal. For example, a labor strike that results in inability to ship products or government regulation precluding importation or shipping of goods bearing the mark will usually excuse nonuse. Similarly, the sale of few products bearing the mark when the products are extremely expensive may excuse nonuse. However, mere economic conditions that make selling the product or service unprofitable do not excuse nonuse.

It is possible that the mark has been so changed by the owner over time that the original mark has become abandoned. As discussed, minor changes will not result in loss of rights, but a material alteration in the mark may result in abandonment of the original mark. For protection, owners should register each version of a mark.

Marks can also be expressly abandoned, such as when a trademark owner cancels or surrenders his or her registration, perhaps as a result of a settlement agreement with another.

Abandonment causes a loss of common law rights as well as rights under the Lanham Act. Resumption of use by the owner after abandonment does not revive the mark but merely establishes a new use date for the new mark. On the other hand, if an applicant inadvertently abandons an application (perhaps because the applicant failed to timely respond to an office action) or a registration (because the registrant forgot to renew the registration), but continues to use a mark, rights to the mark continue and the owner retains common law rights and can reapply for trademark registration.

TRADEMARK USE AND COMPLIANCE POLICIES

trademark compliance policy: A guide to use of a trademark to ensure a mark is not misused or does not become generic or abandoned

Because misuse of a mark by allowing it to become generic or alteration of a mark can cause loss of rights, trademark owners should initiate compliance policies to ensure use of marks is proper. Failure to monitor and actively police a mark may result in abandonment of all rights to the mark. A **trademark compliance policy** will help to ensure that a company's marks continue to enjoy protection both under the Lanham Act and at common law.

Following are some guidelines for proper trademark usage:

- A trademark should be displayed prominently in comparison with its surroundings and should clearly stand out on a label, advertisement, in text, and so forth. Thus, many owners capitalize their marks, display them in some prominent style or larger-than-average typeface, place them in quotation marks, or use distinctive lettering, colors, or the word *brand* after the mark, as in "VASELINE® brand petroleum jelly" to remind consumers that VASELINE is the brand name of a certain product from a certain source.
- Marks should be used in connection with the appropriate goods and services. Companies that have numerous similar marks for similar products and services must exercise care that a mark does not become abandoned because it is no longer used in correlation with the product or service for which it was registered.
- Appropriate designations and notices should be used to inform the public that trademark rights are claimed in the mark. The federal registration symbol ® is most often used for registered marks while the initials "TM" or "SM" are often used in connection with marks that are not yet registered. The symbols are generally placed to the right of and slightly above (or below) the mark, such as in "CAMPBELL'S® condensed cream of chicken soup." The symbol should be large enough to be easily spotted but need not be obtrusive. If a mark is repeated several times in an advertisement or brochure, the symbol can be displayed with the first or most prominent use of the mark. Alternatively, the mark can be displayed with an asterisk. A corresponding footnote at the bottom of the page can provide the information that the mark is a registered trademark owned by the company.
- Marks should be used consistently. The addition of words or symbols to a mark may lead to the conclusion that the company has abandoned its original mark and is now using some nonregistered form of the mark.
- The owner of the mark should be identified. For example, a notice may state "SOUTHRISE® is a federally registered trademark of Hutchins Associates, Inc."
- The mark should not be used in the plural form or possessive form, such as "Excedrins are great pain relievers" or " Shout's spot-removing power is improved." Such uses may result in the mark becoming generic. Marks should be used as adjectives rather than nouns to ensure the mark does not become generic. The mark should not be used to refer to the general type of a product or service or to the owner. Use of a mark as a noun, rather than an adjective, suggests that the mark is the generic name for a product or service rather than a unique trademark for a particular product or service of a particular company.

Correct: SOUTHRISE® juices are refreshing.
                   SOUTHRISE® cranberry juice is the juiciest.
Incorrect: SOUTHRISE® refreshes you.
                   SOUTHRISE® is a sparkling beverage.
                   SOUTHRISE® contains real cranberries.

Famous marks such as COKE® and FORD® are exceptions to this rule, and their owners do not always follow the noun-adjective rule. For example, advertising copy may read, "Have you driven a Ford lately?" This copy would be using the mark as a noun rather than an adjective. Other than these extraordinary cases, marks should always be used as adjectives rather than nouns.

To ensure that trademark use is proper and consistent, many companies provide detailed information sheets to their advertisers, suppliers, vendors, and licensees to instruct them in proper use of trademarks. When marks comprise color or design components rather than mere wording, companies usually supply advertising "slicks" as well so users can faithfully reproduce the mark. Many companies designate a responsible person to regulate use of the company's marks and verify compliance with guidelines and policies regarding use of the marks.

TRADEMARK POLICING AND MAINTENANCE

In addition to ensuring that marks are used properly to avoid genericide or abandonment, trademark owners should initiate active policing and maintenance procedures to avoid infringement of their marks. Among the steps trademark owners should take to protect their marks from infringement are the following:

- Critical dates for required actions with the PTO should be docketed to ensure marks, applications, and registrations are not inadvertently abandoned and then used by others.
- Owners should subscribe to watching or tracking services to monitor marks for potential infringement. Professional service companies will review a number of trademark resources, including applications filed at the PTO, the *Official Gazette,* state trademark registers, Internet domain names, and common law sources. Worldwide watching is also available for marks used internationally. Early notification of potential conflicts allows an owner to take aggressive action to protect a mark. The companies identified in Chapter 3 (Thomson & Thomson, Corsearch, CCH Trademark Research Corporation, and so forth) perform these watching services at varying rates. The most comprehensive watch of all resources previously described might cost $800 per year per mark. However, for a company like McDonald's Corporation that has spent years and substantial amounts of money in building goodwill in its marks, such as its GOLDEN ARCHES® mark, such a sum represents a very reasonable investment. Some trademark owners conduct an annual intellectual property "audit" to review the status of their intellectual property and detect potential infringing uses (see Chapter 24). More limited watches, such as one only of new applications filed at the PTO, might cost approximately $150 per year per mark.
- Company employees should be asked to be alert to competing uses in the marketplace. Trade publications, business press, web sites, and marketing materials of competitors should be monitored to ensure that marks that may be confusingly similar to the company's marks are not being used.

USE OF MARKS OWNED BY THIRD PARTIES

Parties often use their competitors' marks in promotional materials comparing and contrasting the respective goods or services of the parties. A trademark owner does not have an absolute right to prohibit any and all uses of its trademarks. A **collateral use** of another party's marks may be acceptable in some circumstances. For example, it is not trademark infringement for a party to inform consumers truthfully that its products will "fit with" the trademark product of another. Thus, a seller of sponges was able to advertise its sponges fit as replacements in the "O-CEDAR® 76 mop." Many parents are familiar with the announcements that certain blocks "work with LEGOS®."

Statements that one's products are "superior to" or "better than" another's, however, may be actionable as false advertising if the statement is untrue. Courts tend to examine language in advertising to ensure there is no misleading use, product disparagement, or confusion caused to the public. To reduce confusion, a party should always place the registration symbol ® next to another party's registered mark and provide the announcement, "XYZ® is a federally registered trademark owned by XYZ Corp." This will help ensure that consumers are not confused about the source and origin of goods or services offered under the respective marks.

TRANSFER OF OWNERSHIP OR RIGHTS IN TRADEMARKS

Assignment of Marks

A trademark or service mark may be transferred or assigned to another *if* the goodwill symbolized by the mark is assigned with it. Because a mark is used to identify the source of goods and services, rather than existing as an independent object of property, it is inseparable from the goodwill of the business to which it applies. Thus, an arrangement by which a mark is assigned without the business goodwill that the mark symbolizes, called an **assignment in gross,** is ineffective to transfer trademark rights, and the new owner who begins using the mark cannot claim the original owner's use date for purposes of establishing priority in the mark. The new owner, the "assignee," will establish its own first use date upon using the mark. Thus, valuable trademark rights could be lost if a third party begins using a mark *after* the assignor's original use date but *before* the date of an assignment in gross to the assignee. This third party would have priority over the assignee and could prevent use of a confusingly similar mark by the assignee. To prevent such a situation, the parties should enter into a written **assignment** agreement that recites that the mark is being transferred together with the goodwill of the portion of the business associated with the mark. A recitation that goodwill is transferred with the mark is usually sufficient to ensure the assignee can capture or retain the original date of first use.

The transfer of common law rights to a mark does not require a written agreement. If the assignment is oral, its existence may be proven by clear and uncontradicted testimony. However, while an oral agreement to transfer a mark is valid, a written agreement lends certainty and should always be used. Moreover, the assignment document should recite that the mark and the

collateral use: Acceptable use of another's trademark, such as in comparative advertising

assignment in gross: A purported transfer of a trademark without the business goodwill that the mark symbolizes; it is insufficient to transfer trademark rights

assignment: Transfer of all rights in a trademark, copyright, patent, or other property to another

goodwill symbolized by the mark are being transferred to ensure there is no loss of trademark rights. The assignment document itself is a relatively simple agreement (see Figure 5–1).

An entire business need not be transferred with a mark. A trademark owner may assign a mark used in connection with specific goods or services and retain other marks used in connection with other goods or services. If all of the assets of a business are sold, however, it is assumed that all marks and their goodwill pass with the other assets, even if they are not specifically mentioned in the sales documents.

If the mark assigned has been registered or is the subject of a pending use-based application at the PTO, the assignment must be in writing and should be filed or "recorded" with the PTO. Although there is no requirement that the assignment be recorded to be effective, **recordation** is a relatively simple procedure that affords several advantages:

- it clarifies the records of the PTO and affords notice to all of the identity of the owner of the mark;
- it allows the new owner to commence and defend actions at the PTO in its name;
- it ensures that documents and notices issued by the PTO will be sent to and will identify the correct owner;
- it simplifies postregistration procedures inasmuch as section 8 affidavits and applications for renewal will be rejected unless their identification of the trademark owner is consistent with the PTO records; and
- it provides public notice of the fact of the assignment such that later purchasers of the mark are bound by it.

Although common law marks, registered marks, and marks that are the subject of pending use-based applications can be assigned, marks that are the subject of intent-to-use applications cannot be assigned prior to filing an amendment to allege use or a statement of use with the PTO verifying that the mark is in use in commerce, unless the mark is being assigned to a successor of the business of the applicant to which the mark pertains and the business is ongoing and existing (15 U.S.C. § 1060). The purpose of the prohibition against assignment of marks not yet in use is to prevent the sale or trafficking of intent-to-use applications. Additionally, permitting assignment of an application before a mark is used would conflict with the principle that a mark may be validly assigned only with some of the business or goodwill attached to use of the mark. There can be no goodwill attached to a mark that has not been used. An assignment of an intent-to-use application prior to the filing of the verified statement of use is not only invalid but voids the underlying trademark application or any resulting registration.

Recording documents at the PTO requires that a party file a specific PTO form (Form 1618A, Recordation Form Cover Sheet; see Figure 5–2), identifying the conveying and receiving parties, the marks affected by the transfer, and a correspondent to whom the PTO can send notices. The fees for recording are $40 for the first mark being assigned and $25 for each subsequent mark identified in the form. Form 1618A is also used to inform the PTO that a mark has been acquired by a party through a merger (as when a corporation that owns a mark is acquired by another corporation) or in the event the trademark owner changes its name or state of incorporation.

recordation: Filing of certain documents with the PTO, Library of Congress, or other official body to provide public notice of the contents of a document or a transaction, such as an assignment or transfer of intellectual property, a grant of a security interest in intellectual property, or a change in the chain of title of intellectual property

FIGURE 5–1
Assignment of Trademark

WHEREAS, Hollis & Sanders Co., a corporation organized under the laws of the State of California, located and doing business at 890 Second Avenue, San Diego, CA 92117 ("Assignor"), is the owner of U.S. Trademark Registration No. 1,908,457 for the mark SMARTLOCK issued December 14, 1996, in the United States (the "Mark"); and

WHEREAS, Business Consultants, Inc., a corporation organized under the laws of the State of California, located and doing business at Technology Drive, Simi Valley, CA 96607 ("Assignee"), desires to acquire all of Assignor's rights in and to the Mark and the goodwill symbolized thereby;

NOW, THEREFORE, for good and valuable consideration, the receipt and sufficiency of which are hereby acknowledged, Assignor hereby sells, assigns, transfers, and conveys to Assignee all of its right, title, and interest in and to the Mark, together with the goodwill of the business associated with the Mark, the same to be held and enjoyed by Assignee, its successors, assigns, and other legal representatives.

Assignor further assigns to Assignee all right to sue for and receive all damages accruing from past infringements of the Mark herein assigned.

This Assignment shall be binding upon the parties, their successors and/or assigns, and all others acting by, through, with, or under their direction, and all those in privity therewith.

Assignee agrees to cooperate with Assignor and take any further action and execute any documents required to effect the purposes of this Assignment.

Hollis & Sanders Co.   Business Consultants, Inc.

By: _____   By: _____

Title: _____   Title: _____

Date: _____   Date: _____

Licensing of Marks

A party may allow another party to use a mark and yet retain ownership rights in the mark. Such a form of limited transfer is called a **license.** Some of the most common license arrangements occur in franchising. For example, McDonald's Corporation will grant a franchise to a party to open a McDonald's restaurant in a certain territory. In connection with the franchise, McDonald's will grant the party a license to use McDonald's marks on the cups, packaging, signs, and in advertising. McDonald's continues to own the marks; it has merely granted a license to a third party to use its marks for certain specific purposes.

The licensor will lose its rights to the mark, however, if it does not control the nature and quality of the goods or services offered by the licensee under the mark. Thus, license agreements must include "quality control" provisions whereby the licensor protects the mark by ensuring the goods and services offered under it by the licensee are consistent with those offered by the licensor. Failure of the licensor to exercise quality control will result in a **naked license** and a loss of the licensor's rights in the mark. Failure to monitor the goods and services offered under the license may result in abandonment of the mark and may preclude or estop the trademark owner/licensor from challenging use of the mark by the licensee during the period of unsupervised use. License agreements should therefore allow the licensor to conduct periodic inspection of the licensee's facilities and its use of the mark. The licensor may require the licensee to submit samples of how the mark is being applied to the goods or how

license: A limited transfer of rights, such as a permission to another to use a trademark, copyright, patent, or trade secrets subject to some conditions, rather than an outright transfer of all rights

naked license: Granting permission to another to use a trademark and retaining no control over the nature or quality of the goods or services offered under the mark; a naked license results in a loss of the licensor's rights in a mark

FORM PTO-1618A
Expires 06/30/99
OMB 0651-0027

U.S. Department of Commerce
Patent and Trademark Office
TRADEMARK

RECORDATION FORM COVER SHEET
TRADEMARKS ONLY

TO: The Commissioner of Patents and Trademarks: Please record the attached original document(s) or copy(ies).

Submission Type

☐ New

☐ Resubmission **(Non-Recordation)**
   Document ID #

☐ Correction of PTO Error
   Reel #   Frame #

☐ Corrective Document
   Reel #   Frame #

Conveyance Type

☐ Assignment   ☐ License

☐ Security Agreement ☐ Nunc Pro Tunc Assignment
                      Effective Date
                      Month Day Year

☐ Merger

☐ Change of Name

☐ Other

Conveying Party

☐ Mark if additional names of conveying parties attached

Execution Date
Month Day Year

Name

Formerly

☐ Individual   ☐ General Partnership   ☐ Limited Partnership   ☐ Corporation   ☐ Association

☐ Other

☐ Citizenship/State of Incorporation/Organization

Receiving Party

☐ Mark if additional names of receiving parties attached

Name

DBA/AKA/TA

Composed of

Address (line 1)

Address (line 2)

Address (line 3)

City   State/Country   Zip Code

☐ Individual   ☐ General Partnership   ☐ Limited Partnership

☐ Corporation   ☐ Association

☐ Other

☐ Citizenship/State of Incorporation/Organization

If document to be recorded is an assignment and the receiving party is not domiciled in the United States, an appointment of a domestic representative should be attached. *(Designation must be a separate document from Assignment.)*

FOR OFFICE USE ONLY

Public burden reporting for this collection of information is estimated to average approximately 30 minutes per Cover Sheet to be recorded, including time for reviewing the document and gathering the data needed to complete the Cover Sheet. Send comments regarding this burden estimate to the U.S. Patent and Trademark Office, Chief Information Officer, Washington, D.C. 20231 and to the Office of Information and Regulatory Affairs, Office of Management and Budget, Paperwork Reduction Project (0651-0027), Washington, D.C. 20503. See OMB Information Collection Budget Package 0651-0027, Patent and Trademark Assignment Practice. DO NOT SEND REQUESTS TO RECORD ASSIGNMENT DOCUMENTS TO THIS ADDRESS.

Mail documents to be recorded with required cover sheet(s) information to:
Commissioner of Patents and Trademarks, Box Assignments , Washington, D.C. 20231

FIGURE 5–2
PTO Recordation Cover Sheet

FORM PTO-1618B
Expires 08/30/99
OMB 0651-0027

Page 2

U.S. Department of Commerce
Patent and Trademark Office
TRADEMARK

Domestic Representative Name and Address   Enter for the first Receiving Party only.

Name

Address (line 1)

Address (line 2)

Address (line 3)

Address (line 4)

Correspondent Name and Address   Area Code and Telephone Number

Name

Address (line 1)

Address (line 2)

Address (line 3)

Address (line 4)

Pages   Enter the total number of pages of the attached conveyance document including any attachments.   #

Trademark Application Number(s) or Registration Number(s)   ☐ Mark if additional numbers attached

Enter either the Trademark Application Number or the Registration Number (DO NOT ENTER BOTH numbers for the same property).

Trademark Application Number(s)			Registration Number(s)		

Number of Properties   Enter the total number of properties involved.   #

Fee Amount   Fee Amount for Properties Listed (37 CFR 3.41): $

Method of Payment: Enclosed ☐   Deposit Account ☐

Deposit Account
(Enter for payment by deposit account or if additional fees can be charged to the account.)
Deposit Account Number: #

Authorization to charge additional fees: Yes ☐   No ☐

Statement and Signature

To the best of my knowledge and belief, the foregoing information is true and correct and any attached copy is a true copy of the original document. Charges to deposit account are authorized, as indicated herein.

Name of Person Signing	Signature	Date Signed

FIGURE 5–2
PTO Recordation Cover Sheet (continued)

it is used in advertising or may require testing of products offered under the mark. Such measures ensure that the licensee's products and services are of the same level of quality that consumers have come to associate with the licensor's mark. Failure to control and supervise the mark by the owner so as to ensure quality and consistency in the goods or services offered under the mark leads to public deception inasmuch as the function of a mark is to identify the source of goods or services. Thus, a naked license (one without quality control provisions) results in abandonment of the mark.

The license may grant the licensee exclusive rights to use the mark. Alternatively, the licensor may limit the licensee's rights by allowing the licensee to use the mark only in specific geographic areas or may allow others to use the mark. Similarly, the licensor may retain rights to use the mark itself. The license agreement should specify whether the license is an **exclusive** or **nonexclusive license,** indicate whether use is restricted to any geographic territory, and must include adequate quality control provisions. Most license arrangements also recite that the licensee acquires no ownership rights in the mark and cannot challenge the licensor's rights to the mark. A one-time fee may be paid by the licensee for the privilege of using the mark, or the licensee may make periodic royalty payments to the licensor based upon sales of the products. For example, the licensee may be required to pay the licensor 4 percent of its net profits arising out of its use of the mark as **royalties.** On occasion, a trademark owner may assign the entire mark to a party who then "licenses back" to the original owner the right to use the mark for some purpose. Some adversarial proceedings between trademark claimants are resolved by such licensing arrangements. Although a license can be recorded with the PTO (using Form 1618A), there is no requirement of recording, and most parties in the United States do not do so, believing the license is a private agreement of which the public need not be informed. In most foreign countries, however, as discussed in Chapter 8, there is usually a statutory duty to record a license agreement with the appropriate governing body.

(See Figure 5–3 for a sample trademark license agreement.)

Trademarks as Collateral

Trademark owners may use their marks as collateral to secure their promise to perform some obligation. For example, a trademark owner may wish to borrow $400,000 from a bank. The bank may insist that certain property be pledged as collateral so that in the event of a default by the owner, the bank can seize the assets pledged. Trademarks can be used as such collateral. Typically, the parties enter into an agreement called a **security agreement** that contains the terms and conditions of their arrangement. The security agreement will identify the marks being pledged as collateral. The security agreement is typically recorded at the PTO (using Form 1618A) to afford notice to the public that the marks are subject to the security interest. When the trademark owner satisfies its obligations, the security interest is released, again by using Form 1618A. During the existence of the security agreement, the owner retains all rights in the mark. Granting a security interest in a trademark is not a transfer of any present rights in a mark. It allows a party to seize the marks (and then exercise all rights of ownership) only in the event of a default by the owner in

exclusive license: A grant of rights to one party with no other party having any rights

nonexclusive license: A grant of rights to more than one party

royalties: Periodic payments paid by one who uses or licenses property owned or created by another, usually based on sales or licenses of the property

security agreement: In intellectual property law, an agreement by which one party grants an interest to another in its intellectual property, usually in order to obtain or secure a loan; if the owner defaults on the loan, the lender usually obtains ownership of the intellectual property

FIGURE 5–3
Trademark License
Agreement

This Trademark License Agreement (the "Agreement") is entered into and is effective as of this _____ day of _____, 20_____, by and between _____, a _____ corporation with its principal offices at _____ ("Licensor") and _____, a _____ corporation with its principal offices at _____ ("Licensee").

WHEREAS, Licensor is the owner of the trademark DENNISON (& DESIGN) (the "Mark") and U.S. Registration No. 1,789,746 therefor and has the right to license use of the Mark to others;

WHEREAS, Licensor is desirous of licensing and Licensee is desirous of obtaining a license to use the Mark in connection with its business;

NOW, THEREFORE, in consideration of the above, and for other good and valuable consideration, the receipt and sufficiency of which are hereby acknowledged, the parties agree as follows:

1. GRANT OF LICENSE

Licensor grants to Licensee an exclusive, nontransferable, worldwide license to use the Mark in its name in connection with the goods covered by the registration of the Mark.

2. TERM OF LICENSE

Unless sooner terminated as provided in Section 8 hereof, the grant, as specified in Section 1, shall continue for a period of three (3) years from the date of this Agreement. This Agreement may be renewed for additional terms of three (3) years by mutual written agreement of the parties not less than six (6) months prior to the expiration of the initial or any renewal term of this Agreement. Upon expiration of this Agreement:

    a. All rights of the Licensee to the Mark shall terminate and the Licensee shall have no further rights with respect thereto;

    b. Licensee shall not offer any goods in connection with the Mark or any confusingly similar mark and shall cease all use of the Mark or any confusingly similar mark; and

    c. Licensee shall cease any activity that suggests that it has any right to the Mark or that it has any association with the Licensor.

3. OWNERSHIP OF MARK

Licensee acknowledges the ownership of the Mark in Licensor, agrees that it will do nothing inconsistent with such ownership and that all use of the Mark by Licensee shall inure to the benefit of and be on behalf of Licensor, and agrees to assist Licensor in recording this Agreement with any appropriate domestic or foreign government authorities. Licensee agrees that nothing in this Agreement shall give Licensee any right, title, or interest in the Mark other than the right to use the Mark in accordance with this Agreement, and Licensee agrees that it will not attack the title of Licensor to the Mark or attack the validity of this Agreement.

4. QUALITY CONTROL STANDARDS AND MAINTENANCE

    a. Licensee agrees that the nature and quality of all goods offered or sold by Licensee in connection with the Mark shall be of high quality, manufactured free from defects and in full compliance with all laws, and of such style and appearance to be adequately suited to their exploitation to the best advantage and enhancement of the Mark and consistent with the quality control standards established by Licensor.

    b. At reasonable times during the term of this Agreement, Licensor may request Licensee to submit samples of any advertising or promotional materials and specimens of all uses of the Mark. If any such materials fail to meet with Licensor's approval, Licensee shall cease using such disapproved materials or items until such times that it modifies such materials and items and receives approval in writing from the Licensor of such materials and items, as modified.

c. Licensor shall have the right to review the Licensee's use of the Mark and Licensee's business operations at any reasonable time and upon reasonable notice. Upon notice of defects given by Licensor, Licensee shall cure such defects in the use of the Mark or the goods offered thereunder. In the event that Licensee does not take reasonable steps to cure such defects within thirty (30) days after notification by Licensor, Licensor shall have the right to require that Licensee remove the Mark from any products or materials or, at the sole discretion of Licensor, to terminate this Agreement.

d. Licensee shall operate its business in a manner that reflects favorably at all times on the Mark.

5. FORM OF USE

Licensee agrees to use the Mark only in the form and manner and with appropriate legends and notices as prescribed herein and from time to time by Licensor and not to use any other trademark or service mark in combination with the Mark without prior written approval of Licensor.

6. PROPRIETARY RIGHTS AND GOODWILL

a. Licensee acknowledges that the Mark is owned by Licensor, which has the sole and exclusive right to license the Mark. The parties intend that Licensee shall use the Mark only under the terms and conditions of this Agreement. Licensor has the sole and exclusive right to deal with the U.S. Patent and Trademark Office in connection with the Mark, and Licensee will perform any acts reasonably required by Licensor in connection with same. All costs associated with maintenance of the Mark shall be borne by Licensor.

b. Licensee shall use all reasonable precautions and take all necessary steps to prevent the Mark from being acquired or duplicated or used by unauthorized persons. Licensee shall take appropriate action, by instructions, agreements, or otherwise, with any persons permitted access to the Mark to ensure that Licensee satisfies its obligations under this Agreement.

c. Any goodwill arising out of Licensee's use of the Mark shall inure solely and exclusively to the benefit of Licensor, and Licensee shall have no rights therein or claims thereto. Licensee acknowledges that this Agreement does not confer any goodwill or other interest in or to the Mark except the right to use the same in accordance with the terms hereof.

7. INFRINGEMENT BY THIRD PARTIES

Licensee agrees to notify Licensor of any unauthorized use of the Mark by others promptly as it comes to Licensee's attention. Licensor shall have the sole right and discretion to bring infringement or unfair competition proceedings involving the Mark.

8. DEFAULT AND TERMINATION

Licensee shall be deemed to be in default and Licensor may, at its option, terminate this Agreement and all rights granted hereunder, without affording Licensee any opportunity to cure the default, effective immediately upon receipt of notice by Licensee, upon the occurrence of any of the following events:

a. If Licensee ceases to do business or otherwise forfeits the right to do or transact business in any jurisdiction where its business offices are located.

b. If a threat or danger to public health or safety results from the management and operation of Licensee's business conducted in connection with the Mark.

FIGURE 5–3
Trademark License
Agreement (continued)

c. If Licensee is convicted of a crime of moral turpitude or similar felony or is convicted of any other crime or is the subject of any civil action that Licensor reasonably believes is likely to have an adverse effect on the Mark, the goodwill associated therewith, or Licensor's interest therein.

d. If Licensee purports to transfer any rights or obligations under this Agreement to any third party without Licensor's prior written consent.

e. If Licensee fails to maintain any of the quality control standards prescribed by Licensor in this Agreement or otherwise in writing.

f. If Licensee engages in any business or markets any service or product under a name or mark which, in Licensor's opinion, is confusingly similar to the Mark.

9. MISCELLANEOUS

a. This Agreement shall be construed in accordance with the law of the State of _____.

b. Licensee shall not assign, sublicense, encumber, or otherwise transfer its rights and obligations under this Agreement without the prior written consent of Licensor.

c. This Agreement contains the entire agreement between the parties with respect to licensing of the Mark. It supersedes and cancels any prior oral or written understandings or negotiations and may not be modified in any respect except in writing signed by both parties.

d. The terms of this Agreement shall be severable such that if any term hereof is held to be illegal, invalid, or unenforceable, such holding shall not affect the validity of any of the other provisions of the Agreement, unless the severing of such term would defeat the purpose of this Agreement.

e. The failure of any party to exercise any right or option given to it by or to insist upon strict adherence to the terms of this Agreement shall not constitute a waiver of any terms or conditions herein with respect to any other or subsequent breach.

f. Any notice, payment, or statement required by this Agreement shall be either personally delivered or sent by registered or certified mail, postage prepaid, to the addresses indicated above and shall be effective when placed in the U.S. mail, properly addressed and containing the proper postage.

g. This Agreement shall be binding on and shall inure to the benefit of the parties to this Agreement and their successors and assigns, if any.

IN WITNESS WHEREOF, the parties hereto have caused this License Agreement to be executed as of the date provided herein.

LICENSEE   LICENSOR

By: _____   By: _____

Name: _____   Name: _____

Title: _____   Title: _____

regard to some promise or obligation. Because the grant of a security interest is conditional (because it has no effect unless there is a default), a trademark that is the subject of an intent-to-use application can be used as collateral.

ROLE OF INTELLECTUAL PROPERTY PROFESSIONAL

Intellectual property professionals play a significant role in trademark maintenance. Some law firms with large trademark practices maintain separate departments for trademark prosecution and maintenance, with IP professionals taking an active role in every aspect of both. Among the activities participated in are the following:

- docketing dates for the section 8 affidavits of use and the section 9 applications for renewal;
- corresponding with (and often locating) clients to notify them that their registrations will expire unless the section 8 affidavit or the renewal application is filed;
- ensuring the chain of title is continuous so that the party who files the postregistration documents with the PTO is "of record" with the PTO as the owner of the mark and recording changes in ownership of the marks, if required;
- comparing a specimen of the mark as presently used with that in the original registration to ensure a material alteration has not occurred that would preclude the filing of a section 8 affidavit or renewal application;
- conducting due diligence to determine whether a mark has been in such continuous use that the owner can file a section 15 affidavit to obtain incontestable status of its mark;
- preparing, filing, and monitoring section 8 and 15 affidavits and applications for renewal;
- communicating PTO action on affidavits and renewal applications to clients and docketing new date for renewal;
- docketing the fifth anniversary after registration of a mark on the Supplemental Register so the registration can be moved to the Principal Register (due to the presumption that after five years of exclusive and continuous use of a mark, it has acquired distinctiveness);
- assisting clients in drafting trademark compliance policies;
- assisting clients in conducting monitoring of marks to detect possible infringing uses;
- reviewing clients' advertising copy and other materials to ensure display and use of marks is proper and that there is no misuse of another party's marks;
- drafting assignments and licenses; and
- recording assignments, mergers, changes of name, and security interests with the PTO.

CHAPTER SUMMARY

Merely obtaining a federal trademark registration does not guarantee an owner unlimited and perpetual rights to a mark. Because rights to a mark stem from use (rather than mere registration), the Lanham Act imposes certain requirements on registrants to ensure that only active marks remain on the PTO rolls.

Thus, a registration will be canceled unless, between the fifth and sixth year after registration, and in the year before the end of each ten year period after registration, the owner files a section 8 affidavit with the PTO alleging its continued use of the mark and submitting a specimen showing the mark as presently used.

If the mark is registered on the Principal Register, has been in continuous use for five years, and has not been the subject of any adverse action, the owner may file a section 15 affidavit and thereby obtain incontestability status for the mark, severely limiting the grounds upon which attacks on the mark may be made.

At the end of the registration period, and every ten years thereafter, an application for renewal must be filed, submitted with a specimen showing the mark as presently used.

In addition to losing rights to federal registration, a trademark owner can lose rights to the mark if it becomes generic or if it is abandoned with intent not to resume use. Nonuse for three years creates a presumption of abandonment.

To ensure rights to marks are maintained, many trademark owners develop compliance policies that set forth guidelines for proper use and display of the mark. Additionally, many owners monitor use of marks in the marketplace to detect potentially infringing marks.

Finally, rights to marks can be lost by acts that cause the mark to lose significance, such as by an assignment of a mark that does not include its goodwill or a license of a mark without quality control provisions to ensure that a licensee's use will be consistent with the standards of quality the public has come to expect of a mark. Trademarks can be used as collateral to secure a party's obligation to perform a promise. In the event of a party's default, the marks are then seized by the secured party, who is usually a lender of money.

DISCUSSION QUESTIONS

1. The registration certificate for a mark identifies the owner as Blackhawk Inc., a California corporation. A section 8 affidavit identifies the owner as Blackhawk Co., a California corporation. Will the section 8 affidavit be accepted? Discuss.

2. If the original registration certificate identifies a mark as FLEXTONE (STYLIZED—in script) and the specimen supporting use of the mark when it is renewed shows FLEXTONE (STYLIZED—all printed lowercase letters), will the PTO renew the registration?

3. If FLEXTONE (STYLIZED) was registered on October 1, 1995, give all dates for filing documents with the PTO to maintain the registration.

4. At the time the registrant files a combined affidavit under sections 8 and 15 for FLEXTONE (STYLIZED), the mark is the subject of litigation in which another party is claiming rights to the mark. Will the combined affidavit be accepted?

5. Discuss whether the following are advisable uses of marks:
    a. "Xerox your important documents with XEROX copiers."
    b. "KLEENEX brand tissues—the softest touch."
    c. "A FLEXTONE is easily customized for your use."
    d. "WEBCRAFT software is easy to use."
    e. "WEBCRAFT provides answers to all your accounting needs."

6. May the owner of HARTWARE for computer software advertise that "HARTWARE is compatible with MICROSOFT® products"?

7. If the owner of TRUDY'S ICE CREAM PARLORS licenses use of the mark to another party for an ice cream shop, what quality control measures should the license agreement include?

Inter Partes Proceedings, Infringement, and Dilution

Disputes often arise between parties regarding use and ownership of marks. Some proceedings occur at the PTO, and others may be initiated in federal court. There are four categories of actions involving disputes over trademark rights: inter partes proceedings, trademark infringement cases, actions alleging dilution, and actions alleging unfair competition.

Inter partes (literally, "between parties") proceedings fall into four categories: oppositions, cancellations, interferences, and concurrent use proceedings. All of these matters are adjudicated by the Trademark Trial and Appeal Board (TTAB).

A person who believes a mark is being used so as to create a likelihood of confusion in the marketplace with his or her registered mark may initiate an action for trademark infringement under the Lanham Act. Infringement actions are brought in federal court.

The Federal Trademark Dilution Act protects famous marks by prohibiting uses that are not confusingly similar under conventional trademark analysis but may nonetheless dilute the strength of or tarnish another's rights in a mark.

Finally, the Lanham Act provides broad sweeping protection for nearly all forms of unfair competition, including false advertising and infringement of trade dress, which protection is available to those who do not own a registered mark.

INTER PARTES PROCEEDINGS

Inter partes proceedings are those involving disputes between parties regarding rights, use, and ownership of marks. These actions are heard before

inter partes proceedings:
Literally, "between parties"; proceedings handled by the Trademark Trial and Appeal Board; may be oppositions, cancellations, interferences, or concurrent use proceedings

the TTAB, a department of the PTO. Generally, the Federal Rules of Civil Procedure govern these proceedings, making the proceedings substantially similar to actions brought in federal courts.

Oppositions

Timing Requirements   An **opposition** is a proceeding initiated by a person who believes that he or she would be damaged by registration of a mark on the Principal Register. Oppositions may not be initiated against marks sought to be registered on the Supplemental Register those marks may be objected to by way of cancellation proceedings, discussed later. The document initiating the proceeding is called a **Notice of Opposition.** The time for initiating an opposition is triggered by the publication of a mark in the *Official Gazette* (OG). Publication occurs after the examining attorney at the PTO has approved the mark and is intended to provide notice to the public of the pending application so interested persons can oppose the registration.

An opposition must be filed within thirty days after publication of the mark in the OG or, if an extension of time has been granted, within the extended time period. If additional time to oppose is desired, the potential opposer should prepare and file (in triplicate) a written request for extension of time to oppose before the initial thirty days expires. A thirty-day extension will be granted by the TTAB upon request, without any necessity of showing cause why the extension is needed. However, subsequent extensions must be for good cause and, unless the applicant consents, the TTAB will not grant extensions aggregating more than one hundred and twenty days from the date of publication. Typically, alleging that the potential opposer needs additional time to investigate whether the applied-for mark may conflict with his or her mark is sufficient to demonstrate good cause.

For example, if MARTIPPE is published in the OG on March 1, 1999, either a notice of opposition or a request for extension of time must be filed by March 30, 1999. Extensions of time may be granted by the TTAB until June 29, 1999 (one hundred and twenty days from publication). Additional extensions will be granted only if the applicant for MARTIPPE consents. The PTO is fairly liberal in approving extensions, believing that parties should always be given the opportunity to work out disagreements between themselves, much as courts prefer litigants to reach settlement rather than going to trial. There is no fee required for filing a request for extension of time to oppose. (See Appendix D, Form 6, for a sample form for request for extension of time to oppose.)

Notice of Opposition   If the parties themselves cannot reach some resolution, an opposition proceeding will be initiated by the filing (in triplicate) of a notice of opposition. The Lanham Act requires only that the notice of opposition set forth a short and plain statement of the reasons why the opposer believes it will be damaged by registration of the mark and the grounds for opposition. When the TTAB receives the notice of opposition, it forwards it to the applicant for response, much as a defendant in a civil action is provided with a copy of a complaint so the defendant may answer its allegations. The filing fee for a notice of opposition is $300 per class of goods/services identified in the application. (See Appendix D, Form 7, for a notice of opposition.)

Even if the parties ultimately reach resolution of the matter, the filing of a notice of opposition or even a request for extension of time to oppose seriously delays the application process. Thus, IP professionals should use the TRAM line

opposition: A proceeding initiated at the Trademark Trial and Appeal Board by one who believes he or she may be damaged by registration of a trademark

Notice of Opposition: The document that initiates an opposition proceeding and that sets forth a short and plain statement of the reasons why the opposer believes he or she will be damaged by registration of a mark

or TARR, the PTO's online status reporting system, to monitor applications to determine if such proceedings have been initiated and alert clients of such an impediment to registration.

Grounds for Opposition   In brief, an opposer wishes to prevent registration of a mark. The most common reason a person might believe he or she will be damaged if the mark applied for proceeds to registration is that the mark is confusingly similar to the opposer's mark. Opposers are not, however, limited to asserting confusing similarity as a basis for opposition. The opposer is only required to state why he or she believes registration of the mark in question would result in damage. Thus, oppositions can also be initiated on the basis of descriptiveness or that the mark is a surname, contains immoral or disparaging matter, has been abandoned, and so forth. Nevertheless, the vast majority of oppositions allege that the mark in an application should be refused because it is likely to cause confusion with the opposer's mark.

Nature of Proceeding   As soon as either a notice of opposition or a request for time to oppose is filed, the examining attorney at the PTO relinquishes the file to the TTAB, which will handle the matter until its conclusion. Opposition proceedings are somewhat like trials. The notice of opposition (equivalent to a complaint) is filed, and a copy is forwarded to the applicant; the applicant files a response to the notice of opposition (equivalent to an answer); a discovery schedule will be issued by the TTAB and will occur by way of interrogatories, depositions, and the like; briefs are filed by each party; and the TTAB will render a decision. However, the entire opposition proceeding is done by filing of documents with the PTO; no trial or oral presentations of evidence occur, unless the parties request to present oral argument. The schedule in an opposition is faster than that for most trials and the issue is narrow: should the mark be allowed to register? Damages are not awarded, and the opposer cannot force the applicant to stop using the mark. A successful opposition merely results in denial of registration of a mark in a pending application.

Just as most civil cases do not go to trial and conclude by voluntary settlement, opposition proceedings are overwhelmingly concluded by voluntary agreements. Generally, the opposer and the applicant enter into a written **consent agreement** (called a Consent to Use Agreement) whereby they agree on the scope and nature of each party's use of its mark, submit the agreement to the TTAB, and then ask for dismissal of the opposition proceeding. The consent to use agreement is the equivalent of a settlement agreement in a civil action. Until relatively recently, the PTO accorded such agreements little weight; however, since the decision in *In re Four Seasons Hotels Ltd.*, 26 U.S.P.Q. 1071 (Fed. Cir. 1993), such agreements have been given great weight in determining whether confusion is likely to result from coexistence of marks. While the PTO or TTAB can always refuse such an agreement on the basis that the public interest is not served thereby, *Four Seasons* makes it clear that if those parties who have the greatest interest in reducing confusion agree that confusion is unlikely, their decision should be respected by the PTO. If an agreement is reached, the applicant's file wrapper will be returned to the PTO for further processing, namely, registration (if the application was use-based) or allowance (if the application was based on the applicant's intent to use the mark). (See Appendix D, Form 8, for a consent to use agreement.)

consent agreement: Private agreement entered into between two trademark owners whereby each consents to the use of the other's mark, generally with some limitations or restrictions; also called consent to use agreement

Cancellations

As discussed, an opposition can be initiated only within a very limited time period. In fact, if no action is taken within thirty days of publication of the mark in the *Official Gazette,* an opposition proceeding may not be instituted. Because reading the *Official Gazette* and filing a timely notice of opposition can be extremely difficult, the Lanham Act recognizes that additional opportunity to object to registration of a mark should be afforded to those who might be injured by it. Thus, **cancellation** proceedings may be initiated after a mark is registered. The primary difference between oppositions and cancellations relates to their timing: oppositions must be initiated before registration of a mark, while cancellations are initiated after registration.

Timing Requirements   Any person who believes that he or she will be damaged by the continued existence of a registration (whether on the Principal or Supplemental Register) may petition to cancel the registration. If the mark is registered on the Supplemental Register, a **Petition to Cancel** can be filed at any time. If the mark is on the Principal Register, the petition to cancel must be filed within five years of the registration date if the grounds are those that would have justified denial of registration to begin with (such as descriptiveness, that the mark is confusingly similar to that owned by another, and so forth).

After five years, the Lanham Act narrows the grounds for cancellation and the registration may be cancelled only if certain grounds are proven, typically that the mark has become generic, the registration was obtained through fraud, the mark is functional, or the mark has become abandoned through nonuse.

The Petition to Cancel   The petition to cancel must set forth a short and plain statement of the reasons for the petitioner s belief that he or she will be damaged by continued registration of the mark, state the grounds for cancellation, and identify the owner of the registration so a copy of the petition can be forwarded to the owner. The filing fee for a petition to cancel is $300 per class of goods or services covered by the registration, and a duplicate copy must be forwarded to the TTAB so it can be forwarded to the owner of the registration.

Grounds for Petition to Cancel   Just as with notices of opposition, petitions to cancel must be brought by one who believes he or she will be damaged by registration of the mark. Thus, mere intermeddlers who cannot demonstrate they have a real interest (usually, a pecuniary interest) generally have no standing to initiate either an opposition or cancellation proceeding.

Although a variety of grounds may be asserted in a petition to cancel (the mark comprises a flag of another nation, it is primarily merely a surname, it contains immoral or scandalous matter, it includes the name of a living person without consent, or it is disparaging), the most common grounds asserted in a petition to cancel are the ones that must be brought within five years of registration: that the mark is merely descriptive, it is confusingly similar to another mark, or it has become abandoned.

Nature of Proceeding   The proceedings at the TTAB relating to cancellations are nearly identical to those involving oppositions. The petition to cancel will be filed at the TTAB, which will then forward a copy to the registrant. The

cancellation: A proceeding initiated after registration of a trademark seeking to cancel registration of a mark registered on the Principal or Supplemental Register

Petition to Cancel: The document initiating a trademark cancellation proceeding that sets forth a short and plain statement of the reasons a petitioner would be damaged by continued registration of a mark

registrant will file an answer to the petition (typically denying the grounds asserted in the petition and raising various defenses). Discovery will commence and depositions may be taken, interrogatories served, and documents requested. The TTAB will set dates for submission of written briefs and will review those briefs and render a decision.

As with oppositions, the vast majority of cancellations are settled voluntarily by the parties (who will enter into a trademark settlement agreement that is highly similar to the consent to use agreement shown in Appendix D, Form 8) rather than by TTAB decision. (See Appendix D, Form 9, Petition to Cancel Trademark Registration.)

Interferences

If two pending applications conflict or if a pending application conflicts with an existing registration (that is not yet incontestable), the PTO may declare an **interference.** Interferences are rare proceedings and occur only upon a showing of "extraordinary circumstances." Typically, if marks conflict, the parties resolve their differences by way of an opposition (if the potentially conflicting mark is not yet registered) or cancellation (if registration has occurred). Generally, only when an opposition or cancellation proceeding is unavailable to a party or will not adequately protect a party, may a party request an interference proceeding. The TTAB will then determine the rights of the parties if they cannot reach a voluntary settlement arrangement.

Concurrent Use Proceedings

If parties use similar marks in different geographical areas, a **concurrent use proceeding** may be initiated. Generally, these parties have used their marks in their respective areas in good faith and without knowledge of the other's existence. In a concurrent use application, a party requests that the registration that will ultimately issue be restricted geographically, so that on its face the registration will state that the owner has the right to use the mark in certain identified states, cities, or regions in the United States. Once the applicant files an application for concurrent use, the matter is referred to the TTAB. In most instances, the concurrent use proceeding is initiated after an application for registration is refused on the basis the mark is confusingly similar to another. The applicant then often approaches the other party in an effort to reach an accord whereby they each agree to use the mark in certain designated geographic markets. The applicant will then amend its original application to seek concurrent use. The TTAB will allow concurrent use only if confusion is not likely to result.

In brief, in a concurrent use proceeding, the parties "carve up" the United States and each agrees to use his or her mark only in a specific geographical area. Concurrent use proceedings are relatively rare.

If a party is dissatisfied with the decision of the TTAB in an opposition, cancellation, interference, or concurrent use proceeding, an appeal may be taken to the Court of Appeals for the Federal Circuit (CAFC), located in Washington, DC. The Federal Circuit can set aside PTO findings only when the findings are arbitrary, capricious, an abuse of discretion, or unsupported by substantial evidence. *Dickinson v. Zurko,* No. 98-377 (U.S. June 10, 1999). Thereafter, an

interference: A proceeding before the Trademark Trial and Appeal Board when marks in two pending trademark applications are confusingly similar or when a mark in a pending application may be confusingly similar to a registered mark that is not yet incontestable; a proceeding initiated by the PTO to determine which of two or more patents has priority

concurrent use proceeding: A proceeding initiated at the Trademark Trial and Appeal Board to determine specific geographic areas in which parties with confusingly similar marks can each use the mark

appeal may be taken to the United States Supreme Court if the Court, in its discretion, decides to hear the appeal. As an alternative to appealing to CAFC, the party may institute a civil action in the federal district court that will determine the issues *de novo*.

INFRINGEMENT OF TRADEMARKS

Introduction

The Lanham Act (15 U.S.C. § 1114) provides that the owner of a federally registered trademark may bring a civil action in federal court against any person who uses, without the registrant's consent, a mark that is likely to cause confusion with the registrant's mark. Such an action is for "trademark infringement." The central inquiry in an **infringement** action is whether there is a likelihood that an appreciable number of ordinarily prudent purchasers are likely to be misled or confused about the source, affiliation, or sponsorship of goods or services. If consumers, upon encountering the defendant's goods or services, would believe they are produced by or somehow affiliated with a plaintiff's goods or services, the defendant's mark infringes the plaintiff's.

The standard for determining whether there is a likelihood of confusion is the same as that used in the application process when an examining attorney refuses registration of a mark on the basis that it is likely to be confused with that of another prior mark. The standard is also identical to that used in opposition and cancellation proceedings when a party alleges registration of another mark should be denied or canceled because the mark is likely to be confused with that of the opposer or petitioner.

In the typical infringement action, a prior user alleges that a subsequent user is causing confusion in the marketplace by using a confusingly similar mark. In some instances, however, the second user may become so well-known and famous that it dwarfs the prior user and allegedly causes consumers to believe that the prior user's goods come from the subsequent user. The prior owner can then initiate an infringement action for "reverse confusion." (See Appendix D, Form 10, Complaint for Trademark Infringement.)

Standard for Determining Likelihood of Confusion

Various courts in various circuits have enumerated tests for determining whether one mark is likely to be confused with another. Generally, no one factor is determinative; courts examine the totality of circumstances in attempting to determine whether infringement has occurred. In general, pursuant to *E.I. du Pont de Nemours & Co.*, 476 F.2d 1357 (C.C.P.A. 1973), the following factors are considered by courts in determining whether trademark infringement exists:

infringement: A violation of some right; in the intellectual property context, a violation of a party's rights in a trademark, copyright, or patent

- the similarity of the marks in regard to appearance, sound, connotation, and commercial impression;
- the similarity of the goods or services offered under the marks;
- the similarity in the channels of trade in which the goods or services are offered;

- the conditions under which sales are made, namely, whether the purchases are made on impulse or after careful consideration by sophisticated purchasers;
- the strength of the prior mark;
- whether there has been any actual confusion;
- the number and nature of similar marks on similar goods; and
- the length of time during which there has been concurrent use with no confusion.

Sight, Sound, Meaning, and Connotation   With dissimilar marks, there is little likelihood of confusion. The more similar marks are, the more likely it is that confusion will occur. Generally marks are compared in their entireties rather than on the basis of a side-by-side comparison or a dissection of their respective elements inasmuch as courts cannot assume consumers would have the opportunity to make a side-by-side comparison when making a purchase. Some general rules have emerged:

- Marks may be confusingly similar in appearance notwithstanding the addition, deletion, or substitution of letters. Thus, TRUCOOL for synthetic coolant was held likely to be confused with TURCOOL for cutting oil. *In re Lamson Oil Co.,* 6 U.S.P.Q.2d 1041 (T.T.A.B. 1987).
- Similarity may occur due to sound or pronunciation. For example, BONAMINE was held confusingly similar to DRAMAMINE when both were used for medical goods. *G.D. Searle & Co. v. Charles Pfizer & Co.,* 265 F.2d 835 (7th Cir. 1959).
- Similarity in meaning may result in a finding of confusion. Thus, AQUA-CARE (STYLIZED) was held likely to be confused with WATERCARE when both were used for water conditioning products. *Watercare Corp. v. Midwesco Enterprise Inc.,* 171 U.S.P.Q. 696 (T.T.A.B. 1971). Similarly, BUENOS DIAS for soap was held likely to be confused with GOOD MORNING for shaving cream, *In re American Safety Razor Co.,* 2 U.S.P.Q.2d 1459 (T.T.A.B. 1987), and CYCLONE and TORNADO were held confusingly similar for wire fencing because their connotations were the same.
- If the marks include compound words, some courts consider whether there is a dominant portion of the mark and give less weight to common or descriptive elements. Thus, there was no likelihood of confusion between SOLVENTOL and SOLVITE. *Solventol Chemical Prods. v. Langfield,* 134 F.2d 899 (6th Cir. 1943). Because the descriptive prefixes *solvent* and *sol* are so commonly used, the court held that the remaining portions of the marks were distinguishable.
- When marks comprise both words and designs, greater weight is sometimes given to the wording, which would be used by consumers in requesting the goods or services.
- If an owner has a "family" of marks that has achieved public recognition, such as the family of "Mc" marks owned by McDonald's, the mark may be more likely to be infringed. Thus, due to the strong public association by the public of the "Mc" prefix with McDonald's, many attempted uses of a mark including "Mc" have been found to infringe McDonald's marks. For example, McPRETZEL was held to infringe McDonald's

family of "Mc" marks. *J & J Snack Foods Corp. v. McDonald's Corp.,* 932 F.2d 1460 (Fed. Cir. 1991).

Similarity of Goods or Services   Generally, the more similar the goods or services are that are offered under the marks, the less similar the marks need be for confusion to be found, and vice versa. The goods or services need not be identical; confusion may be found if they are related in some manner in that they serve the same purpose, relate to the same activities, or are likely to be encountered by the same types of purchasers. Thus, LAREDO for vehicles was held likely to be confused with LAREDO for tires because both relate to vehicles, *In re Jeep Corp.,* 222 U.S.P.Q. 333 (T.T.A.B. 1984), while LEXUS for vehicles was allowed to register over LEXIS for computer-assisted legal research services (because the goods are unrelated). In a recently filed case, Kellogg Company sued Exxon Corporation for trademark infringement alleging that the energy company's tiger character is likely to be confused with Kellogg's "Tony the Tiger" character used to promote food products. Although the two characters had peacefully coexisted for more than thirty years, when Exxon began selling food products at its gasoline/convenience outlets, Kellogg sued for infringement.

Courts also consider that parties may extend their product lines at some future time. Thus, the mark THE PALM for pasta would likely be refused on the basis of confusing similarity to THE PALM®, already registered for restaurant services, because restaurants often sell their food products, and consumers, upon encountering THE PALM for pasta, might believe it was associated with the restaurant of the same name.

Channels of Trade   In determining likelihood of confusion, courts consider to what extent the parties' respective goods or services are distributed through the same trade channels and advertised in the same media. Thus, if products offered under one mark are marketed to wholesalers while those under the other mark are marketed to retailers, there may be little likelihood of confusion because the goods are offered to different classes of purchasers. For example, no likelihood of confusion was found where one party sold computer services under the mark E.D.S. while the other sold power supplies and battery chargers under EDS. Although the marks were nearly identical and both parties sold in the medical field, the plaintiff sold its E.D.S. data processing services to medical insurers while the defendant sold its EDS batteries to makers of medical equipment. Because purchases would be made by different persons in different departments, coexistence of the marks was unlikely to cause confusion. *Electronic Design & Sales Inc. v. Electronic Data Systems Corp.,* 954 F.2d 713 (Fed. Cir. 1992).

Consumer Care and Sophistication   In determining trademark infringement, everything hinges on whether there is a likelihood of confusion in the mind of an appreciable number of reasonably prudent buyers. The price level of the goods or services is an important factor in determining the amount of care the buyer will use. If the goods or services are relatively expensive, more care is taken and buyers are less likely to be confused. Thus, purchasers of inexpensive items such as snack foods and sodas, which are purchased on impulse, do not give much care to such purchases and are more likely to be confused by items that bear similar marks. If the goods are expensive, however, the discriminating purchaser does not purchase casually or on impulse but only after thoughtful consideration. Thus, confusion is less likely than where the goods are inexpensive.

Strength of Marks   "Strong" marks are afforded greater protection than weak marks. Thus marks that are coined, fanciful, or arbitrary are given greater weight than marks that are suggestive, descriptive, or generic. MUCKY DUCK (& DESIGN) for mustard was held confusingly similar to MUCKY DUCK for restaurant services primarily because MUCKY DUCK was viewed as a unique and memorable mark. *In re Mucky Duck Mustard Co.,* 6 U.S.P.Q.2d 1467 (T.T.A.B. 1988). Thus, the marks EXXON® and XEROX® are given a broad scope of protection inasmuch as these coined or made-up marks had no meaning before their owners built up or developed goodwill in them.

Actual Confusion   Actual confusion is not required to support a case for trademark infringement; the standard is likelihood of confusion. However, plaintiffs who can demonstrate that some significant level of actual confusion has already occurred in the marketplace generally prevail in trademark infringement cases. Conversely, if the marks have coexisted for a number of years with no confusion, such is strongly suggestive that confusion is not likely.

Plaintiffs establish actual confusion in two ways: through testimony by consumers who have been confused about the products and by survey evidence. In the first instance, a party's initial knowledge that a competing mark is in the marketplace and is causing confusion may come about through complaint letters from consumers, misdirected orders, or inquiries and telephone calls sent to the wrong party. If, however, evidence shows that only a few purchasers were confused, such supports a finding that confusion may be unlikely. For example, when determining that SCOTT® (for paper products) and SCOTT'S LIQUID GOLD® (for furniture polish) were unlikely to be confused, the court noted that only nineteen misdirected letters had been received even though some fifty million cans of the furniture polish had been sold during the relevant period. *Scott Paper Co. v. Scott's Liquid Gold,* 589 F.2d 1225 (3d Cir. 1978).

A plaintiff may also demonstrate actual confusion by survey evidence, namely, surveys conducted by experts to determine whether confusion of consumers is likely. However, flaws in survey methodology, the types of questions asked, and the failure to survey the proper universe of purchasers may dilute the impact of a survey.

Existence of Other Similar Marks   If numerous other marks that are similar to the alleged infringer's mark coexist with the plaintiff's mark, this may be evidence that confusion is unlikely. Defendants thus often conduct comprehensive searches to demonstrate that the field is crowded and that numerous other marks all coexist with the plaintiff's mark. For example, in Arizona, marks including the term *Desert* are common, and the owner of a restaurant operating under the mark DESERT SUN might have a difficult time persuading a court that a bar called the DESERT STAR infringes his or her mark. When numerous similar marks coexist, consumers often become adept in distinguishing those marks from each other. Thus, even the slight differences between DESERT STAR and DESERT SUN may be sufficient to obviate confusion when numerous "Desert" marks coexist.

Coexistence of Marks with no Confusion   If the allegedly infringing mark has coexisted with the plaintiff's mark for a period of time and there is no evidence of confusion in the marketplace, courts often find that confusion is unlikely. For example, when STEAMEX DELUXE 15 XL coexisted with Oreck's

XL mark for seventeen months with no instances of confusion, the court held there was no infringement. *Oreck Corp. v. U.S. Floor Systems, Inc.,* 803 F.2d 166 (5th Cir. 1986).

Intent of Alleged Infringer   Proving an alleged infringer's intent or lack of good faith is not required to sustain an action for trademark infringement. However, if a party adopts a confusingly similar mark with the intent of reaping the benefits of the prior user's goodwill, such tends to weigh in favor of confusing similarity; the infringer would not have willingly adopted a similar mark unless he or she intended to trade off another's established reputation and divert customers.

When the alleged infringer had actual knowledge of the plaintiff's mark or had a prior business relationship with the plaintiff, such tends to suggest an intent to cause confusion. On the other hand, conducting a comprehensive search and relying on advice of counsel tend to rebut any inference of an intent to cause confusion.

Defenses to Infringement

There are a variety of defenses that may be raised by one accused of trademark infringement. They include the following:

- the defendant may assert that an *abandonment* of plaintiff's rights in the mark has occurred through nonuse prior to the time the defendant began using the mark;
- the defendant may allege that the plaintiff's mark has become *generic* and is thus undeserving of exclusive appropriation by the plaintiff;
- a defense may be raised that the mark is *merely descriptive* and that it has not acquired secondary meaning, and, thus, it is undeserving of protection;
- the defendant might assert that the plaintiff's registration was procured by *fraud,* is thus invalid, and cannot support an action for infringement;
- the accused infringer might assert **estoppel,** that is, that the plaintiff is *estopped* or precluded from asserting trademark infringement because it led the defendant to believe that it could use the mark (for example, by allowing numerous other similar uses to go unchallenged);
- the defendant might assert that the plaintiff has **unclean hands** and has committed such a serious wrongful act (such as wrongfully using a trademark notice when it had no right to do so) that relief should not be awarded to it;
- the defendant might assert **laches,** namely, that the plaintiff delayed an unreasonable amount of time to bring the action and this delay has prejudiced the defendant (who, during the period of delay, expended significant time and money in promoting the mark and thus should be allowed to continue using the mark);
- the defendant may allege the mark is *functional* and thus unprotectable;
- the defendant might allege that its use is a mere *parody* and is protected by the First Amendment; and/or
- the defendant may assert that its use was a **fair use,** meaning that it did not use the plaintiff's name or mark as a trademark but merely to describe its goods in a general fashion.

estoppel: A defense often raised in infringement actions, alleging the plaintiff is precluded from making certain assertions due to the plaintiff's conduct or acquiescence in the infringement

unclean hands: A defense often raised in infringement actions; an assertion that the plaintiff's own wrongful conduct precludes it from obtaining relief

laches: An unreasonable delay in asserting one's rights that causes prejudice or harm to another; a common defense asserted in intellectual property infringement actions

fair use: A defense asserted in trademark or copyright infringement actions; a non-infringing use of copyrighted work such as a parody or for criticism, scholarly research, or educational purposes

Remedies for Infringement

A plaintiff who is successful in proving trademark infringement might obtain a variety of remedies, including the following:

- an **injunction** preventing the defendant from further use of the confusingly similar mark or ordering the defendant to print a notice (called a *disclaimer*) on its goods that it is not affiliated with the plaintiff;
- *monetary damages* to compensate the plaintiff for the damage it has suffered, including actual damages due to lost sales and injury to its reputation and goodwill (which damages may be trebled, if necessary to compensate the plaintiff), and an accounting of the profits earned by defendant (however, no profits and no damages may be recovered unless the defendant had actual knowledge of the trademark registration—thus, a registrant should always use the registration symbol ® to afford such notice);
- *seizure* or *destruction* of the infringing articles; and/or
- *costs* of the action, including attorneys' fees and actual expenditures.

Resolving an Infringement Dispute

Because an infringement action, like any civil action, is expensive and time-consuming, parties often try to resolve trademark disputes between themselves before or during the pendency of litigation. Typically, a party who believes its mark is being infringed will send a **cease and desist letter** (see Figure 6–1) to the alleged infringer, notifying the infringer of its rights to the mark and demanding that the infringer cease any further use of the confusingly similar mark. Even if the cease and desist letter does not achieve the goal of convincing the infringer to stop use of the mark, it puts the infringer on notice of the prospective plaintiff's rights and thus serves to cut off any defense of good faith or lack of knowledge of the existence of the prior mark the infringer may later attempt to assert. Investigation should be conducted before sending a threatening letter to ensure the alleged infringer is the junior user. Otherwise, the alleged infringer may turn the tables on the sender of the letter.

The accused infringer typically responds to the cease and desist letter by denying its allegations, asserting various defenses, or suggesting a compromise. A compromise might be reached by the parties agreeing to use their marks only in certain geographic areas. The accused infringer might agree to place a prominent notice on its goods that it is not affiliated in any way with the prior user (although called a *disclaimer*, this notice is different from the disclaimer used in the prosecution process when an applicant disclaims or agrees it has no exclusive rights in a descriptive term in a mark). The parties might agree that the defendant should modify its mark in some way or gradually phase out use of the infringing mark. They may enter into a monetary arrangement whereby the infringer pays a sum of money to the senior user to license the mark. One party may acquire the other's mark by outright purchase. One party might agree to assign its interest in the mark to the other who then permits or licenses the original assignor to use the mark. They may agree to have an arbitrator resolve the dispute rather than going to federal court.

injunction: A court order prohibiting or compelling some act

cease and desist letter: Correspondence sent to a party demanding that it cease and desist from certain action (in the intellectual property context, from further use of a trademark, copyright, patent, or trade secret)

FIGURE 6–1
Cease and Desist Letter

Mr. Michael Taylor
InterSys Products, Inc.
2957 Fifth Avenue
New York, NY

    Re: Trademark INTERFILE
         U.S. Reg. No. 1,423,293

Dear Mr. Taylor:

Global Supplies, Inc. ("Global") is the owner of U.S. Trademark Registration No. 1,423,293 for the mark INTERFILE used by Global since 1988 in connection with the sale of divided file folders. A copy of Global's registration certificate for INTERFILE is enclosed. This trademark is a valuable asset of Global, which has expended a great deal of time and effort in establishing and maintaining consumer recognition of the mark.

Global recently became aware that InterSys Products, Inc. ("InterSys") is using the mark INNERFILER in connection with file folders. Your use of the mark INNERFILER is likely to cause confusion, mistake, or deception of the purchasing public and the trade as to the source and origin of the goods offered under the respective marks, thereby causing damage and irreparable injury to Global and diminishing the valuable goodwill associated with Global's mark. Consequently, InterSys's conduct is an infringement and violation of Global's proprietary rights in its mark, unfair competition, false advertising, and false designation of origin under applicable state laws and the U.S. Trademark Act.

Global therefore demands that InterSys immediately cease and desist from using the mark INNERFILER or any other mark confusingly similar to Global's mark and cease and desist from marketing, selling, or distributing any goods or materials bearing the mark of any confusingly similar name or mark.

Because this matter is of significant importance to Global, we request that you respond within ten days of the date of this letter to confirm your intention to cease and desist from any further use of INNERFILER or any other mark confusingly similar to any of Global's marks. If we do not receive a satisfactory response within this time period, we will consider all available remedies under state and federal law, including requesting injunctive relief and the recovery of damages for trademark infringement, which damages may be trebled by a court, and attorneys' fees and costs incurred by Global in protecting its mark.

We sincerely desire a quick and amicable resolution to this matter. Therefore, we look forward to your timely reply.

                     Sincerely,

_____

Typically, the arrangement between the parties is set forth in a written agreement, usually called a "Trademark Settlement Agreement." (See Appendix D, Form 11, for a sample trademark settlement agreement.)

Trademark Infringement Litigation

If the dispute cannot be resolved, the plaintiff will file an action for infringement in federal district court. The action will be governed by the Federal Rules of Civil Procedure relating to federal civil actions generally; these rules set the times for responding to the complaint, matters pertaining to motions and discovery, and any other litigation-related matters. Within one month after the action is commenced (and upon its conclusion), the clerk of the court must provide notice thereof to the Commissioner of Patents and Trademarks so notice of the action and its conclusion can be published in the *Official Gazette* and in the file wrappers relating to the marks.

If the defendant has a cause of action relating to the trademark to assert against the plaintiff, it must be asserted by way of a counterclaim in the litigation so that all disputes between the parties affecting the mark can be resolved at the same time.

A claim may also be made for **contributory infringement** when one party aids another to infringe a party's mark. Thus, assisting in infringement or inducing infringement are also actionable.

After the complaint, answer, and counterclaim have been filed, various motions may be made. Discovery will commence. The plaintiff and defendant will take depositions to obtain testimony of those who may have information about the case (for example, the plaintiff may depose individuals in the defendant's marketing department to determine how the defendant came to adopt its mark); interrogatories may be served on either party to obtain information, such as to inquire about experts either side may intend to call or the existence of documents; and each party may ask the other to produce relevant documents, such as surveys or complaints by consumers indicating confusion.

Ultimately, if the matter cannot be resolved by private agreement, it will proceed to trial. Either party may request a jury trial; otherwise, a judge will render the decision. The decision in the case may be appealed to the United States Court of Appeals for the circuit in which the district court is located. Thereafter, the matter may be appealed to the United States Supreme Court, if the Court decides, in its discretion, to hear the appeal.

DILUTION OF TRADEMARKS

Introduction

In January 1996, the long-awaited Federal Trademark Dilution Act (15 U.S.C. § 1125) was enacted to provide special protection to "famous" marks when the owners of those marks are unable to establish likelihood of confusion and thus avail themselves of the many avenues afforded to protect marks from confusingly similar uses.

Dilution refers to unauthorized acts that tend to blur the distinctiveness of a famous mark or to tarnish the mark by using it in a disparaging or unsavory way. For example, use of the mark TIFFANY® by a restaurant in Boston was found not to be likely to be confused with TIFFANY for jewelry store services in New York, inasmuch as no reasonable consumer would believe the uses were related or that the restaurant services were sponsored by or originated with Tiffany Jewelers. Nevertheless, use by the restaurant was held to be a dilution of Tiffany Jeweler's famous mark and was enjoined. *Tiffany & Co. v. Boston Club, Inc.*, 231 F. Supp. 836 (D. Mass. 1964).

Another well-known case involved the use of DOGIVA in connection with dog biscuits. Clearly, consumers would not be confused upon encountering the mark and believe that the dog biscuits were related to GODIVA® brand chocolates. However, use of DOGIVA on such a product tended to injure or tarnish the plaintiff's business reputation and was enjoined.

contributory infringement: In the intellectual property context, causing, inducing, or assisting in infringement of another's trademark, copyright, or patent

dilution: Unauthorized acts that tend to blur the distinctiveness of a famous mark or to tarnish it

Finally, use of a bottle in the shape of that protected by Coca-Cola Company, for white bubble gum resembling cocaine was held to tarnish Coca-Cola's well-known and famous marks and was enjoined even though, under traditional likelihood of confusion analysis, there would have been no infringement.

The primary focus of the new Dilution Act is to preserve a trademark owner's property rights and goodwill in its famous mark, which might evaporate if junior users were allowed to use the mark even on unrelated goods. Dilution is generally defined as the lessening of the capacity of a famous mark to identify and distinguish goods and services.

Blurring and Tarnishment

Generally, there are two types of unauthorized use that constitute dilution: blurring and tarnishment. **Blurring** is the whittling away of an established trademark's selling power through its unauthorized use upon dissimilar products. Examples might include STARBUCKS PENS, SHELL COFFEE, PEPSI VIDEO, or the use of TIFFANY for restaurant services as described earlier. Such uses would eventually drain away the distinctive power of the original mark even if they did not cause consumer confusion. **Tarnishment** occurs when a mark is linked to products of an inferior quality or when the mark is portrayed in an unwholesome or embarrassing context (such as a poster reading "Enjoy Cocaine" in a script and color identical to that used by Coca-Cola Company or the substitution of an expletive for "Dunkin" in the mark DUNKIN' DONUTS®).

Federal Remedies for Dilution

The new act provides a remedy for owners of famous marks in federal court. The Dilution Act (15 U.S.C. § 1125(c)(1)) lists several factors for courts to consider in determining whether a mark is sufficiently famous that it is protectable under the act, including the duration and extent of use of the mark, duration and extent of advertising and publicity for the mark, the degree of inherent or acquired distinctiveness of the mark, fame of the mark in the parties' respective trading areas, and whether the mark is federally registered. An owner who prevails is entitled to injunctive relief, destruction of all diluting goods, and, if intent to dilute is shown, actual damages, treble damages, the violator's profits, and costs.

Some types of conduct are exempt from liability, such as fair use of a famous mark in comparative advertising, parody for noncommercial purposes, and news reporting. These uses are protected under the First Amendment.

Many of the newer cases discussing dilution relate to the use of Internet addresses that dilute famous marks. Thus, the address "candyland.com" for sexually explicit goods and services was held to dilute the famous CANDY-LAND® mark owned by Hasbro Toys, *Hasbro Inc. v. Entertainment Group Ltd.*, 40 U.S.P.Q.2d 1479 (W.D. Wash. 1996), and the address "adultsrus.com" for sexual paraphernalia was held to dilute the famous TOYS R US® mark owned by Toys "R" Us, Inc. *Toys "R" Us, Inc. v. Akkaouli*, WL 772709 (N.D. Cal. 1996).

blurring: A form of trademark dilution that whittles away the value of a famous trademark through its unauthorized use on a dissimilar product or with a dissimilar service

tarnishment: A form of dilution in which a famous trademark is portrayed in an unsavory or embarrassing manner

RELATED TRADEMARK CLAIMS

Importation of Gray Market Goods

In many instances, U.S. trademark owners grant rights to those in foreign countries to manufacture goods that bear the U.S. trademark. After the goods are distributed in the foreign markets, other parties buy them (often in bulk) and import them back into the United States to resell to others, in competition with the U.S. trademark owner. These goods are called **gray market goods** or **parallel imports.** The law relating to the permissibility of such importation is unsettled, with most courts holding that the import and sale of gray market goods is not infringement because once a mark owner sells goods bearing its mark, it cannot prevent subsequent owners from reselling the goods if: there is no deception or consumer confusion; the goods are physically the same as those sold by the U.S. trademark owner; and the U.S. registrant and the foreign manufacturer are the same or related entities. The situation is analogous to resales in the United States. For example, a consumer who purchases a baby stroller bearing the APRICA® mark can later resell it to another. This doctrine is referred to as the **exhaustion theory** inasmuch as once the first lawful sale is made, the trademark owner's rights are exhausted or extinguished in regard to subsequent sales. Allowing importation of gray market or parallel goods is consistent with the exhaustion theory. As discussed in Chapter 16, recent holdings in the copyright field are also consistent with this theory.

Counterfeiting

Trademark **counterfeiting** is a particularly specious type of infringement. A counterfeiter applies the trademark owner's mark to goods or services that do not originate with the owner. Perhaps the best examples of counterfeiting or "black market" activities involve the unauthorized sale of scarves bearing the HERMES® mark, pocketbooks bearing the GUCCI® or LOUIS VUITTON® marks, watches bearing the ROLEX® mark, and other "high end" or designer items that are sold at flea markets, corner stands, and "on the street." The items sold and which bear the mark are not genuine and are intentionally sold for the express purpose of trading off the owner's established goodwill and reputation.

Universities, athletic teams, and rock bands that own valuable marks often have their marks counterfeited and placed on black market goods, primarily T-shirts, sweatshirts, and jackets. To deter counterfeiters, statutes allow for the immediate impoundment and destruction of the "knockoff" goods; awards of treble damages, actual damages, and attorneys' fees; and criminal penalties. It has been reported that in just the few months prior to the 1996 Atlanta Olympics, $2.5 million worth of infringing merchandise was seized, mostly in the Atlanta area. Unfortunately, however, seizing the goods provides little long-term benefit, inasmuch as the counterfeiter simply moves its stall or stand to some other location the next day.

Unfair Competition

Section 43 of the Lanham Act (15 U.S.C. § 1125) provides that any person injured by a false designation of origin or false representation may bring a civil

gray market goods: Unauthorized importation of goods into the United States for resale after the goods are distributed in foreign markets

parallel imports: See *gray market goods*

exhaustion theory: In trademark and patent law, the extinguishment or exhaustion of a trademark or patent owner's rights once a lawful first sale has been made of trademarked goods or a patented invention; in copyright law, the extinguishment of a copyright owner's right to distribute a copyrighted work once a lawful first sale has been made; also see *first sale doctrine*

counterfeiting: A form of trademark infringement in which a trademark is affixed to goods or services that do not originate with the trademark owner

action against the offending party. This statute is often used as a "catchall" because it is so broadly worded that it prohibits nearly all forms of **unfair competition,** including false advertising and infringement of trade dress. Moreover, a party need not have a registered trademark to invoke its protections. Thus, it affords even broader protection than section 32 of the Lanham Act (15 U.S.C. § 1114), which prohibits infringement of a registered mark. In most instances, parties alleging trademark infringement under section 32 of the Lanham Act also include a cause of action for unfair competition under section 43 (and state consumer protection or unfair competition statutes, if they exist). Unfair competition is fully discussed in Chapter 23.

Customs Regulation

Additional protection is provided to trademark owners through section 42 of the Lanham Act (15 U.S.C. § 1124), which allows owners of registered trademarks to deposit their certificates of registration with the U.S. Customs Department in order to allow Customs to block importation of offending goods. The trademark owner files an application with the Commissioner of Customs in Washington, DC, to have its marks recorded with Customs, deposits one certified copy and five additional copies of its registration certificates with Customs, and pays an application fee of $190 per class. The U.S. Customs will then "post its ports." **Posting of ports** means that customs will monitor ports of entry

unfair competition: A branch of law protecting against deceptive and improper conduct in the marketplace

posting of ports: Monitoring of ports of entry into the United States by the Customs Department for the purpose of seizing unauthorized goods bearing a party's registered trademark

ROLE OF INTELLECTUAL PROPERTY PROFESSIONAL

Intellectual property professionals are typically involved in a variety of interesting and challenging tasks related to trademark protection, including the following:

- reviewing the *Official Gazette* to locate marks that may need to be opposed or reviewing reports from watching services relating to publications of marks that may need to be opposed;
- docketing relevant dates for filing a notice of opposition, request for time to oppose, or petition to cancel;
- preparing or responding to cease and desist letters;
- preparing notices of opposition, petitions to cancel, complaints for infringement, or responses or answers thereto;
- docketing all relevant dates in opposition, cancellation, and infringement proceedings, such as dates for close of discovery, submission of written briefs, and so forth;
- assisting in the discovery process by drafting interrogatories, reviewing documents produced, summarizing depositions, reviewing surveys, and so forth;
- conducting searches and investigations to determine the number and use of other similar marks;
- drafting consent to use or trademark settlement agreements;
- providing general assistance for infringement trials such as locating witnesses, organizing exhibits and documents, conducting research, and preparing jury instructions; and
- preparing applications to U.S. Customs to record trademark registrations to block importation of offending goods.

into the United States and will seize any unpermitted goods bearing the owner's mark. Criminal sanctions may be imposed on the offending party.

CHAPTER SUMMARY

Disputes over use and ownership of trademarks are common. Such disputes typically fall into one of four categories: inter partes proceedings, infringement actions, actions for dilution, and actions alleging unfair competition.

An inter partes proceeding is one brought before the Trademark Trial and Appeal Board and may be categorized as follows:

- an opposition by a party to registration of a mark;
- a petition to cancel an existing registration of a mark;
- an interference; and
- a concurrent use proceeding whereby parties each agree to use their respective marks in specifically designated geographical areas.

An action for trademark infringement can be brought in federal court if a defendant's use of a mark is likely to cause confusion with a registered mark to an appreciable number of reasonably prudent consumers about the source, origin, affiliation, or sponsorship of goods or services. Courts consider a variety of factors in determining whether there is a likelihood of confusion, including the similarity of the marks, the similarity of the goods/services offered under the marks, the similarity of trade channels, the strength of the senior mark, whether the sale is made on impulse or only after careful deliberation, and whether actual confusion has occurred. A trademark infringement action proceeds much like any trial: a complaint is filed, an answer is filed, motions may be made, discovery occurs, and a trial is held.

An action for dilution may be brought even when another's use of a mark is not likely to cause confusion if another uses a mark in a way that blurs the distinctiveness of a famous mark or tarnishes its reputation and goodwill.

If a mark is not registered, an action for unfair competition may be brought against a party who is using a false designation of origin or is engaged in false advertising. Additional protection is afforded by depositing a certificate of trademark registration with the U.S. Customs Service to prohibit offending goods from entering the United States.

Thus, securing a federal registration for one's mark enhances the level of protection for a trademark owner who may then bring a civil action for infringement of the registered mark and may obtain the assistance of U.S. Customs in blocking offending goods from entry into the United States. Owners of unregistered marks may seek protection under section 43 of the Lanham Act for unfair competition, but the remedies provided by infringement actions and posting of ports are not available to them.

DISCUSSION QUESTIONS

1. What is the primary difference between an opposition and a petition to cancel?
2. The mark VALLEY GREENE FARMS was published on April 15. Today is May 14, and you have just discovered this publication and are concerned the mark conflicts with a client's mark. What should you do?
3. Your firm's client has sold expensive computer hardware under the mark COMPUTEL. The product, sales of which are significant, has been exhibited nationwide for at least five years and has been displayed at trade shows with hardware by other vendors, including that offered under the mark COMPUCARE. Your client is unaware of any instances of actual confusion. An action for trademark infringement has been filed by the owner of COMPUCARE seeking to enjoin use of COMPUTEL. Using traditional likelihood of confusion analysis, discuss whether the marks are likely to be confused. Additionally, discuss what defenses the owner of COMPUTEL might assert in an answer.
4. A client has penned a cartoon to be published in *Newsweek* magazine that pokes fun at Microsoft and parodies it. The mark MICROSOFT® will appear in the cartoon. Discuss whether the use would constitute dilution.
5. Classify the following as either blurring or tarnishment:
   VISA Child Care Centers
   GENERAL MILLS CAT VITAMINS
   REEBOK BOOKS
   "Things go Better with Coke," placed on a poster promoting drug use
   MERCEDEZ BENZ CHEDDAR CHEESE SNAK CRACKERS

New Developments in Trademark Law

New issues have arisen in trademark law that were entirely unanticipated just a few years ago. The emergence of the Internet as a tool for electronic communication has resulted in complex intellectual property issues; chief among them are the assignment of Internet domain names and attendant disputes over such domain names. Companies that have invested significant amounts of time and money in their marks have been surprised when they have attempted to use their marks as part of their domain names, only to find the names have been taken by cybersquatters or electronic pirates who register famous domain names in the hopes of ransoming them back to their rightful owners. The issue of domain name assignment and dispute resolution is one that has caused great controversy and cries for reform.

Use of marks on the Internet has also led to various First Amendment issues, especially with regard to the practice of using another party's mark on one's web site as a link to another site. Finally, courts have struggled with the issue whether merely operating a passive web site should expose a party to jurisdiction in all states where the web site can be accessed. Generally, courts have held that passive web sites offering information only should not subject the web site operator to personal jurisdiction in other states.

As use of the Internet continues to increase in ways not yet imagined, intellectual property rights are likely to continue to be affected, requiring courts to be imaginative and flexible in dealing with emerging technologies.

THE INTERNET

Introduction

Trademark owners throughout the world are struggling with new issues presented by increased electronic communication, primarily that occurring through the Internet. The Internet derives from a network set up in the 1970s by the Department of Defense to connect military and research sites that could continue to communicate even in the event of nuclear attack. In the 1980s, the National Science Foundation expanded on the system, and its first significant users were government agencies and universities. In the early 1990s, however, it became apparent that the system could provide a global communication network, allowing people from all over the world to talk with each other; send written messages (electronic mail or "e-mail"), pictures, and text to each other; and establish web pages (also called "home pages") to advertise their wares and provide information to their customers. Thus, the Internet has become a channel of commerce with more than one hundred million users worldwide. It has been estimated that in the United States alone, commerce on the Internet will exceed $300 billion by 2002.

To communicate on the Internet, businesses and individuals are assigned addresses called "domain names." To consumers, these domain names function much like a trademark in that they identify a source of goods or services.

Assignment of Domain Names

The rapid explosion of the Internet has presented two novel trademark issues: how should domain names be registered for use on the Internet, and how should disputes over domain names be resolved? As marks are used more frequently on the Internet, trademark owners need to ensure that their marks continue to serve their key functions of distinguishing an owner's goods and services from those of others and protecting the public from deception and confusion. Moreover, businesses desire domain names that are easy to remember and that relate to their name, products, or services. Owners of famous trademarks, such as Nestle Co., typically register their primary trademark as their domain name, as in "nestle.com." Additionally, consumers who do not definitely know a company's domain name often merely type in the company name, such as "ibm.com" in the hope of locating the company's site. This method is often successful.

A company's presence on the Internet begins with its address or **domain name.** A domain name not only serves as a locator for a company but also functions as a designation of origin and a symbol of goodwill—a trademark. There are two portions to a domain name: the **generic top-level domain,** which is the portion of the name to the right of a period (such as .gov or .com), and the **secondary level domain,** which is the portion of the name to the left of a period (such as "kraft" in "kraft.com"). Disputes frequently arise between owners of registered marks and owners of domain names who use domain names similar or identical to the registered marks. While several parties might have identical trademarks (because their products or services are not confusingly similar), it is not possible for two parties to have identical web addresses. For example, a company might register the mark SHOEBIZ for its shoes. Another party might adopt the domain name "shoebiz.com." When consumers encounter the domain name, they may go to the site seeking information on the shoe products and instead be presented with information from an entirely unrelated company. Moreover, the owner of the SHOEBIZ mark might not be able to secure the domain name for its business even though it has a valid trademark registration because the domain name has already been taken by someone else.

Domain names are appearing as assets in sales of businesses and in bankruptcies. The name "business.com" was recently sold for $150,000, and the art

domain name: Internet address used by a company or individual

generic top-level domain: The portion of a domain name to the right of a period, such as ".com" or ".gov"

secondary level domain: The part of a domain name to the left of a period, such as "ibm" in "ibm.com"

of establishing a value for a domain name is a burgeoning business. Moreover, at least one state, Virginia, has held that domain names are property and can thus be garnished and sold. *Umbro Int'l, Inc. v. 3263851 Canada, Inc.*, Civ. No. 174388 1999 WL 117760 (Va. Cir. Mar. 12, 1999).

At the time of writing of this text, domain names in the United States are assigned by a company called Network Solutions, Inc. (NSI, or sometimes called InterNIC) of Herndon, Virginia, which was selected by the National Science Foundation in 1992 to administer domain names. Network Solutions, Inc., registers or assigns more than 100,000 domain names each month on a first-come, first-served basis for a certain fee. As of mid-1997, more than 1,400,000 domain names had been assigned by NSI—with an estimated $200,000,000 in gross profits earned by NSI. Registration of domain names is fairly straightforward. A party applies with NSI for a desired domain name. If the name has not yet been taken, NSI assigns it to the applicant. In other countries, independent agencies or companies assign domain names using two-letter country codes, such as "ca" for Canada. Thus, a Canadian company's domain name might be "abc.com.ca."

Disputes soon arose when companies discovered they could not obtain their names or marks as domain names because those names had been assigned by NSI to a prior applicant. Network Solutions, Inc., thus instituted the following policy to address these issues:

- In applying to register a domain name, an applicant must represent that, to its knowledge, the name does not infringe the rights of another.
- The applicant must assert that it has a bona fide intent to use the domain name on a regular basis and for a lawful purpose.
- Once a domain name is registered, if a party claims ownership of a trademark embodied in that name and presents evidence to NSI of its priority (by submitting a certified copy of its certificate of registration and a copy of a protest letter to the domain name holder), NSI will request that the owner of the domain name prove it has prior rights to use the domain name by submitting a valid foreign or U.S. trademark registration.
- If the trademark owner has priority (because its registration or date of first use precedes the creation date of the domain name), NSI will not allow the domain name owner to continue its use; NSI will give the domain name registrant ninety days to adopt another name and will then put the disputed name on "hold," making it unavailable for use by anyone, until a court or arbitration order is presented that establishes the rights of the parties.

Network Solutions, Inc.'s policy has stirred much debate inasmuch as it allows one party, the trademark owner, to obtain relief similar to what a court would order by way of injunction, namely, the cessation of use of the domain name, without the necessity of authenticated evidence or proof such as a court would require and with no showing of a likelihood of confusion. As a result of its role in assigning and then freezing domain names, NSI was named in several trademark-related lawsuits alleging that NSI had a duty to screen domain name applications for potential infringement before assigning or registering those names. In 1997, the U.S. district court ruled that NSI did not have a duty to prevent infringement, *Lockhead Martin Corp. v. Network Solutions, Inc.*, 985 F. Supp. 949 (C.D. Cal. 1997), and suits against NSI appear to be on the wane.

Additionally, a suit alleging that NSI was an illegal monopoly because it was the exclusive registrar of domain names was dismissed in mid-1998.

Cybersquatters and the Dilution Doctrine

If the domain name owner uses its site to promote or offer goods or services confusingly similar to those offered by a trademark owner with prior rights and the domain name and mark are confusingly similar, the trademark owner can bring an action for infringement under the Lanham Act just as it would for any act of infringement. More difficult issues have arisen, however, when domain names have simply been registered and are used merely for an e-mail address with no web site associated with them (making the name unavailable as a domain name for the rightful owner) or are used in connection with goods or services that are unrelated to those offered by the trademark owner. In such cases, the trademark owner cannot bring an action for infringement inasmuch as the owner cannot show likelihood of confusion. Enter the dilution doctrine.

When the Federal Trademark Dilution Act (15 U.S.C. § 1125(c)) was being considered, Senator Patrick J. Leahy (D. Vermont) expressed his hope that it would be useful in prohibiting the misuse of famous marks as domain names on the Internet. Since the passage of the act, most trademark owners have in fact relied on the act in disputes over domain names.

A few recent cases have dealt with the issue of parties who register famous marks as domain names without the trademark owners' permission and then attempt to sell the domain name to the owner. Such a practice is called **cybersquatting.** In *Intermatic v. Toeppen,* 947 F. Supp. 1227 (N.D. Ill. 1996), the owner of the well-known mark INTERMATIC® (used on a variety of electronic products) sued Dennis Toeppen, an individual who had registered the domain name "intermatic.com" with NSI. Toeppen did not offer any goods or services on his "intermatic.com" site and acknowledged he intended to "arbitrage" the name, along with more than two hundred and forty other names he had registered as domains, including "deltaairlines.com" and "neiman-marcus.com," which he then offered to sell to their owners for sums ranging between $10,000 and $15,000. The district court held that the act of registering a domain name with the intent to resell it constituted "use in commerce" and was therefore covered by the Federal Trademark Dilution Act. Toeppen's acts were held to have diluted the famous INTERMATIC mark by decreasing the owner's ability to identify and distinguish its goods on the Internet because the domain name registration system does not permit two entities to use the same domain name (unlike marketplace conditions in which similar or identical marks may coexist) and it decreased Intermatic's ability to control the association that the public would make with its mark. In mid-1998, the Ninth Circuit Court of Appeals upheld a summary judgment ruling against Toeppen for trademark dilution arising out of similar acts, namely, attempting to sell Panavision's domain name to it for $13,000. *Panavision Int'l, L.P. v. Toeppen,* 141 F.3d 1316 (9th Cir. 1998).

Similarly, in *Hasbro Inc. v. Internet Entertainment Group Ltd.,* 40 U.S.P.Q.2d 1479 (W.D. Wash. 1996), Hasbro, the owner of the CANDYLAND® mark used in connection with the famous children's board game, was able to enjoin the defendant's use of the domain name "candyland.com" for a web site featuring sexually explicit material. The court held that the defendant's use tarnished the famous CANDYLAND mark under the Federal Trademark Dilution Act.

cybersquatting: A practice in which a person, without permission, registers another's name as a domain name and then attempts to sell the domain name to its true owner

Although the act is intended to protect only "famous" marks from dilution, some courts have shown a tendency to construe that requirement liberally in cases related to Internet use so as to afford relief even to trademark owners whose marks are not famous, primarily because those parties cannot show sufficient likelihood of confusion to support an action for infringement. Courts have often used the dilution doctrine to protect the owners of marks from use of their marks as domain names by others, particularly when evidence shows "cybersquatting," or acts showing a party's piracy or bad faith in registering a domain name.

Because NSI, the domain name registrar, will act only if domain names are identical, some porn operators have reserved a misspelling of a name, such as "newswek.com," as porn sites. Generally, such sites are shut down by courts relying on the dilution doctrine.

Cybersquatting also occurs in Europe, where courts have banned Internet domain name dealers from registering names such as "spice-girls.net" and then selling them to their rightful owners for sums up to the equivalent of $40,000.

Plans for Reform

Concerns over the wisdom of allowing one private for-profit commercial enterprise such as NSI/InterNIC to administer the lucrative domain name registration practice have led to numerous and often competing plans for reform. Moreover, there has been international concern that the United States is dominating the Internet and assignment of domain names. The result has been the formation of a not-for-profit benefit corporation, the Internet Corporation for Assigned Names and Numbers (ICANN). ICANN, a more internationally based organization than NSI, will replace NSI in administering domain names and by late 2000 will decide whether to expand the top-level domain name indicators to accommodate the need for additional domain names (for example, by adding ".arts" for entries related to entertainment and the arts and ".firm" and ".store" for business uses). ICANN also intends to adopt a policy requiring disputes over trademarks to be sent to mandatory arbitration, with the prevailing party obtaining attorneys' fees. ICANN, acting as an oversight board for the Internet, will be governed by a nine-member board composed of individuals from around the world. Its web site is www.icann.org.

HYPERLINKING AND THE FIRST AMENDMENT

Web page owners frequently provide symbols, called **hyperlinks,** that designate other web pages that may be of interest to a user. Thus, a trademark owner's mark may be displayed on thousands of different web sites, allowing users to "click" onto the symbol and be transported to a different location, either to a different page within that same web site or to an entirely different web site on the Internet.

Most companies have no objection to linking, rightfully believing that linking allows more individuals to visit their sites and thus increases commercial use. Thus, most web site owners have not sought permission from others to link to their site.

A recently enacted Georgia statute prohibited the use of any trademark on the Internet that falsely implied that permission to use the symbol had been

hyperlink: A symbol designating another's web page

granted. In striking down the statute as unconstitutional, the United States District Court for the Northern District of Georgia held that the First Amendment protects the linking function as free speech. *ACLU v. Miller,* 43 U.S.P.Q.2d 1356 (N.D. Ga. 1997). Many experts analogize linking with footnoting in written documents, namely, a signal to users that additional information can be sought elsewhere.

At this time, however, it is unknown whether the ruling will apply to **deep linking,** which allows a user at one site to proceed directly to certain information at another site, bypassing the home page at the second site. Because home pages often provide background information and their owners sell advertising on the home pages, arguments have been raised that deep linking that bypasses a home page deprives the second site owners of advertising revenue. Another unresolved issue related to linking is "framing," the retrieval by one web site of content from another web site that is then incorporated into the original web site within a frame.

At this time, there is no certainty on the permissibility of deep linking or framing, and many commentators believe that permission of the original web site owner should be sought by those wishing to deeplink and bypass a home page or those wishing to incorporate others' material by framing. However, those challenged with infringement or other intellectual property violations on the Internet should strongly consider asserting that their acts are protected by the First Amendment.

OTHER CYBERSPACE TRADEMARK ISSUES

Asserting Jurisdiction over Web Site Owners

One of the questions that has troubled courts over the past several years is whether by operating a web site accessible in all fifty states, a web site operator becomes subject to the jurisdiction of courts in each state such that it can be sued in that state. In general, a state can only subject a party to personal jurisdiction if the party has had some minimum contacts with the state such that subjecting him or her to jurisdiction does not offend traditional notions of justice. The most recent analyses of this issue indicate that if a party is merely posting information or advertising its products and services on a passive web site, jurisdiction cannot be exercised over a nonresident defendant. If, however, the defendant is actively conducting business, entering into contracts, or transmitting files over the Internet, jurisdiction can likely be exercised. In sum, the exercise of personal jurisdiction depends on the level of interactivity between the consumer and the web site operator.

deep linking: The process by which an Internet user can proceed directly to certain information at another's web site, bypassing the home page at the second site

Clandestine Trademark Misuse

Another area of growing concern is that of clandestine trademark abuse. This involves embedding a trademark into a web site such that it is not visible to the viewer. The search engine, however, registers the presence of the hidden or clandestine trademark and lures the viewer to another web site, generally that of a competitor. The practice is usually accomplished by the use of "metatags," which are special codes whose function is to emphasize key words, making it easier for search engines to locate the web site. In one case, a defendant embedded the plaintiff's registered trademarks into the keyword section of its web site so that users of Internet search engines seeking to obtain information about the plaintiff were lured to the defendant's site. Although the parties reached a private settlement, the terms included the entry of a permanent injunction prohibiting the defendant from the practice and also requiring the defendant to notify the search engine companies to delete the link between the plaintiff's marks and the defendant's web site.

Trademark Policing on the Internet

Although many companies conduct annual or periodic audits and searches to review possible conflicting marks, the proliferation of use of marks and domains on the Internet adds yet another level of complexity to a trademark owner's duty to monitor and protect its marks. Many search companies review lists or databases of domain names, but further investigation may be called for due to the use of hyperlinking and embedded use of marks on others' sites. A firm in Houston, Texas, idNames.com, conducts worldwide searches and then reports the results from every country offering domain name registration (see www.idnames.com). The database of the top-level domain names administered by NSI is located at http://internic.net. A tutorial is available to help with searching. Another company, Datalytics, offers monitoring of the NSI domain name registry and access to online discussion groups (see www.markwatch.com).

In addition to disclosing potential conflicts, periodic monitoring will reveal "deadwood" domains, namely, those not in actual use, so they may then be applied for and used by others.

Internet Complaint Sites

Irate consumers have often set up their own web sites to complain about certain products or services. In one case, Bally Total Fitness claimed that its BALLY® mark was infringed by a defendant's "Bally Sucks" web site. The court held there was no infringement because consumers would not be confused inasmuch as the addition of the word *sucks* clearly distinguished the defendant's site from Bally's registered mark. The court also held that the web site did not dilute Bally's mark inasmuch as the defendant's use was not commercial and the federal dilution statute was not intended to prohibit noncommercial expression such as parody and satire. There was no tarnishment because the defendant's use was consumer commentary. *Bally Total Fitness Holding Corp. v. Faber,* 29 F. Supp. 2d 1161 (C.D. Cal. 1998). Thus, the use of another's mark on a web site to complain about a product or service is permissible as long as there is no consumer confusion, the remarks are protected parody or noncommercial expression, and the content is neither false nor defamatory.

ROLE OF INTELLECTUAL PROPERTY PROFESSIONAL

Intellectual property professionals can assist in enhancing protection for trademark owners in a variety of ways:

- monitoring new developments in cyberspace by reading articles of interest and visiting web sites devoted to areas of trademark concern;
- filing applications for domain name registrations;
- assisting in periodic audits or reviews of uses of conflicting marks in cyberspace;
- reviewing sites of competitors of clients for embedded marks; and
- checking links from and to clients' web sites to ensure that neither the clients' nor third parties' marks are being infringed.

CHAPTER SUMMARY

The Internet has dramatically changed communication. Along with that change, however, has come conflict over use of domain names and trademarks. The assignment of domain names, or Internet addresses, has resulted in disputes between the owners of domain names and the owners of trademarks. Courts have protected the rights of trademark owners as against "cybersquatters," those who register domain names for the purpose of selling them to their rightful owners rather than for some bona fide use or purpose.

If a dispute arises between parties claiming rights in domain names, the present register of marks, NSI, has the right upon demonstration that another party has a prior registered trademark, to require a domain name holder to cease use of the domain name or to freeze the name, not allowing use by any party. This policy has been severely criticized, and a number of proposals for reform of assignment of domain names and conflict resolution has been made by a variety of organizations.

Use of the Internet also implicates First Amendment rights to freedom of speech. At present, courts have held that merely providing links to another party's web site is permissible. Deep linking (allowing a party to bypass a home page and proceed directly to relevant material) is subject to dispute. The practice of embedding another party's trademarks on a web site may also constitute trademark infringement. In addition, merely having a passive presence or web site on the Internet will likely not subject a party to personal jurisdiction; however, if goods are offered for sale or contracts are entered into through a web site, a court may subject the web site owner to personal jurisdiction. Finally, use of another's mark on a noncommercial web site for the purposes of satire, parody, or consumer commentary is likely permissible as long as there is no likelihood of confusion.

DISCUSSION QUESTIONS

1. Under the current NSI policy, if a domain owner is assigned the name www.acme.com and the owner of a federal registration for ACME for unrelated goods demonstrates it used the ACME mark prior to the domain owner, what may NSI do?

2. Holly Turner, an entrepreneur, has applied for and been assigned two hundred domain names by NSI, including www.revlon.com, www.starbucks.com, and www.cnn.com. What theory may the owners of the marks REVLON®, STARBUCKS®, and CNN® rely on in attempting to protect their marks?

3. Given the facts in question 2, does NSI have any liability to the owners of the REVLON, STARBUCKS, and CNN marks?

4. Harry Hunter, located in California, has a web site that provides information about a line of clothing he offers. The web site is informational only, and viewers cannot interact with the site or order any goods. Can Harry be subject to jurisdiction in New York because his web site can be accessed by New York residents? Discuss.

5. Harry Hunter has links in his web site that connect to a web site of Nordstrom, a store that offers Harry's line of clothing, by displaying the NORDSTROM® mark. Has Harry infringed Nordstrom's mark? What if Harry's link bypasses Nordstrom's home page and proceeds directly to the specific information relating to Harry's goods? Discuss.

CHAPTER
8
International Developments in Trademark Law

Foreign nationals who wish to offer their products and services under a trademark or service mark in the United States can seek registration under the Lanham Act. While foreign applicants can seek federal registration on the same bases as U.S. applicants, namely, based on actual use of a mark in commerce, or based on a bona fide intent to use the mark in commerce, two additional bases are available. First, the foreign applicant may apply for registration of a mark in the United States based on a pending application in a foreign country and, if the application was filed in the foreign country within the previous six months, the applicant will be able to use the earlier filing date as its priority date in the United States. Second, the applicant may apply for registration of a mark in the United States based upon a registration issued by a foreign country. The advantage of using either of these latter two bases for registration is that neither requires use in commerce, thus allowing foreign applicants to secure federal registrations for marks that are not in use in commerce in the United States.

Just as foreign nationals may apply for trademark protection in the United States, U.S. trademark owners should give serious consideration to protecting their marks in foreign countries. Because the trademark laws of various foreign countries are complex and often rapidly changing, most U.S. law firms work in tandem with attorneys in the foreign countries who will prosecute the application on behalf of the U.S. trademark owner. The priority date afforded to foreign applicants in the U.S. is also available to United States trademark owners who wish to seek trademark protection in various foreign countries; if the foreign application is filed within six months of the U.S. application, it will retain the earlier filing date for priority purposes.

A new system, called the Community Trademark System, allows U.S. trademark owners to file one single application for the fifteen member nations of the European Union, thereby saving considerable time, effort, and money.

United States trademark owners who are considering foreign expansion should consider filing trademark applications in the countries in which they intend to do business to protect their marks and to ensure their marks are not "pirated" by unscrupulous third parties who register marks owned by others and then attempt to sell the marks to the rightful owners.

APPLICATIONS IN THE UNITED STATES BASED ON FOREIGN APPLICATIONS AND REGISTRATIONS

In the United States, application for federal registration of trademarks can be made by anyone based on actual use of the mark or a bona fide intent to use the mark in commerce in the future. In addition to these bases, the United States has assumed certain obligations under international agreements in the trademark field, principally the Paris Convention for the Protection of Industrial Property of 1883, briefly mentioned in Chapter 1. The Paris Convention seeks to afford citizens of each member nation protection against unfair competition and trademark infringement and requires that member nations provide the same trademark protection to citizens of other member nations as they do for their own citizens. More than one hundred and thirty-five countries are member nations of the Paris Convention, including Canada, Mexico, most of South America, Europe, and many African and Asian countries. (See Appendix A for a table of treaties and identification of members of the Paris Convention.)

Section 44 of the Lanham Act (15 U.S.C. § 1126) implements these agreements. Section 44 provides significant benefits to any person whose country is a party to a treaty relating to trademarks to which the United States is also a party by allowing the party to file an application for registration of a trademark with the PTO based upon one or both of the following:

- that the applicant filed an *application* in his or her country of origin or a member nation within the previous six months and has a bona fide intent to use the mark in the United States (called a **Section 44(d) Application** after section 44(d) of the Lanham Act); and/or
- that the application in the United States is based upon a *registration* already secured in the applicant's country of origin or in a member nation and the applicant has a bona fide intent to use the mark in the United States (called a **Section 44(e) Application**).

One of the significant benefits of the section 44(d) application is that it affords the applicant a priority filing date; that is, if the applicant files an application in the United States within six months after filing the application in the foreign country, the applicant's priority date in the United States will relate back to the earlier foreign filing date. For example, if Compagnie Le Chat of France files an application in France on March 1, 1999, and files an application under section 44(d) with the PTO anytime before September 1, 1999, the critical date for determining Compagnie Le Chat's priority in the United States with regard to conflicting marks is the foreign filing date of March 1, 1999.

A significant benefit of the section 44(e) application is that it allows those who have secured registrations in a member nation to use that registration as a basis for securing a United States registration *even if the mark has not been*

Section 44(d) Application:
Trademark application filed with the PTO by a non–U.S. citizen based upon an application filed in a foreign country

Section 44(e) Application:
Trademark application filed with the PTO by a non–U.S. citizen based upon a registration secured in a foreign country

used in the United States. The United States principle is that the *first to use* a trademark has rights, while most foreign countries provide that the *first to register* a trademark has rights. Thus, many foreign countries allow registration of marks even though the marks have not been used. Once a registration is secured in the foreign country, it may then serve as a basis for securing a U.S. registration, with no use whatsoever of the mark anywhere in the world (although an intent to use the mark in commerce must be alleged to ensure marks are not warehoused). In this way, foreign applicants receive more favorable treatment than U.S. applicants who can never secure a U.S. registration without a showing of use in commerce.

Contents of Applications Made Under Section 44

Applications made under section 44 must comply with a variety of requirements, some of which are identical to those imposed on other applications and some of which are in addition to those imposed on other applications. One additional requirement is that an applicant who relies on a foreign application under section 44(d) must specifically assert its claim of priority by stating either in the application or before the end of the priority period, "Applicant has a bona fide intention to use the mark in commerce on or in connection with the above-identified goods/services, and asserts a claim of priority based upon a foreign application in accordance with 15 U.S.C. § 1126(d), as amended. The application was filed in [country] on [date] and was assigned the serial number [application filing or serial number]."

An applicant who relies on an existing foreign registration under section 44(e) must submit a certified copy of the foreign registration during the prosecution process and state in the application, "Applicant has a bona fide intention to use the mark in commerce on or in connection with the above-identified goods/services and will submit a certification or certified copy of a foreign registration in accordance with 15 U.S.C. § 1126(e), as amended. The mark was registered in [country] on [date] and was assigned the registration number [registration number]." A certified copy of the foreign registration (not merely a photocopy) must be submitted before the PTO will issue a registration. If the foreign registration is not in English, a translation must be provided together with a signature by the translator.

Applications filed under section 44 must also include a "Designation of Domestic Representative," which designates some person in the United States, typically a law firm, as the **domestic representative** to whom the PTO can direct notices and correspondence regarding the mark (see Figure 8–1). In many instances, law firms in the United States have developed relationships with law firms in foreign countries, generally referred to as "foreign associates." Each firm sends applications and business to the other to assist its own clients in securing trademark protection in foreign countries. Because United States lawyers are not experts in the trademark laws and procedures of foreign nations, these relationships allow United States law firms to refer business to respected attorneys in other countries. Similarly, the United States law firms usually expect that the foreign associates will refer trademark matters to them as well. The Trademark Data Sheet found in Figure 3–1 that is used to gather information from domestic applicants can be easily modified to gather information from foreign clients who wish to register their marks.

domestic representative: A person or law firm in the United States designated by a foreign applicant to receive documents and notices affecting a trademark application

FIGURE 8–1
Designation of Domestic
Representative

The law firm of Bailey & Bailey, L.L.P., 4890 Terrace Place, Minneapolis, MN 09847, is designated the Applicant's representative upon whom notices or process in proceedings affecting the mark may be served, and all prior appointments in connection herewith are hereby revoked.

MAISON BLANC, L.C. of the
United Kingdom _____

By: _____

Title: _____

Date: _____

Applicants under section 44 must submit a drawing of the mark applied for in the United States, just as is required of other applicants, and the drawing must conform to the drawing shown in the foreign application or registration. Applicants under section 44 also must identify the goods and services applied for and specify the international class for the goods or services. Many foreign countries allow applicants to claim all goods in an entire class or allow broad identifications of goods (such as "computer goods in I.C. 9"), but that would not be permissible in the United States, and the examining attorney at the PTO may request a more specific identification in accordance with general PTO policy. Because an application filed under section 44 does not require use of the mark in commerce, such an application will generally not state a date of first use. Similarly, because the mark need not be in use, specimens are not usually filed with the applications.

Examination of Applications Made Under Section 44

Although applications made under section 44(d) (based upon a pending application in a member nation) and section 44(e) (based upon an existing registration in a member nation) are exempt from the use requirements of the Lanham Act, they must meet all other requirements for registration set forth in the Lanham Act. Securing registration in the country of origin does not guarantee registration in the United States because section 44 applications are subject to the same review as other applications and may be refused on the basis they are scandalous or immoral, merely descriptive, or confusingly similar to a registered mark or a mark in a pending application. Office actions may be issued and must be responded to in six months, just as is required for other applications. If a mark that is the subject of a section 44 application is refused registration on the basis that it is merely descriptive, the section 44 applicant may assert (just as its U.S. counterpart would) that the mark has acquired distinctiveness or secondary meaning through its long-standing and continuous use such that consumers, upon encountering the mark, recognize it as the applicant's mark and have come to associate the mark with the applicant. However, such a claim of acquired distinctiveness must be based upon use in commerce in the United States; the applicant may not rely on use solely in a foreign country to show the mark has acquired such distinctiveness or secondary meaning that it is not merely descriptive.

For applications filed under section 44(d) (based upon a pending foreign application), the applicant will eventually be required to submit a certified copy of the resulting registration issued by the foreign country before it can be published in the *Official Gazette.* A translation may be necessary if the registration is in a foreign language. If the foreign application is subject to delays, the PTO may suspend action on the U.S. application until the foreign registration is issued. The PTO generally requires that the applicant submit written status reports every six months informing the PTO of the status of the pending application and when registration in the foreign country is expected.

Registration of Marks Applied for Under Section 44

After publication of the mark in the *Official Gazette,* and assuming there is no opposition made to registration of the mark, the mark will proceed to registration. Once issued, the U.S. registration exists independently of the underlying foreign application or registration and is subject to all provisions of the Lanham Act that apply to all other registrations, such as affidavits of use, renewals, assignments, and similar matters. When submitting any other documents, the foreign applicant or registrant will be required to designate a domestic representative in the United States upon whom notices and documents affecting the mark may be served (see Figure 8–1).

SECURING TRADEMARK PROTECTION IN FOREIGN COUNTRIES

Introduction

The globalization of the world economy and ever-expanding markets in other countries for goods and services from the United States has made trademark protection abroad an increasing interest of many U.S. companies. In many instances, a vital part of a company's market strategy includes penetration of foreign markets with a concomitant need to protect the trademarks and service marks under which goods and services will be offered. Similarly, a trademark owner may need to consider registering its marks in countries in which trademark piracy is common so that if and when it decides to enter a foreign market, its name is available to it.

One of the first treaties or "conventions" designed to address trademark protection in foreign countries was the Paris Convention of 1883, adopted to facilitate international patent and trademark protection. As discussed, the Paris Convention is based on the principle of reciprocity so that foreign trademark owners may obtain in member countries the same legal protection for their marks as can citizens of those member countries.

Perhaps the most significant benefit provided by the Paris Convention is that of priority. An applicant for a trademark has six months after filing an application in a member nation to file a corresponding application in other member countries and obtain the benefits of the first filing date.

Initial Considerations

Once a decision has been made to adopt a mark, consideration should be given to whether the mark should be applied for in any foreign countries. One of the first factors to consider is the meaning of the mark in various foreign languages. One of the classic international trademark stories is that of Chevrolet's adoption of the mark NOVA® for a compact car. While NOVA connotes "new" or perhaps "star" in English, the literal translation in Spanish of "no va" is "it does not go," immediately dooming the product to ridicule or failure. Thus, if a trademark owner intends to "go global," the assistance of trademark experts in foreign countries is necessary even before a mark is adopted to ensure the mark's translation into the respective foreign language is acceptable.

Once a mark, or perhaps several alternatives, has been selected, international searches should be conducted. Although the search companies identified in Chapter 3 are capable of conducting extensive international searches, many law firms prefer to ask their foreign associates to conduct the search, believing they are most capable of reviewing the results, interpreting the results of the search, and providing an opinion regarding availability of the mark for registration. Once again, the relationships between U.S. trademark counsel and their foreign counterparts can be long-standing and intimate. Some trademark firms have established relationships with foreign law firms that date back for several generations and are based on mutual respect and business interests.

The Foreign Application

Just as foreign applicants can file an application with the PTO and claim priority based on a pending foreign application, so too can U.S. applicants claim such benefits afforded by the Paris Convention. Therefore, upon filing an application for a client, many U.S. law firms confirm the filing particulars and inform the client that if protection for the mark is desired in any foreign country, such a decision should be made within six months from the PTO filing date in order to claim priority in the member nation and secure the benefit of the earlier U.S. filing date (see Figure 8–2). Similarly, just as foreign applicants can use a foreign registration as a filing basis in the United States, U.S. companies can use registrations issued by the PTO as a basis to secure registration of marks in any of the more than one hundred and thirty-five member nations of the Paris Convention.

Trademark owners who are considering global expansion should file trademark applications in any countries in which they anticipate they may do business. Because most countries do not require that a mark be in use to be registered, filing applications in foreign countries allows U.S. trademark owners to protect their marks in anticipation of future expansion and may deter others from using similar marks for similar goods or services. In many countries, because use is not required to secure a registration, third parties often attempt to register marks in anticipation of the entrance of a trademark owner. These "trademark pirates" then attempt to sell the marks to their true owners. Alternatively, pirates register copycat marks, such as registrations secured for "Pizza Hot" and "Sharaton Hotels" in Cambodia. Thus, filing applications in foreign countries preempts trademark piracy and reserves the mark for its rightful owner. Recently, the United States has been pressing its trading partners to strengthen their laws to prevent such acts of piracy and provide stronger protection to the intellectual property rights of U.S. citizens.

The progress of an application filed in a foreign country varies dramatically based upon the country. Some countries have an expeditious procedure, and others take several years. Some countries do not yet recognize service marks.

FIGURE 8-2
Letter to Client Advising of
Foreign Priority Dates

March 30, 20xx
Mr. Thomas Anderson
American Tablet Association
1820 South Santa Ana Street
Santa Ana, CA 96601

   Re: Mark: TABSTRIP
         Serial No.: 75/011,193
         Filing Date: January 3, 20xx

Dear Mr. Anderson:
   We are pleased to enclose the official filing receipt issued by the United States Patent and Trademark Office (PTO) in connection with the application filed for TABSTRIP on January 3, 20xx. We have reviewed the official filing receipt and it appears to be correct; however, if you notice any errors, please inform us so we can ensure the PTO records are corrected.
   In view of the backlog of applications at the PTO, no action in connection with this application should be expected for approximately four to six months.
   If protection for this mark is desired in any foreign country, or if you plan to expand your business and offer products and services in any foreign country, please notify us immediately. In many countries, it is possible to obtain the benefit of the United States application's filing date if the foreign application is filed within six months of the United States filing date. In your case, applications in foreign countries must be filed by July 3, 20xx in order to claim priority.
   We will continue to keep you informed of any further developments in connection with this application.

                              Sincerely,

                              David N. Bailey
                              Bailey & Bailey, L.L.P.

Therefore, if a client is engaged in hotel or restaurant services, rather than forego the opportunity to secure any trademark protection, the owner may seek registration in I.C. 16 for its printed matter, menus, and brochures relating to the hotel or restaurant services. Some countries, such as Saudi Arabia, have nearly prohibitive filing fees. Others, such as Italy, have more reasonable fees but take nearly three years to process the application. Searching can be speculative inasmuch as many countries lack sophisticated databases and are unable to search for phonetic equivalents of marks and the like. Just as learning the rules and processes of the PTO requires patience and determination, learning the vagaries of international trademark offices requires the same. In almost all instances, the services of reputable foreign counsel should be retained. To determine counsel with experience in trademark matters, consult *Martindale-Hubbell Law Directory,* which provides information and biographical sketches of foreign counsel, or contact the International Trademark Association (INTA), an association of approximately 3,200 trademark owners and practitioners from all over the world, at 1133 Avenue of the Americas, New York, NY 10036-6710 (212/768-9887).

   The nature and type of examination of an application pending before a foreign trademark office varies greatly, with some countries subjecting the mark to strict scrutiny and issuing refusals similar to the office actions issued by the PTO, while other countries merely review the form of the application and then issue a registration unless there is a prior identical mark or nearly identical mark. Registrations are usually valid for ten years and may be renewed for like periods. Proof of use often must be submitted after the third or fifth year of registration in many foreign countries. If use is not proved, the registration will be canceled, similar to the U.S. practice of canceling registrations if the section 8 affidavit of use is not submitted between the fifth and sixth years after registration.

If the owner of a foreign trademark registration allows or licenses another to use the registered mark, most countries require that a **registered user agreement** be filed with the foreign trademark office, providing information about the owner of the mark, the licensee, and various other license terms.

The European Community Trademark

In 1996, a new **Community Trademark (CTM) System** was established by the fifteen member countries of the European Union (Austria, Belgium, Denmark, Finland, France, Germany, Greece, Ireland, Italy, Luxembourg, Netherlands, Portugal, Spain, Sweden, and the United Kingdom). The new system makes it possible for an applicant to file an application for one trademark or service mark that can be protected in each of the fifteen member countries of the **European Union (EU).** A single application may cover any number of classes of goods or services, although the initial fee (U.S. $1,265) covers up to only three classes of goods/services. The CTM blanket application covering the fifteen member nations of the EU provides significant protection at a considerable savings over filing fifteen separate applications in the member nations. Consistent with the philosophy of many foreign countries, actual use is not required to secure a registration. The CTM System does not replace the trademark offices in the fifteen member nations but coexists with them.

Another distinct advantage to the new CTM application is that there is no need to perform a search prior to filing the application. An examining attorney at the central office in Alicante, Spain, is charged with the responsibility of clearing the mark in each of the member countries, providing additional savings of time and money. Moreover, in the event that an examiner's search discloses a conflicting mark in a nation, a separate application can be filed in that nation, using the earlier filing date of the CTM application. After examination, the mark will be published for opposition purposes. If there is no opposition, the mark will proceed to registration. Once registered, the CTM registration is valid for ten years from the date of filing and may be renewed for successive ten-year periods.

Among the other advantages afforded by the CTM System are the following:

- an attractive fee structure is provided, both in terms of the official fees and the reduction in the number of trademark attorneys required;
- the unitary filing simplifies licensing or assigning the mark;
- a single infringement action may be brought to cover all countries in the European Union;
- priority can be claimed if an application was filed within the previous six months in a member nation of the Paris Convention, allowing the CTM application to capture the earlier priority date;

registered user agreement: Agreement by which an owner of a registered mark allows or licenses another to use its mark and is required to be filed by many foreign trademark offices for the grant to be effective

Community Trademark (CTM) System: A trademark system allowing trademark owners to file one single trademark application that covers all 15 members of the European Union

European Union (EU): An association of 15 European nations

- protection of a mark is possible throughout all of the European Union countries that may not have previously been possible due to some countries' strict examination of marks (for example, surnames are considered to be *prima facie* distinctive in a CTM application, while these are generally refused registration in the Scandinavian countries);
- use in any of the member nations of the European Union will protect a CTM registration throughout all of the European Union against cancellation of a registration due to nonuse of a mark; and
- a user-friendly filing system allows applications to be filed by facsimile or e-mail.

In just the short period of time since the CTM System was established, it has been an overwhelming success. In its first month of existence, nearly thirty thousand applications were filed, with one-third being filed by U.S. applicants. At present, there is some discussion of expanding the European Union to include other countries, particularly some of the eastern European countries.

The Madrid Protocol

In April 1996, the Madrid Protocol came into existence, allowing trademark protection for nearly thirty countries and all of the European Union countries by a single trademark application. However, the United States is not yet a party to the Madrid Protocol, and American trademark owners cannot take advantage of this new trademark filing procedure unless the owner is domiciled in or has a real place of business in one of the Madrid Protocol countries, which include the European Union nations, Brazil, Czech Republic, Hungary, Israel, Poland, Slovakia, and Turkey. Thus, if a U.S. company maintains an office in Poland, it could take advantage of the Madrid Protocol by depositing a trademark registration secured in the United States with a Central Registration Bureau in Berne, Switzerland. The bureau will register the mark and then apply for registration in the other member countries.

Legislation is presently pending in Congress that would make the United States a party to the Madrid Protocol. This treaty, when fully implemented, will facilitate a one-stop, low-cost, efficient system for the international registration of trademarks by permitting a U.S. trademark owner to file for registration in any number of member countries by filing one single standardized application form with the PTO, in English, with a single set of fees. (See Appendix A for identification of Madrid Protocol members.)

Developments in Eastern Europe

The disintegration of the Communist Bloc into independent republics greatly changed trademark practices in Eastern Europe and the former Soviet Union. The Soviet Union, once a single nation, has now become fifteen countries, each of which is attempting to achieve some degree of free market economic development. Many of these countries have their own trademark offices, and it is now possible to file applications in each country.

The breakup of Czechoslovakia led to the creation of two trademark offices, one in the Czech Republic and one in Slovakia. Each has adopted its own trademark laws, and each accepts trademark applications. It is also possible to file trademark applications in Croatia, Slovenia, and Macedonia. Some countries, such as Serbia and Montenegro, are presently subject to U.S. embargo, and U.S. citizens are not permitted to file applications there, much as U.S. citizens cannot file applications in other restricted countries, such as Cuba.

EFFECTS OF NEW INTERNATIONAL AGREEMENTS (NAFTA AND GATT)

The North American Free Trade Agreement (NAFTA) came into effect on January 1, 1994, and is adhered to by the United States, Canada, and Mexico. The most significant change in U.S. trademark law resulting from NAFTA is that trademarks that are geographically misdescriptive cannot be registered in the United States, even if they have acquired secondary meaning.

The General Agreement of Tariffs and Trade (GATT) was concluded in April 1994 and is adhered to by the United States and most of the major industrialized nations of the world. The first of two key changes to U.S. trademark law resulting from GATT is that nonuse of a mark for three years must be shown for a registration to be canceled for such nonuse. Prior to GATT, the United States followed a rule that two years of nonuse of a mark resulted in a presumption of abandonment. The second change is that GATT precludes registration of marks for wines and spirits that contain misleading geographical indicators. For example, a wine bearing the mark SONOMA must originate in that region of the United States.

INTERNATIONAL ASSOCIATIONS

There are a variety of international associations devoted to protecting the rights of trademark owners. The best known are the International Trademark Association (INTA) and the World Intellectual Property Organization (WIPO).

International Trademark Association (INTA)

INTA was founded in 1878 as the United States Trademark Association and is dedicated to the advancement and support of trademarks as valuable items of world commerce. It is a not-for-profit association that serves its members and actively pursues private and public policy matters concerning trademarks. More than 3,200 companies and firms in more than 115 countries belong to INTA, together with others interested in promoting trademarks such as law firms practicing in the field of trademarks and advertising agencies that deal with trademarks.

INTA has played a significant role in trademark legislation, including promotion of the passage of the U.S. Trademark Act in 1946 and the 1988 Trademark Law Revision Act, designed to bring U.S. trademark law into conformity with that of the international community. In 1993, a name change from United States Trademark Association to International Trademark Association was effected to reflect the association's broader focus. INTA offers a variety of educational seminars and publications, including many worthwhile materials available for free on the Internet (see INTA's home page at www.inta.org). INTA is located at 1133 Avenue of the Americas, New York, NY 10036-6710 (212/768-9887).

World Intellectual Property Organization (WIPO)

WIPO, founded in 1883, is an intergovernmental organization headquartered in Geneva, Switzerland. Since 1974, WIPO has been a specialized agency of the United Nations. Its purposes are to promote intellectual property throughout the world through cooperation among nations and to administer various multilateral treaties dealing with intellectual property, including the Paris Union, Madrid Union, the Trademark Law Treaty, and the Berne Convention. WIPO encourages new treaties and modernization of national legislative bodies, disseminates information, and provides technical assistance to developing nations. More than 170 nations are members of WIPO. (See Appendix A for identification of WIPO members.)

Additionally, WIPO has an Arbitration and Mediation Center whose purpose is to offer binding arbitration or nonbinding mediation services to resolve intellectual property disputes between parties. These services are available to any person, regardless of nationality.

WIPO promotes protection of all aspects of intellectual property (trademarks, copyrights, and patents), while INTA is devoted exclusively to promoting trademarks. WIPO offers a variety of useful information on the Internet including the list of international classifications for trademarks, texts of treaties administered by WIPO, and information on publications offered by WIPO (see WIPO's home page, located at http://www.wipo.int/eng/index/htm).

ROLE OF INTELLECTUAL PROPERTY PROFESSIONAL

International trademark work can be interesting and challenging. Working with clients and attorneys from foreign countries provides an international perspective on trademark law. Individuals with fluency in other languages should emphasize such skills to potential employers, who are often in need of translations of foreign documents and correspondence.

Among the tasks IP professionals will undertake in the area of international trademark law are the following:

- assisting clients and foreign associates in completing a trademark data worksheet to determine what marks should be protected in the United States;
- preparing applications based on section 44 and securing either filing particulars about a pending foreign application or a certified copy of the foreign registration;
- monitoring the progress of section 44 applications and corresponding with foreign associates regarding the same;
- notifying U.S. clients of the advantages of filing applications in Paris Convention nations within six months of the date an application is filed with the PTO;
- working with foreign associates in filing applications for marks in foreign countries;
- maintaining dockets to track the progress of foreign applications;
- providing status reports to clients regarding the progress of foreign applications; and
- reviewing registration certificates and docketing same for maintenance and renewal.

CHAPTER SUMMARY

A foreign national may file an application for trademark registration with the PTO on the basis of actual use of the mark in commerce in the United States, a bona fide intent to use the mark in commerce in the United States, or on the bases of a pending application or existing registration in a foreign country. If the application is filed with the PTO within six months of its filing in the foreign country, it will retain its earlier foreign filing date for purposes of determining priority rights in the mark. Once filed, the application will proceed similarly to other applications, although to secure a U.S. registration, the applicant must submit to the PTO a certified copy of the registration issued by the foreign country. One significant difference is that while U.S. applicants can receive a registration only upon a showing of actual use, foreign nationals can obtain registrations without ever using the mark (inasmuch as their U.S. registration is based upon their foreign registration, which may not have required use).

Just as foreign nationals may seek protection for their marks in the United States, U.S. trademark owners may seek protection for their marks in various foreign countries. The assistance of a foreign associate who is expert in trademark law in the relevant country is nearly always required. As with applications filed by foreign nationals in the United States, applications filed in countries that are members of the Paris Convention filed within six months of the date of a U.S. application retain the earlier United States filing date for priority purposes. United States trademark owners should file applications in countries in which they intend to do business and in any countries that have a history or tradition of trademark piracy, namely, countries in which third parties attempt to register marks for goods or services they will not be offering in anticipation of the entrance of a foreign trademark owner to whom they can then sell the mark.

DISCUSSION QUESTIONS

1. Conform Industries Inc. is a corporation of France. It filed an application in France for its CONFORM mark on September 15th. The company wishes to file an application in the United States, although it has no present intent to use the mark in the United States. What type of application should it file and when should the application be filed?
2. Tenleyshire Company is a company of the United Kingdom. It owns a registration issued by the United Kingdom in 1995. It intends to enter the U.S. market at some time and wishes to protect its mark in the United States. What bases should the U.S. application claim?
3. Truck-Tel Inc., a Minnesota corporation, filed an application for its TRUCK-TEL mark, used in connection with transportation services, with the PTO on June 8th. It intends to do business in France, Germany, and Austria within the next few years. What type of application should be filed and when?
4. What are some disadvantages to a U.S. law firm in conducting searches of foreign registers for its clients who may wish to file applications in foreign countries?

PART

III

The Law of Copyrights

CHAPTER
9
Foundations of Copyright Law

Copyright is a form of protection arising from the Patent and Copyright Clause of the U.S. Constitution. Copyright protects the works of authors and artists to ensure their products are not unlawfully reproduced, distributed, performed, or displayed, acts that would deprive them of revenue and discourage further creative work. As new technologies have developed, copyright law has evolved to keep pace, thereby affording protection to works not originally contemplated by the framers of the Constitution, such as computer programs.

The present act governing copyrights in the United States is the Copyright Act of 1976, which provides protection upon creation of a work in a fixed form rather than requiring publication of a work as a prerequisite to protection as did the previous Copyright Act of 1909. Rights arise automatically upon creation of a work, and no publication or registration with the Copyright Office is required to secure copyright, although there are several advantages to registration.

INTRODUCTION TO COPYRIGHTS

Just as medieval merchants in guilds in England used trademarks on their wares to indicate the source of those products, mercantile interests in England prompted the first insistence upon protection for publication of books. When the invention of the printing press in about 1440 resulted in the ability to produce books by machine rather than by hand, bookbinders and printers demanded protection from copying of books. Authors also began to demand protection from unauthorized copying and demanded to share in the financial rewards the publishers were winning. Finally, in 1710, Parliament enacted the first copyright statute, the Statute of Anne, which limited the formerly perpetual rights publishers enjoyed to a period of fourteen years. Under the statute, damages for infringement were set at one penny for every sheet found in the infringer's custody, one-half to go to the author, and one-half to go to the Crown. Authors were thus granted the right to control copying of their books. This grant of rights was called a *copyright*.

Just as trademark law protects the investment by merchants in the marks under which their goods are sold, copyright law protects the creators of books, music, and art by providing them with the exclusive right to reproduce their works and derive income from them. Protecting these rights fosters creative effort—there would be little to be gained from investing and pouring effort into composing a song or writing a novel if others could reproduce the song or book at will without compensating its creator.

Not only is copyright at the center of the creative soul of artists, but it has a significant financial impact in the United States as well. Approximately 5 percent of the gross domestic product in the United States derives from copyright industries, including software, films, music, and television shows. Additionally, copyright piracy costs U.S. businesses an estimated $12.4 billion each year in lost revenues.

Copyright law in the United States stems from the Patent and Copyright Clause of the Constitution, which provides that Congress shall have the power "to promote the progress of science and useful arts, by securing for limited times to authors and inventors the exclusive rights to their respective writings and discoveries." U.S. Const. art. I, § 8. Under this clause, Congress has the power to enact legislation to provide copyright protection for authors for limited periods. Over time, the wording in the clause has been liberally interpreted to incorporate new technologies and protect new forms of expression as varieties of "writings."

Congress enacted the first copyright act in 1790, and the first federal copyright registration was issued that same year to author John Barry for *Philadelphia Spelling Book*. Since 1790, the act has been subject to major revision on four occasions: in 1831, 1870, 1909, and 1976. The 1790 act provided copyright protection to maps, charts, and books, and set damages for infringement of published works in the sum of fifty cents for every sheet found in the infringer's possession, one-half of the damages to go to the copyright owner, one-half to the federal government. Subsequent revisions to the 1790 act reflect a gradual expansion of the categories of works or "writings" that are entitled to protection. Thus, musical compositions, dramatic compositions, photographs, paintings, and sculpture were eventually included within the definition of copyrightable material. The present act provides protection to nearly anything that can be expressed in tangible form, including sound recordings, videotape, and computer software.

Copyright law strives to balance two competing interests: the interests of authors in protecting their works from unauthorized copying and the interest of the public in having the greatest possible access to works of authorship. United States copyright law is intended to stimulate the creation of new works of art, literature, music, sculpture, and other tangible forms of expression.

COMMON LAW RIGHTS AND RIGHTS UNDER THE 1976 COPYRIGHT ACT

Until January 1, 1978 (the effective date of the 1976 Copyright Act), the United States had a dual system of copyright protection in that a distinction was drawn between unpublished works and those that were published. Until 1978, authors had a perpetual common law right to their unpublished works.

Thus, the author of an unpublished manuscript could exclude others from copying the material forever. Once the work was published, however, the common law perpetual copyright was extinguished and protection was afforded by virtue of the 1909 act, which then provided a period of protection up to fifty-six years. **Publication** is the distribution of copies of a work to the public for sale or other transfer of ownership, by rental, lease, or lending.

Because this dual nature of copyright protection was complex, and the point at which works became published often led to controversy, the 1976 act eliminated the distinction between unpublished and published works and provides simply that a work is protected from its **creation,** that is, as soon as it is created or fixed in some tangible form. Thus, even an unpublished manuscript is governed by the 1976 act inasmuch as it is created when the author sets the words down onto paper or types them into a computer.

Works published before the 1976 act, for example, Ernest Hemingway's *A Farewell to Arms* (published in 1929), are governed by the act in existence on the date of their publication. Hemingway's book would thus be governed by the 1909 act.

Just as trademark rights arise from use and not from registration with the PTO, copyright rights arise from the creation of a work in fixed form and not from publication or registration or other action in the United States. No permission or application with the U.S. Copyright Office is required to secure copyright protection; however, just as securing a trademark registration from the PTO provides certain advantages to trademark owners, securing a copyright registration from the Copyright Office provides certain advantages to authors of works, including the following:

- registration establishes a public record of the copyright claim;
- before an infringement suit may be filed in court, registration is necessary for works of U.S. origin;
- if made before or within five years of publication, registration will establish *prima facie* evidence in court of the validity of the copyright and of the facts stated in the certificate; and
- if registration is made within three months after publication of the work or prior to an infringement of the work, statutory damages and attorneys' fees will be available to the copyright owner in court actions (otherwise, only an award of actual damages and lost profits is available to the copyright owner).

Copyright protection generally lasts until seventy years from the death of the author. The 1976 Copyright Act is found at 17 U.S.C. §§ 101–1101. (See Appendix E.)

The 1976 Copyright Act has been amended several times. In 1980, specific protection was afforded to computer programs as works entitled to copyright protection. In 1989, the United States joined the Berne Union, an organization now comprising more than one hundred and thirty-five nations, by entering into an international treaty called the Berne Convention for the Protection of Literary and Artistic Works. Just as the Paris Convention requires member nations to treat citizens of member nations as they do their own citizens with regard to trademarks, the Berne Convention requires member nations to treat citizens of member nations as they do their own citizens with regard to copyrights. To satisfy our obligations under the Berne treaty, Congress once again

publication: The distribution of copies of a work to the public for sale or other transfer of ownership by rental, lease, or lending

creation: In copyright law, the fixation of a work in a copy or phonorecord for the first time

amended the 1976 Copyright Act by eliminating any requirement for a copyright notice (©) to be used with a work (although use of the notice is recommended) and by requiring copyright applicants to submit two copies of a published work in which copyright is claimed when they apply for copyright registration. In 1990, the Copyright Act was again amended to bring U.S. copyright law more into conformity with that of other Berne Union members, particularly with respect to rights of attribution and integrity for certain works of visual arts (see Chapter 11). The most recent significant amendment to the 1976 Copyright Act was enacted in late 1998, when Congress extended the duration of copyright to seventy years from an author's death rather than fifty years from death as was previously the case. References in this text to the Copyright Act are references to the 1976 act.

THE UNITED STATES COPYRIGHT OFFICE

The U.S. Copyright Office is a division of the Library of Congress and is located in Washington, DC. Its address and telephone number are as follows: Register of Copyrights, Copyright Office, Library of Congress, 101 Independence Avenue SE, Washington, DC 20559-6000 (202/707-3000). Its chief officer is the Register of Copyrights, and its powers and procedures are established in the 1976 Copyright Act. The primary function of the Copyright Office is to issue copyright registrations and serve as a depository for materials in which copyright is claimed. The Copyright Office is not permitted to give legal advice and will not offer guidance on matters such as disputes over the ownership of a copyright, suits against possible infringers, or other matters related to copyrights. It does, however, provide a variety of information, publications, circulars (information packets), and forms related to copyright, most of which are provided free of charge. Among the more useful publications and materials are the following:

- forms for copyright registration;
- Circular 1, "Copyright Basics";
- Circular 2, "Publications of the Copyright Office";
- Circular 3, "Copyright Notice";
- Circular 4, "Copyright Fees";
- Circular 15, "Renewal of Copyright";
- Circular 15a, "Duration of Copyright";
- Circular 38a, "International Copyright Relations of the United States";
- Circular 61, "Copyright Registration for Computer Programs";
- Kit 109, containing material, announcements, and forms relating to copyright registration for books; and
- Kit 113, containing material, announcements, and forms relating to copyright registration for computer programs.

To order copyright publications, write to:

Publications Section, LM-455
Copyright Office
Library of Congress
101 Independence Avenue SE
Washington, DC 20559-6000

ROLE OF INTELLECTUAL PROPERTY PROFESSIONAL

At this stage of copyright protection and prosecution, IP professionals will typically be engaged in general legal research relating to copyrightability of clients' works. Additionally, IP professionals should contact the Copyright Office and begin creating form files for forms and publications related to copyrights. The files should be maintained in a central location, and indexes to the forms and publications should be circulated to all other IP professionals. Finally, IP professionals should routinely monitor the Copyright Office web site to keep informed of new developments in copyright law, check fee schedules, and determine whether the Copyright Office has implemented new procedures.

Alternatively, you may call the Copyright Office "Forms and Circulars Hotline" at (202) 707-9100 (twenty-four hours a day). Orders are recorded automatically and materials will be mailed to you as quickly as possible, usually within two weeks.

Selected circulars and announcements are available via facsimile. Call (202) 707-2600 from any touch-tone telephone. Key in your fax number at the prompt and the document number of the item(s) you want. The item(s) will be transmitted to your fax machine. If you do not know the document number of the item(s) you want, you may request that a menu be faxed to you. You may order up to three items at a time. Copyright applications are not available by fax.

Finally, frequently requested Copyright Office circulars, announcements, application forms, and the most recent proposed and final regulations are now available over the Internet. These documents may be examined and downloaded through the Library of Congress campuswide information system "LC Marvel." To connect through the World Wide Web, enter http://lcweb.loc.gov/copyright. This web site gives you access to information created by the Copyright Office and links to a wide variety of other copyright resources. LC Marvel and World Wide Web access are available twenty-four hours a day, and no fees are charged to connect to these Internet resources.

The Copyright Office is in the process of implementing an electronic registration system that will enable applicants for registration to file their applications electronically and that will reduce processing time for registration.

CHAPTER SUMMARY

In the United States, copyright law arises under the Patent and Copyright Clause of the Constitution. The U.S. copyright laws have been amended several times, and the current governing statute is the Copyright Act of 1976. Copyright ensures that an author or creator of a work will derive benefits from his or her creation and will be protected from unauthorized use or copying of a work. Under the Copyright Act of 1909, a work had to be published to be protected under the act. The 1976 act eliminated the requirement of publication and provides that copyright is secured automatically when the work is created.

No publication or registration is necessary to secure copyright protection, although there are certain advantages to registration of a copyright with the U.S. Copyright Office.

DISCUSSION QUESTIONS

1. Classify whether the following works would be protected under the 1909 Copyright Act and/or under the 1976 Copyright Act:

    a journal maintained by an author and never published

    a published manuscript

    a painting by an artist hung in the artist's private study

2. List two advantages to securing registration of a copyright with the U.S. Copyright Office.

3. If a new technology were developed, would it be protected under the 1976 act or would an amendment to the act be necessary in order to provide copyright protection to it?

The Subject Matter of Copyright

To be eligible for copyright protection, matter must be original, it must be fixed in some tangible form, and it must qualify as a "work of authorship." The requirement of originality does not mean the work must be new or novel; it must merely be created independently by its author. The most common subjects of copyright protection are literary works; musical works; dramatic works; pantomimes; choreographic works; pictorial, graphic, and sculptural works; motion pictures and other audiovisual works; sound recordings; and architectural works. Not all printed or communicable matter can be the subject of copyright protection. For example, useful articles, facts, ideas, titles, and U.S. government works cannot be copyrighted. In some instances, material that itself is not copyrightable (such as facts) may be subject to protection if it is arranged or compiled in such a way that shows creativity, for example, arrangement of facts into a book of lists.

INTRODUCTION TO COPYRIGHTABILITY

The limits of copyrightability are dictated by statute. According to 17 U.S.C. § 102, copyright protection exists in original works of authorship fixed in any tangible medium of expression, now known or later developed. Thus, there are three basic requirements for copyrightability:

- a work must be original;
- a work must be fixed in a tangible form of expression; and
- a work must be a work of authorship.

Each of these requirements will be discussed in this chapter.

ORIGINALITY OF MATERIAL

To be eligible for copyright protection, material must be original, meaning that it must have been independently created and must possess a modicum of creativity. The requirement of **originality** should not be confused with novelty, worthiness, or aesthetic appeal. The requirement is rather that the material must be an independent product of the author and not merely some copy or minimal variation of an existing work.

A work can be original even if it is strikingly similar or identical to that of another. The Copyright Act only requires originality, meaning independent creation by the author. Thus, if two photographers each take photographs of the Washington Memorial, each will have copyright protection for the work (as long as one did not copy another). Similarly, if two authors independently write novels that are strikingly similar, each will have copyright protection (again, assuming there was no copying). In a famous copyright case, *Feist Publications, Inc. v. Rural Telephone Service Co.,* 409 U.S. 340, 345–46 (1991), the Court held:

> Originality does not signify novelty; a work may be original even though it closely resembles other works so long as the similarity is fortuitous, not the result of copying. To illustrate, assume that two poets, each ignorant of the other, compose identical poems. Neither work is novel, yet both are original, and, hence, copyrightable.

"Originality" thus does not mean "first"; it merely means "independently created."

In regard to the level of creativity required for copyright protection, the threshold is quite low. Even a slight amount of "creative spark" will suffice. In order to be protected by copyright, however, a work must contain at least a certain minimum amount of original expression. Thus, copyright does not extend to blank forms, column headings, names, titles, or lists of ingredients. In *Feist,* the Supreme Court held that telephone white page listings did not satisfy the requirement inasmuch as they lacked minimal creativity. The Court held that the names, towns, and telephone numbers were all merely facts, and as such, and arranged in alphabetical order, an age-old practice, were uncopyrightable. Although facts are not copyrightable, an author's original selection and arrangement of those facts may be copyrightable as a compilation (see the section in this chapter entitled "Compilations, Collections, and Derivative Works").

FIXATION OF MATERIAL

The Copyright Act protects works of authorship that are "fixed in any tangible medium of expression." A work is "fixed" when it is embodied in a copy or phonorecord and is sufficiently permanent or stable to permit it to be perceived, reproduced, or communicated for a period of more than transitory duration. 17 U.S.C. § 101.

There are thus two categories of tangible expression in which works can be fixed: "copies" and "phonorecords." A **copy** is a material object (other than a phonorecord) from which a work can be perceived, reproduced, or communicated, either directly by human perception or with the help of a machine. Thus, according to the Copyright Act, a famous photograph by Ansel Adams that appears on a book cover, a calendar, a T-shirt, a tie, and a coffee mug is a "copy" in each case. The scope of "material object" is broad enough to encompass writings on paper, images on marble, and even designs on fabric.

originality: In copyright law, a work that is independently created (not copied) and that exhibits a minimal amount of creativity

copy: In copyright law, a material object (other than a phonorecord) from which a work can be perceived, reproduced, or communicated, either by human perception or with the help of a machine

A **phonorecord** is a material object in which sounds (other than those accompanying a motion picture or other audiovisual work) are fixed and from which the sounds can be perceived, reproduced, or communicated either directly by human perception or with the help of a machine. Thus, a record, a cassette tape, and a CD recording of a song by the Rolling Stones are all considered to be "phonorecords."

Because the definition of **fixation** requires that a work be embodied in some sufficiently stable or permanent form to be perceived, an oral presentation, lecture, or live performance is not fixed (unless it is reduced to writing or placed on film or tape). However, by virtue of 17 U.S.C. § 101, which defines the word *fixed,* a live broadcast of a television or radio show is viewed as fixed *if* it is recorded simultaneously with its broadcast transmission. Thus, an impromptu stand-up comedy routine by Jerry Seinfeld is not fixed; however, a recording and transmission of the same routine is fixed. Fixation occurs when a work is reduced to words, numbers, sounds, or shapes and placed on some permanent or stable medium. Thus, literary works are fixed when they are typed or processed into a computer or put onto a disk; sound recordings are fixed when they are recorded and placed on tape; and photographs are fixed when they are captured on film.

Prior to the 1976 act, works were protected only if they were fixed in a form that was perceptible to the human eye (although special rules existed for sound recordings, protecting records). One famous case held that the rolls of music for a player piano were not subject to copyright protection because they could not be read by humans as sheet music could. *White-Smith Music Publishing Co. v. Apollo Co.,* 209 U.S. 1 (1908). The 1976 act (17 U.S.C. § 102), however, provides that copyright protection subsists in original works of authorship fixed in *any* tangible medium of expression, now known or later developed, from which they can be perceived, reproduced, or otherwise communicated, either directly or with the aid of a machine or device, thus allowing protection for works that are perceived by machines as well as humans, such as CDs, video games, and videotapes.

WORKS OF AUTHORSHIP

The Copyright Act provides that copyright protection subsists in original works of authorship fixed in any tangible medium of expression, *now known or hereafter developed,* from which they can be perceived, reproduced, or otherwise communicated, either directly or with the aid of a machine. 17 U.S.C. § 102. Section 102 then lists eight categories of protectable works. The list is preceded by the phrase that copyright "includes" those categories, demonstrating that the listed categories are not the only types of works that can be developed, but are illustrative only. Thus, it has been held that fabric designs and toys are copyrightable even though they are not specifically listed in section 102. Moreover, the provision that copyright protection exists in works "now known or hereafter developed" indicates congressional intent to protect new forms of expression that are not yet existent. The eight enumerated categories are as follows:

1. literary works;
2. musical works (including accompanying words);

phonorecord: A material object in which sounds (other than those accompanying a motion picture or other audiovisual work) are fixed and from which the sounds can be perceived, reproduced, or communicated by human perception or with the help of a machine

fixation: The embodiment of a work in a sufficiently permanent or stable form to permit it to be perceived, reproduced, or communicated for more than a transitory period

3. dramatic works (including accompanying music);
4. pantomimes and choreographic works;
5. pictorial, graphic, and sculptural works;
6. motion pictures and other audiovisual works;
7. sound recordings; and
8. architectural works.

Literary Works

A **literary work** is one expressed in words, numbers, or other verbal or numerical symbols, regardless of the nature of the material objects, such as books, periodicals, manuscripts, phonorecords, film, tapes, disks, or cards, in which they are embodied. This broad category includes works of fiction and non-fiction, poetry, catalogs, reports, speeches, pamphlets, and manuscripts. Works such as computer programs are also treated as literary works because they are expressed in letters and numbers. Literary works can include dictionaries, an employee handbook, an instruction manual, or an advertisement. The fact that many people would not regard an advertisement or an instruction manual to be *literary* in the sense the word is usually used is of no significance. If the material is original, in fixed form, and can be expressed in letters or numbers, it is "literary" even though it may be entirely lacking in artistic merit to most people.

Musical Works (Including Accompanying Words)

A **musical work,** together with its accompanying words, is copyrightable. A musical work or composition may be in the form of a notated copy (such as sheet music) or in the form of a phonorecord (such as a record, a cassette tape, or a CD). The author of a musical work is usually the composer, and the lyricist, if any.

The lyrics or words to a musical composition are not protected as a literary work, but rather as a musical work. Both elements of a composition are separately protected. Thus, if someone writes the lyrics to "Yesterday" in a novel, without permission, it is a violation of the author's copyright. Similarly, an unauthorized performance of the musical arrangement for "Yesterday" on stage, even without singing of lyrics, is also a copyright violation.

Dramatic Works (Including Accompanying Music)

A **dramatic work** is usually a theatrical performance or play performed for stage, movie, television, or radio. Dramatic works usually include spoken text, plot, and directions for action. The music accompanying a dramatic work is protected as a dramatic work rather than as an independent musical work. Examples of dramatic works include the well-known plays *Phantom of the Opera, Cats,* and *Death of a Salesman.*

Pantomimes and Choreographic Works

Pantomime or *mime* is a performance using gestures and expression to communicate with no accompanying sound. An impromptu street performance of mime would not be protected (because it is not fixed in some stable or permanent medium of expression), but a filmed performance of the famous mime Marcel Marceau would be protected.

literary work: A work expressed in words, numbers, or other verbal or numerical symbols, such as a book or computer program

musical work: Original musical compositions or arrangements, including lyrics

dramatic work: A theatrical performance or play performed for stage, movies, television, or radio

pantomime: A performance using gestures as expression to communicate with no accompanying sound

The 1976 act was the first statute to include choreography as a copyrightable work. Choreography is the composition and arrangement of dance movements and patterns. Simple dance routines and social dance steps such as the waltz, the fox trot, and the second position of classical ballet are not copyrightable in and of themselves; however, once these steps are incorporated into an otherwise choreographic work, they are protected, much like words are protected once they are incorporated into a work of fiction or nonfiction. A **choreographic work** does not need to tell a story in order to be protected by copyright; however, the work must be fixed in a tangible medium of expression from which the work can be performed, such as a recorded or notated choreographic work. In one case, still photographs of a George Ballanchine ballet performance were held to infringe his copyrighted choreographic work *The Nutcracker. Horgan v. MacMillan, Inc.,* 789 F.2d 157 (2d Cir. 1986).

Pictorial, Graphic, and Sculptural Works

Pictorial, graphic, and sculptural works include two-dimensional and three-dimensional works of fine, graphic, and applied art. This category of copyrighted works is extremely broad and includes the following: photographs; prints, posters, and art reproductions; maps; globes; charts; diagrams; artwork applied to clothing; bumper stickers; cartoons and comic strips; dolls; toys; jewelry designs; mosaics; patterns for sewing; record jacket artwork; tapestries; fabric, floor, and wallcovering designs; games; puzzles; greeting cards, postcards, and stationery; stencils; sculptures (including carvings, figurines, and molds); models; and technical drawings, including blueprints. A minimal threshold of creativity is required. Thus, a simple shape such as a drawing of a circle or square may not be protected; however, even a drawing of a bowl of chili on the label of a can is copyrightable as a pictorial work.

Copyright law does not protect useful articles. A **useful article** is one having an intrinsic utilitarian function. Examples of useful articles are clothing (including costumes), vehicular bodies, furniture, machinery, appliances, dinnerware, and lighting fixtures. Toys, dolls, and stuffed animals are not useful articles and can be copyrighted, even if they portray a utilitarian product. Thus, a toy airplane was held not to be a useful article in *Gay Toys, Inc. v. Buddy L. Corp.,* 703 F.2d 970 (6th Cir. 1983). The intent of Congress was to exclude from copyright protection industrial products such as cars, appliances, and electronic products. In one case, the court of appeals affirmed that automobile wire-spoke wheel covers were useful and were not subject to copyright protection. The creator argued that the wheel covers were ornamental and were intended to beautify and embellish the wheels, but the court held that the wheel covers were mere utilitarian articles serving to protect lugnuts, wheels, and axles from damage. *Norris Indus. v. International Tel. & Tel. Corp.,* 696 F.2d 918 (11th Cir. 1983).

The Copyright Act provides, however, that the design of a useful article shall be considered a pictorial, graphic, or sculptural work if such design incorporates pictorial, graphic, or sculptural features that can be identified separately from and are capable of existing independently of the utilitarian aspects of the article. Thus, the famous statuette that adorns the hood of a Rolls Royce can be protected by copyright inasmuch as it can exist as a sculpture independently from the hood and the car. Similarly, a carving on the back of a

choreographic work: The composition and arrangement of dance movements and patterns

useful article: An article having an intrinsic utilitarian value

chair, animal foot slippers, or a floral relief design on silver flatware is protectable by copyright, but the design of the chair, slipper, or flatware itself is not.

Motion Pictures and Other Audiovisual Works

A **motion picture** is an audiovisual work consisting of a series of related images that, when shown in succession, impart an impression of motion, together with accompanying sounds. These works are typically embodied in film, videotape, or videodisk. Music accompanying a movie (the motion picture soundtrack) is protected as part of the motion picture.

An **audiovisual work** is a work that consists of a series of related images that are intended to be shown by the use of machines or devices such as projectors, viewers, or electronic equipment, together with accompanying sounds. Thus, a photograph of a mountain is protected as a pictorial work. If the photograph is made into a slide, it remains a pictorial work; however, when the photograph is made into a slide that becomes part of a presentation about mountains of the world, the resulting slide show is an audiovisual work.

Sound Recordings

A **sound recording** is a work that results from the fixation of a series of musical, spoken, or other sounds, regardless of the nature of the material objects, such as disks, tapes, or other phonorecords, in which they are embodied. Thus, a sound recording could be a narration by Meryl Streep of a book played on a cassette tape, a CD of a live performance by Garth Brooks, or an album by Sugar Ray. Sound recordings, however, do not include the sounds accompanying a motion picture or other audiovisual work.

There is a distinction between a "musical work" and a "sound recording." A musical work consists of music, including any accompanying words. The author of a musical work or composition is generally the composer, and the lyricist, if any. A musical composition may be in the form of sheet music or a cassette tape, album, or CD. A sound recording results from the fixation of a series of musical, spoken, or other sounds. The author of a sound recording is the performer whose performance is fixed, or the record producer who processes the sounds and fixes them in the final recording, or both.

For example, the song "You Are the Sunshine of My Life" by Stevie Wonder is frequently recorded by other artists. The original music and lyrics are copyrighted by Stevie Wonder as a musical work. If Celine Dion performs the song "You Are the Sunshine of My Life," she cannot claim copyright in the lyrics and music because she did not create them. However, her particular arrangement of the lyrics and song is copyrightable as a sound recording by her and her record producer. If a later artist wishes to perform "You Are the Sunshine of My Life," permission must be sought from Stevie Wonder (or the present copyright owner). Permission need not be sought from Celine Dion or her record company because the new artist will not be copying Celine Dion's particular arrangement (unless the new artist wishes to extract or "sample" some of the Celine Dion arrangement into the new version, in which case permission must be sought from Celine Dion and/or the record company for the part sampled).

motion picture: Audiovisual work consisting of a series of related images that, when shown in succession, impart an impression of motion, together with accompanying sounds

audiovisual work: A work consisting of a series of related images intended to be shown by the use of a machine such as a projector together with its accompanying sounds

sound recording: A work that results from the fixation of a series of musical, spoken, or other sounds

Architectural Works

An **architectural work** is the design of a building as embodied in any tangible medium of expression, including a building, architectural plans, or drawings. The work includes the overall form and arrangement and composition of spaces, but not individual standard features such as windows, doors, and other standard components of buildings, which cannot be registered. The term *building* includes not only permanent and stationary structures for human habitability (such as houses and office buildings) but also gazebos and garden pavilions. Structures other than buildings (such as bridges, tents, and mobile homes) are not subject to protection.

Before 1990 and the United States's adherence to the Berne Convention, architectural plans and models were protected only as graphic and sculptural works. Because buildings were useful articles, they could not be protected. Protection was allowed only for nonuseful portions, such as decorative moldings, murals, friezes, and so forth.

In 1990, however, Congress expressly amended the 1976 Copyright Act to include "architectural works." A claim to copyright in an architectural work is distinct from a claim in technical drawings of the work. If registration is sought for both an architectural work (such as a building) and technical drawings of the work, separate applications must be submitted to the Copyright Office.

If the building is ordinarily visible to the public, anyone can take pictures of it or display it in a painting or movie. One recent case demonstrates the difficulties inherent in protecting architectural works. The recent movie *The Devil's Advocate* with Al Pacino displayed a frieze, which a noted sculptor claimed was an infringement of his work, placed over the doorway of the National Cathedral in Washington, DC. The sculptor sued, alleging copyright infringement. The producers of the movie claimed the frieze was independently created and was merely part of a building ordinarily visible to the public. The case settled out of court, and thus there was no determination of the rights of the parties.

EXCLUSIONS FROM COPYRIGHT PROTECTION

Not all works are protected by copyright. In addition to articles that are purely useful and which cannot be copyrighted, a number of other works are not protected under copyright law, including ideas, blank forms, short phrases, titles, works in the public domain, facts, and computing devices.

Ideas, Methods, or Systems

Section 102 of the Copyright Act not only lists eight categories of works that are protected by copyright, but also states that the following are specifically excluded from copyright protection: ideas, procedures, processes, systems, methods of operation, concepts, principles, and discoveries, regardless of the form in which they are described, explained, or illustrated. This statutory prohibition sets out in long form a well-established copyright principle: copyright protects expression, not ideas.

The rule that copyright protection extends only to the expression of ideas, and not to ideas themselves, derives from a famous Supreme Court case, *Baker*

architectural work: The design of a building as embodied in any tangible medium of expression

v. Selden, 101 U.S. 99 (1879). In that case, Selden published a book explaining a bookkeeping system that included blank forms with ruled lines and columns for using the new system. Baker later published a book with additional forms for using Selden's system. Selden sued for copyright infringement. The Court denied relief, holding that a copyright on a book explaining a system does not prevent another party from explaining the same system; otherwise, the bookkeeping system or method itself would be monopolized by the first to explain it. The Court held that Baker had copied only Selden's unprotectable idea and not any protectable expression of the idea. The discussion by the Court is often referred to as the **idea-expression dichotomy** and results in a well-known copyright principle: ideas are not protectable, although the expression of those ideas is subject to copyright protection. The Court also held that the forms were not writings and were thus unprotectable, thereby giving rise to the rule that mere blank forms are not copyrightable.

The Copyright Office itself states that copyright protection is not available for the following: ideas or procedures for doing, making, or building things; scientific or technical methods or discoveries; business operations or procedures; formulas of mathematical principles; algorithms; or any other concept, process, or method of operation.

Generally, if there are a number of ways of explaining a topic or subject, the original expression will be protected against copying; however, if there are no or few alternative ways of expressing something, only literal copying (rather than mere paraphrasing) will likely result in infringement. In such cases, it is said that the expression merges with the idea, and copyright protection is denied to the merged expression because ideas are not copyrightable. This principle is known as the **merger doctrine.** Thus, in a case involving alleged infringement of contest rules, the court held that because there were a limited number of ways of expressing the rules, given their straightforward nature, only exact copying was prohibited. Otherwise, the first to express the idea would be able to prohibit all later users. *Morrissey v. Procter & Gamble Co.,* 379 F.2d 675 (1st Cir. 1967).

Blank Forms, Titles, Short Phrases, and Common Property

In order to be protected by copyright, a work must contain at least a certain minimum amount of original literary, pictorial, or musical expression. Copyright does not extend to names, titles, short phrases, slogans, clauses such as column headings, or simple checklists. Thus, many books and even movies may share the same title. For example, there are numerous textbooks that share the title *Introduction to Mathematics.* If one person could appropriate a title to the exclusion of others, creativity would be hindered rather than encouraged. Similarly, neither a title nor a slogan such as "You deserve a break today" may be copyrighted (although it may qualify for protection as a trademark).

Mere variations in typeface, familiar symbols or designs, lettering or coloring, and mere lists of ingredients or contents are not protected by copyright. Similarly, blank forms (such as forms for bank checks, time cards, account books, diaries, scorecards, report forms, address books, and order forms) that are used primarily for recording information rather than conveying information lack sufficient creativity to be copyrightable. Although mere listings of ingredients as in recipes, formulas, or prescriptions are not subject to copyright

idea-expression dichotomy: Doctrine that ideas are not protectable by copyright although the expression of those ideas is copyrightable

merger doctrine: The principle that if there are few alternative ways of expressing something, only literal copying will infringe because the expression merges with the idea and ideas are uncopyrightable

protection, when the recipe or formula is accompanied by substantial literary expression in the form of an explanation or directions, or when there is a combination of recipes (as in a cookbook), there may be a basis for copyright protection.

Finally, copyright protection does not extend to works consisting entirely of information that is common property containing no original authorship, such as standard calendars, height and weight charts, tape measures and rulers, schedules of sporting events, and lists or tables taken from public documents or other common sources. Thus, a Sierra Club Calendar or Far Side Calendar would be protected to the extent of the photographs or cartoons accompanying the calendars, but the calendars themselves with their standard and readily ascertainable information are not copyrightable.

Public Domain Works

A variety of works are not subject to appropriation by copyright inasmuch as they are said to be in the **public domain,** meaning they are free for all members of the public to use and exploit. The two primary types of works in the public domain are those that arise from expired copyrights and works of the U.S. government.

Expired and Forfeited Copyrights Copyrights have always been subject to some period of limited duration. Once a copyright expires, or it is forfeited by its owner, it resides in the public domain and is free for all to use. Under the 1909 act, copyrights were subject to an initial period and a period of renewal. Failure to renew the copyright at the appropriate time resulted in a forfeiture of the copyright with the work being placed in the public domain. For works created on or after January 1, 1978, the copyright duration is the life of the author and an additional seventy years. If the work is the product of corporate authorship, it will last for ninety-five years from publication, or one hundred and twenty years from its creation, whichever occurs first. These time periods have recently been changed. Until October 1998 and the passage of the Sonny Bono Copyright Term Extension Act, each period of duration was twenty years shorter.

United States Government Works Pursuant to section 105 of the Copyright Act, copyright protection is not available for any work of the U.S. government or any of its agencies if that work is prepared by an officer or employee of the U.S. government as part of that person's official duties. Thus, federal laws and cases may be freely reproduced and distributed, together with federal regulations, and information and forms from agencies such as the Internal Revenue Service, PTO forms, and forms provided by the Copyright Office.

If the U.S. government commissions special work by an independent contractor, for example, a sculpture for a national park commissioned by an artist not employed by the federal government, the independent contractor will retain copyright in the work (unless he or she agrees that the government can own the copyright). The U.S. government is not precluded from receiving copyrights transferred to it by a third party. Thus, the artist could assign or transfer the copyright to the government.

Works produced by state governments and local governmental bodies are not covered by the Copyright Act, although they may be covered under relevant state law. Nevertheless, certain information such as cases, statutes, regulations,

public domain: A work or invention that is free for all members of the public to use

and ordinances are not copyrightable inasmuch as the public needs free access to such information.

Facts

Facts are not protected by copyright because one who uncovers a fact is not an author or creator. Facts are viewed as "discoveries" and are thus excluded from copyright protection under section 102 of the act. Moreover, according to *Feist*, facts are not original to a researcher and are not created by a researcher, even if the researcher is the first to reveal them. For example, statistics relating to population, dates of birth and death, and other ascertainable matters cannot be protected by copyright. Thus, the protection afforded to purely factual works, such as books that merely gather statistics or that provide biographies, is relatively narrow. Although a newscast content may be protected by copyright, the facts recited by newscasters themselves cannot be appropriated by one party to the exclusion of others.

Computing and Measuring Devices

Devices and similar articles designed for computing and measuring cannot be copyrighted. Examples of uncopyrightable works are slide rules, wheel dials, and perpetual calendar systems. The printed material on the device (numbers, symbols, calibrations, and their arrangements) is not capable of copyright protection because the material is dictated either by the underlying idea (which is uncopyrightable) or some standard formula (which is uncopyrightable). Moreover, a computing or measuring device does not contain a minimum amount of creative authorship—it is merely a means for arriving at a result or reading.

Other Copyright Issues: Characters, Scenes a Faire, and Immoral Works

A variety of interesting issues have arisen in copyright law regarding the protectability of characters (both graphical and literary), scenes a faire, and immoral works.

Characters and Scenes a Faire   Generally, graphical characters, such as cartoon figures like Superman, Mickey Mouse, Dick Tracy, and Doonesbury, are protectable separate and apart from the cartoon strips, films, and books in which they appear. Thus, in one case, a party was enjoined from using a "Wonderman" character on the basis that it infringed the copyright in Superman when the only significant difference between the two characters was the color of their uniforms. *Detective Comics Inc. v. Bruns Publications, Inc.*, 111 F.2d 432 (2d Cir. 1940). On the other hand, the concept of a hero who bravely saves people and the planet from destruction and peril is merely an idea that cannot be protected by copyright. Other heroes with similar characteristics would be permissible as long as they did not appropriate the details of Superman's persona. Cartoon strips, films, and books are also protectable as pictorial works, motion pictures, and literary works, respectively.

In regard to literary characters or characters depicted in a television series or movie, such as James Bond in the Ian Fleming books and movies, Jack Ryan in the Tom Clancy novels, or the Terminator in the *Terminator* movies, if those characters are specifically described and presented, they may be protectable. In 1988, the Ninth Circuit was called upon to determine whether the television series *The A-Team* infringed a screenplay called *Cargo*. Noting that both shared a common approach (adventure actions portraying Vietnam veterans), the court held that this idea alone was unprotectable. There was little similarity in terms of plot, dialogue, or setting. The fact that both involved action-adventure heroes was not sufficient to show infringement. *Olson v. NBC*, 855 F.2d 1446 (9th Cir. 1988). This reasoning is a further illustration of the rule that ideas are not protectable while the expressions of those ideas are. In sum, basic character types are not copyrightable; characters that are uniquely developed and display some level of novelty, however, such as Rocky Balboa, are copyrightable.

Certain standard or stereotypical characters and incidents, called **scenes a faire** (literally, "scenes which must be done"), are generally excluded from copyright protection. For example, stock characters, standard literary devices, common expressions, and incidents are viewed as uncopyrightable scenes a faire. For example, in one case involving police fiction, a court held that foot chases, morale problems of police officers, and the "familiar figure of the Irish cop" are common themes in such works and are thus unprotectable scenes a faire. Similarly, the mazes, scoring table, tunnels, and dots of the "Pac-Man" computer game have been held to be scenes a faire, protectable only from identical copying.

Immoral Works Although the Trademark Act forbids registration of immoral, disparaging, or scandalous works, no such prohibition exists in the Copyright Act. Generally, Congress has been reluctant to place restrictions on the copyrightability of certain matter believing it would chill First Amendment rights.

COMPILATIONS, COLLECTIONS, AND DERIVATIVE WORKS

Compilations

An author often selects certain items and groups them together in a new presentation. For example, a book may be published that presents lists of Oscar winners or tables of statistics and data that are not themselves copyrightable. Such a work is called a **compilation.** According to section 101 of the Copyright Act, a compilation is a work formed by the collection and assembling of preexisting materials or of data that are selected, coordinated, or arranged in such a way that the resulting work as a whole constitutes an original work of authorship. Compilations are protected by copyright if there is original authorship in the selection or arrangement of the material.

Thus, although the material that comprises the compilation is not original (and therefore is not copyrightable), the manner of its selection and arrangement results in an original work. For example, a type of day planner that consists of calendars, blank forms for appointments, entries, maps, lists of area codes, and time zones may be copyrightable as a compilation due to its unique arrangement, even though the parts that comprise it (calendars, blank forms, and so forth) are not copyrightable because they lack originality or are standard devices. As

scenes a faire: Literally, "scenes which must be done"; stock characters and devices in a work that are uncopyrightable

compilation: A work formed by the collection of preexisting material arranged in such a way that the resulting work is original; includes *collective works*

another example, a book of lists or an information-based almanac is likely comprised merely of facts or raw data that are not copyrightable in and of themselves; however, the unique arrangement of those facts into a select and coordinated system is copyrightable. The author has reviewed certain facts, selected the particular facts to include, and then arranged or presented the facts so that they are interesting or useful to the reader. It is this selection that shows sufficient creativity that copyright protection is provided for that arrangement or selection. The underlying facts themselves, however, remain uncopyrightable.

As seen in *Feist,* in which an alphabetically arranged telephone directory was held not copyrightable, not every selection of facts or compilation will pass muster. As always, a certain level of creativity, namely, "originality," is required. In *Feist,* the Supreme Court recognized that while the requirement of originality is not stringent, the arrangement of facts cannot be so mechanical and routine as to demonstrate no creativity whatsoever.

Collections

According to section 101 of the Copyright Act, the term *compilation* includes collective works. A **collective work** is a work, such as a periodical issue, anthology, or encyclopedia, in which a number of contributions, constituting separate and independent works in themselves, are assembled into a collective whole. Thus, a CD containing musical compositions by various artists and called *The Golden Age of Rock* would be a collective work, as would a book of selected short stories dealing with sports, an anthology of poems by twentieth-century American poets, or selected film clips showing the greatest comedy routines of the 1950s. Even when the works assembled into the collection are public domain works (for example, folk songs or spirituals), the resulting work qualifies for protection as a collection.

The difference between a compilation and a collection is that the matter comprising the compilation is not copyrightable (think lists of facts, such as an almanac), while the matter comprising the collective work (think short stories, photos, or poems) is copyrightable.

Derivative Works

A **derivative work** is one that is based on (or derived from) one or more already existing works, such as a translation, dramatization, fictionalization, or any other form in which a work may be recast, transformed, or adapted. Thus, the author of a derivative work transforms or somehow changes a preexisting work (while the author of a compilation or collective work assembles or arranges preexisting materials). The resulting work is copyrightable if it includes original work of authorship and if the original material was not used unlawfully.

Derivative works, also known as *new versions,* include such works as musical arrangements, motion picture versions, abridgments, and condensations. Additionally, any work consisting of editorial revisions, annotations, elaborations, or other modifications that, as a whole, represent an original work, is a derivative work subject to copyright protection.

The following examples show some of the many different types of derivative works:

collective work: A work such as a periodical issue or anthology in which a number of contributions, constituting separate and independent works, are assembled into a collective whole

derivative work: A work based on one or more preexisting works, such as a translation, fictionalization, revision, or abridgment; also called a *new version*

- a television drama of *The Glass Menagerie* based on the earlier play by Tennessee Williams;
- a motion picture of *Fried Green Tomatoes* based on the earlier novel by Fannie Flagg;
- a play of *In Cold Blood* based upon the work by Truman Capote;
- a television dramatization of *The Gambler* based upon the song by Kenny Rogers;
- a novel in English, such as *Doctor Zhivago* (translated from a book originally published in Russian);
- words and music, such as the musical *Cats* based upon the poems of T. S. Eliot; and
- the movie *Rocky II* based upon the original *Rocky* movie.

To be copyrightable, the derivative work must be different enough from the original to be regarded as a new work or must contain a substantial amount of new material. Making minor changes or additions of little substance to a preexisting work will not qualify the work as a new version for copyright purposes. The new material must be original and copyrightable in itself.

The copyright in a derivative work covers only the additions, changes, or other new material appearing for the first time in the work. It does not extend to any preexisting material and does not imply a copyright in that material. The copyright in the derivative work does not affect or extend the nature, scope, or duration of copyright protection for the original work. Thus, if a new preface or foreword is prepared for a new printing of John Grisham's novel *The Rainmaker,* only the new material is independently protected and owned by the new author. John Grisham retains the rights in the original work. One cannot extend the length of protection for a copyrighted work by creating a derivative work. A work that has fallen in the public domain (that is, one that is no longer protected by copyright) may be used for a derivative work, but the copyright in the derivative work will not restore or revive the copyright of the public domain material; neither will it prevent anyone else from using the same public domain material for another derivative work.

Only the owner of copyright in a work has the right to prepare or to authorize someone else to create a new version of that work. The owner is generally the author or someone who has obtained rights from the author.

ROLE OF INTELLECTUAL PROPERTY PROFESSIONAL

The role of an IP professional prior to preparing a copyright application will likely be limited to legal research relating to copyrightability so that clients can be advised about whether works created by them qualify for copyright protection and to ensure clients do not infringe the rights of others. Research may focus on any of the following topics:

- whether a work is an original, fixed work of authorship;
- what type of work of authorship an author's work is, for example, a literary work, dramatic work, musical work, or pictorial work;
- whether the work is subject to protection as an expression rather than a mere idea, system, or process;
- whether the work is excluded from copyright protection because it consists of blank forms, titles, slogans, common property, or facts;
- whether the work is excluded from copyright protection as a work of the U.S. government; and
- whether the author's work is a compilation, collective work, or derivative work.

CHAPTER SUMMARY

Copyright protects original works of authorship that are fixed in a tangible form of expression such that they can be perceived, communicated, or reproduced either directly or with the aid of a machine or device. The requirement of originality means that the work must be independently created by the author; it need not be the only work of its kind. Copyrightable works include the following categories: literary works; musical works (including any accompanying words); dramatic works (including any accompanying words); pantomimes and choreographic works; pictorial, graphic, and sculptural works; motion pictures and other audiovisual works; sound recordings; and architectural works.

Some matter is uncopyrightable, such as ideas, useful articles, blank forms, titles, short phrases, common property (such as height and weight charts), lists of ingredients, facts, and matters in the public domain, including works whose copyrights have expired and works of the U.S. government.

A compilation of otherwise uncopyrightable material may be protectable (such as a book of lists). Similarly, a collection of other copyrightable material (such as a collection of photographs showing poverty in America) may itself be copyrightable as a new work. Finally, a work that is recast (such as a movie made from a book) is copyrightable, in regard to the new material, as a derivative work.

DISCUSSION QUESTIONS

1. Classify the following as likely copyrightable or not copyrightable:

   - the slogan "Nobody does it like Sears"
   - a doctoral thesis
   - a promotional brochure advertising a car
   - the body of a car
   - blueprints for a museum
   - blueprints for a footbridge
   - a list setting forth deaths in U.S. wars since 1900
   - the federal statute governing awards of the Medal of Honor

2. Would a graceful vase made of pewter be copyrightable? Discuss.
3. Would a lecture given by your instructor be copyrightable? Discuss.
4. Two authors independently write a screenplay relating to a love triangle. Can each obtain a copyright on the screenplay? Discuss.
5. Is the character Darth Vader protected by copyright? Discuss.
6. Classify the following as a compilation, a collection, or a derivative work:

   - a cookbook of recipes
   - a book displaying photos taken by photographers and journalists covering Bosnia
   - a movie based upon the book *Cold Mountain*
   - a directory listing lawyers practicing in the field of intellectual property
   - the American movie *Cousins* based upon the French movie *Cousin, Cousine*

The Rights Afforded by Copyright Law

Under the Copyright Act, a copyright owner has a "bundle" of rights: the right to reproduce, adapt, distribute, perform, and display the work to the exclusion of others. Thus, copyright owners have a full complement of ways to commercially exploit their works. There are, however, some limitations on these exclusive rights. For example, once certain works have been distributed, under the "first sale doctrine," the subsequent owner is free to use or resell the item without liability for infringement. Similarly, some activities do not constitute infringement, for example, uses for certain educational activities, noncommercial fund-raising, or for religious worship. Rights for sound recordings are considerably more limited than rights for other works, such as literary or musical works. Authors of fine arts such as paintings and sculptures may also have "moral rights," meaning rights personal to themselves that survive the sale of their work so that authorship of the work is forever attributed to them and the work is not mutilated or altered, which would prejudice their reputation as artists and creators.

INTRODUCTION

Section 106 of the Copyright Act provides that, subject to certain exceptions, the owner of a copyright has the exclusive rights to do and to authorize any of the following:

- to reproduce the copyrighted work in copies or phonorecords;
- to prepare derivative works based on the copyrighted work;
- to distribute copies or phonorecords of the copyrighted work to the public;
- to perform the copyrighted work publicly (in the case of certain works);
- to display the copyrighted work publicly (in the case of literary, musical, dramatic and choreographic works, pantomimes, and pictorial, graphic, or sculptural works); and

- to perform the copyrighted work publicly by means of a digital audio transmission (in the case of sound recordings).

Unauthorized exercise of any of these rights by another is an infringement of the owner's copyright in the work, whether or not the owner has secured a copyright registration and whether or not the owner has published the work.

These exclusive rights, usually referred to as a "bundle," will be examined in this chapter.

RIGHTS OF REPRODUCTION

The most fundamental of the rights granted to copyright owners is the right to reproduce the work, thereby excluding others from reproducing the work. A violation of the Copyright Act occurs whether or not the violator profits by the reproduction. Consider the warning displayed at the beginning of every video movie you rent that reproduction is a violation of the Copyright Act. Thus, making a copy of the movie *Men in Black* violates the owner's right to reproduction, even if you only intend to view the movie privately.

Only the owner has the right to reproduce the work. Secretly taping a concert, taking pictures at a performance, or recording a simultaneously recorded speech all violate the owner's right to reproduce the work even if there is no later sale or distribution of the work.

At the suggestion of Congress, in 1978 a group of authors, publishers, and users established a not-for-profit entity called Copyright Clearance Center (CCC) to serve as a clearinghouse granting rights to reproduce and distribute books and periodicals. Authors register their works with the CCC, which then grants licenses to academic, government, and corporate users to copy and distribute the works. The CCC grants permission or licenses to use works and then collects royalty fees, which are distributed to the authors. Companies that photocopy articles from journals and magazines often enter into licensing arrangements with the CCC so they can make copies of articles for internal distribution within the company and remain in compliance with copyright law. The CCC is located at 222 Rosewood Drive, Danvers, MA 01923. Its telephone number is (508) 750-8400, and its Internet address is http://www.copyright.com.

RIGHTS TO PREPARE DERIVATIVE WORKS

Section 106 of the Copyright Act provides that the owner of a copyright has the exclusive right to prepare derivative works based upon the copyrighted work. This right is often referred to as the right to adapt the original work.

As discussed in Chapter 10, a derivative work is broadly defined as a work based upon one or more preexisting works, such as a translation, dramatization, fictionalization, motion picture version, abridgment, condensation, or any other form in which a work may be recast, transformed, or adapted. A work consisting of editorial revisions, annotations, elaborations, or other modifications is also a derivative work, if the new material represents original work of authorship.

The copyright owner thus has the right to exclude others from adapting his or her work or creating works based on the owner's work. For example, George Lucas has the right to exclude others from making other movies based upon his original *Star Wars* works. Stephen King can exclude others from making a play or a television movie based upon his books. John Mellencamp can prevent another from making a movie based upon his songs. Of course, if the authors of the works consent, others may be granted rights to adapt a work. Thus, many of author Danielle Steel's works of fiction have been made into television movies, and the novel *The Horse Whisperer* was made into a motion picture. The new derivative work is separately copyrightable in regard to its new elements. Copyright in the derivative, however, does not affect the copyright in the original. Thus, the new elements, lines, characters, and so forth that are added to the movie *The Horse Whisperer* are separately copyrightable as a derivative work, while the original author retains rights to any material in the novel *The Horse Whisperer*.

RIGHTS OF DISTRIBUTION AND THE FIRST SALE DOCTRINE

Section 106(3) of the Copyright Act provides that the owner of a copyright has the exclusive right to distribute copies or phonorecords of the work to the public by sale or other transfer of ownership, or by rental, lease, or lending. A violation of the distribution right can arise solely from the act of distribution itself even if the distributor did not make an unlawful copy or know the copy being distributed was unauthorized. Thus, Blockbuster Video stores can be liable for violating an owner's right to distribute a movie, even if Blockbuster does not know that the movie was placed on videocassette without the owner's authority. Authors often grant permission to others to distribute their works, including granting licenses through entities such as the Copyright Clearance Center discussed earlier.

One limitation on a copyright owner's sole right of distribution is found in section 109 of the Copyright Act, which provides that once the author has parted with ownership of copyrighted material, the new owner of a lawfully made copy can treat the object as his or her own and can then freely use, sell, lease, or lend the work to another. Just as in trademark law (see Chapter 6), where the first sale "exhausts" the trademark owner's right to a mark, in copyright law, the copyright owner's sale of an item exhausts his or her exclusive right to distribute the work. Thus, purchasing a copy of the book *Midnight in the Garden of Good and Evil* or purchasing a videocassette of the movie *Jurassic Park* gives the new owner the right to lend the book or movie to a friend, resell the work at a garage sale, or even destroy it. The **first sale doctrine** does not apply to or limit the author's exclusive rights to prepare derivative works or rights of public performance and display.

The copyright owner, however, while having parted with distribution rights, retains other rights, such as the right to reproduce the work, adapt it, and prepare derivative works based on it. Thus, in the above example, the purchaser of the book *Midnight in the Garden of Good and Evil* does not have the right to make a movie of the book or to prepare a second updated version of the book based upon the original. The original owner, the author, retains such derivative rights, having lost only the right to distribution through the first sale doctrine.

Courts have struggled with the question whether the first sale doctrine applies to goods imported into the United States. Section 602 of the Copyright Act provides that importing copies or phonorecords of a work acquired abroad

first sale doctrine: In copyright and patent law, the principle that once the owner of copyrighted material or a patented item sells it, the buyer can treat the object as his or her own and freely sell, lease, or lend the work to another; also see *exhaustion theory*

into the United States without the copyright owner's authorization is an infringement of the copyright owner's exclusive right to distribute his or her works. In a 1998 decision, the United States Supreme Court held that once a first sale occurs, even abroad, the copyright owner's right to distribute is exhausted. Thereafter, the owner of the work or product can resell the item freely, without permission of the copyright owner. *Quality King Distributors v. L'anza Research International*, 523 U.S. 135 (1998). See Chapter 16 for further discussion of this topic.

Exceptions to the First Sale Doctrine

There are some exceptions or limitations to the doctrine that once a copyright owner parts with ownership he or she has lost the right to distribute his or her work.

- The first sale doctrine applies only to lawfully made copies and phonorecords. Thus, if Border's Books comes into possession of a pirated or unauthorized version of *Memoirs of a Geisha,* resale to others would violate the author's rights of distribution, even if Border's Books did not know it possessed a pirated version of the book.
- Due to a special statutory exception, enacted largely at the urging of the music industry, the first sale doctrine does not apply to commercial rentals of records and certain computer programs. Those works cannot be commercially rented. Thus, Barbra Striesand can prohibit the purchaser of her records or albums from renting those works commercially, generally because commercial renting of sound recordings would seriously undermine creativity and deprive copyright owners of revenue. Nonprofit libraries and other similar institutions may, however, lend or rent out sound recordings and computer programs. Additionally, if the computer program is incapable of being copied, it can be rented. Thus, Blockbuster Video can rent out computer video games to consumers because consumers are generally unable to duplicate or copy the video games. Finally, this limitation does not apply to computers that are part of other machines or products. Thus, a car can be rented by a consumer inasmuch as the computer programs, such as an onboard navigational system that makes up part of the car, cannot be readily copied and are integrated into the car itself.

The *Droit de Suite* Doctrine

Droit de suite is a doctrine recognized in many foreign countries, but not generally in the United States, that allows authors of works of fine art to share in the appreciation of the value of a work. Under this doctrine, if a painter sells a painting for $25,000 and the painting is later sold for $100,000, the painter would be able to share in the $75,000 appreciation of the work. California has enacted a statute called the California Resale Royalties Act (Cal. Civ. Code § 986), which accomplishes the same goal, by allowing artists residing in California to collect 5 percent of any resale price for their works, if the work (which must be an original painting, sculpture, drawing, or an original work of art in glass) is sold for at least $1,000 and is sold for more than the reseller paid for it.

droit de suite: A doctrine in foreign countries that allows the authors of fine works to share in the appreciation of those works, even after they have parted with ownership of those works

Thus, in California, the first sale of a work of fine art does not exhaust the owner's distribution right because the original owner can share in the proceeds of a later sale. Many experts have questioned the constitutionality of the California statute inasmuch as the Constitution provides exclusive authority to Congress (not the individual states) to promote science and arts through copyright law.

RIGHTS TO PERFORM THE WORK PUBLICLY

Section 106(4) provides that in the case of literary, musical, dramatic, and choreographic works, pantomimes, and motion pictures and other audiovisual works, the copyright owner has the exclusive right to perform the copyrighted work publicly. The word *perform* means to recite, render, play, dance, or act a work, either directly or by means of a device or process to show its images in any sequence or to make the sounds accompanying it audible. Thus, if an individual reads the copyrighted novel *Angela's Ashes* on the Oprah Winfrey show, there have been two performances: one in the reading of the work before the live audience and the other in the transmission of it by the television show.

The copyright owner's right to perform is limited to public performances. To perform a work publicly means to perform the work at a place open to the public or at any place where a substantial number of persons outside of a normal circle of a family and its social acquaintances is gathered or to transmit or communicate the work to the public or to a place open to the public (again, outside of a small family or social setting), whether the performance is live or recorded. Performances at places such as clubs, lodges, schools, and summer camps are "public performances" subject to copyright protection. Thus, if Van Morrison sings a song copyrighted by Bob Dylan at a nightclub, theatre, in concert, on Howard Stern's radio show, or on the *Tonight* television show, he has violated Bob Dylan's right of public performance. Note that if Howard Stern's radio show is live in New York City but taped for later transmission in Los Angeles, there have been two separate public performances. The transmission by radio or television broadcast is a public performance even though listeners receive the transmission at different times and places and in the privacy of their own homes or cars. If Van Morrison sings the same song for a small group of friends and family gathered at his home, there is no violation because there has been no public performance.

If a room or facility is open to the public and a copyrighted movie or song is performed therein, there has been a violation of the owner's exclusive right to public performance of his or her work. Courts have held, however, that a private viewing or transmission of a rented movie in a guest's hotel room is not a public performance, and such a viewing is treated the same as rental of a movie for home viewing. *See Columbia Pictures Indus., Inc. v. Professional Real Estate Investors, Inc.,* 866 F.2d 278 (9th Cir. 1989).

Exception for Sound Recordings

The exclusive right of a copyright owner to perform his or her work publicly does not extend to sound recordings. Recall from Chapter 10 that a sound recording usually protects the arrangement or production of a song, while a musical work is a musical composition and its accompanying words. When a radio station plays or transmits a record of Frank Sinatra singing "My Way," a song written by Paul Anka, there is no violation of Frank Sinatra's or the record company's rights; however, there has been a violation of Paul Anka's right to perform the work publicly because he is the author of the underlying musical composition (assuming Paul Anka did not authorize the performance).

Other Exceptions

According to section 110 of the Copyright Act, the following performances, many of which relate to nonprofit educational or charitable activities, do not violate a copyright owner's exclusive right to perform his or her work publicly:

- performances or displays of a work by instructors or pupils in the course of face-to-face teaching activities of a nonprofit educational institution and certain instructional or educational broadcasting by governmental bodies or nonprofit educational institutions engaged in systematic instructional activities. Thus, students in a drama class can perform a copyrighted play without liability. The Copyright Office has recommended to Congress that this provision be amended to allow for distance learning as well as face-to-face instruction (see Chapter 15);
- performances of a nondramatic literary or musical work in the course of services at a place of worship or other religious assembly;
- performances of nondramatic musical works (namely, the playing of recorded music) at retail stores, such as record stores and stores that sell radios and CD players, to promote sales;
- live (not transmitted) performances of nondramatic literary or musical works for noncommercial purposes if there are no admission charges or, if there are charges, the net proceeds are used for charitable purposes and the author is notified so he or she can object prior to the performance (thus promoting benefit and fund-raising concerts for educational, religious, or other charitable purposes);
- performances of nondramatic literary or musical works at social functions organized by a nonprofit veterans' organization or a nonprofit fraternal organization to which the public is not invited and the proceeds of which are used for charitable purposes and not for financial gain;
- performances of a nondramatic musical work by a governmental body or nonprofit agricultural or horticultural association in the course of an annual agricultural or horticultural fair or exhibition;
- transmissions of radio and television broadcasts in small businesses, restaurants, and bars (less than 2,000 square feet for noneating establishments and less than 3,750 square feet for eating establishments), thus allowing such establishments to play radios and televisions without obtaining licenses, as long as no direct fee is charged and there is no further retransmission. Note that this exception applies to transmissions— setting up a CD player and playing a tape or CD would be prohibited as a violation of the copyright owner's exclusive rights. Businesses whose square footage exceeds the stated amounts also qualify for the exemption if they use six or fewer speakers;
- certain transmissions for the benefit of blind and deaf persons; and

- displays of electronic audiovisual games by coin operated equipment (17 U.S.C. § 109(e)).

Note that many of the exceptions relate to "nondramatic literary or musical works," meaning books and records and excluding plays, motion pictures, and operas. Thus, showing a motion picture at a religious service (even if it is related to religion) violates the owner's rights of performance and is prohibited.

Performing Rights Societies

Because the playing of music by CDs and radio in theatres, clubs, or large establishments is a public performance (requiring permission of the copyright owner of the music) and because the copyright owner of the music would have a difficult time keeping track of each time his or her musical work is publicly performed to enforce his or her copyright rights, performing rights societies came into existence to reduce the administrative burdens for both those seeking to perform the work and copyright owners.

Composers, lyricists, and publishers usually join one of three performing rights societies that grant licenses to others to publicly perform the works of their members. The societies then collect and distribute fees for the licenses granted.

A **performing rights society** acts as an agent for musical copyright owners and issues licenses in their behalf. The best known of the performing rights societies are ASCAP (Association for the Society of Composers, Authors, and Publishers) and BMI (Broadcast Music, Inc.). ASCAP and BMI are the dominant organizations in the field, and together their repertoires include nearly all the world's copyrighted music. A smaller society is SESAC (Society of European Stage Authors and Composers). These societies issue blanket licenses to commercial establishments, radio and television stations, and clubs, allowing them to play any of the works in the societies' repertoires or inventories for a fixed fee, thus eliminating the need for a large commercial establishment or radio station to negotiate thousands of separate licenses to play music owned by others. The societies charge license fees and then distribute the fees to the thousands of composers, authors, and publishers they represent. ASCAP and BMI monitor and visit radio stations, clubs, restaurants, skating rinks, conventions, shopping malls, gyms, and other commercial establishments to ensure that copyrighted works are not being publicly performed without license. ASCAP, BMI, and SESAC function in granting licenses to perform music the way the Copyright Clearance Center does in granting licenses to others to reproduce and distribute written works. Information about the societies can be found at their web sites, www.ascap.com, www.bmi.com, and www.sesac.com, respectively.

Commercial establishments such as hotels, stores, and other businesses may also be engaged in public performances when they "pipe in" music throughout the establishment or play music when callers are placed on hold, whether the music is from the owner's own record or CD or is music being simultaneously played on the radio. Although smaller commercial establishments are exempt, as discussed earlier, if larger enterprises pipe in such music, there has been a public performance for which permission or a license must be sought. Thus, in *Sailor Music v. Gap Stores, Inc.,* 516 F. Supp. 923 (S.D.N.Y), *aff'd,* 688 F.2d 84 (2d Cir. 1981), the Gap Stores were held to have

performing rights society:
An organization of copyright owners (such as ASCAP or BMI) that licenses the rights to use copyrighted music to third parties, collects fees therefor, and remits those fees to its members, the authors of the works

publicly performed musical works in violation of the owners' copyrights where two stores had several speakers recessed in their ceilings that broadcast songs and the stores encompassed an average of 3,500 square feet of space.

Generally, fees charged by ASCAP and BMI are determined by square footage, room capacity, or the number of trunk lines a company has coming into its offices that play music on hold.

RIGHTS TO DISPLAY THE WORK PUBLICLY

Section 106(5) of the Copyright Act provides that in the case of all copyrighted works other than sound recordings and works of architecture, the copyright owner has the exclusive right to display the work publicly. A display is "public" under the same circumstances in which a performance is "public," namely, if it occurs at a place open to the public or at a place where a substantial number of persons outside of the normal circle of a family and its social acquaintances is gathered or if it is transmitted or communicated to the public or to a place open to the public (again, outside of a small family or social setting), whether the display is live or recorded.

Exception for Owners of Lawful Copies

Just as the first sale doctrine allows the owner of a lawful copy of a book to sell it or lend it to another, a similar right allows the owner of a lawful copy of a work (other than a sound recording or architectural work) to display that copy publicly, either directly or by the projection of no more than one image at a time, to viewers present at the place where the copy is located. Thus, the lawful owner of a painting or sculpture may display that work in a museum or gallery but may not display it by multiple displays, such as displays on multiple computer screens, or by some other method of transmission (for example, closed circuit television transmission) to viewers at another location. By way of illustration, a department store cannot have a bank of screens that display several multiple slide projections of a painting even if it has purchased the painting. Only one image at a time can be displayed to viewers present at the place where the copy is located. Thus, as an exception to the first sale doctrine, the original painter, sculptor, or other author retains the right to display the copy in a way that makes it available either in multiple images or to persons in places other than where a lawfully sold copy is located.

Other Exceptions

Other exceptions to the copyright owner's exclusive right to display are identical to certain of the exceptions to the copyright owner's exclusive right to perform discussed earlier, namely, the following:

- displays in face-to-face teaching activities of nonprofit educational institutions and certain transmissions that are part of systematic instructional activities of a governmental body or nonprofit educational institution;

- displays in the course of religious worship and services;
- displays in small establishments.

RIGHTS TO PERFORM COPYRIGHTED SOUND RECORDINGS

The rights in sound recordings (the author of which is the performer whose performance is fixed or the record producer, or both) are quite limited and are far different from the rights in musical works (composed music including words, on sheet music, in records, or on CDs). The exclusive rights given to owners of copyrighted works in section 106 of the Copyright Act to perform and display their works do not extend to sound recordings. Once a sound recording exists, others may perform the recording without liability. Thus, radio and television stations can play sound recordings without liability (although they likely have entered into blanket licenses with ASCAP and BMI so that the composers and authors of the underlying musical works are being compensated inasmuch as the owners of copyright in musical works are granted exclusive unlimited rights to perform their works).

Although the owner of a sound recording has the exclusive right of reproduction, this right is quite limited and allows the owner merely to produce actual physical copies and thereby prohibits pirates from making bootleg copies of a record.

Some experts believe these limited rights available to the owners of copyrighted sound recordings are meant to relieve those who would pay royalties (such as radio and television stations) from the multiple burdens of having to pay royalties to the composer or author of the underlying musical work as well as to the record companies that produce the sound recording and the performer who performs the work.

One protection afforded to the owners of copyright in sound recordings is protection against public performances of their sound recordings by subscription services (such as transmission by a cable service that charges recipients for the service) and interactive services (such as services that allow a person to request by telephone or e-mail and then receive a digital transmission of a sound recording). However, the owner of a sound recording cannot preclude others from publicly performing the work (other than by digital audio transmission) because the owner does not have rights of performance.

OTHER LIMITATIONS ON EXCLUSIVE RIGHTS

In addition to the exemptions to copyright owners' exclusive rights already discussed (namely, exemptions for use of works for certain educational purposes, religious worship, noncommercial charitable purposes, limited transmission for small establishments, performances at fairs, and performances for the handicapped), there are a few other limitations on a copyright owner's exclusive rights to his or her work:

- libraries or archives may reproduce and distribute copyrighted works and maintain a copy for preservation if there is no commercial advantage, the library is open to the public, and a copyright notice is placed on the work;

- libraries and archives are not liable for infringement for unauthorized photocopying of copyrighted works as long as a notice is placed on the equipment warning that the making of copies may be subject to copyright law;

- secondary transmissions whereby hotels and other establishments relay radio and television transmissions to private guest rooms without charge are acceptable; and

- radio and television stations that have entered into lawful arrangements to perform works may make a temporary or "ephemeral" recording of the work so that it is easier for them to transmit it and may preserve it for archival purposes (for example, a radio station may copy a compact disc onto a cartridge so it can be readily played).

In addition to the exceptions described, certain uses of copyrighted works are not infringement, for example, quoting lyrics of a song or narrative from a book in reviews of the material or parodying works. Such a use is called a "fair use" and is discussed in Chapter 14 as a defense to copyright infringement.

MORAL RIGHTS

Introduction

Many countries recognize certain personal and noneconomic rights of authors in their works to protect their honor and reputation, even after they have sold their work. Such personal rights are referred to as **moral rights.**

There are two primary moral rights: the right of **attribution,** which ensures the author's right to be known as the author of a work, and the **right of integrity,** which ensures that the work not be distorted, mutilated, or misrepresented in a way that would injure the author's reputation.

The Berne Convention, to which the United States is a signatory, requires that member nations protect authors' moral rights of attribution and integrity. In 1990, Congress enacted the Visual Artists Rights Act (17 U.S.C. § 106A) in order to comply with its Berne Convention obligations. Prior to this legislation, authors generally protected their moral rights through actions for breach of contract, defamation, misrepresentation, or unfair competition.

Definition of Visual Arts

The Visual Artists Rights Act is quite limited and applies only to works of visual arts, namely, paintings, drawings, prints, photographs (produced for exhibition purposes), or sculptures that exist in a single copy or in a limited edition of two hundred or fewer copies, if those copies are signed and consecutively numbered. Works of visual art do not include posters, maps, globes, charts, technical drawings, motion pictures, books, magazines, newspapers, electronic information services or publications, or merchandising, promotional, packaging material, works made for hire, and works not subject to copyright protection (such as useful articles). Thus, the term *visual arts* generally refers to what is commonly called *fine art*.

moral rights: Personal rights retained by authors in their works (often works of fine arts) to protect their honor and reputation even after they no longer own the copyright in the work

attribution: The right of an author to be known as the author of a work

right of integrity: A personal right of a copyright author to ensure that his or her work not be distorted, mutilated, or used in a way that would injure the author's reputation

Rights of Attribution and Integrity

The author of a work of visual art has the following rights of attribution:

- to claim authorship of the work;
- to prevent the use of his or her name as the author of any work of visual art that he or she did not create; and
- to prevent the use of his or her name as the author of a work of visual art that has been distorted, mutilated, or otherwise modified such as to prejudice his or her honor or reputation.

The author of a work of visual art has the following rights of integrity:

- to prevent intentional distortion, mutilation, or other modification that would be prejudicial to his or her honor or reputation; and
- to prevent any destruction of a work of recognized stature, whether through intentional or gross negligence.

Thus, authors of fine arts have the right to be identified as the creator of their works and to prevent mutilation of their works, such as intentional distortions of their paintings or removal of limbs from sculptures. Modifications that are the result of the passage of time (such as chipping and fading), conservation, or presentation to the public (such as occurs when paintings in museums fade due to exposure to light) are not violations of the statute. The California statute discussed earlier also prohibits the destruction or mutilation of works of fine art and recognizes the right of attribution.

Extent and Duration of Moral Rights

The artist who creates the covered work owns the moral rights in it, even after selling the work to another. The moral rights reside with the author and, because they are personal rights, cannot be assigned or transferred to another, although the owner can waive his or her moral rights if the waiver is in writing. Joint authors of a work jointly own the moral rights.

For works created after June 1, 1991, moral rights endure for the author's life. Moral rights in works created jointly last until the death of the last surviving author.

Other Ways to Protect Moral Rights

Because the Visual Artists Rights Act applies to such a narrow category of works, namely, fine arts, authors of other works often use other remedies to achieve a level of protection equivalent to moral rights. Authors can agree by contract when they sell their works that they are entitled to future attribution and integrity rights. If the purchaser later removes the author's signature from the work or destroys it, a breach of contract has occurred. Authors may also be able to bring an action for violation of their exclusive right to prepare derivative works if a subsequent owner of a work defaces it or edits it. Finally, section 43 of the Lanham Act prohibits persons from making a false designation about the origin of goods. Thus, failure to give attribution by naming the author of a work or implying that an author is the creator of a revised or edited work likely violates this prohibition.

COMPULSORY LICENSES

In the early days of music recording, under the 1909 Copyright Act, once a composer authorized a sound recording, the composer was automatically entitled to a compulsory license or royalty fee of two cents per copy. Another producer was free to copy the sound recording as long as the statutorily set fee was paid. This arrangement, known as a **compulsory license,** allowed certain copyrighted works to be used, provided that the fixed fees were paid, eliminating the need for the user to contact each and every copyright owner for permission to use works. Compulsory licenses are governed by 17 U.S.C. § 115.

The provisions of section 115 of the Copyright Act do not prohibit a party from entering into a voluntary license arrangement with a copyright owner but rather provide a method of licensing when voluntary arrangements are not pursued, the copyright owner is unwilling to negotiate, or the copyright owner cannot be located.

Once a nondramatic musical work (such as a song) has been distributed to the public on a phonorecord under the authority of the copyright owner, any other person may make or manufacture other phonorecords for distribution to the public as long as notice is given and the set fees are paid to the copyright owner. A compulsory license may be obtained only if the primary purpose in making the phonorecords is to distribute them to the public for private (not commercial) use. A compulsory license is not available for phonorecords intended for use in background music systems, jukeboxes, broadcasting, or any other commercial use. Proprietors of establishments that allow patrons to make selections on coin-operated jukeboxes are required to enter into voluntary (rather than compulsory) license agreements and typically do so through one of the performing rights societies, such as BMI or ASCAP.

Generally, compulsory licensing requires that users register with and pay the royalty fees to the copyright owner or to the Licensing Division of the Copyright Office, which then remits the payments to Copyright Arbitration Royalty Panels administered by the Copyright Office that determine and distribute the royalty fees to the copyright owners.

compulsory license: The imposition of a statutorily set fee for use of a copyrighted work

ROLE OF INTELLECTUAL PROPERTY PROFESSIONAL

Intellectual property professionals may need to participate in copyright audits to ensure that clients are not infringing copyrighted works, even innocently. Common activities include the following:

- surveying clients to determine if music is played on hold for telephone callers or if music is piped into clients' business establishments;
- contacting ASCAP and BMI and obtaining sample license agreements and royalty fee schedules so arrangements can be made for performance of copyrighted works; and
- preparing newsletters and copyright fact sheets for distribution to clients advising them of possible copyright violations in the photocopying and distribution of literary works (such as magazine and journal articles), use of copyrighted materials including songs and movie clips in presentations, and playing of music on hold or throughout the clients' places of business.

CHAPTER SUMMARY

Owners of copyright are granted a bundle of exclusive rights:

- rights to reproduce the work;
- rights to prepare adaptations or derivative works based on the original work;
- rights to distribute the work;
- rights to perform the work; and
- rights to display the work.

Exercise of any of these rights without permission of the copyright owner will constitute infringement of copyright, even if there is no intent to infringe and the use is innocent. There are, however, certain exceptions to the exclusive rights granted to copyright owners, such as rights to use certain copyrighted works in certain instructional and educational activities, during religious worship services, for noncommercial fund-raising, for the handicapped, and for transmission of works in small commercial establishments. Moreover, according to the first sale doctrine, once a copyrighted work has been lawfully distributed by the owner, the new purchaser is free to further distribute the work by sale or lending.

A copyright owner's rights in sound recordings are significantly more limited than rights granted for other works, especially nondramatic literary and musical works.

Finally, authors of fine arts such as paintings and sculptures are granted "moral rights" in those works, allowing them to be identified as the author of the work and prohibiting destruction or alteration of the work, even after the creator has sold it.

DISCUSSION QUESTIONS

1. Is photocopying a chapter of this textbook a violation of copyright law? If so, which of the exclusive rights granted to the copyright owner is violated by such photocopying?
2. Given the facts in question 1, is the library at which the photocopying took place liable for copyright infringement? Discuss.
3. If you purchase the book *Chicken Soup for the Soul,* may you resell the book to another? What principle governs your answer?
4. If you purchase the book *The Royal Windsors,* may you prepare a television screenplay or treatment of it? What principle governs your answer?
5. May the owner of a large nightclub play records (using a sophisticated sound system with twenty speakers) so patrons can dance to the music? Discuss.
6. May the owner of a jewelry store consisting of less than one thousand square feet bring his home radio onto the premises so customers can listen to music? Discuss.
7. May the owner of the small business described in question 6 bring his "boom box" onto the premises and play CDs of Billy Joel? Discuss.
8. May a college professor teaching a music class have his students sing (in class) the song "Don't Cry for Me Argentina"? What if the performance is done at the college's annual winter chorale that members of the public and parents attend?

9. May the movie *The Ten Commandments* be shown at a youth group gathering at a church without the copyright owner's permission?

10. In 1995, a painter created an original signed painting and then produced three hundred and fifty reproductions of it, all of which are signed and numbered. The painter later produced one hundred posters of the painting. What rights to attribution does the painter have once the painting, the reproductions, and the posters are sold?

Copyright Ownership, Transfers, and Duration

Copyright ownership vests in the author of a work. Special issues arise when more than one person creates a work, when a derivative work based upon an underlying work is created, or when existing works are combined into a collection, such as an anthology. Determining ownership is critical because the exclusive rights of reproduction, performance, display, and so forth belong to the copyright owner. The person who creates a work is the author; however, if a work qualifies as one "made for hire," the author is not the creator but the employer or commissioning party. A work qualifies as a work made for hire if the work is created by an employee within the scope of employment or if the work falls within one of nine enumerated types of works and the parties agree in writing that the work is one made for hire. The exclusive rights ordinarily granted to the work's creator will instead be owned by the employer or commissioning party.

Copyright rights may be transferred. A transfer of exclusive rights must be in writing, while a nonexclusive grant, or license, need not be in writing. To protect copyright authors, even absolute or exclusive transfers can be set aside by the author or certain heirs during a five-year period beginning in the thirty-sixth year after a transfer.

Duration of copyright rights for works created after the 1976 act is for the author's life plus seventy years. For joint works, the duration is for seventy years after the last survivor's death. For works made for hire, the duration is generally ninety-five years from first publication or one hundred and twenty years from creation, whichever is shorter. Works copyrighted before the 1976 act are subject to special rules.

COPYRIGHT OWNERSHIP ISSUES

Copyright in a work protected under the Copyright Act vests in the **author** or authors of the work. 17 U.S.C. § 201(a). Issues about ownership arise when more than one person creates a work, when the work has multiple parts (such as a song consisting of a melody composed by one person and lyrics composed by another), or when work is created by an employee. Determining ownership is critical because it affects other rights, such as the ability to transfer or license a work and the duration of the copyright in a work.

Ownership of a physical object is separate and distinct from ownership of the copyright embodied in the material object. 17 U.S.C. § 202. Thus, the purchaser of choreographic notations for a ballet written by Mikhail Baryshnikov acquires only the written document. Baryshnikov, as the copyright owner, retains the exclusive rights granted under section 106 of the act, such as rights to perform the work and prepare derivative works based on it. Similarly, purchasing a manuscript, handwritten lyrics to a song scratched on an envelope, or letters written by a famous person gives the purchaser ownership only of those physical objects. Unless copyright has been explicitly conveyed with those physical articles, the original authors generally retain all other rights associated with the works, including the rights to perform and reproduce them and any other exclusive rights granted to copyright owners under section 106 of the Copyright Act.

JOINT WORKS

Intent to Create a Unitary Whole

A **joint work** is a work prepared by two or more authors with the intention that their contributions be merged into inseparable or interdependent parts of a unitary whole. 17 U.S.C. § 101. Only one copyright exists in the created work. Examples of joint works are books that are coauthored by individuals; plays that are composed of narrative written by one party, music by another, and lyrics to the music by a third; songs such as "Don't Cry for Me Argentina," in which the music was written by Andrew Lloyd-Webber and the lyrics by Tim Rice; and books comprising narrative written by one person and illustrations by another.

It is the intent of the parties at the time a work is created that determines whether it is a joint work. Thus, if two persons sit at a piano and collaborate on a melody and lyrics, the resulting song is a joint work. More difficult issues arise when parts to a work are created at different times, for example, when a melody is composed by itself and lyrics are added later. The parties' intent governs. If the first composer intended the work to be complete at the time he or she composed it, the copyright in the melody is owned solely by him or her. Merely changing one's mind at some later date and allowing another to add lyrics to a completed work does not convert the work into a joint work. In such a case, the first composer owns the copyright to the melodic composition, and the lyricist has created a derivative work based on the first and owns rights in the newly created lyrics alone. Unless both parties intend at the time they make their contributions that the parts be combined or absorbed into an integrated unit, there is no joint work.

author: For copyright purposes, a person who creates a work or, if the work is one made for hire, the employer or commissioning party

joint work: A copyrightable work created by two or more authors with the intent that their contributions be merged into a unitary whole

Merely making suggestions or giving directions to one creating a work is not sufficient to make one a joint author. For example, giving an architect instructions that a house to be designed by the architect should have a certain amount of living space and giving other directions does not make one a joint author. Although the contributions of coauthors need not be equal, each must make some significant contribution.

In regard to dividing profits arising out of joint works, courts presume the parties contributed equally unless they provide otherwise. Thus, if three individuals coauthor a book, the profits or royalties will be divided in equal thirds unless the parties agree to some other division. Agreements regarding division of revenue among joint authors should be in writing to avoid later disputes.

Ownership Rights in Joint Works

If individuals are authors of a joint work, each owns an equal undivided interest in the copyright as a tenant in common, meaning that each has the right to use the work, prepare derivative works based on it, perform it, display it, and so forth, without seeking the other coauthor's permission. Because each coauthor has rights in the work, one cannot exclude another from using the work or exercising the rights of copyright ownership. Nevertheless, if profits arise out of such uses, an accounting must be made so that each author shares in the benefits or proceeds.

Any coauthor may grant a *nonexclusive* license to another party to use the joint work without permission from the other coauthors; however, the granting of an *exclusive* license (one in which rights are granted solely to one party with no other party having any rights to use the work) requires consent from all coauthors of a joint work.

Upon the death of a coauthor, his or her rights pass to his heirs who then own the rights in common with the other coauthor(s). Joint ownership of a single work often arises in this fashion. A book may be authored by one person. Upon that person's death, the copyright may pass to several heirs who now own the work jointly.

Duration of Works of Joint Ownership

A copyright generally lasts for the author's life plus seventy years. 17 U.S.C. § 302. If the work is a joint work, however, the copyright lasts until seventy years after the last surviving coauthor's death. Additionally, as discussed in a later section in this chapter entitled "Termination of Transfers of Copyright," each joint author has the ability to terminate his or her transfers.

OWNERSHIP IN DERIVATIVE OR COLLECTIVE WORKS

If a work such as a book is created by one person who intends it to be complete at the time and illustrations are later added to it by another, the work cannot be a joint work because there was no intention of the parties to create a unitary whole at the time of their creation. In such a case, the new work, consisting of text and illustrations, is a derivative work (assuming the original author authorized the illustrator to use the earlier work).

The author of the original book has rights only to his or her work and cannot reproduce or perform the derivative work without permission. Similarly, the author of the derivative work cannot create further works based on the original book without permission and cannot reproduce the original work (or exercise other copyright rights) without permission.

Copyright to the first work (the book alone) will last until seventy years after its author's death, and copyright to the derivative work (book and illustrations) will last until seventy years after its author's death.

Multiple ownership rights may also arise if separately copyrightable works are compiled into a collection. For example, if essays written by Jerry Seinfeld, Ellen DeGeneres, and Paul Reiser are collected into a humor anthology by Bill Jones (with permission of the original authors), the original authors retain their exclusive rights (such as rights to reproduce, distribute, and perform) in their respective essays. No joint work is created because there was no intent at the time the separate essays were created to merge them into a unitary whole. No derivative work is created because the original works have not been transformed in any way and nothing new has been added to them. The anthology by the compiler, Bill Jones, is a collective work and pursuant to section 201(c) of the act, Jones acquires only the right to reproduce and distribute the contributions as part of the particular collective work or any revision of the collective work.

WORKS MADE FOR HIRE

Introduction

Although the general rule is that the person who creates a work is the author of that work and the owner of the copyright therein, there is an exception to that principle: the copyright law defines a category of works called **works made for hire.** If a work is "made for hire," the author is considered to be the employer or commissioning party and not the employee or the actual person who created the work. The employer or commissioning party may be a company or an individual.

There are two types of works that are classified as works made for hire: works prepared by an employee within the scope of employment and certain categories of specially ordered or commissioned works.

Works Prepared by Employees in the Scope of Employment

Copyright in works prepared by employees are presumptively owned by their employers. For example, if an employee is tasked with creating a computer program by his or her employer, the resulting work is owned by the employer who is treated as the author of the work for purposes of copyright law. Oftentimes, however, questions arise whether the person creating the work is an "employee" (such that his or her creations belong to the employer) or whether the person is an "independent contractor" (such that his or her creations belong to him or her as the owner/author). This question often arises when freelance artists prepare works for others.

In *Community for Creative Non-Violence v. Reid*, 490 U.S. 730 (1989), the Supreme Court held that the term *employee* for purposes of determining

work made for hire: A work that is presumed to be authored by an employer because it was created by an employee on company time or authored by a commissioning party when the parties have agreed the commissioning party will own the copyright and the work falls into one of nine statutorily enumerated categories

authorship of works made for hire should be interpreted according to general common law agency principles. If the person doing the work is an employee under common law agency principles and the work was done in the scope of employment, the employer (not the employee) is the copyright owner/author.

The Court identified certain factors that characterize an employer-employee relationship:

- **Control by the employer over the work.** If the employer has a voice in how the work is done, has the work done at the employer's location, and provides equipment and tools to the person to create the work, such tends to show an employer-employee relationship.
- **Control by the employer over the employee.** If the employer controls the worker's schedule in creating work, has the right to have the worker perform other assignments, determines the method of payment, and/or has the right to hire the worker's assistants, such evidences an employer-employee relationship.
- **Status of employer.** If the employer is in business to produce such works, provides the worker with benefits similar to those received by other workers, and withholds taxes from the worker's compensation, such is supportive of an employer-employee relationship.

These factors are not exhaustive; for example, courts can also consider the duration of the relationship of the parties (a long-term relationship is indicative of employment) and the skill level of the employee. Moreover, no one factor is determinative. All or most of these factors, however, characterize a regular, salaried employment relationship, and works created by employees in the course and scope of such a relationship are works made for hire, authorship and copyright of which vests in the employer (unless the parties agree in writing otherwise).

The Copyright Office has provided the following examples of works made for hire:

- a software program created by a staff programmer for Creative Computer Corporation;
- a newspaper article written by a staff journalist for publication in a daily newspaper; and
- a musical arrangement written for XYZ Music Company by a salaried arranger on its staff.

Note that the work must be created *within the scope of employment* to be a work made for hire. Thus, if the software program was created by a person before joining Creative Computer Corporation, the company has no rights to the work. Similarly, if an employee employed by Creative Computer Corporation writes a book about computers in the evenings and weekends, the work is likely not a work made for hire because it was not created in the course of the employee's duties.

Many employers ask that employees sign agreements acknowledging that works created by the employees will be works made for hire. Such agreements may be considered by courts, but an agreement alone is not controlling. Other factors may be considered in determining the nature of the parties' relationship. One approach may be to recite in an agreement that the relationship is one of employer-employee, that works created by the employee are works made for hire owned by the employer, and that in the event it is later determined by a court that the work is not one made for hire, the employee irrevocably and immediately assigns all rights to the work to the employer. Such an agreement will likely be given effect by a court. If the employee desires to retain ownership of works created in the course of employment that otherwise would be works made for hire, the parties must expressly agree in a written instrument signed by both parties. (See Appendix D, Form 12, for sample provisions in employment agreements relating to works made for hire.)

Specially Commissioned Works

If the work is not one prepared by an employee but, rather, is one prepared by an independent contractor, it can be deemed a work made for hire if three conditions are met: it is a specially ordered or commissioned work; the parties agree in writing that the work is one made for hire; and the work falls into one of nine specially enumerated categories. 17 U.S.C. § 101. All three of these elements must be satisfied if the work is to be one made for hire. The nine categories of works are as follows:

1. a contribution to a collective work;
2. part of a motion picture or other audiovisual work;
3. a translation;
4. a supplementary work (a work prepared for publication as a secondary adjunct to a work by another author for the purpose of introducing, illustrating, or explaining the work, such as forewords, pictorial illustrations, tables, editorial notes, bibliographies, appendices, and indexes);
5. a compilation;
6. an instructional text (a literary, pictorial, or graphic work prepared for publication with the purpose of use in systematic instructional activities);
7. a test;
8. answer material for a test; and
9. an atlas.

Although the parties can agree in writing that the commissioning party owns the work, this agreement will not convert a work that does not fit within one of the nine statutorily designated categories into one made for hire. Therefore, the safest approach is for the parties to agree in writing that the work is one made for hire and that if for some reason the work is determined not to be one made for hire, by the same document, the work is automatically assigned and transferred to the person who commissioned the work.

For example, if a museum hires a graphic artist to create a painting and an audiovisual slide presentation for a museum opening, and the parties agree in writing that the works are to be owned by the museum and are to be considered works made for hire, the agreement is sufficient to vest ownership and certain other rights in the physical painting and the slide presentation in the museum. However, while the audiovisual slide presentation is a work made for hire (it was specially commissioned, the parties agreed in writing it would be considered a work made for hire, and it fits the statutory definition), the painting is not a work made for hire despite what the parties agreed because it does not fit the statutory definition. Thus, a safety net clause should be added conveying all of the author's rights in the painting in the event it is not a work made for hire.

This would allow the museum to create derivative works based on the painting, display it, and so forth.

Effects of Works Made for Hire

There are several effects if a work is classified as one made for hire:

- **Ownership.** The owner/author of a work made for hire is the employer or commissioning party. The artist who created the work has no more rights in the work than any stranger, and the artist cannot reproduce, distribute, or perform the work, or prepare derivatives based on it, without being liable for copyright infringement.
- **Duration.** Copyrights in works made for hire endure for ninety-five years from publication or one hundred and twenty years from creation, whichever is shorter. Copyrights in other works generally endure for the author's life plus seventy years thereafter.
- **Reversion of transfers.** Rights in works that are not made for hire revert back to the author after thirty-five years, even if there has been an unconditional transfer or sale to another. (See the section entitled "Termination of Transfers of Copyright" later in this chapter.)
- **Moral rights.** There are no moral rights (rights of attribution and integrity) in works made for hire.

TRANSFERS OF COPYRIGHT

Divisibility of Ownership

Any or all of the exclusive rights of the copyright owner (rights to reproduce, prepare derivative works, distribute the work, and perform and display the work publicly) can be transferred or licensed to another party. 17 U.S.C. § 201(d). Thus, the author of a book may grant the right to prepare derivative works based on the book to one party and yet transfer the rights to distribute the book to another party. The grants or licenses can be perpetual or for limited terms. Similarly, they can be limited to certain geographic areas, such as when one party is granted the right to distribute a work in the western region of the United States and another party is granted the right to distribute the work in the eastern region of the United States.

Copyright rights are divisible, meaning they can be subdivided, such as occurs when the copyright owner of a book carves up his or her rights to prepare derivative works by granting one party the right to translate the book, granting another party the right to make a motion picture based on the book, and granting a third party the right to prepare a sequel to the book.

Granting rights to others is a way for copyright owners to exploit their works to the fullest extent. The copyright owner will grant rights and generally require payment therefor, such as periodic royalties on the sales of each book or song exploited by the licensee.

Requirement of Writing for Transfer of Exclusive Rights

A transfer of exclusive rights (meaning that only one party is granted rights rather than several parties) other than a transfer by operation of law is not valid unless the transfer is in writing and signed by the owner of the rights conveyed (or his or her exclusive agent). 17 U.S.C. § 204(a). Granting rights on a nonexclusive basis (for example, allowing several parties to reproduce the work) is not considered a "transfer" under the Copyright Act and thus need not be in writing. Such an arrangement is generally called a license, and although there is no requirement that there be a written document, such is advised because it lends certainty to the terms of the transaction. (See Figure 12–1, Assignment of Copyright.)

Like other property rights, copyrights can be transferred by operation of law, generally meaning the law can require a transfer. For example, transfers by operation of law occur when, in a bankruptcy, the bankrupt's property is transferred to the bankruptcy trustee or to a creditor; when a court orders the sale of a copyright in a divorce proceeding; or when an owner dies without leaving a will and the laws of intestate succession govern who acquires the decedent's property. Copyrights can also pass by will to one's specified beneficiaries.

Just as trademarks can be used to secure obligations, copyrights can serve as secured property. If Carly Simon wishes to borrow money from a bank, the bank may require her to pledge certain copyrights in her songs as security for repayment of the debt. If she fails to repay the debt, the bank can seize the copyrights and all rights therein. In fact, some entertainers, including David Bowie and the group Iron Maiden, have sold bonds backed by predicted revenues from future recordings and performances. Bowie financed one of his tours with the money raised from the sale of such bonds.

Recordation of Transfers

There is no requirement that transfers or licenses of copyright or grants of security interests in copyright be recorded with the U.S. Copyright Office. Recordation is prudent, however, because it provides notice of rights in copyrights and may establish priorities of conflicting transfers. The Copyright Office does not make or participate in the transfer but merely records the document in its files. Recordation can be made whether the work is published or unpublished and whether or not it has been registered with the Copyright Office. Other documents pertaining to copyrights can also be recorded. For example, a will that bequeaths a copyright can be recorded with the Copyright Office. The current basic fee for recording a document covering one work is $50. An additional charge of $15 is made for each group of ten additional titles or fewer. In certain circumstances (generally when litigation is pending or threatened), special handling may be requested and recordation will be expedited (usually within five business days) upon the payment of an additional fee and a showing of the necessity for special handling.

TERMINATION OF TRANSFERS OF COPYRIGHT

Introduction

In many instances, young artists, songwriters, and other creators transfer or license rights in their copyrighted works at a time when they do not truly have an idea about the value of the works transferred. The works may be exploited by the new owners who may collect astounding amounts of money, and yet the original creators of the works may not realize any economic gain

FIGURE 12–1
Assignment of Copyright

WHEREAS, Kathryn Sherman ("Assignor"), an individual residing at 1010 Canyon Glen Terrace, Phoenix, AZ 22098, is the owner of all copyrights in that literary work entitled *The Challenge* (the "Work") and is the author of such Work; and

WHEREAS, Blake Publishers, Inc. ("Assignee"), a corporation organized under the laws of the State of New York, located and doing business at 555 Avenue of the Americas, New York, NY 96607, desires to acquire all of Assignor's rights in and to the Work;

NOW, THEREFORE, for good and valuable consideration, the receipt and sufficiency of which are hereby acknowledged, Assignor hereby irrevocably sells, assigns, transfers, and conveys to Assignee the entire right, title, and interest in and to the Work, including any copyrights and registrations, the same to be held and enjoyed by Assignee, its successors, assigns, and other legal representatives.

Assignee shall have the right to register the copyright in the Work in its own name and shall have the exclusive rights to develop, exploit, publish, reproduce, distribute, perform, display, and prepare derivative works based thereon throughout the world.

Assignor represents and warrants that she created the Work independently, the Work is the result of her original effort, and that she is the owner of all copyrights and other rights in the Work and that no other party has any rights in or to the Work.

Assignor further assigns to Assignee all right to sue for and receive all damages accruing from past, present, and future infringements of the Work herein assigned.

This Assignment shall be binding upon the parties, their successors and/or assigns, and all others acting by, through, with, or under their direction, and all those in privity therewith.

Assignee agrees to cooperate with Assignor and take any further action and execute any documents required to effect the purposes of this Assignment.

Kathryn Sherman   Blake Publishers, Inc.

_____   By: _____

                                                    Title: _____

                                                    Date: _____

whatsoever from these early works and may not be able to exercise any control with regard to reproduction, distribution, preparation of derivative works, performance, or display of the works. To remedy this situation, section 203 of the Copyright Act provides that transfers of copyrights can be terminated after thirty-five years so that the original author can recapture his or her works.

The Copyright Act's termination of transfer provisions are highly unusual and are contrary to general principles of contract law, which hold that once a valid contract has been entered into, it cannot be set aside (except in extreme cases, such as those involving fraud). When an individual sells a house, he or she is not allowed to cancel the sale and reclaim the house if it later appreciates. Bad decisions made on the stock market cannot be set aside. Yet transfers of copyrights can be set aside or terminated, reflecting Congress's intent to protect artists and authors from exploitation.

Grants Executed After January 1, 1978

Statutory Authority   Section 203 of the Copyright Act sets forth the procedures for terminating grants or transfers of copyrights that occurred after the

1976 Copyright Act became effective on January 1, 1978. Section 203 refers to transfers that occur after January 1, 1978, regardless of when the work was created.

According to section 203(a), in the case of any work *other than a work made for hire,* an exclusive or nonexclusive grant of a transfer or license of a copyright or of any right under a copyright, executed by an author after January 1, 1978, and other than a grant made by will, is subject to termination. Grants of copyright that occur by way of a will cannot be terminated, apparently because Congress saw no exploitation of the author in such cases. The author's right to reach back in time and terminate an earlier transfer cannot be waived, and any provision attempting to waive the protections afforded by section 203 is void.

Who May Effect Termination   In the case of grants by a single author, the author may terminate. If the author has died, his or her termination rights may be exercised by the surviving spouse and his or her children and grandchildren. These successors may terminate in the author's place if they hold more than 50 percent of the author's termination rights.

Section 203(a)(2) sets forth an elaborate scheme for determining who may exercise the rights of a deceased author. In brief, the following apply:

- If a spouse survives the death of the author, and there are no children or grandchildren, the spouse owns all of the termination right.
- If the author leaves both a spouse and surviving children or grandchildren by a deceased child, the spouse owns one-half of the termination rights and the surviving children and grandchildren share the remaining one-half.
- If there is no surviving spouse, the author's living children and any children of a deceased child own all of the termination rights.
- Each surviving child gets his or her percentage share. Children of a deceased child of the author take the share that would have gone to their parent and, in casting their votes to effect a termination, must act as a unit. A majority vote controls. Children of surviving children have no rights.
- If the author leaves no surviving spouse, children, or grandchildren, his or her executor owns the author's termination interest.

Example: Author Smith dies, leaving a widow (*W*), one living child (*LC*), and four grandchildren (*GC*) by way of a deceased son. Their termination rights are as follows: *W* owns 50 percent; *LC* owns 25 percent; and the *GC*s collectively own 25 percent. To terminate a transfer, more than 50 percent approval is needed. *W* must be joined either by *LC* or the *GC*s (three of whom must approve the transaction) in order to terminate.

In the case of a transfer by joint authors of a work, the transfer may be canceled by a majority of the authors who made the transfer. If any of the joint authors has died, his or her termination rights are exercised according to the scheme just described.

Effecting a Termination   Generally, termination of the prior grant may be effected at any time during a period of five years beginning in the thirty-sixth year after the date of execution of the grant. To effect the termination, those who own the rights of termination (or their authorized agents) must sign and serve a written notice to the grantee two to ten years before the transfer is to be terminated. The notice must set forth the date of termination and must describe the grant being terminated. A copy of the notice must be recorded with the Copyright Office. Upon the effective date of the termination, the rights in the work automatically revert to the author or the author's successors (including those who voted against the termination). The author (or successors) must follow this statutory procedure in order to effect a termination.

After the effective date of termination, the author (or successors who have recovered his or her rights) may make a new grant of rights to a different party. If the author (or successors) wishes to regrant rights to the original grantee, such can be done once the notice of termination has been served. In fact, once the notice of termination is served, the grantee will often commence negotiations with the author (or successors) so the grantee can continue to exercise the rights originally granted to him or her. Typically, new fee payments are negotiated. The new grant or regrant must be signed by the same number and proportion of owners as are required to terminate the grant.

Grants Prior to January 1, 1978

Grants made by copyright authors prior to January 1, 1978, the effective date of the 1976 Copyright Act, are governed by section 304 of the act. Most of the rules and procedures relating to termination of transfers granted after the Copyright Act of 1976 also apply to transfers granted under the previous 1909 act. One difference, however, is that under the 1976 act, only grants made by the author of a work in his or her lifetime may be terminated. Under section 304, grants made by the author, or certain of his or her beneficiaries or executor if the author was dead, may be recaptured. Most other rules relating to notice, recordation of the notice with the Copyright Office, effect of termination, inability to waive termination rights, and so forth remain the same.

Under section 304, termination can be effected of rights (other than copyrights in works made for hire or those transferred by will) at any point during a five-year period that begins at the end of fifty-six years from the date copyright was originally secured. For a copyright in its renewal term, if a termination right had expired, under the new Sonny Bono Copyright Term Extension Act, a termination of a transfer may be effected at any time during the five years beginning at the end of seventy-five years from the date copyright was secured. Identical to rights terminated under the 1976 act, rights that have been recaptured may be granted to a new party after the termination is effective, and an agreement to regrant rights to the original transferee may be effected as soon as the notice of termination is served.

DURATION OF COPYRIGHT

Introduction

The duration of a copyright depends upon whether the copyright was created after January 1, 1978, the effective date of the 1976 Copyright Act, or before that date. Under the Copyright Act of 1909, federal copyright protection commenced upon publication of the work. Prior to publication, common law copyright principles controlled. Under the 1976 act, federal copyright protection commences upon creation of the work in a fixed form, whether the work is published or not. Because works under the 1909 act may still be subject to copyright protection, it is important to understand the periods of duration for works created under both acts.

Duration Under the 1909 Copyright Act

Under the 1909 act, the copyright in a work lasted for a first term of twenty-eight years from the date it was secured. During the last year of the term, the copyright was eligible for renewal either by the author or specified heirs. If renewed, the copyright was extended for a second term of twenty-eight years. If not renewed, the copyright expired at the end of the first twenty-eight-year term. Thus, the maximum allowable length of copyright protection under the 1909 act was fifty-six years.

Duration Under the 1976 Copyright Act

For works that are created and fixed in a tangible medium of expression after January 1, 1978, the Copyright Act of 1976 does away with the burdensome renewal requirements and establishes a single copyright term. There are three basic categories of works:

- for works created after January 1, 1978, copyright extends for the lifetime of the author plus seventy years (this term is similar to that of many foreign countries);
- for joint works, the term lasts for seventy years after the last surviving author's death; and
- for works made for hire and for anonymous works (those in which no natural person is identified as the author on the copies or phonorecords of the work) and pseudonymous works (those in which the author is identified by a fictitious name on the copies or phonorecords of the work), the duration of copyright is ninety-five years from the first publication of the work, or one hundred and twenty years from creation, whichever is shorter (although if the anonymous or pseudonymous author discloses his or her name to the Copyright Office, the duration will convert to life plus seventy years).

Until recently, duration of each of these copyrights was twenty years shorter. To harmonize U.S. law with that of many foreign countries, Congress passed the Sonny Bono Copyright Term Extension Act in late 1998, which extended the duration of copyright terms as set forth herein. This legislation was subject to much debate, with critics complaining that extending the duration of copyright protection benefits only copyright owners and deprives the public of having works enter the public domain for ready dissemination at the earliest possible date. To respond to fears by libraries and archives that the extended copyright duration would inhibit their educational functions, a provision was added to allow, during the last twenty years of any term of copyright of a published work, a library or archives to make certain uses of copyrighted materials for preservation, scholarship, or research purposes, if those works are not commercially available.

Effect of 1976 Copyright Act on Preexisting Works

Any copyright still in its renewal term on October 27, 1998 (the date the new Sonny Bono Copyright Term Extension Act became effective) now has a copyright term of ninety-five years from the date copyright was originally secured.

Works that were in existence but were not published or copyrighted on January 1, 1978 (for example, an unpublished manuscript that had no copyright protection under the 1909 act and was governed by common law principles) are automatically given protection as if they were created after January 1, 1978 (the life-plus-seventy or the ninety-five- and one-hundred-and-twenty-year terms, as applicable) or until December 31, 2002, whichever occurs last. To encourage publication, Congress provided that if the work is published before December 31, 2002, an additional forty-five years of protection will be granted, until December 31, 2047.

In many instances, owners of copyrights that were in their first terms on January 1, 1978, did not apply to renew their copyrights and their copyrights expired after only twenty-eight years. To avoid similar situations, in 1991 Congress amended the Copyright Act of 1976 to provide for automatic renewals for works in their first term. There is now no requirement to file a renewal application to extend the original twenty-eight-year copyright term to the full term of ninety-five years. Although the renewal term is automatically extended, there are a number of incentives that encourage the filing of a renewal application (using Copyright Office Form RE), especially during the twenty-eighth year of the copyright term (for example, the Copyright Office will issue a renewal certificate that constitutes *prima facie* evidence of the validity of the facts stated in the renewal certificate and the copyright in the extended term).

(See Figure 12–2 for a chart illustrating duration of copyright.)

FIGURE 12–2
Copyright Duration

Date of Work	Duration of Copyright
Works created after 1/1/1978	Author's life plus 70 years (or if a joint work, 70 years after last survivor's death); if work is "work made for hire" (or anonymous or pseudonymous work), copyright lasts for 95 years from publication or 120 years from creation, whichever is shorter
Work created before 1/1/1978, but not published	Author's life plus 70 years or until 12/31/2002, whichever is longer (if work is published before 12/31/2002, copyright extended until 12/31/2047)
Copyright secured under 1909 act and in first or renewal term on 1/1/1978	Term automatically extended to give a total length of copyright of 95 years from publication of work

Calculating Dates for Copyright Duration

The act provides that all terms of copyright will run through the end of the calendar year in which they would otherwise expire. For example, if an author of a work created in June 1980 died in June 1990, protection would extend until December 31, 2060.

No Restoration of Lost Copyrights

Neither the 1976 act nor any amendments provide for revival or restoration of lost copyrights. If a work fell into the public domain because its author failed to renew the work under the 1909 act, it is not restored by any statutory provision.

ROLE OF INTELLECTUAL PROPERTY PROFESSIONAL

There are numerous tasks for IP professionals to be involved in relating to ownership, transfer, and duration of copyrights. Commonly performed tasks are as follows:

- legal research to determine whether a work is a joint work, derivative work, or collective work;
- drafting agreements between or among joint authors in regard to divisions of royalties and other rights;
- investigating circumstances of employment to determine whether an individual is an employee or an independent contractor;
- drafting provisions for employment agreements relating to ownership of works created by employees;
- drafting agreements relating to specially commissioned works confirming the works are "made for hire," and providing that if they are later determined not to be works made for hire, the creator assigns all rights to the commissioning party;
- drafting agreements transferring or assigning copyright rights to others;
- drafting agreements subjecting copyrights to security interests;
- recording transfers of copyright ownership with the Copyright Office;
- docketing transfers of copyright so dates for termination of transfers can be tracked;
- drafting notices for termination of transfers of copyright and recording notices with Copyright Office;
- docketing dates for duration of copyright so owners can be informed that copyright protection will terminate; and
- renewing copyrights for works protected under the 1909 act to obtain benefits of voluntary renewal.

CHAPTER SUMMARY

Determining ownership of a copyright is critical because a wide variety of rights flow from copyright ownership, including rights to reproduce, adapt, distribute, perform, and display the work. Moreover, the duration of copyright depends upon its ownership. When two or more people create a work with the intent that their separate contributions be merged into the completed work, the work is a joint work and the authors each have rights to distribute, perform, reproduce, or display the work. A derivative work is one based upon an underlying work. The author of the underlying work has exclusive rights in his or her work, and the author of the derivative work has rights in his or her newly created work that exist independently from any rights in the original work.

Although the general rule is that the person who creates a work is the author of that work, there is an exception to that rule: the copyright law defines a category of works called "works made for hire." If a work is one "made for hire," either the employer or commissioner of the work is the author for copyright purposes and possesses the exclusive rights of a copyright owner. A work made for hire is one prepared by an employee in the scope of employment or one of nine specially enumerated types of commissioned works that the parties have agreed in writing will be a work made for hire.

Because copyrights are property, they may be transferred. Moreover, the rights of a copyright owner (including rights to reproduce, adapt, distribute, perform, and display the work) are divisible, meaning that the author may transfer some rights and retain others. Transfers of exclusive rights must be in writing. Transfers of copyright can be terminated either by the author or certain of his or her heirs during a statutorily defined period beginning the thirty-sixth year after the transfer. This unusual provision in copyright law is intended to protect authors who transfer rights before they fully understand the value of their works.

Copyrights created after the 1976 act last for the author's life plus seventy years or seventy years from the last survivor's death in the case of joint works. For works made for hire and anonymous and pseudonymous works, the duration of copyright is ninety-five years from first publication of the work or one hundred and twenty years from its creation, whichever first occurs.

DISCUSSION QUESTIONS

1. Janet is an author who wrote a novel in 1988. In 1990, she granted exclusive rights to Fox Studios to make a movie based on the novel (the movie was created in 1990), and in 1991, she granted nonexclusive rights to Penguin Books to distribute the novel in the area west of the Mississippi River.
   a. Must the grants of rights to Fox and Penguin be in writing? Discuss.
   b. Can Janet terminate the rights she granted to Fox and Penguin? If so, when?
   c. When do the copyrights in the novel and movie expire?
2. Kim Hunter and John Taylor have collaborated on a song comprising melody and lyrics. Who owns the work? When does the copyright expire?
3. Susan Farrell works out of her home as a freelance computer programmer. She was hired by TNI Computers to create a computer program. Susan worked on the project exclusively from her home and worked for other companies during this same time. She paid her own taxes and received no benefits from TNI Computers. Who is the author of the computer program? Why?
4. Warner Brothers Studios hired Sam, an independent filmmaker, to prepare a movie based on the life of President Reagan. The parties orally agreed Warner Brothers would own the movie. Who is the author of the movie? Why? Would your answer be different if the agreement was in writing?
5. Greg, a noted author of children's books, wrote a book in 1994. Three years later he allowed Dave to illustrate the second edition of the book. Is the finished project a joint work?
6. Harry and Barbara are authors of a joint work, which is a song. May Barbara, by herself, grant exclusive rights to Whitney Houston to perform the song? If Barbara collects royalties arising out of a nonexclusive grant to a party to reproduce the work, what are Barbara's duties to Harry, if any?
7. What is the period of duration for the following works?
   a. a song created by Susan Blake in 1990
   b. a book written by Judith and Michael Smith in 1995
   c. a work created by an employee in the scope of his or her employment in 1985
   d. a work created in 1975 that has never been published
   e. a novel that was published in 1940 and that was in its renewal term on January 1, 1978, when the 1976 Copyright Act went into effect
   f. a song published in 1890
   g. a movie created in 1970 and that was in its first term when the Copyright Act of 1976 went into effect

Copyright Registration, Searching Copyright Office Records, and Notice of Copyright

In the United States, copyright protection exists from the time a work is created. Thus, applying for and securing a copyright registration is not a condition of copyright protection. Nevertheless, copyright registration provides several benefits, such as establishing a public record of the claim of copyright, allowing a claim of infringement to be brought in federal court, and resulting in availability of statutory damages and attorneys' fees if a registered work is infringed. The Copyright Office provides all forms necessary for registration, and the process typically takes about sixteen weeks. The Copyright Office also is open for searching of records, and its information specialists will help conduct searches of records for a fee. Although notice of copyright is optional since March 1, 1989, use of a notice is recommended. A copyright notice consists of the symbol © (or the word "Copyright" or the abbreviation "Copr."), the date of first publication of the work, and the name of the copyright owner.

INTRODUCTION

As discussed in Chapter 9, neither publication of a work nor registration or other action in the U.S. Copyright Office is required to secure copyright protection under federal law. Copyright is secured automatically when the work is created. A work is "created" when it is fixed in a copy or phonorecord for the first time. Although not required to provide copyright protection for a work, registration of copyright with the Copyright Office is inexpensive, easy, and provides several advantages. The relative ease with which works may be registered is chiefly due to the fact that there is no substantive examination of applications for registration of copyrights (as there is for trademarks and patents). To register a work, the applicant must send the following three elements to the Copyright Office: a properly completed application form, a filing fee, and a deposit of the work being registered. Registration may be made at any time within the life of the copyright.

THE APPLICATION FOR COPYRIGHT REGISTRATION

Parties Who May File Applications

The following persons are entitled to submit an application for registration of copyright:

- the author (either the person who actually created the work or, if the work is one made for hire, the employer or commissioning party);
- the copyright claimant (either the author or a person or organization that has obtained ownership of all of the rights under the copyright originally belonging to the author, such as a transferee);
- the owner of exclusive rights, such as the transferee of any of the exclusive rights of copyright ownership (for example, one who prepares a movie based on an earlier book may file an application for the newly created derivative work, the movie); and
- the duly authorized agent of the author, claimant, or owner of exclusive rights (such as an attorney, trustee, or anyone authorized to act on behalf of such parties).

Application Forms

Types of Forms   The Copyright Office provides forms for applications for copyright registration. Each form is one 8½- by 11-inch sheet, printed front and back. An applicant may use photocopies of forms. Because the Copyright Office receives more than six hundred thousand applications each year, each application must use a similar format to ease the burden of examination. The type of form used is dictated by the type of work that is the subject of copyright. For example, one form is used for literary works, while another is used for sound recordings. Following are the forms used for copyright applications.

- **Form TX.** Form TX is used for registration of published or unpublished nondramatic literary works, excluding periodicals or serial issues. This class includes a wide variety of works: fiction, nonfiction, essays, poetry, textbooks, reference works, catalogs, advertising copy, compilations of information, and computer programs.
- **Form PA.** Form PA is used for works of the performing arts (namely, those to be performed before an audience), including plays, pantomimes, choreographic works, operas, motion pictures and other audiovisual works, musical compositions, and songs.

- **Form VA.** Form VA is used for registration of published or unpublished works of visual arts, including two- and three-dimensional works of fine, graphic, and applied art, such as cartoons, comic strips, dolls, toys, fabric and wallcovering designs, games and puzzles, greeting cards, jewelry designs, maps, original prints, photographs, posters, sculptures, and technical drawings including architectural plans and blueprints.
- **Form SR.** Form SR is used for sound recordings.
- **Form SE.** Form SE is used to register each individual issue of a serial, such as periodicals, newspapers, magazines, newsletters, annuals, and journals.
- **Short forms.** The Copyright Office offers a short version of some of its application forms to make registering a copyright claim easier. The information requested is minimal and the instructions are brief. Short forms may be used if the application is by a living author who is the sole author and owner of the work, the work is completely new, and the work is not one made for hire. The following forms are available in short form: Short Form PA (for works of the performing arts), Short Form TX (for literary works), and Short Form VA (for works of the visual arts).
- **Group forms.** Group forms may be used for certain applications comprising several parts, such as the following: Form Group/DN (for registering copyrights in a group of daily newspapers); Form Group/CP (for submission with Forms TX, PA, or VA when a group of works such as short stories or a series of sculpture figurines is being applied for); Form Group/SE (for applying for a group of serials, such as several issues of a magazine).

The Copyright Office provides other forms as well, namely, forms for renewals for works under the 1909 act (Form RE); forms for continuation when, due to length, the application cannot be completed on one page (Form CON); and a form to correct or amplify information given in the Copyright Office record of an earlier registration (Form CA).

Obtaining Application Forms   There are a variety of ways to obtain application forms from the Copyright Office. Application forms are provided free of charge.

- **Forms and circulars hotline.** A person can call the Copyright Office (202/707-9100) and leave a recorded message asking for forms by name and leaving a mailing address. The forms will be sent within a week or two.
- **Ordering by mail.** Copyright applications can be obtained by mailing a request to Library of Congress, Copyright Office, Publications Section LM-455, 101 Independence Avenue SE, Washington, DC 20559-6000.
- **Internet.** All Copyright Office application forms are now available on the Internet. They may be downloaded and printed for use in registering or renewing copyrights. Connect to the Library of Congress home page on the World Wide Web and select the copyright link. The address is http://www.loc.gov. Alternatively, you may connect through the Copyright Office home page at http://lcweb.loc.gov/copyright. You must have Adobe® Acrobat® Reader installed on your computer to view and print the forms. The free Adobe Acrobat Reader may be downloaded

from Adobe Systems Incorporated through links from the same Internet site at which the forms are available. Print the forms head to head (the top of page 2 must be directly behind the top of page 1) on a single sheet of 8½- by 11-inch white paper.

Preparing the Application Form   Although there are a variety of application forms to be used in applying for registration, the information required of an applicant and the format of the forms are nearly identical from form to form. Generally, there are several sections or "spaces" that must be completed. In order to obtain the information needed for the copyright application, many law firms ask clients to complete copyright questionaires so information will be complete and accurate (see Figure 13–1 for a sample questionnaire).

Space 1: Title.   Every work submitted for copyright registration must be given a title to identify it. If the copies or phonorecords of the work bear a title or any identifying phrase that could serve as a title, this wording should be used in its exact and complete form. Indexing of the registration and future identification of the work depends on its title. If the work is a collective work (such as a collection of songs), the overall title of the collection should be given.

The applicant must also indicate if the work has been known under a previous title or if there is an additional title under which someone searching for the registration might be likely to look. For example, if a movie title is changed in the course of filming, the previous title should be given. Similarly, the song "My Heart Will Go On" is also known as the "Theme Song from Titanic." Both titles should be given.

Space 2: Author(s).   A variety of information must be given about the author(s) of the work. The fullest form of the author's name should be given, unless the work is a work made for hire, in which case the name of the employer or commissioning party should be given as author. If there is more than one author (such as may be the case in a joint work consisting of a book and its accompanying illustrations), all should be identified.

The application must indicate if the author's contribution is anonymous or pseudonymous. An author's contribution to a work is **anonymous** if a natural person is not identified on the copies or phonorecords of the work. An author's work is **pseudonymous** if the author is identified under a fictitious name, such as the books written by Stephen King under the pseudonym Richard Bachman.

If the author is dead, the application requires that the date of death be given (because copyright protection for most works lasts for life plus seventy years, the author's date of death determines copyright duration). The author's birth date is requested, although it is not required. If the work is one made for hire, the date of birth space should be left blank. The author's nationality or domicile must be given in all cases.

Finally, a brief description of the nature of authorship must be given. For example, the following terms are usually acceptable: *entire text, illustrations, computer program, words and music, sculpture, photographs, lyrics,* and *motion picture.* Conversely, the following terms should be avoided because they suggest lack of copyrightable material: *idea, concept, typeface, title, system, method,* and *layout.*

Space 3: Creation and Publication.   Space 3 of each copyright application requires an identification of the year in which creation of the work was

anonymous work: A copyrighted work in which the author is not identified

pseudonymous work: A copyrighted work in which the author is identified under a fictitious name, such as the name "Mark Twain" used by Samuel Clemens

FIGURE 13–1
Copyright Questionnaire

The following questions are intended to help determine whether a work is entitled to copyright registration and the particular form to be used in applying for registration. Complete the questions to the best of your knowledge. If you do not know the answer to a question, indicate such and we can address outstanding issues together.

1. Describe your work. Is it a book? A short story? A song? A painting?
2. What is the title of your work?
3. Has the work had any previous or alternative titles? If so, list the titles.
4. Is the work part of a contribution to a periodical, such as a magazine or other serial? Has it been published in the magazine or is it scheduled to be published?
5. Who created the work? Give full name(s). Did anyone else participate in creating the work as a joint effort? If so, identify all joint authors. What part did each author play in the creation of the work (for example, one author may create text and another illustrations for a book or one author may compose a melody and another the lyrics for a song)?
6. Did you create the work in the scope of your employment as an employee of another?
7. Are you an employer whose employee created the work in the scope of employment? Was the creator of the work your employee or was the creator acting as an independent contractor for you?
8. Was the work created as a result of a special order or commission? If so, describe.
9. Give the date(s) of birth, and if applicable, date(s) of death of the author(s) of the work. What is the nationality or domicile of the author(s)?
10. Will the author be identified on the work or is the author anonymous? Is the author known by a pseudonym or fictitious name?
11. In what year was the work created (what year was it fixed in a tangible form)?
12. Has the work been published ("publication" refers to distribution of the work to the public by sale, transfer, sale, lease, or lending, or an offering to distribute it to a group of persons for purposes of further distribution, public performance, or display)? If the work has been published, give the exact date and nation in which it was first published.
13. Who is the owner of the copyright in the work? Has it been transferred by its author to anyone?
14. Have any licenses been granted to others to use the work, reproduce it, distribute it, or perform it? If so, are these licenses exclusive or nonexclusive? Were the licenses in writing?
15. Has registration for this work or an earlier version of this work already been sought in the Copyright Office? If so, please provide a copy of the earlier registration and describe how this version of the work differs from the earlier version.
16. Does the work include contributions by others, such as photographs or text by others? Does the work include any material owned by the U.S. Government?
17. Is this work based upon another work? For example, is this work a translation of another work? Is it based upon another work such as a book, song, movie, or play? Is it a condensation or abridgment of another work? Does it consist of revisions or editorial modifications? Describe.
18. If the work contains both original and preexisting material, identify and describe the new material.

Give the full name, address, and telephone number of the individual completing this questionnaire.

completed. Under the Copyright Act, a work is "created" when it is fixed in a copy or phonorecord for the first time. Generally, when a work is prepared over a period of time, such as is the case with a novel, the date of creation is the date of completion of the finished project.

If the work has been published, Space 3 requires that the month, day, and year of the first publication be provided together with an identification of the country in which publication first occurred. "Publication" of a work is the distribution of copies or phonorecords of a work to the public by sale, transfer of ownership, or by rental, sale, or leasing. A work is also published if there has been an offering to distribute copies or phonorecords to a group of persons for purposes of further distribution, public performance, or public display. Thus, a novel is published when it has been offered to bookstores for further sale to the public.

Space 4: Claimant(s).   The names and addresses of the copyright claimant(s) of the work must be given even if they are the same as those of the author(s). The copyright claimant is either the author of the work or a person or organization to whom the copyright has been transferred. For example, if Beverly Young is the author of a novel who has sold all rights to the novel to ABC Inc., Beverly Young would be listed as "author" and ABC Inc. would be identified as the claimant. If the claimant is not the author, a brief statement of how the claimant obtained ownership must be given. It is sufficient to state that the claimant obtained ownership "by written contract," "by transfer of all rights by author," "by assignment," or "by will."

Space 5: Previous Registration.   The questions in Space 5 are intended to show whether an earlier registration has been made for the work and, if so, whether there is any basis for a new registration inasmuch as only one basic copyright registration can be made for the same version of a particular work.

If the version of the work subject to the application is substantially the same as the work covered by a previous registration, a second registration is generally impermissible.

If the work has been changed and a new registration is being sought to cover the additions or revisions, a new registration can be sought for these changes. Thus, if a movie is published in 1990 and a new version of it with additional scenes and footage is published in 1995, a second registration can be sought for the new version. Similarly, a new version of a computer program is eligible for copyright registration. The applicant must briefly describe the changes made to the work and give the number and date of the latest registration, if any.

Space 6: Derivative Work or Compilation.   Space 6 requires the applicant to indicate if the work is a derivative work or compilation. A derivative work is a work based on a preexisting work (such as a movie based on a novel, a translation, editorial revisions, or a condensation). A compilation is a work formed by collecting and assembling preexisting materials or data that are selected and arranged in such a way that they constitute an original work (such as an almanac or a collection of short stories). If the work is a derivative work, the applicant must identify the preexisting work upon which the derivative work is based, for example, by stating "French translation of *Silent Witness*." Whether the work is a derivative work or a compilation, the applicant must give a brief description of the new material covered by the copyright claim. For example, the applicant may state "foreword, editing, and annotations" for a derivative work, or may state "compilation of short stories by twentieth-century feminists" for a compilation.

Remaining Spaces. The remaining portions of copyright application forms ask for a variety of miscellaneous information.

- **Reproduction for use by handicapped persons.** For applications for literary works, the Copyright Office allows applicants to voluntarily grant a license for reproduction and distribution of literary works for the exclusive use of the blind and physically handicapped, permitting the Library of Congress to reproduce and distribute the work without further paperwork. The license is entirely voluntary, nonexclusive, and may be terminated upon a ninety-day notice.

- **Deposit account.** Individuals who file many copyright applications (at least twelve transactions each year) can establish a deposit account with the Copyright Office by depositing at least $250, eliminating the burden of sending in a fee with each application filed. If a deposit account is established, the applicant indicates the deposit account number so fees can be automatically withdrawn from the account. The Copyright Office sends monthly statements showing charges so individuals can replenish the account. If no deposit account has been established, the applicant merely sends in the fee with the application.

- **Correspondence.** The applicant should provide a name, address, and telephone number of a person to be consulted in the event correspondence about the application is necessary.

- **Certification.** The application cannot be accepted unless it bears the date and handwritten signature of the author or other copyright claimant or of the owner of exclusive rights or the duly authorized agent of such. The signature certifies to the Copyright Office that the information provided in the application is correct to the best of the applicant's knowledge. Making a false representation of a material fact can subject the signatory to a fine up to $2,500.

- **Address for return of certificate.** The address to which the certificate of registration should be sent must be given. The address space should be completed legibly because the certificate will be sent in a window envelope and this information will appear in the window.

(See Figure 13–2 for a sample of a completed copyright application.)

Filing Fee

Section 708 sets forth the fee schedule for fees charged by the Copyright Office. Effective through June 30, 2001, the nonrefundable fee for filing an application is $30. Check the Copyright Office web site or call (202) 707-3000 for the latest fee information. The fee for a copyright application may be paid by check or money order payable to Register of Copyrights. Cash is not accepted. Electronic transfers and credit card charges are generally not permissible.

DEPOSIT MATERIALS

Introduction

Section 407 of the Copyright Act requires that the owner of copyright or of the exclusive right of publication in a work published in the United States deposit, within three months after publication, two complete copies of the best

FIGURE 13–2
Completed Copyright
Application

FORM TX
UNITED STATES COPYRIGHT OFFICE

REGISTRATION NUMBER

TX   TXU
EFFECTIVE DATE OF REGISTRATION

Month   Day   Year

DO NOT WRITE ABOVE THIS LINE. IF YOU NEED MORE SPACE, USE A SEPARATE CONTINUATION SHEET.

1 TITLE OF THIS WORK ▼
The Prophet

PREVIOUS OR ALTERNATIVE TITLES ▼
none

PUBLICATION AS A CONTRIBUTION If this work was published as a contribution to a periodical, serial, or collection, give information about the collective work in which the contribution appeared.   **Title of Collective Work ▼**

If published in a periodical or serial give: Volume ▼   Number ▼   Issue Date ▼   On Pages ▼

2
a NAME OF AUTHOR▼
Angeline Bach

DATES OF BIRTH AND DEATH
Year Born ▼   Year Died ▼
7-30-44

Was this contribution to the work a "work made for hire"?
☐ Yes
☑ No

AUTHOR'S NATIONALITY OR DOMICILE
Name of Country
OR { Citizen of ▶ *USA*
Domiciled in ▶

WAS THIS AUTHOR'S CONTRIBUTION TO THE WORK
Anonymous?   ☐ Yes ☑ No
Pseudonymous?   ☐ Yes ☑ No
If the answer to either of these questions is "Yes," see detailed instructions.

NOTE
Under the law, the "author" of a "work made for hire" is generally the employer, not the employee (see instructions). For any part of this work that was "made for hire" check "Yes" in the space provided, give the employer (or other person for whom the work was prepared) as "Author" of that part, and leave the space for dates of birth and death blank.

NATURE OF AUTHORSHIP Briefly describe nature of the material created by this author in which copyright is claimed. ▼
text

b NAME OF AUTHOR ▼

DATES OF BIRTH AND DEATH
Year Born ▼   Year Died ▼

Was this contribution to the work a "work made for hire"?
☐ Yes
☐ No

AUTHOR'S NATIONALITY OR DOMICILE
Name of country
OR { Citizen of ▶
Domiciled in ▶

WAS THIS AUTHOR'S CONTRIBUTION TO THE WORK
Anonymous?.   ☐ Yes ☐ No
Pseudonymous?   ☐ Yes ☐ No
If the answer to either of these questions is "Yes," see detailed instructions.

NATURE OF AUTHORSHIP Briefly describe nature of the material created by this author in which copyright is claimed. ▼

c NAME OF AUTHOR ▼

DATES OF BIRTH AND DEATH
Year Born ▼   Year Died ▼

Was this contribution to the work a "work made for hire"?
☐ Yes
☐ No

AUTHOR'S NATIONALITY OR DOMICILE
Name of Country
OR { Citizen of ▶
Domiciled in ▶

WAS THIS AUTHOR'S CONTRIBUTION TO THE WORK
Anonymous?   ☐ Yes ☐ No
Pseudonymous?   ☐ Yes ☐ No
If the answer to either of these questions is "Yes," see detailed instructions.

NATURE OF AUTHORSHIP Briefly describe nature of the material created by this author in which copyright is claimed. ▼

3
a YEAR IN WHICH CREATION OF THIS WORK WAS COMPLETED This information must be given in all cases.
1998 ◀ Year

b DATE AND NATION OF FIRST PUBLICATION OF THIS PARTICULAR WORK
Complete this information ONLY if this work has been published.
Month ▶ *April* Day ▶ *10* Year ▶ *1999*
United States ◀ Nation

4 COPYRIGHT CLAIMANT(S) Name and address must be given even if the claimant is the same as the author given in space 2.▼
Angeline Bach
604 Calvert Court
Raleigh, NC 08714

See instructions before completing this space.

TRANSFER If the claimant(s) named here in space 4 are different from the author(s) named in space 2, give a brief statement of how the claimant(s) obtained ownership of the copyright.▼

APPLICATION RECEIVED

ONE DEPOSIT RECEIVED

TWO DEPOSITS RECEIVED

REMITTANCE NUMBER AND DATE

DO NOT WRITE HERE
OFFICE USE ONLY

MORE ON BACK ▶ • Complete all applicable spaces (numbers 5–11) on the reverse side of this page.
• See detailed instructions.   • Sign the form at line 10.

DO NOT WRITE HERE
Page 1 of_____pages

edition of the work or, if the work is a sound recording, two complete phonorecords of the best edition. Deposits are to be made into the Library of Congress so that it can continue its tradition of cataloguing and collecting works published in the United States by ensuring that it receives copies of every copyrightable work published in the United States. The Copyright Act presumes that individuals will make the deposit voluntarily.

Although this deposit requirement can be fulfilled through application for copyright registration (because deposit materials are required to be submitted with the application), the requirement is mandatory whether or not an application is ever filed (although certain works such as greeting cards, postcards, stationery, technical drawings, and advertising materials are exempt). Failure to deposit the materials does not cause a loss of copyright protection, but it may

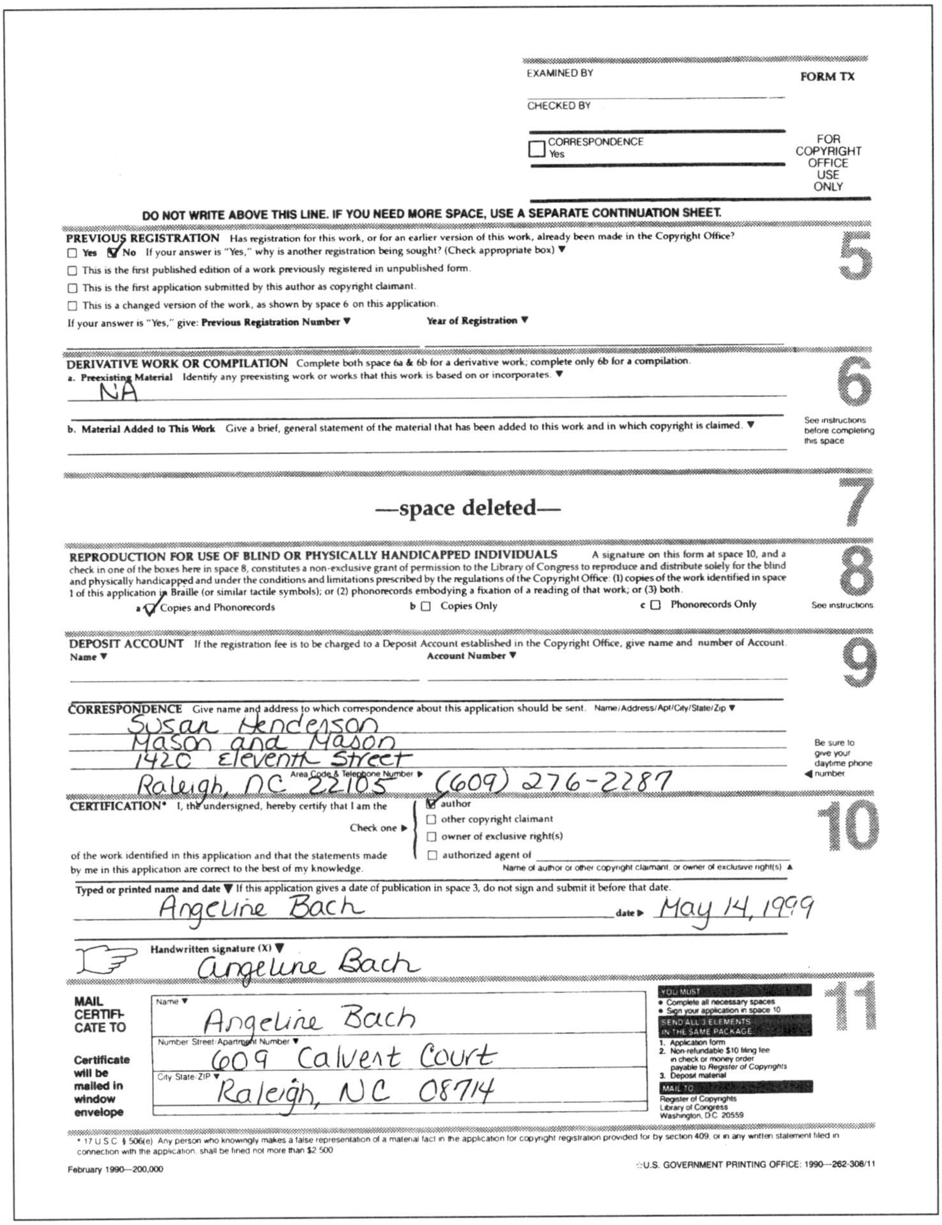

FIGURE 13-2
Completed Copyright
Application (continued)

subject a party to fine if the Copyright Office requests the deposit and the copyright owner fails to supply the materials within three months.

Deposit Materials Accompanying Copyright Applications

An application for a copyright registration must be accompanied by a nonreturnable **deposit** of the work being registered. Although the deposit requirements vary in particular situations, the general requirements are as follows:

- if the work is unpublished, one complete copy or phonorecord; or
- if the work was first published in the United States on or after January 1, 1978, two complete copies or phonorecords of the best edition.

deposit: The best edition of a work provided to the Copyright Office in support of an application to register a copyright for the work

The "Best Edition" Requirement

The Copyright Act requires that copies or phonorecords deposited be of the **best edition** of the work. The "best edition" requirement is intended to discourage inferior deposit materials. Generally, the best edition is one that is larger rather than smaller; color rather than black and white; and printed on archival-quality rather than less permanent paper. For example, for books, hardcover rather than softcover copies are the best edition, and sewn rather than glue-only binding is preferred; for photographs, unmounted rather than mounted photographs are the best edition; for phonorecords, compact digital discs rather than vinyl discs are the best edition; for motion pictures, film rather than videotape formats are the best edition.

If the depositor cannot deposit the best edition, a request for special relief may be made, stating why the applicant cannot send the required deposit and what the applicant wishes to submit in place of the required deposit.

Deposit Requirements for Specific Works

Following are the deposit requirements for specific works:

- **Visual arts materials.** Because it would be impracticable or impossible to submit large sculptures, paintings, and posters, photographs are generally acceptable for these works. For fabrics and wallcoverings, swatches showing the design repeat are acceptable. For games, a complete copy of the game must be submitted unless it is large, in which case a photograph is permissible.
- **Literary works.** Copies of the text, book, advertising copy, and so forth must be submitted.
- **Performing arts works.** For plays, cinema, radio, and television scripts, the scripts themselves should be deposited. For pantomimes and choreographic works, a film or video recording showing the work is permissible, or the works may be described in written text.
- **Architectural works.** The required deposit for an architectural work, whether or not the building has been constructed, is one complete copy of an architectural drawing or blueprint. If the building has been constructed, the deposit must also include photographs showing the work (preferably 8- by 10-inch photos showing interior and exterior views).
- **Motion pictures.** For motion pictures, one copy of the work as first published is required (one of the first prints or tapes made from the master, clear, undamaged, and unspliced). Additionally, a separate description of the work is required, such as a script or summary.
- **Musical compositions.** For vocal and instrumental music, generally the sheet music or full score must be submitted.
- **Sound recordings.** The deposit for sound recordings is two complete phonorecords of the best edition plus any text or pictorial matter published with the phonorecord (compact discs, albums, or cassettes). Examples of the textual material include all phonorecord packaging, record sleeves, and separate leaflets or booklets enclosed with the phonorecords.
- **Computer programs.** Generally, the first and last twenty-five pages of source code must be submitted as the deposit for computer programs;

best edition: The deposit edition of a copyrighted work most suitable for purposes of the Library of Congress; generally, clean, legible, and superior deposit materials

however, as discussed in Chapter 15, the Copyright Office permits authors to "block out" portions of the source code if it constitutes a trade secret.

- **Multimedia works.** A multimedia work is a work that combines forms of authorship, such as a book including charts or a slide presentation to be shown with accompanying narration or music on a cassette tape. A single application can be used if the copyright claimant is the same for each element of the work and the elements of the work, if published, are published as a single unit. Generally, the deposit should be a complete multimedia kit containing all elements covered by the registration.

THE APPLICATION PROCESS AND REGISTRATION OF COPYRIGHT

Filing the Application

After the correct application form has been selected and completed and the correct deposit materials have been identified, the application may be filed with the U.S. Copyright Office. Despite the apparent complexity of the numerous forms and deposit requirements, for those with familiarity with copyright law and procedure, completing the application form often takes thirty minutes or less.

Although not required, it is a good idea to send a cover letter accompanying the application. The cover letter can confirm the contents of the package and provide a name and phone number of a person to contact in the event the Copyright Office has questions. Many applicants also include a "come-back" card, a self-addressed and stamped postcard so the Copyright Office can confirm the filing of the application because the Copyright Office itself does not issue any acknowledgment that an application has been received.

Examination of the Application and Copyright Registration

The Copyright Office will assign the application to a specialist; however, the examination of the application is not substantive, as is the case with trademark and patent applications. Generally, a copyright application is examined only to ensure that the material in which copyright is claimed is copyrightable (for example, a copyright claim in facts, a recipe, or a blank form will be refused) and that the material deposited complies with statutory requirements.

There are four major examining sections in the Copyright Office: one for literary works, one for works of the performing arts, one for works of visual arts, and one for renewals. The examiner will review the application to ensure all information is complete and compare the application and deposit for consistency.

It is nearly impossible to determine the status of an application that has been filed. The Copyright Office Certifications and Documents Section may have information, but such information is provided only upon payment of applicable fees. Due to the volume of applications filed each year (more than six hundred thousand), the Copyright Office does not provide free information about the status of an application.

Nevertheless, within approximately sixteen weeks of filing the application, the Copyright Office will either issue a certificate of registration or contact the applicant by letter or phone asking for additional information or explaining why the application has been rejected. If the Copyright Office has questions, the applicant usually has one hundred and twenty days to respond. Failure to respond within the time required generally results in closing of the file without further notification. If registration is later desired, a new application, deposit, and fee must be submitted.

If the application is acceptable, the Copyright Office will register the copyright by returning a certificate of registration, namely, a copy of the application stamped with a seal, a registration number, and date of registration. A copyright registration is effective on the date the Copyright Office receives a complete application package in acceptable form, regardless of how long it may take to process the application. In general, Copyright Office policy is to resolve questionable cases in favor of the applicant under the **rule of doubt,** meaning that although the Copyright Office has doubts about copyrightability, it will resolve doubts in favor of the applicant and allow a court to make a final determination in the future if questions arise regarding copyrightability.

The Copyright Office is in the process of implementing an electronic filing system called the Copyright Office Electronic Registration, Recordation, and Deposit System (CORDS). The CORDS project aims to develop and implement a totally electronic system of receipt and processing of copyright applications, deposited works, and related documents over communications networks such as the Internet. In early 1996, the Copyright office received its first electronic application (an unpublished dissertation by a student). The application was completed using a specially developed online form, and the dissertation was transmitted with the application over the Internet in a few minutes. The application and dissertation were "signed" using encryption technology. The CORDS system will enable the Copyright Office to complete its review and processing and issue a registration certificate within a few days or weeks rather than the four-month period usually experienced. Testing and implementation will continue over the next several years.

Refusal of Registration

If registration is refused by the Copyright Office, reexamination can be requested. The applicant "appeals" the adverse decision by making a written request for reexamination or reconsideration and paying the appeal fee of $200. A response in writing will be made by a Copyright Office section head. Further reconsideration may be requested of the Chief of the Examining Division upon payment of an additional fee of $500. If registration is still refused, the applicant may seek judicial review in the United States District Court for the District of Columbia.

Because copyright registration is a prerequisite for an infringement suit for works originating in the United States, refusal of registration would put a party who believes his or her work has been infringed in the untenable situation of being unable to initiate action in federal court for infringement. Thus, if registration has been applied for and refused, the applicant may still file an infringement action but must provide notice of the action and a copy of the complaint to

rule of doubt: Policy followed by the Copyright Office to resolve doubts about copyrightability in favor of a copyright applicant

the Register of Copyrights. The Register may become a party to the court action but only with regard to registrability of the work.

The Copyright Office can cancel a registration if it is determined that a work is not copyrightable or the check for the filing fee is returned for insufficient funds. Prior to cancellation, the Copyright Office will provide notice to the registrant so the registrant has an opportunity to respond to the cancellation procedure.

Special Handling

In some instances, applicants may not be able to wait sixteen weeks to receive notification that a copyright has been registered. For example, before a copyright infringement suit may be filed in court, registration is necessary for works of U.S. origin. Thus, a party who wishes to commence an infringement action upon short notice must have assurance that a copyright has been registered. To expedite the processing of applications for registration (or the recordation of documents relating to copyrights), the Copyright Office has established **special handling** procedures.

Special handling is granted only in special circumstances. These are:

- pending or prospective litigation;
- customs matters; or
- contract or publishing deadlines that necessitate the expedited process.

Special handling is typically requested by a letter stating the reasons why special handling is needed. The request must also include a signed statement certifying that the information contained in the request is correct to the best of the requestor's knowledge. Once a request for special handling is approved, every effort is made to process the application or request for recordation within five working days. The present fee for a special handling request is $500 (plus the usual application filing fee of $30 or the usual fee for recording documents).

Supplementary Copyright Registration

If information in a registration is incorrect or incomplete, an application may be filed for **supplementary copyright registration** to correct the error or amplify the information given. Supplementary registration can be made only if a basic copyright registration for the same work has already been issued. Form CA is used, and the filing fee is $65. No deposit materials should be included.

Supplementary registration is not necessary for minor typographical errors or omission of articles, such as the word *the*. Some of the more common reasons a supplementary copyright registration is requested are the following:

- the original application identified an incorrect author;
- the work was registered as published when publication had not yet taken place;
- a coauthor was omitted; or
- a change in the name or title of the work has occurred (for example, a book or movie title has been changed).

If the supplementary registration is issued, there will be two registrations on file with the Copyright Office. The original registration will not be expunged

special handling: Expedited processing of copyright applications and other documents for specified reasons upon payment of a fee

supplementary copyright registration: An application to correct an error or amplify information in a copyright registration

or canceled, but the supplementary registration will direct the public's attention to an error or omission in the basic registration and will place the correct facts or additional information on official record.

Benefits of Securing Registration

Because copyright protection exists from the time a work is created, securing a registration from the Copyright Office is not necessary to protect copyright material. Nevertheless, federal copyright law provides several inducements to encourage copyright owners to secure registration. Among these advantages are the following:

- Registration establishes a public record of the claim of copyright.
- Before an infringement suit may be filed in courts, registration is necessary for works of U.S. origin and for foreign works not originating in a Berne Union country.
- If made before or within five years of publication, registration constitutes *prima facie* evidence of the validity of the copyright and of the facts given in the certificate.
- If registration is made within three months after publication or prior to an infringement of an unpublished work, statutory damages and attorneys' fees will be available to the copyright owner in court actions. Otherwise, only an award of actual damages and lost profits is available to the copyright owner.
- Registration allows the owner of the copyright to record the registration with the U.S. Customs Service for protection against the importation of infringing copies.

SEARCHING COPYRIGHT OFFICE RECORDS

It may become necessary to determine whether copyright for a work has been registered or what copyrights are registered to a company or individual. For example, if a company is selling all of its assets to another, the buyer will typically conduct **due diligence** and review records of the PTO and the Copyright Office to determine what patents, trademarks, and copyrights are registered in the seller's name so these can then be transferred to the buyer.

Conducting searches prior to applying for copyright registration is not nearly as critical as conducting searches prior to applying for trademark or patent protection. Because copyright protection exists once a work is created and independent creation is permissible, the fact that another party has a copyright registration for a work will not preclude registration for another similar or identical work (as long as the works do not copy from each other). Nevertheless, although titles are not copyrightable, an author may wish to select a unique title for a book or movie, and a search would reveal similar or identical titles.

There are a variety of ways to search Copyright Office records:

- The records of the Copyright Office are open for inspection and searching by the public. The Copyright Office, however, cannot give legal advice, answer questions on possible infringement, recommend publishers, or enforce contracts. The records freely available to the public

due diligence: A type of audit of intellectual property, usually conducted when a company is sold, when it borrows money, or when it acquires another company

include an extensive card catalog (for registrations from 1870 through 1977) and an online catalog (for registrations since 1978) that provide an index to more than 40 million registered copyrights. Searching can be done by the title of the work, author(s), claimant(s), date of publication, or registration number.

• The Library of Congress card catalog can be searched; however, only a portion of the works deposited for copyright are selected for inclusion in the Library's collections, and the Library does not always fully catalog those works it selects.

• Most copyright records since 1978 can be searched by Internet. The Internet site address for the Copyright Office files is: http://lcweb.loc.gov/copyright.

• The Copyright Office itself will conduct searches for $65 per hour. The Reference and Bibliography Section of the Copyright Office will conduct a search and provide a factual report on the results of the search. Searches can be initiated by writing to this section or by calling (202/707-6850). The Copyright Office will estimate the total search fee and initiate the search upon receiving the fee. Upon payment of additional fees, the search can be expedited. A search request form is provided in Copyright Office Circular 22.

• Private companies can conduct searches. Just as companies will search PTO records and provide reports of trademarks, they will conduct searches of Copyright Office records, file applications and other documents, and provide copies of documents. Contact Thomson & Thomson, 500 E Street SW, Suite 970, Washington, DC 20024 (800/356-8630 or 202/488-2900) or CCH Trademark Research Corporation, 300 Park Avenue S., New York, NY 10010 (800/872-6275 or 212/228-4084).

OBTAINING COPYRIGHT OFFICE RECORDS AND DEPOSIT MATERIALS

Upon request, the Copyright Office will prepare certified or uncertified copies of certain public records. Applications, registrations, assignments, licenses, and other documents pertaining to copyrights can be obtained. Generally, these records can be obtained for minimum fees (for example, $25 for an additional copy of a certificate of registration). Certified copies are usually requested as evidence of the authenticity of a document when litigation involving the copyright is involved. Upon payment of additional fees, expedited service is possible.

Obtaining copies of deposit materials is considerably more difficult than obtaining copies of records. Moreover, not all deposits are retained. The Copyright Office policy is to retain deposits for published works for five years (ten years for works of visual arts). Unpublished deposits are generally kept for the full copyright term. Registrants who wish to ensure the Copyright Office retains their published deposits for the duration of a copyright term must pay a fee of $365 to cover storage costs.

Assuming the material is available, the Copyright Office will provide certified or uncertified copies of the actual works deposited with the Copyright Office only when one of the following three conditions has been met:

- written authorization is received from the copyright claimant of record or his or her agent (or the owner of any of the exclusive rights upon written documentation of the transfer);
- a Copyright Office Litigation Statement Form is completed and received from an attorney or authorized representative stating there is actual or prospective litigation involving the copyrighted work, giving assurance that the material will be used only in connection with the litigation, and providing detailed information about the parties, the controversy, and the court; or
- a court order is issued for reproduction of a deposited article that is the subject of litigation.

Rather than providing the actual deposit material, the Copyright Office may provide a reproduction, such as photographs or photocopies or a reproduction of a sound recording. A fee will be quoted by the Copyright Office when the request for deposit material is made.

COPYRIGHT NOTICE

Introduction

Since March 1, 1989 (the date of adherence by the United States to the Berne Convention), use of a **notice of copyright** (usually the symbol © together with the date of first publication and copyright owner's name) is no longer mandatory, although it is recommended and offers some advantages. Use of the notice informs the public that the work is protected by copyright, identifies the copyright owner, and shows the year of first publication. Furthermore, if a work is infringed, if a proper notice of copyright appears on a published work to which the defendant had access, the defendant cannot assert that infringement was innocent (an innocent infringement defense may result in a reduction of damages). Use of the notice is the responsibility of the copyright owner and does not require advance permission from or registration of copyright with the Copyright Office.

Works published before January 1, 1978, are governed by the 1909 Copyright Act. Under that act, if a work was published under the copyright owner's authority without a proper notice of copyright, all copyright protection for that work was permanently lost in the United States. Many works fell into the public domain merely because the owner failed to include the copyright notice. To align the United States with the laws of most other foreign countries, the United States joined the Berne Convention in 1989 and agreed to eliminate any requirement for copyright notice. With regard to works published between January 1, 1978, and March 1, 1989, omission of a notice was generally excused if the notice was omitted from a small number of copies and a reasonable effort was made to add the notice after discovery of its omission.

notice of copyright: A mark informing the public that a work is protected by copyright and identifying its owner and year of publication

Form of Notice for Visually Perceptible Copies

The form of notice used for visually perceptible copies—those that can be seen or read either directly (such as books) or with the aid of a machine (such as movies)—is different from the form used for sound recordings (such as records or cassettes).

The form for visually perceptible copies includes three elements that should appear together or in close proximity. The elements are:

1. the symbol © (the letter C in a circle), the word "Copyright," or the abbreviation "Copr.";
2. the year of first publication (the year can be omitted when a pictorial, graphic, or sculptural work is reproduced on greeting cards, stationery, jewelry, dolls, or toys); and
3. the name of the owner of copyright in the work, or an abbreviation or alternative designation by which the name can be recognized.

Recall that *publication* is defined as the year of distribution of copies or phonorecords of a work by sale, transfer, rental, lease, or lending or an offering to distribute copies or phonorecords to a group of persons for purposes of further distribution, public performance, or display. If there are joint owners, all of their names should be given.

Examples of acceptable copyright notices are "© 1995 John Andrews," "© 1997 ABC Inc.," and "Copr. 1997 Madonna."

Form of Notice for Sound Recordings

Because audio recordings such as audio tapes and phonograph discs are not "copies" but are "phonorecords" under the Copyright Act, the form of copyright notice is different from that used for visually perceptible copies. Copyright in a sound recording protects the particular series of sounds fixed in the recording against unauthorized reproduction, revision, and distribution. Phonorecords may be records (such as LPs and 45s), audiotapes, cassettes, or discs. Notice for phonorecords should contain the following three elements:

1. the symbol "P" placed inside a circle;
2. the year of first publication; and
3. the name of the owner of copyright or an abbreviation or alternative designation by which the owner can be recognized.

Special Notice Requirements

Questions about the form of copyright notice arise in a variety of cases. Some commonly encountered problems are as follows:

- **Contributions to collective works.** A single copyright notice applicable to the collective work (such as an anthology or magazine) as a whole is sufficient protection for all the contributions in the collective work (except advertisements). Nevertheless, the separate contributions to the collective work may bear their own notices of copyright (primarily to inform the public of the identity of the owner of the contribution).
- **Publications incorporating U.S. government works.** Any work published before March 1, 1989, that included government works should have included a special notice identifying the portions of the work that incorporated government works. Thus, if a 1985 textbook reproduced the U.S. Constitution, the notice should state "© 1985 Penguin Books. Copyright is not claimed as to the U.S. Constitution reproduced in Chapter 14." For works published after March 1, 1989, the notice is not required but is recommended.

- **Derivative works.** In the case of a derivative work (one based on an underlying work, such as a sequel to a preexisting book), the information in the notice should relate to the new work, not the underlying work. The symbol © (or the word "Copyright" or the abbreviation "Copr."), the year of first publication of the new work, and the name of the copyright owner of the new work should be given.
- **Unpublished works.** There has never been a requirement for use of a copyright notice for unpublished works, although a notice may be used. An example would be: "Unpublished work © 1996 Daniel Donoghue."

Location of Notice

The Copyright Act does not dictate exact placement of the copyright notice but requires only that it be placed in such a way that it gives reasonable notice of the claim of copyright. According to 37 C.F.R. § 201.20, the following placements are acceptable:

- **Works published in book form.** The notice may be placed on the title page, the page immediately following the title page, either side of the front or back covers, or the first or last page of the work.
- **Single-leaf works.** The notice may be placed anywhere on the front or back of the leaf.
- **Contributions to collective works.** The notice may be placed under the title or elsewhere on the same page if the contribution consists of one page. If the contribution spans more than one page, the notice may be placed under the title, on the first page of the contribution, or at the end of the contribution.
- **Works published as periodicals or other serials.** The notice may be placed at any of the locations acceptable on books, near the masthead or on the same page as the masthead, or adjacent to a prominent heading near the front of the issue.
- **Computer programs and works produced in machine-readable copies.** The notice may appear with or near the title or at the end of the work, on visually perceptible printouts, at the user's terminal at sign-on, on continuous display on the terminal, or reproduced durably on a label securely affixed to the copies or to a container used as a permanent receptacle for the copies.
- **Motion pictures and other audiovisual works.** The notice may be placed with or near the title, with the credits information, at or immediately following the beginning of the work, or at or immediately preceding the end of the work. If the work is distributed to the public for private use (such as rental of videotaped movies), the notice can also be placed on the permanent container for the videotape.
- **Pictorial, graphic, and sculptural works.** For works embodied in two-dimensional copies (such as paintings and posters), the notice may be affixed to the front or back of the copies or any backing or mounting material. For works reproduced in three-dimensional copies (such as sculptures, globes, and dolls), the notice may be affixed to any visible portion of the work or any base or mounting for the work. If it is impracticable to affix a notice to the copies directly (such as is the case with

jewelry), a notice may be placed on a tag or label. For sheeting such as fabrics and wallcoverings, the notice may appear on the margin selvage or reverse side of the material in frequent and regular intervals. For games and puzzles, the notice may be reproduced on the container.

- **Sound recordings.** The notice may be placed on the surface of the phonorecord or on the phonorecord label or container.

Omission of and Errors in Notice

Under the 1909 Copyright Act (and until 1989), copyright notices were mandatory; failure to give the notice resulted in permanent loss of copyright. There were no provisions to cure omissions of notice. The 1976 act attempted to lessen the harshness of prior law and allowed for cure of omissions of notice or certain errors as long as cure occurred within five years of publication. For works published after March 1, 1989 (the effective date of the Berne Convention Implementation Act), use of the notice of copyright is optional, and omissions and errors in the notice are less important. Nevertheless, the 1909 act still applies to works published while it was in effect. For example, if copies of a work first published in 1987 omit or have errors in the copyright notice, the owner risks losing copyright protection if the defect is not cured.

Some errors are considered so serious that they are viewed as equivalent to omitting the notice entirely. These errors include failing to include the symbol ©, the word "Copyright," or the abbreviation "Copr."; dating a notice more than one year later than the date of publication; giving a notice without a name; and locating a notice so that it does not give reasonable notice of the claim of copyright. Omission of a notice does not affect copyright protection and no corrective action is required if the work was published after March 1, 1989.

Under section 406, if an error in the date occurs for works distributed before March 1, 1989, it may affect copyright duration. For example, if a work for hire is published in 1985 and yet the copyright notice gives the year as 1984, the term will be measured from 1984 and the copyright will last until 2079 (ninety-five years from 1984). If the year date is more than one year later than the year of publication, the work is considered to be published without any notice.

Surplusage in Copyright Notice

Many copyright owners and publishers place notices or information in addition to the three elements of a copyright notice. For example, the following information is often seen: "Not for reproduction," "All Rights Reserved," and "No portion of this work may be reproduced, displayed, broadcast, or disseminated in any form without prior written consent." Such additional information may be included on the copyrighted work; however, it is mere surplusage and provides no rights beyond those already provided for by the Copyright Act. The phrase *all rights reserved* is often seen inasmuch as it is commonly used in many foreign countries. Surplusage should never take the place of the actual copyright notice and serves primarily to offer a certain level of comfort to the author or copyright owner.

ROLE OF INTELLECTUAL PROPERTY PROFESSIONAL

Intellectual property professionals are more actively involved in applying for copyright registration than in any other aspect of copyright law. Among the many activities in which IP professionals are engaged are the following:

- obtaining forms and circulars from the Copyright Office so the office has a ready supply of application forms and information;
- assisting copyright owners in completing copyright questionnaires so applications can be prepared;
- preparing applications and sending them to clients for review and signature;
- assisting clients in collecting deposit materials to accompany copyright applications;
- establishing deposit accounts with the Copyright Office and monitoring those accounts to ensure they are routinely replenished;
- filing copyright applications with come-back postcards;
- working with clients to determine if special handling is needed for applications;
- docketing dates of filing of applications and monitoring progress of the typical sixteen-week application process;
- responding to requests for information or clarification from the Copyright Office;
- reviewing certificates of registration for errors and preparing supplementary registration to correct or amplify information in copyright records;
- preparing letters confirming registration, indicating duration of copyright, and giving instructions for providing notice of copyright;
- searching or requesting searches of Copyright Office records;
- requesting copies, certified and uncertified, of Copyright Office records;
- reviewing client materials to ensure copyright notices are in compliance with law and are placed properly; and
- monitoring the Copyright Office web site to keep abreast of changes in copyright law and procedure.

CHAPTER SUMMARY

Copyright protection exists from the time a work is created in fixed form. No publication or registration or other action in the Copyright Office is required to secure copyright. There are, however, several advantages to securing registration, namely, the ability to initiate suit in federal court for copyright infringement, the ability to recover statutory damages and attorneys' fees in infringement actions, and the creation of a public record of one's claim to copyright.

Because there are many advantages to copyright registration, copyright owners should be encouraged to complete an application for copyright registration. Three elements are required to register a work: a properly completed application form; a nonrefundable filing fee of $30; and supporting deposit materials. The Copyright Office provides forms for applications. The registration process takes approximately sixteen weeks, although it can be expedited if certain conditions are met. Existing registrations can be corrected or amplified if needed.

Searches of Copyright Office records can be conducted at the Copyright Office, online, or by requesting search assistance from the Copyright Office or a private company. The Copyright Office provides copies (both certified and uncertified) of records upon request and payment of fees.

Although use of a copyright notice is optional for works created on or after March 1, 1989, use of the notice is recommended. The notice consists of three elements: the symbol © (or the word "Copyright" or abbreviation "Copr."); the year of first publication of the work; and the name of the copyright owner. The notice should be affixed to copies or phonorecords in such a way as to give reasonable notice of the claim of copyright.

DISCUSSION QUESTIONS

1. Jim Gray, an employee of ABC Inc., created advertising brochures and materials for the company in 1990 during the scope of his employment. The company wishes to secure a registration for the materials. Who is the author of the work and what form should be used?

2. Assume that significant revisions were made to the advertising material in 1995. Should a new registration be secured? What form should be used?

3. ABC Inc. is considering suing XYZ Company for infringement of ABC's copyrighted advertising materials. What advantages has securing registration for the materials afforded ABC Inc.?

4. In the course of discovery in the infringement suit, ABC Inc. learns that XYZ Company filed for copyright registration of certain advertising materials first published in 1988. May ABC obtain copies of the deposit materials submitted by XYZ when it secured its registration? Discuss.

5. After ABC Inc. obtains XYZ's deposit materials, it discovers that XYZ did not place a copyright notice on the 1988 materials. What effect does this omission of notice have? What if the omission occurred for materials first published in 1992?

6. May ABC Inc. obtain deposit materials for copyright registrations secured by its competitors because it is simply curious to see what competitors have filed with the Copyright Office?

7. If a book created as a work for hire was first published in 1988 but mistakenly bears a copyright notice giving the year as 1986, when does the copyright expire?

Copyright Infringement

A copyright owner who has a registered copyright may bring an action for infringement when any of his or her exclusive rights have been infringed by another. Generally, to prevail in an infringement action, a plaintiff must show ownership of copyright and impermissible copying. Copying is generally proven by demonstrating that the defendant had access to the work and the defendant's work is substantially similar to that of the copyright owner.

There are various defenses a defendant may assert in an infringement action. One of the most common defenses is that the defendant's use of the work is a "fair use." A fair use is generally a use for scholarly, research, or educational purposes. Courts examine four factors in determining whether a defendant's use of a copyrighted work is a fair use: the purpose and character of the use, including whether the use is of a commercial nature or is for nonprofit educational work; the nature of the copyrighted work (with factual works receiving less protection than works of fiction or fantasy); the amount and substantiality of the portion taken by the defendant; and the effect of the defendant's use on the market for the plaintiff's work. Other defenses include laches, unclean hands, and the statute of limitations, which is three years from the infringing act. Remedies available to a plaintiff include injunctive relief, impoundment of the infringing goods, actual damages and the defendant's profits, statutory damages, costs, and attorneys' fees. Criminal sanctions can be imposed for certain willful infringements.

INTRODUCTION TO COPYRIGHT INFRINGEMENT

Registration of a copyright is a requirement for initiating an action for infringement, 17 U.S.C. § 411, although registration is not required for works not originating in the United States. Moreover, prompt registration is a prerequisite for certain remedies for infringement. 17 U.S.C. § 412. Thus, although registration is not required to obtain copyright protection for a work, the failure to register will preclude a copyright owner from seeking redress for infringement. If registration of a work is refused by the Copyright Office, an action for infringement may still be brought if the author notifies the Copyright Office of the action. The Register of Copyrights then has the right to become a party to the action with respect to the issue of registrability of the copyright claim. 17 U.S.C. § 411.

Section 501 of the Copyright Act provides that anyone who violates any of the exclusive rights of a copyright owner (rights of reproduction, adaptation, distribution, performance, and display), or of the author (as provided in the Visual Artists Rights Act), or who imports copies or phonorecords into the United States in violation of copyright law, is liable for direct infringement of the copyright or right of the author. For example, the following may constitute infringement: playing copyrighted music in a large store without permission; failing to provide attribution for a painting or other work covered by the Visual Artists Rights Act; and photocopying material from a copyrighted book.

ELEMENTS OF INFRINGEMENT

Ownership of Copyright

To prevail in an infringement action, a plaintiff must prove two things: his or her ownership of the copyright and copying or some other impermissible invasion by the defendant of one of the five exclusive rights afforded to copyright owners. Ownership is usually more easily established than copying. A party may prove ownership by demonstrating that he or she is the author of the work or that the copyright in the work has been transferred to him or her. A certificate of copyright registration (made before or within five years of first publication of the work) will establish *prima facie* evidence in court of the validity of the copyright and of the facts stated in the certificate, including identity of the author or copyright owner. Ownership issues often arise in the context of work made for hire disputes, particularly when a party claims he or she is not an employee and thus a work cannot be owned by an employer or when a party claims there was no written agreement relating to the status of a specially commissioned work and thus he or she has retained copyright ownership.

If the copyright has been transferred to another, that party is now the owner of the transferred rights and has the right to protect the work by an infringement action. For example, if a copyright author has transferred exclusive rights to perform a work to another and the work is infringed by impermissible performance, the transferee's rights have been infringed. If there has been unauthorized reproduction rather than unauthorized performance, the original copyright author's rights have been infringed and he or she may initiate an infringement action. Courts will insist the plaintiff prove the transfer and show how the plaintiff acquired rights. Additionally, the plaintiff must have been the owner at the time his or her rights were infringed. If a copyright owner has transferred a work to another and yet retains some connection with the work, for example, by receiving periodic royalty payments, the owner as well as the transferee's rights have been infringed because both are affected by an infringement that would reduce the value of the work; therefore, both have standing to initiate an infringement suit.

Upon introduction of the registration (or transfer of copyright) into evidence, the court will presume that the work is protected under copyright law (although that presumption can be rebutted or defeated by the defendant) and that the plaintiff has ownership rights in the work such that it is the proper party to bring the infringement action.

Copying

Introduction   Proving copying generally requires that the plaintiff in an infringement action show that there is substantial similarity between his or her work and that of the defendant and that the defendant had access to the copyrighted work. The infringing work must derive from the copyrighted work. An independently created work cannot infringe even if it is identical to the copyrighted work.

Innocent Infringement Is Not a Defense   Infringement does not require an intent to infringe; even **innocent infringement** gives rise to liability. For example, assume *A* is given a book that *B* claims *B* wrote. The book was actually the creation of *C*. If *A* copies the book, *A* has infringed *C*'s copyright even though *A* did not intend to infringe and did not know *C* had any copyright interest in the book. Thus, neither intent to infringe nor knowledge of copyright is required for infringement to occur, although innocence may have a bearing on the amount of damages for which a defendant is liable. Moreover, merely attributing the material copied to the owner by stating that copies of chapters of a text are the product of their author will not protect an infringer. Attribution may reduce damages, but a party cannot escape liability for infringement by merely acknowledging the work is owned by another.

Additionally, infringement can be "subconscious," as was the case in *Bright Tunes Music Corp. v. Harrisongs Music, Ltd.,* 420 F. Supp. 177 (S.D.N.Y. 1976), *aff'd,* 722 F.2d 988 (2d Cir. 1983), in which a court held George Harrison's song "My Sweet Lord" infringed the song "He's So Fine" performed by The Chiffons. In that case, the court held that Harrison did not deliberately plagiarize the earlier song but that he subconsciously recollected the copyrighted song when he composed "My Sweet Lord." On appeal, the Second Circuit reaffirmed that intent to infringe is not essential and that to allow a defense of innocent infringement would undermine the protections Congress intended copyright owners to possess.

Access   **Access** is generally interpreted to mean that a party had the opportunity to perceive or review a work, either directly or indirectly. Access can be inferred if the copyrighted work has been widely disseminated. Moreover, if the two works are identical or nearly so, it may be presumed that the defendant had access to the plaintiff's work. Generally, the greater the similarity between two works, the less access must be shown. Conversely, if the works are entirely dissimilar, no amount of access will result in a finding of copying.

In some cases, where there has been no evidence of access, courts have nevertheless found infringement if the two works are strikingly similar. Access will be inferred where the works are so similar that the possibility of independent creation or coincidental creation is precluded.

Access has been shown where copies of the plaintiff's work have been sent to the defendant, where the defendant has visited the plaintiff's place of business, where the plaintiff's works have been displayed at events attended by the

innocent infringement: Infringement of another's intellectual property rights without any intent to infringe; not a valid defense in copyright or patent infringement actions

access: Availability of a copyrighted work to a defendant so that the defendant had a reasonable opportunity to copy it

defendant, and where access occurred through a third party, such as a manufacturer, connected to both the plaintiff and the defendant.

Substantial Similarity of Works   Because it is seldom possible to prove copying by direct evidence (such as testimony from a witness who saw the defendant copy from the plaintiff's book), copying is usually proven through circumstantial evidence. Thus, infringement is usually shown by demonstrating that the allegedly infringing work is substantially similar to the copyrighted work. In some instances, map makers and directory authors purposely include fictitious entries in their works; when the same erroneous matter is found in a defendant's work, copying is generally found to exist.

The test used, often referred to as the ordinary observer test, focuses on whether the accused work is so similar to the copyrighted work that an ordinary reasonable person or lay observer would recognize that the copyrighted work was appropriated by the defendant.

The lay observer test has been refined to take into account the intended market for the works. Thus, where infringement of a video game was alleged, and the target market was young men, a court found that the intended purchasers (seventeen-and-a-half-year-old males) were a knowledgeable and discerning group and would not regard the works as substantially similar. *Data East USA, Inc. v. Epyx, Inc.,* 862 F.2d 204 (9th Cir. 1988). Another refinement of the lay observer test occurs when the works are complex, such as computer programs. In such cases, expert testimony is often used to prove or disprove substantial similarity inasmuch as computer programs are highly technical and unfamiliar to most of the general public.

Many courts use a two-step analysis to determine if infringement has occurred. The first step analyzes whether there has been copying. Once copying has been established, the second step requires that a determination be made whether the copying constitutes an impermissible appropriation, namely, whether the copying of the protected material was so extensive that it rendered the offending and copyrighted works substantially similar. In the first stage, some courts compare the works element by element and create lists of similarities and dissimilarities, in essence, "dissecting" the works. Other courts criticize dissection and prefer to focus on the overall similarities or the "total concept and feel" of the works, especially when only some of the work is protectable.

Courts have continually struggled in assessing "substantial similarity." In *Nichols v. Universal Pictures Corp.,* 45 F.2d 119 (2d Cir. 1930), Judge Learned Hand commented that copyright protection cannot be limited literally to the text; otherwise a plagiarist would be able to make immaterial variations with impunity. When only a part of a work is taken, such as one scene from a play, Judge Hand stated that the question is whether the part taken is substantial. Even more difficult questions, however, arise when the plagiarist does not copy a block of material but rather abstracts the whole work. In these two instances (**literal copying** of some of a work and nonliteral copying of an entire work), Judge Hand remarked that "Nobody has ever been able to fix that boundary [of protection], and nobody ever can." *Id.* at 121.

If part of a work is copied or taken, courts usually examine not only the quantity of the work taken but also its characteristics and the nature of the work itself. Infringement has been found even if language is not identical when

literal copying: Identical duplication or copying of another's copyrighted work

recognizable paraphrases have been taken. There is no precise answer to the question "how much is too much?" In one case, the taking of fragments from three sentences in a book of more than two hundred pages was found to be infringement. Moreover, if the part taken is the "heart" of the material, there may be an infringement. Thus, a love story about lovers from different economic classes with a tragic ending might not infringe the book *Love Story;* however, using the well-known line, "Love means never having to say you're sorry," might well constitute an infringement because the statement is a substantial portion of or the "heart" of the work copied.

Once copying is shown, examination must focus on whether the elements taken were protected by copyright. It is permissible to take ideas but impermissible to appropriate expression of those ideas. Works in the public domain may be examined, and the defendant may attempt to prove that both the plaintiff's work and the defendant's work share elements and similarities with works in the public domain. If all similarities arise from use of common ideas or works in the public domain, there can be no substantial similarity and no infringement.

Some courts use a test known as the "abstraction-filtration-comparison" test to separate protectable expression from unprotectable ideas in copyright infringement cases. First, a court dissects the allegedly infringing work and isolates each level of abstraction in it. Second, unprotectable elements, such as ideas, processes, facts, and public domain information, are filtered out. Third, a comparison is made of the remaining protectable elements to determine if the second work misappropriates substantial elements of the first. *Gates Rubber Co v. Bando Chem. Indus., Ltd.,* 9 F.3d 823 (10th Cir. 1993). The abstraction-filtration-comparison test is used most frequently in determining whether infringement of computer programs has occurred.

CONTRIBUTORY INFRINGEMENT AND VICARIOUS INFRINGEMENT

Courts have held persons and companies liable for the infringing acts of others. If a person, with knowledge of an infringing activity, induces, causes, or contributes to infringing conduct, he or she will be liable for infringement as a contributory infringer. **Contributory infringement** occurs when photo shops reproduce or duplicate photographs bearing a copyright notice, when copy shops reproduce or allow customers to photocopy books and other protected materials, when operators of flea markets or swap meets allow pirated works to be sold, or when an individual sells specially formatted blank cassettes and tape duplicating equipment to pirates with knowledge they are engaging in acts of infringement. In the famous case *Sony Corp. of America v. Universal City Studios Inc.,* 464 U.S. 417 (1984), the Supreme Court was called upon to determine whether videotaping of copyrighted works for later private viewing (for example, taping the movie *The American President* shown on television so one can watch it at a more convenient time, commonly referred to as "time-shifting") constituted infringement and whether the defendant Sony was contributorily liable for making the videocassette recorders used to make the allegedly infringing copies. The Court held that time-shifting did not constitute infringement and that the sale of copying equipment, like the sale of other articles of commerce, does not constitute contributory infringement if the product is

contributory infringement: In the intellectual property context, causing, inducing, or assisting in infringement of another's trademark, copyright, or patent

widely used for legitimate and unobjectionable purposes. Sony was held not liable for contributory infringement.

Vicarious infringement occurs when one party is responsible for infringement conducted by another when the two parties share a special relationship, such as that of employer-employee. One who is in a position to control the use of copyrighted works by others and authorizes use without permission of the copyright owner will be liable for vicarious infringement, even if he or she had no knowledge the infringement was occurring. For example, universities may be held liable for the infringing activities of teachers who photocopy copyrighted materials for distribution to students. The universities are in a position to control and direct the activities of teachers and should implement policies refusing photocopying unless the teachers obtain copyright releases or permission forms from the authors. Similarly, the operator of a swap meet was held vicariously liable for the sale of counterfeit recordings by a vendor who rented space from the operator on the basis that the operator had the right and ability to supervise the direct infringer and derived a financial benefit from the infringer's activities.

DEFENSES TO INFRINGEMENT

There are a variety of defenses a defendant charged with copyright infringement may assert. As stated, however, the infringer's intent is not relevant and infringement can be found whether or not the defendant intended to infringe copyrighted works. Intent, however, may be relevant in assessing damages.

Fair Use

Section 107 of the Copyright Act provides that the fair use of a copyrighted work for purposes such as criticism, comment, news reporting, teaching, scholarship, or research is not an infringement. Fair use is thus a privilege to use copyrighted material without permission of the copyright owner. The rationale for allowing certain uses of copyrighted material is to benefit the public and promote the arts and sciences.

The Copyright Office has given examples of activities that courts have regarded as fair use, including the following:

- quoting excerpts from copyrighted materials in a review or criticism of the work;
- quotation of short passages in scholarly or technical works for illustration or clarification of the author's observations;
- use in a parody of some of the parodied work;
- reproduction of a small portion of a work by a teacher to illustrate a lesson; and
- a summary of an address or article, with brief quotations, in a news report.

Thus, reviewers critiquing a song may quote lyrics from it, and parodies may be made of other works.

The act identifies (and courts consider) four factors in determining whether a use is fair and is thus permissible:

vicarious infringement: Liability imposed for copyright infringement on a party due to its special relationship (such as employer-employee) with another infringer

1. the purpose and character of the use, including whether such use is of a commercial nature or whether it is a nonprofit educational use;
2. the nature of the copyrighted work;
3. the amount and substantiality of the portion used in relation to the copyrighted work as a whole; and
4. the effect of the use upon the potential market for or value of the copyrighted work.

None of the four factors identified in section 107 are meant to be conclusive. Courts will examine each factor and weigh all considerations in determining whether a use is a permissible fair use or an infringing use. No one test is applied, and each case is determined on its own merits.

The Purpose and Character of the Use   One factor considered by courts focuses on the purpose for which reproduction, adaptation, distribution, performance, or display of a copyrighted work is undertaken and the use that is made of it. Generally, use for comment, criticism, and so forth is acceptable because it benefits the public and advances the public good; however, if a for-profit motive underlies any of these purposes, a different conclusion may be reached. Although commercial use will not automatically defeat a defense of fair use, use of another's work for a commercial purpose is less likely to be permitted than use for a noncommercial purpose.

Courts also examine whether the defendant's use adds something new with a new purpose or different character. Addition of new material benefits the public. Failure to transform a work in any way weighs against a finding of fair use.

Finally, a use that is merely incidental is more likely to be determined to be a fair use. For example, if a news reporter stands in front of a copyrighted painting while reporting on theft of works of art, such a use is incidental and may support a finding of fair use, even though it violates the copyright owner's right to display the work.

The Nature of the Copyrighted Work   Courts consider the degree of creativity in the copyrighted work in determining whether a use is fair. Generally, the more creative the work, the more protection it is afforded. Conversely, the more informational or functional the work, the less protection it receives. Thus, the fact that a second work is factual or informational in nature tends to support a finding of fair use. Once again, use and dissemination of factual and informational material tends to advance research and scholarship and is thus encouraged.

Whether the work is published or unpublished is important. Unauthorized use of an owner's work prior to publication severely affects the owner's right to determine the timing of entry into the market and be the first "on the scene." Thus, works that are unpublished generally receive more protection than those that have been published.

Amount and Substantiality of the Portion Used   In determining whether use of another's copyrighted work is fair, courts consider the quantitative as well as the qualitative portion of the work that is reproduced. Generally, it is not a fair use to reproduce an entire work. When less than all of a work is reproduced, whether the use is fair depends on the importance of the portion used, namely, whether the reproduced portion is the "heart" of the copyright owner's work. Even when the amount taken is quantitatively small, the use may still be impermissible if what is taken is the central or pivotal portion of the work.

The Effect of the Use on the Market for the Copyrighted Work   Most courts agree that the effect of the defendant's use on the potential market for the copyright owner's work is the most important of the four factors considered in determining whether a use of another's work is a permissible fair use. If the defendant's use causes a loss of revenue to the copyright owner, such argues against a finding of fair use. If the work will supplant the market for the copyright owner's work or diminish the potential market, the use is likely not a fair one.

Overview of Fair Use Cases   A brief review of some fair use cases will help demonstrate the balancing of the fair use factors engaged in by courts.

- *Sony Corp. of America v. Universal City Studios, Inc.,* 464 U.S. 417 (1984). In this case, Universal alleged that use of VCRs sold by the defendants violated the 1976 Copyright Act and that sale of the VCR machines constituted contributory infringement. The Court focused on the fourth factor of the fair use doctrine (the effect of the use on the potential market for the copyrighted work). The Court held that the practice of using a VCR to record a program for later private viewing ("time-shifting") was a fair use because it was noncommercial and there was little likelihood of harm to the potential market for the copyrighted works.

- *Harper & Row Publishers, Inc. v. Nation Enterprises,* 471 U.S. 539 (1985). In this case, President Ford granted Harper & Row exclusive rights to publish his memoirs and to license prepublication serialization of those memoirs. *Time* magazine then purchased from Harper & Row the right to publish certain excerpts from the book before its publication. Before *Time* could publish the excerpts, someone provided a copy of the manuscript to *Nation* magazine, which then published an article about the forthcoming book and included approximately three hundred words of direct quotes from the book. Because it had been "scooped," *Time* abandoned its plans to publish excerpts from the book and refused to pay the balance of its license fee to Harper & Row. Harper & Row sued *Nation* for copyright infringement. The Court held that the use was not a fair one: the publication in *Nation* was commercial in nature; the amount copied, though small quantitatively, captured the "heart" of the book; and the publication had an adverse effect on the potential market for the book.

- *Basic Books, Inc. v. Kinko's Graphics Corp.,* 758 F. Supp. 1525 (S.D.N.Y. 1991). For many years, Kinko's, a copy shop, had prepared course packets consisting of photocopies of assigned reading for college students. Publishing houses sued Kinko's, alleging that Kinko's practice of copying portions of books without permission and without payment violated the publishers' copyrights. The court found that Kinko's use was not fair use. Although the students' use of the materials was educational, Kinko's purpose in copying them was commercial. The amount and substantiality of the portions copied also weighed against a finding of fair use, and the potential market for the copyrighted materials was harmed in that Kinko's offered the materials at a lower cost and thus students refrained from buying the books.

- *Consumers Union of United States, Inc. v. General Signal Corp.,* 724 F.2d 1044 (2d Cir. 1983). In *Consumers Union,* the defendant's commercials included excerpts from the magazine *Consumer Reports,* which favorably rated defendant's product. The court held the use was fair and concluded that the purpose of the use was to report factual information and that the commercials made relatively insignificant use of the work. Use of reviews containing significant original analysis and conclusions from the first work rather than primarily factual material, however, might not be a fair use.

- *American Geophysical Union v. Texaco, Inc.,* 37 F.2d 881 (2d Cir. 1994). In this case, publishers of several scientific journals brought suit against Texaco, alleging that the company's practice of copying articles from journals and then routing or distributing the articles to its more than four hundred researchers was infringement. The researchers placed copies of the articles in their files for later use and reference. The publishers alleged the practice infringed their rights in the articles. The court held that Texaco's copying was not a fair use. Although the for-profit motive of Texaco was relevant, the court stated the focus should be on the use of the material itself rather than the user. The fact that the materials were used for an archival purpose—they were merely placed in files and not transformed in any way—weighed against a finding of fair use. On the second factor (the nature of the work), the court found the articles were scientific and factual, and this weighed in favor of Texaco. The third factor (amount of work copied) weighed against Texaco because entire separately copyrighted articles were copied. In regard to the last factor (impact of the copying on the potential market for the copyrighted materials), the court found against Texaco because the publishers lost subscription revenue and because Texaco could have entered into a license with the Copyright Clearance Center (CCC), a central clearinghouse established by publishers at the suggestion of Congress to license the copying of materials, much like ASCAP and BMI license the performance of music. By bypassing CCC, Texaco's copying caused a loss of revenue to the publishers. Texaco appealed to the United States Supreme Court, which granted *certiorari;* however, before the Court heard the case, the parties entered into a settlement with Texaco agreeing to pay more than $1 million and an additional retroactive license fee to CCC. Texaco also agreed to enter into a five-year licensing arrangement with CCC.

The *Texaco* case has caused much consternation inasmuch as it has been common practice for many companies to purchase only a limited number of subscriptions to journals and then copy articles as needed for distribution to employees. Without a ruling by the Supreme Court, users are left with the Second Circuit's holding that the practice is infringement. Many issues remain unresolved, including whether there is a difference between the archiving of articles by researchers funded by government grants and archiving by those funded by private company grants and what result should be reached when copying is done by an institution that serves both the commercial sector and the educational sector. The safest course appears to be to enter into private licensing arrangements with the publishers or to obtain a license through CCC. The CCC also offers guidelines for creating copyright compliance policies. Call (978) 750-8400 or access CCC's web site at http://www.copyright.com.

Parody

Parodies of works of literature, art, and music are viewed as a productive form of social commentary and criticism. Because copyright owners are highly unlikely to grant permission to another to parody their work, parodists often rely on the fair use defense when infringement is alleged by the owner of the parodied copyrighted work. Generally, no more than is necessary to accomplish the parody may be taken from the original work. The parodist's work must "conjure up" the copyright owner's work and link the parody with that of the original to make social comment or criticism. If the parodist merely copies a work to make social comment on some other topic, fair use is not available.

In *Campbell v. Acuff-Rose Music, Inc.,* 510 U.S. 569 (1994), Acuff-Rose, a music company, brought suit against the rap group 2 Live Crew claiming that the group's rap version of the song "Pretty Woman" infringed its copyright in the famous Roy Orbison song, "Oh, Pretty Woman." The Supreme Court held the parody was a fair use. In regard to the first fair use factor, the Court held that although the use was commercial, the new work added something new with a new expression and meaning. The second factor (the nature of the copyrighted work) was held to be of little use in the context of a parody because a parody, by definition, almost always copies known works such as the Orbison song. As for the amount and substantiality of the work copied, the Court stated that even if 2 Live Crew copied the "heart" of the Orbison song, it is the heart that most readily conjures up the original for the parody. Regarding the fourth factor, there was no evidence that the 2 Live Crew song had any impact on the market for nonparody or nonrap versions of the original Orbison song. Persons interested in the original song were unlikely to purchase the parody version in its place.

Conversely, in *Dr. Seuss Enterprises, L.P. v. Penguin Books USA, Inc.,* 924 F. Supp. 1559 (S.D. Cal. 1996), the district court held that a poetic account of the O. J. Simpson double murder trial presented in the style of the famous *Cat in the Hat* rhyming book was not protected parody inasmuch as it did not target or parody that book itself but merely copied its general style to make comments regarding society as a whole.

Reproduction of Copyrighted Works by Educators and Librarians

Pursuant to section 108 of the Copyright Act, libraries can reproduce a work for distribution and for preservation purposes. Similarly, libraries are protected from liability for infringement for unpermitted photocopying by their patrons as long as a notice is displayed on the photocopy equipment that the making of copies may be subject to copyright law.

In 1975, Congress urged educators and publishers to meet to reach an agreement regarding permissible educational uses of copyrighted material. The result was the "Agreement on Guidelines for Classroom Copying in Not-for-Profit Educational Institutions with Respect to Books and Periodicals." These guidelines were made part of the legislative history of the 1976 act. Some of the more notable provisions of the guidelines follow:

- Single copies of copyrighted materials (such as chapters from books, short stories, charts, or articles from a journal) may be made by teachers for scholarly research or use in teaching.
- Multiple copies (not to exceed more than one copy per pupil in a course) may be made if the copying meets specified tests for brevity (the guidelines include stated criteria for the amount of work that may be copied, for example, a poem may be copied if it is less than two hundred and fifty words) and spontaneity (the decision to use the material is made so close to the time the material is needed that it would be unreasonable to expect a reply to a request to the author to use the material); each copy includes a copyright notice; and the cumulative effect of the copying is limited (for example, no more than nine instances of multiple copying for one course during one class term can be made).

Similarly, music teachers and publishers met and developed "Guidelines for Educational Use of Music" to state the standards of educational fair use of music. The guidelines for books and for music are available as Circular 21 from the Copyright Office and are also available on the Internet (http://lcweb.loc.gov. copyright/circs/circ21).

Other Defenses to Infringement

Although fair use is one of the most widely asserted defenses in actions for infringement, a number of other defenses are also available.

Invalidity of Copyright A defendant may assert that the material sought to be protected by the plaintiff is uncopyrightable. Even if a certificate of copyright registration has been issued, the defendant may rebut the presumption of validity arising from registration and prove that the work lacks sufficient originality to be protectable and that the Copyright Office erroneously registered the work. Thus, the defendant may assert that the works are useful articles, public domain matter, common facts not subject to copyright protection, or scenes a faire (common or stock themes) that flow naturally from a premise or setting and are thus unprotectable. Moreover, works are not protected merely because they result from hard work. To be protectable, works must contain copyrightable expression. Thus, in *Feist Publications, Inc., v. Rural Telephone Service Co.,* 499 U.S. 340 (1991), the Supreme Court held that although a telephone company had invested a great deal of hard work or "sweat of the brow" into compiling its telephone directory, the directory was unprotectable because it was merely factual. A similar result was reached in 1998 when the Second Circuit held that West Publishing Company's addition of certain features, such as attorney information, parallel citations, and star pagination, to cases in the public domain did not result in original copyrightable work entitled to protection. A defendant may also show that the plaintiff failed to disclose certain facts to the Copyright Office (such as that the plaintiff's work was a derivative work or a useful article), thus rendering the registration invalid.

Estoppel A copyright owner who knows of an infringing use and acquiesces in it may be estopped or precluded from later claiming the use is an infringement, particularly when the defendant has expended sums in marketing the work.

Misuse or Unclean Hands A plaintiff may be precluded from obtaining relief in an infringement action if it is guilty of inequitable conduct, unclean hands, or **misuse** of its copyright. For example, requiring a defendant who licenses one copyrighted work to license another or coupling a copyright license with a restrictive covenant precluding a party from developing its own copyrighted works may be such misuse as to preclude the licensor from later asserting infringement of copyright.

Improper Copyright Notice   Section 406 of the Copyright Act provides a complete defense to infringement if the alleged infringer is misled by a pre-Berne copyright notice that misidentifies the copyright owner. In one case, the plaintiff created a video and licensed it to another, the licensee, for use in schools. The video contained a copyright notice that improperly identified the licensee as the copyright owner (rather than the plaintiff, the true owner). The licensee sold copies of the video to the defendant. The defendant successfully defended the action on the basis that the copyright notice identified the licensee as the owner and that he therefore had the right to assume that such party could sell the video to him. The court agreed and found no infringement by the defendant.

Statute of Limitations and Laches   Section 507(b) of the Copyright Act provides a three-year statute of limitations on civil copyright infringement actions. The time period may be tolled or suspended if the defendant has fraudulently concealed his or her copyright infringement from the plaintiff such that the plaintiff did not know to bring an action. The three-year period is measured from the time the infringement occurred. If there are separate acts of infringement or the infringement is continuing in nature, the plaintiff may initiate suit at any time within three years of the last infringing act.

Even if the plaintiff is within the three-year statute of limitations, the defendant may assert a defense of laches, namely, that the plaintiff unjustifiably delayed in bringing suit and this delay caused prejudice to the defendant. Laches typically does not excuse infringement but may preclude a plaintiff from obtaining injunctive relief.

INFRINGEMENT ACTIONS

Generally, a party who believes its copyrighted work has been infringed will send a cease and desist letter to the other party (much like the cease and desist letter used in trademark infringement matters shown in Chapter 6, Figure 6–1). If the parties cannot resolve their dispute amicably, they may proceed to arbitration or litigation.

The federal courts have exclusive jurisdiction over copyright infringement cases. Thus, infringement cases can be brought only in federal district courts, and not in state courts. Like any civil action, the proceeding is initiated by the filing of a complaint by the plaintiff. The clerk of the court must report the action to the Register of Copyrights. The defendant typically answers the complaint and asserts various defenses or challenges to the complaint. If the defendant has claims against the plaintiff, they must be made in the same action. This promotes judicial economy because the court can resolve all differences between the parties at the same time.

The action is governed by the Federal Rules of Civil Procedure. The plaintiff has the burden of proving all elements of an infringement action: ownership of

misuse: A defense often asserted in infringement actions alleging that the owner of an intellectual property right has so misused its rights as to be precluded from recovery

copyright; copyrightable subject matter; and unauthorized use, copying, repro-duction, adaptation, performance, or display of material expression by the defendant. Discovery will be scheduled by the court, and the parties may take depositions, propound interrogatories to each other, and request that various documents and other materials be produced. If settlement is not reached, the matter will proceed to trial. Either party may demand a jury trial. Expert wit-nesses may testify. Ultimately, the fact finder (either the jury or the judge) will render a decision. An appeal may be filed in the appropriate U.S. Court of Appeals by the losing party if a prejudicial error of law occurred at the trial. Further review may be sought in the U.S. Supreme Court, although it has dis-cretion to deny *certiorari* and refuse to hear the case.

REMEDIES FOR INFRINGEMENT

Plaintiffs in infringement actions may seek both monetary and nonmone-tary relief. In some instances, the plaintiff may be more interested in ensuring the infringing activity ceases than in recovering damages. Courts can use a vari-ety of remedies to ensure the copyright owner is adequately protected:

- **Injunctive relief.** Section 502 of the Copyright Act provides that a court may grant both temporary and final injunctions to prevent or restrain infringing activities. To secure an injunction before trial, gener-ally a plaintiff must prove that it is likely to succeed on the merits of its case, that it will suffer irreparable injury unless injunctive relief is ordered, that the threatened injury to it outweighs possible damage to the defendant, and that monetary damages will not provide sufficient relief. If a plaintiff has delayed in seeking injunctive relief, such tends to show that there is no irreparable harm occurring and injunctive relief may be denied.
- **Impoundment.** Courts can order the **impoundment** of infringing copies during the pendency of an infringement action and may order their destruction as part of a final judgment. The plaintiff usually must post a bond so that if no infringement is found, the defendant is recom-pensed for the seizure of the goods.
- **Compensatory damages and profits.** Plaintiffs may recover **compen-satory damages**—the actual damages suffered as a result of the infringe-ment—and any profits received by the defendant arising out of the infring-ing activities. Actual damages should compensate the plaintiff for lost sales and revenues. To recover the infringer's profits, the plaintiff must present proof of the infringer's gross revenue, and the infringer may then prove deductible expenses and profits attributable to factors other than the infringing work. Even indirect profits may be recovered. For example, in one case, a plaintiff recovered a portion of the defendant's hotel and gam-bling revenue on the basis that the performance of an infringing show in the hotel drew additional business to the hotel and casino.
- **Statutory damages.** In lieu of actual damages, if the copyright owner has secured registration within three months after publication or, for unpublished works, before the defendant's infringement, a plaintiff may elect an award of **statutory damages** under section 504(c) of the act.

impoundment: Seizure, generally of infringing goods

compensatory damages: Damages awarded to a plaintiff to compensate it for injury suffered

statutory damages: Damages awarded by a court in an infringement action as specified by statute, generally elected when a plaintiff will have difficulty proving actual damages

The statutory damages are set by the judge or jury in their discretion in a sum of not less than $500 and not more than $20,000 for infringement of one work (all the parts of a compilation or derivative work are viewed as one work). If willful infringement is shown, statutory damages may be awarded in an amount not exceeding $100,000. If the court finds that infringement was innocent (the infringer was not aware his or her acts were infringing and had no reason to know such), the court can reduce statutory damages to an amount not lower than $200. The election can be made at any time prior to entry of final judgment and is usually made in cases in which the plaintiff has difficulty proving actual damages. In one recent case, it was held that each unauthorized airing of a television series program by a different station controlled by the defendant was a separate act of infringement. Because the defendant's acts were willful, damages were fixed at just over $70,000 per act multiplied by 440 separate airings, for a total damage award to the copyright owner of $31.7 million (plus costs and attorneys' fees). This award was made by a jury in April 1999 and is believed to be the highest ever award of statutory damages. *Feltner v. Columbia Pictures Television, Inc.,* 106 F.3d 284 (9th Cir. 1997), *rev'd and remanded on other grounds,* 118 S. Ct. 1279 (1998). In *Feltner,* the Supreme Court also held that under the Seventh Amendment, if a party demands, there is a right to a jury trial on all issues pertinent to an award of statutory damages, including the amount itself.

- **Costs and attorneys' fees.** If registration has been secured within three months after publication of the work or, for unpublished works, before the defendant's infringement, the plaintiff may recover an award to compensate it for its costs incurred (expert witness fees, court filing fees, photocopy charges) and attorneys' fees. If the defendant prevails, reasonable attorneys' fees may be awarded to him or her in the discretion of the court.

- **Criminal sanctions.** Under the No Electronic Theft Act (the NET Act) signed into law in late 1997 (P.L. 105-147), persons who willfully infringe copyright for commercial advantage or by the reproduction or distribution during any 180-day period, by electronic means or otherwise, of one or more copies or phonorecords of one or more copyrighted works, which have a value of more than $1,000, may be subject to criminal penalties of fines and up to three years of imprisonment in some cases, up to six years of imprisonment for a second or subsequent offense, and up to one year of imprisonment in certain other cases. 18 U.S.C. § 2319. Fines up to $250,000 can be imposed. The NET Act strengthens the prior criminal provisions to make serious copyright piracy subject to criminal penalties even if there is no profit motive. Its primary purpose was to close the "LaMacchia Loophole," named for David LaMacchia, a student at MIT who set up an electronic bulletin board from which users downloaded approximately $1 million of free software. A copyright piracy case against LaMacchia was dismissed because LaMacchia had received no monetary compensation for the software he distributed. The NET Act also extended the statute of limitations in which criminal action may be brought from three years to five years. The Register of Copyrights testified before Congress in support of enhancing criminal penalties for copyright violations, stating that advances in technology have increased the potential for copyright piracy because it is easy and inexpensive to make and distribute pirated copies without a major investment in equipment and facilities. Thus, more serious penalties were needed to deter infringers.

- **Fines.** A fine up to $2,500 may be imposed when a copyright notice is fraudulently used or removed. Making a knowingly false statement of a material fact in a copyright application may subject a person to a fine up to $2,500.

ROLE OF INTELLECTUAL PROPERTY PROFESSIONAL

The role of IP professionals in infringement matters is similar to the role played by legal professionals in other litigation matters. Intellectual property practitioners may be engaged in the following activities:

- obtaining certified copies of certificates of registration or other documents to prove a plaintiff's ownership of copyright;
- obtaining certified copies of applications for registration of copyrights to examine applications for misstatements to prove misuse of the copyright application procedure by a plaintiff;
- conducting research regarding defenses that may be asserted by a defendant, especially the fair use defense;
- preparing a cease and desist letter (or response to same);
- drafting complaints, answers, motions, and other pleadings in infringement actions;
- assisting in the discovery process in infringement actions (summarizing depositions, drafting interrogatories and responses to interrogatories, reviewing documents produced, examining statements related to defendant's revenues, and so forth); and
- assisting at the trial (preparing and maintaining exhibits and lists of witnesses, preparing a trial notebook, preparing jury instructions, and assisting in preparing trial brief).

CHAPTER SUMMARY

An infringement action may be brought by an owner of a registered copyright whenever any of his or her exclusive rights have been violated. Infringement requires that a plaintiff prove copyright ownership and impermissible copying. Copying is usually demonstrated by showing that the defendant had access to the copyrighted work and there is substantial similarity between the copyrighted work and defendant's work.

A defendant in an infringement action may assert a variety of defenses. The most common defense raised is that the defendant's use was a "fair use" of the copyrighted work. The fair use doctrine developed to promote scholarly and educational use of certain works. Courts examine four factors in determining whether a defendant's use is fair: the purpose and character of the use, including whether the use is for commercial or nonprofit purposes; the nature of the work (with factual and scholarly works receiving less protection than works of fiction or fantasy); the amount and substantiality of the portion of work taken by the defendant (even a small taking may constitute infringement if it is the "heart" of the work); and the effect of the defendant's activities on the potential market for the copyrighted work. No one factor is conclusive; courts examine and weigh all factors in reaching a conclusion about infringement. Parody is a form of fair use, as are certain uses by libraries and educators.

Other defenses to infringement are invalidity of the plaintiff's copyright; estoppel to allege infringement due to the plaintiff's acquiescence in infringement; misuse or unclean hands by the plaintiff; and the statute of limitations, which provides that a civil infringement action must be brought within three years of the infringing activity.

Remedies available to a plaintiff include injunctive relief, actual damages and the defendant's profits, statutory damages, costs, and attorneys' fees. Criminal penalties may be imposed in the case of certain willful infringements.

DISCUSSION QUESTIONS

1. Andersen has transferred the exclusive right to reproduce a copyrighted work to Smith. The work is being infringed. Who should bring the action?

2. Frank sent the manuscript for his novel to a literary agent. The agent refused to represent the work and returned it to Frank. The agent also represents Susan. One year after Frank sent the work to the agent, Susan published a novel that Frank believes is substantially similar to his work. Discuss whether Frank can prove access to the work by Susan.

3. Frank has sued Susan for infringement. Susan has asserted that there is no infringement and that any resemblance between the two works is merely in paraphrasing and that there is no identical copying of language. Can paraphrasing constitute infringement?

4. Sam is a freelance instructor who teaches classes in self-defense for which he charges fees. As part of his instruction, Sam photocopies articles and chapters from books about self-defense theories from various published works and distributes them to the attendees. Sam is sued for copyright infringement and asserts a fair use defense. Discuss and analyze the four fair use factors.

5. Jean is a reviewer for her community newspaper. As part of her review of a recently published novel, Jean would like to include excerpts and quotes from the novel. Is such reproduction infringement?

6. A local comedy troupe in your area is performing a skit poking fun at the novel *The Bridges of Madison County*. Discuss whether the skit is infringement of the copyrighted work.

15

New Developments in Copyright Law and the Semiconductor Chip Protection Act

Technological advances have created new forms of copyright authorship that in turn have created new issues relating to protection and dissemination of these new works. Although it is clear that computer programs and automated databases are copyrightable literary works, issues relating to copying computer programs continue to present challenges to the courts. The literal portions of computer programs (source code and object code) are protectable, but the nonliteral portions are often viewed as unprotectable useful articles, scenes a faire, or merged ideas and expressions. Reverse engineering of computer programs to create compatible programs may be acceptable, but creating identical or substantially similar programs may be infringement.

No subject in copyright law is subject to as much debate as copyright in the electronic age. The ease with which works can be viewed, copied, reproduced, displayed, and transmitted using electronic means, particularly the Internet, has given rise to serious concern by authors that their works will be subject to wholesale infringement and piracy. Although some advocate that there should be no restrictions on information on the Internet, others are furiously working to develop encryption and metering devices that can track and monitor electronic use of works and charge for that use. A number of bills are pending in Congress to address these issues. Nevertheless, many experts believe the solutions to technology-related issues lie with technology rather than the courts or the legislature and that copyright protection on the Internet will be advanced by encryption and coding devices rather than piecemeal legislation or court decisions.

Protection for semiconductor chips stems from the Semiconductor Chip Protection Act of 1984. The act establishes a new form of intellectual property protection for the "masks" used to create the electronic circuitry of semiconductor chips. Although this form of protection is said to be *sui generis* (literally, "one of a kind"), mask protection draws upon many copyright principles.

INTRODUCTION

Developments in technology create new industries and new opportunities for reproduction and dissemination of works of authorship. A number of new issues have arisen relating to the growth of electronic publishing, distribution, and viewing of copyrighted works. Along with new and expanded markets for works comes the ever-increasing challenge of protecting works from piracy or infringement. For example, in 1998, an advance copy of the first single from Madonna's newest album was released to foreign radio stations. Almost immediately, unauthorized copies were placed on web sites allowing anyone with Internet access to download a copy weeks before the single was released for sale or radio play in the United States.

Both the courts and Congress continue to be faced with issues that were unimagined just a decade ago. More "high-tech" legislation was introduced in the 105th Congress than in any previous Congress. Courts struggle with the complexity and balance between protecting the rights of authors and promoting the progress of science and useful arts as is mandated by the Constitution. This chapter is intended to introduce some of the copyright cutting edge and bleeding edge issues presently confronting authors, users, legislators, and judges.

COPYRIGHT PROTECTION FOR COMPUTER PROGRAMS

Protectable Elements of Computer Programs

Computer programs have been accepted for copyright registration since the mid-1960s. In 1974, Congress created the Commission on New Technological Uses of Copyrighted Works (CONTU) to analyze various technology-related issues and report to Congress on several topics, including copyrightability of computer programs. The CONTU recommended that the 1976 Copyright Act be expressly amended to make clear that computer programs are copyrightable. In 1980, Congress followed CONTU's recommendations and added a definition in the Copyright Act for the term *computer program* and a limitation on the exclusive rights of computer program authors in order to allow users to make certain adaptations to programs and to make archival copies of programs.

According to section 101 of the Copyright Act, a **computer program** is a set of statements or instructions to be used directly or indirectly in a computer in order to bring about a certain result. Copyright protection extends to all of the copyrightable expression embodied in the program. Copyright protection is not available for ideas, program logic, algorithms, systems, methods, concepts, or layouts. Computer programs are copyrightable as literary works, and applicants seeking registration of computer programs should generally use application Form TX (the same form used for books and other literary materials). However, if pictorial or graphic authorship predominates, registration may be made using Form PA (for audiovisual works).

computer program: A set of instructions used directly or indirectly in a computer to produce a certain result

Computer languages are written in specialized alphanumeric languages called **source code** that are human-readable. In order to operate a computer, source code must be translated into machine-readable **object code,** consisting of only two symbols, 0 and 1, which represent the alphanumeric characters of the source code. Both source code and object code are copyrightable.

Copyright protection extends to screen displays as well, if they possess copyrightable material. Screens consisting of mere menus or blank forms usually are not protectable, either because they lack original expression or because they are useful articles. In *Lotus Development Corp. v. Borland International, Inc.,* 49 F.3d 807 (1st Cir. 1995), *aff'd,* 516 U.S. 233 (1996), the First Circuit held that the menu command hierarchy of the Lotus 1-2-3 spreadsheet was uncopyrightable subject matter inasmuch as it was a mere method of operation. The court held that highlighting a "p" for "print" on a computer screen was really no different from pressing a "play" button on a VCR. Such was not protectable expression.

A single registration is sufficient to protect the copyright in a computer program, including related screen displays, without a separate registration for the screen displays or a specific reference to the displays in the application. Acceptable identifications of the work include "computer program," "entire text of computer program," "entire program code," and "text of user's manual and computer program." These identifications will cover any copyrightable authorship contained in the computer program and screen displays. The Copyright Office will refuse registration if the claim of authorship is based only on "encrypting," "firmware," "formatting," "functions," "printout," "software methodology," or "system."

Because most computer programs are accompanied by user manuals, the manuals may be included as part of the computer program registration, thus eliminating the need for a separate application for the manuals.

Deposit Requirements for Computer Programs

For published or unpublished computer programs, the first twenty-five and last twenty-five pages of source code should be submitted in a form visually perceptible without the aid of a machine or a device. If the program is less than fifty pages in length, all of the source code should be deposited.

Because computer programs often contain proprietary information and trade secrets, the Copyright Office has developed alternative deposit requirements for such works. Where a computer program contains trade secret material, a cover letter should accompany the application, stating that the claim contains trade secrets. One of the following must then be deposited:

- first twenty-five and last twenty-five pages of source code with portions containing trade secrets blocked out; or
- first ten and last ten pages of source code alone, with no blocked-out portions; or
- first twenty-five and last twenty-five pages of object code plus any ten or more consecutive pages of source code, with no blocked-out portions; or
- for programs less than fifty pages in length, entire source code with trade secret portions blocked out.

Some applicants are reluctant to deposit even blocked-out portions of source code. They may therefore apply for a registration under the Copyright

source code: An alphanumeric computer language that is human-readable

object code: A computer language consisting of zeroes and ones that is machine readable

Office's "rule of doubt" by submitting object code together with written confirmation that the material does contain copyrightable authorship. The Copyright Office will issue a registration on the basis of the information given by the applicant even though it is unable to examine the deposited material and determine the existence of copyrightability. If questions arise later regarding copyrightability, a court will determine whether the material is copyrightable.

Notice of Copyright

Although the form of copyright notice is the same for computer-related works as for other works (the symbol ©, the year of first publication, and the name of the owner), the location of the notice presents special problems. The Copyright Office has stated the following are acceptable placements of the notice:

- a notice embedded in the copies in machine-readable form in such a manner that on visually perceptible printouts it appears either with or near the title, or at the end of the work;
- a notice that is displayed at the user's screen or terminal at sign-on;
- a notice that is continuously on the screen or terminal display; or
- a legible notice on a label securely affixed to the copies or to a box, reel, cartridge, cassette, or other container used as a permanent receptacle for the copies.

Video Games

Although the ideas underlying some video games (such as a solitaire game) are not copyrightable, certain elements of video games, such as a sequence of sounds and images, are copyrightable as audiovisual works apart from the underlying computer program. Some infringers alleged early on that video games were not copyrightable inasmuch as player participation causes variations in games and different outcomes, and thus the works are not "fixed," but courts have held that many of the game elements remain constant and that the memory devices of games satisfy the requirement of fixation.

Revisions and Modifications to Computer Programs

Computer programs are frequently updated and revised by their authors, generally to provide additional features to users. Substantive revisions will result in a new work for which a new copyright registration should be sought. Thus, each separately published version of a computer program should be separately registered, assuming each contains a sufficient amount of new or revised authorship to sustain a claim of copyright. The Copyright Office will accept the following claims of authorship: "new modules," "revised modules," "revised program," "new routines," and "revised routines."

Copyright owners have the exclusive right under section 106 of the Copyright Act to reproduce their works and to prepare derivative works based on their copyrighted works. Section 117 of the act, relating exclusively to computer programs, limits these exclusive rights by allowing a backup copy to be made and allowing some modifications of programs for an owner's own use, such as improving the program or increasing its speed of performance.

Section 117 provides that notwithstanding the otherwise exclusive rights of a copyright owner, it is not an infringement for the owner of a copy of a computer program to make an additional copy or to adapt a program if the new copy or adaptation is created as an essential step in the utilization of the computer program or is used for archival purposes only. Thus, section 117 authorizes some modifications to computer programs for a purchaser's own use under the theory that having paid for a computer program, "the consumer may experiment with the product and create new variations of play, for personal enjoyment, without creating a[n] [infringing] derivative work." *Lewis Galoob Toys, Inc. v. Nintendo of America, Inc.*, 780 F. Supp. 1283, 1291 (N.D. Cal. 1991). Thus, converting a program from one language to another to facilitate its use or adding features to a computer program for one's own needs is permissible. *Foresight Resources Corp. v. Pfortmiller*, 719 F. Supp. 1006 (D. Kan. 1989). Section 117 applies to "owners," and thus its provisions are inapplicable to licensees of software or those who are in possession of software unlawfully.

Infringement of Computer Programs

Some of the most complex copyright cases involve the extent of protectability for computer programs. A number of litigants have asserted that computer operating systems are not protectable inasmuch as they are uncopyrightable "processes" or "systems," expressly excluded from protection according to section 102 of the Copyright Act. Courts generally have held otherwise, reasoning that if other programs can be written or created that perform the same functions, then an operating system is an expression of an idea and is therefore copyrightable. If the idea cannot be expressed in any other way, however, then it is purely necessary to the purpose and is functional, and hence not copyrightable. This is the merger doctrine, discussed in Chapter 10, that provides that if an idea in a work can be expressed in only one way or a very limited number of ways, it is unprotectable inasmuch as it would be unfair to allow one party to appropriate an idea and exclude all others from using it. When an idea and its expression are so merged or inseparable that the unprotectable idea cannot be used without also using protectable expression, then use is not infringement.

Courts have struggled with infringement issues in computer-related cases in part because the issues are often technical, unfamiliar, and complex. Thus, experts are often relied upon rather than the "ordinary observer" commonly referred to in other infringement actions. Moreover, unlike songs and books, which are highly creative, computer programs are usually task-oriented, performing very specific functions. Historically, "useful articles" are excluded from copyright protection.

Some courts have expressly recognized that many computer programs are by nature utilitarian articles inasmuch as their purpose is to accomplish tasks. *See Computer Associates International, Inc. v. Altai, Inc.*, 982 F.2d 693 (2d Cir. 1992). Thus, functional commands and aspects are unprotectable. Based on the merger doctrine, courts have held that when specific instructions are the only means of accomplishing a given task, another may use them without infringing the original work.

Moreover, many cases involving computer-related works have held that certain elements are unprotectable inasmuch as they are standard or stock scenes a faire (literally, "scenes which must be done"). Thus, hardware and software standards, mechanical specifications, industry programming practices, and compatibility requirements have been held to be unprotectable scenes a faire, since they are expressions dictated by external factors and their creation is the natural product of such external considerations.

Some courts have used the "abstraction-filtration-comparison" test discussed in Chapter 14 in determining whether infringement of computer programs has occurred. A court will abstract or dissect the allegedly infringed program's structure, filter out the unprotectable elements (such as processes, facts, merger material, and scenes a faire), and then compare the remaining elements of the two works to determine whether infringement exists. *Gates Rubber Co. v. Bando Chem. Indus., Ltd.,* 9 F.3d 823 (10th Cir. 1993). Other courts focus on the idea-expression dichotomy and hold that only those elements not necessary to the purpose or function of the work are protectable expression.

Early cases often involved nearly identical copying of code (often referred to as "literal copying"), and courts found it easy to determine that in such cases infringement had occurred. Analogizing computer programs to other textual works, such as books, which could be infringed even without literal copying (namely, by paraphrasing), courts then extended copyright protection to the structure, sequence, and organization of programs, namely the nonliteral elements of a program.

Later cases have involved less clear-cut issues, such as copying functional elements of programs. Many of these cases involve **reverse engineering,** or disassembling a computer program to understand its functional elements. In *Sega Enterprises Ltd. v. Accolade, Inc.,* 977 F.2d 1510 (9th Cir. 1993), the defendant reverse engineered Sega's video game programs in order to make its own video games that would be compatible with Sega's console into which the defendant's game cartridges were inserted. The Ninth Circuit held that such was permissible because the defendant had copied Sega's software solely in order to discover the functional elements for compatibility with Sega's console, elements of Sega's programs that were not protectable by copyright. The court held that where disassembly is the only way to gain access to the ideas and functional elements embodied in a copyright program and where there is a legitimate reason for seeking such access, such disassembly is a fair use of the copyrighted work.

Many experts interpret *Sega* as part of a growing trend of courts to limit the scope of copyright protection for computer programs, particularly for the functional elements of programs. Thus, many owners are now seeking patent protection for their computer programs (see Chapter 21). Nevertheless, although efforts can be undertaken to understand a work's ideas, processes, and methods of operation (all unprotectable functional aspects of a computer program), if the final program produced by the "engineer" is substantially similar to the original work, infringement may be found.

Licensing of Computer Programs

reverse engineering: Disassembling an object, usually a computer program, to understand its functional elements

Due to the ease of copying computer programs (allowing numerous users to share one purchased program) and due to the first sale doctrine (allowing the owner/purchaser of a copy to sell or rent it to others), makers of software programs became concerned over piracy and potential loss of revenues. To remedy the problem, they implemented the practice of licensing their programs.

Software purchased over the counter is thus not "sold" by the maker but rather "licensed" by the maker to the user/purchaser. Such a license is often called a **shrink-wrap license** because opening the plastic wrapping on the package immediately subjects the user/purchaser to the terms of the license agreement. A notice to this effect is placed on the box or packaging, and a method for returning the software is usually provided if the user/licensee objects to the license terms. Courts generally have held that such licenses are valid contracts enforceable under the principles of contract law unless their terms are unconscionable. *ProCD, Inc. v. Zeidenberg,* 86 F.3d 1447 (7th Cir. 1998).

The license agreements contain warranties and the terms and conditions under which the user/licensee can use the software and make it clear that violation of any of the terms, such as loading the software into more than one computer or decompiling it, constitutes infringement. Because the transaction is a license rather than a sale, no "first sale" concerns are implicated, and the user/licensee cannot resell or rent the software to another inasmuch as there was no sale to him or her in the first instance. In some cases, software is licensed electronically; this license agreement is referred to as a **click-wrap license**, since the license terms and conditions come into existence when the user/licensee clicks an icon displayed on a computer screen to indicate "purchase" or license of the work per the stated terms.

Section 117 of the Copyright Act, allowing owners of copies of computer programs to make a new copy or adaptation if necessary to use the program and to make an archival or backup copy, is limited to "owners" and is thus not applicable to licensees under shrink-wrap or click-wrap license agreements. Most software makers/licensors, however, typically include as a term of the license a provision substantially similar to section 117, allowing the user/licensee to make a new copy or adaptation if necessary to enable the use for which the software was obtained or for archival purposes.

Piracy of Software

In addition to the complex legal issues surrounding protection and infringement of computer-related works, there are significant economic issues as well. It has been estimated that software piracy causes a loss of revenue of nearly $3 billion annually in the United States alone. One expert has estimated that there may be nearly thirty thousand sites on the Internet that offer software illegally. Just the day after the film *Titanic* won several Oscar awards, fifty separate web sites offered illegal video copies of the film. One of the most common types of software piracy is "softlifting," or making unauthorized copies of a licensed software program (often for a home computer, fellow employee, family, or friends). The economic effect of computer piracy is reportedly more than $11 billion worldwide per year, costing 130,000 jobs in the United States alone. Consequently, many companies, notably Microsoft Corporation, are stepping up their crusades against software piracy, both through educational programs and legal action. One counterfeiting operation in early 1999 in California resulted in a seizure of $30 million of pirated MICROSOFT® software.

Software makers often join one of two associations, the Software Publishers Association (SPA) or the Business Software Alliance (BSA) that exist to educate businesses about copyrights in software and to locate infringers. The SPA has twelve hundred members and represents the software industry. The BSA was

shrink-wrap license: A license of software that comes into existence by the opening of the plastic wrapping on the software and by which act the licensee agrees to terms governing use of the software

click-wrap license: A license of software that comes into existence by the clicking of a computer keystroke, by which act the licensee agrees to terms governing use of the software

formed in the late 1980s, and some of its members are Apple, Borland, Novell, Lotus, and Microsoft. Generally, it represents the interests of the leading makers of software for personal computers. It has filed hundreds of lawsuits for software infringement, asking for restraining orders and audits of a company's computers to locate pirated software. Most lawsuits are settled out of court, with the infringers paying the retail value of the software and replacing the pirated software. In other cases, damages have been assessed in the millions of dollars. Both BSA and SPA have hotline numbers to report infringement, and in many instances, disgruntled former employees report infringement by their former employers. The SPA reports that it receives about thirty calls per day on its hotline. Visiting technicians to companies and temporary employees also tend to report infringement.

The BSA offers a publication to help businesses implement antipiracy programs. Call (800) 688-2721 and ask for *The Guide to Software Management.* The SPA offers a free self-audit kit to help determine if a company is in violation of any copyrights. Write to SPA at 1730 M Street NW, Washington, DC 20036.

Although software piracy is of great concern in the United States, it is estimated that most loss from computer piracy arises in foreign countries due to their lax enforcement practices and laws. For example, until 1998, software piracy was not a crime in Argentina or Brazil. The SPA has rated China as having a piracy percentage of 98 percent, meaning that for every one hundred programs sold, ninety-eight are pirated. Similarly, in May 1998 alone, Hong Kong officials seized more than ten million pirated CDs. The United States Trade Representative attempts to work with these countries to secure their commitment to protect copyrighted works by placing countries on intellectual property "watch lists," which can lead to trade restrictions and sanctions. Countries currently on the priority watch list include India, Israel, and the Philippines. Once a country is placed on a watch list, an investigation is initiated to determine whether tariffs or trade restrictions should be imposed on the offending country.

COPYRIGHT PROTECTION FOR AUTOMATED DATABASES

According to the Copyright Office, an **automated database** is a body of facts, data, or other information assembled into an organized format suitable for use in a computer and comprising one or more files. An automated database is usually a compilation. Although there is no specific reference to automated databases anywhere in the Copyright Act, they are viewed as types of literary works subject to copyright protection. An example of an automated database is WESTLAW's database of federal court cases. Although the cases themselves are government works in the public domain, West Group's arrangement of those cases qualifies for copyright protection as a compilation.

Automated databases will not receive protection if there is no original authorship in the selection and ordering of the data, such as is the case in merely transferring data from hard copy to computer storage. Registration is secured using Form TX. If the material in the database has been previously published, previously registered, or is in the public domain, the claim should be described as "compilation." If the material is original, the claim should be described as "text."

automated database: A body of facts, data, or other information assembled into an organized format suitable for use in a computer and comprising one or more files

For a single-file database (one in which the data records pertain to a single common subject matter, such as bankruptcy cases), the deposit should consist of the first and last twenty-five pages or data records. For a multiple-file database (one in which there are separate and distinct groups of data records, such as bankruptcy cases, federal regulations, and state statutes), the deposit should consist of fifty data records from each file, or the entire file, whichever is less. The Copyright Office also requires a descriptive statement from the applicant, giving the title of the database, identifying the copyright claimant, describing each separate file in the multiple-file database, and giving information about the nature and frequency of changes within the database and information about the copyright notice to be used. The Copyright Office will consider requests for relief from the deposit requirements if the database contains trade secrets or the applicant is unable to deposit the materials.

The Copyright Office provides specific information about copyright registration for automated databases in its Circular 65, obtainable from the forms hotline (202/707-9100) and on the Internet at http://www.loc.gov/copyright.

In April 1998, the United States sponsored a conference on database protection to discuss providing additional protection to databases. Additionally, the 106th Congress is considering legislation (H.R. 354) that would protect databases created through a substantial investment of time and money (a provision that would effectively overrule *Feist,* which held that a database work, namely, a telephone directory, was not protectable merely because it was the result of "sweat of the brow"). Thus, protection would be provided for realtors' home listings, stock quotations, and certain case reports. Certain databases containing information for educational, scientific, research, and news-gathering purposes would be exempt from the act. Such protection would harmonize U.S. law with that of many of the European Union countries, which provide some protection to noncreative compilations of material. As discussed in Chapter 16, the issue of providing enhanced protection to databases is the subject of both national and international debate and discussion, with no present resolution in regard to the extent to which databases should be protected.

COPYRIGHT IN THE ELECTRONIC AGE

Introduction

There is a dynamic tension inherent in copyright law: the rights of authors and creators to protect their works and reap the benefits of their creations must be balanced against the right of the public to have access to information. Nowhere is that tension more pronounced than in the discussion of copyright in cyberspace. It is amazingly easy to make electronic copies of works and then transmit those works to others using digital media. Using our computers, we are capable of retrieving, storing, revising, and disseminating vast amounts of information created by others with a single keystroke. There are few mechanical or economic restrictions precluding or restricting the free flow of information in cyberspace.

On one side of a vigorous debate are the adherents to the "Dyson model," named after Esther Dyson who heads the Electronic Frontier Foundation, who believe that "information wants to be free," meaning that the logical product of the Internet and our global communications capacities is unrestricted dissemination of information. Widespread access to information is beneficial to the research, educational, and scientific communities, all benefiting the public interest. On the other side of the debate are authors and creators of works who fear that unrestricted access to their works on the Internet will impair the value of their works, cause a loss of revenue to them, and ultimately discourage creation of work. If authors fear loss of protection, they will not create work, and the public will then receive no benefit.

The Copyright Act has been liberally written to encompass new technologies as seen in the reference in section 102 that copyright protection subsists in original works of authorship fixed in any tangible medium of expression, *now known or later developed.* Nevertheless, although the Copyright Act anticipates emerging technologies, developments of the past several years have been so unexpected and rapid that many experts believe some amendments to the Copyright Act may be necessary.

Issues Confronting Cyberspace Users

Some of the issues presently facing authors, consumers, and Internet service providers (such as America Online or Mindspring) are the following:

- Should individuals browsing information offered on the Internet be required to obtain the author's permission before: viewing the information; saving the information; transmitting it to others; revising the material; making a hard copy of or printing the information; or reproducing the information in another form, such as in a newsletter? At least one court has held that a company that downloaded copyrighted material from a web site to post on an internal intranet was liable for copyright infringement. *Marobie-FL v. National Ass'n of Fire Equipment Distributors,* 983 F. Supp. 1167 (N.D. Ill. 1997).
- Should the owner of a digital version of a copyrighted work be permitted to disseminate that information to another under the "first sale" doctrine?
- Is placing information (or "uploading") on the Internet a dedication to the public domain such that anyone can thereafter use, reproduce, adapt, or display the information for any purpose?
- Is posting information on a bulletin board system a "performance" of a copyrighted work?
- Is quoting material from others in a chat room infringement?
- Should the U.S. government be able to restrict exports of the most powerful encryption software unless the maker of the software provides the government with a decoding key or "back door" so the government can fight organized crime and terrorism?

A common thread running through all of these issues is whether the Copyright Act should be amended to address these issues or whether the courts should resolve these questions on a case-by-case basis.

The National Information Infrastructure

In 1993, President Clinton formed the Information Infrastructure Task Force to study the complex issues posed by posting and disseminating information in cyberspace and to develop guidelines for a National Information Infrastructure (NII). The NII encompasses digital interactive services now available, such as the Internet, as well as those that may be developed in the future.

The NII is not restricted to copyright issues. The NII, combining computer technology and communications technology, can support our education systems by connecting students and educators all over the world, advance cultural and entertainment opportunities, and increase participation in the democratic process by making available speeches, bills, and other government works. However, the NII has a direct impact on copyrighted works. Two-dimensional works are easily converted to digitized form (a series of zeroes and ones) and can then be easily and rapidly reproduced (with each "copy" identical in quality to the original) and transmitted to others with just a few keystrokes. They may be posted on a bulletin board where thousands of individuals can have access to them. These works can be changed by modifications and by combining them with other works (such as the addition of lyrics written by one party to music written by another), blurring ownership rights. Just one unauthorized uploading of an author's work onto a bulletin board could have a devastating effect on the market for that author's work. Thus, appropriate systems must be put into place to protect authors' rights.

After holding hearings and examining a variety of issues, the task force determined that although some minor modifications and amendments may be needed to the 1976 Copyright Act to reflect the realities of the NII, the act is capable of resolving the new issues and challenges presented by advances in technology. The task force also concluded that no revisions are needed to trademark, patent, or trade secret law at this time. Its final report, however, "The White Paper on Intellectual Property and the National Information Infrastructure," has engendered much criticism. Opponents of the recommendations set forth in the White Paper have formed the "Digital Future Coalition," which believes that the White Paper recommends far too much protection to authors at the cost of drying up information that should be freely accessible to the public.

Copyright Notices in the Electronic Age

Authors concerned about unauthorized reproduction and dissemination of their works by electronic means can include notices with their works to remind users that further reproduction or transmission is unauthorized and may constitute infringement. Some notices are as follows:

- © 1996 John Doe. Copying, transmitting, reproducing, or archiving this work in any media or by any means for other than personal use without express permission of John Doe is prohibited and may constitute copyright infringement.
- Access to and use of this web site is subject to the following terms and conditions: you may browse this site only for information and entertainment use; you may not modify, transmit, or revise the contents of this site without the owner's written permission; any communication you post to this site will be treated as nonconfidential; you may not post or transmit any unlawful or defamatory material; your use of the site constitutes acceptance of these terms.

- This web site contains links to other sites. Such links are not affiliations with or endorsements of other sites or the products or services offered by or through such sites.
- © 1998 Jane Roe. The user or viewer of this work is hereby granted an express nonexclusive license to reproduce the work, display, transmit, and distribute it by all means and in any media.
- Those individuals who post messages or works to this list own the copyrights to the messages or works; however, they grant a nonexclusive license to the list owner to reproduce, transmit, forward, and archive any messages or works posted to this list.

Although these notices will not preclude infringement, they may assist an author in obtaining damages for willful infringement or, alternatively, clarify that the work may be freely disseminated.

Copyright Rights Management

A number of proposals have been advanced to protect works from unauthorized and global reproduction, transmission, and distribution over the Internet. These proposals are generally referred to as "copyright rights management." Some of the proposals include the following:

- "metering" each use of a copyrighted work so that viewers are required to pay for viewing or distributing the work, with proceeds going to the author and Internet service provider (note that "metering" works substantially similar to "pay per view" television viewing);
- developing secure processors, encryption techniques, and digital watermarking technologies that preclude copying of digital works unless authorized;
- developing secure containers for digital works, sometimes called "cryptelopes," that operate as lock boxes, requiring users to secure permission or pay a fee before works can be decrypted for use and viewing;
- protecting information through the use of passwords and requiring users to agree to certain terms and conditions (for example, the *New York Times* does not charge a fee for users to access its web site, although it requires users to register by selecting a password and agreeing to abide by the terms of the *Times'* subscriber agreement);
- developing models based on those used by the Copyright Clearance Center (discussed in Chapter 14) whereby a broad library of information would be preauthorized for digital use and licenses and permissions would be granted to use and reproduce the digital works for preset fees much the same way licenses and permissions are granted by clearinghouses to use works printed in conventional hardcopy form. In this model, clearinghouses would allow customers to purchase software on the Internet through the use of a secure "envelope" that could not be opened until payment is received or confirmed (note that this method allows no protection against downstream infringement because the first authorized user could readily distribute copies to others, both by electronic and conventional means);
- developing devices that monitor and track digital usage (comparable to the way telephone companies determine telephone charges) by embedding

chips into works that meter usage as soon as information is accessed and then produce monthly statements or bills; and

- introducing fingerprint readers or iris-scanning software (the field of biometrics) to recognize authorized users and protect network security.

Practical Do's and Don'ts

Because of the uncertainty inherent in viewing, archiving, transmitting, reproducing, downloading, uploading, and otherwise using digital information, following are some practical pointers and guidelines for copyright compliance in the electronic age:

- Even attributing quotes to their authors may not protect against a claim of infringement. When on the Internet, do not quote from, transmit, copy, archive, or reproduce others' works without permission (unless such use is a fair use).
- Review material placed on the Internet for permissions; in many cases, authors have already granted limited permissions or licenses for others to use and view the materials. Unless permission is given, all material on the Internet, especially software, should be considered copyrighted work. Therefore, software should not be downloaded or modified without permission from the copyright holder. Similarly, downloading and printing an article you find for your personal use may be appropriate; however, printing multiple copies of the article and distributing them to others without permission likely violates the owner's exclusive copyright rights. Although such acts are infringements, copyright violations are common. For example, the developer of the popular computer games "Quake" and "Doom" estimates that 50 percent of the versions of Quake now being played are unlicensed, having been downloaded from unauthorized web sites.
- Do not place any documents or materials from clients or your employer on the Internet without permission and without including a copyright notice.
- Newsgroup and e-mail postings are not always in the public domain. The safest course may be to forward postings only with permission (although a number of people believe that posting messages is an implied license to either archive or to forward those messages to others).
- Do not copy material (whether text or graphics) from another's web page without permission, and do not combine items from others' web pages to create a web page.
- Ask permission before establishing links to others' sites, and indicate that links to unaffiliated sites are so unaffiliated to avoid presumed sponsorship of others.
- Place copyright notices on all web sites and on all original works.

RECENT DEVELOPMENTS IN COPYRIGHT LAW

As is apparent from the foregoing discussion, copyright law continues to evolve with technology. Some of the more recent and interesting developments are as follows:

- While acknowledging that clothing is a useful article and thus not subject to copyright protection, a New York federal court ruled that lace designs, copyrighted as writings and incorporated into wedding dresses, were protectable and enjoined another maker of wedding dresses from making or marketing copies. Similarly, detailed embroidery or some other two-dimensional drawing or graphic work affixed to a portion of a garment may be copyrightable.

- A federal court in California recently held that while type fonts themselves are not protectable under copyright law, a software program that generated and created the typefaces was protectable.

- Two recent cases held Internet service providers and electronic bulletin boards liable for copyright infringement when their users or customers posted infringing works to the Internet. Contributory infringement was found in regard to bulletin board operators based on the fact they provided the facilities to store and access copyrighted works (photos owned by Playboy Enterprises, see *Playboy Enterprises v. Frena,* 839 F. Supp. 1552 (M.D. Fla. 1993)) and in regard to an Internet service provider because it provided facilities, direction, knowledge, and encouragement to copy copyrighted SEGA® games. *Sega v. Maphia,* 857 F. Supp. 679 (N.D. Cal. 1994).

- Perhaps in response to the cases holding Internet service providers and bulletin board operators liable for contributory infringement, the Digital Millenium Copyright Act was passed by the 105th Congress (17 U.S.C. § 512 (c)) providing that online providers will be liable for copyright infringement for storage and transmission of material though their networks only if they profit from violations and have actual knowledge of such infringement. The statute also creates criminal penalties for those who circumvent antipiracy protections.

- The Digital Era Copyright Enhancement Act introduced in the House in the 105th Congress (H.R. 3048) is intended to confirm that the first sale doctrine applies in digital networked environments, allowing the owner of a lawfully acquired digital copy of a work to transmit it to another as long as the owner simultaneously destroys or erases his or her copy. The act would amend the Copyright Act to provide that it is not an infringement to make an ephemeral digital copy of a work if such copying is incidental and in the course of an otherwise lawful use of the work, thereby allowing users to view a copyrighted work posted on the Internet even though an ephemeral copy is made in the course of so viewing the work. Another provision in the act addresses shrink-wrap and click-wrap licenses and would make it unlawful for terms in those licenses to narrow or abrogate certain rights granted under the Copyright Act. The act also confirms that the fair use defense is applicable to digital works and may be raised by a user of conventional or electronic works. Finally, the act would impose liability on any person who knowingly deactivates or circumvents technology designed to preserve authors' exclusive rights to reproduce their works. Due to the complexity of the issues raised by the act, few expect rapid passage.

- As discussed in Chapter 14, in late 1997 President Clinton signed into law the No Electronic Theft (NET) Act (amending 18 U.S.C. § 2319) to enhance criminal penalties for copyright infringement, even if the infringer does not profit from the transaction. The act also extends the statute of limitations for criminal copyright infringement from three to five years, and allows law enforcement officers to use federal copyright laws against online copyright violation, thereby extending the same copyright protection to the Internet that is provided to other media.

- In September 1999, the Clinton administration relaxed government restrictions on the export of encryption products and simultaneously introduced new legislation to give law enforcement agencies greater authority to combat the use of computers by terrorists and criminals and to create a new code-cracking unit within the FBI.

- BMI, the music licensing society, has developed a Web robot (sometimes called a "spider") to track transmission and sales of music on the Internet so it can eliminate electronic infringement of music by requiring users to either cease infringement or enter into licensing and royalty agreements with BMI.

- As further evidence of the seriousness of copyright piracy, in 1999, a father and son accused of conspiracy to sell more than $20 million in stolen Microsoft software were sentenced to five years and one year in prison, respectively.

- In August 1999, the National Conference of Commissioners on Uniform State Law passed a model law, called the Uniform Computer Information Transaction Act, to regulate electronic commerce, including shrink-wrap and click-wrap licenses. The act, the product of three years of work, is intended to provide a uniform law for software and other computer information transactions and will now be presented to the various state legislatures for consideration and adoption. The act, however, is already subject to much dispute and controversy, with its opponents saying it favors the software, Internet, and banking industries. Attorneys general from twenty-four states oppose the act as presently written, and thus, its adoption in all states is highly uncertain.

- The Copyright Office has recommended that Congress amend section 110 of the Copyright Act to grant educators the right to transmit copyrighted works for distance learning if certain conditions are met (the educational institution must be nonprofit, only officially enrolled students may view the material, and so forth).

- In *Tasini v. New York Times Co.*, Nos. 97-9181 and 97-9650 (2d Cir. Sept. 24, 1999), the court held that the conversion of articles that had appeared in the *Times* in print form to electronic form was a republication of the works such as would entitle authors to additional compensation.

- The U.S. Supreme Court rejected West Publishing Company's appeal from a Second Circuit ruling that West was not entitled to copyright protection for its database of judicial opinions, using its pagination systems. The Second Circuit had held that West's star pagination system and additions of attorney information and parallel citations to cases in the public domain were not sufficiently original to qualify for copyright protection. As a consequence of this ruling, West and other database publishers are now looking toward Congress rather than the courts, hoping that Congress will pass some form of database protection law (see earlier discussion of "Copyright Protection for Automated Databases" in this chapter) that will result in protection for its compilations of judicial opinions.

- Copyright experts are debating whether file retrieval by "intelligent agents," akin to web robots, that monitor the Internet, search for files on behalf of users, and copy the files for later viewing and use, constitutes infringement.
- Many Internet service providers are now introducing privacy policies, allowing customers to prohibit or limit distribution of information about themselves to others and prohibiting collection of information relating to children unless parental permission is granted.

One of the music industry's greatest concerns is the development of technology called MP3 ("Moving Picture Experts Group 1, Audio Layer 3") that allows consumers to download music from the Internet and store it on pager-size devices or play it on a computer's speakers with vivid clarity. The Recording Industry Association of America is leading the effort to develop a copyright-secure format for downloading music from the Internet to protect the rights of performers. A similar method for distributing and downloading movies over the Internet is causing controversy and debate, with motion picture companies concerned that the format will lead to unprecedented piracy on the Internet.

While many authors and copyright owners are justifiably concerned over infringement of their works by electronic means, a number of other experts compare the situation to that faced by the music industry several years ago when it became possible to make copies of tapes and CDs. For years people have been able to borrow books and tapes from friends and libraries, and yet there remains a strong market for the sale of books and music. Thus, many experts believe that although some measures and controls are needed to reduce electronic infringement and piracy, there is no need for panic, at least not yet.

TERMS OF THE TRADE

Following is a glossary of some terms currently used in discussing availability of works in the electronic age:

softlifting: The act of software piracy by which one makes unauthorized copies of computer software

copyhoarding: Retaining all rights in a work and refusing to allow others to use it

shareware: Copyrighted software that has been released under the condition that if the user likes it, the user will pay a license fee therefor

copylefting: Licensing users of software to use it for any purpose

- **Softlifting.** Loading unauthorized copies of software into other computers, a practice frequently encountered in small businesses that do not wish to incur the expense of buying software for each computer and by consumers who share software with friends and family.
- **Copyhoarding.** Retaining all rights in a work, especially software, and refusing to allow others to view it, reproduce it, display it, or use it in any way.
- **Shareware.** Releasing copyrighted software under the condition that if the user likes what he or she sees, the user will pay a license fee.
- **Copylefting.** Licensing all users of software to have free and unfettered access and rights for any purpose and requiring that any improvements or adaptations they make to the work be similarly treated. This concept is even more permissive than that allowed for works in the public domain, which, although not protected, may serve as the source for derivative works that can then be copyrighted and protected from

unauthorized use. Copylefting ensures that any derivative works based on the original work remain as freely available as the underlying work.

- **Freeware.** Allowing others to use software for free but retaining rights to ensure the work is not reverse engineered or disassembled.
- **Downstream infringement.** Infringement by users who obtain copyrighted items from legitimate users. Thus, if a licensee allows X to make an unauthorized copy of a software program, X is a downstream infringer (and the licensee is likely liable for contributory infringement).

SEMICONDUCTOR CHIP PROTECTION

Introduction to the Semiconductor Chip Protection Act

Semiconductor chips are used in wide array of products, including watches, microwave ovens, televisions, automobiles, and computers. Development and engineering of the complex chips can cost millions of dollars, yet once created, chips can be easily copied. Copyright law does not provide adequate protection for the chips inasmuch as they are useful products and cannot be copyrighted (although the design drawings of chips are copyrightable). Neither does patent law provide adequate protection because the chips generally do not meet the strict standards that patentable material be nonobvious (see Chapter 17). Furthermore, issuance of a patent typically takes two years, and given the rapidity of technological advances, chips are often nearly obsolete by the time a patent might issue.

In 1984, Congress fashioned a solution to the lack of protection for semiconductor chips by enacting the Semiconductor Chip Protection Act. The act creates an entirely new form of intellectual property right in semiconductor chips, one that is different from either copyright law or patent law. As such, it is said to be *sui generis* (literally, "the only one of its kind"). Nevertheless, many of the concepts relating to protection, registration, and infringement of chips draw from copyright law. The act is found in title 17 of the United States Code, after the copyright statutes (17 U.S.C. § 901 *et seq.*). The Copyright Office offers Circular 100, entitled "Federal Statutory Protection for Mask Works," to provide information about semiconductor chip protection and registration of mask works. The circular can be downloaded from the Copyright Office's web site.

Protectable Matter

The act protects **mask works,** which are the stencils used to etch, pattern, or encode an electronic circuit on a semiconductor chip. A **semiconductor chip** is defined as any product "having two or more layers of metallic, insulating, or semiconductor material, deposited or otherwise placed on, or etched away or otherwise removed from, a piece of semiconductor material . . . and intended to perform electronic circuitry functions." 17 U.S.C. § 901(a)(1).

To be protected, the mask work must be "fixed," meaning that it must be capable of being perceived or reproduced for more than some transitory period. Additionally, the mask work must be original. It must be independently created and cannot consist of some commonplace variation of an already existing design.

freeware: Software that is allowed to be used for free but in which certain rights are maintained to ensure the work is not reverse engineered

downstream infringement: Infringement by users who obtain copyrighted items from legitimate users

mask works: Stencils used to etch or encode an electronic circuit on a semiconductor chip

semiconductor chip: A product having two or more layers of metallic, insulating, or semiconductor material placed on or removed from semiconductor material and intended to perform electronic circuitry functions

Duration of Protection and Exclusive Rights

Protection for a mask work commences on the date the mask work is registered with the Copyright Office or on the date on which it is first commercially exploited (generally meaning the offer, sale, or distribution to the public) anywhere in the world, whichever occurs first. Protection lasts for ten years from the date protection begins.

The mask work owner has the following exclusive rights:

- to reproduce the mask work;
- to import or distribute a semiconductor chip product that embodies the mask work; and
- to induce or knowingly to cause another to do the foregoing acts.

The mask owner's rights are infringed by copying of the work. The House Report relating to the act explicitly recognized that the concepts used to determine infringement of copyright (such as substantial similarity and the protection of expression rather than ideas) are applicable to mask works. Thus, a mask work that is substantially similar to a protected work infringes even if it is not an identical copy.

Limitations on the Rights of Mask Works Owners

There are several notable limitations on the exclusive rights granted to mask work owners.

- Similar to copyright law, there is no protection if another mask work is independently created. The act prohibits copying, not independent creation.
- It is not an infringement to reproduce a mask work for teaching, analyzing, or evaluating the concepts or techniques embodied in the mask work. Moreover, it is not an infringement to incorporate the results of this analysis in another original mask work. Thus, mask works can be lawfully reverse engineered.
- Also similar to copyright law, protection does not extend to ideas, systems, processes, or methods of operation, but only to the expression of those ideas in the mask work.
- In another borrowing from copyright law, the "first sale" doctrine applies such that a person who lawfully obtains a semiconductor chip product may later use, sell, or otherwise dispose of it (as long as the work is not reproduced). Thus, after lawfully purchasing the product, the owner may thereafter also sell, import, distribute, use, or dispose of the semiconductor chip product.

Registration and Notice of Protection

Registration of a mask work is highly similar to that of registration of copyrights. An application is made with the Copyright Office (using Form MW), identifying matter must be deposited with the application. The fee is $75. However, an application must be made within two years after the work is first commercially exploited. Protection for a mask work terminates if an application is not made with the Copyright Office within that two-year period. Thus,

registration is encouraged by providing a longer period of protection for registered works (ten years) than for nonregistered works (two years).

The registration process for mask works is nearly identical to that for copyrights in that the examination by the Copyright Office is not exhaustive. If the
application is correctly completed, the deposited materials are sufficient, and
the fee is paid, the registration will be issued, generally within four months.
Few refusals are made.

The mask work owner may affix a notice of protection to the mask work and
to masks and semiconductor chip products embodying the mask works. The
notice is not a prerequisite for protection, although it constitutes *prima facie*
evidence of notice of protection. The notice consists of the words "mask work,"
the symbol "M," or the letter "M" in a circle, and the name of the owner of the
mask work. No date is needed. The notice is usually placed on a label attached
to the packaging for the product.

Infringement of Mask Works

A person who violates any of the exclusive rights of a mask work owner may
be sued for infringement. To bring an action in federal court for infringement,

ROLE OF INTELLECTUAL PROPERTY PROFESSIONAL

Because copyright issues confronting users, authors, legislators, and judges are continuing to
evolve, the primary task of IP professionals may be simply to monitor the issues by continuing
research. Specifically, practitioners may be involved in the following tasks:

- preparing and monitoring copyright applications for computer programs and automated databases;
- tracking legislation relating to copyright using LEXIS or WESTLAW or the free and accessible Internet sites THOMAS (http://thomas.loc.gov), Government Printing Office Access offering access to public laws and various congressional documents at http://www.access.gpo.gov,
  or the Senate and House home pages at http://www.senate.gov and http://www.house.gov;
- monitoring articles, bulletin boards, and other postings on the Internet for information relating to copyrights in the electronic age;
- reviewing legal periodicals and journals for articles relating to emerging copyright issues;
- assisting in preparing newsletters and bulletins for clients to inform them of developments in
  the field;
- assisting clients in developing copyright compliance policies to ensure their employees do not
  infringe copyrights of others;
- reviewing clients' web sites and other electronic materials to ensure copyright notices are displayed at those sites;
- reviewing web sites of competitors of clients to ascertain whether clients' copyrighted materials are being infringed or whether links to clients' sites are being improperly used;
- preparing and monitoring applications for registration of mask works; and
- ensuring that clients' mask works (or the containers therefor) contain the proper mask work
  notice.

however, the owner must have registered the mask work (or been refused registration by the Copyright Office). The action must be brought within three years after the claim accrues. Actual damages and the infringer's profits may be awarded to the mask work owner. Alternatively, similar to copyright actions, the owner may elect statutory damages (up to $250,000). A court may enjoin further infringement and may impound and destroy infringing works and the drawings by which infringing chips are reproduced. Attorneys' fees and costs may be awarded.

CHAPTER SUMMARY

Computer programs and automated databases are copyrightable and may be registered with the Copyright Office as literary works. As original works of expression, computer programs are protectable against infringement. Nevertheless, a number of cases have held that purely functional elements of programs, stock or standard scenes a faire, and merged ideas and expressions cannot be protected. To hold otherwise would grant developers of computer programs a monopoly and would discourage creative expression. Computer programs may be reverse engineered in certain instances, for example, when it is necessary to gain access to unprotected elements of a program.

The ease with which works may be copied, stored, reproduced, and disseminated by electronic means, primarily the Internet, has caused much debate among authors and owners of works who are concerned about infringement of their works and those who believe that information "needs to be free." The Clinton administration implemented a task force to examine the issues, and its recommendations have been set forth in proposed legislation that would amend the Copyright Act. Other pending legislation would also amend the act. Some experts believe that technology itself can solve the challenges of the electronic age: devices can be constructed that would encrypt or protect works and prevent them from being copied or transmitted unless permission or royalties are first obtained. In the interim, the Copyright Act is sufficiently muscular to protect works from infringement by electronic means. Thus, copying and transmitting works over the Internet is subject to risk.

Because neither patent law nor copyright law afforded sufficient protection for complex and expensively developed semiconductor chips, Congress enacted the Semiconductor Chip Protection Act of 1984. The act creates an entirely new form of intellectual property protection for mask works, the stencils used to pattern or encode semiconductor chips. Mask works may be registered with the Copyright Office and are protected against infringement.

DISCUSSION QUESTIONS

1. Where should a copyright notice for a computer program appear?
2. Greg has purchased a software program at a local store. It is subject to a shrink-wrap license stating the program is licensed to Greg but owned by the maker. Is the first sale doctrine applicable so that Greg, having purchased the program, can now sell it to another? Discuss.
3. A computer program for a financial management system can be expressed in only one way. Is it copyrightable? Discuss.
4. Why is the "ordinary observer" test not used in cases involving infringement of computer programs?
5. An automated database created by Sandra exactly reproduces a list of sports statistics found in Sandra's earlier published book. Is the automated database copyrightable? Discuss.
6. Is it advisable to link one's web site to another's? Discuss.
7. Why should a notice of copyright be placed on works that will be placed on the Internet?
8. MX Development Corporation began marketing and selling its semiconductor chip in May 1996. May the company secure a mask work registration for the chip embodying the mask work?

16

International Developments in Copyright Law

There is no international copyright law that protects copyrighted works in every country. More than one hundred and thirty-five nations, however, adhere to the Berne Convention, the terms of which require members to treat nationals of other member countries like their own nationals for purposes of copyright. By joining the Berne Convention in 1989, the United States was required to make some changes to its copyright laws, notably, eliminating the requirement that works be accompanied by a copyright notice in order to receive protection and allowing owners of works not originating in the United States to sue in federal court for copyright infringement even if they did not possess a copyright registration. New treaties supplementing the Berne Convention ensure that copyrighted works are protected from infringement by any means, including electronic means, and prohibit attempts to defeat encryption or protection of copyrighted works. The United States is also a party to the Universal Copyright Convention and the Uruguay Round Agreements Act.

INTRODUCTION

Nearly one million books and other literary titles, five thousand feature films, and three million songs are published worldwide each year. Yet there is no such thing as "international copyright" that will protect an author's work throughout the world. Protection generally is afforded on a country-by-country basis. However, most countries offer protection to foreign works under international conventions and treaties. There are two principal international copyright treaties or conventions: the Berne Convention for the Protection of Literary and Artistic Property (Berne Convention) and the Universal Copyright Convention (UCC).

Authors who desire protection for their works in foreign countries should first determine the scope of protection available to works of foreign authors in that country. Determination should be done prior to publication of the work in any country inasmuch as the extent of protection afforded to a work may depend on facts existing at the time of first publication anywhere. The laws of most countries provide that copyright protection exists independently of any formalities and that it is not necessary to register a copyright to achieve protection for a work.

If the country in which protection is sought is a party to one of the international copyright conventions, the work generally may be protected by complying with the conditions of that convention. Even if the work cannot be protected under an international convention, protection may still be available under the specific laws of a foreign country. Some countries, however, offer little or no copyright protection to foreign works.

THE BERNE CONVENTION

The Berne Convention was created in 1886 under the leadership of Victor Hugo to protect literary and artistic works and has more than one hundred and thirty-five member nations (see Appendix A for a table of nations adhering to the Berne Convention). In 1989, the United States became a party to the Berne Convention by entering into an international treaty called the Berne Convention for the Protection of Literary and Artistic Works. The Berne Convention is administered by the World Intellectual Property Organization (WIPO), an organization whose objective is to promote the protection of intellectual property throughout the world. The Berne Convention is based on the precept that each member nation must treat nationals of other member countries like its own nationals for purposes of copyright (the principle of **national treatment**).

Moreover, the Berne Convention has established certain minimum levels of copyright protection to which all member nations must adhere (such as specifying that all members must recognize that authors have the exclusive rights to perform, broadcast, adapt, and reproduce their works), ensuring that copyright laws in the member nations will share many features. The Berne Convention also provides that copyright protection cannot be conditioned upon compliance with any registration formalities, thus clarifying that works are automatically protected without requiring notice of copyright or registration. Finally, the Berne Convention provides that works are protected independently of the existence of protection in the country of origin of the work. If a work originates in one of the more than one hundred and thirty-five member nations of the Berne Union, it is entitled to protection in all other member nations. A work's "country of origin" is usually the place of its first publication. Generally, works are protected under the Berne Convention for a minimum of fifty years after the author's death, though member nations may provide for a longer term, as has the United States.

In order to fulfill its obligations under the Berne Convention, the United States made certain changes in its copyright laws, effective after March 1, 1989, the date the United States acceded to the Berne Convention. Perhaps the most

national treatment: Principle that member countries adhering to a treaty guarantee to the citizens of other member adherents the same rights in intellectual property matters that they provide to their own citizens

significant change to U.S. copyright law was that the mandatory notice of copyright (for example, © 1988 John Doe) that was previously required in the United States was abolished so that failure to place a notice on copyrighted works would no longer result in the loss of copyright. Thus, for all works published after March 1, 1989, use of a copyright notice is voluntary (although it is strongly recommended, since use of a notice will preclude a party from asserting its infringement was innocent, which claim might reduce damages in an infringement action).

The Berne Convention also recognizes "moral rights" (the rights of authors to claim authorship of their works and to object to any mutilation or modification of the work that would be prejudicial to the author's reputation or honor). In 1989, in order to become a party to the Berne Convention, the United States for the first time recognized moral rights; however, the scope of moral rights afforded in the United States is less extensive than in many other countries inasmuch as the Visual Artists Rights Act (17 U.S.C. § 106A) provides moral rights only to works of fine arts.

As discussed in Chapter 14, before a copyright infringement suit is brought for a work of U.S. origin, the work must be submitted to the Copyright Office for registration. Works originating in Berne Union countries are exempt from the requirement to register before bringing suit. Authors whose works originate in the United States, however, are still subject to the requirement of registering their work (or showing they attempted to register but registration was refused).

TREATIES SUPPLEMENTING THE BERNE CONVENTION

In December 1996, WIPO convened in Geneva, Switzerland, to work on the first amendment to international copyright laws in twenty-five years, action that was primarily spurred by concern over piracy of copyrighted works through the Internet. Authors, of course, are concerned that the value of their works will be diminished by unauthorized reproduction and transmission, and Internet service providers are concerned they may face liability for contributory or vicarious infringement based on the fact that their services are used to carry out infringing activities.

Two treaties, the WIPO Copyright Treaty and the WIPO Performances and Phonograms Treaty, were adopted at the Geneva conference and are now being considered for ratification by individual countries. In late 1998, in the Digital Millenium Copyright Act (17 U.S.C. § 1201 *et seq.*), the United States agreed to be bound by the treaties. The WIPO Copyright Treaty expressly states that computer programs are protected by copyright as literary works and makes it clear that authors' rights of distribution extend to electronic distribution by granting authors the exclusive right to distribute, sell, or rent their works via electronic means. The Copyright Treaty also requires adhering nations to provide remedies against any person who removes or alters electronic rights management information (information about copyright works, authors, and owners that is appended or attached to works in electronic form) and to provide adequate legal protection against the circumvention of security or encryption devices used by authors to protect their works. The act prohibits both the use of circumvention methods and the manufacturing or offering of circumvention devices. Circumvention is permissible for computer security testing, encryption research, certain library uses, and for law enforcement activities. The WIPO Performance Treaty provides similar rights, granting protection to sound recordings first fixed in a treaty member country.

Neither treaty addresses liability of Internet service providers for copyright infringement using the Internet, although legislation passed in late 1998 in the United States (17 U.S.C. § 512(c)) as part of the Digital Millennium Copyright Act clarifies that Internet services providers are not liable for infringement if they do not know of such acts and if they do not profit from them. Upon receiving notification of claimed infringement, the service providers must expeditiously take down or remove access to the material. Finally, although much discussion occurred relating to whether databases resulting from a substantial investment of time and effort should be protected, the parties could not reach agreement; however, they did agree that databases consisting of original work could be protected. Recall that the United States expressly rejected the "sweat of the brow" doctrine in *Feist Publications v. Rural Telephone Service Co.,* 499 U.S. 340 (1991), holding that a telephone directory consisting merely of facts could not be copyrighted even if it was the result of much effort. The conference adopted a recommendation calling for another session to further discuss database protection inasmuch as many experts fear that extending database protection rights to compilations resulting from effort and time would result in sports statistics, weather information, stock market information, and transportation schedules all being monopolized by the first to compile the data. As discussed in Chapter 15, Congress is considering extending copyright protection to databases produced through investment of substantial time and money (although databases generated with government funding would likely remain available for all to use, and the fair use of information in databases would be protected). If passed, the bill (H.R. 354) would create an entirely new form of copyright protection for databases and would nullify *Feist* to some extent because it would protect collections of information or data that might not otherwise be copyrightable. The bill is subject to much debate and an uncertain future.

THE URUGUAY ROUND AGREEMENTS ACT

In December 1994, President Clinton signed the Uruguay Round Agreements Act (URAA) that implements the Uruguay Round General Agreement on Tariffs and Trade (GATT), which itself includes an agreement on Trade-Related Aspects of Intellectual Property (TRIPS).

The URAA amended federal copyright law in several ways, including the addition of civil and criminal penalties to provide remedies for "bootlegging" sound recordings of live musical performances and music videos. Prior to this amendment, U.S. copyright law generally protected only the fixed work (such as the song being performed) rather than the live performance itself. The new provisions prohibit unauthorized recording or broadcasts of live performances and reproduction or distribution of unauthorized fixations of the work.

Equally important, the URAA also provided for the automatic restoration of copyright in certain foreign works (but not U.S. domestic works) that had fallen into the public domain in the United States but were protected by copyright in their countries of origin. Typically, works from eligible countries had fallen into the public domain because their authors failed to comply with formalities required by the United States, such as including a notice of copyright on the work or renewing the work (during the time when the United States required copyright notice and had a renewal period for copyrighted works).

Eligible copyrights are restored automatically and remain protectable for the term they would have enjoyed had they not entered the public domain. However, the URAA directs that the owner of a restored work notify "reliance parties" (parties who, relying on the public domain status of the work, were using the work prior to its automatic restoration under the URAA) if the owner of rights in a restored work intends to enforce his or her rights. Either actual notice may be given to a reliance party, or constructive notice may be given through filing a "Notice of Intent to Enforce" with the Copyright Office. The reliance party then has a grace period of twelve months to sell off its existing stock, publicly perform the work, or phase out its reproduction, distribution, performance, or display of the work.

The **World Trade Organization (WTO)** was established in 1995 to implement the Uruguay Round Agreements, serve as a forum for trade negotiations, handle trade disputes, and monitor national trade policies. It has more than one hundred and thirty members. (See Appendix A.) The United States has been a member of the WTO since 1995. The WIPO and the WTO cooperate to provide assistance to developing countries with respect to intellectual property rights and laws.

THE UNIVERSAL COPYRIGHT CONVENTION

The United States became a party to the **Universal Copyright Convention** (UCC) in 1955, more than thirty years before the United States became a party to the Berne Convention; thus, the UCC was the first international convention relating to copyright to which the United States was subject. Similar to the Berne Convention, the UCC requires that works originating in a member nation must be given the same protection in each of the other member nations as is granted by the laws of the country of origin. The UCC imposes fewer minimum standards on its members than does the Berne Convention. The UCC provides that use of a copyright notice in a prescribed form (the © symbol, accompanied by the year of first publication and the name of the copyright owner) will satisfy notice requirements in all other member nations. Because the Berne Convention imposes requirements that are stricter than those of the UCC, to ensure members would not drop out of the Berne Convention and rely strictly on the UCC, the UCC provides that no Berne member may withdraw from Berne and later rely on the UCC in its relations with other Berne members. Additionally, the Berne Convention takes precedence over the UCC inasmuch as the terms of the Berne Convention, rather than those of the UCC, apply to relationships among Berne members, even though those parties may also be members of the UCC. Some Berne member countries joined the UCC to establish relations with nations that are not members of Berne (such as British Virgin Islands, Gibraltar, and Saint Helena).

World Trade Organization (WTO): An international organization established in 1995 with more than one hundred and thirty member countries, created by the Uruguay Round negotiations to handle trade disputes and monitor national trade policies

Universal Copyright Convention (UCC): An international convention relating to copyright requiring that works originating in a member nation must be given the same protection in all member nations as is granted by the country of origin of the work

GRAY MARKET GOODS

Section 602(a) of the Copyright Act bars importation of copyrighted goods into the United States without the authority of the copyright owner (the goods are referred to as "gray market" goods because they are lawfully made as opposed to pirated "black market" goods). In 1998, the Supreme Court held that a copyright holder loses control over subsequent sales of material produced in the United States once a "first sale" has occurred anywhere. In *Quality King Distributors, Inc. v. L'anza Research International,* 523 U.S. 135 (1998), a product was manufactured in the United States and then exported for exclusive sale outside the United States. The product was then imported back into the United States without the copyright owner's permission. The copyright owner alleged that such importation violated its exclusive right to distribute the product. The defendant contended that once a first sale of the product occurred abroad, the copyright owner's exclusive right to distribute was exhausted. The Supreme Court agreed that once the first sale occurred, even abroad, the owner of the work or product could resell the item anywhere without permission of the copyright holder.

Copyright holders are concerned over this ruling, and some experts believe they will attempt to use provisions in their contracts barring importation of goods into the United States, move their manufacturing or production abroad, or lobby Congress for a change in the law to ensure their domestic revenues are not undercut by identical goods intended for export only.

SUMMARY OF UNITED STATES RELATIONS WITH FOREIGN NATIONS

The United States is a party to various copyright conventions, agreements, and treaties with other nations. Following is a summary of some of the agreements and treaties to which the United States is a party:

- **Berne Convention.** The United States is a party to the Berne Convention as of March 1989. The Berne Convention provides protection to literary and artistic works, including computer programs.
- **Universal Copyright Convention.** The United States has been a party to the Universal Copyright Convention since September 16, 1955.
- **WIPO Copyright Treaties.** The United States implemented the WIPO Copyright Treaty and WIPO Performances and Phonograms Treaty in late 1998.
- **World Trade Organization.** The United States has been a member of the World Trade Organization, established to implement the Uruguay Round Agreements, since 1995.

ROLE OF INTELLECTUAL PROPERTY PROFESSIONAL

Unless a client sells or distributes its products or works abroad, involvement by IP practitioners with international copyright issues will be minimal. Nevertheless, inasmuch as works can now be sold or distributed in foreign countries merely by the touch of a computer key, some familiarity with international copyright protection is needed. Intellectual property professionals will likely be involved in the following tasks:

- monitoring issues related to international copyright by reading journals, articles, and other materials;
- gathering information and publications from the United States Copyright Office related to international copyright protection, such as Circular 38a entitled "International Copyright Relations of the United States" and Circular 38b entitled "Highlights of Copyright Amendments Contained in the Uruguay Round Agreements Act";
- retrieving the text of treaties to which the United States is a party either by locating them in conventional print form at law libraries or locating them on the Internet (the Berne Convention and its supplementary treaties can be located through WIPO at http://www.wipo.org, and the Universal Copyright Convention can be located through the United Nations site at http://www.un.org); and
- routinely monitoring various web sites (see the resources in Appendix C) related to intellectual property to keep abreast of new developments in the international arena.

CHAPTER SUMMARY

There is no one treaty or agreement governing copyright throughout the world. More than one hundred and thirty-five nations, however, belong to the Berne Convention, which is based on the principle of national treatment: each member nation must treat works originating in other member nations as it does its own domestic works. Recent supplements to the Berne Convention clarify that computer programs are protectable literary works, that unauthorized reproduction or distribution of a work by electronic means is infringement, and that devices that defeat copyright security measures such as encryption are prohibited. The international copyright community is struggling with the issues presented by the ease and rapidity of electronic communications, just as is the United States.

To comply with its commitments under the Berne Convention, the United States was required to modify its copyright law, primarily to eliminate any requirement for a copyright notice for a work to be protectable and to allow owners of works not originating in the United States to sue in federal court for copyright infringement even if they did not possess a U.S. registration for their work.

The United States is also a party to the Universal Copyright Convention and the Uruguay Round Agreements Act that required the United States to amend its copyright law to allow restoration of copyright for works that had fallen into the public domain due to lack of copyright notice or failure to renew the work during the time the United States required renewal.

DISCUSSION QUESTIONS

1. France and Spain are both members of the Berne Convention. Assume a work originated in France. Its author now wishes to distribute the work in Spain. Can Spain treat the work differently than it does works originating in Spain? Discuss.
2. May Norway, a member of the Berne Convention, require registration of copyright in Norway as a prerequisite to protecting a work originating in the United States? Discuss.
3. May Chile, a member of the Berne Convention, provide that protection for literary works extends for the author's life plus thirty years? Discuss.
4. Why would a country join the Universal Copyright Convention when it is based on the principle of national treatment, just as is the Berne Convention?
5. The owner of a work originating in Austria, a member of the Berne Convention, secured a copyright registration in the United States in 1950. The owner failed to renew the work, and the work fell into the public domain. A third party, knowing the work was in the public domain, began distributing the work. The owner would like to restore the copyright. What agreement governs and what will happen to the rights of the third party?
6. ABC, a U.S. author, manufactured a copyrighted work in the United States. The work was then sold abroad and is being imported back into the United States at a lower price. Can ABC stop the importation of the goods? Discuss.

PART
IV

The Law of
Patents

CHAPTER
17
Foundations of Patent Law

A patent is a legal right granted by the federal government that permits its owner to prevent others from making, using, or selling an invention. There are three types of patents: utility patents, design patents, and plant patents. The great majority of patents are utility patents, granted for useful objects or processes. Patents are generally granted to the first to invent, assuming the invention or discovery is not known or used by others in the United States or patented or described in a printed publication in the United States or elsewhere.

Not all discoveries or inventions are eligible for utility patent protection. Patent protection is available only for a new and useful process, machine, manufacture, or composition of matter, or any new and useful improvement thereof. Thus, an inventor must demonstrate that the invention or discovery is useful, novel, and nonobvious. Generally, patent law prohibits the patenting of an invention that is merely an insignificant addition to or alteration of something already in existence or already known.

Some items are excluded from patent protection. For example, a mere arrangement of printed matter, a naturally existing substance, some methods of doing business, and a scientific principle are unpatentable subject matter.

Applications for patents are filed with the U.S. Patent and Trademark Office (PTO), and protection begins only when a patent is issued by the PTO (as opposed to trademark protection, which arises from first use rather than registration with the PTO, and copyright protection, which arises from creation of a work rather than from registration with the Copyright Office).

INTRODUCTION TO PATENTS

The word *patent* is a shorthand expression for "letters patent." A **patent** is a grant from the United States government to exclude others from making, using, or selling another person's new, nonobvious, and useful invention in the United States for the term of patent protection. After this period of exclusive

patent: A grant from the U.S. government permitting its owner to exclude others from making, selling, or using an invention for a limited period of time

protection (twenty years from filing for utility and plant patents and fourteen years from grant for design patents), the invention falls into the public domain and may be used by any person without permission. This right of exclusion is far different from the rights provided under copyright law. Under patent law, inventors can enjoin the making, using, or selling of an infringing invention *even if it was independently created.* In contrast, copyright law protects only original works of authorship. If two writers independently compose the same poem, both are protected under copyright law. A patent allows its owner to exclude others from using the owner's invention; it does not provide any guarantee that its owner can sell the invention.

To obtain a patent, an inventor must file an application with the PTO, the same agency of the Department of Commerce that issues trademark registrations. The application must describe the invention with specificity. The application will be reviewed by a PTO examiner, and, if approved, the patent will issue. The patent is a written document that fully describes the invention.

Just as U.S. copyright law derives from the Constitution, so does patent law. The U.S. Constitution provides that Congress shall have the power "to promote the progress of science and useful arts, by securing for limited times to authors and inventors the exclusive right to their respective writings and discoveries." U.S. Const. art. I, § 8. The wording applicable to patents is *science, useful arts, inventors,* and *discoveries.*

Patents promote the public good in that patent protection incentivizes inventors. If inventors of useful discoveries could not protect their works from use or exploitation by others, there would be little motivation to expend effort, time, and money in creating inventions. The introduction of new products and processes benefits society. In return for the full disclosure to the public of the specifics of the invention, thus advancing science and technology, the inventor is given a limited period of time within which to exploit his or her invention and exclude others from doing so. Inventors are thus incentivized to create new products, and the public benefits from inventions that ultimately will fall into the public domain.

RIGHTS UNDER FEDERAL LAW

As stated, patent law derives from the Constitution. In 1790, pursuant to the direction provided in the Constitution, Congress passed the first patent statute, which in large part relied upon English law. Just three years later, the statute was replaced with a new act authored by Thomas Jefferson. These early acts provided the structural framework for U.S. patent law and specified the four basic conditions, still existing, that an invention must satisfy to secure patent protection:

1. the invention must be a utility, design, or plant patent;
2. it must be useful (or ornamental in the case of a design patent or distinctive in the case of a plant patent);
3. it must be novel in relation to the prior art in the field; and
4. it must not be obvious to a person of ordinary skill in the field.

Revisions of federal patent statutes occurred in 1836 when the Patent Office was created and again in 1870 and 1897. Thereafter, in 1952, Congress enacted a new patent act, codified in title 35 of the *United States Code*. This was the last major revision to federal patent statutes. Issues relating to patents are resolved solely by federal law. Moreover, development of patent law has evolved primarily through federal court decisions rather than the legislature. Just as seen in copyright law, where the term *writings* has been held to be broad enough to cover emerging technologies such as computer programs, the language in the 1793 act relating to the protectability of machines, manufactures, art (later changed to *process*), and composition is broad enough to cover new developments such as computers and electronics. In 1982, Congress created a new court, the Court of Appeals for the Federal Circuit (CAFC), to exercise exclusive jurisdiction over all cases involving patent issues and to promote uniform interpretation of the U.S. patent statutes, which until then had been interpreted in often inconsistent ways by the various federal courts of appeals throughout the nation.

Unlike trademark and copyright law, both of which recognize common law rights in marks and works of authorship even without federal registration, patent law requires that an inventor secure issuance of a patent to protect and enforce his or her rights against infringers. Inventors, however, may also secure some protection for their works under trade secret law (see Chapter 22). Moreover, some inventions, such as computer programs, are protectable under copyright law as well as patent law.

UNITED STATES PATENT AND TRADEMARK OFFICE

Patents exist only by authority of government grant. The department of the government responsible for granting patents is the Department of Commerce, acting through the PTO. The PTO receives applications, reviews them, and issues or grants patents. The PTO also publishes and disseminates patent information, records assignments of patents, maintains files of U.S. and foreign patents, and maintains a search room for public use in examining issued patents and records. The address and information given in Chapter 2 for the PTO for trademark applications, namely, Commissioner of Patents and Trademarks, Patent and Trademark Office, Washington, DC 20231, are also used for patent applications and information. Additionally, the PTO web site (http://www.uspto.gov) offers a wealth of general information, forms for downloading, patent statistics, news updates about issues affecting the PTO and patent practice, schedules of patent fees, and other valuable information.

As secretary of state, Thomas Jefferson was the first head of the Patent Office. Legend has it that the reason the files in which patents are kept and maintained are called *shoes* is that the first patent applications were stored in Jefferson's shoeboxes.

The rules and regulations relating to examination and issuance of patents are found in the PTO publication *Manual of Patent Examining Procedure* **(MPEP)**, which most practitioners keep handy to serve as a reference tool for patent issues and questions. The entire text of the MPEP is available for viewing and downloading at the PTO web site.

A variety of methods for locating patents are available. The Franklin Pierce Intellectual Property Mall (http://www.ipmall.fplc.edu) provides links to a variety of patent-related sites, including one listing famous patents, from Eli Whitney's cotton gin, to the application by Orville and Wilbur Wright for the

Manual of Patent Examining Procedure **(MPEP):** A PTO publication containing rules and regulations relating to examination and issuance of patents

FIGURE 17–1
Famous U.S. Patents

Patent Number	Inventor	Description	Date of Issuance
None	Eli Whitney	Cotton gin	3/14/1794
None	Samuel Colt	Revolver	2/25/1836
1,647	Samuel F.B. Morse	Telegraph	6/20/1840
3,630	Linus Yale	Door lock	6/13/1844
6,281	Walter Hunt	Safety pin	4/10/1849
6,469	Abraham Lincoln	Buoying boats over shoals	5/22/1849
13,661	Isaac Singer	Sewing machine	10/9/1855
22,186	John Mason	Mason jar	11/30/1858
127,568	Richard Chesebrough	VASELINE®	6/4/1872
140,245	Samuel Clemens	Scrapbook	6/24/1873
174,465	Alexander Graham Bell	Telephone	3/7/1876
182,346	Melville Bissell	Carpet sweeper	9/19/1876
223,898	Thomas Edison	Electric light	1/27/1880
388,850	George Eastman	Roll film camera	9/4/1888
473,653	Sarah Boone	Ironing board for sleeves	4/26/1892
504,038	Whitcomb Judson	Zipper	8/29/1893
644,077	Felix Hoffman	Aspirin	2/27/1900
686,046	Henry Ford	Automobile	11/5/1901
775,135	King Gillette	GILLETTE® safety razor	11/15/1904
821,393	Wilbur and Orville Wright	Airplane	5/22/1906
1,102,653	Robert Goddard	Two-stage rocket	7/7/1914
1,242,872	Clarence Saunders	Supermarket	10/9/1917
1,370,316	Harry Houdini	Diver's suit	3/1/1921
2,071,250	Wallace Carothers	Nylon	2/16/1937
2,177,627	Richard Drew	SCOTCH® cellophane tape	10/31/1939
2,682,235	Buckminster Fuller	Geodesic dome	6/29/1954
2,799,619	Seifter, Monaco, & Hoover	Tranquilizer	7/16/1957
4,270,182	Satya Asija	First computer program (software)	5/26/1981

airplane, to the first application for a computer program. Another site identifies the "wacky patent of the month" and references issued patents for oddities such as hay fragrance and eye protectors for chickens. Numerous other links are provided to articles and information of interest to IP practitioners. Another way of locating and retrieving issued patents is through the PTO patent database, which provides links to all patents issued since 1976 and allows searching by patent number or by topic (using Boolean connectors).

Nearly six million patents have been issued since the first patent in 1790. The patent office is increasingly busy. In 1998, two hundred and fifty thousand applications were filed. Many experts attribute the onslaught of filings to applications for software and Internet-related inventions.

(See Figure 17–1 for a list of famous patents issued in the United States.)

PATENTABILITY

An invention must satisfy four basic requirements to be eligible for patent protection:

1. the invention must be one of the types specified by statute as patentable subject matter (namely, a utility, design, or plant patent);
2. the invention must be useful;
3. the invention must be novel; and
4. the invention must be nonobvious.

Patentable Subject Matter—Utility Patents

There are three distinct types of patents: utility patents, design patents, and plant patents. Utility patents are the most common and cover a wide variety of inventions and discoveries including the typewriter, the automobile, the sewing machine, the geodesic dome, the helicopter, sulfa drugs, gene sequences, and genetically altered mice. Design patents cover new, original, and ornamental designs for useful articles such as furniture and containers. Plant patents cover new and distinct plant varieties, such as hybrid flowers or trees. Because the vast majority of patents are utility patents, they will be discussed first. Design and plant patents will be discussed later in this chapter.

Federal law establishes the subject matter that can be protected by a **utility patent:** "Whoever invents or discovers any new and useful process, machine, manufacture, or composition of matter, or any new and useful improvement thereof, may obtain a patent therefor . . . ." 35 U.S.C. § 101.

Although ideas are not patentable, processes are. A **process** is a method of doing something to produce a given result. According to *Cochrane v. Deener,* 94 U.S. 780, 787–88 (1877), a process is "an act, or series of acts, performed upon the subject-matter to be transformed and reduced to a different state or thing. If new and useful, it is just as patentable as is a piece of machinery." A patent may be issued for a newly developed process or a new use of an already known process. Some examples of patented processes are the process for chrome plating; the process for making synthetic diamonds; processes for vulcanizing India rubber, smelting ore, tanning, and dyeing; Louis Pasteur's 1873 patented yeast process; and Clarence Birdseye's process for packaging frozen food. In fact, the first patent issued in the United States, to Samuel Hopkins in 1790, was entitled "improved potash process." In some instances, not only the process but also the result of the process is patentable, such as U.S. Pat. No. 5,658,991 for "toner resin composition and a method of manufacturing it," which combines a process (the method of manufacturing) with a composition of matter (the toner resin).

The other types of utility patents (machines, manufactures, and compositions of matter) are all products or items. A **machine** is a device that accomplishes a result, such as a sewing machine or a typewriter. A **manufacture** includes anything under the sun that is made by humans; the term is broad enough to include a pitchfork and the patented Monopoly game. It is often said

utility patent: A patent for a useful article, invention, or discovery

process: A patentable method of doing something to produce a given result

machine: In patent law, a device that accomplishes a result

manufacture: In patent law, anything made by humans

that the category of "manufactures" is a type of catchall category to encompass devices or items not easily classified as machines, compositions of matter, or processes. A **composition of matter** is a combination of two or more chemical or other materials into a product, such as a synthetic diamond or the fabric known as polyester. An invention can also consist of some new use of a process, machine, manufacture, or composition of matter as long as that new use demonstrates significant change from the original invention.

Usefulness

The Constitution itself provides that patent protection is available for "*useful* arts," and 35 U.S.C. § 101, in defining what is patentable, states that patents are available for *useful* processes, machines, manufactures, and compositions of matter. Although **usefulness** is not a stringent standard, the invention must be of some benefit to humanity to be "useful." Mere novelties or inventions that conflict with scientific principles, such as a perpetual motion machine, are not patentable because they are not useful. Similarly, inventions whose only purpose is detrimental or dangerous or would promote illegal ends cannot be patented inasmuch as, by definition, they are not useful. For example, a patent was denied for a process of making a low-cost tobacco leaf that resembled a more select leaf on the basis that its only purpose was to deceive consumers. *Richard v. Du Bon*, 103 F. 868 (2d Cir. 1900).

The usefulness required of an invention must be present usefulness, not usefulness purely for research purposes. Thus, patent protection will be denied to a drug whose usefulness cannot yet be shown or to a process, the result of which produces an article that has no current use. The fact that a drug, invention, or result of a process might show some benefit or usefulness at some time in the future is generally not sufficient and a patent therefor will be denied. Nevertheless, even if an invention or discovery shows no benefit to humans, it will be protected by patent law if usefulness for animals can be shown. Thus, drugs or compounds whose effectiveness has been demonstrated for animals can be patented even though their usefulness for humans cannot yet be shown. *In re Brana*, 51 F.3d 1560 (Fed. Cir. 1995). Applications that claim some drug or other substance is useful for humans must be accompanied by supporting evidence, usually results of tests or trials, and must show the substance is reasonably safe. To secure a patent, an invention need not meet the stricter standards of regulatory agencies such as the Food and Drug Administration; it need only be "reasonably safe."

To ensure that the invention is useful, the application must disclose or specify the usefulness of the invention. To allow a patent that does not specify its utility would be to grant a patent on an entire range of unknown applications, thereby allowing an inventor to obtain a monopoly on an entire field of knowledge. Thus, patent applications must describe their specific advantage or usefulness so the public can benefit from the invention. Similarly, a patent will be denied when an invention fails to operate as described or claimed in the application.

Novelty

Section 101 of the Patent Act requires that an invention (or any improvement to an invention) be "new" or novel. Section 102 of the Patent Act elaborates on the requirement of **novelty** by setting forth certain situations that

composition of matter: In patent law, a combination of two or more chemical or other materials into a product

usefulness: In patent law, a process or invention that is of some present value to humanity

novelty: In patent law, a new invention; one not known or used by another

demonstrate the invention is not novel. Most codify the basic principle that the first to invent will be granted a patent. If an invention is known or used by others, is the subject of an existing patent, or has been described or sold, then it is not novel and, accordingly, is not eligible for patent protection.

Inventions Known or Used by Others—Section 102(a)   Section 102(a) provides that a patent application must be denied if the invention was known or used by others in the United States or patented or described in another's printed publication in the United States or elsewhere before the applicant invented the item or process. In such a case, it is deemed that the applicant's invention was anticipated and an application will be denied. Often called the **doctrine of anticipation,** this principle is intended to ensure that a second or junior inventor does not secure a monopoly on an invention that a senior inventor owns or that is in the public domain.

An invention is "described in a printed publication" when it is printed in nearly any kind of document by any means (including electronic means) and has been made available to the public. Such availability can occur by circulating copies of a document at a conference, releasing advertising brochures, or by disseminating a thesis. Internal business documents or documents provided to others under conditions of confidentiality are not publications within the meaning of the statute.

Invention Is the Subject of a Prior Application—Section 102(e)
Pursuant to section 102(e), an application will be denied if the invention was the subject of a patent granted on an application filed in the United States before its invention by the applicant. Thus, if inventor *A* invents a new type of scissors and files an application for patent for it on June 1, 1998, and *B* invents the same scissors one month later, *A* will have priority (if *A*'s application matures into a patent registration) and inventor *B*'s application will be denied, even if *A*'s invention was not known or used in the United States or described in a printed publication. Because patent applications filed at the PTO are maintained in confidence, inventor *A*'s scissors may not have been known to or used by others, and section 102(e) preserves the rights of the first inventor. Inventor *B*'s invention cannot be novel if it is the subject of an existing patent.

Inventions First Invented by Others—Section 102(g)   Under section 102(g), an application for a patent will be denied if before the applicant's invention, the invention was made in this country by another who had not abandoned, suppressed, or concealed it. Sections 102(a), (e), and (g) are all intended to ensure patents are granted to the first inventor. The second or junior inventor's product or process is not novel in such circumstances.

Abandonment typically requires an express intention to relinquish rights to a patent. Merely failing to file a patent application does not constitute abandonment, suppression, or concealment. Similarly, use of the product under agreements with others to protect the invention as a confidential trade secret is not necessarily concealment or suppression as long as the public is receiving some benefit from the invention. Typically, inventors are required to engage in diligent efforts to bring the invention to the marketplace. Such efforts will help counter a claim the invention has been abandoned, suppressed, or concealed. Because abandonment, suppression, and concealment of information that could be valuable and beneficial to the public are contrary to patent law policy, patent

doctrine of anticipation:
Theory that an invention was known or used by others such that its invention was anticipated

law punishes such acts by allowing the second inventor to secure a patent even though another previously invented the item or process.

In determining priority of invention, the statute provides that the dates the inventors conceived of the invention, the dates they reduced their inventions to practice, and their reasonable diligence in reducing the invention to practice will be considered. As discussed in Chapter 19, reduction to practice can be actual (making or building the invention or a prototype) or constructive (filing an application for a patent after invention).

Invention Is in Use or on Sale—Section 102(b)

A patent will not be granted unless an application is filed less than one year from the time the invention is in public use or on sale in the United States or described by the applicant in a printed publication in any country. This requirement, typically called the **on sale bar,** is intended to ensure that inventors act promptly to secure protection for their inventions. Once an invention is in public use or offered for sale or sold in the United States or is patented or described in a printed publication anywhere, the inventor has a one-year **grace period** or statute of limitations to file an application. Failure to file an application in a timely manner will bar issuance of a patent.

An invention is "in use" if it is being used in the manner intended by the inventor without any confidentiality restrictions. Although primarily experimental use (to test or perfect the invention) or private use by the inventor will not trigger the one-year limitation period, an invention that is "ready for patenting" will start the one-year grace period if there is a commercial offer for sale of the invention. *Pfaff v. Wells Electronics, Inc.,* 119 S. Ct. 304 (1998). In *Pfaff,* the one-year sale bar applied although the inventor had made only engineering drawings and had not yet made the invention although he had accepted an offer to sell the invention. An invention is deemed "on sale" if it is offered for sale, even though no actual sales occur. An invention is "described in a printed publication" if it has been printed by any manner and described in such a way that a person of ordinary skill in the art could make the invention, just as is the case under section 102(a).

Invention Has Been Abandoned—Section 102(c)

A person cannot obtain a patent if he or she has abandoned the invention. As discussed, abandonment is shown when the inventor expressly or impliedly demonstrates an intent to abandon his or her right to a patent.

Invention Is the Subject of a Foreign Patent—Section 102(d)

A patent will be denied to an applicant if the invention was the subject of a patent application in a foreign country filed twelve months before an application in the United States and the patent issued in the foreign country before application was made in the United States.

Inventor Did Not Invent the Invention—Section 102(f)

Only the inventor is entitled to a patent for the invention or discovery. The inventor is the person who conceived the specific invention. An employee who invents an item while on the job remains the inventor. Although the employer may have a contractual right to own any inventions created by employees, a patent application must be filed by the individual inventor. It can, however, be assigned to the employer or another concurrently with filing. Parties who work jointly on an

on sale bar: The doctrine precluding granting of a patent unless a patent application is filed less than one year from the time the invention is in public use, on sale in the United States, or described in the inventor's printed publication anywhere

grace period: A period within which late documents are accepted by the PTO; in patent law, the one-year period within which a patent application must be filed after the invention is in public use, on sale, or described in the inventor's printed publication

invention may be joint inventors even though their contributions are not equal or simultaneous. An application for the resulting invention must name all inventors.

Nonobviousness

Merely because an invention is useful and novel does not automatically entitle it to patent protection. To qualify for a grant of patent, the invention must be nonobvious to those having skill in the field or art to which the subject matter pertains. 35 U.S.C. § 103. The subject matter sought to be patented must be sufficiently different from what has been used or described before that it may be said to be nonobvious to a person having ordinary skill in the area of technology related to the invention. For example, the substitution of one material for another in an invention and mere changes in size are ordinarily not patentable because they are obvious. A distinct improvement, however, is patentable even if the new invention improves matter in the public domain. Similarly, a new use of a known process is patentable.

Determining whether an invention is nonobvious is one of the most difficult tasks in patent law. After all, a disposable razor, a safety pin, and a retractable tape measure all seem obvious now, yet none of these items were obvious at the time they were invented.

Until the 1952 Patent Act, courts generally required than an invention result from a "flash of genius" or some sudden insight. The view was that an invention must have been so nonobvious that no amount of diligent research would have produced it. The act now states that "patentability shall not be negatived by the manner in which the invention was made." 35 U.S.C. § 103. Thus, whether an invention is produced by dint of arduous research or a flash of genius does not determine whether it is nonobvious. The present method of determining **nonobviousness** is by reference to the prior art.

The* Graham *Factors   In *Graham v. John Deere Co.*, 383 U.S. 1 (1966), the Supreme Court articulated the following factors to consider in determining whether an invention is nonobvious and thus deserving of a patent:

- **Pertinent prior art.** One must review the scope and content of the prior art in the pertinent field to determine if an invention is nonobvious. The term **prior art** refers to the circumstances set forth in sections 102 and 103, namely, the generally available public knowledge relating to the invention for which a patent is sought and which was available prior to invention. Thus, information contained in existing patents, printed publications, and inventions that were known and used before the subject invention will be considered.
- **Differences between the prior art and the invention.** In determining whether an invention is nonobvious, consideration must be given to differences between the prior art and the invention at issue. Applicants themselves may include statements in their applications in regard to how their inventions differ from and are improvements over prior art. An invention that achieves superior results is likely not obvious.
- **Level of ordinary skill in the prior art.** If the invention would be obvious to a person having ordinary skill in the art to which the invention pertains, it cannot be patented. A person of "ordinary skill" is

nonobviousness: In patent law, the requirement that subject matter sought to be patented be sufficiently different from what has been used or described before such that it may be said to be nonobvious to a person having ordinary skill in the area of technology related to the invention

prior art: In patent law, the generally available public knowledge relating to an invention at the time of its creation

neither a highly sophisticated expert or genius in the art nor a layperson with no knowledge of the field of art but rather some hypothetical person who is aware of the pertinent prior art.

Secondary Considerations   In *Graham,* after enumerating the factors evaluated in determining whether an invention is nonobvious, the Court suggested that some **secondary considerations,** all of which are nontechnical and objective, could be considered in determining nonobviousness. Some of the secondary considerations include the following:

- **Commercial success.** An invention that is a commercial success may be nonobvious because acceptance by the marketplace tends to show that an invention is significant; moreover, if the invention were obvious, someone would already have attempted to commercialize it for his or her own financial gain.
- **Long-felt need.** If there has been a long-standing need for a device or process that has gone unresolved despite the efforts of others to solve the problem, and the invention satisfies this need, it tends to show the invention is nonobvious. If the invention were obvious, others would have been able to discover it readily.
- **Commercial acquiescence.** If competitors seek to enter into licenses with the owner so they may use or sell the invention to others, such tends to show nonobviousness because otherwise the third parties would have challenged the patent as invalid based on nonobviousness.
- **Copying.** Copying or infringement of the patent by another suggests nonobviousness because otherwise the infringer would have been able to independently develop the invention.

Conversely, the independent and near-simultaneous invention of like products or processes tends to suggest obviousness. If it is easy for a number of people in the field to invent the same product or process, it is likely obvious to those with ordinary skill in the art.

To ensure that courts do not overrely on the secondary considerations (commercial success, long-felt need, commercial acquiescence, and copying), the Federal Circuit requires that a party demonstrate some link or *nexus* between the secondary characteristic and the invention. For example, if an inventor argues that an invention is nonobvious because it is commercially successful, the inventor must demonstrate that commercial success is due to some property inherent in the invention, rather than due to some external factor such as aggressive marketing or the renown of the inventor.

Combination Patents   One area that has caused debate over obviousness relates to new inventions consisting of a combination of older, known elements. The unique combination of the elements may make the invention novel, but the combination must be nonobvious to receive patent protection. A factor sometimes used in determining whether these patents, called **combination patents,** are nonobvious is *synergism:* the newly combined elements must result in some different function or some result that is different or unexpected such that one who possesses ordinary skill in the art would not have predicted the result of the combination of the known elements. If there is such a new result, the invention is nonobvious and is patentable.

secondary considerations: In patent law, nontechnical and objective factors considered in determining whether an invention is nonobvious, namely, its commercial success, the long-felt need for the invention, commercial acquiescence to it by others, and copying of it by others

combination patents: New inventions consisting of a combination of older, known elements

There is overlap between the requirements of novelty and nonobviousness. Both depend on examination of prior art. To ensure novelty, one must examine the prior art (what others know, use, and publish) to determine if the invention could have been anticipated. Similarly, to ensure nonobviousness, one must examine the scope and content of pertinent prior art to determine if the invention would be obvious to a person having ordinary skill in the field.

Exclusions from Patent Protection

There are a variety of items, products, and processes that cannot be patented. The following are excluded from patent protection either by statutory prohibition or judicial interpretation:

- **Products of nature.** Only human-made inventions can be patented. Naturally occurring substances cannot be protected by patent even if they have previously been unknown to others. For example, a new plant or mineral that is discovered cannot be patented. On the other hand, genetically altered living organisms can be patented as "manufactures" or "compositions of matter." In *Diamond v. Chakrabarty,* 447 U.S. 303 (1980), the Court held that a live, human-made microorganism (in that case, a genetically engineered bacterium capable of breaking down crude oil) was patentable as a human-made "manufacture" or "composition of matter," and stated that "anything under the sun made by man" is patentable. Thus, genetically altered oysters and mice have been held patentable.
- **Laws of nature.** Laws of nature, physical phenomena, scientific truths, and abstract ideas cannot be patented. As the Court remarked in *Chakrabarty,* "Einstein could not patent his celebrated law that $E = mc^2$; nor could Newton have patented the law of gravity." *Id.* at 310. Generally, mere chemical or mathematical formulas or algorithms cannot be patented as such; however, chemical substances can be patented, systems using formulas can be patented as processes, and items that are produced as the result of formulas can be patented. Thus, a machine or product that depends on some law of physics or the law of gravity can be patented. A process is not unpatentable merely because it contains a law of nature or a pure mathematical algorithm. Similarly, computer programs, although they consist of algorithms, can be patented in many instances. In *Diamond v. Diehr,* 450 U.S. 175 (1981), a patent was upheld for the process of molding rubber products with the aid of a computer. The Court noted that although mathematical formulas as such are not patentable, a process employing a well-known mathematical equation was patentable. Additionally, the use of a computer to improve an otherwise patentable process did not preclude the process from being patented. Thus, incorporating a computer program as a step in a process or as a component in a machine or manufacture may be acceptable. See Chapter 21 for additional discussion on protection of computer programs under patent law.
- **Printed matter.** Printed forms cannot be patented.
- **Atomic weapons.** Under the Atomic Energy Act of 1954, atomic weapons cannot be patented.

- **Business methods and mental steps.** Systems for the operation of businesses cannot be patented unless they produce a useful, tangible, and concrete result. Thus, in one case, a method for maintaining restaurant records to prevent fraud by employees was held unpatentable. A useful and novel business system or idea is not patentable unless there is a product or process to effect it. Similarly, processes consisting solely of mental steps, meaning human thought and deliberation, cannot be patented. See Chapter 21 for additional discussion.

In a novel case initiated in 1999, Amazon tribes asked the PTO to revoke a patent granted on a plant (PP 7,751) sacred to the tribes and believed to have medicinal qualities used in religious rituals. Experts are divided on the possible outcome of the case. Additional information may be available at the PTO web site.

DESIGN PATENTS

The Patent Act provides that whoever invents any new, original, and ornamental design for an article of manufacture may obtain a patent. 35 U.S.C. § 171. Comparing the scope of this provision to that of section 101 relating to utility patents, it is clear that the requirement of "usefulness" for utility patents has been replaced by a requirement of "ornamentality." The design must be novel and nonobvious. Just as a person may obtain a patent for a chemical compound and one for the process utilizing the chemical compound, a person may obtain a utility patent and a design patent for one article of manufacture because a useful article may be ornamented with a design. A **design patent** can be obtained for articles as diverse as jewelry, furniture, trash receptacles, and clothing.

Recognizing that while authors could seek protection for their works under copyright law and inventors could seek protection for their works under patent law, no protection was afforded for the creators of decorative arts, Congress allowed design patents in 1842. One of the first design patent cases related to a claim by Gorham Manufacturing that its spoon and fork handle design patents had been infringed. *Gorham Mfg. v. White,* 81 U.S. (14 Wall.) 511 (1871). In *Gorham,* the Court noted that the intent of the design patent statute was to encourage the decorative arts.

To be protectable, a design must satisfy the following four requirements:

1. **It must be an "article of manufacture."** An article of manufacture is nearly anything made by a human and may consist of a manufactured article's configuration (the particular shape of a chair), surface ornamentation (the design on the handle of tableware), or a combination of both (a uniquely shaped fork with two irregularly sized tines, embossed with a leaf design).
2. **It must be new.** The requirements of novelty for utility patents discussed in the previous section on patentability under the hearing "Novelty" apply equally to design patents.
3. **It must be original.** The requirement of originality is the equivalent of the requirement of nonobviousness for utility patents. A design cannot be patented if a designer of ordinary skill who designs articles similar to the one applied for would consider the design obvious in view of the prior art.

design patent: A patent covering new, original, and ornamental designs for useful articles

4. **It must be ornamental.** To be patentable, a design must be primarily ornamental rather than utilitarian. The article may serve a useful purpose (for example, a spoon and a chair serve a useful purpose), but its primary purpose cannot be functional. If there are several ways that an item could be designed and yet still remain functional, then any one design is likely ornamental rather than functional. An article may qualify for design patent protection if at some point in its life cycle its appearance is a factor even if, when ultimately used, the article is hidden. Thus, caskets and artificial hip prostheses have been given design patent protection. Although both are certainly useful, the appearance of the article is of importance at some point even though when put to their intended use, the articles are hidden from view.

There is some overlap between design patents and copyright. It has been held that the same work can qualify for protection under both copyright law and patent law. For example, the drawing of a cartoon character can be protected under copyright law; when the character is embossed on some article, such as china plates, it may be protected under patent law. Similarly, the same item may qualify for protection under trademark law and patent law. For example, in a case involving the shape of a bottle of Mogen David wine, the court stated the design qualified for both patent and trademark protection. *In re Mogen David Wine Corp.*, 328 F.2d 925 (C.C.P.A. 1964). Finally, there is overlap between trade dress protection and patent law such that the ornamental appearance of an item may be protected under trade dress law and as a design patent.

Securing copyright protection is generally the easiest and least expensive method of protecting certain designs. Although copyright registration is not required, a copyright registration may be obtained for a filing fee of $30 within four to five months, and protection will last for the life of the author plus seventy years. Trademark registrations last only as long as they are renewed, and patent protection comes into being only once the patent issues, a process that may take two to three years from the date of application. Moreover, the nonrenewable term of a design patent is fourteen years from the date of issuance of grant. Thus, a combination of intellectual property strategies may be needed to secure the broadest possible scope of protection for certain articles.

PLANT PATENTS

Patents for plants have been recognized only since the passage of the Plant Patent Act in 1930. Prior to that time, the philosophy was that plants were natural products not subject to patent protection. Section 161 of the Patent Act now provides that whoever invents or discovers and asexually reproduces any distinct and new variety of plant may obtain a patent therefor. Just as design patents substitute the requirement of "ornamentality" for the "usefulness" required of utility patents, plant patents substitute the requirement of "distinctiveness" in place of "usefulness."

Congress allowed patents for plants to provide the benefits of the patent system that were then available to manufacturing and industry to the agriculture business in order to incentivize growers and protect their plant products from infringement. Without patent protection, copies of plants could be produced by grafting techniques. Thus, a **plant patent** affords its owner the right to exclude others from reproducing the plant. The term *plant* is construed in its ordinary meaning and does not include bacteria. The use of the term *discovery* means a discovery by asexual propagation; plants discovered in nature cannot be patented.

There are four requirements that must be satisfied before a plant can be patented:

1. **The new variety must be asexually reproduced.** A grower or discoverer of a new and distinct variety of plant must be able to reproduce the plant by asexual means. Generally, this is accomplished by taking cuttings of the original plant and placing them in soil or by grafting so as to create a new plant. **Asexual reproduction** involves growing something other than from a seed.

2. **The plant must be distinctive.** The new plant must be clearly distinguishable from existing varieties. Features that show distinctiveness are color, odor, flavor, shape, ability of the plant to grow in a different type of soil, its productivity, its factors of preservation, or immunity to disease. The requirement of distinctiveness imposes only a requirement that the plant be different from, rather than superior to, other varieties. A new color of a rose may be different from other roses but may not be better than some other variety. Nevertheless, it may be patented. There is a great deal of overlap between nonobviousness for utility patents and distinctiveness for plant patents. One patent for a variety of bluegrass recites that the plant is a "new and distinct variety of Kentucky Bluegrass characterized by its excellent tolerance to drought, low fertilizer requirements, deep rooting system, excellent tolerance to Fusarium blight, and good to excellent shade tolerance. The plant tolerates a close cut, is highly resistant to most common bluegrass diseases, is extremely aggressive, has a medium to coarse leaf texture and consistently maintains excellent turf quality." U.S. Plant Pat. No. 4,704.

3. **The plant must be novel.** The new variety of plant must not have previously existed in nature. The bars to novelty set forth in section 102 and discussed in the earlier section on patentability under the heading "Novelty" apply equally to plant patents.

4. **The plant must be nonobvious.** Although section 161 of the Patent Act providing for statutory protection for plant patents does not specifically state that patents for plants must be nonobvious, the section does provide that the provisions of the act relating to utility patents apply equally to plant patents unless otherwise specified. Generally, the standards set forth in *Graham v. John Deere Co.,* discussed in the earlier section on patentability under the heading "Nonobviousness" apply equally with regard to plant patents.

Although the most common means of securing protection for plants is through application for a plant patent, two other methods of protection exist for plants. In 1970, Congress enacted the **Plant Variety Protection Act** (7 U.S.C. § 2321), allowing quasipatent protection for certain sexually reproduced plants, meaning plants bred through seeds. Sexually reproduced plants could not receive protection under the 1930 Plant Patent Act because new varieties could

plant patent: A patent covering asexually reproduced and distinct plant varieties

asexual reproduction: Growing something other than from a seed, often by grafting or placing cuttings in soil

Plant Variety Protection Act: Federal law allowing quasipatent protection for certain sexually reproduced plants

not be reproduced true-to-type through seedlings. The new variety was not always stable, and its new characteristics could not be passed uniformly from one generation to the next. By 1970, however, it was generally recognized that true-to-type sexual reproduction of plants is possible, and the Plant Variety Protection Act was passed.

These new varieties, produced through the use of seeds, are awarded "plant variety protection certificates" by the Department of Agriculture, rather than letters patents issued by the PTO. The primary purpose of the Plant Variety Protection Act is to encourage the development of novel varieties of sexually reproduced plants. The certificate owner may exclude others from selling, offering, reproducing, or trading infringing plants.

Finally, a plant may qualify for protection as a utility patent, even though it also qualifies for protection under the Plant Patent Act as a plant patent or under the Plant Variety Protection Act for patentlike protection. An application for a utility patent for a plant must satisfy the requirements for utility patents generally, namely, usefulness, novelty, and nonobviousness.

In some cases, matters of tactics and strategy may dictate whether an inventor seeks protection for a plant under the Plant Patent Act of 1930, the Plant Variety Protection Act of 1970, or as a general utility patent. Although the most significant determinant is how the plant can be reproduced (asexual reproduction is required under the Plant Patent Act while sexual plant reproduction is protected under the Plant Variety Protection Act), other factors should be considered. For example, the requirement that an invention be nonobvious applies to utility patents and plant patents reproduced asexually, but not to the Plant Variety Protection Act. Thus, an inventor who cannot demonstrate nonobviousness might seek protection under the Plant Variety Protection Act. Similarly, fees to maintain the patent are due on utility patents but not on plant patents. Assuming applications do not claim identical subject matter, it is possible that a patent could be obtained for a plant both under the Plant Patent Act and under the Patent Act as a utility patent.

DOUBLE PATENTING

The **double patenting** principle prohibits the issuance of more than one patent for the same invention or for an invention that is substantially the same as that owned by an inventor. The intent of this bar is to ensure that inventors do not make some insignificant change to an invention near the end of its term of existence in order to secure another twenty-year monopoly on the invention or discovery. Nevertheless, design and utility patents may coexist because they relate to arguably distinct subject matter. A utility patent claims protection for the usefulness of the object while a design patent covers its ornamentality. Inventors often insert a **terminal disclaimer** into their applications, agreeing that the term of protection for a second invention will terminate upon expiration of the patent for the first invention and that the patent claim to the second invention will be valid only as long as both inventions are owned by the same person or entity. Such a disclaimer will enable an inventor to overcome a rejection based on double patenting. Double patenting is discussed further in Chapter 18.

double patenting: In patent law, a principle prohibiting the issuance of more than one patent for the same invention

terminal disclaimer: An agreement by an inventor that the term of protection for a second patented invention will terminate upon expiration of the term for the first patented invention

THE ORPHAN DRUG ACT

Just as the Plant Variety Protection Act grants rights somewhat similar to patents, the Orphan Drug Act (21 U.S.C. §§ 360aa–360ee) provides rights for certain drugs that are similar to patent rights, namely, an exclusive right for seven years to market an **orphan drug** that is necessary to treat a disease that affects fewer than two hundred thousand people. Protection under the act is triggered when the Food and Drug Administration determines that unless such protection is granted, the drug would likely not be made or available to those in need of it. The act applies whether or not the drug can be patented (thus affording protection for drugs that may lack novelty or nonobviousness). The act thus provides incentives to pharmaceutical companies to develop drugs for rare diseases or conditions when otherwise they might not invest the time and effort in developing a drug for a small target group if patentability could not be assured.

ROLE OF INTELLECTUAL PROPERTY PROFESSIONAL

Until patent searching begins and an application is filed, the role of an IP professional will be fairly limited. Typically, tasks may consist of conducting research to help assess and satisfy the required elements of usefulness, novelty, and nonobviousness. If a law firm does not have a general information letter available that can be sent to clients who have basic questions about patent law, one should be drafted. Similarly, a "Frequently Asked Questions" sheet can be prepared for distribution to clients. Flowcharts showing the patent process can be made, and charts comparing types of patents (for example, plant patents and utility patents for plants) can be prepared.

An IP professional may also be involved in conducting some type of audit of clients to inquire whether they have invented any processes or products that may qualify for patent protection. A questionnaire should be prepared to assess whether clients' intellectual property is being fully protected. See Chapter 24 for sample questions for an intellectual property audit.

CHAPTER SUMMARY

A patent is a grant from the federal government allowing an inventor to exclude others from producing, using, or selling the inventor's discovery or invention for a limited period of time, generally twenty years from the filing date of a patent application. Patent laws are aimed at fostering and promoting discoveries. There are three types of patents: utility patents, design patents, and plant patents. The vast majority of patents are utility patents, which must satisfy the requirements of usefulness, novelty, and nonobviousness in order to secure protection. An invention or discovery that is merely an insignificant addition to or alteration of something already known or in existence is unpatentable. Protection is allowed for processes, machines, human-made articles of manufacture, and compositions of matter.

orphan drug: A drug needed to treat a disease affecting fewer than two hundred thousand people

Not all inventions or discoveries may be patented. Generally, patents are awarded to the first to invent. Additionally, patents are not available for scientific or mathematical principles, some business methods, printed matter, or substances existing in nature.

Design patents protect original, new, and ornamental designs for articles of manufacture. Plant patents protect new and distinct varieties of asexually reproduced plants.

DISCUSSION QUESTIONS

1. Two individuals independently create a new invention, one in June and one in August of the same year. Because the inventions were independently created, are both works protectable under patent law? Discuss.
2. *A* invents a new lawnmower in September. He files his patent application in October of the same year. The patent issues in November two years later. When do *A*'s patent rights come into existence?
3. Can an invention whose only purpose is harmful or deceptive be patented? Discuss.
4. Smith invents a new exercise machine in January. In February of the same year, he posts an article on the Internet describing the invention. The next month he files an application for a patent for the machine. Is the invention subject to patent protection? Discuss.
5. Why does commercial success of a product or process tend to show nonobviousness?
6. Jones discovers a new plant growing in the rain forest. Discuss the following:
   a. Is the plant patentable?
   b. By grafting, Jones is able to produce a variety of the plant with a distinctive fragrance. Can the new variety be patented?
   c. By a novel process, Jones produces a beneficial medicine from the plant. What type of protection will Jones receive?
7. Andrews invents a trash receptacle with highly decorative fluted legs. What type of protection is the receptacle entitled to?
8. Hendrix invents a new chemical compound for which there is no present use, although Hendrix and others strongly believe the compound has significant research value and may lead to important breakthroughs in the field. Is the compound patentable? Discuss.
9. Ellen Novak invents a new type of fountain pen. She offers the pen for sale through a catalog on January 1, 1998. No sales are made. Ellen applies for a patent for the pen on January 10, 1999. Is the invention eligible for a patent? Discuss.

Patent Searches and Applications

Before an application for a patent is filed, a search should be conducted to ensure that the invention is novel and nonobvious. If the search results suggest that an invention may be patentable, an application is then prepared. An application consists of two parts: the specification (describing the invention) and the inventor's oath or declaration. Applications must be filed by individual inventors, although the application can be assigned to another at the same time it is filed. After the application is filed at the PTO, it will be examined for patentability. All application proceedings at the PTO are confidential. The examiner may issue office actions, requiring amendment of some of the claims of the invention. No new matter can be added to an application. When an application is allowed by an examiner, a notice of allowance is issued and an "issue fee" must be paid to the PTO for the patent to be granted. The term of utility and plant patents is twenty years from the date of filing of the application therefor. The term of design patents is fourteen years from the date of grant. Maintenance fees must be paid at three intervals during the term of a utility patent to maintain it in force. Once the patent is issued, its owner may exclude others from making, selling, or using the invention for the term of the patent.

PATENT SEARCHING

The Need for a Search

Patentability requires novelty and nonobviousness. The only predictable method of determining whether an invention is new and nonobvious is to conduct a search of the prior art. The patentability search, sometimes called a **novelty search,** will help determine whether the differences in the subject matter sought to be patented and the prior art are such that the subject matter as a whole would have been obvious to a person having ordinary skill in the art. Moreover, because 35 U.S.C. § 102 excludes from patent protection inventions that have been known or used by others in the United States or patented or

novelty search: A search of prior art to determine if an invention is new and nonobvious

described in a printed publication in the United States or elsewhere, a search will disclose whether such bars to protection exist. Finally, if an invention has fallen into the public domain because its patent has expired, anyone can use it and no one can obtain a patent for it. Searching will disclose the existence of such expired patents. Thus, although not required prior to filing a patent application, a search is recommended to determine the feasibility of obtaining a patent. Otherwise, an inventor may incur costs of several thousands of dollars in prosecuting a patent application only to have an examiner determine that the invention fails to satisfy the requirements of novelty and nonobviousness. An additional benefit of conducting a search is that it may provide ideas for drafting the application itself.

A novelty search is somewhat limited in scope and is designed to disclose whether an application will be rejected on the basis of lack of novelty or obviousness. A novelty search can usually be completed for less than $1,000. If an invention is intended for immediate commercial use or sale, an additional search, called an infringement search or investigation, is often conducted concurrently with the novelty search. An invention may be patentable as a significant improvement over an existing invention and yet still infringe a patent. An infringement search or full patentability search is far more extensive than a novelty search and is thus more expensive, often costing between $1,000 and $2,000. Conducting a search and obtaining an opinion relating to infringement is critical inasmuch as persons have affirmative duties of due care to avoid patent infringement. Obtaining advice of competent counsel may protect a person from having punitive damages imposed against him or her in an action for patent infringement because it demonstrates exercise of the duty of due care (see Chapter 20).

Searching Methods

The PTO provides a public search room for patent searching. Searching is free and the PTO allows searchers to review issued patents, complete with drawings. The patent search room contains copies of all U.S. issued patents from 1790 to present as well as many foreign patents. Searching can be done either in the main public search room or in the examiners' search areas where examiners will assist in searching.

The PTO employs a classification system that provides for the storage and retrieval of patent documents. Although the system is primarily designed to be used by patent examiners in the course of examining patent applications, the system is also used by searchers. The classification files are divided into smaller searchable units called subclasses. Most classes have approximately three hundred subclasses. One approach divides art on the basis of the industry employing the art or the use to which an art is put. All relevant patents for a given technology are grouped together. For example, all of the materials relating to butchering are grouped together and all of the materials related to bee culture are classed together. Another approach classifies inventions or art based on their function. Thus, all heat exchange devices are grouped together, whether they are milk coolers or beer coolers. The patents are stored in "shoes" stacked one atop the other. Explanations of the Patent Classification System and suggestions for searching are provided on the PTO's web site at http://www.uspto.gov.

Searching can also be done on the Internet. The PTO itself offers free searching at its site (see end of previous paragraph). The PTO has now published the full text of two million patents (all patents since 1976) on the

Internet, allowing users to view, download, and print the images they desire. Searching can be done by patent number or through the use of topic names using Boolean connectors. Another resource that is free and that many inventors find helpful is the patent searching site offered by IBM at http://www.patents.ibm.com. The site includes nearly thirty years of patent descriptions and images, allowing access to more than two million patents. Searching can be done by key words, phrases, patent number, inventor name, title of patent, or attorney or agent. A mechanism is provided for immediate ordering by mail or fax of a full copy of a patent.

In many major cities throughout the United States, public libraries receive copies of issued patents and trademarks. Called Patent and Trademark Depository Libraries, these libraries store patents on microfiche or microfilm, and the collections are available for use by the public free of charge. Unless an inventor is nearly certain that his or her invention is new and nonobvious, searching through the Patent and Trademark Depositories is usually not recommended inasmuch as records are often not updated and review by microfiche or microfilm is cumbersome. Additionally, the scope of the collections varies from library to library, with some offering patents from 1790 and others offering patents only from recent years. Nearly one hundred libraries have been designated Patent and Trademark Depositories. See the PTO web site for a listing of the patent and trademark depository libraries.

Patent searching is also offered by LEXIS. Charges are assessed by time spent online. Call (800) 543-8682. Dialog Information Services also offers searching for a fee. Contact (800) 3-DIALOG. Dialog's database is very comprehensive and includes the full text of utility patents in the United States as well as patents issued in several foreign countries.

Because searching is so difficult and typically requires knowledge of the prior art, many inventors employ professional search firms, similar to those that conduct trademark searches, to determine availability of a mark prior to filing an application for registration. The results are usually reviewed by a patent attorney who will then provide an opinion on the possibility of obtaining patent protection and/or the likelihood that an invention infringes another invention. The opinion should disclose the method of search, the databases covered by the search, whether foreign patents were reviewed, and the classifications searched. The opinion typically states that apparently favorable results from a search do not necessarily guarantee that a patent can be obtained and that due to human error and mistakes in filing, it is possible that not all relevant patents were disclosed.

THE PATENT APPLICATION PROCESS

Overview of the Application Process

The process of preparing, filing, and shepherding a patent application through the PTO toward issuance is called "prosecution" (just as is the process of obtaining a trademark registration). An application may be filed by the inventor himself or herself or, as is more usual, by a patent attorney. Only 20 percent of all applications are filed by inventors without the assistance of attorneys. After the application is filed with the PTO, it will be assigned to an examiner having experience in the area of technology related to the invention who will review the application and conduct a search of patent records to ensure the application complies with the statutory requirements for patents (including novelty, usefulness, and nonobviousness). Generally, there will be some objection made by the examiner, which will be set forth in an "office action." The applicant or attorney typically responds to the office action either by telephone or in writing. The process may continue for several rounds. If the rejections cannot be overcome, the application may be abandoned or the examiner's refusal may be appealed to the Board of Patent Appeals and Interferences. Alternatively, the examiner will accept the response(s) to the office action(s) and allow the application. An **issue fee** must then be paid to the PTO in order for the patent to be granted. During prosecution, the application is not subject to public review. All patent applications received by the PTO are maintained in confidence. Once a patent issues, however, the entire application file (the "file wrapper") becomes a matter of public record. Patents are granted for roughly 65 percent of all applications filed.

It generally takes anywhere from one to three years to prosecute a patent (although the PTO goal is to reduce this "cycle time" to twelve months or less by 2003), and costs and fees can range from $5,000 to more than $30,000, with fees generally ranging from $10,000 to $12,000. Because of the time and the high costs involved in obtaining a patent, inventors should conduct a cost-benefit analysis to determine whether the invention merits the effort and expense of obtaining a patent. If the invention will have limited application, it may not be worth securing a patent for it. On the other hand, if the invention is likely to be a commercial success, the time and expense involved in obtaining patent protection will be a worthwhile investment.

Patent Practice

While preparing trademark and copyright applications is relatively straightforward, preparing a patent application requires skillful drafting as well as knowledge in the relevant field, whether that is biotechnology, chemistry, mechanical engineering, physics, computers, pharmacology, electrical engineering, and so forth. Because patent practice is highly technical, law firms that provide patent services to clients generally have a number of attorneys with different skill sets, and the patent department itself may be divided into different groups, such as a mechanical group, a biotech group, and an electrical group. Many **patent attorneys** possess both a law degree and an advanced degree in engineering, physics, chemistry, or the like. Due to the highly skilled nature of patent work, patent attorneys are highly marketable and often command salaries significantly higher than other attorneys. Similarly, other experienced IP professionals are also in high demand.

To represent patent applicants before the PTO, an attorney must be registered to practice with the PTO. An attorney must pass the Patent Bar, which requires the attorney to demonstrate background in science or engineering. The examination is very difficult, and the pass rate tends to hover around one-third. The examination includes a multiple-choice section as well as a written claim-drafting section. Generally, the test-taker can elect to draft a claim for one of three types of inventions: mechanical, chemical, or electrical. In a recent examination, most applicants chose to draft a claim for a mechanical patent for a corkscrewlike apparatus used to remove champagne corks.

issue fee: A fee required by the PTO for a patent to be granted

patent attorney: A licensed attorney who passes a PTO exam testing patent knowledge and who may engage in patent prosecution, give legal advice, and appear in court

In addition to the inventor himself or herself and registered patent attorneys, individuals called registered **patent agents** can prosecute patent applications. Patent agents are not attorneys but rather skilled engineers and scientists who take and pass the patent agent's examination. Attorneys may also take the patent agent's examination, which is designed to test knowledge in science and engineering. Although patent agents can engage in patent prosecution, they may not engage in activities that constitute the practice of law, such as representing parties in patent infringement actions or providing legal advice.

A list of attorneys and agents registered to practice before the PTO is available from the Government Printing Office located in Washington, DC. Alternatively, the PTO web site (http://www.uspto.gov/web/offices/dcom/olia/oed/roster/) provides an index to the more than eighteen thousand attorneys and agents who are licensed to practice before the PTO. Many cities also have attorney referral services that can recommend patent attorneys or agents. Finally, a local or state bar association may have associations of patent attorneys and agents.

Confidentiality of Application Process

Under 35 U.S.C. § 122, applications for patents are kept in confidence by the PTO, and no information concerning a pending application may be given without the specific authority of the applicant or the applicant's representative. Once an application matures into an issued patent, however, the file wrapper containing the application and all correspondence leading up to the issuance of the patent is available.

Types of Applications

Although the prosecution of patents is essentially the same for any type of patent application, there are different types of applications. They are as follows:

- **Provisional application.** Effective in 1995, and as a result of the adherence of the United States to the General Agreement on Tariffs and Trade (GATT), it is possible to file a **provisional patent application** with the PTO. A provisional application is less formal than a full utility patent application. It is intended as a relatively inexpensive and expeditious way of embarking on patent protection. A provisional application need not include any claims, and the filing fee is inexpensive ($150 for large entities and $75 for small entities). The applicant must, however, file for a standard utility patent within twelve months of filing the provisional application or the provisional application will be deemed abandoned. If the final day falls on a nonbusiness day or holiday, the application must be filed on the previous business day (this rule is quite different from most statutory time requirements, which provide that if the last day for doing an act falls on a holiday or weekend, the period is extended to the next business day). A provisional application is most useful when an inventor is in a race with a competitor and wishes to be the first to file an application. Filing a provisional application allows the inventor to mark the invention with the notice "patent pending." The twenty-year term for a utility patent begins with the filing of the actual utility patent. Thus, filing a provisional application allows an inventor to

patent agent: A nonattorney engineer or scientist who passes a PTO exam testing patent knowledge and may engage in patent prosecution but may not give legal advice or appear in court

provisional patent application: A patent application that is less formal than a utility patent application; within twelve months of its filing, it must be following by a standard utility patent application at the PTO

delay the start of the twenty-year period of patent protection. Moreover, it provides the inventor a simplified filing with a lower initial investment with one full year to assess the invention's commercial potential before committing to the higher costs of filing and prosecuting a standard utility patent. Although there are obvious advantages to filing a provisional patent application, there are disadvantages as well, primarily that the application will not be reviewed by an examiner during its twelve-month pendency. Thus, the inventor is left without any indication regarding the ultimate protection for his or her invention.

- **Utility application.** An inventor may file a utility application for a new, useful, and nonobvious process, machine, article of manufacture, or composition of matter or some improvement thereof. If a provisional application has previously been filed by an inventor, a **utility application** must be filed within twelve months of the filing date of the provisional application.

- **Design application.** A **design application** protects new, original, and ornamental designs for articles of manufacture.

- **Plant application.** A **plant application** protects new and distinctive asexually reproduced plants.

- **Continuation application.** A **continuation application** claims priority from a previously filed application. There are two types of continuation applications: the *continuation application* or *file wrapper continuation application* (a continuation patent filed when an examiner issues a final office action rejecting some claims in an application and the inventor wishes to allow the permitted claims to proceed and continue to pursue the rejected claims in a separate application) and the **continuation-in-part application** (which contains some matters in common with the original or "parent" application but also adds new matter, usually because an improvement to the invention was developed subsequent to the filing of the parent application).

- **PCT application.** A **PCT** (Patent Cooperation Treaty) **application** allows an applicant to file one application that may be relied upon for later filing in countries that are members of the **Patent Cooperation Treaty,** to which nearly one hundred nations belong, including the United States. PCT applications are administered by the World Intellectual Property Organization (WIPO). Because section 102 of the Patent Act bars patents that are the subject of patents in foreign countries, an inventor wishing to protect a discovery or invention would be required to file simultaneous applications in every country in which he or she desires patent protection in order to avoid the statutory bar of section 102. Such filings would be an extremely expensive gamble inasmuch as the applications might be denied in various countries or the inventor might discover there is no market for the invention in some countries and might wish to abandon the process. The PCT application process allows an inventor to file one application and then postpone filing in other member nations for twenty months or longer. The filing date for each foreign country is deemed to be the date identified in the original application. Although often called an "international application," the application does not automatically result in registration in member nations of the PCT. The application must still be prosecuted

utility application: A patent application for a new, useful, and nonobvious process, machine, article of manufacture, composition of matter, or some improvement thereof

design application: An application for a design patent

plant application: An application for a patent for a plant

continuation application: A patent application that claims priority from a previously filed application and contains no new information

continuation-in-part application: A patent application that adds new matter to a previous patent application

PCT application: A patent application that has applicability and effect in designated member nations adhering to the Patent Cooperation Treaty

Patent Cooperation Treaty (PCT): A 1978 treaty adhered to by approximately one hundred countries that provides a centralized way of filing, searching, and examining patent applications in several countries simultaneously

separately in each individual nation in which the inventor desires protection. The primary purpose of a PCT application is to allow an inventor to delay filing in foreign countries until a determination is made about whether protection is desirable in those countries. Patent Cooperation Treaty (PCT) applications are discussed in Chapter 21.

- **Divisional application.** After an application is filed, the examiner may determine that the application covers more than one invention. Because each patent application can cover only one invention, a **divisional application** will be created to carve out a new application for the additional invention. The new divisional application typically retains the filing date of the original or parent application.

Preparing the Application

A utility patent application has two required components: a specification and an oath. If needed to understand the invention, a drawing is also required. A filing fee must also accompany the application. Although these elements are few, their importance cannot be underestimated. Drafting the specification (describing the invention) is difficult and painstaking work. For a complex invention, it may take forty hours or more. The level of detail and specificity imposed on applicants is a trade-off: in return for obtaining a twenty-year monopoly during which they may exclude others from selling, making, or using their inventions, inventors must fully disclose to the public what the invention is and exactly how it works.

Specification   The **specification** is the part of the application that describes the invention and the manner and process of making it and using it. It must be made in "such full, clear, concise, and exact terms as to enable any person skilled in the art . . . to make and use the same, and shall set forth the best mode contemplated by the inventor of carrying out his invention." 35 U.S.C. § 112.

Section 112 requires that the specification must be so complete as to enable one skilled in the art to make and use the invention. Thus, a general description such as "the invention is a high-speed drill" will be insufficient. In many instances, an application is rejected because of a **nonenabling specification,** meaning the specification is not sufficient to teach or enable another to make or use the invention. Simply put, stating what the invention is, is insufficient; the application must describe how the invention works. A specification may incorporate by reference other materials such as pending or issued patents, publications, and other documents as part of the enabling requirement.

In addition to the enabling requirement, the application must set forth the "best mode" contemplated by the inventor for making the invention.

The specification itself is composed of several distinct elements:

- **Title.** The invention must be given a short and specific title that appears as a heading on the first page of the application. Examples of titles are "Track Ball for Computer System Cursor Control," "Nail Gun," and "Combined Refrigerator and Microwave Oven with Timed Overload Protection."
- **Cross-references to related applications.** If the application seeks the benefit of the filing date of a prior invention applied for by the same inventor or claims an invention disclosed in an earlier application by the

divisional application: A patent application separated from another application when the original or parent application covers more than one invention

specification: The part of a patent application that describes an invention and the manner and process of making and using it

nonenabling specification: A specification in a patent application rejected by the PTO on the basis that it is not sufficient to teach or enable another to make or use the invention

same inventor, the second application must provide a cross-reference to the earlier application and identify it by serial number and filing date.

- **Background.** The **background** section of the specification should identify the field of the invention and discuss how the present invention differs from the known art. Generally, this section critiques other inventions and demonstrates the need and worth of the invention being applied for. A typical background section might discuss the shortcomings of existing similar inventions and itemize the benefits of the subject invention.

- **Summary of invention.** The summary section provides a short and general statement of the nature and substance of the invention. Because the summary and the background section are highly similar, some applications merge the two together into one called "Background and Summary of the Invention."

- **Brief description of drawings.** If drawings are included, they should be briefly described.

- **Description of the preferred embodiments.** This section must teach another skilled in the art the manner and process of making and using the invention.

- **Claims.** A specification must include at least one **claim.** The claims define the scope of the invention. Although the language is precise, the inventor's goal is to draft the claims in such a way as to achieve the broadest possible scope of protection for the invention and yet comply with the statutory requirement of specificity. The claims are the most significant part of the application. The claims will be compared against the prior art to determine whether the invention is entitled to be patented. If the inventor later alleges another has infringed his or her invention, a court will compare the claims set forth in the patent with the alleged infringer's invention in determining whether infringement has occurred. There are two types of claims: independent claims, which describe the invention in a general manner, and dependent claims, which are more narrowly stated and incorporate all elements of the more broadly stated independent claim. Claims are often compared to the descriptions of real estate found in deeds that describe the "metes and bounds" of a parcel of property. A patent claim similarly describes the boundaries of the claimed invention. One specific type of claim, called a **Jepson claim,** is used for improvements to existing inventions and identifies what is new to the invention. Design patent applications have only one claim, for example, "the ornamental design of a child's chair, as shown and described." Plant patents also have only one claim inasmuch as the entire plant is claimed as the inventive material. (See Figure 18–1 for a sample of claims.)

- **Abstract.** Strictly speaking, the abstract is not part of the specification but is rather a concise statement of the invention. The **abstract** should be a single short paragraph. The abstract for U.S. Pat. No. 5,682,931, entitled "Baby Feeding Bottle" is as follows:

    A baby food jar is directly attachable to the top of a squeezable baby bottle so that the baby food jar can be inverted on the squeezable bottle to gravitationally transfer the baby food without spilling. Thereafter, a feeding member includes a nozzle which attaches directly to the squeezable baby bottle. The nozzle terminates in a

background: The portion of a specification in a patent application that discusses how the invention differs from the prior art

claim: The portion of a specification in a patent application that defines the scope of the invention

Jepson claim: A type of claim in a patent specification used for improvements to existing inventions that identifies what is new to the invention

abstract: A concise statement of an invention

FIGURE 18–1
Claims for Utility Patent
(U.S. Pat. No. 5,682,931)

What is claimed is:

1. A baby feeding bottle comprising:
   - A baby feeding bottle, said baby feeding bottle being made of resilient material so that it is squeezable to help in expelling the contents, said baby feeding bottle having a top and having an opening at said top, said baby feeding bottle being configured so that it can rest on a horizontal flat surface with said opening directed upwardly;
   - means integral with said baby feeding bottle at said opening being nonremovable therefrom for detachably attaching a baby food jar thereto with the baby food jar in an inverted position when said baby feeding bottle is in an upright position; and
   - a feeding structure, means for detachably attaching said feeding structure to said squeezable baby bottle at said opening thereof, said feeding structure having a spoon thereon sized for feeding a baby and an opening through said feeding structure from said attachment means to said spoon so that baby food can be delivered from said squeezable baby bottle to said spoon for one-handed feeding of a baby.

baby feeding spoon. Squeezing the bottle delivers baby food directly to the spoon.

An abstract for a plant patent might read, "A hybrid tea rose having two-toned blossoms of pink with a white reverse."

Drawings, Models, and Specimens If drawings are needed to understand the invention, they must be included. Nearly all patent applications are accompanied by drawings. The drawings must also be described so that the viewer knows whether the drawing is a cross-section, a side view, and so forth. For example, the drawings might be described as follows: "Figure 3 is a right-hand perspective view of the child's chair. Figure 2 is a front plan view thereof." The PTO has stringent requirements relating to the size, symbols, and format of drawings, and usually a graphic artist or patent draftsperson is retained to prepare the drawings. Many law firms that practice patent law employ draftspersons on a full-time basis. Informal drawings (photocopies) may be submitted if they are legible, but the examiner will usually impose a requirement that formal pen and ink drawings be submitted.

Applicants were formerly required to submit a working model of the invention, but this requirement was eliminated in the late 1800s (although an examiner does have the authority to require that a working model be submitted). If the invention relates to a composition of matter, the PTO may require the applicant to furnish specimens or ingredients for the purpose of inspection or experiment.

Oath of Inventor The applicant must sign an oath or declaration that he or she believes himself or herself to be the original and first inventor of the process, machine, manufacture, or composition of matter, or improvement thereof. The applicant must also identify his or her country of citizenship and provide an address. The applicant must acknowledge that he or she has reviewed and understands the contents of the application and understands the duty to disclose all information known to be relevant to the application.

The Patent Act requires that the person claiming the patent must be the original inventor. 35 U.S.C. § 111. The applicant cannot be an assignee of the inventor. Thus, a review of the several million applications on file with the PTO will disclose that in nearly every case, the application has been made by an individual. Applications are not made by General Electric, Ford Motor Company, Westinghouse, or any other corporation or business entity. Although these companies may employ the inventors and may, in fact, own the invention (due to agreement between the parties that the employer will own any invention made by the employee), the application itself must be signed by the individual inventor. This requirement helps to ensure that inventions are not stolen by others. If an inventor cannot be found or refuses to file an application, an assignee may file the application upon showing such facts. If an inventor has died or is subject to some incapacity, his or her estate or legal representative may file the application. If an invention has been made by two or more persons jointly, they must file the application jointly. A **joint application** may be made even if the inventors did not physically work together at the same time, did not each make the same type or amount of contribution, or did not each make a contribution to the subject matter of every claim in the patent. Accurate records should be kept regarding each inventor's contributions so that if one inventor's contributions are refused or dropped from the claims, he or she can be removed from the application. An application can be assigned to another person or company concurrently with the execution of a patent application or at any time thereafter. Concurrent assignments usually take place when companies own the inventions created by their employees. All assignments should be recorded with the PTO to provide public notice of the owner of the patent rights even though recordation is not required to make an assignment valid.

If anyone other than the actual inventor is filing the application, a power of attorney will be needed to authorize the patent attorney or patent agent to act on the inventor's behalf. The power of attorney may be a separate form or may be included as part of the oath or declaration.

The requirements for preparing and filing design and plant patents are nearly identical to those discussed earlier for utility patents. Design patent applications, however, require a preamble stating the name of the applicant and the title of the design, and plant patent applications require the inventor's oath or declaration to confirm that the plant was reproduced asexually.

An oath is made before a notary, while a declaration is a statement by the applicant acknowledging that willful false statements are punishable by law. Either an oath or a declaration is acceptable.

Filing the Application   After the application has been thoroughly reviewed to ensure it complies with PTO regulations (such as requirements relating to the size of the paper used and that all pages be line-numbered and double-spaced), the application package should be assembled for filing with the PTO. A transmittal letter should be prepared (the PTO provides a form), and it should reference the following documents:

- the application (consisting of the background, summary, specification and claims, abstract, and drawings, if any);
- the enclosed filing fee (or instructions to the PTO to charge a deposit account maintained by the firm or agent for patent filings); and

joint application: An application for a trademark, copyright, or patent registration made by more than one person

a self-addressed stamped postcard (so the PTO can stamp the filing date and serial number of the application and return it to the applicant for verification of filing).

If the application is being simultaneously assigned at the same time it is filed, a recordation form should be included. (The recordation form used for patent assignments is nearly identical to that used for trademarks shown in Chapter 5 as Figure 5 2.)

To obtain a filing date for an application, all that is needed is the specification (including claims) and drawings, if needed. The oath and fee can be submitted later, although an additional fee will be assessed as a surcharge.

Although most other documents can be sent to the PTO by regular mail, new patent applications must be filed in person or sent by express mail. Any document sent by regular or express mail should include a certificate consisting of a single sentence verifying the date the document was placed in the mail/express mail. In the event of a later dispute about filing dates of documents, the certificate of mailing will be accepted as proof of mailing on the date alleged. If there is no certificate of mailing, the filing date of the document will be deemed to be the date the PTO received it.

Fees In order to provide encouragement to individual inventors, small entities or businesses, universities, and not-for-profit organizations, fees for these applicants are reduced by 50 percent of the standard fees (except those in connection with PCT or international patent applications). A **small entity** is one with fewer than five hundred employees. While the small business cannot be the inventor, it is possible that, due to assignment, it is the owner of the patent rights, including the right to prosecute the application.

To claim the benefit of the reduced fees, the party must prepare a small entity statement (see Figure 18 2) and verify its status as an independent inventor, university, not-for-profit organization, or small business. A small entity statement can be prepared and filed at the same time as the application and the reduced fee paid at that time. Alternatively, the small entity statement can be prepared and filed later and a refund will be made. If a party s small entity status changes during the prosecution of the application (often due to an outright assignment to a nonqualified party or internal growth of the applicant), full fees will be due from and after the date of change.

Effective November 10, 1998, the filing fee for a utility patent is $690. Small entities will pay $345. If there are independent claims in excess of three, claims in excess of twenty, or multiple dependent claims, additional fees are charged. The fee for filing a design patent is $310/$155, and the fee for filing a plant patent is $480/$240. The PTO web site provides a fee schedule. Because the fees are subject to change, it is a good idea to check the site periodically. (See Figure 18 3 for a schedule of patent fees.)

Duty of Candor Patent applicants are subject to a **duty of candor** and good faith in their dealings with the PTO and must therefore disclose to the PTO any information that is relevant to the patentability of a claimed invention. Violation of this duty may result in loss of patent rights. The applicant must therefore disclose prior art references that bear on the novelty or nonobviousness of the invention, printed publications that describe the invention, any possible use or sale of the invention, related domestic or foreign applications or

small entity: A business with fewer than five hundred employees, an individual inventor, a university, or a not-for-profit organization entitled to a 50 percent reduction in standard patent fees

duty of candor: Requirement that patent applicants disclose to the PTO any information that is material to the patentability of a claimed invention

PTO/SB/10 (1-99)
Approved for use through 09/30/2000. OMB 0651-0031
Patent and Trademark Office; U.S. DEPARTMENT OF COMMERCE
Under the Paperwork Reduction Act of 1995, no persons are required to respond to a collection of information unless it displays a valid OMB control number.

STATEMENT CLAIMING SMALL ENTITY STATUS (37 CFR 1.9(f) & 1.27(c))--SMALL BUSINESS CONCERN	Docket Number (Optional)

Applicant, Patentee, or Identifier: _____

Application or Patent No.: _____

Filed or Issued: _____

Title: _____

I hereby state that I am

☐   the owner of the small business concern identified below:

☐   an official of the small business concern empowered to act on behalf of the concern identified below:

NAME OF SMALL BUSINESS CONCERN _____

ADDRESS OF SMALL BUSINESS CONCERN _____

_____

I hereby state that the above identified small business concern qualifies as a small business concern as defined in 13 CFR Part 121 for purposes of paying reduced fees to the United States Patent and Trademark Office. Questions related to size standards for a small business concern may be directed to: Small Business Administration, Size Standards Staff, 409 Third Street, SW, Washington, DC 20416.

I hereby state that rights under contract or law have been conveyed to and remain with the small business concern identified above with regard to the invention described in:

☐   the specification filed herewith with title as listed above.

☐   the application identified above.

☐   the patent identified above.

If the rights held by the above identified small business concern are not exclusive, each individual, concern, or organization having rights in the invention must file separate statements as to their status as small entities, and no rights to the invention are held by any person, other than the inventor, who would not qualify as an independent inventor under 37 CFR 1.9(c) if that person made the invention, or by any concern which would not qualify as a small business concern under 37 CFR 1.9(d), or a nonprofit organization under 37 CFR 1.9(e).

Each person, concern, or organization having any rights in the invention is listed below:

☐ no such person, concern, or organization exists.

☐ each such person, concern, or organization is listed below.

Separate statements are required from each named person, concern or organization having rights to the invention stating their status as small entities. (37 CFR 1.27)

I acknowledge the duty to file, in this application or patent, notification of any change in status resulting in loss of entitlement to small entity status prior to paying, or at the time of paying, the earliest of the issue fee or any maintenance fee due after the date on which status as a small entity is no longer appropriate. (37 CFR 1.28(b))

NAME OF PERSON SIGNING _____

TITLE OF PERSON IF OTHER THAN OWNER _____

ADDRESS OF PERSON SIGNING _____

SIGNATURE _____ DATE _____

Burden Hour Statement: This form is estimated to take 0.2 hours to complete. Time will vary depending upon the needs of the individual case. Any comments on the amount of time you are required to complete this form should be sent to the Chief Information Officer, Patent and Trademark Office, Washington, DC 20231. DO NOT SEND FEES OR COMPLETED FORMS TO THIS ADDRESS. SEND TO: Assistant Commissioner for Patents, Washington, DC 20231.

FIGURE 18-2
Small Entity Statement

FIGURE 18 3
Schedule of Patent Fees

Description	Fee	Small Entity Fee
Utility application filing fee	$690	$345
Design application filing fee	$310	$155
Plant application filing fee	$480	$240
Submission of IDS	$240	$240
Reissue filing fee	$690	$345
Provisional application filing fee	$150	$75
Issue fee for utility patent	$1,210	$605
Issue fee for design patent	$430	$215
Issue fee for plant patent	$580	$290
Maintenance fee due at 3‰ years	$830	$415
Maintenance fee due at 7‰ years	$1,900	$950
Maintenance fee due at 11‰ years	$2,910	$1,455
Statutory disclaimer	$110	$55
Notice of appeal	$300	$150
Filing brief in support of appeal	$300	$150
Request for oral hearing	$260	$130
Request for reexamination	$2,520	$2,520

patents, litigation involving the invention, and any other matter that bears on patentability. The PTO does not have the capabilities of fully researching all patent applications and thus relies on applicants to disclose prior art and other matters material to patentability.

Under PTO rules, information is material to patentability when it is not cumulative to information of record and (1) it establishes a *prima facie* case of unpatentability of a claim or (2) it refutes or is inconsistent with a position taken by the applicant. To comply with this duty, applicants file an **Information Disclosure Statement (IDS)** with the PTO listing and identifying material information. The PTO provides a form (Form 1449; see Figure 18 4) for such disclosure. The IDS can be filed with the application or within three months of its filing. If the IDS is not filed during these time limits, it may be filed later, but generally additional fees will be charged and other documents may be required. If a party discovers additional material information during the course of the application process, the new information must be disclosed. In many instances, an application may be withdrawn so the newly disclosed information can be considered in a continuation-in-part application.

Breach of the duty to disclose may result in refusal to issue a patent, invalidity of the patent, and possible sanctions against the patent attorney.

PROSECUTING THE APPLICATION

Examination of the Application

Once the application is filed and a **filing receipt** is sent by the PTO to the applicant, the application will be assigned to a patent examiner who is trained

Information Disclosure Statement (IDS): A document filed by an inventor with the PTO identifying information material to patentability of an invention

filing receipt: Document mailed by the PTO to an applicant to confirm filing and details of an application

Please type a plus sign (+) inside this box → ☐

PTO/SB/08B (10-96)
Approved for use through 10/31/99. OMB 0651-0031
Patent and Trademark Office: U.S. DEPARTMENT OF COMMERCE
Under the Paperwork Reduction Act of 1995, no persons are required to respond to a collection of information unless it contains a valid OMB control number.

Substitute for form 1449B/PTO

INFORMATION DISCLOSURE STATEMENT BY APPLICANT

(use as many sheets as necessary)

Complete if Known	
Application Number	
Filing Date	
First Named Inventor	
Group Art Unit	
Examiner Name	
Attorney Docket Number	

Sheet		of	

OTHER PRIOR ART – NON PATENT LITERATURE DOCUMENTS

Examiner Initials*	Cite No.¹	Include name of the author (in CAPITAL LETTERS), title of the article (when appropriate), title of the item (book, magazine, journal, serial, symposium, catalog, etc.), date, page(s), volume-issue number(s), publisher, city and/or country where published.	T²

Examiner Signature		Date Considered	

*EXAMINER: Initial if reference considered, whether or not citation is in conformance with MPEP 609. Draw line through citation if not in conformance and not considered. Include copy of this form with next communication to applicant.

¹ Unique citation designation number. ² Applicant is to place a check mark here if English language Translation is attached.

Burden Hour Statement: This form is estimated to take 2.0 hours to complete. Time will vary depending upon the needs of the individual case. Any comments on the amount of time you are required to complete this form should be sent to the Chief Information Officer, Patent and Trademark Office, Washington, DC 20231. DO NOT SEND FEES OR COMPLETED FORMS TO THIS ADDRESS. SEND TO: Assistant Commissioner for Patents, Washington, DC 20231.

FIGURE 18–4
Information Disclosure Statement

Please type a plus sign (+) inside this box → ☐

PTO/SB/08A (10-96)
Approved for use through 10/31/99. OMB 0651-0031
Patent and Trademark Office: U.S. DEPARTMENT OF COMMERCE
Under the Paperwork Reduction Act of 1995, no persons are required to respond to a collection of information unless it contains a valid OMB control number.

Substitute for form 1449A/PTO	*Complete if Known*	
INFORMATION DISCLOSURE STATEMENT BY APPLICANT *(use as many sheets as necessary)*	Application Number	
	Filing Date	
	First Named Inventor	
	Group Art Unit	
	Examiner Name	
Sheet ___ of ___	Attorney Docket Number	

U.S. PATENT DOCUMENTS

Examiner Initials*	Cite No.¹	U.S. Patent Document Number	Kind Code² (if known)	Name of Patentee or Applicant of Cited Document	Date of Publication of Cited Document MM-DD-YYYY	Pages, Columns, Lines, Where Relevant Passages or Relevant Figures Appear

FOREIGN PATENT DOCUMENTS

Examiner Initials*	Cite No.¹	Office³	Foreign Patent Document Number⁴	Kind Code⁵ (if known)	Name of Patentee or Applicant of Cited Document	Date of Publication of Cited Document MM-DD-YYYY	Pages, Columns, Lines, Where Relevant Passages or Relevant Figures Appear	T⁶

Examiner Signature		Date Considered	

*EXAMINER: Initial if reference considered, whether or not citation is in conformance with MPEP 609. Draw line through citation if not in conformance and not considered. Include copy of this form with next communication to applicant.

¹ Unique citation designation number. ² See attached Kinds of U.S. Patent Documents. ³ Enter Office that issued the document, by the two-letter code (WIPO Standard ST.3). ⁴ For Japanese patent documents, the indication of the year of the reign of the Emperor must precede the serial number of the patent document. ⁵ Kind of document by the appropriate symbols as indicated on the document under WIPO Standard ST. 16 if possible. ⁶ Applicant is to place a check mark here if English language Translation is attached.

Burden Hour Statement: This form is estimated to take 2.0 hours to complete. Time will vary depending upon the needs of the individual case. Any comments on the amount of time you are required to complete this form should be sent to the Chief Information Officer, Patent and Trademark Office, Washington, DC 20231. DO NOT SEND FEES OR COMPLETED FORMS TO THIS ADDRESS. SEND TO: Assistant Commissioner for Patents, Washington, DC 20231.

FIGURE 18–4
Information Disclosure Statement (continued)

in the field to which the invention pertains. The examiner will review the application, conduct a search in the patent files of the prior art, and determine if the invention is patentable. If the examiner finds defects in the application or rejects some of the claims, he or she will issue an office action (similar to the office action issued by trademark examiners in rejecting trademark applications). If the examiner determines there are no bars to patentability, a notice of allowance will be issued for the application. Relatively few applications are allowed as filed.

It is far more likely that at least one office action will be issued, often indicating that based on the prior art, the subject matter claimed is either not novel or is obvious or that not enough information is disclosed in the application to enable another to practice what is claimed. The maximum time limit to respond to an office action is six months. Typically, however, the examiner demands that a response be filed within three months. The applicant may then obtain one-month extensions, up to a total of three, upon filing a petition asking for an extension and payment of a fee. If a written response to an office action is not timely filed, the application will be abandoned. If the final day for a response falls on a nonbusiness day or holiday, the applicant has until the next business day to file the response. The applicant may also request either a telephonic or in-person interview with the examiner to discuss the office action.

An applicant's response to an office action may include amendments to claims, drawings, or portions of the specification. Although amendments may be added to make explicit a disclosure that was implicit in the application as originally filed, amendments adding "new matter" are normally not allowed. Thus, claims may be amended and even added as long as they are supported by the original specifications in the application. If the applicant believes the examiner's rejection of some claims to be sound, those may be canceled and the applicant may proceed on the remainder. Alternatively, the applicant may submit argument attempting to demonstrate patentability and may submit evidence of secondary considerations, such as evidence of commercial success of the invention or its long-felt need.

The process of office action by the examiner and response by the applicant will continue either until the application is allowed or the examiner enters a **final action** rejecting one or more of the claims. An applicant may appeal a final action (or may initiate an appeal when his or her claims have been rejected twice) to the Board of Patent Appeals and Interferences in the PTO. An appeal fee ($300/$150) is required, and the applicant must file a brief to support his or her position. An oral hearing will be held, if requested, upon payment of a specified fee ($260/$130). If the board affirms the examiner's decision, the applicant may file an appeal with either the U.S. District Court for the District of Columbia or with the Court of Appeals for the Federal Circuit (CAFC), located in Washington, DC. Many experts believe the Federal Circuit defers too readily to the board, noting that CAFC affirms between 75 and 90 percent of the board's determinations. The Federal Circuit can set aside PTO findings only when the findings are arbitrary, capricious, an abuse of discretion, or unsupported by substantial evidence. *Dickinson v. Zurko,* No. 98-377 (U.S. June 10, 1999). Decisions by CAFC may be appealed to the United States Supreme Court; however, the Supreme Court has the discretionary power to deny *certiorari* and refuse to hear the case.

final action: Action by the PTO refusing a trademark or patent application; also called *final refusal*

Restriction Requirements

If an inventor claims two or more independent and distinct inventions in one application, the examiner will issue a **restriction requirement,** requiring the applicant to restrict or limit the application to one invention. The other invention may be pursued in a divisional application for which a separate application fee must be paid. Independent inventions are those that are unconnected in their design, operation, or function. For example, combining a bread-maker with a hair dryer, two articles that are not capable of being used together, would result in a restriction requirement. An applicant may argue against the examiner's requirement that an application be restricted to one invention. Such an argument is called a **traverse.**

Divisional Applications

If the applicant agrees with the examiner that the application includes two independent and distinct inventions and agrees to restrict the application to one invention, the second invention is usually protected or covered by the creation of a divisional application, a separate and distinct application. The divisional application retains the filing date of its **parent application.** It is possible that creation of the divisional application may require changes in inventors inasmuch as the claims in the newly created divisional application may be the product of different inventors from those claims set forth in the original parent application.

Continuation Applications

If the examiner continues to refuse some claims in an application while accepting others, the applicant may wish to divide the application and allow the approved claims to proceed to issuance while continuing to do battle with the examiner on the rejected claims. Such a "continuation application" requires a separate filing fee. Because patents cannot be enforced until they are issued, and the period of protection runs for twenty years from the date of application, an applicant should consider the strategy of moving forward with whatever he or she can to obtain patent protection as soon as possible. Filing a continuation application affords the applicant the opportunity to continue argument on the disputed claims while allowing the permitted claims to proceed to issuance. Moreover, because the continuation application retains the same date as the earlier "parent" application, the continuation application may be able to circumvent "prior art" that came into being after the original filing date and that would bar an entirely new application. A continuation application contains no new material.

If an applicant wishes to proceed on allowed claims and pursue rejected and additional matter that differs from that in the parent application, the applicant will file a "continuation-in-part" application. Because the continuation-in-part application includes additional information not in the original application (often, new improvements recently discovered), it requires a new oath and declaration. A continuation-in-part application may have two filing dates: the original filing date for the original material and a new filing date for the newly added material.

restriction requirement: Requirement by the PTO that a patent applicant limit a patent application to one invention when two or more distinct inventions are claimed in one application

traverse: Arguments made in response to objections by the PTO to a trademark or patent application

parent application: An original trademark or patent application that is the source or parent of a later separate application

The distinction between a continuation application and a continuation-in-part application is that the former contains no new information while the latter includes new matter.

Double Patenting

Another basis for refusal to issue a patent is double patenting. An applicant may not obtain two patents for the same invention. The doctrine prohibiting double patenting is an attempt to ensure that inventors do not apply piecemeal for patents in an effort to extend the term during which they may preclude others from making, selling, or using the invention. A rejection based on double patenting may arise because of an applicant's related application or already issued patent for the same subject matter or subject matter that is an obvious variation of that in the application.

If the subject matter is identical, the applicant must cancel one set of claims. If the examiner states that the subject matter is not identical but is rather an obvious variation of that in another application or issued patent, and the examiner cannot be persuaded otherwise, the applicant may enter a terminal disclaimer, agreeing that the term of the second patent will not extend beyond the term of the first. Both patents will simultaneously terminate. A terminal disclaimer will remedy a refusal based on double patenting only if the refusal alleges that the second invention is an obvious variation of another. A refusal alleging that two identical inventions have been applied for or patented cannot be remedied by a terminal disclaimer. The duplicate claims in the second application must be canceled.

Interference Practice

In the course of examination, an examiner may discover that another party's pending application or issued patent conflicts with the application in that the subject matter claimed in the application under examination is substantially the same as that claimed in a prior application or existing patent. In such cases, an **interference** will be declared or initiated by the PTO, and a determination will be made regarding priority of invention by the Board of Patent Appeals and Interferences. About one percent of applications filed with the PTO become involved in an interference proceeding. In many of those cases, interferences are declared because, due to the confidentiality of PTO application proceedings, applicants may not know of other conflicting inventions at the time they file their applications. Because patents are typically issued to the "first to invent," a determination must be made by the PTO in regard to which invention has priority.

Generally, the inventor who proves to be the first to conceive the invention and the first to reduce it to practice either by filing the application (constructive reduction to practice) or by making and testing an embodiment of the invention (actual reduction to practice) will be held to be the first inventor. If an inventor is the first to conceive of the invention but the second to reduce it to practice, he or she may still prevail upon a showing that diligent efforts were made to reduce the invention to practice.

After holding a hearing and receiving testimony, the board will issue a decision. Appeal may be made to CAFC. A dissatisfied party also has the option of initiating a civil action to determine the matter. Alternatively, during the course

interference: A proceeding before the Trademark Trial and Appeal Board when marks in two pending trademark applications are confusingly similar or when a mark in a pending application may be confusingly similar to a registered mark that is not yet incontestable; a proceeding initiated by the PTO to determine which of two or more patents has priority

of any interference proceeding, the parties may reach a private settlement that will be binding on the PTO if they file their agreement resolving the matter with the PTO.

Notice of Allowance and Issuance of Patent

If the examiner allows the claims, a notice of allowance will be issued to the applicant. Within three months, the applicant must pay an "issue fee" to the PTO for the patent to be granted. At present, the issue fee for a utility patent is $1,210 ($605 for a small entity), $430/$215 for a design patent, and $580/$290 for a plant patent. When the issue fee is paid, the patent will be granted and a patent number and issue date will be given to the application. The applicant, now the **patentee,** may enforce its rights to exclude others from making, selling, or using the invention. Furthermore, once a patent is issued, there is a statutory presumption of its validity. 35 U.S.C. § 282. On the date of the grant by the PTO, the patent file becomes open to the public. Failure to pay the issue fee when due will result in abandonment of the application (unless late payment was unavoidable or unintentional and a showing is made demonstrating such).

It generally takes between two and three years for a patent to be issued, compared with four to five months for registration of a copyright and approximately eighteen months to secure trademark registration.

(See Figure 18–5 for a flowchart illustrating the patent prosecution process.)

Portions of the issued patent will be published in the *Official Gazette,* the weekly publication of the PTO. While the purpose of publishing trademarks in the *Official Gazette* is to provide notice so those who may be damaged by registration of a mark may oppose registration, publication of patents in the *Official Gazette* is done merely to provide information about patents, including patents that may be available for sale or license. The *Official Gazette* will include a claim and a selected figure of the drawings of each patent granted on that date, notices of patent lawsuits, a list of patents available for license or sale, and other general information such as changes in patent rules.

Utility patents are assigned numbers such as 4,999,904. Design patents are assigned a number as well as the letter "D," such as D39704. Plant patents are assigned a number and the letters "PP," as in PP4074.

(See Figure 18–6 for a sample of an issued patent.)

Notice of Patent

During the time that the application for the patent is pending, an inventor may mark the invention with the term *patent pending* or *patent applied for.* These notices have no legal effect, although they do provide notice that a patent application has been filed with the PTO. Use of these terms or any other implying that an application for a patent has been made, when it has not, is a violation of statute and is punishable by fine. 35 U.S.C. § 292.

Once a patent has been issued, its owner may give notice that an article or invention is patented by using the word *patent* or its abbreviation *pat.,* together with the number of the patent. The notice may be placed on the article or on a label attached to the article. Use of the notice is not mandatory; however, in the event of failure to use the notice, no damages may be recovered by the patentee in

patentee: The owner of a patent issued by the PTO

FIGURE 18–5
Patent Prosecution
Flowchart

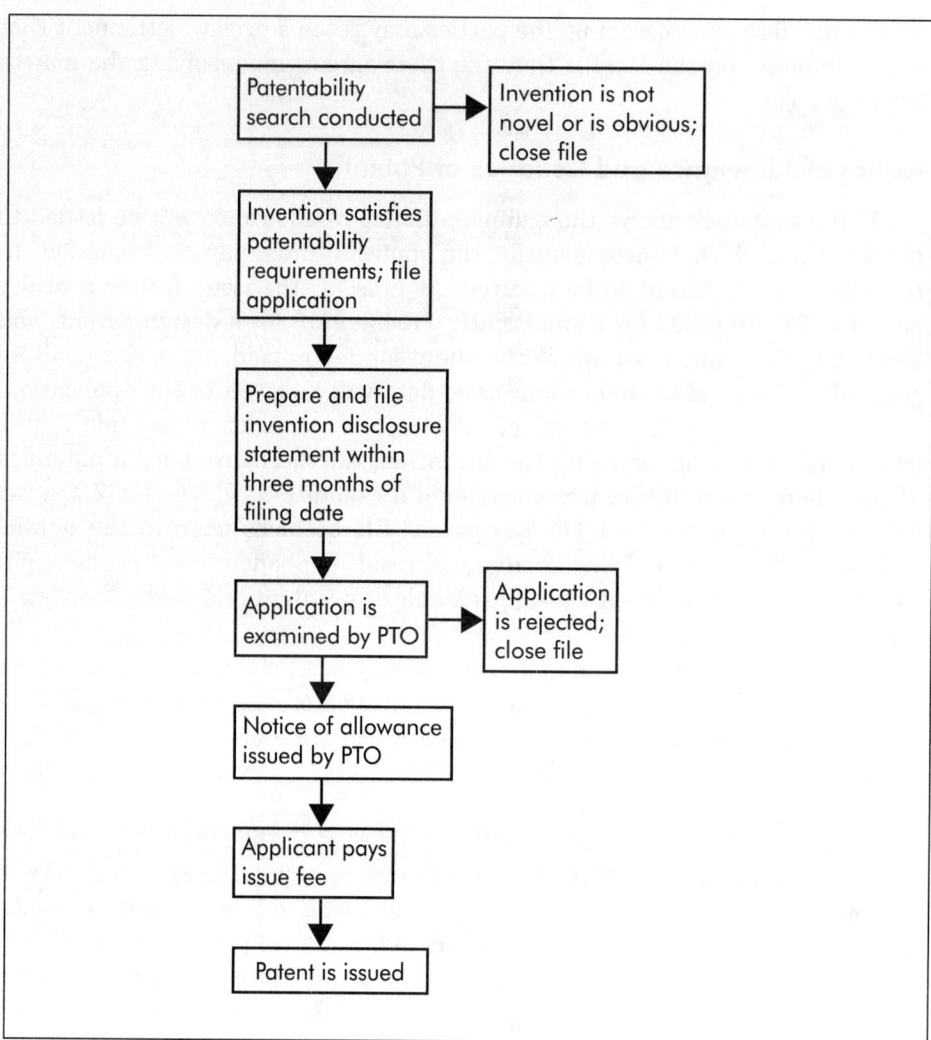

any infringement action, unless it is proved that the infringer was notified of the infringement and continued to infringe thereafter. Marking of the patented invention constitutes such notice. Thus, although use of the notice is not required, it is always recommended. False marking is prohibited and is punishable by fine.

POSTISSUANCE ACTIONS

Correction of Defective Patents: Certificates of Correction and Reissue Patents

Errors occurring through the fault of the PTO, minor errors (such as typographical errors), and errors in the naming of inventors can be corrected by asking the PTO to issue a "Certificate of Correction." Mistakes made by the PTO will be corrected without charge. Mistakes made by the applicant will be corrected upon the payment of a $100 fee.

Errors that are more significant, such as defects in the specifications or drawings, that cause the patent to be partially or wholly inoperative or invalid

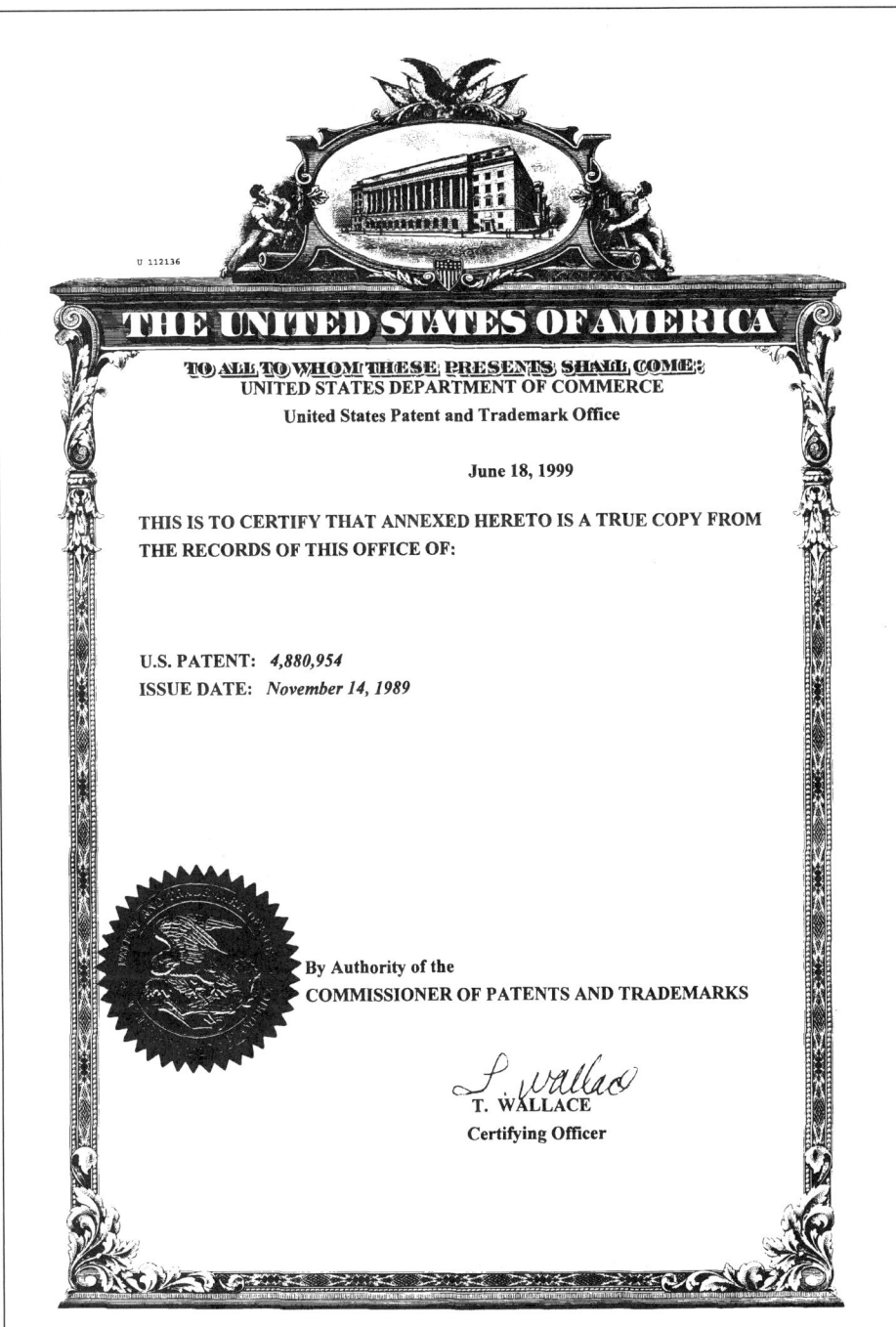

FIGURE 18–6
Issued Patent

are corrected by a **reissue patent.** A reissue patent may also be sought for the purpose of enlarging claims. The patentee's attorney may have failed to state the claims broadly enough or the patentee may discover that the claims stated in the issued patent are narrower than the prior art would require the patentee to make. In cases in which the patentee seeks to broaden claims, a reissue application must be filed within two years of the grant of the original patent. A reissue application can be made only if the error was committed without deceptive

reissue patent: A proceeding to correct defects in an issued patent or to enlarge the claims of an issued patent

FIGURE 18–6
Issued Patent (continued)

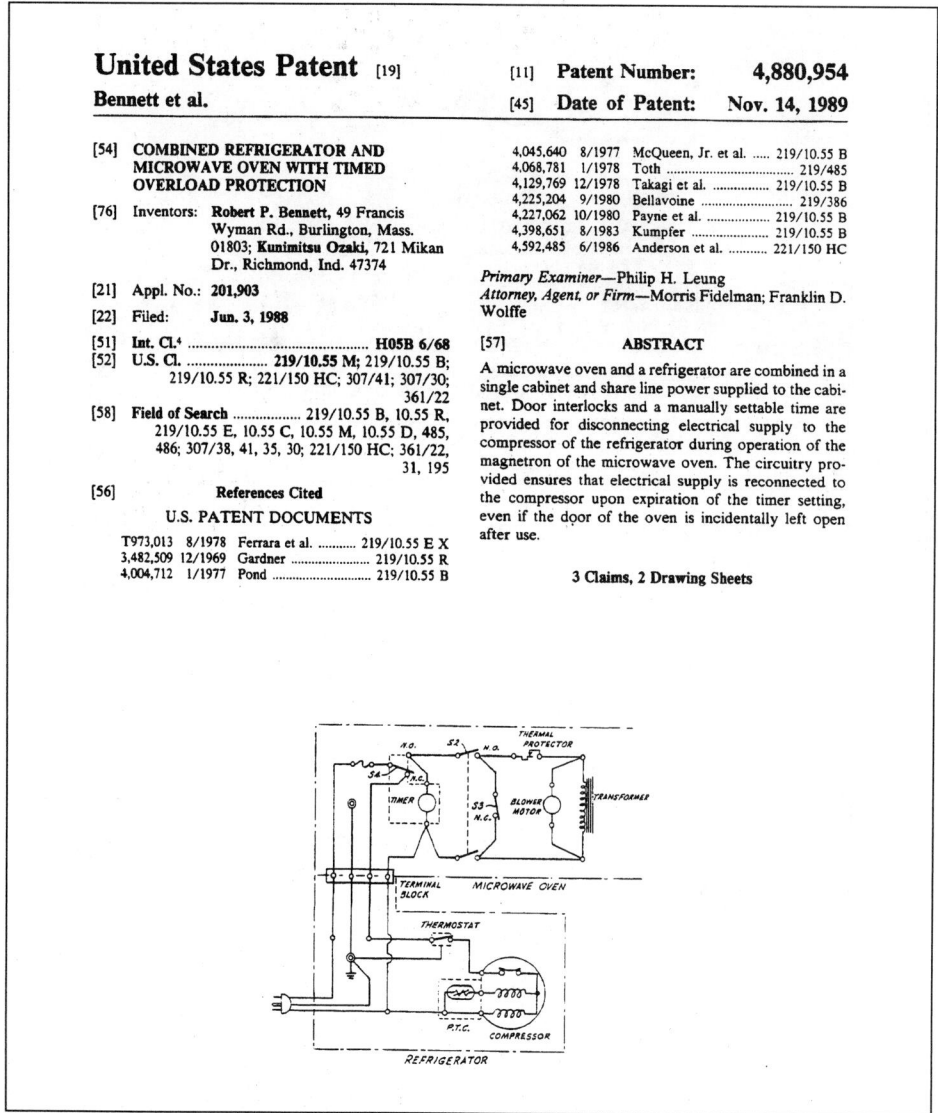

United States Patent [19]

Bennett et al.

[11] Patent Number: **4,880,954**

[45] Date of Patent: **Nov. 14, 1989**

[54] **COMBINED REFRIGERATOR AND MICROWAVE OVEN WITH TIMED OVERLOAD PROTECTION**

[76] Inventors: **Robert P. Bennett**, 49 Francis Wyman Rd., Burlington, Mass. 01803; **Kunimitsu Ozaki**, 721 Mikan Dr., Richmond, Ind. 47374

[21] Appl. No.: **201,903**

[22] Filed: **Jun. 3, 1988**

[51] Int. Cl.⁴ H05B 6/68
[52] U.S. Cl. .... **219/10.55 M**; 219/10.55 B; 219/10.55 R; 221/150 HC; 307/41; 307/30; 361/22
[58] Field of Search .... 219/10.55 B, 10.55 R, 219/10.55 E, 10.55 C, 10.55 M, 10.55 D, 485, 486; 307/38, 41, 35, 30; 221/150 HC; 361/22, 31, 195

[56]   **References Cited**

U.S. PATENT DOCUMENTS

T973,013   8/1978   Ferrara et al. .... 219/10.55 E X
3,482,509 12/1969 Gardner .... 219/10.55 R
4,004,712   1/1977 Pond .... 219/10.55 B

4,045,640 8/1977   McQueen, Jr. et al. ..... 219/10.55 B
4,068,781 1/1978   Toth 219/485
4,129,769 12/1978 Takagi et al. .... 219/10.55 B
4,225,204 9/1980   Bellavoine 219/386
4,227,062 10/1980 Payne et al. .... 219/10.55 B
4,398,651 8/1983   Kumpfer .... 219/10.55 B
4,592,485 6/1986   Anderson et al. .... 221/150 HC

Primary Examiner—Philip H. Leung
Attorney, Agent, or Firm—Morris Fidelman; Franklin D. Wolffe

[57]   **ABSTRACT**

A microwave oven and a refrigerator are combined in a single cabinet and share line power supplied to the cabinet. Door interlocks and a manually settable time are provided for disconnecting electrical supply to the compressor of the refrigerator during operation of the magnetron of the microwave oven. The circuitry provided ensures that electrical supply is reconnected to the compressor upon expiration of the timer setting, even if the door of the oven is incidentally left open after use.

3 Claims, 2 Drawing Sheets

intent. While claims may be enlarged because the patentee originally claimed less than he or she had a right to claim, no new matter may be allowed.

An oath or declaration must be filed and facts must be set forth showing the grounds for the application for reissue. The filing fee for a reissue application is $760/$380 (the same as that for an original application). A reissue application is examined under the same procedures as any application. If the application is granted, the original patent is surrendered. The reissue patent is identified by the prefix "RE" in the PTO records, for example, RE4,901,804, and its term is the same as that of the original patent inasmuch as it is granted to replace the original patent.

It is possible that during the two-year period before a reissue application is made, a third party has begun offering a device that does not infringe the original patent claims but which now infringes the reissue patent with its broader claims. In such a case, the third party may continue offering the device without liability for infringement. According to 35 U.S.C. § 252, no reissued patent shall affect the right of such an intervening party to continue to use or sell a device or invention unless the device or invention infringes a valid claim of the reissued

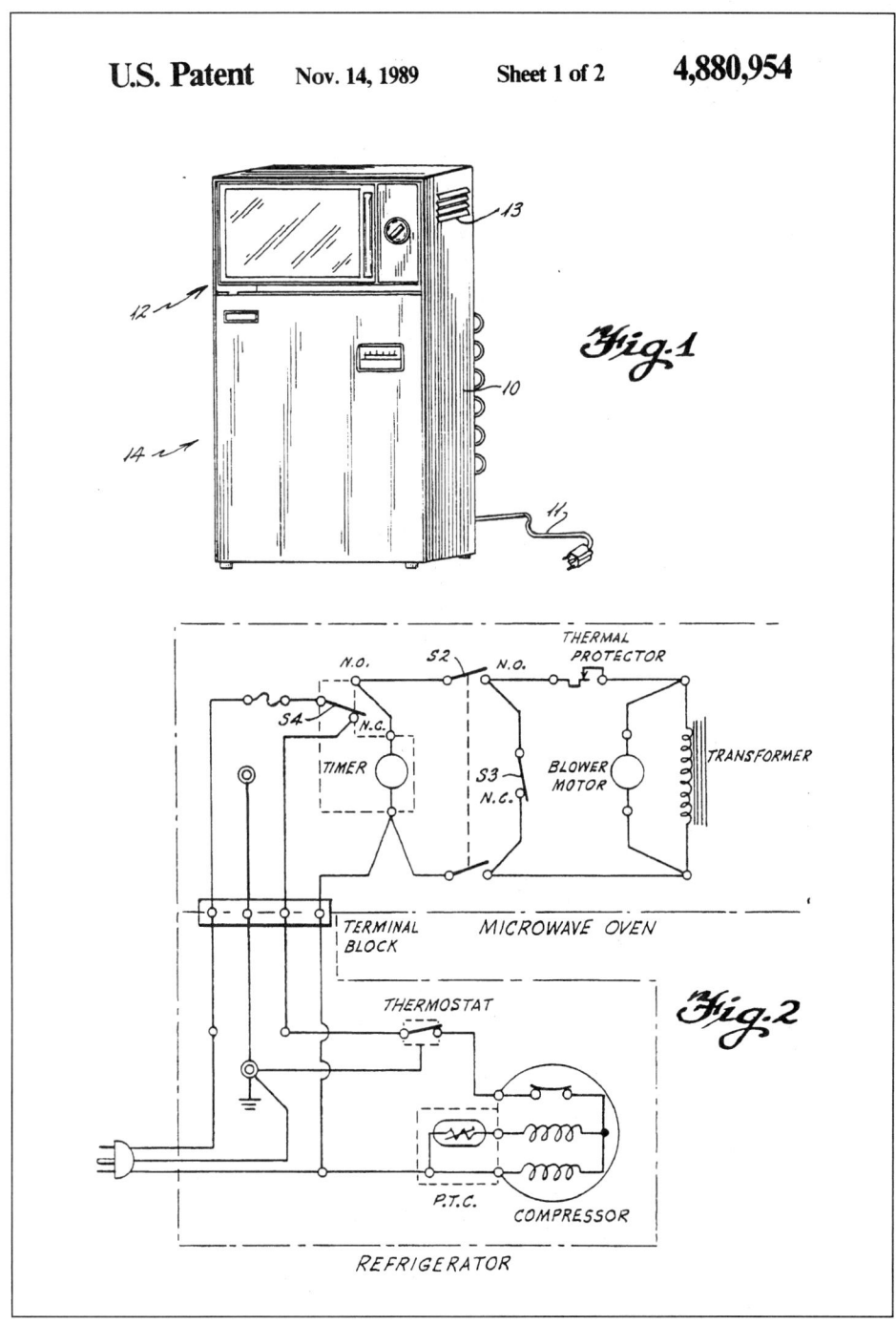

FIGURE 18–6
Issued Patent (continued)

patent that was in the original patent as well; otherwise, the significant investment an innocent third party might make in bringing a product to market would be lost. The intervening party, however, may continue to make or sell only the same specific thing; no additional devices can be offered.

Reexamination

When trademarks are published for opposition in the *Official Gazette,* third parties who believe they may be harmed by registration of the mark may oppose registration of the mark. Similarly, even after trademark registration, a

FIGURE 18–6
Issued Patent (continued)

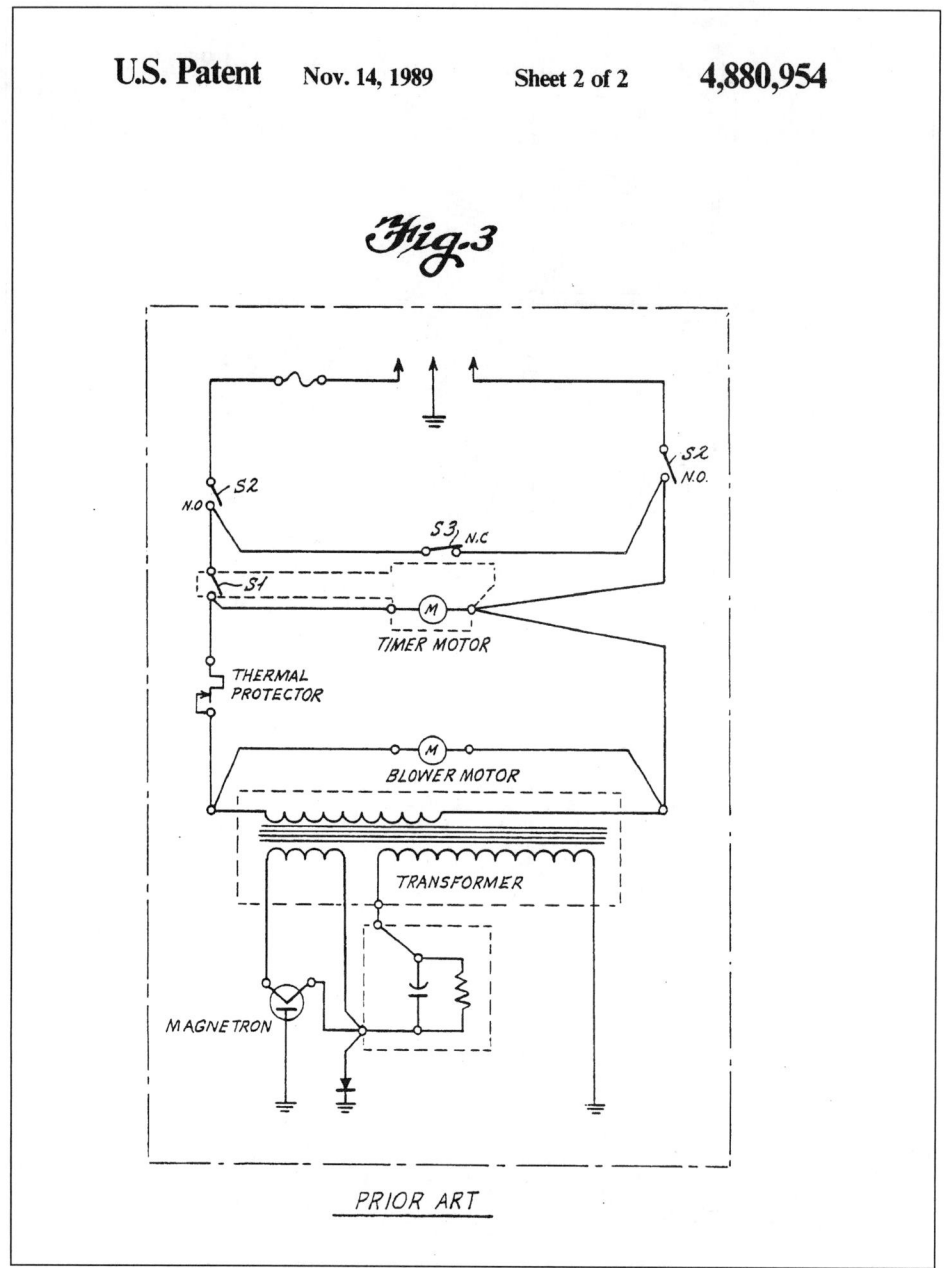

U.S. Patent   Nov. 14, 1989   Sheet 2 of 2   4,880,954

Fig.3

PRIOR ART

registration may be canceled on certain grounds, including confusing similarity to a prior mark. Federal law affords no equivalent rights to a party to oppose the issuance of a patent or to cancel a patent on the basis he or she would be harmed by its issuance. In fact, because pending patent applications are kept confidential, parties seldom know whether an application has been filed for a patent.

Nevertheless, 35 U.S.C. §§ 301 and 302 provide that any person, including either the patent owner or an accused infringer of a patent, may file a request for reexamination of any claim in an issued patent based upon the prior art, namely, patents or printed publications that may have a bearing on the patentability of a claim. A request for reexamination may be made at any time during the term of the patent and must be accompanied by a filing fee of $2,520.

FIGURE 18-6
Issued Patent (continued)

4,880,954

1

COMBINED REFRIGERATOR AND MICROWAVE OVEN WITH TIMED OVERLOAD PROTECTION

PRIOR ART CROSS REFERENCES

U.S. Pat. No. 3,482,509 Gardner, SANDWICH COOKING AND DISPENSING MACHINE, issued Dec. 9, 1969.

U.S. Pat. No. 4,225,204—Bellavoine. CUPBOARD FOR STORING PREPARED MEALS, WITH COLD-STORAGE AND REHEATING BY MICROWAVES, issued Sept. 30, 1980.

U.S. Pat. 4,398,651 Kumpfer, MICROWAVE FOOD DISPENSING MACHINE, issued Aug. 16, 1983.

U.S. Pat. No. 4,592,485—Anderson, et al, MEAL VENDING APPARATUS, issued June 3, 1986.

U.S. application Ser. No. 097,680—Bennett, REFRIGERATOR AND MICROWAVE OVEN AND OVERDEMAND INTERRUPT CIRCUIT, filed Sept. 17, 1987.

BACKGROUND OF THE INVENTION

This invention relates to a refrigerator and microwave oven enclosed in the same cabinet with unique electrical circuitry, so as to provide the convenience of storing and cooking food simultaneously in the same unit, while avoiding the peak power demands of simultaneous operation of the refrigerator compressor and the microwave magnetron. The invention finds particular application in buildings having older wiring and fewer circuits, by minimizing the possibilities of overloading such circuits while providing safe uninterrupted service. It also prevents overloading a more modern circuit which is "dedicated" to the apparatus by preventing start-up of the compressor during operation of the magnetron.

Microwave ovens are now commonly available in quick stop grocery stores and lunch rooms for heating and cooking foodstuffs purchased across the counter and from vending machines. Prior to the above-referenced Bennett application though, it had not been proposed to combine a microwave oven and refrigerator on a smaller scale in the same cabinet, particularly with provision for limiting the peak instantaneous power consumption so as to make the combination useful and attractive for use by students in dorm rooms, resort hotel rooms, tractor trailer cabs, recreational vehicles, so-called pullman efficiencies and the like.

The remaining prior art teaches refrigerated storage and a microwave oven combined in the same vending machine cabinet, and provision for transporting a selected item to the microwave oven for heating and subsequent removal from the machine. In particular, U.S. Pat. No. 4,398,651 discloses a switch, associated with a stack of food containers and actuated upon insertion of the uppermost container from the stack into a microwave oven, which causes a motor to drive a screw which, in turn, raises the stack until the next uppermost container changes the state of the switch. The amount of time that it takes for the switch to be changed by the raising stack determines the time of de-energization of a relay 56 which, in turn, determines how long the refrigerator is off and the microwave oven is on.

It is among the objects of the instant invention to combine prior art appliances into a single more convenient apparatus by utilizing a single molded, insulated shell containing both a microwave oven and a refrigera-

2

tor, while at the same time providing adequate ventilation of both and limiting instantaneous peak power consumption by the combination.

SUMMARY OF THE INVENTION

A microwave oven and a refrigerator are combined in a single cabinet and share line power supplied to the cabinet. Door interlocks and a manually settable time are provided for disconnecting electrical supply to the compressor of the refrigerator during operation of the magnetron of the microwave oven. The circuitry provided ensures that electrical supply is reconnected to the compressor upon expiration of the timer setting, even if the door of the oven is incidentally left open after use.

BRIEF DESCRIPTION OF THE DRAWINGS

FIG. 1 is an isometric view of a microwave oven and refrigerator sharing a common housing.

FIG. 2 is a schematic diagram illustrating an electrical circuit providing features of the instant invention.

FIG. 3 is a schematic circuit diagram of a conventional microwave oven.

DETAILED DESCRIPTION OF THE INVENTION

Referring to the drawings, cabinet 10 houses a microwave oven upper section 12 and a refrigerator lower section 14, with louvers 13 for venting the microwave section and cord 11 for supplying power to the combined refrigerator and microwave device from the standard receptacle.

The basic housing 10 comprises molded inner and outer shells with appropriate insulation therebetween, and these shells may be comprised of several panels defining sides, top, bottom, front and back of the device. The construction of the refrigerator section generally is well known and includes a freezer compartment. Below or at the rear of the refrigerated compartment and above the bottom panel is a refrigeration unit including condenser coils (not shown), while heat transfer mesh or screen is attached at the rear of the unit.

Above refrigerator section 14, and thermally insulated therefrom, is the microwave oven section 12 having the cooking compartment thereof surrounded by an absorptive layer. The absorptive layer is for preventing microwave energy from (1) reflecting from the outer wall and back to the magnetron of the microwave oven and thus damaging the magnetron, (2) warming foodstuffs in adjacent refrigerator compartments, and (3) escaping from the unit to the surrounding environment.

Of particular importance in the invention is the provision of a timing circuit 30 for controlling power to the magnetron and the compressor of the refrigerator.

Referring to FIG. 3, the magnetron of a conventional microwave is supplied with power via a transformer. In FIG. 3, the door of the oven is open and, upon closing thereof, the interlock switches S2 are closed and switch S3 is opened. Thus, the door must be closed in order for line power to be supplied to the timer switch S1 and to the transformer.

However, in order to combine a microwave oven and refrigerator in the same cabinet, while sharing line power supplied to the cabinet in the least costly and most efficient manner, it is necessary to ensure that the magnetron of the oven and the compressor of the refrigerator are not operated at the same time.

Within three months following the filing of a request for reexamination, the PTO will determine whether a substantial new question of patentability affecting any claim of the patent has been raised. If the PTO determines that a substantial question is raised, **reexamination of the patent** will be ordered so the question may be resolved. Reexamination procedure is identical to the procedure for initial examination of a patent application. The patent owner is permitted to amend his or her claims to distinguish them from the prior art, although no new matter enlarging or broadening the scope of a claim is permitted. If a reexamined claim is determined to be unpatentable, it will be canceled. If a reexamined claim is confirmed as

reexamination of patent:
Proceeding initiated at the PTO to review or reexamine a claim in an issued patent to determine its validity

FIGURE 18–6
Issued Patent (continued)

4,880,954

3

As seen in FIG. 2, the instant invention provides that the manually settable timer of a microwave oven interrupts line power to the refrigerator compressor by means of switch S4 whenever the timer is operating, while providing that same line power to the microwave oven and magnetron thereof in a manner that ensures the availability of line power to the refrigerator compressor upon completion of the timing function, even if the door of the microwave has been left open. In other words, with the timer manually set and actuated so that power is supplied to the timer motor via switch 54 according to a desired cooking time by the microwave oven, and with the door of the oven closed so that the interlock switches S2 and S3 allow supply of line power to the transformer of the microwave, opening the door of the prior to completion of the timing function will open switches S2 and interrupt power to the magnetron, but not to the timer. Thus, if the door is left open, line power can again be supplied to the compressor via switch S4 at the end of the previously selected timing period.

Having described the invention, it will be seen that the objects set forth above, among those made apparent from the preceding description, are efficiently obtained and, since certain changes may be made in carrying out the above method and in the construction set forth without departing from the scope of the invention, it is intended that all matter contained in the above description or shown in the accompanying drawings shall be interpreted as illustrative and not in a limiting sense.

It is also to be understood that the following claims are intended to cover all of the generic and specific features of the invention hereindescribed, and all statements of the scope of the invention which, as a matter of language, might be said to fall therebetween.

Now that the invention has been described, I claim:

1. In a method of operating a compressor of a refrigerator and a magnetron of a microwave oven, said re-

4

frigerator and microwave oven being combined in a single cabinet, the improvement comprising the steps of:

providing said microwave oven with manually settable means for timing supply of operating power to said magnetron for different, selectable periods of time;

setting said timing means according to each desired period of operation of said magnetron;

starting and operating said timing means according to said setting; and

preventing operation of said refrigerator compressor by and during said operating of said timing means.

2. In an electrical supply control circuit for a compressor of a refrigerator and a magnetron of a microwave oven, said refrigerator and microwave oven being combined in a single cabinet and sharing line power supplied to said cabinet, the improvement comprising:

manually settable means for timing supply of operating power to said magnetron for different, selectable periods of time; and

means for interrupting a power path to said refrigerator compressor during said operating of said timing means.

3. In an electrical supply control circuit for a compressor of a refrigerator and a magnetrom of a microwave oven, said refrigerator and microwave oven being combined in a single cabinet and sharing line power supplied to said cabinet, said microwave oven being provided with a door having interlock means for interrupting power to said magnetron when said door is open, the improvement comprising:

manually settable means for timing supply of operating power to said magnetron for different, selectable periods of time;

means for interrupting a power path to said refrigerator compressor during said operating of said timing means; and

circuitry means for reestablishing said power path upon cessation of said timing means even when said door is open.

* * * * *

patentable, a certificate of confirmation will be issued by the PTO. The Patent Act requires that reexamination procedure be conducted with "special dispatch."

The reexamination procedure can provide an alternative to litigation. Prior to commencing an infringement action, either the patent owner or the potential defendant may request reexamination of an issued patent. Reexamination is less expensive and more expeditious than patent infringement litigation, confirms that claims are patentable, and may thus provide impetus for the parties to settle a dispute.

Disclaimers

A patent owner who discovers that a claim in a patent is invalid may cancel the claim by filing a *disclaimer.* 35 U.S.C. § 253. The other claims remain valid and are unaffected by the disclaimer of the affected claim. A patent owner is not required to cancel an invalid claim, but cannot recover costs in an infringement suit alleging infringement of the valid claims unless the invalid claim is canceled prior to commencement of the lawsuit.

TERM AND MAINTENANCE OF PATENTS

Term of Patents

For a number of years, the term of a utility patent was seventeen years from the date of issuance. To align the U.S. patent system with that of most European countries and Japan, effective June 8, 1995, the term of utility and plant patents was changed from seventeen years from issuance to twenty years from the date of filing of the application. The new provisions thus encourage inventors to prosecute applications in a timely manner. Under special statutory provisions, patents in existence or issued under applications filed before June 8, 1995, have a term of seventeen years from issuance, or twenty years from filing, whichever is longer. The term for design patents is fourteen years from the date of issuance. After the term for any patent expires, anyone in the public has a right to make, use, or sell the invention or process (assuming no other government agency approval, such as that of the FDA, is required).

There are some rare exceptions to the twenty-year term. For example, if the application has been subject to an interference action, the term is extended for the period of delay (assuming the delay does not extend more than five years). Similarly, because certain patented items, such as drugs, cannot be marketed until they are reviewed by agencies such as the FDA and such review may take considerable time, the patent term may be extended, generally by a time equal to the regulatory review period. Patent terms can also be extended if the patent application was subject to a successful appellate review or if a **secrecy order** (orders generally imposed by the government to protect inventions relating to national security) delayed issuance of the patent.

Maintenance Fees

To maintain a utility patent in force, certain fees must be paid to the PTO at three times throughout the term of the patent. **Maintenance fees** are due at the 3‰-, 7‰-, and 11‰-year anniversaries of the date of issuance. If the maintenance fees are not paid on or within six months before the due date or within a six-month grace period thereafter, the patent will expire at the end of the grace period. A surcharge is assessed if payment is made within the six-month grace period. Patents that expire for nonpayment of maintenance fees can be revived only upon a showing of unavoidable or unintentional delay.

At present, the maintenance fees are as follows:

Due Date	Regular Fee/Small Entity Fee
Due at 3‰ years:	$830/$415
Due at 7‰ years:	$1,900/$950
Due at 11‰ years:	$2,910/$1,455

The surcharge for late payments made within six months of the due date is $130/$65.

No maintenance fees are due for design or plant patents.

secrecy order: An order issued by the PTO requiring that an invention be kept secret and prohibiting publication of it or patent applications for it in another country, generally for national security reasons

maintenance fees: Fees due at 3‰, 7‰, and 11‰ years after issuance of a utility patent required to keep it in force

ROLE OF INTELLECTUAL PROPERTY PROFESSIONAL

Intellectual property professionals are involved in a variety of tasks in the patent prosecution process, including the following:

- conducting online searches to locate and retrieve patents that may bar a client's application for a patent;
- drafting claims and preparing patent applications;
- coordinating and assembling drawings for application;
- verifying small entity status;
- assisting in the patent application process by drafting and securing inventor's oath or declaration, drafting descriptions of drawings, and preparing small entity statement, if applicable;
- assembling the application packet and preparing the transmittal letter;
- preparing assignment of patent application and invention and recordation document for same, if applicable;
- preparing and filing information disclosure statements;
- docketing dates for responding to office actions and preparing requests for extensions, if necessary;
- assisting in preparing responses to office actions;
- amending application to omit inventors if their claims have been dropped from the application;
- notifying clients of status of patent prosecution;
- preparing terminal disclaimers if a double patenting rejection is made;
- assisting in preparing divisional, continuation, and continuation-in-part applications;
- reporting notice of allowance to client and docketing date for payment of issue fee;
- reviewing issued patent and making requests for correction, if necessary;
- assisting in notifying client of issuance of patent, term of duration, and necessity to maintain patent; and
- docketing dates for maintenance fees for utility patents.

CHAPTER SUMMARY

Once a patent search has been conducted to determine an invention is novel and nonobvious, a patent application can be prepared. The patent application consists of a specification describing the invention and the inventor's oath or declaration. Applicants have a duty of candor in their dealings with the PTO and must disclose anything that bears on the patentability of the invention. Applications filed at the PTO are maintained in confidentiality during the application process. Once a patent issues, however, the entire file wrapper is available for review and copying. Once the application is filed, it will be examined by an examiner who will review the specification and determine patentability. One or more office actions may be issued to amend or clarify the claims. No new matter can be added to a pending application. Once the examiner allows the application, an issue fee must be paid for the patent to be granted. Utility and plant patents have a term of twenty years from the date of application while design patents have a term of fourteen years from the date of grant. Patentees must pay fees at three different intervals to maintain a utility patent. The invention may be marked with a notice of patent, which will assist the inventor in recovering damages from infringers. After a patent has been issued, the patentee may request reissuance to correct a defective patent or to broaden claims if the application for reissuance is filed within two years after the original patent was granted. Either the patentee or a third party may request reexamination of a patent at any time during its term to determine if the patent or any of its claims are invalid.

DISCUSSION QUESTIONS

1. Tom, the inventor of an improved mountain bike, is concerned that a competitor, Nan, is nearing completion of a similar bike. Tom, however, does not have sufficient funds to file and prosecute a utility patent. What course of action should Tom consider?
2. Assume Tom has filed an application for a utility patent for the bike. Nan would like to review Tom's application and the claims in it. May she do so? Discuss.
3. Assume that after Tom filed his application, Tom entered into an agreement with ABC Company to sell the rights in the invention. ABC Company has three hundred employees. Is it entitled to the benefits of the reduced filing fees for small entities? Discuss.
4. At the time Tom filed his application, he was aware of certain prior art references that possibly related to the patentability of the invention. What is Tom's duty with regard to the information?
5. After Tom filed his application, he discovered a significant improvement to the mountain bike. How can the improvement be protected?
6. Within three months after Tom's patent was issued, Tom discovered that the claims in the patent could have been drafted more broadly. What should Tom do?
7. Five years after Tom's patent issued, Tom discovered a competitor, Ned, selling Tom's invention. Ned has informed Tom that Ned believes Tom's patent is invalid. Neither Ned nor Tom wishes to engage in litigation. Is there some alternative to them whereby their rights can be determined?
8. Perri has invented a new vegetable peeler and a new bread-kneading tool to be attached to a mixer. Perri filed one application for these inventions. What is the examiner likely to determine with regard to the application?

Patent Ownership and Transfer

Because patents have the attributes of personal property, they may be sold, licensed, or made subject to security agreements. Patent applications must be signed by the inventor of the discovery, namely, the person who conceived the invention. In many instances, inventions are the product of more than one inventor. Joint inventorship exists even when the contributions are not equal and the parties do not work in the same physical location. Disputes over ownership of invention are typically determined by the principle that the first to invent is presumed to be the one who first reduced the invention to practice. Laboratory notebooks kept by inventors assist in determining the efforts inventors have made in reducing the invention to practice. Inventions made by an employee are owned by the employee, subject, however, to a "shop right," a nonexclusive royalty-free license to use the invention in favor of the employer. In most cases, employees and employers enter into written agreements by which employees agree that any inventions will be owned by and assigned to the employer. Patents may be assigned to others (an outright sale) or may be licensed to others, in which case permission to use the invention is granted to another.

OWNERSHIP RIGHTS

Patents are items of personal property and thus may be owned, sold, licensed, or devised by will. Applications for patents must be filed by the inventor of the article, process, design, or plant. If there is more than one inventor, the application must be signed by all inventors. Although the application must be signed by the actual inventor(s), it is possible that another party may already own the invention and any rights arising from it. In many instances, employees are required to sign agreements with their employers whereby they agree that any invention or discovery invented by them while on the job will belong to the employer and that they will agree to assist and cooperate in any manner, including signing applications for patents, to ensure the employer's rights are protected. (See Appendix D, Form 13, for an agreement including provisions relating to ownership of inventions and work product by employers.)

SOLE AND JOINT INVENTORS

Sole Inventors

An invention may be the product of one person or more than one person. If one person conceives of the invention, he or she is the sole inventor. A directive given by an employer to an employee to solve a problem does not make the employer an inventor. It is finding a solution to a problem rather than articulating it that determines whether one is an inventor. Similarly, giving suggestions, making minor contributions, or helping to build a model or embodiment of the invention do not make a person an inventor.

Joint Inventors

When more than one person contributes to an invention, they are **joint inventors.** Persons may be joint inventors even though they do not physically work together or at the same time, do not make the same type or amount of contribution to the invention, or do not make a contribution to the subject matter of every claim of a patent. Each, however, must have made some contribution of inventive thought to the resulting product.

Joint inventors must each sign an application for their patent. If one of the joint inventors cannot be found or refuses to join the application, the application may be made by the others on behalf of themselves and the omitted inventor. The PTO will grant the patent to the inventor making the application, but the patent will remain subject to the rights of the omitted inventor. Errors in the naming of inventors can be readily corrected by amendment to the application or by correction to an issued patent as long as the errors occurred without any deceptive intent. Similarly, amendments occurring during prosecution that result in deletion of certain claims may require changing the named inventors if certain inventors contributed only to the deleted claims.

joint inventors: Two or more people who contribute to an invention

conception of an invention: The completion of the devising of the means for accomplishing an invention's result

actual reduction to practice: Construction of an invention in physical form, making or testing an invention or its prototype

constructive reduction to practice: The filing of a patent application that fully discloses an invention

DISPUTES OVER INVENTORSHIP

Generally, in the United States, patent rights are awarded to the first to invent. Disputes over inventorship are usually determined in interference proceedings, as described in Chapter 18. When a dispute occurs over inventorship, generally, the first to conceive the invention and to reduce it to practice (either actually or constructively) will be held to be the prior inventor. **Conception of an invention** refers to the completion of the devising of the means for accomplishing the invention's result. **Actual reduction to practice** involves construction of the invention in physical form or making or testing the invention or a prototype thereof. **Constructive reduction to practice** occurs when an application for a patent, completely disclosing the invention, is filed with the PTO.

A person who reduces the invention to practice second may prevail and be found to be the first inventor only by showing that he or she conceived the invention first and made continual diligent efforts to reduce it to practice.

Under TRIPS, and effective January 1, 1996, inventive activity abroad may be considered in determining who is the first to invent.

To determine when an invention is reduced to actual practice and which inventors worked on which claims, inventors should keep **laboratory notebooks.** Inventors should make routine entries and sketches in notebooks as work on an invention progresses and as contributions are made by others. The safest course is to have the entries witnessed by the signature of a disinterested third party. Documents relating to the work, such as telephone bills, copying charges, and expenses for materials and supplies, should also be maintained with the notebook. Such notebooks are often critical pieces of evidence in determining conception, reduction to practice, diligence, and collaboration by joint inventors.

An inventor may also file an **Invention Disclosure Document** with the PTO. The invention disclosure document is not a patent application. It is an informal document filed with the PTO that describes the invention and includes sketches or photographs. Its purpose is to provide evidence of dates of an inventor's conception of an invention, the invention's **reduction to practice,** and the inventor's diligent efforts in reducing the invention to practice. The PTO imposes no requirements in regard to the content of the document, and formal claims need not be stated. The PTO filing fee is $10. The document should be signed by the inventor or his or her attorney or agent. The document is kept in confidence by the PTO, although it will be available to the public when an application referencing it matures into an issued patent. While the PTO will retain the document for two years, the inventor is still bound by the one-year grace period and other provisions of 35 U.S.C. § 102 requiring an inventor to file an application within one year of using or offering the invention for sale in the United States or describing it in a printed publication anywhere in the world. After two years, the PTO generally destroys the invention disclosure document.

INVENTIONS MADE BY EMPLOYEES AND INDEPENDENT CONTRACTORS

Employers engaged in the business of developing inventions, drugs, processes, and other matter subject to patent protection typically require their employees to sign agreements by which the employees agree that anything discovered or invented by the employee during employment will be owned by the employer. The employee also usually agrees to assign the invention and any patent rights therein to the employer and to cooperate in filing documents and taking any other action to assist the employer in obtaining a patent. If the employee later refuses to sign an application for a patent as the inventor, the employer may do so upon a showing of his or her proprietary interest in the invention, and a patent will issue in the employer's name. (See Appendix D, Form 13).

If an employer and employee do not agree in advance about which party will own inventions conceived by the employee during the course and scope of employment, the general rule is that the employee retains ownership rights, subject to a **shop right** in favor of the employer. A shop right is a nonexclusive, royalty-free, non-transferable license of the employer to make and use the invention in the employer's business whether or not the employee remains employed by the employer. The employee may grant other licenses, may file a

laboratory notebooks: Books and notes kept by inventors as work progresses on an invention, often used in determining conception of invention and reduction to practice of an invention

Invention Disclosure Document: A document filed with the PTO that describes an invention and is intended to provide evidence of the dates of conception and reduction to practice of an invention

reduction to practice: Construction of an invention in physical form (called actual reduction to practice) or filing a patent application for an invention (called constructive reduction to practice)

shop right: An employer's non-exclusive royalty-free license to use an invention or trade secret when the employer and employee do not agree in advance as to who will own the invention or trade secret conceived by the employee while on company time

patent application and own any issued patent, and may sue for infringement by parties other than the employer. If an employee is specifically hired to solve a certain problem, however, and an invention results from the employee's work, the employee must assign the invention and any patent rights to the employer, regardless of the existence of any express agreement between the parties.

Companies that engage or commission independent contractors to work on projects or create inventions should always require that the contractor assign all inventions, discoveries, and any other intellectual property rights to the company.

Inventions made by federal employees while working for the U.S. government are generally owned by the employee. Nevertheless, the government will have a shop right to use the invention. Inventions made by companies or individuals working for the federal government pursuant to contract are usually governed by the terms of the contract. Typically, the government has the burden of demonstrating that it owns the invention. In many instances, particularly for educational, not-for-profit, or small business organizations, the government waives its patent rights. Government contracts relating to energy, nuclear propulsion, weapons programs, and other special topics generally provide that the government retains title to inventions arising from such contracts.

ASSIGNMENT OF PATENT RIGHTS

Because patents have the attributes of personal property, they may be transferred or assigned, just as may other items of personal property, and may be bequeathed by will. Patents or applications for patents may be assigned to another; a written instrument is required. 35 U.S.C. § 261. The written instrument should identify the patent by application or issue number, date, and title of the invention. An assignment is a transfer of all the rights in the patent or application, with the inventor retaining no rights (see Figure 19–1).

Although recording the assignment with the PTO is not required for an assignment to be valid, recording is recommended because an assignment is void as against a subsequent purchaser of a patent or patent application who gave valuable consideration without notice of the earlier assignment unless the first assignment is recorded with the PTO within three months from its date or prior to the time of a subsequent assignment. The PTO provides forms for recording assignments, and the patent recordation form is highly similar to that used for recording assignments of trademarks.

Pursuant to 35 U.S.C. § 262, in the absence of agreement to the contrary, each of the joint owners of a patent may make, use, license, offer to sell, or sell the patented invention without the consent of and without accounting to the other owners. Thus, similar to copyright law, each owner has the right to assign or license the patent to a third party without agreement of the other co-owners. Unlike copyright law, however, which requires accounting of profits, patent law does not require a joint owner to account to the others for monies received from such sale. Thus, it is critical that joint inventors be subject to a written agreement detailing their rights to use, make, sell, and license the invention to others.

PTO/SB/41 (8-96)
Approved for use through 9/30/98. OMB 0651-0027
Patent and Trademark Office; U.S. DEPARTMENT OF COMMERCE
Under the Paperwork Reduction Act of 1995, no persons are required to respond to a collection of information unless it displays a valid OMB control number.

ASSIGNMENT OF PATENT	Docket Number (optional)

Whereas, I, _____ of _____ , hereinafter

referred to as patentee, did obtain a United States Patent for an improvement in _____

_____

No. _____ , dated _____ ; and whereas, I am now the sole

owner of said patent, and,

Whereas, _____

of _____

hereinafter referred to as "assignee" whose post office address is _____

_____

City of _____ , and State of _____ .

is desirous of acquiring the entire right, title and interest in the same;

Now, therefore, in consideration of the sum of _____ dollars ($ _____), the receipt whereof

is acknowledged, and other good and valuable consideration, I, the patentee, by these presents

do sell, assign and transfer unto said assignee the entire right, title and interest in and to the said

Patent aforesaid; the same to be held and enjoyed by the said assignee for his own use and

behoof, and for his legal representatives and assigns, to the full end of the term for which said

Patent is granted, as fully and entirely as the same would have been held by me had this

assignment and sale not been made.

Executed this _____ day of _____ , 19 _____ ,

at _____ .

_____
(Signature)

State of _____)
County of _____)   SS:
Before me personally appeared said _____
and acknowledged the foregoing instrument to be his free act and deed this _____ day
of _____ , 19 ____ .

_____

Seal   (Notary Public)

Burden Hour Statement: This form is estimated to take 0.1 hours to complete. Time will vary depending upon the needs of the individual case. Any comments on the amount of time you are required to complete this form should be sent to the Chief Information Officer, Patent and Trademark Office, Washington, DC 20231. DO NOT SEND FEES OR COMPLETED FORMS TO THIS ADDRESS. SEND TO: Commissioner of Patents and Trademarks, Washington, DC 20231.

FIGURE 19–1
Patent Assignment

LICENSING OF PATENT RIGHTS

A license differs from an assignment in that it is not an outright grant or transfer of ownership. A license is merely a permission to use. The permission or license may be limited in its scope, duration, terms, or territory. Licenses may be exclusive (meaning that only one party has the ability to exploit the invention) or may be nonexclusive (meaning that more than one party may be given rights in the invention or patent). Similarly, they may be for the term of the patent (twenty years from the date of filing) or may be for a limited time period. Licenses may be granted to one party to make the invention and to another party to sell the invention. They may be restricted to specific geographical areas, so that one party has rights west of the Mississippi while another (or the patent owner) has rights east of the Mississippi. Licenses are not usually recorded with the PTO because they are viewed as private contractual relationships between parties that do not affect the ultimate ownership of the patent.

The patent owner may charge a one-time lump-sum payment for the license or may receive royalties or periodic payments during the term of the license. Typically, royalty payments are based upon sales of the invention. For example, an owner might receive 5 percent of the sales price of each patented item sold. Restrictions may be imposed on the licensee requiring the licensee to sell a certain number of units or forfeit the license or pay an increased amount therefor.

Security interests may also be granted in patents to secure an obligation so that in the event of a default, the patent may be seized by the secured party. For example, the owner of a patent may wish to borrow money from a lender. The lender may be unwilling to lend money without some property being pledged as collateral for the loan. If a patent is pledged as collateral, and the patent owner defaults in any payments due to the lender, the lender may seize all rights in the patent. Although recordation with the PTO of security interests in patents is not required, recordation is advised inasmuch as it provides notice to the public of the various interests claimed in a patent.

INVENTION DEVELOPERS AND PROMOTERS

Many individual inventors do not have the funds necessary to prosecute a patent application, make the invention, and promote it. To avoid or reduce these costs, many inventors attempt to sell or license their rights to established companies. The invention must be protected during any period of negotiation. (See Appendix D, Form 14, for an Evaluation Agreement that will protect information and inventions disclosed for the purpose of discussing future business transactions.) Alternatively, there are a number of private organizations, usually referred to as **invention developers** or *invention promoters,* that assist inventors in bringing a discovery to market and negotiate with others for assignment or licensing of an inventor's patent rights. Although many of these developers are reputable, others have poor rates of success in bringing an invention to market. Inventors need to exercise caution in dealing with invention promoters or developers, particularly those that demand significant advance payments or guarantee success. The Better Business Bureau can check the background of an invention promoter or developer. Similarly, the Small Business Administration may be of assistance. Finally, for $25, the PTO will publish a notice in the *Official Gazette* that a patent is available for licensing or sale.

invention developer: One who assists an inventor in bringing a discovery to market or negotiates with others for assignment or licensing of an inventor's rights; also called an invention promoter

ROLE OF INTELLECTUAL PROPERTY PROFESSIONAL

Intellectual property professionals typically engage in the following activities related to owner-ship of patents:

- monitoring the progress of patent prosecution and the addition and deletion of claims to ensure inventorship is accurate for all claims;
- reviewing issued patents to confirm all inventors are correctly identified;
- preparing and filing invention disclosure documents;
- assisting in drafting clauses for employment contracts confirming that inventions developed by employees will be owned by and assigned to employers;
- reviewing the *Official Gazette* to determine whether clients should be informed of patents offered for sale or license;
- assisting in drafting assignments and security agreements relating to patents and recording same with the PTO and assisting in drafting licenses of patent rights; and
- checking the chain of title of records at the PTO to determine ownership of patents.

CHAPTER SUMMARY

Because patents have the attributes of personal property, they may be sold, licensed, or bequeathed by will. A person who conceives of an invention and reduces it to practice is a sole inventor. In many cases, however, more than one person will work on an invention. Those parties may be joint inventors even though they do not contribute equal efforts to the invention and do not physi-cally work together. If a dispute over priority of inventorship arises, the general rule is that the first to invent is the one who conceived of the invention and first reduced it to practice, either actually (by building a model or embodiment of the invention) or constructively (by filing a patent application for the invention). Notebooks describing work done by inventors often assist in determining prior-ity disputes.

Generally, inventions discovered by employees (who are not subject to agreements granting rights to employers) are owned by employees, subject, however, to a "shop right," namely a nonexclusive royalty-free license in favor of the employer to use the invention. In most instances, however, employers require employees to enter into agreements assigning any inventions and rights therein to the employer. Nevertheless, even without a written agreement, if an employee is hired specifically to create a certain work, the employer will own the resulting work.

As items of personal property, patents may be assigned or sold to others, as long as the instrument is in writing. Recordation with the PTO is not required for an assignment to be valid but is recommended. Patents may also be licensed by agreements granting another the right to use, make, or sell the invention for a specified period in a specified territory in return for which the licensee will give consideration (usually in the form of periodic royalty payments) to the licensor. Patents may also be used to secure obligations so that in the event of a default by the patent owner, the secured party may seize the patent and exercise all rights of ownership.

DISCUSSION QUESTIONS

1. Tom and Mark are long-time friends who have often discussed inventing a new type of camera. Conversations have been informal and nonspecific. Last year, after considerable work and effort, Mark invented a new type of high-speed film. Tom is claiming rights as a joint inventor. Discuss the rights of Mark and Tom.

2. Barbara and Toni are sisters living in different states. For years, they have discussed inventing a new type of home security system. Each has prepared drawings and collaboration has been periodic and routine, although Barbara's efforts comprise roughly 65 percent of the finished system. Are the sisters joint inventors? Discuss.

3. Keith is employed by Galloway Enterprises. While on the job, Keith discovered an improved process for microwaving foods. There is no agreement between Keith and Galloway Enterprises regarding any inventions or discoveries made by Keith. Who owns the invention? What rights, if any, does the other party have?

4. Greg, an inventor, assigned his invention to Philip by a written agreement. Philip did not record the assignment with the PTO. Is the assignment valid? Discuss.

5. Susan has granted Talbot Company the right to market her invention for ten years in any states west of the Mississippi River. What is the nature of the arrangement between the parties? Who owns the patent?

Any person who, without authority, makes, uses, offers to sell, or sells any patented invention infringes the patent. Innocence is not a defense to a claim of infringement, although it may serve to ensure punitive damages are not assessed. A person can also be liable for encouraging or inducing infringement or for contributory infringement by selling a component of a patented invention knowing it will be used to infringe a patent.

In determining whether infringement has occurred, the infringing device will be compared against the claims of a patent. If the accused invention falls within the language used in a patent claim, infringement is literal. Even if the accused invention differs from the claims in some way, it may still infringe under the doctrine of equivalents if it performs substantially the same function in substantially the same way to reach substantially the same result as the patented invention. A patentee is bound by the prosecution history of the patent process and cannot assert a position inconsistent with one taken during prosecution of the patent. In an infringement action, a defendant may raise a variety of defenses, including asserting that there was no infringement, that the patent is invalid or was procured by fraud, that the patentee has misused the patent to abuse his or her position, that the alleged infringer is using the invention solely for research purposes, laches, or estoppel. If infringement is found, a court may order injunctive relief, compensatory damages in an amount necessary to compensate the patentee for injury, costs, interest, and, if bad faith is shown, punitive damages up to three times the amount of compensatory damages and attorneys' fees. If parties cannot resolve infringement disputes amicably, litigation takes place in federal district court and is governed by the Federal Rules of Civil Procedure.

DIRECT INFRINGEMENT, INDUCEMENT TO INFRINGE, AND CONTRIBUTORY INFRINGEMENT

Direct Infringement

A patent issued by the PTO does not grant a party any right to make, use, offer to sell, or sell an invention but rather *excludes* others from engaging in such acts. Under the Patent Act, any person who, without authority, makes, uses, offers to sell, or sells any patented invention within the United States or imports into the United States any patented invention during the term of its patent, infringes the patent. 35 U.S.C. § 271(a). A patent is effective and enforceable only after it is issued. Thus, making, using, or selling devices prior to the time of a patent's issuance do not constitute acts of infringement. Violations of 35 U.S.C. § 271(a), namely, making, using, or selling patented inventions, are referred to as acts of **direct infringement.** Direct infringement can occur even if the infringer does not intend to infringe and is an "innocent" infringer with no knowledge that his or her acts will infringe a patented invention.

The Patent Act prohibits importing into the United States, or selling, offering to sell, or using in the United States a product made abroad by a process patented in the United States. Thus, a company cannot use a patented process abroad to make a product and then bring those products into the United States to compete with the patent owner. Although using the process abroad is not an infringement, subsequent importation of an article produced by a process patented in the United States is infringement. As an alternative to suing for patent infringement, a patent owner may bring a proceeding before the International Trade Commission to block the infringing device from entry into the United States. A patent owner may also order an import survey from the U.S. Customs Service to determine the address of any importer whose goods may infringe a patent. The survey will not stop infringement or importation, but it does provide information relating to the importer, who can then be sued for infringement.

Inducement to Infringe

Liability for infringement can arise from inducing another to infringe a patent. 35 U.S.C. § 271(b). Thus, if a person actively and intentionally encourages a third party to infringe a patent, and the patent is so infringed, the person who solicited the infringement will be liable. For example, selling a product with instructions on how to use the product in a manner that would infringe is **inducement of infringement.** Similarly, if a corporation encourages and assists an employee in making another's patented invention, the corporation (together with the officer or director who induced the act) will be liable for infringement.

The Patent Act also provides that a person who supplies from the United States all or a substantial portion of a patented invention in a manner that actively induces combination of the components abroad is liable for infringement. Liability is also imposed if a person knowingly supplies from the United States a material component of a patented invention that has no substantial use apart from its role in the invention and intends that the component will be combined with other components abroad in a manner that would be infringement if done in the United States. These provisions are intended to ensure that patent laws are not circumvented by shipping parts outside of the United States for assembly abroad into infringing articles.

Contributory Infringement

If a person offers to sell or sells within the United States or imports into the United States a component of a patented invention or process, or material for use in practicing a patented process (and the component has no substantial use

direct infringement: In patent law, making, using, or selling another's patented invention

inducement of infringement: In patent law, actively and intentionally encouraging another to infringe a patent

apart from use in the patented invention or process), knowing the same to be especially made or adapted for use in an infringement of such patent, he or she will be liable for contributory infringement. 35 U.S.C. § 271(c). Selling some common or staple article that can be used for purposes other than in the invention does not constitute contributory infringement. Thus, a seller may successfully defend a claim of contributory infringement by proving that he or she had no knowledge that the goods sold had no substantial use other than in the patented invention. Moreover, to be liable for contributory infringement, a person must know that his or her component or material will be used by a buyer to infringe a patent.

In sum, while liability can be imposed for direct infringement (making, using, or selling a patented invention) without regard to the infringer's intent, liability for inducing infringement or contributory infringement requires that the defendant infringer know that infringement will occur because of his or her inducement or contribution.

THE FIRST SALE DOCTRINE

In copyright law, once a copyrighted work, such as a book, is sold, the owner may then resell it or lend it to another without infringing the copyright under the first sale doctrine. The same principle applies with regard to lawful sales of trademarked goods. Similarly, this principle applies to patented inventions. Once the patent owner sells a patented item, the buyer has the right to resell it or use it as desired. As in copyright and trademark law, it is said that the first sale "exhausts" the rights of the patent owner. Along with the right to resell the invention, the buyer may repair it in order to prolong its use. Courts generally draw a distinction between repair, which is permissible, and reconstruction, which is impermissible infringement. While an owner of a patented invention has the right to repair and restore the article, activities that amount to rebuilding it such that the invention is being made anew are infringements. For example, if a party lawfully acquires a television, replacing components or reconditioning it is acceptable as a repair of the invention as long as the complete invention is not reconstructed.

CLAIMS INTERPRETATION

The claims in a patent determine its exclusive rights. The skill required in claims drafting comes into play both before and after a patent is issued. Drafting a claim in a patent application is done to demonstrate patentability of an invention by distinguishing the invention from prior art. If the inventor later believes the invention is being infringed, the claims are again examined for this purpose. Thus, determining infringement requires interpreting the claims language in the patent and then comparing and contrasting the allegedly infringing article against those claims.

Literal Infringement and the Doctrine of Equivalents

If the accused invention, device, or process falls within the language used in a patent claim, there is **literal infringement** because the accused invention is the

literal infringement: An accused invention that falls within the language used in a claim in an issued patent

same as that protected by the grant of patent. In some cases, however, a party has made some change to a patented invention, for example, substituting one ingredient known to be an equivalent to that used in the patented invention. Because such a change would not constitute a literal infringement inasmuch as a claim has not been exactly copied, courts developed the **doctrine of equivalents** to protect the true invention from misappropriation and ensure that a fraud is not committed on a patent. Courts will thus examine the accused invention to determine if it is "equivalent to" the patented invention in that it performs substantially the same function in substantially the same way to reach substantially the same result as the patented invention. If so, the two inventions are the same even though they may differ in name, form, or shape, and the second invention will be held to infringe the patent. *See Warner Jenkinson Co. v. Hilton Davis Chem. Co.,* 520 U.S. 17 (1997). Thus, a minor and obvious improvement on a patented invention can be an infringement.

For a device to infringe under the doctrine of equivalents, it must have an equivalent of each element of the patented invention. Thus, if one element of a claim in the patented invention is not present in or has no equivalent in the accused invention, there is no infringement, even if the accused device as a whole performs substantially the same function in substantially the same manner as the patented invention.

The doctrine of equivalents reflects the tension between two competing policies. While claims should be drafted clearly and interpreted somewhat strictly so that the patentee is not given a broader scope of protection than that set forth in the patent itself, a patentee's efforts and invention should not be allowed to be circumvented by another person who makes some minor change in the invention or process.

Determining equivalency is a difficult task and generally depends upon the facts of each particular case rather than any set formula or rules. Moreover, the range of equivalents varies according to the significance of the patented invention: a **pioneer patent** (one that is an important advance or significant breakthrough in the art) is usually given a wide range of equivalents so that protection is broader; if the accused invention is generally equivalent to the patented invention, it infringes. Similarly, a patented invention that represents a marked improvement over prior art is given a wide range of equivalents. Conversely, a patented invention that is only a modest improvement is given a limited range of equivalents; the accused invention must be convincingly equivalent to the patented invention for infringement to be found. This theory is somewhat comparable to the one used in trademark infringement cases that holds that distinct and unique trademarks such as XEROX® or EXXON® are given a broader scope of protection than weak or descriptive ones such as TASTEE BITES.

Reverse Doctrine of Equivalents

An accused device may fall within a claim's literal language and yet not infringe if it is so changed in principle from the patented article that it performs the same or similar function as the patented invention but in a completely different way. *Graver Tank & Mfg. Co. v. Linde Air Products Co.,* 339 U.S. 605 (1950). Known as the **reverse doctrine of equivalents,** this theory holds that despite literal infringement of claims, if the resulting device is different from the patented device, there is no infringement.

doctrine of equivalents: Principle that if an accused invention is equivalent to a patented invention in its purpose and achieves the same result, it infringes the patent, although a claim in the patent is not literally copied

pioneer patent: A patent representing an important advance or significant breakthrough

reverse doctrine of equivalents: In patent law, the principle that even if there is literal infringement of claims, if the accused resulting device differs from the patented device, there is no infringement

Prosecution History Estoppel

During the patent application process, the inventor or applicant may amend his or her claims and make various arguments to the examiner relating to the claims in the application. In the course of the patent prosecution, the applicant may omit certain claims or narrow them to avoid rejection on the basis they are precluded by prior art. The inventor/patentee is bound by this prosecution history in a later action alleging infringement under the doctrine of equivalents and is estopped from alleging that the claim was intended to be broader or asserting a position inconsistent with one taken earlier. The principle is inapplicable to literal infringement cases inasmuch as literal infringement exists when the accused invention copies the actual claims in an issued patent; what occurred during the course of prosecution is thus not relevant.

The doctrine, variously called **prosecution history estoppel** or **file wrapper estoppel,** applies not only to prosecution of the original patent but to reissue and reexamination proceedings. Underlying the doctrine is the principle that an applicant who disagrees with an examiner's position should appeal. The applicant is the one who drafts the claims, submits arguments, and makes amendments and should therefore be bound by his or her own actions, even if it is later determined that the examiner's position was incorrect.

DEFENSES TO INFRINGEMENT

Defendants in infringement actions generally assert one or more of several affirmative defenses. The most commonly asserted defenses are noninfringement, patent invalidity, fraud, patent misuse, experimental or research use, laches, and estoppel.

A defendant may assert that its acts do not constitute infringement, either literally or under the doctrine of equivalents. An accused infringer may also assert that the patent is invalid and thus cannot be infringed. An invalidity defense alleges that the invention fails to meet statutory subject matter, is not novel or useful, or is obvious, such that the patent for the invention should not have been issued by the PTO. Because issued patents are presumed to be valid, a defendant asserting invalidity must prove invalidity by clear and convincing evidence. A party using an invention under a license from the patentee may assert patent invalidity and is not estopped from raising such a defense even though he or she has agreed in a license agreement not to contest the validity of the patent, primarily because the policy favoring the negation of invalid patents outweighs contract law policy.

Fraud or inequitable conduct by a patentee during prosecution will render a patent resulting therefrom unenforceable. Such conduct may consist of omissions or material misrepresentations during the patent application process.

An accused infringer may assert patent misuse, namely, that the patent owner has abused his or her position to exploit a patent improperly and thus should be precluded from suing for infringement. Common examples of patent misuse include price fixing, tying arrangements (generally, tying or conditioning the sale or license of a patented item to the sale of another item), and other antitrust violations. Other examples of patent misuse that will preclude a patentee from suing for infringement are threatening or initiating patent infringement suits without

prosecution history estoppel: The principle that an inventor or patentee is bound by acts taken and statements made during the prosecution of a patent and cannot later take an inconsistent position; also called file wrapper estoppel

file wrapper estoppel: See prosecution history estoppel

probable cause or attempting to extend a patent beyond its term by requiring a licensee to pay license fees even after expiration of a patent.

A person accused of infringement may assert that unauthorized making or using of a patented invention was solely for research or experimental purposes. Making or using the patented invention for commercial purposes will defeat this defense.

Although there is no statute of limitations in the Patent Act requiring that suits for infringement be instituted within any set time period, 35 U.S.C. § 286 provides that no recovery may be had for any infringement committed more than six years prior to the filing of a claim of infringement. Although action may be initiated for infringement after six years (perhaps to enjoin further acts of infringement), monetary damages cannot be awarded for infringing acts committed more than six years before litigation is begun.

Even if the patentee initiates suit within six years after infringement, an action may still be barred by the doctrines of laches or estoppel. Laches is an unreasonable delay in bringing suit that causes prejudice to the defendant. A laches defense might be successfully asserted if a patentee knew of infringement and its delay in acting allowed the infringer to build up its business, market its accused device, and expend time and money expanding its business. An estoppel defense might be successfully asserted if a patentee knew of infringement and yet led the infringer to believe it would not enforce the patent. Mere silence will not amount to estoppel. In the typical case, a patentee who informs an infringer that it objects to the infringer's activities and then fails to take action, leading the infringer to believe the patentee has decided not to enforce his or her patent rights, may be estopped or precluded from asserting infringement.

Some specific acts do not constitute infringement. For example, 35 U.S.C. § 271(e) allows persons to make, use, offer to sell, and sell certain patented inventions relating to genetic manipulation techniques for the purpose of submitting information to federal regulatory agencies such as the FDA. Thus, using certain patented inventions to perform experiments in order to obtain FDA approval of certain drugs is permissible. Similarly, use of another's patented biotechnical invention is not an infringement if the use is strictly for research purposes. Medical practitioners may perform certain medical activities (such as the performance of medical or surgical procedures) that do not constitute infringement as long as the performance has no commercial application.

REMEDIES FOR INFRINGEMENT

A plaintiff who is successful in a suit for patent infringement may obtain injunctive relief, monetary damages, attorneys' fees, interest, costs of litigation, and, possibly, triple damages.

- **Injunctive relief.** In many instances, a patentee is as interested in ensuring that infringing activities cease as in recovering damages. A court may grant a preliminary injunction pending the final judgment in the case upon a showing that the patentee is reasonably likely to prevail in the action and that irreparable harm would result to the patentee unless an injunction were granted. If a patentee prevails in an infringement action, a permanent injunction is usually issued, enjoining the infringer from further infringing acts.

- **Compensatory damages.** The Patent Act provides that upon finding infringement, a court shall award a claimant damages adequate to compensate for infringement, but in no event less than a reasonable royalty for the use made of the invention by the infringer, together with an award of interest and costs. 35 U.S.C. § 284. If a patentee can prove actual damages, such as lost profits, those damages will be awarded. If such damages are highly speculative or cannot be proven because the infringer has only made rather than sold the invention, courts will then use the reasonable royalty rate as the measure of damages. Amounts paid as royalties by authorized licensees using the invention or other comparable inventions will be used to determine the rate to be paid by the infringer. Under 35 U.S.C. § 287, if a patented product is not marked with a notice of patent, no damages may be recovered by the patentee in an infringement action, unless there is proof that the infringer was notified of the infringement and continued to infringe thereafter, in which case damages are recoverable only for infringement occurring after notice. Filing an action for infringement constitutes notice. The patentee should always mark the invention with a notice of patent so he or she may recover damages from the time the patent is first infringed. To compensate a patentee fully, prejudgment interest is usually awarded, meaning interest from the date of actual infringement rather than from the date judgment is entered by the court. Costs of litigation are awarded to a successful patentee. However, if the patent includes an invalid claim together with a valid claim, no costs may be recovered unless a disclaimer of the invalid claim is entered with the PTO before suit for infringement is commenced.

- **Punitive damages.** Under 35 U.S.C. § 284, courts are authorized to increase compensatory damages up to three times the amount assessed. An award of such **punitive damages** (those meant to punish the defendant rather than compensate the plaintiff) is made only upon a showing of willful infringement or bad faith by the defendant. Persons have affirmative duties to use due care in avoiding infringement of another's rights. This duty can be satisfied by obtaining advice of counsel that a patent is invalid or that defenses exist to a claim of patent infringement. Thus, reliance on counsel may be used to defend against a claim of willful infringement or bad faith. Bad faith infringement might occur when an infringer duplicates a patented invention or obtains a sham opinion of counsel only for the purpose of using it as a shield against a later charge of willful infringement. Such conduct might justify the imposition of punitive damages. Thus, obtaining an infringement opinion (see Chapter 18) is critical because it may protect an infringer from punitive damages by showing an exercise of due care to avoid infringement.

- **Attorneys' fees.** A court may award reasonable attorneys' fees to the prevailing party "in exceptional cases." 35 U.S.C. § 285. If the patentee is the prevailing party, attorneys' fees might be awarded when the infringer's conduct is willful or in bad faith. If the accused infringer is the prevailing party, he or she may be able to recover attorneys' fees if the patentee instituted or continued the litigation in bad faith or was guilty of inequitable conduct, either in procuring the patent or in the

punitive damages: Damages intended to punish a defendant rather than to compensate a plaintiff

course of litigation. Attorneys fees awarded in some cases have reached $1,000,000.

- **Design patents.** In addition to the usual remedies available for infringement, one whose design patent has been infringed is entitled to recover all of the total profit of the infringer (but not less than $250). 35 U.S.C. § 289.

RESOLVING AN INFRINGEMENT DISPUTE

Lawsuits for patent infringement are among the most expensive and time-consuming of all litigation cases. Not only must the acts of the defendant be evaluated, but the entire file wrapper and prosecution history of the patent are open for examination. Moreover, because the subject matter of most patents is highly technical, experts and professionals must be retained for claim interpretation. If infringement is found, damages can run into the millions of dollars. For example, one case relating to a Hughes Aircraft Company patent for satellites produced sixteen separate decisions, took more than twenty-five years to resolve, and resulted in an award of more than $100,000,000. Thus, many parties try to resolve patent disputes between themselves either before or during the pendency of litigation.

Typically, a party who believes its patent is being infringed will send a "cease and desist" letter to the accused infringer, notifying the infringer of its rights to the patent and demanding that any further infringing activities cease. (The sample cease and desist letter shown in Chapter 6, Figure 6–1, may be easily modified for purposes of patent infringement.) Even if the cease and desist letter does not achieve the goal of convincing the infringer to cease his or her activities, it provides actual notice of the patent so that if the patented invention is not marked with a patent notice, the patent owner may recover damages for infringement after the date of letter notice. Moreover, the cease and desist letter generally triggers the accused infringer's duty of due care to avoid patent infringement so that failure to obtain advice of competent counsel in the face of an allegation of infringement might result in the imposition of punitive or increased damages against the infringer if infringement is found.

The accused infringer often responds to the cease and desist letter by denying its allegations, asserting various defenses, or suggesting a compromise. The parties might agree that the accused infringer should modify the invention in some way or gradually phase the invention out of use. They may enter into a licensing arrangement whereby the accused infringer pays royalties to the patent owner to be able to make, use, or sell the patented invention. One party might acquire the other's rights by outright purchase. The parties may agree to have an arbitrator resolve the dispute rather than go to federal court. One of the parties may initiate a reexamination proceeding before the PTO to have the patent reexamined to determine the validity of any claim in a patent on the basis of prior art. A determination by the PTO that a claim is valid (or, conversely, that it is unpatentable) may give the parties some impetus to settle their dispute inasmuch as the determination constitutes another full review of the patent and its validity. As another alternative to a patent infringement action, either party involved in an actual controversy may initiate an action in federal court for declaratory relief, asking a court to review the matter and declare the parties' respective rights and obligations with respect to the patent.

PATENT INFRINGEMENT LITIGATION

If the parties cannot resolve their dispute, the plaintiff will file an action for infringement in federal district court. Federal courts have exclusive jurisdiction over patent law cases, although if the matter only peripherally relates to a patent (for example, a case involving whether a patent licensee has paid its license fees under the terms of a written contract), the matter may be heard in state court. Questions relating to validity of the patent and infringement must be initiated in federal court. Moreover, state regulation of intellectual property must yield to the extent it conflicts with federal patent law. *Bonito Boats, Inc. v. Thunder Craft Boats, Inc.,* 489 U.S. 141 (1989).

The action will be governed by the Federal Rules of Civil Procedure relating to federal civil actions generally. These rules set the times for responding to the complaint, matters pertaining to motions and discovery, and any other litigation-related matters. The action should be filed in the federal district court where the defendant resides or where the defendant committed the acts of alleged infringement and has an established place of business. After the complaint for infringement is filed, the defendant will respond by filing an answer, generally denying that infringement has occurred and asserting various defenses. If the defendant has a cause of action to assert against the plaintiff relating to the patent, it must be asserted by way of a counterclaim in the litigation so that all disputes between the parties relating to the patent can be resolved at the same time. Claims for inducing patent infringement or contributory infringement may also be asserted.

Within one month after the filing of an action for patent infringement, the clerk of the court must provide notice of the suit to the PTO, identifying the parties, name of the inventor, and the patent number of the patent at issue. Similarly, within one month after judgment is entered in the case, the clerk must provide notice thereof to the PTO.

After the complaint, answer, and counterclaim have been filed, various motions may be made. Discovery will commence. The plaintiff and defendant will take depositions to obtain testimony from those who may have information about the case. For example, the plaintiff may depose individuals in the defendant's company to determine whether they were instructed to copy the patented invention. Interrogatories may be served on either party to obtain information, such as to inquire about experts either side intends to call, how damages such as lost profits were calculated, or to determine the existence of pertinent documents.

Ultimately, if the matter cannot be resolved by private agreement, it will proceed to trial. The patent owner must prove infringement by a preponderance of the evidence. Either party may request a jury trial; otherwise, a judge will render the decision. Although juries determine whether infringement has occurred, the issue of claims construction is determined by the trial judge, not the jury. *Markman v. Westview Instruments, Inc.,* 517 U.S. 370 (1996). The need for uniformity in patent law requires that courts, not juries, interpret patent claims, including terms of art used within those claims. The testimony of witnesses may be received when needed, but per *Markman,* judges, not juries, are "better suited" to find the acquired meaning of patent terms. *Id.* The losing party may appeal the decision to the Court of Appeals for the Federal Circuit, established in 1982 in the District of Columbia to bring about consistency in patent cases, which hears all appeals from infringement cases brought in any of the federal district courts. Thereafter, the matter may be appealed to the United States Supreme Court if the Court, in its discretion, grants *certiorari* and decides to take the case.

If the United States government has allegedly infringed a patent, action is brought in the United States Court of Federal Claims in Washington, DC. Although the patentee is entitled to obtain compensation for use by or for the government, an injunction cannot be ordered against the government to compel it to cease making, using, or selling the invention. If a patent is infringed by a state, a patentee may obtain the same remedies (including injunctive relief) as may be obtained against other infringers.

As technology progresses and the value of certain communication and entertainment inventions increases, patent litigation is becoming an increasingly common and high-stakes occupation. Patent infringement cases have increased 80 percent since 1991. Damage awards may run into the millions. For example, in 1997, a court awarded Procter & Gamble Company $178.4 million in lost profits and royalties arising out of the sale of diapers that infringed Procter & Gamble's. Legal fees for both companies exceeded $10 million. In 1994, Microsoft was ordered to pay $120 million in an infringement suit relating to patents for software. Microsoft and the patent owner later agreed to a reduction of damages.

To protect against such suits, which can be costly to a litigant even when no infringement is found, many companies now procure insurance—either to cover the costs of defending a patent infringement suit or for the costs of prosecuting a suit to enforce a patent. Such insurance is extremely expensive, especially for companies owning several patents or patents in high-tech areas.

A recent suggestion advanced by in-house counsel for Procter & Gamble Company, designed to decrease both the time and expense of full-scale patent litigation, is a private forum to resolve patent disputes. The "Patent Court," funded by the National Patent Board, a private organization of attorneys and patent agents that promotes patent law, would hold a one-day hearing within six months of the filing of a dispute. The hearing would be informal and would result in a nonbinding written ruling. A losing party could "appeal" to court; however, if the loser fails to prevail in court, he or she would bear the costs of the private patent hearing. The Patent Court is modeled after the Council of Better Business Bureaus's National Advertising Division, which resolves private commercial disputes and is so well respected that only about one percent of its decisions are appealed. The National Patent Board is presently reviewing the feasibility of establishing the Patent Court.

ROLE OF INTELLECTUAL PROPERTY PROFESSIONAL

Intellectual property professionals are typically involved in a variety of interesting and challenging tasks related to patent infringement, including the following:

- ordering and reviewing file wrappers from the PTO to review patent claims and prepare a summary of the prosecution history (because prosecution history will bind a patentee from later taking an inconsistent position);
- reviewing client materials to ensure patented items are properly marked with notice of patent;
- preparing or responding to cease and desist letters;
- preparing requests for reexamination of patents, complaints for infringement, or responses or answers thereto;
- docketing all relevant dates in infringement proceedings, such as dates for close of discovery, submission of written briefs, and so forth;
- assisting in discovery by drafting interrogatories, reviewing documents produced, summarizing depositions, and so forth;
- conducting patent searches and investigations to determine the existence of other patents and whether a patent is a pioneer patent and thus entitled to a broader scope of protection than one that represents only a modest improvement in the art;
- drafting settlement agreements; and
- providing general assistance in infringement trials such as locating witnesses, organizing exhibits and documents, conducting research, and preparing jury instructions.

CHAPTER SUMMARY

A patent can be infringed even if the infringer does not intend to infringe and does not know a patented invention exists. Liability for inducing infringement or contributory infringement, however, requires intent.

If parties cannot resolve a patent dispute amicably, litigation will be instituted in federal court. The claims of the patent will be construed and the accused invention will be compared against the claims to determine if infringement has occurred. If the accused invention falls within the language used in a patent claim, literal infringement exists. Under the doctrine of equivalents, infringement can also exist if the accused invention performs substantially the same function as the patented invention in substantially the same way to reach substantially the same result. The patentee is bound by arguments made and amendments entered during the history of prosecution of the patent and cannot later argue a position inconsistent with one reflected by the file wrapper.

An accused infringer may assert that there is no infringement, that the patent is invalid, that the patent was procured by fraud, that the patentee is guilty of patent misuse, that the accused device is being used solely for research purposes, or that the patentee is barred by laches or estoppel.

Remedies in infringement actions may include injunctive relief, compensatory damages, costs, interest, and, if bad faith is shown, attorneys' fees and increased damages of up to three times compensatory damages.

DISCUSSION QUESTIONS

1. Mike, a young college student, purchases patented videocassette recorders from a retail seller. Mike has changed the timing mechanism on the VCRs and is reselling them. Mike has no intent of infringing and is unaware of patent law. Is Mike liable for infringement? Because Mike has made a change in the invention, can there be infringement? Discuss.

2. Assume the VCRs purchased by Mike are not marked with a notice of patent. Does failure to mark have any implications for the patentee?

3. Assume that upon discovering Mike's actions, the patentee sends a cease and desist letter to Mike setting forth information about the patent, informing Mike that Mike's actions are patent infringement, and demanding Mike cease further sales. Mike ignores the letter and continues to make sales. Do Mike's actions have any effect on remedies that may be imposed against him?

4. Elizabeth has purchased a patented food processor. After a period of time, the machine has become worn and Elizabeth has repaired the item by replacing two of its many parts. Do such actions constitute infringement? Discuss.

5. Gregory owns a parts store and as part of his inventory he sells a variety of hardware items, including a bolt that can be used for a variety of purposes. A patentee whose invention includes the bolt has discovered that Sam, an infringer who has copied the patentee's invention, purchases the bolt from Gregory. Is Gregory liable for contributory infringement? Discuss.

6. During the course of the patent application process, and to overcome a prior art reference, Andy dropped Claim Number 4 from his application. Andy has now discovered that a device infringes his patented invention, particularly Claim Numbers 4 and 5. What is the effect of Andy's action taken during the prosecution process? May he sue for infringement? Discuss.

New Developments and International Developments in Patent Law

Most of the new developments in patent law relate to the increasing number of patent applications filed for computer software, reflecting the somewhat more limited scope of protection afforded to software under copyright law. Other new developments relate to medicine, science, and pharmacology.

In regard to international patent law, because patents granted in the United States have no effect outside U.S. territorial borders, inventors desiring patent protection in foreign countries must comply with the laws of the countries in which they desire patent protection. Alternatively, however, they may rely on three treaties to which the United States adheres. Under the Paris Convention, a U.S. inventor who files a patent application in any of the more than one hundred and thirty-five Paris member nations has twelve months to file applications in any of the other member nations and yet claim the priority date of the first filing. Under the Patent Cooperation Treaty (PCT), an inventor may file one "international" application, thereby receiving the benefit of one centralized filing, searching, and examination process and receiving protection in any PCT member nation, as long as the application is ultimately prosecuted in those nations. Prosecution in the other countries may be delayed for up to thirty months, affording the inventor significant time to gather funds, consider the commercial application of the invention, and evaluate market conditions. Under the Uruguay Round Agreements on Trade-Related Aspects of Intellectual Property Rights (TRIPS), member nations must afford patent protection to citizens of member nations on the same basis they do for their own citizens. Foreign inventors may apply for patents in the United States as long as they comply with the provisions of the Patent Act.

NEW DEVELOPMENTS IN PATENT LAW

The Patent Act has proven remarkably flexible in accommodating changes and developments in technology. Thus, advancements in technology generally have not necessitated changes in the statutes governing patent protection. This situation is somewhat different from that encountered in trademark law with the conflict over domain names creating much turmoil and in copyright law with the ramifications of publication on the Internet creating similar turmoil.

Many of the cutting edge issues in patent law relate to patents for computer software. For several years, the conventional wisdom has been that unless a computer program had significant commercial value and application, patent protection was often counterproductive or ineffective in that the PTO often took two years to issue a patent, roughly the same time it took for the software program to become obsolete. Thus, protection of the program under copyright law was often viewed as the most effective means of protection for software.

Some experts believe that in 1995, when the First Circuit held in *Lotus Development Corp. v. Borland International Inc.,* 49 F.3d 807 (1st Cir. 1995), *aff'd,* 516 U.S. 233 (1996), that Lotus's menu command system did not constitute copyrightable expression (being an unprotectable method of operation), courts clearly signaled that copyright law provides little protection for computer software. Major companies apparently felt the same way: more than one-third of the patents issued to IBM in 1998 were software-related and nearly one-fourth related to network computing. Similarly, in the wake of losing a $120 million patent infringement suit (see Chapter 20), Microsoft received nearly two hundred patents for software in 1997 alone. The PTO has reported that software-related patent applications nearly doubled in just the two years between 1995 and 1997.

The courts have struggled with the issue of patentability for software programs. Programs that are "processes" or "machines" are patentable; programs that are purely mathematical principles or algorithms are not. Nevertheless, in what many observers believe to be a ground-breaking decision, in *State Street Bank & Trust Co. v. Signature Financial Group Inc.,* 147 F.3d 1368 (Fed. Cir. 1998), *cert. denied,* 119 S. Ct. 851 (1999), the Federal Circuit held that a data processing system designed to make financial calculations (calculating daily changes in the allocation of certain assets and tracking data relevant to determining year-end income, expenses, and capital gains and losses) was patentable because the calculations produced a useful, concrete, and tangible result. In 1996, certain guidelines for computer-related inventions were adopted by the PTO to aid examiners in determining the patentability of software. Under the guidelines (available at the PTO web site at http://www.uspto.gov), the following are patentable: a machine that is directed by a computer program; a computer-readable memory; and a computer-implemented process. Algorithms that manipulate only abstract ideas remain unpatentable. In brief, patent applications for computer-related inventions must be carefully drafted by attorneys knowledgeable in the art, the developing case law, and the new PTO guidelines.

New patents are being applied for and granted for e-commerce technologies, such as Priceline.com's patent for its dutch auction system and Amazon.com's patent for processing credit card orders securely.

In sum, *State Street* is seen as a death blow to the older view that business methods were not patentable. Under *State Street,* software, mathematical algorithms, and business methods are patentable as long as they produce a useful, tangible, and concrete result. In fact, since *State Street,* the PTO has seen a 700% increase in applications for software and business-method patents.

Medicine, science, and pharmacology present the other cutting edge issues in patent law. Patents have been issued for gene sequences that may offer cures for diseases. With cloning now possible, more patents than ever are expected in fields related to gene manipulation. In 1998, a patent application was filed for a method of making creatures that are part human and part animal. The inventor has stated that he does not intend to make such creatures but rather intends to provoke public debate on the morality of patenting life forms. In March 1999, the application was rejected by the PTO on the basis that the claimed invention, a chimera, "embraced a human being." Many experts believe the rejection was also based on the fact the invention was either contrary to public policy or injurious to the well-being of society and thus not "useful." The inventor has resubmitted the application and has stated he intends to obtain a patent or appeal all the way to the U.S. Supreme Court. Similar debate focuses on a patent recently issued for a new strain of basmati rice, a product identified with the cultural heritage of India, with some people contending that the patent commercializes a national heritage. The development of strains of plants and crops that are resistant to drought and disease has also led to an increasing number of patents issued, and attendant litigation, in the field of "agbiotech."

The intersection of the Patent Act's requirements that an invention be "useful" with patents in the biotech and chemical fields has led to much discussion. If drugs are experimental, how can their utility be proven to satisfy the Patent Act? Thus, drugs aimed at the most difficult diseases, such as AIDS and cancer, often face the most difficult challenges in meeting the requirements of utility. New PTO guidelines now provide that sufficient utility is shown when a patent application explicitly describes a use for a drug that is credible to a person ordinarily skilled in the art.

Nearly insatiable consumer demand continues to fuel activity in the biotech arena. Just two years ago, drugs were known by name only to the physicians who prescribed them. Today, patients routinely request or demand prescriptions for CLARITIN®, PROZAC®, or VIAGRA®, all patented products, whose effects are advertised with as much vigor as any other consumer product. Pharmaceutical companies invested nearly $21 billion in 1998 to discover and develop new medicines. Without patent protection for drugs, the pharmaceutical industry could not exist. The process of drug invention is lengthy, costly, and risky. Unless protection were provided by patent, manufacturers would not expend the time and effort in developing drugs that ultimately support public health. Thus, the public is benefited by the limited monopoly a patent gives to pharmaceutical companies.

INTRODUCTION TO INTERNATIONAL PATENT PROTECTION

The rights granted by a U.S. patent extend only throughout the United States and have no effect in a foreign country. Therefore, an inventor who desires patent protection in other countries must apply for a patent in each of the other countries or in regional patent offices. Nearly every country has its own patent law, and a person who wishes to obtain a patent in a particular country must make an application for patent in that country, in accordance with its requirements. A directory of more than one hundred foreign patent offices can be found at www.piperpat.co.nz, which also provides direct links to the home pages for the foreign patent offices. See also www.patents.com for contact information for more than twenty foreign patent offices.

The laws of many other countries differ in various respects from the patent law of the United States. In most foreign countries, publication of the invention before the date of the application will bar the right to a patent, while in the United States, the one-year grace period applies so that if the invention was described by the inventor in a printed publication, the inventor has one year thereafter to file the patent application for the invention. Most foreign countries require that the invention be manufactured in that country within a certain period of time, usually three years, after grant of the patent or the patent will be void, while in the United States there is no requirement that the invention ever be manufactured, used, or sold. Additionally, most foreign countries grant patents to the "first to file" the application. In the United States, however, a patent is usually granted to the "first to invent."

There are several **international patent** treaties to which the United States adheres, primarily the Paris Convention, the Patent Cooperation Treaty, and the Agreement on Trade-Related Aspects of Intellectual Property Rights.

THE PARIS CONVENTION

The Paris Convention for the Protection of Intellectual Property of 1883 is a treaty adhered to by more than one hundred and thirty-five nations and is administered by WIPO, discussed in Chapter 8. The Paris Convention requires that each country guarantee to the citizens of the other member adherents the same rights in patent and trademark matters that it provides to its own citizens (the principle of "national treatment"). The treaty also provides for the right of priority in the case of patents, trademarks, and industrial designs (design patents). The right of priority means that, on the basis of a patent application filed in one of the member countries, the applicant may, within one year, apply for protection in any of the other member countries. These later applications will then be regarded as if they had been filed on the same day as the first application in the first country, assuming the first application adequately disclosed the invention. (See Appendix A for a table of the countries adhering to the Paris Convention.)

Recall from Chapter 8 that after a trademark application is filed in the United States (or any Paris Convention member country), the applicant has six months to file an application for the same mark in any Paris Convention member country. The later-filed application captures the filing date, called the "priority date," of the earlier-filed application. The same principle is true for patents, although the time period for filing a patent application is one year (six months for a design patent). Thus, a later application will have priority over an application for the same invention that may have been filed during the twelve-month period of time. For example, if an inventor files a patent application in the United States on January 1, 1998, he or she will have until January 1, 1999,

international patent: A patent filed under the Patent Cooperation Treaty

to file an application for the same invention in any Paris Convention member country, which application will then be treated as if it were filed in that country on January 1, 1998. Filing either a provisional application or a standard utility patent begins the Paris Convention priority year.

Additionally, the later-filed application, because it is based on the date of the first application, will not be invalidated by some act accomplished in the interval, such as publication or use of the invention. Similarly, the earlier priority date is the date of invention for determining whether prior art precludes granting of a patent for the invention. Finally, for purposes of determining priority of inventorship, the earlier priority date will be deemed to be the date of constructive reduction to practice of the invention.

There are, however, a few conditions that must be satisfied if an applicant is to be allowed to claim the date he or she first filed an application in a foreign country as the priority date in a later-filed U.S. application:

- the foreign country in which the application was first filed must afford similar privileges to citizens of the United States or to applications first filed in the United States;
- no patent will be granted on any application for patent for an invention that has been patented or described in the inventor's printed publication in any country more than one year before the date of the actual filing of the application in the United States or that has been in public use or on sale in the United States more than one year prior to such filing. Thus, if A offers an invention for sale in the United States on January 1, 1998, files an application in Spain on April 1, 1998, and then files an application in the United States on February 1, 1999, claiming the foreign priority date of April 1, 1998, the application will be barred because the invention was offered for sale in the United States more than one year prior to the filing of the application in the United States, regardless of the fact that A is entitled to the benefit of the priority date of April 1, 1998;
- the applicant must submit a certified copy of the original foreign application, specification, and drawings to the PTO; and
- the priority application must be for an invention by the same inventor(s) as named in the later U.S. application.

The priority right is based on the filing of the application in the foreign country and timely filing in the United States. The prosecution status or history of the application in the foreign country is irrelevant. If the foreign country refuses to grant a patent, or the applicant abandons the application, such is irrelevant to the later U.S. application.

The Paris Convention affords patent applicants the opportunity to file a patent application in a member country and then take twelve months to determine whether foreign protection will be sought. An applicant may determine that the invention is not marketable in certain countries and thus decide not to apply for patents in those countries. In this way, the Paris Convention saves an applicant the time and expense of having to file simultaneous patent applications in several nations before it has had an opportunity to evaluate the likelihood of obtaining patent protection and exploiting the invention commercially.

THE PATENT COOPERATION TREATY

Introduction to the Patent Cooperation Treaty

While the Paris Convention allows applicants to defer decisions about filing in member countries for twelve months, it still requires that applicants file separate applications in each country in which they desire protection. For an inventor who wishes to market his or her invention on a global basis, this process is time-consuming and expensive in the extreme. The Patent Cooperation Treaty (PCT), which was negotiated in 1970 and came into force in 1978, responds to these concerns by providing a centralized way of filing, searching, and examining patent applications in several countries simultaneously. Moreover, a standardized application format is used, saving applicants substantial time and money that is ordinarily incurred in ensuring that a patent application complies with the procedural and formatting requirements imposed by each country. The PCT is adhered to by nearly one hundred countries, including the United States, and is administered by WIPO. In sum, the PCT allows an inventor to file one "international" application and seek protection for the invention simultaneously in several countries. (See Appendix A for a table of the countries adhering to the PCT.)

The one application filed with the PCT does not automatically mature into a patent that affords patent rights in several countries. The application must designate the countries in which protection is desired, and eventually the applicant must prosecute separate applications in those designated countries (the **national phase**). The PCT process, however, affords a significant window of time for the applicant to keep his or her options open while a determination is made whether protection should be sought in various foreign countries. The PTO web site (http://www.uspto.gov) provides a great deal of information about the PCT process, including a map showing PCT member countries, fee schedules and PCT fees, and tutorials relating to the PCT application process.

The Patent Cooperation Treaty Application Process—Chapter I

The "international" application may be filed with the patent office of the member country of which the applicant is a national or resident or, if the applicant desires, with the International Bureau of WIPO in Geneva, Switzerland. When filed with a national patent office, such as the PTO, the office is said to act as a PCT **receiving office.** The application designates those countries in which the applicant desires patent protection. For example, a citizen of the United States could file a PCT application with the PTO and designate Spain, Brazil, and the United Kingdom as countries in which he or she also desires patent protection. When the application is filed with the PTO as the receiving office, the effect is the same as if the applicant had simultaneously filed applications in Spain, Brazil, and the United Kingdom. Only one filing fee is paid for filing the PCT application, which is called an "international patent application." The amount of the filing fee generally depends upon the length of the application and how many countries are designated in the application. The application is similar in form to utility patent applications in that it contains claims and drawings of the invention.

A PCT application may claim priority, under the Paris Convention, of an earlier patent application for the invention. Thus, if an application was filed in

national phase: The final phase of a patent application filed under the Patent Cooperation Treaty consisting of prosecution of the patent in countries designated in the application

receiving office: A patent office in which a patent application prepared in accordance with the Patent Cooperation Treaty is filed

Hungary on January 4, 1999, and an international PCT application was filed with the PTO on June 4, 1999, designating Spain, Brazil, and the United Kingdom, the effective filing date for the PCT application for all of those countries will be January 4, 1999. If priority is not claimed under the Paris Convention (usually because no prior application has been filed in any foreign country), the priority date will be the date the PCT application was filed.

Many applicants file a standard patent application with their home patent office and then, near the end of the twelve-month period afforded by the Paris Convention, file a PCT application with their home office (now acting as a "receiving office"), designating the various foreign countries in which they seek patent protection.

The filing of the international patent application triggers the first phase of the PCT process, called **Chapter I.** During Chapter I, the international application is subjected to an international search by an "international searching authority," experienced patent offices designated by WIPO to conduct searches. The international searching authorities designated by WIPO are the national offices of Australia, Austria, China, Japan, the Russian Federation, Spain, Sweden, the United States, and the European Patent Office. The applicant elects the international searching authority it desires, and it may be different from the office that is serving as the receiving office. The international searching authority will conduct an extensive search of the relevant prior art. The results of the search are set forth in an "international search report" that is provided to the applicant several months after the international application is filed. Although the international search report does not provide an opinion on patentability in the various countries designated in the international patent application, its citations of prior art enable an inventor to evaluate the likelihood of obtaining patents in the designated countries and to amend claims in the international patent application, if necessary to avoid prior art. The applicant is generally given two months to amend its claims. If the report discloses prior art that would bar the application, the applicant may decide to abandon the PCT application.

The PCT application will be published eighteen months after its filing date or priority date. Publication serves to notify the public that an international patent application has been filed for the invention and affords an opportunity for third parties to obtain copies of the application. This publication date should be docketed so that the inventor can ensure applications are timely filed in countries that are not members of the Paris Convention or are not designated in the PCT application inasmuch as this publication will foreclose patent applications in those countries that bar applications for inventions that have been published (unless they have a one-year grace period such as the United States). Until publication, the application is maintained in confidence. In a later infringement case, in most PCT countries, a patent owner may recover damages arising from the date of publication (rather than the date the patent issues).

The Chapter I phase of the PCT process lasts for twenty months from either the filing date of the international patent application with the receiving office or the claimed priority date if the application claims priority under the Paris Convention. This twenty-month period affords the inventor the opportunity to evaluate the marketability of the invention in the designated countries and gather funds in order to enter foreign markets.

Chapter I: The first phase of a patent application filed under the Patent Cooperation Treaty, consisting of a search of the application and generally lasting for 20 months

The Patent Cooperation Treaty Application Process—Chapter II

If the applicant has not yet decided to pursue the patent application in the designated countries, he or she may elect to enter **Chapter II** of the PCT process. Chapter II must be entered twenty months after the date the PCT application was filed or twenty months after the filing date of an application claiming Paris Convention priority. Upon entering Chapter II, the applicant may further extend the time before it must prosecute the applications in each designated nation by requesting that the application undergo an "international preliminary examination," a process that takes ten months and requires payment of a fee. Nearly 80 percent of PCT applicants request international preliminary examination. A written opinion on patentability is prepared by an "international preliminary examining authority" having qualifications similar to those of the international searching authorities. The examining authorities are identical to the searching authorities, except that Spain is not an examining authority. The examining authority will review the prior art citations listed in the earlier search report and provide an opinion on patentability, novelty, and usefulness of the invention in the various countries designated in the PCT application. The applicant will have an opportunity to respond to the written opinion and may amend claims or delete claims in the application based upon the examining authority's opinion. The examining authority then issues an "international preliminary examining report," which is a formal report on patentability in the designated nations. Although the report is not binding on any specific nation, it is highly authoritative.

The additional time afforded by the PCT process (twenty months from filing of the application plus an additional ten months if a preliminary examining report is requested) is significantly more than the twelve months afforded under the Paris Convention. This additional time is useful for allowing inventors to determine whether the invention is commercially exploitable in various countries and whether protection is needed in certain countries.

The Patent Cooperation Treaty Application Process—The National Phase

If, after the duration of Chapter I (and the international preliminary examining report, if elected through Chapter II), the applicant decides to go forward with the application in the countries designated in the application, the applicant commences the "national phase" of the PCT application process. National fees must be paid to each country in which protection is desired, and often translations must be obtained of the PCT application. In many instances, the applicant will decide to forego protection in some countries and will not pursue the patent application in those countries. Thus, the application will lapse in those countries. Each national office in which the application is pursued will now conduct its own search and examination procedure, although the process is both easier and faster due to the fact that the highly credible international search report and international preliminary examination report have already provided interpretations regarding the patentability of the invention. Each of the countries designated in the PCT application will either grant or reject the application. The term of a patent designating the United States is twenty years from the filing date of the PCT application.

Chapter II: The second phase of a patent application filed under the Patent Cooperation Treaty during which an International Preliminary Examination is conducted of the application, generally lasting ten months

Advantages of the Patent Cooperation Treaty Application Process

The most significant advantage provided by the PCT application process is time. If an application is filed in the United States, and the applicant wishes to file an application for the same invention in Japan, under the Paris Convention, the applicant has only twelve months from the United States filing date to file in Japan. The filing in Japan will require filing fees, translations, and the costs of prosecution as the process proceeds in Japan. On the other hand, under the PCT, the applicant can file one application in the United States and designate Japan in the application. The applicant then has twenty months during Chapter I while a search is done, and if the applicant requests examination, an additional ten months under Chapter II, for a total of thirty months before it must decide whether to pursue the application in Japan and pay the filing fee, arrange for a translation, and prosecute the application in Japan. In addition to the benefits afforded by this time, the PCT process also affords the benefits of a single application format and a centralized filing, searching, and examination system. The PCT, however, is not applicable to design patents, and therefore, the maximum delay afforded an applicant for a design patent to decide whether to make foreign patent applications is the six months provided for design patents under the Paris Convention.

The time afforded by the PCT allows an inventor additional opportunity to reflect on whether protection is actually desired in certain countries and to gather funds necessary to prosecute the applications during the national phase and to market and exploit the invention. Additionally, due to the highly author-itative nature of the international search report and international preliminary examination report, the PCT process provides an indication to the inventor about the likelihood whether a patent will be granted in various countries. Finally, the time and costs involved in the national phase are likely to be signif-icantly reduced because much of the searching and examination work required has already been conducted in Chapters I and II.

The success of the PCT process is demonstrated by the fact that in 1979, only 2,625 PCT applications were filed, while in 1998, the number had grown to 67,007. The number filed in 1997 grew more than 15 percent over the previous year. The average number of countries designated in each application grew from 6.6 in 1979 to 35 in 1997. The United States is the country of origin for more than 40 percent of PCT applications, followed by Germany (14 percent), Japan (9 percent), the United Kingdom (7 percent), and France and Sweden (5 percent each).

THE EUROPEAN PATENT ORGANIZATION

The **European Patent Organization** was founded in 1973 to provide a uniform patent system in Europe. A European patent can be obtained by filing a single application with the European Patent Office headquartered in Munich (or its subbranches in The Hague or Berlin or with the national offices in the twenty-four contracting nations). Once granted, the application is valid in any of the European Patent Organization countries designated in the application and has the same force as a patent granted in any one of the contracting nations. The European Patent Organization contracting nations are Albania,

European Patent Organization: An organization with 24 member nations founded in 1973 to provide a uniform patent system in Europe

Austria, Belgium, Cyprus, Denmark, Finland, France, Germany, Hellenic Republic (Greece), Ireland, Italy, Latvia, Liechtenstein, Lithuania, Luxembourg, Monaco, Netherlands, Portugal, Romania, Slovenia, Spain, Sweden, Switzerland, and the United Kingdom.

After the application is filed, a search will be conducted and the application will be published. Within six months after publication, the applicant must decide whether to pursue the application by requesting an examination. It generally takes nearly four years to obtain a European patent. Within nine months following the date of grant of the patent, a party may oppose the grant on the basis the patent does not comply with the substantive provisions of the European Patent Convention. A binding decision will be issued by the opposition division of the European Patent Office. The European patent is valid for twenty years from the date the application was filed. Since the filing of the first European patent application in 1978, more than 300,000 European patents have been granted.

An applicant who is a national or resident of a nation that is a party to the European Patent Convention may file a PCT application with the European Patent Office. A party from outside the European Patent Convention countries who designates a contracting state in a PCT application may opt for the effect of a European patent application. Thus, if a citizen from the United States files a PCT application and desires patent protection in Germany, the applicant may opt for the effect of a European patent application to cover all of the European contracting nations, rather than merely designating Germany.

FOREIGN FILING LICENSES

To ensure that national security is not impaired, a person may not file a patent application in another country for an invention made in the United States unless the commissioner of the PTO grants a license allowing the foreign filing or until six months from the filing of the United States application for the invention. The six-month waiting period allows the PTO to review applications that might affect matters of national security.

Filing an application with the PTO is deemed to be a request to the commissioner for a license to file an application in a foreign country. The official PTO filing receipt will indicate to the applicant whether the license is granted or denied. If the inventor does not wish to file an application in the United States but prefers to file immediately in a foreign country, he or she may file a petition to the commissioner of the PTO requesting that a **foreign filing license** be granted.

If the foreign filing license requirements are violated, any corresponding U.S. application is invalid. Additionally, criminal penalties and fines may be imposed. The violation may be cured, however, and a retroactive foreign filing license may be granted if failure to obtain the license was through error and without deceptive intent.

It is possible that the commissioner may refuse the applicant permission to file an application in a foreign country and may order that the invention be kept secret. A secrecy order prohibits publication or filing in another country until the order is lifted. No patent can issue on an application subject to a secrecy order. The applicant may, however, obtain compensation from the

foreign filing license: The grant by the PTO of permission to an inventor to file a patent application in another country for an invention made in the United States, required before a foreign application may be filed

government for damages caused due to his or her inability to secure a patent for the invention.

AGREEMENT ON TRADE-RELATED ASPECTS OF INTELLECTUAL PROPERTY RIGHTS

The General Agreement on Tariffs and Trade, Uruguay Round Agreements on Trade-Related Aspects of Intellectual Property Rights (TRIPS) was accepted by the United States in 1994. In addition to providing enhanced protection for trademarks (by requiring all adhering nations to allow registration of service marks as well as trademarks and prescribing an international standard for determining likelihood of confusion of marks) and copyrights (by specifying that computer programs must be protected as literary works), TRIPS also strengthens international patent law.

To comply with its obligations under TRIPS, the United States was required to amend the Patent Act in several respects. The most significant change was the revision relating to the term of a patent. Until adherence to TRIPS, the U.S. utility patent term was seventeen years from the date the patent was issued. Because the term of the patent did not start until issuance, applicants in some instances delayed prosecution of their patents (sometimes called "submarine patents" because they lurked below public view) while they tested the market, gathered funds, and made plans to bring the invention to the marketplace. To harmonize U.S. law with that of most foreign nations, the term of a utility patent was changed to twenty years from the date of filing of the application, thus encouraging applicants to pursue prosecution diligently. Another significant change in U.S. patent law related to determining the first to invent in priority disputes. Until TRIPS, the United States ignored evidence of inventive activity abroad, thus discriminating against foreign inventors. TRIPS requires the United States to make patent rights available without discrimination in regard to the place of invention. Thus, the United States now generally considers evidence of inventive activity abroad equivalent to evidence of inventive activity in the United States in determining which party is the first to invent for purposes of priority.

APPLICATIONS FOR UNITED STATES PATENTS BY FOREIGN APPLICANTS

The patent laws of the United States make no discrimination with respect to citizenship of the inventor. Any inventor, regardless of his or her citizenship, may apply for a patent in the United States on the same basis as a U.S. citizen. Compliance with U.S. patent law is required; thus, no U.S. patent can be obtained if the invention was patented abroad on an application filed by the inventor more than twelve months before filing of the application in the Untied States.

If the applicant is a citizen of a Paris Convention nation and has first filed the application in a foreign country, the applicant may claim the filing date of the earlier filed application (as long as the U.S. application is filed within twelve months after the filing of the foreign application). The U.S. application will then be treated as if it were filed on the earlier filing date.

An oath or declaration must be made with respect to the U.S. application. This requirement imposed on all applicants for U.S. patents is somewhat different from that of many foreign nations in that foreign nations often require neither the signature of the inventor nor an oath of inventorship.

ROLE OF INTELLECTUAL PROPERTY PROFESSIONAL

Intellectual property professionals may be involved in a variety of activities relating to international protection of patents. Some of the more common tasks include the following:

- docketing filing dates and notifying clients that they have twelve months from the filing date of a patent application in the United States to file applications in Paris Convention nations and claim the earlier filing date as a priority date;
- docketing filing dates and ensuring clients are notified that foreign applications cannot be filed without receipt of a foreign filing license;
- preparing PCT applications and surveying clients for designations of countries to be specified in the PCT applications;
- docketing critical dates involved in PCT applications to ensure rights to pursue patents in foreign countries are preserved;
- reviewing PCT search reports and assisting in reporting results of the reports to clients;
- docketing critical dates to ensure the option to pursue Chapter II of the PCT process is preserved, if desired by clients;
- reviewing PCT examination reports and assisting in reporting results of the reports to clients;
- assisting clients in eliminating countries from PCT designation if patent protection is not desired in those countries; and
- assisting in prosecution of national phase for PCT applications in desired countries.

CHAPTER SUMMARY

The most significant new development in patent law is likely the Federal Circuit's decision in *State Street* to largely discard the business method exception to patentability. So long as they produce a useful, concrete, and tangible result, mathematical algorigthms, software, and business methods are patentable. In the wake of *State Street,* patents for Internet business systems and e-commerce technologies are being applied for in tremendous numbers. Other new developments in patent law relate to inventions in the areas of medicine, pharmacology, and agbiotech.

Because patents granted by the PTO have no effect in a foreign country, inventors desiring patent protection in other countries must apply for patents in each of the countries in which protection is desired. Because applying for and prosecuting patents on a country-by-country basis is expensive and cumbersome, inventors often rely on the protection afforded by the Paris Convention, a treaty adhered to by nearly one hundred and forty nations. On the basis of an application filed in one of the member countries, the applicant may, within one year, apply for protection in any or all of the other member countries, and claim as its priority date the date the application was first filed. This twelve-month period of time allows inventors to gather funding and engage in marketing analysis to determine in which countries patent protection should be sought.

Another treaty, the Patent Cooperation Treaty, facilitates the filing of applications for patents in member countries by providing a centralized filing procedure and standardized application format. The filing of an "international" application under the PCT affords applicants an international filing date in each country that is designated in the application and provides a later time period (up to thirty months) within which individual national applications must be filed.

Other international conventions also exist, principally the European Patent Organization (a centralized patent system affording patent protection in as many of the twenty-four member countries as the applicant designates in a single patent application), and TRIPS, by the terms of which the United States revised the duration of utility patent protection from seventeen years from date of grant to twenty years from the date of filing of a patent application.

Under U.S. law, it is necessary to obtain a license from the commissioner of the PTO before applying for a patent in a foreign country. Filing an application in the United States is equivalent to requesting a license, and when the PTO issues a filing receipt, it will indicate whether the request is granted or denied. The PTO may order an invention to be kept secret if national security concerns are implicated.

DISCUSSION QUESTIONS

1. Smith files an application for a utility patent in the United States on August 1. Six months later, Smith decides to file for patent protection in Spain and Portugal, members of the Paris Convention. What is the last date Smith can file applications in Spain and Portugal and obtain the benefit of the Paris Convention?

2. Jones has not filed an application for patent in the United States but would rather seek patent protection in Japan. What is Jones required to do before applying for patent protection in Japan? Why?

3. Anderson believes his invention has significant commercial application and is considering filing for patent protection in more than thirty countries. What advantages does the PCT offer over the Paris Convention?

4. Assume Anderson has completed Chapter I of the PCT process. What factors might determine whether Anderson proceeds to the national phase of the PCT process or elects to enter Chapter II proceedings?

5. Harrison, a national of France, desires patent protection only in France, Germany, and Switzerland. What alternative methods may Harrison pursue to secure patent protection?

6. Tanaka, a national of Japan, filed a design patent application in Japan on February 1. If Tanaka wishes to claim priority under the Paris Convention and file an application for the same invention in the United States, what is the latest date he may do so?

7. In what way does TRIPS encourage diligent prosecution of patent applications?

The Law of Trade Secrets and Unfair Competition

22

Trade Secrets Law

Trade secrets consist of any valuable business information that, if known by a competitor, would afford the competitor some benefit or competitive advantage. To be protected, trade secrets must be protected by their owner from unauthorized discovery. If properly protected, trade secrets may last forever.

Although many companies and employers require employees to sign agreements promising to keep key information confidential, trade secrets can be protected even in the absence of written agreement if parties occupy a relationship of trust and confidence to each other, as is the case in the employer-employee relationship. Thus, employees who learn trade secrets while in the scope of their employment cannot misappropriate those secrets, even after termination of their employment.

Trade secrets are also protected from being appropriated by improper means, such as theft or espionage. Employers typically require certain employees, generally those with access to the employer's valuable information, to sign agreements promising not to disclose confidential information and not to compete with the employer after leaving the job. Covenants not to compete restrict an employee's ability to earn a living and are strictly scrutinized by courts to ensure they are reasonable in regard to time, scope, and subject matter.

A company whose trade secrets are misappropriated may seek injunctive relief to prohibit further use or disclosure of the information as well as monetary damages. Defendants typically assert that trade secret protection has been forfeited due to the owner's failure to employ reasonable efforts to protect the information.

INTRODUCTION TO TRADE SECRETS LAW

Definition of Trade Secret

Legend has it that the formula or recipe for COCA-COLA® is locked in a vault with no one person having access. Similar stories exist relating to the recipe for the seasoning for KFC® chicken. Whether true or not, these legends illustrate a critical business reality: information that is proprietary to a company and gives it certain advantages over competitors must be protected. Release or dissemination of the information to others may cause economic hardship to (or even total elimination of) the first owner who would then be faced by competitors trading off and using the information to compete with the owner. The type of information that must be kept confidential in order to retain its competitive advantage is generally called a *trade secret*.

A trade secret is any information that can be used in the operation of a business or other enterprise that is sufficiently valuable and secret to afford an actual or potential economic advantage over others. Restatement (Third) of Unfair Competition § 39 (1995). A recipe, a formula, a method of conducting business, a customer list, a price list, marketing plans, financial projections, and a list of targets for a potential acquisition can all constitute trade secrets. Even negative information can be protectable as a trade secret. For example, information that a certain operating process or technique is *not* effective or that a product is *not* profitable can qualify for protection. There is no requirement that a trade secret be unique or complex. Even something simple and nontechnical, such as a list of customers, can qualify as a trade secret as long as it affords its owner a competitive advantage and is not common knowledge.

The rapid pace of technology advances, the ease with which information can now be rapidly disseminated, and the mobility of employees require businesses to devote significant effort to protecting their trade secrets. One survey showed that within 246 responding companies, there were 589 incidents of trade secret theft, representing nearly $2 billion in combined losses.

If trade secrets were not legally protectable, companies would have no incentive for investing time, money, and effort in research and development that ultimately benefits the public at large. Trade secret law not only provides an incentive for companies to develop new methods and processes of doing business but also, by punishing wrongdoers, discourages improper conduct in the business environment.

The Law Governing Trade Secrets

While trademarks, copyrights, and patents are all subject to extensive federal statutory schemes for their protection, there is no federal law relating to trade secrets, and no registration is required to obtain trade secret protection. Most trade secret law arises from common law 5principles, namely, judge-made case law. The first reported trade secret case in the United States was decided in 1837 and involved manufacturing methods for making chocolate. *Vickery v. Welch,* 36 Mass. 523 (1837). In 1939, the Restatement of Torts adopted a definition of a trade secret, and many states relied on that in developing their body of case law, leading to greater consistency in the development of trade secrets law. Trade secrets are now discussed in the Restatement (Third) of Unfair Competition, which restates in a simple and clear fashion the law relating to trade secrets. Additionally, in 1979, the National Conference of Commissioners on Uniform State Law drafted the Uniform Trade Secrets Act (UTSA) to promote uniformity among the states with regard to trade secrets law. The UTSA has been adopted in more than forty states. Although modifications to the UTSA have been made by various states, in general, most states now share similar trade secret legislation largely patterned after the UTSA. There are some differences between the Restatement and the UTSA. For example, the Restatement requires that for trade secret protection, information must be in continuous use while the UTSA has never imposed such a requirement. For the most part, however, the Restatement position and the UTSA are consistent in their treatment of trade secrets law.

In sum, the law related to trade secrets is derived from case law, state statutes modeled after the UTSA, and the various pronouncements made on trade secrets law by the Restatement.

In addition to the various state statutes and cases that provide a body of trade secrets law, additional protection is often gained through contractual arrangements. Companies routinely require employees with access to confidential information to sign agreements promising not to disclose that information to others and to refrain from using that information to compete with the employer, even after employment has terminated. Similarly, companies that enter into business relationships with each other generally require contractual confidentiality obligations to ensure neither party will use confidential information gained through their business relationship for improper purposes. Terms and breaches of those agreements (variously called "confidentiality agreements" or "nondisclosure agreements") are generally governed under standard contract law principles. (See Appendix D, Form 15, for a sample confidentiality agreement.)

Interplay of Trade Secrets Law with Copyright and Patent Law

Copyright rights often intercept with trade secrets. For example, a company may be in the process of developing a new software program. While the program is being developed, any documents or material relating to it are likely trade secrets. Employees of the company might be required to sign agreements promising not to disclose information about the software to others. If software is developed for internal use only or is intended for limited distribution, it may retain its character as a trade secret. Once the program is completed or "fixed," it is automatically protected under copyright law. If the owner wishes to apply for copyright registration, certain deposit materials must be supplied to the Copyright Office. The Copyright Office, however, expressly recognizes that the source code for a computer program might constitute a trade secret and allows the copyright owner to deposit less than all of the source code or to deposit blocked-out portions of the source code, thereby preserving the trade secret status of the program. Similarly, marketing materials for the program might constitute trade secrets while they are being developed. Once created, they are subject to copyright protection and the owner may apply for copyright registration for the written materials and advertisements. Once the marketing materials are distributed to consumers, they will lose their status as trade secrets but will remain protectable as copyrighted works.

In regard to patents, patent applications remain confidential until a patent issues (which might take two years or more). Thus, during the patent application process, an invention might well be protected by trade secret law. Once a patent issues, however, the invention is fully disclosed, and it cannot be a trade secret. Any protection for the invention arises under patent law. Information that is properly protected as a trade secret may maintain that status indefinitely. In contrast, patents are of a definite duration (twenty years from the date of filing of a utility application). Thus, the formula for COCA-COLA® is well protected under trade secret law and protection can last indefinitely, while under patent law, the formula or process would be disclosed upon issuance of the registration and would be protected for only twenty years from the date of filing of the patent application.

Like patents and copyrights, trade secrets can be transferred outright to others or may be licensed to others for use under specified conditions, generally in regard to territory and duration. Such license agreements, however, must contain adequate provisions to protect the confidential nature of the information or its trade secret status will be lost.

DETERMINATION OF TRADE SECRET STATUS

Restatement of Torts § 757 cmt. b lists six factors to be considered in determining whether information qualifies as a trade secret. Courts routinely examine these factors to determine whether a company's information constitutes a trade secret. None of the factors alone are determinative; courts balance these factors and weigh them against each other in determining whether information qualifies as a protectable trade secret:

- **The extent to which the information is known outside the company.** Although information may be known to others outside the company and still qualify as a trade secret, the greater the number of people who know the information, the less likely it is to qualify as a trade secret. Secrecy need not be absolute. The owner of a trade secret may, without losing protection, disclose it to a licensee or a stranger if the disclosure is made in confidence. However, the more widely disseminated the information is, the less likely courts are to protect it.

- **The extent to which the information is known within the company.** Although an employer or company is permitted to disclose confidential information to those with a demonstrated "need to know" the information, if the information is widely known within the company, especially among those who have no business need to know the information, it may not qualify as a trade secret. Companies should implement policies to prevent the inadvertent disclosure of trade secret information and limit dissemination of the material to those who need it to do their work. Thus, while the information may no longer be technically a "secret," as long as those in possession of the information need to know it to be able to perform their duties, such limited disclosure will not preclude information from trade secret protection.

- **The extent of the measures taken by the company to maintain the secrecy of the information.** One claiming trade secret protection must take reasonable precautions to protect the information. Courts are unlikely to protect information a company has not bothered to protect. A company is not obligated to undertake extreme efforts to protect information, but reasonable precautions are required. Thus, companies that require employees to sign nondisclosure agreements, keep confidential information in locked desks or rooms, restrict access to the information, and mark information with legends relating to its confidentiality are more likely to demonstrate successfully that information is a trade secret than those that fail to take such ordinary and reasonable precautions against inadvertent disclosure. Some experts predict that courts will likely require advanced security measures to protect trade secrets transmitted via e-mail, including encryption and protocols to ensure confidentiality of messages, authentication of the source of the message, and devices that ensure the recipient cannot deny receiving the message.

- **The extent of the value of the information to the company and its competitors.** If information has little value either to its owner or to the owner's competitors, it is less likely to qualify as a trade secret. Conversely, information that is valuable to a company, such as the recipe for its key menu product, and that would be of great value to the company's competitors is more likely to be a protectable trade secret.
- **The extent of the expenditure of time, effort, and money by the company in developing the information.** The greater the amount of time, effort, and money the company has expended in developing or acquiring the information, the more likely it is to be held to be a protectable trade secret.
- **The extent of the ease or difficulty with which the information could be acquired or duplicated by others.** If information is easy to acquire or duplicate, it is less likely to qualify as a trade secret. Similarly, if the information is readily ascertainable from observation or can be easily reproduced, it is less likely to be a trade secret. If it would be a straightforward matter to reverse engineer the product, it may not qualify for trade secret protection. On the other hand, if it can be reverse engineered only with significant expenditures of time, effort, and money, the product may retain its status as a trade secret.

LIABILITY FOR MISAPPROPRIATION OF TRADE SECRETS

Misappropriation of a trade secret occurs when a person possesses, discloses, or uses a trade secret owned by another without express or implied consent and when the person:

- used improper means to gain knowledge of the trade secret;
- knew or should have known that the trade secret was acquired by improper means; or
- knew or should have known that the trade secret was acquired under circumstances giving rise to a duty to maintain its secrecy.

The term *improper means* includes bribery, theft, misrepresentation, breach or inducement of a breach of duty to maintain secrecy, and espionage through electronic or other means. Thus, misappropriation occurs either when a trade secret is lawfully acquired but then improperly used or when the trade secret is acquired by improper means.

Absence of Written Agreement

While a written agreement prohibiting misappropriation of trade secrets can be enforced through an action for breach of contract, a company's trade secrets can be protected against misappropriation even in the absence of any written agreement between the parties. A party owning trade secrets can bring an action in tort for breach of the duty of confidentiality, which duty can arise

misappropriation: The taking or using of property created or secured at great effort by another

even without an express agreement. Courts will impose a duty of confidentiality when parties stand in a special relationship with each other, such as an agent-principal relationship (which includes employer-employee relationships) or other fiduciary or good faith relationships (such as relationships among partners, or between corporations and their officers and directors, or between attorneys and clients). Courts have consistently held that employees owe a duty of loyalty, fidelity, and responsibility to their employers. Other persons found to be subject to a duty of confidentiality are customers, suppliers, trainees and students, licensees, and independent contractors. In fact, more trade secret cases are brought in tort for breach of confidentiality than in contract for breach of written agreements.

Similarly, courts can find that the parties had an implied contract arising out of their common understanding. For example, if ABC Company is attempting to make a sale to Jones and informs Jones that the ABC product is superior to that of competitors because it involves a new breakthrough in technology and explains the trade secret, courts would likely find that Jones is subject to a duty not to disclose the information. Similarly, if ABC Company explains its trade secrets to its bankers in an attempt to obtain financing, the bankers would likely be precluded from disclosing or using the information. Such implied contracts to protect the information generally arise when the parties' conduct indicates they intended the information to be kept confidential or impliedly agreed to keep it confidential.

Misappropriation by Third Parties

A number of other parties may also have liability for misappropriation of trade secrets if they knew or should have known they were the recipients of protected information. For example, assume Lee is employed by XYZ Company. In the course of his employment with XYZ Company, Lee learns valuable trade secret information. If Lee leaves his employment with XYZ Company and begins working for New Company, Lee and New Company may be prohibited from using the information. Lee may not misappropriate the information because he was in an employee-employer relationship with XYZ Company, and New Company may be prohibited from using the information if it knows or should know that the information was acquired by Lee under circumstances giving rise to a duty to maintain its secrecy or limit its use. In such cases, XYZ Company would generally prefer to sue New Company inasmuch as it is far likelier to have "deep pockets," meaning it is more able to pay money damages than is an individual such as Lee.

If New Company has no reason to know the information was secret or that Lee may not reveal it, New Company would not have liability for such innocent use of the information. Similarly, if trade secret information were innocently obtained by New Company by mistake (for example, by a misdirected package or letter), New Company would have no liability for subsequent use or disclosure of the information. However, once New Company receives notice of the secrecy of the information (for example, by a letter from XYZ Company informing New Company of the nature of the trade secret and demanding that New Company cease use), it may not thereafter use the information unless New Company has so changed its position based on the information that to preclude New Company from further use would be unjust. For example, assume that after acquiring information from Lee, New Company, mistakenly believing it may use the information, incurs great expense in building a new plant facility so it may use the information in a complex manufacturing process. In such cases, courts often attempt to fashion relief for both parties by requiring the party in New Company's position to pay a royalty or license fee to XYZ for continued use of the information. Companies in New Company's position should protect themselves by requiring employees to verify in writing that they will not use information gained in confidence from previous employers.

One who obtains trade secrets by improper means, such as espionage, theft, bribery, or placing one's own employees at a competitor's place of business, cannot use or disclose the information. For example, in one case, a court prohibited a party from using information gained by hiring a plane to make a low-altitude flight over a competitor's half-completed plant to determine its layout and features. While the plane was properly flying in public airspace, the court held that improper means, namely, means that fell below the generally accepted standards of commercial morality and reasonable conduct, subjected the actor to liability. To require the owner of the plant to erect a roof over the half-completed plant would impose an unreasonable burden and expense on the owner, and thus the measures it took to protect its plant at ground level were reasonable and sufficient. *E.I. Du Pont De Nemours & Co. v. Christopher*, 431 F.2d 1012 (5th Cir. 1970).

Finally, a recipient of trade secrets may be liable for misappropriation even if modifications or improvements are made to the original confidential information if the resulting product or information is substantially derived from the owner's original trade secret.

EMPLOYER-EMPLOYEE RELATIONSHIPS

Ownership of Trade Secrets in the Absence of Written Agreement

Use or disclosure of trade secrets by employees and former employees is a frequently litigated area. While employers should require employees who will have access to trade secrets to sign agreements promising not to disclose the information, even employees who may not be subject to written nondisclosure agreements have a duty not to use an employer's trade secrets learned by the employee within the scope of employment. Moreover, this duty survives termination of the employment relationship. Generally, the higher the level of expertise possessed by the employee, the more likely it is that a confidential relationship exists between the employer and employee. Thus, senior executives, engineers, and scientists are typically subject to a higher duty of trust and confidence than more junior employees, such as file room clerks. In no event, however, may an employee steal an employer's trade secret.

If confidential information is learned by or disclosed to an employee in the course and scope of employment, the employee is subject to an implied agreement to maintain the information in secret. Information discovered by the employee on his or her "own time" (for example, on weekends or in the evenings) or before or after the employment relationship is owned by the employee. In many cases, courts find that if an employee makes a discovery during employment that is related to his or her duties (even if the employee was not hired for that specific task), the employer is automatically granted a nonexclusive "shop right" in the discovery or trade secret, such that the employer can use the information, royalty-free, both during and after the employee's employment. Because the license to the employer is nonexclusive, the employee is free to market or license the information to others.

Written Agreements

Employers are generally free to require employees, independent contractors, and consultants to sign express agreements relating to the confidentiality of information. These agreements are usually enforced by courts as long as they are reasonable. The agreements usually include four specific topics: (1) ownership of inventions; (2) nondisclosure provisions; (3) nonsolicitation provisions; and (4) noncompetition provisions.

Ownership of Inventions Most agreements expressly state that any information, inventions, or material created by the employee in the course of employment are owned by the employer. Better agreements go one step further and state that if for some reason such a clause is not sufficient to vest ownership in the employer, by the terms of the agreement, the employee irrevocably assigns the information or invention to the employer.

Nondisclosure Provisions The agreement should prohibit the employee from using or disclosing the employer's trade secrets or confidential information whether during or after employment. The agreement should describe with specificity the information that is to be protected.

Nonsolicitation Provisions Most agreements prohibit employees from soliciting or encouraging other employees from leaving the employer's business and from soliciting or attempting to "poach" clients or customers of the employer.

Noncompetition Provisions Most agreements include provisions prohibiting employees from competing against the employer both during and after the term of employment. Noncompetition clauses are also referred to as *restrictive covenants,* and they are enforceable in most states if they are reasonable. Because a covenant precluding an employee from exercising his or her only trade and earning a livelihood can be so detrimental to an employee, restrictive covenants are strictly construed by courts. In California, **noncompetition agreements** are automatically void as a restraint against trade because they preclude people from engaging in their lawful professions (unless they occur in connection with the sale of a business). A variety of factors are taken into account in determining whether such covenants are enforceable.

noncompetition agreement: An agreement prohibiting an employee from competing against the employer during and after the term of employment; also called restrictive covenant

- **Purpose.** Courts often consider whether the restriction is related to a legitimate business purpose of the employer. A restriction by McDonald's Corporation that its food handlers could not later work for other restaurants would likely be unenforceable, while a restriction by United Airlines that its senior engineers could not later work for other competitor airlines would likely be enforced by a court. The restriction by McDonald's serves no legitimate public purpose and no legitimate business need of McDonald's. On the other hand, if United Airlines has carefully recruited its top personnel, trained them, and invested time and money in teaching them its techniques and processes, it would be inequitable for a competitor to reap the advantage of this investment of time and money.

- **Reasonableness.** The restriction must be reasonable in regard to scope, duration, and geographic area. Thus, a prohibition by United Airlines that its senior engineers could not work for any other airlines in the United States in any capacity for twenty years would likely be struck down as unconscionable. A prohibition that senior engineers could not work for other competitor airlines for two years in a competitive capacity within a two-hundred-mile radius of any United Airlines facility would be more likely to be enforced.

- **Consideration.** Many states require that a covenant not to compete be supported by adequate consideration. Thus, noncompetition agreements are often entered into when the employee enters the employment relationship. In some instances, when employers award bonuses or salary increases, they use the award as an opportunity to bargain for a noncompetition clause.

If a noncompete clause is struck down by a court (because it is too broad in regard to scope or territory or too long in duration), some courts will reform the covenant (a technique often called **blue penciling**) and enforce it in regard to a more reasonable territory or length, thus making it fit the parties' intentions rather than striking the entire covenant. Many noncompete clauses contain such built-in protection by providing that if the covenant is found to be unenforceable, a court may fashion an appropriate covenant or that if part of the covenant is struck down, the remainder will be valid. In the event of any doubt or ambiguity, the covenant not to compete will be construed against the employer and in favor of the employee.

Even those states that strictly scrutinize noncompete agreements will enforce them in certain situations, such as one bargained for in connection with the sale of a business. For example, if Long purchases Crosby's business at a substantial sum, it would be inequitable to allow Crosby to immediately reenter the market and compete against Long. Thus, a court would enforce a noncompete covenant made by Crosby.

Noncompete clauses must be carefully drafted to ensure they comply with state statutory and case law. Similarly, careful drafting is needed to ensure the employee does not find a loophole to circumvent the restriction. For example, if the covenant merely precludes employment with a competitor, the employee could establish his or her own business or could serve as a consultant to a competitor. Thus, the provisions in a noncompetition agreement or clause should be drafted to afford the employer the protection it needs.

Finally, courts generally will not enforce a restrictive covenant if the employee has left employment due to the employer's breach of the employment agreement. Otherwise, an employer could hire uniquely talented individuals, have them sign covenants not to compete, refuse to pay them, and still reap the benefits of precluding them from working for others. (See Appendix D, Form 13, for a sample nondisclosure and noncompetition agreement.)

blue penciling: The revision of a noncompetition clause by a court to make it enforceable, generally because it is unreasonable in regard to scope, territory, or duration

PROTECTION FOR SUBMISSIONS

Submissions to Private Parties

In many instances individuals wish to submit an idea for an invention, process, game, or entertainment show to a company or business in the hope that the company will market and develop the idea and the individual will be compensated for the idea. For example, assume that Sanders has developed an idea for a new board game that he believes has great potential. Because Sanders cannot mass-produce and mass-market the game, he decides to write a letter and submit the idea to Milton-Bradley, a well-known company in the game and entertainment field. Because ideas are not protected under copyright law, Sanders faces a dilemma: to pique Milton-Bradley's interest, he must describe the game in sufficient detail that it can fully evaluate the game; yet, by describing the game, he runs the risk that Milton-Bradley will appropriate the idea and develop it on its own, cutting him out of the picture.

Idea submission disputes frequently arise in the entertainment industry. In one case, an individual claimed that the producers of the *Cosby Show* misappropriated her idea for a television program portraying a wholesome and loving African American family. A court held there was no misappropriation inasmuch as Bill Cosby had earlier discussed the concept with a number of other people and the idea was so general as to lack the element of concreteness to be protectable. *Murray v. NBC,* 844 F.2d 988 (2d Cir. 1988). In another case, writer Art Buchwald claimed that the movie *Coming to America* with Eddie Murphy misappropriated his written submission for a similar movie, for which Paramount Pictures had agreed to pay him a royalty if a movie was made based upon his idea. Although the idea was changed slightly by the studio, the court held that the studio had misappropriated Buchwald's submission and entered judgment for Buchwald.

The solution to such a dilemma is for the "inventor" to submit the idea pursuant to an evaluation agreement, whereby the other party agrees to evaluate the idea only for the purpose of considering a future transaction between the parties and further agrees not to circumvent the submitter or to disclose the idea to others. The parties agree that if the recipient decides to develop and use the idea, the parties will negotiate further for compensation to the submitter. (See Appendix D, Form 14, for a sample evaluation agreement.)

Unsolicited manuscripts and ideas present unique problems. Many producers and companies do not accept unsolicited submissions for fear of lawsuits and often return packages unopened. In many cases involving unsolicited ideas that arrive with no contractual terms or language limiting their future use, courts allow the recipient to develop and market the idea, based on the concept that a person who discloses an idea without first seeking protection has only himself or herself to blame. Other courts find an implied contract exists, and hold that the recipient has impliedly agreed that he or she will compensate the submitter if the idea is used. Still other courts rely on a theory of unjust enrichment, holding that the recipient would be unjustly enriched if he or she could take the idea, develop it, market it, and make a profit from it, all without compensating the submitter. In those cases, courts award some reasonable compensation or royalty to the submitter. Finally, some courts consider industry practice and custom and if submitters are routinely compensated in the industry, even for

idea submission: The submission of an idea for an invention, process, game, or entertainment show in the hope it will be developed and marketed by the recipient

unsolicited submissions, courts may find an implied contract to compensate the submitter. In any event, the idea must be sufficiently developed or concrete that it can be protected, and it must be something novel rather than something so ordinary that anyone could have conceived of it. In sum, the only way for a submitter to be assured protection for an idea is by written agreement.

Submissions to Government Agencies

Private companies that present bids to government agencies in the hope of obtaining a government contract are often required to disclose confidential or trade secret information to the agency. Under freedom of information acts (both at the state and federal levels), the proposal might later be released to any member of the public requesting the document, thus resulting in loss of confidential information to possible competitors. To protect companies against such disclosure, many freedom of information acts contain exceptions so that parties can designate certain information as a trade secret and thus prevent its release. The protected information is usually blocked out. If a government agency discloses trade secret information, the owner may have a cause of action for an unconstitutional taking of private property and may be awarded compensation if the owner had a reasonable expectation of confidentiality.

DEFENSES TO TRADE SECRET MISAPPROPRIATION

A variety of defenses may be raised by a party accused of misappropriating another's trade secrets. The most commonly asserted defenses are as follows:

- **Lack of secrecy.** A defendant may assert that the owner of the trade secret failed to take appropriate and reasonable measures to protect the trade secret and the information has thus entered the public domain. Courts will then examine the measures taken by the trade secret owner and determine if they were reasonable under the circumstances. If the information could have been readily protected but was not, courts are likely to hold the owner has lost its rights to the information. Thus, discussions of information at conferences or in publications may result in loss of trade secret protection. Some recent cases have examined whether memorization of information is a defense, holding that reconstruction of a trade secret, such as a customer list, through memorization (as opposed to physically taking or copying the list) is not a defense and is another form of misappropriation.
- **Independent creation.** Just as independent creation is a defense to a claim of copyright infringement, independent creation of information that is a trade secret of another is permissible. As long as a party did not breach a duty of confidentiality or an agreement to hold information in confidence, and did not use improper means in acquiring the information, independent creation will be a defense to a claim of misappropriation. Reverse engineering, namely, the inspection or analysis of a product to determine the method by which it was developed, is generally a protected form of independent creation. An assertion that the information lacks protection because it *could have been* reverse engineered is

generally successful only when others have in fact reverse engineered the item or when reverse engineering could be easily accomplished.

- **Privilege.** A party may be compelled to disclose a trade secret in the course of some judicial or administrative action. Such disclosure is privileged and is nonactionable. Many written confidentiality agreements require that one called to testify about a trade secret provide notice to the owner of the trade secret so it may attempt to protect itself by seeking some judicial relief, such as exclusion of bystanders and the media from the courtroom during disclosure.

- **Unclean hands or laches.** A defendant may assert that the trade secret owner's conduct is so reprehensible that its "unclean hands" bars any recovery. Additionally, a defendant may assert that the trade secret owner has so delayed in bringing the action that the defendant has been prejudiced by such delay and thus the action should be barred. Laches (an unreasonable delay that prejudices the other party) is often asserted when a defendant has innocently acquired the trade secret and then expended a great deal of time and money in promoting or marketing the information. To require the defendant to cease use in such circumstances may be inequitable.

REMEDIES FOR MISAPPROPRIATION

A trade secret owner may request a variety of remedies from a court. Among them are the following:

- **Injunctive relief.** In many cases, a trade secret owner is more interested in ensuring the defendant cease use of the trade secret (or is precluded from commencing use) than in recovering damages. In cases in which money damages are not sufficient to protect a trade secret owner, a court may issue an injunction. Injunctions can be issued to prohibit a party from further using or disclosing the information or to ensure the party does not begin to use or disclose the information if disclosure is threatened, imminent, or inevitable. A court may issue a preliminary injunction during the pendency of the action; if the plaintiff prevails, the injunction may be made permanent. A court may also issue an injunction to compel the defendant to surrender or destroy trade secret information. In fact, courts may issue injunctions to prevent "inevitable disclosure," reasoning that even if a former employer cannot show a particular secret has been taken, it is inevitable that key employees will eventually disclose what they know to a new employer. In such cases, even in the absence of a covenant not to compete, courts have enjoined employees from working on particular projects, imposed time limits during which the new employee cannot work for another, or even prohibited employees from working for a new company in any capacity.

- **Money damages.** A trade secret owner whose information has been misappropriated may recover money damages from the defendant. The plaintiff may recover its lost profits as well as the profits made by the defendant. Alternatively, the plaintiff may seek and recover a reasonable royalty arising from defendant's use of the trade secret. Punitive

damages may also be awarded in cases in which the defendant's conduct
is reckless, willful, and intentional. The UTSA provides that punitive
damages not exceed more than twice the compensatory damages
awarded.

- **Attorneys' fees and costs.** In most cases, the parties bear their own
  attorneys' fees and costs. The UTSA, however, provides that reasonable
  attorneys' fees and costs may be awarded to the prevailing party.

TRADE SECRET LITIGATION

If a trade secret is disclosed in violation of a written confidentiality agreement, and the parties cannot resolve the dispute themselves, an action for
breach of contract may be brought, similar to any other breach of contract
action. The plaintiff may add other causes of action as well, for example, for
misappropriation in violation of a state trade secret law. If no written agreement exists, the plaintiff must rely upon case law or state statutes protecting
trade secrets, or both.

To protect itself against a lawsuit by another alleging trade secret violations, companies should require new employees who will have access to confidential information to acknowledge in writing that accepting employment with
the new company does not violate any other agreement or violate any other obligation of confidentiality to which the employee may be subject. Additionally,
employees should be required to represent that work they perform for the
employer will be original work and will not infringe any other party's rights.

If grounds for federal jurisdiction exist (the parties have diverse citizenship
and the claim exceeds $75,000), the action may be brought in federal court. If
the action also involves copyright or patent, it must be brought in federal court.
Otherwise, the action will be brought in a state court. If the action is instituted
in federal court, a federal court will apply state law inasmuch as there is no federal trade secret law.

In federal court, the action will be governed by the Federal Rules of Civil
Procedure relating to federal civil actions generally. These rules set the times
for responding to the complaint, matters pertaining to motions and discovery,
and any other litigation-related matters. Most states have rules relating to civil
procedure that are modeled substantially after the Federal Rules of Civil
Procedure and likewise govern the litigation. After the complaint is filed, the
defendant will respond by filing an answer, usually denying that any breach of
agreement or misappropriation has occurred and asserting various defenses. If
the defendant has a cause of action to assert against the plaintiff relating to the
trade secret, it must be asserted by way of a counterclaim in the litigation so
that all disputes between the parties relating to the information can be resolved
at the same time.

After the complaint, answer, and counterclaim have been filed, various
motions may be made. Discovery will commence. The plaintiff and defendant
will take depositions to obtain testimony from those who may have information
about the case. For example, the plaintiff may depose individuals in the defendant's company to determine whether they were instructed to use the plaintiff's
information. Interrogatories may be served on either party to obtain information, such as to inquire about experts either side may intend to call, how

damages such as lost profits were calculated, or to determine the existence of pertinent documents.

Ultimately, if the matter cannot be resolved by private agreement, it will proceed to trial. The trade secret owner must prove misappropriation by a preponderance of the evidence. Either party may request a jury trial; otherwise, a judge will render the decision. Appeals may follow.

One of the difficult issues in trade secret litigation arises from the fact that the trade secret sought to be protected often must be disclosed in the litigation so the judge or jury can evaluate whether the information is sufficiently valuable that it affords its owner a competitive advantage. Similarly, the owner's methods of protecting the information often must be disclosed so the fact-finder can determine whether the owner has taken reasonable measures to protect the alleged trade secrets. Thus, the dilemma faced by trade secrets owners in litigation is that they must disclose the very information they seek to protect. Courts can fashion a variety of means to protect the information, from issuing protective orders (prohibiting the parties and their counsel from any further disclosure), to holding private hearings in the judge's chambers, to sealing court records.

As technology progresses and the value of certain communication and entertainment inventions increases, trade secret litigation is becoming an increasingly common and high-stakes occupation. Damage awards may run into the millions. For example, the *National Law Journal* reported in September 1997 that the U.S. Court of Appeals upheld a $45.6 million judgment against Polaris Industries for the theft of a design for a fuel-injection engine for snowmobiles. *Injection Research Specialists, Inc. v. Polaris Indus., L.P.,* No. 90-Z-1143 (D. Colo. 1997).

TRADE SECRET PROTECTION PROGRAMS

Because trade secrets are legally fragile and may be lost by inadvertent disclosure or failure to reasonably protect them, companies should implement trade secret protection programs to safeguard valuable information. While it is common for businesses to assume that only scientific and technical data constitute trade secrets, protection is available for a much broader range of subjects, such as customer lists, marketing plans, hiring tactics, and other information that would be valuable to a competitor, and that are common to many companies, not merely those engaged in scientific endeavors.

Because trade secret protection can last indefinitely, businesses should devote proper attention to the methods used to ensure confidentiality of information. Companies that value their trade secrets should implement trade secret protection programs. Developing programs and measures to protect trade secrets is an easy way to demonstrate to a court that an owner values its information and takes appropriate measures to maintain its secrecy. Such programs consist of several elements.

Physical Protection

There are a variety of tangible measures a company can implement to protect trade secrets, including the following:

- safeguarding information under lock and key;
- protecting the information from unauthorized access;
- forbidding removal of protected information from the company premises or certain rooms;
- retaining adequate security during evenings and weekends either through alarm systems or security services;
- ensuring tours of the company premises do not expose outsiders to valuable processes or information;
- marking materials with legends or stamps such as "Confidential—Trade Secret Information";
- using check-out lists when valuable equipment or information is removed from its normal location;
- monitoring activities of former employees who had access to confidential information and monitoring trade journals for articles that may show a competitor has gained access to company trade secrets;
- implementing inventory control systems (such as numbering each copy of valuable written materials and retaining a log showing which employee received which document);
- securing computers with password or encryption protection;
- requiring use of paper shredders for disposal of sensitive documents;
- designating a responsible person to be responsible for trade secret information and release to others (including the media), and for reviewing bids, proposals, and marketing materials;
- implementing photocopying policies and maintaining log books or electronic monitoring of copying;
- monitoring employees' use of e-mail and the Internet to ensure confidential information is not being disseminated (as long as employees are notified beforehand that use of e-mail and the Internet must be for business purposes only and that the employer may monitor use);
- conducting exit interviews with employees to remind them of their obligations not to use or disclose proprietary company information;
- including notices on facsimile cover sheets and e-mail communications that the communication is intended only for the designated recipient and if it is received in error, the party who mistakenly received it must return it to the sender;
- using encryption technology and antivirus protection programs to protect information stored on computers;
- requiring visitors to the premises to sign in and wear badges; and
- ensuring information retained on computers is available only on company networks so that access can be easily tracked.

Contractual Protection

Another method of protecting trade secrets is by contract, namely, requiring those with access to the information to agree in writing not to disclose the information to others or use it to the owner's detriment. Similarly, in licensing arrangements, trade secret owners should ensure the license agreements contain sufficient protection for trade secret information. Employers should use noncompetition agreements to ensure former employees do not use material gained on the job to later compete against the employer. Even without formal contracts, a company should include protection policies in its employee handbooks, routinely publish reminders about confidentiality in company newsletters and through e-mail messages, and remind employees of their duties during their initial orientations and during exit interviews conducted when the individuals leave the company's employment.

Intellectual Property Protection

Companies can also rely on other methods of protection to safeguard trade secrets. Any material that qualifies for copyright protection should be protected by registration, or at a minimum, by ensuring a copyright notice is placed on the material or document to afford notice to others of the owner's right and interest in the material. Inventions should be subject to patent protection, and trademarks should be fully protected by applying for registration.

NEW AND INTERNATIONAL DEVELOPMENTS IN TRADE SECRETS LAW

New Developments

Perhaps the newest developments in trade secret law have arisen out of the ease of electronic communication. Because information can be readily obtained by computer and then similarly disseminated to others with a stroke of the keyboard, companies are investing greater time and money in ensuring their communications systems are secure. While physical methods of protecting trade secrets (such as locked drawers, restricted access to information, marking information with legends, and so forth) have always been favored by courts, companies should now consider protecting their information by electronic security measures. Use of passwords, encryption and coding of documents, and restricting access to information placed on computers are now being examined by courts in attempting to determine whether an owner has taken sufficient measures to protect its proprietary information.

Another newer development in trade secrets law is the use of criminal statutes to punish wrongdoers. In 1996, Congress enacted the Economic Espionage Act of 1996 (18 U.S.C. § 1831), which provides criminal penalties for the theft or attempted theft of trade secret information that will benefit foreign governments and for the theft of trade secrets related to products produced or placed in interstate commerce. Theft of information by physical as well as electronic means is prohibited. The United States Attorney General can initiate a civil action to enjoin threatened theft, violators may be imprisoned, and fines can be imposed of up to $10 million for foreign espionage and $5 million for other trade secret theft.

Similarly, theft of tangible property containing trade secrets (such as documents or disks) and transporting it across state lines may be a violation of the National Stolen Property Act (18 U.S.C. § 2314). Federal mail and wire fraud statutes are also used to punish theft of trade secrets. Many states have similar statutes that are used to deter and punish misappropriation of trade secrets.

International Developments

Because trade secret information is generally lost once it is disclosed (assuming proper precautions have not been taken), companies intending to do business internationally must ensure that their trade secrets are protected in foreign countries so that inadvertent disclosure abroad does not cause world-wide loss of protection. Just as is the case in the United States, theft of trade secrets is a crime in most foreign countries. Moreover, the North American Free Trade Agreement (NAFTA), entered into by the United States, Canada, and Mexico in 1991, complements U.S. trade secret law and requires member countries to protect trade secrets from unauthorized disclosure or use. In response to NAFTA, Mexico amended its laws to allow litigants to bring civil actions to enjoin threatened or existing trade secret violations.

In 1994, the General Agreement on Tariffs and Trade (GATT) was concluded by the major industrialized nations of the world, including the United States. GATT provides for adjudication of trade secret disputes, and under TRIPS (Trade-Related Aspects of Intellectual Property Rights), promulgated in accordance with GATT, member countries must provide effective remedies for misappropriation of trade secrets owned by residents of other member countries. Thus, all member nations of GATT have measures similar to those in the United States for protecting trade secrets, thereby ensuring that companies that wish to do business in other GATT member countries can do so with the knowledge that their valuable trade secret information will be protectable.

Finally, the Economic Espionage Act of 1996 discussed earlier applies not only to conduct within the United States but also to conduct occurring outside the United States if the offender is a natural person who is a citizen or

ROLE OF INTELLECTUAL PROPERTY PROFESSIONAL

Intellectual property professionals can engage in numerous activities related to trade secret protection, including the following:

- conducting trade secret audits to ensure confidential information is protected;
- drafting guidelines for clients to follow in implementing trade secret protection programs;
- reviewing client documents to ensure materials are clearly marked with notices regarding their confidentiality;
- drafting notices for clients to place in newsletters, near photocopy machines, and in prominent locations throughout offices reminding employees of the need to keep company information confidential;
- reviewing confidentiality clauses and employment agreements entered into with key employees to ensure client information will be maintained in confidence;
- drafting nondisclosure and noncompete agreements; and
- conducting state-by-state research regarding enforceability of noncompete clauses.

permanent resident alien of the United States or if an act in furtherance of the offense was committed in the United States.

Additionally, safeguards such as employment and nondisclosure agreements and limiting access to confidential information through both internal and physical measures may help to maintain the status of trade secrets in foreign countries.

CHAPTER SUMMARY

A trade secret consists of any information that its owner has reasonably protected and that, if known by a competitor, would afford some advantage or benefit. If properly protected, trade secrets may exist forever. Trade secrets are protectable even in the absence of written agreement if the parties enjoy a relationship of trust and confidence (as is the case in employer-employee relationships). Trade secrets are also protected from appropriation by improper means such as theft, bribery, or espionage.

Although trade secrets can be protected even without a written agreement, such an agreement is advisable. Agreements with key employees should also include noncompete clauses. While strictly scrutinized by courts as possible restraints against trade, such noncompete provisions are enforceable in most states as long as they are reasonable in time, territory, and scope.

A trade secret owner may obtain injunctive relief or monetary damages, or both, if a trade secret has been misappropriated. Criminal penalties may also be assessed against the violator. A trade secret, however, will not be protected by a court if its owner has not exercised reasonable efforts to maintain its secrecy.

Companies should implement aggressive trade secret protection programs to ensure the protectability of valuable information. Information can be protected by physical barriers (such as lock and key), contractual provisions prohibiting disclosure, and by taking advantage of protection available under copyright and patent laws.

DISCUSSION QUESTIONS

1. ABC Inc. is the owner of a training manual used to train its employees and containing a number of valuable forms. Can the manual constitute a trade secret?

2. Assume ABC Inc. keeps the manual in its reception area with a number of company brochures and other literature and where visitors routinely view all of the materials. Discuss whether the manual can be protected under trade secret law.

3. TriTech Company has recently hired a senior researcher to work on a new computer chip. There is no written agreement between the parties. The researcher recently discovered valuable information relating to development of the chip. Who owns the information? May the researcher be precluded from disclosing it even after he leaves TriTech's employment?

4. Adams & Baker Co., an engineering analysis firm, insists that all of its employees sign agreements promising not to compete with the company after they leave its employment. Discuss whether the following agreements are likely to be enforceable:
   a. an agreement forbidding clerical workers from engaging in similar occupations, for one year following termination of employment, anywhere in the United States
   b. an agreement forbidding engineers from engaging in any engineering work, for two years following termination of employment, anywhere in the United States
   c. an agreement forbidding engineers from engaging in engineering work similar to that performed while at Adams & Baker, for one year following termination of employment, within one hundred miles of any Adams & Baker office
   d. an agreement forbidding key executives from working for competitor companies, for one year following termination of employment, anywhere in the United States

5. AmCard Inc. owns a proprietary software program related to financial and accounting methods. One of its competitors has lawfully obtained a copy of the program and has been able to reverse engineer the program and is now selling it to some of AmCard's customers. Discuss whether misappropriation of trade secrets has occurred.

6. Assume the facts in question 5, except that the program was acquired by an individual who posed as an employee of AmCard but was actually employed by AmCard's competitor. Discuss whether misappropriation of trade secrets has occurred.

7. Assume the facts in question 6, except that AmCard has been aware for the past two years that its competitor reverse engineered the program and has been marketing it and selling it during that period of time. AmCard recently filed suit against the competitor for misappropriation of trade secrets. Discuss whether AmCard is likely to prevail in the action.

Unfair Competition

The term *unfair competition* is a broad term covering a wide variety of deceptive practices in the marketplace. The law of unfair competition continues to evolve with changes in the marketplace so that deceptive infomercials and false advertising on the Internet can be prohibited, just as their earlier print counterparts are.

The most commonly alleged forms of unfair competition are: passing off (selling one's goods as those of another); misappropriation (the taking of another's intangible commercial property right); infringement of the right of publicity (appropriating another's identity or persona for commercial purposes); false advertising (making false or deceptive representations about the nature of one's own goods or services); product disparagement (making false or deceptive representations about another's goods or services); dilution (weakening or tarnishing the value of another's trademark or service mark even though the use does not cause a likelihood of confusion); and infringement of trade dress (causing confusion with the distinctive product image or overall appearance of another's product or service).

There is considerable overlap in the theories used by injured parties to protect their business property interests against deception and fraud, and the same act may give rise to several causes of action. Thus, a misleading advertisement may constitute passing off, false advertising, and product disparagement. For example, the Fifth Circuit Court of Appeals held in 1998 that a tavern's unauthorized use of the name "The Velvet Elvis" constituted trademark infringement, unfair competition, trademark dilution, and violation of the right of publicity. *Elvis Presley Ent. Inc. v. Capece,* 141 F.3d 188 (5th Cir. 1998). Moreover, section 43 of the Lanham Act (15 U.S.C. § 1125), often referred to as a "national unfair competition statute," also protects against a wide variety of false and misleading commercial practices. Finally, the Federal Trade Commission (FTC) may also take action to protect consumers from false and deceptive trade practices. Thus, injured parties often rely upon a wide variety of theories to protect their business goodwill or intellectual property from unfair tactics in the commercial arena.

INTRODUCTION TO UNFAIR COMPETITION

The law of unfair competition is based upon the notion that individuals should be protected from deceptive and improper conduct in the marketplace.

The law of unfair competition is found in case law, in state statutes prohibiting unfair business practices, in specific federal statutes, and in regulations promulgated by the FTC, the federal regulatory agency charged with protecting consumers from unfair or deceptive acts and practices. The law of unfair competition continues to evolve as new methods of conducting business arise, such as electronic offers and sales through telemarketing, television infomercials, and the Internet.

There are a number of theories and actions that can be used by injured parties to protect against unfair competition. For the most part, the remedies are designed to protect intangible interests, such as one's interest in one's business reputation, goodwill, and so forth. For that reason, unfair competition law often protects "intellectual" property rather than real property or personal property and promotes a well-functioning marketplace.

In many instances, actions for unfair competition will be combined with other actions (such as those alleging trademark, copyright, or patent infringement) to provide a plaintiff a wide array of possible remedies. In other instances, a plaintiff may not have a protectable trademark, copyright, or patent, and thus must rely entirely on unfair competition theories to provide relief against unscrupulous business practices. For example, a designer of scarves imprinted with fanciful designs may decide against applying for a design patent due to the expense involved and the short life cycle of fashion products. Protection against copying of the design may thus be available under the umbrella of unfair competition rather than under design patent law.

Section 43 of the Lanham Act (15 U.S.C. § 1125) provides a federal cause of action to protect consumers against unfair competitive business practices. It is effectively a national unfair competition statute prohibiting a broad range of wrongful business activities and providing a wide array of remedies to plaintiffs. Moreover, section 43(a) protects unregistered marks and names, such as those that do not qualify for federal trademark registration because they are descriptive or perhaps used only in intrastate commerce.

The most common types of unfair competition are discussed more fully in this chapter but can be briefly summarized as follows:

- **Passing off (or palming off).** "Passing off" occurs when one party attempts to pass off his or her goods or services as those of another.
- **Misappropriation.** Misappropriation exists when one party takes or uses another's property that the original owner created or secured at effort and expense.
- **Right of publicity.** A person's identity, voice, likeness, or persona is protected against unauthorized commercial exploitation through the right of publicity.
- **False advertising.** Making false or deceptive representations about the nature of one's goods or services is actionable as false advertising.
- **Product disparagement.** Making false representations about the nature of another party's goods or services is actionable as product disparagement.
- **Dilution.** Either tarnishing another's mark or causing it to lose its distinctiveness through "blurring" is actionable as dilution.
- **Infringement of trade dress.** Adopting the overall concept of another's distinctive packaging or product image, generally called its

"trade dress," so as to deceive consumers is an infringement of trade dress.

Generally, injured parties notify the wrongdoer prior to initiating litigation. A cease and desist letter is usually sent, detailing the wrongdoer's acts and demanding that the wrongdoer cease and desist its activities. (See Chapter 6, Figure 6–1, for a sample cease and desist letter used in trademark infringement matters.) If there is no resolution, the injured party may initiate legal action. In many instances, a plaintiff will allege several causes of action. For example, if a competitor of Nike uses a "swoosh" symbol similar to that registered to Nike, Nike may allege trademark infringement, passing off, dilution of its famous mark, and violation of section 43(a) of the Lanham Act, prohibiting a false designation of origin. If another shoemaker sells an athletic shoe that copies the overall appearance or image of Nike's shoes, such conduct may be prohibited as infringement of trade dress.

PASSING OFF

Passing off (also referred to as *palming off*) occurs when one party attempts to pass off its goods under the pretense that they are the goods of another. Passing off may exist when one party affixes another's trademarks to its goods, adopts a trademark or trade name that is so similar to that of another that consumers are deceived about the source of the product or service, or copies features of another's goods so that its goods are confusingly similar to those of the other. The essence of the action is some representation by a defendant, whether direct or indirect, that causes consumers to be deceived about the source of their purchases.

Actions alleging passing off are often brought when a case of trademark infringement does not lie. For example, a business owner may not be able to secure trademark protection for his or her business name because the name is primarily a surname or it is so descriptive it does not qualify for protection as a trademark. The use of a similar name by another party in connection with similar products and services that causes confusion and deception may thus be remedied by bringing an action alleging that the second party is passing off his or her goods as those of the plaintiff. Passing off may be enjoined and damages may be awarded to compensate the plaintiff for damages suffered, including lost profits.

Passing off is the earliest form of unfair competition, and the term is used to describe a wide variety of deceptive trade practices. Passing off can occur when a party suggests that its products or services are somehow associated with or sponsored by another, as when a retailer advertises that it is "an authorized dealer of Maytag® products," when it is not. Such conduct is harmful to Maytag, which has not only lost a sale but may suffer damage to its reputation inasmuch as improper conduct by the retailer could reflect badly on Maytag. Such a blatantly untrue statement also constitutes false advertising as well as a violation of section 43(a) of the Lanham Act, which prohibits false designations of origin. In fact, because much of the conduct formerly attacked as passing off is also prohibited by section 43 of the Lanham Act, the federal unfair competition statute, fewer actions alleging passing off are brought nowadays, inasmuch as those

passing off: Attempting to sell one's goods or services as those of another; also called *palming off*

actions are dependent upon individual state court interpretations of cases. An action brought under the Lanham Act, however, is federal in nature and provides expanded remedies to plaintiffs such as enhanced damages and attorneys' fees, which are generally unavailable under state law.

In sum, passing off one's goods or services as those of another is a form of unfair competition. Actions alleging palming off or passing off are brought less frequently now, since most plaintiffs prefer to bring actions under section 43 of the Lanham Act, which statutorily prohibits such conduct and provides a federal cause of action with expanded remedies.

MISAPPROPRIATION

The doctrine of misappropriation first arose in *International News Service v. Associated Press,* 248 U.S. 215 (1918), in which the Supreme Court held that an unauthorized taking of another's property, in that case, news information, that it invested time and money in creating was actionable as misappropriation of property. In *INS,* news information originally gathered by the Associated Press relating to World War I was pirated by International News Service and sold to its customers. Because the news itself, as factual matter, could not be copyrighted, the plaintiff could not sue for copyright infringement. Instead it alleged that its valuable property right had been taken or misappropriated by the defendant. The Supreme Court agreed, noting that the defendant was "endeavoring to reap where it has not sown, and . . . is appropriating to itself the harvest of those who have sown." *Id.* at 239–40. Because the defendant was not attempting to convince its subscribers that its news reports were from the plaintiff, an action for passing off would not lie. The defendant was misappropriating rather than misrepresenting.

In recent years, the doctrine of misappropriation has fallen into disfavor due to its somewhat amorphous nature, and many courts have followed *INS* only when nearly identical fact patterns are presented, namely, cases involving the taking of news, event results, mathematical formulae (such as golf handicapping systems), and indices (such as stock market index reports and averages) that are not addressed by copyright or patent law.

RIGHT OF PUBLICITY

Introduction

Some of the most interesting cases in the intellectual property field relate to the rights of individuals to protect their identities from unauthorized commercial use. The **right of publicity** gives individuals, not merely celebrities, the right to control commercial use of their identities or personas. Nevertheless, because the right of publicity protects a commercial interest, the vast majority of cases involve celebrities inasmuch as they can readily show economic harm when their names, photographs, or identities are used to sell products or suggest a sponsorship of merchandise.

Publicity rights are governed by state law. Many states have specific statutes dealing with the right of publicity. Others recognize the right through

right of publicity: Protection of a person's identity, voice, likeness, or persona against unauthorized commercial exploitation

case law. Some states do not recognize any right of publicity. On the other hand, California, with its large population of celebrities, has extensive statutes and significant case law recognizing the right of publicity.

The right of publicity has evolved from the right of privacy, which protected against unreasonable invasions upon another person's solitude and provided remedies for the disclosure of private information. While the right of privacy, however, protects one's *personal* interests against indignity, hurt feelings, and invasion, the right of publicity protects one's *commercial* interests against wrongful exploitation. The right of publicity allows individuals to protect the marketability of their identities (a property right) and punishes those who would unjustly enrich themselves by appropriating another's fame for profit-making purposes. Unpermitted commercial exploitation of an individual's persona would dilute the value of the persona, making it more difficult for the individual to commercialize his or her identity. Thus, remedies for infringement include injunctions to prevent further exploitation and monetary relief to compensate the individual whose right of publicity has been appropriated (including damages for injury to reputation, recovery of the defendant's profits, and punitive damages in extreme cases).

Courts have articulated a number of reasons for upholding an individual's right to publicity, including the need to protect against confusion that would arise if consumers were led to believe individuals sponsor or approve products when they do not, the need to incentivize performers who provide entertainment and benefit to society and should thus be provided with a protectable property right in their identities, and the need to prevent unjust enrichment of those who seek to profit from another's talent and often hard-earned fame.

The right of publicity does not apply to noncommercial uses; thus, using another's name, likeness, or identity for news reporting, scholarship, or research is permissible (as long as there is no invasion of privacy or defamation). Most cases relate to unauthorized use of another's identity to promote some product or service, thus suggesting that the individual sponsors or approves the item being advertised.

Appropriation of Identity

Most states protect more than just a person's name. Thus, unauthorized use of a nickname, voice, likeness, portrait, signature, appearance, identity, or personal attribute (such as customary gestures, clothing, or hairstyle) is prohibited if that use is understood to identify a particular person. Neither intent to deceive nor consumer confusion must be proved. The essence of an action for misappropriation of one's right to publicity is that one's identity was used without permission. Nevertheless, wrongfully using a celebrity's name to advertise a product may also be actionable as false advertising and unfair competition.

Although it is clear that unauthorized use of a person's name or picture is actionable, there are a variety of other ways in which the right of publicity can be infringed.

- **Phrases and nicknames.** In *Carson v. Here's Johnny Portable Toilets,* 698 F.2d 831 (6th Cir. 1983), a court prohibited a portable toilet company from using the phrase *Here's Johnny* in connection with advertising its services, holding that the phrase had become sufficiently identified with the entertainer Johnny Carson to be protected, even though neither his full name nor his picture was used. Disguising a name, such as varying a few letters, will not protect a defendant. Even nicknames are protectable if they are understood to identify the plaintiff. For example, in *Hirsch v. S.C. Johnson & Sons, Inc.*, 280 N.W.2d 129 (Wis. 1979), the use of the word *Crazylegs* to advertise moisturizer was held to infringe the right of publicity of football star Elroy "Crazylegs" Hirsch.

- **Likeness.** A person's "likeness," including a variety of physical features, is protectable against unauthorized use, whether by drawing, cartoons, or lookalikes. Thus, in *Ali v. Playgirl, Inc.*, 447 F. Supp. 723 (S.D.N.Y 1978), a cartoon drawing of a black man in a boxing ring that included the phrase *The Greatest* was held to have identified the boxer Muhammad Ali and violated his right of publicity. Similarly, in *Allen v. National Video, Inc.*, 610 F. Supp. 612 (S.D.N.Y. 1985), Woody Allen was able to prohibit the use of a lookalike in advertisements for video rental stores inasmuch as the advertisements falsely suggested that Woody Allen endorsed the advertised services.

- **Voice.** In *Midler v. Ford Motor Co.*, 849 F.2d 460 (9th Cir. 1988), the Ford Motor Company's use of an impersonator to imitate the singer Bette Midler's vocal style in advertisements for Ford's cars was held to be unlawful. The Ninth Circuit held that while it would "not go so far as to hold that every imitation of a voice to advertise merchandise is actionable, . . . when a distinctive voice of a professional singer is widely known and is deliberately imitated in order to sell a product, the sellers have appropriated what is not theirs . . . ." *Id.* at 463.

- **Roles and associated objects.** Imitating a distinctive performing style or persona is actionable. Thus, the roles associated with Groucho Marx and Charlie Chaplin (the "Little Tramp" persona) have been protected from unauthorized commercial exploitation. In *White v. Samsung Electronics America, Inc.*, 971 F.2d 1395 (9th Cir. 1992), the use of a mechanical robot wearing a wig, jewelry, and evening wear posed near a game board similar to that used on the television game show *Wheel of Fortune* was held to create a triable issue of fact regarding whether such use violated game show hostess Vanna White's right of publicity because the display evoked her identity. Similarly, in a recent case, Fred Rogers ("Mister Rogers") sued a store for selling T-shirts showing him wearing his well-recognized sweater and bearing a pistol, arguing that the image was wholly inconsistent with his child-friendly persona and violated his right of publicity.

Duration and Descendibility of Right to Publicity

The duration of the right of publicity is subject to much variation. Some states do not provide any protection for deceased individuals. For example, in New York, the right can be asserted only by a living individual. Many experts believe that this view stems from the association of the right of privacy with the right of publicity. Because the right of privacy is personal to the individual and does not survive death, some states similarly hold that there is no postmortem right of publicity.

The majority of states, however, recognizing that the right of publicity is an economic property right, hold that just as one can pass one's other property to one's heirs so that they receive the fruit of one's labors, so too the right of publicity should survive death. To hold otherwise allows others, generally advertisers, to reap a windfall upon the death of a celebrity. Moreover, because an individual can license the right to another to use his or her name or likeness (for example, the use of athletes' names or photos on sporting goods equipment), clearly indicating the nature of the right of publicity as a property right, the better-reasoned view appears to be that of the majority: the right of publicity is a property right, and like other property rights, it should pass to one's heirs upon death.

On the other hand, there is no real need for the right to exist in perpetuity. It serves little purpose today for the heirs of Benjamin Franklin to be able to control the use of his likeness or name. Thus, in most states, the right of publicity survives death for a stated period of time. For example, in California, the right survives for seventy years after a person's death. Other states recognize varying terms for protection, ranging from twenty years to one hundred years. Still other states, however, that recognize postmortem rights allow heirs to allege infringement only when the individual commercially exploited his or her identity during life. In those states, unless a person has exploited his or her likeness or identity during lifetime, heirs cannot sue for infringement after the person's death.

State laws that do not recognize postmortem rights of publicity can often be circumvented. For example, New York will apply the law of a deceased individual's domicile at death. Thus, celebrities often make sure to claim California or some other state as their domicile. Indiana, another state that is highly protective of the right of publicity, authorizes application of its law as soon as an advertisement enters the state. Not surprisingly, a company that represents the estates of more than one hundred deceased celebrities is headquartered in Indiana. Similarly, in today's climate of national communication and advertising, heirs of celebrities may be able to avoid states that do not recognize postmortem rights by asserting that the infringing act was committed in some other state and therefore its laws should apply.

Defenses in Right of Publicity Cases

A variety of defenses may be asserted in actions alleging infringement of one's right of publicity. One defense raised is that the plaintiff is not specifically and readily identified by the usage. For example, in *T.J. Hooker v. Columbia Pictures Industries, Inc.*, 551 F. Supp. 1060 (N.D. Ill. 1982), the plaintiff, a woodcarver named T. J. Hooker, was unable to prove he was the specific person identified in defendant's television program concerning a fictional police officer.

Another defense asserted is that the usage is protected speech under the First Amendment. News reports using a person's name or identity are protected by the First Amendment's freedom of speech clause as long as the use does not extend beyond what is necessary to inform the public of a newsworthy event. Similarly, use in connection with research and scholarship, because it is not commercial use, is permissible. Courts have clearly held that false or misleading commercial speech is not protected under the First Amendment. Thus, once falsity or deception is shown, a First Amendment defense is generally eliminated.

Use of a person's name, identity, or likeness for purposes of satire, commentary, or parody is protected "fair use." Thus, the biting portrayals of

President Clinton and Frank Sinatra by the late comic Phil Hartman on *Saturday Night Live* would likely not support actions for infringement of the right of publicity.

Because individuals can license the right to use their names, likenesses, and signatures to others, defendants often assert that use was authorized. Actors typically grant studios the right to use their names and identities to promote movies in which they appear. The right generally extends to future re-releases of the movie, even on television, and may extend so far as to allow the studio to use the individual's name or likeness in connection with collateral products, such as toys and other related merchandise. Similarly, athletes often grant or license sporting goods and card companies the right to reproduce their names, signatures, and photos on goods in return for license or royalty fees.

New Developments in the Right of Publicity

As is common with intellectual property rights in today's society, some of the new issues relating to the right of publicity stem from increasing technological advances. Through digital technology, President Clinton appeared in the movie *Contact,* John Wayne sells beer, and Fred Astaire dances with a vacuum cleaner. Some actors, such as Tom Cruise, already insist that their contracts prohibit the modification of their digital images without prior permission. Vanna White's success in presenting a triable issue of fact in seeking to enjoin the use of a robot that evoked her likeness indicates that the right of publicity can extend beyond conventional infringement to misappropriation through digital and electronic means.

In another new development, the International Trademark Association has proposed amending the U.S. Trademark Act to create a federal right of publicity with postmortem rights (although such rights would be limited to some specific period of duration after death). Similarly, the American Bar Association is studying a proposed federal right of publicity. Such federal laws would promote uniformity and eliminate the variation presently existing among the various states.

Another issue is whether the Copyright Act preempts (or takes precedence over) individual state statutes relating to the law of publicity. In some instances, the two fields coexist. For example, if a scene from a movie with Harrison Ford (protected by copyright) is later used without permission in another movie, Harrison Ford's copyright rights as well as his right to publicity have been violated. At least one court has held that in such a case, federal copyright preempts state laws relating to rights of publicity. *Fleet v. CBS,* 50 Cal. App. 4th 1911 (1996). In the Bette Midler case, because voices cannot be copyrighted, Midler sued solely for violation of her right to publicity. Similarly, names, gestures, and likenesses are unprotectable under copyright law because they are titles or ideas rather than expressions. Thus, in some instances, federal copyright law may control a plaintiff's rights, while in other instances, only the right to publicity will provide protection. In another new development, California recently passed the Astaire Celebrity Image Protection Act to allow heirs of celebrities to block commercial uses of deceased celebrities' likenesses while allowing a "safe harbor exemption" to artistic uses, such as the digital insertion of President Kennedy into the movie *Forrest Gump.*

FALSE ADVERTISING

Introduction

In 1943, the federal trademark law, the Lanham Act, was passed. Section 43(a) of the act (15 U.S.C. § 1125) prohibited false designations of origin, namely, descriptions or representations tending falsely to describe or represent goods or services. Until the passage of the Lanham Act, actions involving unfair competition tended to allege passing off or trade disparagement. Passing off, however, was limited to instances in which a party misrepresented the *source* of goods or services. Thus, it was not an effective vehicle to use when a party made misrepresentations relating to the *nature* or *quality* of goods or services. Moreover, until the passage of the Lanham Act, plaintiffs were generally required to prove that the defendant's acts were the direct cause of loss of sales and profits, an element that was often difficult to demonstrate. Finally, courts were reluctant to let business competitors bring actions against each other to assert what was often a harm done to consumers and not to them. In *Ely-Morris Safe Co. v. Mosler Safe Co.*, 7 F.2d 603 (2d Cir. 1925), *rev'd on other grounds*, 273 U.S. 132 (1927), Judge Learned Hand stated that the law did not allow a plaintiff-competitor to sue as a "vicarious avenger" of the defendant's customers.

Although the individual states enacted statutes prohibiting **false advertising,** these statutes varied from state to state and were often ineffective to prohibit false advertising that was national in scope. The expansive language of section 43 of the Lanham Act, however, soon began to be used to protect not only against unregistered trademarks but also against nearly all forms of false advertising. In 1989, Congress amended the Lanham Act and broadened the scope of section 43. As presently written, one portion of the statute allows parties to bring actions in federal courts for infringement of trademarks (both registered and unregistered marks) and trade dress, while the other portion of the statute allows the assertion of claims for false advertising and trade libel.

Under section 43(a), whoever uses a false or misleading description or representation of fact or false designation of origin in commercial advertising or promotion or misrepresents the nature, qualities, or geographic origin of his or her or another person's goods, services, or commercial activities is liable to any person likely to be injured by such act (if the act is committed in interstate commerce). Thus, the statute protects competitors as well as consumers and allows recovery if the plaintiff can show he or she is *likely* to be damaged, thereby eliminating the prior requirement that a plaintiff show *actual damage*. Most plaintiffs are business competitors, injured celebrities, and others who can show direct injury.

The broad and sweeping scope of section 43 has been used to protect the distinctive uniform of the Dallas Cowboys cheerleaders, the color and shape of a drug capsule, the overall look of a line of greeting cards, and the sound of singer Tom Waite's voice from use by a sound-alike to falsely suggest Waite endorsed DORITOS® chips.

Remedies for false advertising include injunctive relief to prohibit further false statements or to correct falsities as well as monetary relief.

Examples of False Advertising

An advertisement that is literally false is clearly actionable. Even advertisements that are implicitly false or unclear, however, are actionable if they are

false advertising: False or deceptive representations about one's own goods or services

nevertheless likely to mislead or deceive consumers. In many cases, surveys of consumers are used to prove that the message conveyed, even if literally true, is deceptive to the public at large. Courts generally require, in cases involving implicit rather than literal falsity, that an "appreciable" or "substantial" number of consumers must be misled by a claim. If scientific, medical, or technical claims are made in an advertisement, experts are usually called to demonstrate truth or falsity. Following are some examples of advertising held to be false:

- a failure to disclose that advertised prices did not include additional charges;
- a statement that a pregnancy test kit would disclose results in "as fast as ten minutes" when a positive result would appear in ten minutes but a negative result might take thirty minutes;
- a claim that a certain motor oil provided longer life and better engine protection than a competitor's product when that claim could not be substantiated;
- a claim that orange juice was pure, pasteurized juice as it came from the orange and showing a celebrity squeezing an orange and pouring the juice directly into the carton when the juice was heated and sometimes frozen prior to packaging;
- a false claim that automobile antifreeze met an automobile manufacturer's standards;
- falsely claiming a whiskey to be "scotch" whiskey when it was not; and
- covering up a label stating "Made in Taiwan" that appeared on goods.

Many cases involve **comparative advertising** claims in which one party claims its products are superior or equivalent to those of a competitor. The competitor need not be specifically identified for an action to lie. In comparative advertising cases, a plaintiff must in fact show that the claimed product is inferior or not equivalent. Claiming that a product is "compatible with" or "works with" another product is permissible as long as the claim is true.

Defenses to False Advertising

Clearly, the truth is a defense to a claim that an advertisement is false or misleading. Truth can be shown by survey evidence (showing consumers are not misled), statistical evidence, or expert opinion. Another common defense asserted in false advertising cases is **puffing.** Puffing is an exaggerated and highly subjective statement upon which no reasonable person would rely. Courts generally hold that such puffing is vague and is opinion only rather than misrepresentation and is thus not actionable. Thus, stating that elves make KEEBLER® cookies is not false advertising because no reasonable person would believe such a statement to be true. Vague statements such as that a product is a "major breakthrough" or represents "new technology" are likewise permissible puffing inasmuch as they are more in the nature of boasting than representation. Similarly, general statements that a product is "superior" are usually held to be nonactionable puffing; however, if a statement purports to rely on test results that demonstrate superiority, such a claim may be false advertising if superiority cannot be proven.

Another defense often raised is that the speech involved in an allegedly false advertisement is protected speech under the First Amendment. Courts have typically held, however, that commercial speech is not constitutionally

comparative advertising:
Advertising that compares one product or service with another or that states that one product works with or is compatible with another

puffing: An exaggerated and highly subjective statement upon which no reasonable person would rely; generally, nonactionable opinion

protected from regulation and that the government has the right to ban deceptive and false speech.

Regulation by the Federal Trade Commission

The **Federal Trade Commission (FTC)** is charged with enforcing a comprehensive law, section 5 of the FTC Act (15 U.S.C. § 45), which prohibits unfair and deceptive acts and practices in or affecting commerce. Similar to section 43 of the Lanham Act and most state statutes relating to false advertising, section 5 requires that objective claims made in advertising and marketing be truthful and substantiated. The FTC will not pursue subjective claims or puffing, such as a claim that a suntan lotion is the "best in the world," but will pursue claims that include an objective component, such as "our suntan lotion lasts longer than other popular brands." Almost all states have statutes similar to section 5 of the FTC Act that prohibit deceptive and unfair trade practices. The state statutes are usually referred to as **little FTC acts.**

Most of the advertising cases challenged by the FTC involve health and safety claims inasmuch as these pose the most risk to consumers. Alcohol and tobacco advertising is subject to particular scrutiny. Many recent cases involve health and nutrient claims for foods. Health and safety claims typically require competent and credible scientific evidence. Claims such as "clinical studies show that our brand is better than . . ." are permissible only if they are true. If other studies exist that contradict claims or if the methodology of the studies is defective, there is likely a violation of the FTC Act.

The FTC also vigorously pursues fraudulent telemarketing tactics and has been paying increased attention to consumer protection on the Internet. Section 5 of the FTC Act applies to electronic commerce and thus the FTC is charged with prohibiting unfair and deceptive practices on the Internet. FTC staff routinely monitor the Net and online services. In 1995, the FTC brought its first case involving an online scam, and with the cooperation of the Internet service provider (America Online), the FTC shut the scam down and achieved complete redress for injured consumers.

The FTC has a wide array of remedies it uses to protect consumers. While cease and desist orders, injunctions, and monetary penalties are common, the FTC is increasingly using more innovative remedies designed to protect consumers. For example, the FTC often requires that restitution be made to injured consumers, rescinds contracts that are deceptive, and has required corrective advertising and affirmative disclosures about product safety claims. In one case involving false claims relating to sunscreen, the FTC required that the respondent design, produce, and print brochures about the importance of sunscreen usage by children. The FTC itself uses the Internet to protect consumers. By accessing the FTC's home page (http://www.ftc.gov), consumers can obtain consumer protection information electronically and participate in online seminars regarding selected topics.

PRODUCT DISPARAGEMENT

At common law, an action can be brought for making intentional and untrue statements about another company or its products or services that cause

Federal Trade Commission (FTC): The federal regulatory agency charged with protecting consumers from unfair or deceptive acts and practices

little FTC acts: State statutes that prohibit deceptive and unfair trade practices

monetary harm to the company. The action is variously called **product disparagement,** *commercial disparagement,* or *trade libel.*

The statements, which can be written or oral, must be false and must clearly communicate a disparaging message about the plaintiff. Mere puffing does not give rise to an action for product disparagement. Most jurisdictions require that the defendant act with intent to injure the plaintiff or, at the least, with a reckless disregard for the truth or falsity of its statements. Finally, specific economic harm must be pleaded and proven. It is not sufficient for a plaintiff to show that it is likely to be harmed by a defendant's false representations. The plaintiff must generally demonstrate specific economic harm, such as the loss of a contract or loss of customers.

Actions for product disparagement are seen less frequently today inasmuch as plaintiffs would generally prefer to rely upon section 43(a) of the Lanham Act. Relying on section 43 rather than individual state judicial decisions affords a plaintiff several advantages, chiefly that the plaintiff need not prove specific economic harm inasmuch as relief is provided to anyone who is *likely* to be damaged. Moreover, under section 43, a plaintiff need not prove that a defendant had the specific intent to injure the plaintiff or that the defendant acted in reckless disregard of the truth or falsity of misrepresentations.

In defending an action for product disparagement (whether brought under common law or section 43(a)), a defendant may allege that its statements are permissible comparative advertising (as long as the statements are true), that its statements are mere puffing, or that its statements are protected as speech under the First Amendment. As discussed earlier, however, commercial speech is provided a lower level of protection than other forms of speech.

DILUTION

Dilution is another form of unfair competition. Dilution occurs when a famous trademark loses its distinctive quality due to tarnishment or blurring. As previously discussed in Chapter 6, the new Federal Dilution Act (15 U.S.C. § 43(c)) provides remedies for the dilution of famous marks. Under the act, effective in 1996, the owner of a famous mark is entitled to an injunction against another person's use in commerce of a mark or trade name if such use begins after the mark has become famous and causes dilution of the distinctive quality of the famous mark.

The Dilution Act is intended to provide a remedy for the owners of famous marks when the owners of those marks would not otherwise be able to establish likelihood of confusion and thus avail themselves of the many avenues available to protect marks from confusingly similar uses. In one famous case, the use of TIFFANY for a restaurant was prohibited inasmuch as it diluted the famous TIFFANY® mark used in connection with jewelry. The court noted that confusion was not likely inasmuch as no reasonable person would believe that the restaurant services were somehow affiliated with or sponsored by the jewelers. Nevertheless, the use of the famous mark TIFFANY, even in connection with unrelated services and goods, whittled away or diluted the strong association consumers make between the TIFFANY mark and fine jewelry. The goodwill inherent in the famous TIFFANY mark would evaporate if junior users were allowed to use the mark even on unrelated goods. *Tiffany & Co. v. Boston Club Inc.,* 231 F. Supp. 836 (D. Mass. 1967).

product disparagement:
Making false representations about another's goods or services; also called *trade libel*

Dilution can occur in two ways: blurring or tarnishment. Blurring occurs when a mark's distinctive quality is eroded through use on dissimilar products. Examples of blurring would be TIFFANY RESTAURANT, KODAK BICYCLES, or CHRYSLER SOUP. Tarnishment occurs when a mark is linked to products of inferior quality or when the mark is portrayed in an unsavory manner, such as a poster reading "Enjoy Cocaine" in the distinctive colors and script used in the famous "Enjoy Coca-Cola" advertisements.

Many of the recent cases involving dilution focus on uses of Internet addresses. For example, the address "candyland.com" for sexually explicit services and goods was held to dilute the famous CANDYLAND mark owned by Hasbro Toys. *Hasbro Inc. v. Internet Entertainment Group, Ltd.*, 40 U.S.P.Q.2d 1439 (W.D. Wash. 1996). Similarly, the address "adultsrus.com" used for sexual paraphernalia was held to dilute the famous TOYS "R" US mark owned by Toys "R" Us, Inc. *Toys "R" Us, Inc. v. Akkaouli,* 1996 WL 772709 (N.D. Cal.).

One of the difficult tasks presented to courts is determining what constitutes a "famous" mark. The act provides some factors for courts to consider in determining whether a mark is distinctive and famous, including the following: the degree of distinctiveness of a mark; the duration and extent of use of the mark; the duration and extent of advertising and publicity of the mark; the degree of recognition of the mark; the nature and extent of use of the same or similar marks by third parties; and whether the mark is federally registered. If a plaintiff can show willful intent by the defendant to trade on the plaintiff's famous mark or to cause dilution of a famous mark, a plaintiff can obtain monetary relief, the defendant's profits, costs, and attorneys' fees, in addition to injunctive relief. Some courts have afforded protection even when marks are not nationally famous but have fame in a "limited circle," such as regionally or in a niche market. Thus, in *Wawa Inc. v. Haaf,* 40 U.S.P.Q.2d 1629 (E.D. Pa. 1996), *aff'd,* 116 F.3d 471 (3d Cir. 1997), the court held that the WAWA mark, used for convenience stores in five mid-Atlantic states, deserved protection against dilution.

Under the act, some uses of famous marks are not actionable, such as fair use of a famous mark in comparative advertising, noncommercial use of a famous mark, and use of a famous mark in news reporting and commentary.

Finally, under new legislation passed in 1999, a mark in a pending trademark application that would cause dilution can be refused registration through an opposition proceeding or canceled through a cancellation proceeding, thus allowing the holders of famous marks to prevent harm before it occurs. (See Chapter 6 for discussion of oppositions and cancellations.)

INFRINGEMENT OF TRADE DRESS

The total image and overall appearance of a product or service is protectable as its "trade dress." Trade dress refers to the distinctive appearance of a business or product and may include a product's distinctive packaging, the interior design of a restaurant, the layout of a business, and other nonfunctional features of a product or service. Trade dress may include features such as size, shape, color or color combinations, texture, graphics, and even particular sales techniques. Trade dress protection does not extend to utilitarian or functional aspects of a product or service inasmuch as such would tend to reduce or stifle competition. Functional products may be protected under patent law (assuming they meet the tests of patentability, such as novelty and nonobviousness), which provides a limited period of duration for utility patents. To allow a functional product or service to be protected as trade dress would allow a monopoly on a useful feature or product in perpetuity.

In *Two Pesos Inc. v. Taco Cabana, Inc.*, 505 U.S. 763 (1992), the Supreme Court held that the inherently distinctive trade dress of a Mexican restaurant could be protected under section 43(a) of the Lanham Act against infringement by another restaurant that used confusingly similar décor and design elements. The trade dress included the shape and general appearance of the exterior of the restaurant, the signage, the interior kitchen plan, the décor, the menu, the equipment, servers' uniforms, and other features that reflected the total image of the restaurant. The Court held that as long as a party's trade dress is distinctive, it will be protected against a junior user's use that is likely to cause confusion among consumers. The Court expressly noted that protection of trade dress, like protection of trademarks, serves the Lanham Act's purpose of securing to owners the goodwill of their businesses and protecting the ability of consumers to distinguish among competing goods and services.

In a recent case, *Samara Bros. Inc. v. Wal-Mart Stores, Inc.*, 165 F.3d 120 (2d Cir. 1998), the plaintiff was awarded $1.2 million against Wal-Mart for selling (under Wal-Mart labels) knockoffs of the plaintiff's children's clothing line. The court held that the clothing, which displayed large collars and bold appliques of hearts and flowers on seersucker, was sufficiently distinctive to be entitled to trade dress protection. Thus, although clothing per se is not protectable under copyright law because it is a useful article, distinctive elements of clothing can be protected under trade dress theory. Moreover, clothing design embellishments, such as the hearts and flowers, can be protected under copyright law, although the scope of protection for such familiar elements will be narrow and only nearly identical copying will be prohibited.

Legislation has been introduced in Congress to amend the Trademark Act to allow trade dress (defined as the "total image or overall appearance of a product or service") that functions as a mark to be registered and protected just like any other mark. If the legislation passes, trade dress could be registered as a trademark, thus affording even broader protection to owners of distinctive product images.

INTERNATIONAL PROTECTION AGAINST UNFAIR COMPETITION

The United States has assumed certain obligations under international agreements in the arena of unfair competition, chiefly under the Paris Convention. The Paris Convention seeks to afford citizens of each of the more than one hundred and thirty-five member nations protection against unfair competition and trademark infringement and requires that member nations provide the same level of protection against unfair competition to citizens of other member nations as they do for their own citizens. (See Appendix A for a table of countries adhering to the Paris Convention.)

The Paris Convention expressly prohibits acts that create confusion by any means with a competitor, false allegations that discredit a competitor, and indications that mislead the public in regard to the nature or characteristics of goods.

Section 44 of the Lanham Act (15 U.S.C. § 1126) implements the Paris Convention and expressly provides that any person whose country of origin is a party to any convention or treaty relating to the repression of unfair competition, to which the United States is also a party, is entitled to effective protection against unfair competition, thus affording citizens of Paris Convention member nations the wide variety of protection afforded under section 43 of the Lanham Act.

ROLE OF INTELLECTUAL PROPERTY PROFESSIONAL

There are a number of tasks in which IP professionals are engaged in the unfair competition arena. Some of those activities are as follows:

- reviewing advertisements and publications to alert clients to possible instances of passing off, misappropriation, false advertising, product disparagement, or dilution;
- reviewing the products and services of competitors of clients to ensure that the trade dress of clients is not being infringed;
- preparing and responding to cease and desist letters that demand the cessation of unfair competitive practices;
- conducting legal research relating to unfair competitive practices;
- preparing and responding to complaints alleging acts of unfair competition;
- engaging in the discovery process in unfair competition actions, including preparing and responding to interrogatories and requests for production of documents and preparing notices of depositions;
- assisting in trial preparation by preparing exhibits and jury instructions and assisting in the preparation of briefs for court; and
- assisting in the drafting of settlement agreements.

CHAPTER SUMMARY

The term *unfair competition* refers to a wide variety of acts and practices that constitute improper commercial conduct. Because the property interests being protected are often intangible, such as reputation, image, and goodwill, the interests are classified as "intellectual property."

Injured parties can rely on a host of theories to protect their commercial interests: passing off (selling one's goods as those of another); misappropriation (the taking of another's valuable commercial interests); false advertising (making false representations about the nature or quality of one's own goods or services); the right of publicity (protecting one's image or persona from commercial appropriation); product disparagement (making false representations about another's goods or services); dilution (weakening another's trademark or service mark); or infringement of trade dress (causing a likelihood of confusion with the overall appearance or image of another's product or service).

Additionally, section 43 of the Lanham Act provides a federal cause of action for a broad range of anticompetitive activities. Finally, the FTC regulates commercial acts and practices. Under the Paris Convention, the United States is required to protect citizens of member nations against unfair competition, and U.S. citizens are treated in other countries equivalently to nationals of those member nations with regard to unfair competition.

DISCUSSION QUESTIONS

1. Discuss whether a claim that a pain reliever has "an active ingredient our competitors' doesn't" is actionable when the ingredient is merely the coating on the pain reliever tablet.

2. Discuss whether a claim that "our computers represent state of the art technology" may constitute false advertising.

3. What actions might Patrick Ewing allege if an unauthorized photograph of him is displayed next to a Harley-Davidson motorcycle in an advertisement? What if the photograph appears on "NBC Nightly News" in a story about a team trade involving Ewing?

4. What objection might McDonald's Corporation raise to the use of the phrase "You deserve a brake today" by an auto repair shop?

5. Tim Howard imports perfume made and packaged in Taiwan, removes the "Made in Taiwan" label, and repackages the perfume in boxes identical to those used for Calvin Klein's "Obsession" perfume. Discuss what causes of action might be alleged by Calvin Klein Companyf.

6. The makers of toy blocks advertise that their products "work with Legos." The statement is true and consumers buy the new product, causing loss of sales for Lego. Discuss whether such a claim is actionable.

7. Discuss whether a claim that a yogurt is "lower in fat than ice cream" is actionable when the yogurt is lower in fat than a few ice cream products but contains more fat than nearly all ice cream products.

Intellectual Property Audits and Due Diligence Reviews

Clients are often unaware of the importance of their intellectual property. To help clients realize the value of such assets and exploit them, law firms often conduct intellectual property audits for clients. The audit reveals the intellectual capital owned by a client and assists in developing a strategy so the client can maintain its valuable intellectual capital. Once clients fully understand *what* they own, they can then protect it, license it, or sell it. The audit should be repeated on a periodic basis to reflect the changing nature of intellectual property. Audits are also conducted when a company is sold, when it borrows money, or when it acquires another company. This type of audit is usually referred to as a "due diligence" review.

INTRODUCTION TO INTELLECTUAL PROPERTY AUDITS AND DUE DILIGENCE REVIEWS

Clients are often unaware that they own valuable assets: their intellectual property. They may use distinctive names for certain products or services, may possess creative marketing materials, or may have developed a novel method of conducting business. All of these developments are assets that can and should be protected as intellectual property. Distinctive names should be registered as trademarks, written materials should be protected by copyright notices and registration, and trade secrets should be protected so they can endure perpetually.

If intellectual property is not protected, it may be lost. Failure to monitor and police infringing activities may also lead to a loss of rights. Competitors may acquire rights to valuable property that formerly provided a competitive edge to a company, resulting in a loss of market share and profits. Companies not only should protect their intellectual property in order to ensure business survival but also should use their intellectual property to create revenue. Trademarks, copyrights, patents, and trade secrets can all be licensed to others. The owner of intellectual property can achieve a continual revenue stream through licensing of rights to others for either a fixed sum or recurrent royalty payments. Alternatively, intellectual property may be sold outright to another. Intellectual property can also be used as collateral so its owner can secure a loan from a bank or other institution. Just as real property or personal property such as inventory is pledged as collateral when money is borrowed, so too can intellectual property (trademarks, copyrights, and patents) serve as collateral.

The failure to capitalize on the value of intellectual property is generally caused by a lack of awareness of just what can be protected. Many companies believe that copyright extends only to important literary works and therefore fail to secure protection for their marketing brochures or other written materials. Similarly, companies often fail to implement measures to ensure valuable trade secrets maintain their protectability. Because clients are often unaware of the great potential and value of this property, law firms often offer their clients an **intellectual property audit** to uncover a company's protectable intellectual property. The IP audit is analogous to the accounting audit most companies conduct on an annual basis to review their financial status.

Another type of intellectual property investigation is usually conducted when a company acquires another entity. At that time, a thorough investigation should be conducted of the intellectual property of the target company to ensure the acquiring company will obtain the benefits of what it is paying for and will not inherit infringement suits and other problems stemming from the target's failure to protect its intellectual property. This type of intellectual property investigation is generally called a "due diligence" review inasmuch as the acquiring company and its counsel have an obligation to duly and diligently investigate the target's assets. Due diligence reviews are also conducted when a company offers its securities for public sale inasmuch as potential investors must be informed of the offeror's assets (including its intellectual property) and any claims that may arise against the offeror. Similarly, when a company is being sold, it is generally required to identify its intellectual property and make certain representations and warranties that it owns the property being sold and there are no defects in title or pending claims involving the property. Thus, due diligence must be conducted to ensure these representations and warranties can be made with respect to a seller's intellectual property.

PRACTICAL ASPECTS OF INTELLECTUAL PROPERTY AUDITS

Intellectual property audits come in all shapes and sizes. Most importantly, the audit must fit the client and respond to its needs. If a client owns a small retail shop or provides auto repair services from only one location, the sole intellectual property may consist of the business name (which may be protectable as a trademark), any logos or designs used by the client, customer lists, and marketing materials, if any. On the other hand, if a client is engaged in software development, information technology, or telecommunications services, it may possess a wealth of intellectual property assets.

In many cases, the first IP audit is the most extensive and expensive. Some clients conduct periodic audits, and law firms typically docket the dates for

intellectual property audit:
A review of the trademarks, copyrights, patents, and trade secrets owned by a person or company

annual reviews and send reminder notices to clients. The annual reviews can focus on changes since the previous audit. While there is some expense involved in conducting any audit, the benefit of the audit outweighs the expense involved. Moreover, there are often intangible benefits to the audit. If the client later wishes to obtain a loan or sell some of its assets, the preceding audit need only be updated, eliminating costly delays in a transaction. If the client is adequately prepared for the audit and actively assists in the audit, costs can be reduced.

Before the audit is conducted, the law firm and the client should agree on its scope and nature. Consideration should be given in regard to whether the firm will conduct the audit on an hourly fee basis or for a fixed fee. In most instances, the law firm will need to send IP professionals to the client site, resulting in disruption to the client's operations. Again, with careful preparation, such disruption can be kept to a minimum.

The following issues should be clearly addressed before the audit begins:

- Who will conduct the audit? Usually, counsel (inside or outside), together with other IP professionals, will conduct the audit, relying on company representatives for assistance. The law firm and the client should each designate a person who will serve as the team leader and to whom questions and concerns can be addressed. If a client is unusually large, it may designate various leaders, for example, one from its research and development department, one from its marketing department, and so forth.
- What scope will the audit have? Should only U.S. rights be explored? Should consideration be given to protecting intellectual property on an international basis?

CONDUCTING THE AUDIT

The first step in the audit should be a face-to-face meeting of the legal team and company managers. The legal team should make a brief presentation on what intellectual property is, why it is important to the company, and why and how the audit will be conducted. Managers will be more likely to cooperate if they fully understand the importance of the audit. Obtaining this kind of "buy in" from the client's managers and employees will speed the audit and reduce costs. Moreover, education about the importance of intellectual property helps ensure managers consider ways to further protect a company's valuable assets and remain alert to possible infringements of the company's intellectual capital or infringements by the company of others' rights. Finally, having outside counsel involved in the process will ensure that communications related to the audit are protected by the attorney-client privilege.

Once the company's mangers have been advised of the need for the audit, the legal team should provide a worksheet or questionnaire (see Figure 24–1) to the company specifying the type of information that the firm is looking for so that company files can be reviewed and materials assembled for inspection by the firm and its representatives. Although it is not strictly necessary that the client do this kind of preparatory work, the more work the client does, the faster, cheaper, and less disruptive the audit will be.

Once the materials that are responsive to the questionnaire are gathered, the legal team can review them. The review is generally done at the client site.

FIGURE 24–1
Intellectual Property Audit
Questionnaire

Identified below is a list of subjects to be covered in connection with our review of the intellectual property rights of your company (the "Company"). Please gather any materials and documents relevant to the subjects listed below so they can be reviewed. If no materials or documents exist with respect to a particular subject, please confirm that in writing next to the relevant question.

For all relevant questions, give the name of the person who assisted in the design, development, or implementation of any intellectual property rights; describe the nature of the relationship between the person and the Company (for example, employee, independent contractor, and so forth); and indicate whether the person signed any confidentiality or nondisclosure agreements with the Company.

A. General

1. Has the Company ever acquired another entity or the business or assets of another entity or person? (This party may have owned intellectual property that is now owned by the Company.)
2. Has the Company ever sold any assets or business to another entity or person?
3. Is the Company engaged in the development or design of any useful products or parts for useful products?
4. Is the Company engaged in the development, design, or modification of computer software?
5. Are there any individuals who may have developed or designed products or software for the Company who have left employment with the Company? If so, indicate whether each such person signed a confidentiality, nondisclosure, or employment agreement with the Company.
6. Does the Company have a web site or are there links from other parties' sites to the Company's site? If so, provide web site addresses.

B. Trademarks and Service Marks

1. Does the Company use any trademarks, service marks, logos, slogans, or designs (collectively "Marks") in connection with the offer and sale of its products or services? These Marks may have been displayed on products, labels, packaging, letterhead, business cards, in advertisements, brochures, or other marketing materials, including a web site.
2. Has the Company ever applied for registration of any Marks with the United States Patent and Trademark Office (PTO) or any state trademark agencies?
3. Has the Company ever allowed another party (such as a client, vendor, or competitor) to use any of the Company's Marks?
4. Does the Company use any Marks that are owned by any third party? Review Company marketing materials, web site, and other written documents to determine whether the Company displays or uses Marks belonging to another.

C. Copyrights

1. What written materials does the Company use to advertise its products and services? These may be written materials, scripts or copy for radio or television advertisements, or web site materials. Were these developed by Company employees or by independent contractors working for the Company? What agreements exist relating to the development of such materials?
2. What written materials does the Company use internally, such as employee handbooks, training materials, company policies, or manuals relating to the way the Company conducts its business?
3. Do Company employees prepare written materials when presentations are made within the Company and outside the Company? If so, describe.

FIGURE 24–1
Intellectual Property Audit
Questionnaire (continued)

    4. Do Company employees submit articles for publication to any journals, periodicals, or other publications? If so, describe.

    5. Has the Company ever applied for registration of any copyrights with the U.S. Copyright Office?

    6. Are articles from periodicals, magazines, trade journals, and other related written materials photocopied for distribution within the Company?

    7. What policies exist regarding reproduction of books, articles, journals, and other materials that may be subject to copyright?

    8. Is any music piped in through the Company's offices (whether through the use of CDs or music being simultaneously transmitted by a radio station)?

    9. Is music played when callers to the Company are placed on hold?

D. Patents

    1. Has the Company or its employees ever invented any useful article, product, method, process, or software? If so, do any inventor or laboratory notebooks exist that document the development of the invention? Does the Company have any present plans for any such inventions?

    2. Has the Company ever made any improvements to another party's useful article, product, or invention?

    3. Has the Company ever engaged in the reverse engineering or decompilation of another company's product or software?

    4. Has the Company ever applied with the PTO for issuance of any patent?

E. Trade Secrets

    1. What information does the Company possess that would be harmful to the Company if it were discovered by a competitor? Consider proprietary information relating to research and development plans; calculations and financial data; employee manuals and handbooks and personnel information; information relating to the Company's clients and customers; the Company's methods of recruiting; methods and processes of production; test results for Company products and services; data concerning the pricing for Company products and services; sales forecasts; research information; manufacturing information; marketing materials; surveys and data relating to customer needs and preferences; and business plans and forecasts.

    2. Do employment or other agreements exist that protect such proprietary materials?

    3. Does the Company conduct employee orientation for new employees and exit interviews for departing employees to ensure employees understand the need to maintain confidentiality of Company trade secrets?

    4. What measures does the Company take to protect confidential and proprietary information? Are documents marked "Confidential"? Are proprietary materials kept in locked cabinets? Are restrictions placed on the access to and copying of such materials?

    5. What measures does the Company take to ensure electronic communications are protected and secure? Are any encryption methods in place for electronic communications? Describe restrictions on access to the Company's computer systems.

    6. Are any legal notices or disclaimers provided at sign-on when Company employees access the Company server or network?

F. Software

    1. Has the Company designed, developed, or modified any software?

    2. Does the Company have the right to use any software designed or developed by another party?

FIGURE 24–1
Intellectual Property Audit
Questionnaire (continued)

G. Claims
1. Are there any presently pending claims relating to any of the Company's intellectual property? Has any person alleged or claimed that the Company has violated or infringed its intellectual property rights?
2. What claims have been made (whether or not resolved or compromised) within the past five years against the Company relating to alleged infringement or violation by the Company of the intellectual property rights of others?
3. Has the Company observed or made any claims relating to any possible infringements by others of the Company's intellectual property rights?

H. General Documents
1. Please assemble all applications and registrations, and all license, royalty, security agreements or other agreements relating to trade names, Marks, copyrights, patents, trade secrets, software, licenses, or other similar rights relating to the Company's intellectual property rights.
2. Please assemble all agreements entered into by employees (including officers and directors) and any Company handbooks, manuals, or policies relating to Company employees.
3. Please assemble all agreements entered into between the Company and any consultants or independent contractors.
4. To the extent not already covered, please assemble all agreements or licenses entered into between the Company and any other parties that relate to the Company's intellectual property, which are essential for the operation of the Company's business, or by which the Company is allowed to offer or use another party's Marks, copyrights, patents, processes, software, or other related property.
5. Does the Company offer its products or services in any foreign countries? If no, does the Company have any plans to offer its products or services in foreign countries within the next three years?

Files are pulled, brochures gathered, and contracts assembled. The legal team will review these materials and often make copies of pertinent documents, marking them as confidential.

After review of the materials is completed, another face-to-face meeting should be held to ensure that all of the materials were gathered and that there are no other contracts, license agreements, or other documents that should be reviewed. Questions may have arisen during the course of the audit for which the legal team needs responses. For example, the legal team may ask whether a certain brochure or trademark is still in use or whether the company logo was designed in-house or by another company. The legal team will generally check the records of the PTO and the Copyright Office to determine whether there are any records on file showing the company's ownership of trademarks, copyrights, and patents. A follow-up questionnaire may be sent to the client to obtain the answers to questions that arose in the course of the audit.

POSTAUDIT ACTIVITY

After the inspection is completed, the legal team will usually prepare a written report identifying the specific items of intellectual property owned by the company, reviewing their status, and making recommendations for protection.

The IP audit team may then proceed to take the following actions: filing applications for registration of trademarks, service marks, copyrights, and patents; drafting contracts to be used when the company retains independent contractors (to ensure that all work created by the independent contractors is "work made for hire" or is owned by or assigned to the company); preparing license agreements so the company can license its intellectual property to others; preparing nondisclosure and noncompetition agreements; and preparing policies for the protection of trade secrets.

The IP audit team may also assist the client's human resources department and provide instructions on conducting exit interviews and may redraft the employee manual to include a trade secret policy, Internet use policy, and instructions regarding use of the company's trademarks.

The company is usually advised to initiate an aggressive campaign to locate others who may be infringing the company's intellectual property by reviewing competitors' materials and trade publications and by monitoring applications filed at the PTO for marks that may be confusingly similar to those owned by the company. The legal team may help the company initiate a docketing system for reminder dates for renewals of licenses and trademark registrations or may be retained to perform the docketing functions itself.

ROLE OF INTELLECTUAL PROPERTY PROFESSIONAL

Intellectual property professionals generally play an active and vital role in planning and conducting IP audits. Using nonattorney IP practitioners also helps reduce the costs associated with audits. In many instances, a paralegal serves as the liaison between the law firm and the client and coordinates all activities related to the audit. Intellectual property professionals are generally involved in the following tasks:

- preparing the audit questionnaire and ensuring a company representative completes the questionnaire;
- coordinating the time and manner of the audit by scheduling a convenient date for all team members and ensuring a conference room or office near a photocopy machine is set aside for the audit team;
- reviewing client files and documents;
- preparing a follow-up questionnaire, if needed;
- reviewing the records of the PTO and Copyright Office to determine if trademarks and copyrights have been applied for or registered and whether patents have issued;
- reporting the results of IP audit;
- preparing applications for registration of marks, copyrights, and patents; drafting policies for trade secret protection; drafting contracts, licenses, and assignments;
- assisting in setting up a docket or calendar for maintenance of intellectual property; and
- providing reminders to clients of the need for annual or periodic updates to the IP audit.

CHAPTER SUMMARY

Because clients can be unaware of the value of the intellectual property they own, law firms often conduct intellectual property audits for clients. The audit reveals valuable intellectual property assets that can then be exploited for the client's benefit. Audits should be conducted on a periodic basis to reflect the changing nature of intellectual property. Audits or reviews are also conducted when companies are sold, when they borrow money, or when they acquire other companies. In such instances, the review is often called "due diligence." Because almost all types of intellectual property can be lost through lack of protection (including nonuse, failure to monitor licensees properly, failure to renew or maintain registrations, and failure to protect against infringing activities), the IP audit is a crucial tool that allows a company to understand and exploit the value of its intellectual property portfolio.

DISCUSSION QUESTIONS

1. In the course of conducting an intellectual property audit, the audit team discovers a marketing brochure used by the client company to advertise a product that will be discontinued by the company next year. Should the company protect the material by filing a copyright application for the brochure?
2. Why are exit interviews conducted with departing employees valuable tools for a company?
3. Identify some policies that can be discussed in a company's employee manual to enhance protection of its intellectual property.

Appendices

Appendix A — Table of Treaties

Appendix B — State Trademark
                      Registration Provisions

Appendix C — Resources

Appendix D — Forms Appendix

Appendix E — Selected Statutes

Please note the Internet resources are of a time sensitive nature and URL address may often change or be deleted.

	Paris Convention (as of 7/8/1998)	Berne Union (as of 6/22/1998)	Madrid Agreement (A) and Protocol (P) (as of 8/18/1998)	Patent Cooperation Treaty (as of 6/22/1998)	World Trade Organization (as of 10/22/1997) *Observer governments	World Intellectual Property Organization (as of 2/20/1997)
Albania	X	X	X (A)	X	*	X
Algeria	X	X	X (A)		*	X
Andorra					*	X
Angola					X	X
Antigua and Barbuda					X	
Argentina	X	X			X	X
Armenia	X		X (A)	X	*	X
Australia	X	X		X	X	X
Austria	X	X	X (A)	X	X	X
Azerbaijan	X		X (A)	X	*	X
Bahamas	X	X				X
Bahrain	X	X			X	X
Bangladesh	X				X	X
Barbados	X	X		X	X	X
Belarus	X	X	X (A)	X	*	X
Belgium	X	X	X (A & P)	X	X	X
Belize					X	
Benin	X	X		X	X	X
Bhutan					*	X
Bolivia	X	X			X	X
Bosnia and Herzegovina	X	X	X (A)	X		X
Botswana	X	X			X	X

	Paris Convention (as of 7/8/1998)	Berne Union (as of 6/22/1998)	Madrid Agreement (A) and Protocol (P) (as of 8/18/1998)	Patent Cooperation Treaty (as of 6/22/1998)	World Trade Organization (as of 10/22/1997) *Observer governments	World Intellectual Property Organization (as of 2/20/1997)
Brazil	X	X		X	X	X
Brunei Darussalam					X	X
Bulgaria	X	X	X (A)	X	X	X
Burkina Faso	X	X		X	X	X
Burundi	X				X	X
Cambodia	X				*	X
Cameroon	X	X		X	X	X
Canada	X	X		X	X	X
Cape Verde		X			*	X
Central African Republic	X	X		X	X	X
Chad	X	X		X	X	X
Chile	X	X			X	X
China	X	X	X (A & P)	X	*	X
Colombia	X	X			X	X
Congo	X	X		X	X	X
Costa Rica	X	X			X	X
Cote d'Ivoire	X	X		X	X	X
Croatia	X	X	X (A)	X	*	X
Cuba	X	X	X (A & P)	X	X	X
Cyprus	X	X		X	X	X
Czech Republic	X	X	X (A & P)	X	X	X
Democratic Republic of the Congo	X	X		X	X	X
Denmark	X	X	X (P)	X	X	X
Djibouti					X	
Dominica					X	X
Dominican Republic	X	X			X	
Ecuador		X			X	X
Egypt	X	X	X (A)		X	X
El Salvador	X	X			X	X
Equatorial Guinea		X				X
Eritrea						X
Estonia	X	X	X (P)	X	*	X
Ethiopia					*	X
Fiji		X			X	X
Finland	X	X	X (P)	X	X	X
France	X	X	X (A & P)	X	X	X
Gabon	X	X		X	X	X

	Paris Convention (as of 7/8/1998)	Berne Union (as of 6/22/1998)	Madrid Agreement (A) and Protocol (P) (as of 8/18/1998)	Patent Cooperation Treaty (as of 6/22/1998)	World Trade Organization (as of 10/22/1997) *Observer governments	World Intellectual Property Organization (as of 2/20/1997)
Gambia	X	X		X	X	X
Georgia	X	X	X (P)	X	*	X
Germany	X	X	X (A & P)	X	X	X
Ghana	X	X		X	X	X
Greece	X	X		X	X	X
Grenada	X	X		X	X	X
Guatemala	X	X			X	X
Guinea	X	X		X	X	X
Guinea-Bissau	X	X		X	X	X
Guyana	X	X			X	X
Haiti	X	X			X	X
Honduras	X	X			X	X
Hong Kong	X	X		X	X	
Hungary	X	X	X (A & P)	X	X	X
Iceland	X	X	X (P)	X	X	X
India	X	X			X	X
Indonesia	X	X		X	X	X
Iran	X					
Iraq	X					X
Ireland	X	X		X	X	X
Israel	X	X		X	X	X
Italy	X	X	X (A)	X	X	X
Jamaica		X			X	X
Japan	X	X		X	X	X
Jordan	X				*	X
Kazakhstan	X		X (A)	X	*	X
Kenya	X	X	X (A & P)	X	X	X
Korea, Democratic People's Republic of	X		X (A & P)	X	X	
Korea, Republic of	X	X		X	X	X
Kuwait					X	X
Kyrgyzstan Republic	X		X (A)	X	X	X
Laos	X				*	X
Latvia	X	X	X (A)	X	X	X
Lebanon	X	X				X
Lesotho	X	X		X	X	X
Liberia	X	X	X (A)	X		X
Libya	X	X				X
Liechtenstein	X	X	X (A & P)	X	X	X
Lithuania	X	X	X (P)	X	*	X

	Paris Convention (as of 7/8/1998)	Berne Union (as of 6/22/1998)	Madrid Agreement (A) and Protocol (P) (as of 8/18/1998)	Patent Cooperation Treaty (as of 6/22/1998)	World Trade Organization (as of 10/22/1997) *Observer governments	World Intellectual Property Organization (as of 2/20/1997)
Luxembourg	X	X	X (A & P)	X	X	X
Macau					X	
Macedonia	X	X	X (A)	X	*	X
Madagascar	X	X		X	X	X
Malawi	X	X		X	X	X
Malaysia	X	X			X	X
Maldives					X	
Mali	X	X		X	X	X
Malta		X			X	X
Mauritania	X	X		X	X	X
Mauritius	X	X			X	X
Mexico	X	X		X	X	X
Moldova, Republic of	X	X	X (A & P)	X	*	X
Monaco	X	X	X (A & P)	X		X
Mongolia	X	X	X (A)	X	X	X
Morocco	X	X	X (A)		X	X
Mozambique	X		X (A & P)		X	X
Myanmar					X	
Namibia		X			X	X
Nepal					*	X
Netherlands	X	X	X (A & P)	X	X	X
New Zealand	X	X		X	X	X
Nicaragua	X				X	X
Niger	X	X		X	X	X
Nigeria	X	X			X	X
Norway	X	X	X (P)	X	X	X
Oman					*	X
Pakistan		X			X	X
Panama	X	X			X	X
Papua New Guinea					X	X
Paraguay	X	X			X	X
Peru	X	X			X	X
Philippines	X	X			X	X
Poland	X	X	X (A & P)	X	X	X
Portugal	X	X	X (A & P)	X	X	X
Qatar						X
Romania	X	X	X (A & P)	X	X	X
Russian Federation	X	X	X (A & P)	X	*	X
Rwanda	X	X			X	X
Saint Kitts and Nevis	X	X			X	X

	Paris Convention (as of 7/8/1998)	Berne Union (as of 6/22/1998)	Madrid Agreement (A) and Protocol (P) (as of 8/18/1998)	Patent Cooperation Treaty (as of 6/22/1998)	World Trade Organization (as of 10/22/1997) *Observer governments	World Intellectual Property Organization (as of 2/20/1997)
Saint Lucia	X	X		X	X	X
Saint Vincent and the Grenadines	X	X			X	X
Samoa					*	X
San Marino	X		X (A)			X
Sao Tome and Principe	X					X
Saudi Arabia					*	X
Senegal	X	X		X	X	X
Seychelles					*	
Sierra Leone	X		X (A)	X	X	X
Singapore	X			X	X	X
Slovakia	X	X	X (A & P)	X	X	X
Slovenia	X	X	X (A & P)	X	X	X
Solomon Islands					X	
Somalia						X
South Africa	X	X			X	X
Spain	X	X	X (A & P)	X	X	X
Sri Lanka	X	X		X	X	X
Sudan	X		X (A)	X	*	X
Suriname	X	X			X	X
Swaziland	X		X (A & P)	X	X	X
Sweden	X	X	X (P)	X	X	X
Switzerland	X	X	X (A & P)	X	X	X
Syria	X					
Taipei					*	
Tajikistan	X		X (A)	X		X
Tanzania	X	X			X	X
Thailand		X			X	X
Togo	X	X		X	X	X
Tonga					*	
Trinidad and Tobago	X	X		X	X	X
Tunisia	X	X			X	X
Turkey	X	X		X	X	X
Turkmenistan	X			X		X
Uganda	X			X	X	X
Ukraine	X	X	X (A)	X	*	X
United Arab Emirates	X				X	X
United Kingdom	X	X	X (P)	X	X	X
United States	X	X		X	X	X
Uruguay	X	X			X	X
Uzbekistan	X		X (A)	X	*	X

	Paris Convention (as of 7/8/1998)	Berne Union (as of 6/22/1998)	Madrid Agreement (A) and Protocol (P) (as of 8/18/1998)	Patent Cooperation Treaty (as of 6/22/1998)	World Trade Organization (as of 10/22/1997) *Observer governments	World Intellectual Property Organization (as of 2/20/1997)
Vanuatu					*	
Vatican	X	X			*	X
Venezuela	X	X			X	X
Viet Nam	X		X (A)	X	*	X
Yemen						X
Yugoslavia	X	X	X (A & P)	X		X
Zambia	X	X			X	X
Zimbabwe	X	X		X	X	X

APPENDIX

B

State Trademark Registration Provisions

Each of the fifty states maintains a web site offering valuable information, addresses, and, in many cases, trademark application and renewal forms. In each state, the state agency responsible for trademark registration is the secretary of state, usually an elected official. Access to each state's web site can be gained through www.nass.org/welcome.htm, the home page for the National Association of Secretaries of State. Follow the directions given and you will be presented with links to each of the fifty member states and the District of Columbia. Alternatively, the site www.nasire.org/stateSearch/displayCategory.cfm?Category=states provides links to each of the official state web sites.

Following is a chart identifying the web site and physical address for each secretary of state, together with a citation to the pertinent state trademark statute and a reference to the duration of a trademark registration in each state. Note that there is no entry for the District of Columbia inasmuch as it has no trademark statutes and trademarks are registrable under the Lanham Act.

State Trademark Registration Agencies and Statutes

State and Web Site	Address	Trademark Statute	Registration Term (years)
Alabama www.sos.state.al.us/	Alabama Secretary of State P.O. Box 5616 Lands and Trademark Division, Room 127 Montgomery, AL 36103-5616 (334) 242-5325	Ala. Code § 8-12-6 et seq.	10
Alaska www.state.ak.us/	Secretary of State Division of Banking, Securities, and Corporations P.O. Box 110807 Juneau, AK 99811-0801 (907) 465-2521	Alaska Stat. § 45.50010 et seq.	5
Arizona www.state.az.us/	Secretary of State Trademarks Division 1700 W. Washington Phoenix, AZ 85007 (602) 542-4285	Ariz. Rev. Stat. Ann. § 44-1441 et seq.	10

State and Web Site	Address	Trademark Statute	Registration Term (years)
Arkansas www.sos.state.ar.us/	Secretary of State 256 State Capitol Building Little Rock, AR 72201-1094 (501) 682-1010 or (501) 682-3409	Ark. Code Ann. § 4-71-101 *et seq.*	5
California www.ss.ca.gov.	Secretary of State 1500 11th Street Sacramento, CA 95814-5701 (916) 653-6814	Cal. Bus. & Prof. Code § 14200 *et seq.*	10
Colorado www.state.co.us/	Secretary of State 1560 Broadway Denver, CO 80202 (303) 894-2251	Colo. Rev. Stat. § 7-70-102 *et seq.*	10
Connecticut www.state.ct.us/	Secretary of State Commercial Recording Division 30 Trinity Street Hartford, CT 06106 (860) 509-6003	Conn. Gen. Stat § 35-11a *et seq.*	5
Delaware www.state.de.us/	Department of State Division of Corporations Trademark Filings John G. Townsend Building P.O. Box 898 Dover, DE 19903 (302) 739-4111	Del. Code Ann. tit. 6, § 3301 *et seq.*	10
District of Columbia		Trademarks registrable under Lanham Act only	
Florida www.dos.state.fl.us/	Department of State Division of Corporations P.O. Box 6327 Tallahassee, FL 32314 (850) 487-6051	Fla. Stat. Ann. § 495.011 *et seq.*	10
Georgia www.sos.state.ga.us/	Secretary of State 315 West Tower 2 Martin Luther King, Jr., Drive Atlanta, GA 30334 (404) 656-2817	Ga. Code Ann. § 10-1-440 *et seq.*	10
Hawaii www.hawaii.gov/	Department of Commerce and Consumer Affairs Business Registration Division P.O. Box 541 Honolulu, HI 96809 (808) 586-2727	Haw. Rev. Stat. § 482-2 *et seq.*	10
Idaho www.state.id.us/	Secretary of State Trademark Division 700 W. Jefferson, Room 203 P.O. Box 83720 Boise, ID 83720-0080 (208) 334-2300	Idaho Code § 48-501 *et seq.*	10

State and Web Site	Address	Trademark Statute	Registration Term (years)
Illinois www.sos.state.il.us/	Secretary of State Department of Business Services, Trademark Division Room 328, Howlett Building Springfield, IL 62756 (217) 524-0400	765 Ill. Comp. Stat. § 1036/1 *et seq.*	5
Indiana www.state.in.us	Secretary of State Business Services 302 W. Washington Room E-018 Indianapolis, IN (317) 232-6540	Ind. Code § 24-2-1-1 *et seq.*	10
Iowa www.state.ia.us/	Secretary of State Corporations Division Hoover Building Des Moines, IA 50319 (515) 281-5204	Iowa Code § 548.101 *et seq.*	5
Kansas www.kssos.org/	Secretary of State Business Services State Capitol 2nd Floor 301 SW 10th Avenue Topeka, KS 66612-1594 (785) 296-7456	Kan. Stat. Ann. § 81-111 *et seq.*	10
Kentucky www.sos.state.ky.us/	Secretary of State Trademarks and Service Marks Room 86, State Capitol Frankfort, KY 40601 (502) 564-2848 (#401)	Ky. Rev. Stat. Ann. § 365.561 *et seq.*	5
Louisiana www.sec.state.la.us/	Department of State Commercial Division 3851 Essen Lane Baton Rouge, LA 70809-9125 (225) 925-4704	La. Rev. Stat. Ann. § 51:211 *et seq.*	10
Maine www.state.me.us/	Secretary of State Division of Corporations 101 State House Station Augusta, ME 04333-0101 (207) 287-4195	Me. Rev. Stat. Ann. tit. 10, § 1521 *et seq.*	10
Maryland www.sos.state.md.us/	Secretary of State Trademark Division State House Annapolis, MD 21401 (410) 974-5531	Md. Bus. Reg. Code Ann. § 1-401 *et seq.*	10
Massachusetts www.magnet.state.ma.us/	Secretary of the Commonwealth Corporations Division Room 1711 One Ashburton Place Boston, MA 02108 (617) 727-8329	Mass. Ann. Laws ch. 110B, § 1 *et seq.*	10

State and Web Site	Address	Trademark Statute	Registration Term (years)
Michigan www.cis.state.mi.us/	Michigan Department of Commerce—Corporations, Securities, and Land Development Bureau Corporation Department P.O. Box 30222 Lansing, MI 48909 (517) 334-6327	Mich. Comp. Laws § 429.31 et seq.	10
Minnesota www.state.mn.us/	Secretary of State Business Services Division 180 State Office Building 100 Constitution Avenue St. Paul, MN 55155-1299 (651) 296-2803	Minn. Stat. Ann. § 333.001 et seq.	10
Mississippi www.sos.state.ms.us	Secretary of State P.O. Box 136 Jackson, MS 39205-0136 (601) 359-1350	Miss. Code Ann. § 75-25-1 et seq.	10
Missouri www.state.mo.us/	Secretary of State Corporations Division P.O. Box 784 Jefferson City, MO 65102 (573) 751-4756	Mo. Rev. Stat. § 417.005 et seq.	10
Montana www.mt.gov/sos/	Secretary of State Corporations Bureau Montana State Capitol Helena, MT 59620 (406) 444-3665	Mont. Code Ann. § 30-13-301 et seq.	10
Nebraska www.nol.org.home/sos	Secretary of State State Capitol Building Lincoln, NE 68509 (402) 471-4079	Neb. Rev. Stat. § 87-111 et seq.	10
Nevada www.state.nv.us/	Secretary of State 101 N. Carson Street, Suite 3 Carson City, NV 89710-4786 (775) 684-5708	Nev. Rev. Stat. §§ 598.0935 et seq., 600.250 et seq.	5
New Hampshire www.state.nh.us/sos/	Secretary of State Corporations Division State House Annex, 3rd Floor Concord, NH 03301 (603) 271-3244	N.H. Rev. Stat. Ann. § 350A:1 et seq.	10
New Jersey www.state.nj.us/state/	Secretary of State P.O. Box 300 Trenton, NJ 08625-0300 (609) 777-0884	N.J. Stat. Ann. § 56:3-13.1a et seq.	5
New Mexico www.sos.state.nm.us/	Secretary of State State Capitol, Room 420 Santa Fe, NM 87503 (505) 827-3600	N.M. Stat. Ann. § 57-3-1 et seq.	10
New York www.dos/state/ny.us/	Secretary of State Miscellaneous State Records 41 State Street Albany, NY 12231-0001 (518) 474-0050	N.Y. Gen. Bus. Law § 360 et seq.	10

State and Web Site	Address	Trademark Statute	Registration Term (years)
North Carolina www.secstate.state.nc.us/secstate	Secretary of State Trademarks Section P.O. Box 29622 Raleigh, NC 27626-0622 (919) 733-4129	N.C. Gen. Stat. § 80-1 *et seq.*	10
North Dakota www.state.nd.us/sec/	Secretary of State Business Information/ Registration Division State Capitol 600 E. Boulevard Avenue Bismarck, ND 58505-0500 (701) 328-4284	N.D. Cent. Code § 47-22-01 *et seq.*	10
Ohio www.state.oh.us/sos/	Secretary of State 30 E. Broad Street, 14th Floor Columbus, OH 43266-0418 (614) 466-2655	Ohio Rev. Code Ann. § 1329.54 *et seq.*	10
Oklahoma www.state.ok.us/~sos/	Secretary of State 2300 N. Lincoln Boulevard, Room 101 Oklahoma City, OK 73105-4897 (405) 522-3043	Okla. Stat. Ann. tit. 78, § 21 *et seq.*	10
Oregon www.sos.state.or.us/	Secretary of State Corporation Division Public Services Building 151 255 Capitol Street, NE Salem, OR 97310-1327 (503) 986-2200	Or. Rev. Stat. § 647.005 *et seq.*	5
Pennsylvania www.state.pa.us/	Department of State Corporation Bureau P.O. Box 8722 Harrisburg, PA 17105-8722 (717) 787-1057	54 Pa. Cons. Stat. Ann. § 1101 *et seq.*	10
Rhode Island www.sec.state.ri.us/	Secretary of State Trademarks Division 100 N. Main Street Providence, RI 02903-1335 (401) 277-1487	R.I. Gen. Laws § 6-2-1 *et seq.*	10
South Carolina www.state.sc.us	Secretary of State Edgar Brown Building, Suite 525 P.O. Box 11350 Columbia, SC 29211 (803) 734-2470	S.C. Code Ann. § 39-15-1105 *et seq.*	5
South Dakota www.state.sd.us/	Secretary of State Trademarks Division Capitol Building, Suite 204 500 East Capitol Avenue Pierre, SD 57501-5070 (605) 773-5666	S.D. Codified Laws § 37-6-1 *et seq.*	4
Tennessee www.state.tn.us/	Secretary of State Suite 1800 James K. Polk Building Nashville, TN 37243 (615) 741-0531	Tenn. Code Ann. § 47-25-501 *et seq.*	10

State and Web Site	Address	Trademark Statute	Registration Term (years)
Texas www.sos.state.tx.us	Secretary of State Trademark Office 1100 Congress Capitol Building, Room 1E.8 Austin, TX 78711-2697 (512) 463-5576	Tex. Bus. & Com. Code Ann. § 16.01 *et seq.*	10
Utah www.commerce.state.ut.us/	Division of Corporations and Commercial Code 160 E. 300 South Salt Lake City, UT 84111 (801) 530-6701	Utah Code Ann. § 70-3-1 *et seq.*	10
Vermont www.cit.state.vt.us	Secretary of State Corporations Division 26 Terrace Street, Drawer 09 Montpelier, VT 06509-1101 (802) 828-2363	Vt. Stat. Ann. tit. 9, § 2521 *et seq.*	10
Virginia www.cns.state.va.us/	State Corporations Commission Division of Securities Tyler Building 1300 E. Main Street Richmond, VA 23219 (804) 371-9967	Va. Code Ann. § 59.1-92.1 *et seq.*	5
Washington www.secstate.wa.gov/corps/default.htm	Secretary of State Corporations Division 505 E. Union, 2nd Floor P.O. Box 40234 Olympia, WA 98504-7115 (360) 753-7115	Wash. Rev. Code § 19.77.010 *et seq.*	6
West Virginia www.state.wv.us/	Secretary of State Building 1, Suite 157-K 1900 Kanawha Boulevard E. Charleston, WV 25303-0770 (304) 558-8000	W. Va. Code § 47-2-1 *et seq.*	10
Wisconsin www.wisgov.state.wi.us/	Secretary of State Government Records Division/ Trademarks P.O. Box 7848 Madison, WI 53707-7848 (608) 266-5653	Wis. Stat. § 132.01 *et seq.*	10
Wyoming www.state.wy.us/	Secretary of State Corporations Division/ Trademarks State Capitol Building Cheyenne, WY 82002 (307) 777-7378	Wyo. Stat. § 40-1-101 *et seq.*	5

APPENDIX
C
Resources

WEB SITES

There are innumerable web sites that offer tremendous information about intellectual property. Most offer the advantage of providing links to other relevant sites. Some of the most useful web sites follow. Please note the Internet resources are of a time sensitive nature and URL address may often change or be deleted.

Government sites

www.uspto.gov	General information about trademarks and patents, fee schedules, forms, list of patent and trademark database libraries, databases of trademarks and issued patents, information about the PTO, text of *Trademark Manual of Examining Procedure* and *Manual of Patent Examining Procedure,* links to related web sites, information and maps relating to the PCT, and access to *pto bulletin,* an informational newsletter relating to the PTO and its procedures
www.lcweb.gov/copyright	General information about copyrights and registration procedures, access to copyright records, general information about the Copyright Office, access to forms and circulars, links to copyright law and legislation, and updates regarding pending legislation affecting copyrights
www.access.gpo.gov/su_docs	Home page of the Government Printing Office, providing direct links to the *Federal Register, Congressional Record,* and *Code of Federal Regulations,* as well as access to congressional bills and documents
www.usdoj.gov/criminal/cybercrime	Computer Crime and Intellectual Property Section home page of the Department of Justice, offering information relating to computer and high-tech crimes

Organization Sites

www.inta.org	Home page for International Trademark Association, offering a wealth of information relating to trademarks and links to other useful sites
www.wipo.org	Home page of the World International Property Organization, providing full text of treaties affecting intellectual property, such as the Paris Convention, Berne Convention, Madrid Protocol, Patent Cooperation Treaty, and other useful international agreements

www.epo.co.at/epo/	Site of the European Patent Office offering information relating to the EPO, its members, and patent registration procedures
www.aipla.org	Home page of the American Intellectual Property Law Association, providing general information about trademarks, copyrights, and patents; links to other IP-related sites; notices of PTO rules changes; and access to the AIPLA newsletter
www.abanet.org/intelprop/	Web site for American Bar Association's Section of Intellectual Property Law, offering general information relating to intellectual property and links to numerous IP-related sites, including those of many foreign patent and trademarks offices
www.icann.org	Home page of Internet Corporation for Assigned Names and Numbers, the organization that will take over assignment of domain names by 2000
www.spa.org	Home page of the Software Publishers Association, providing sample Internet usage policies and other related information

Educational Institution Sites

www.law.cornell.edu	Cornell Law School's site offering easy access to the *United States Code* (for trademark and patent statutes) as well as recent Supreme Court decisions; a primer on trademark, copyright, and patent law; and links to the Lanham Act, the Copyright Act, the Patent Act, international conventions, and many other primary sources
www4.law.cornell.edu/uscode/	Cornell Law School's site offering easy searching techniques for the *United States Code,* searching by popular name, key word, or specific section cite
www.law.cornell.edu/copyright/ regulations/regs.overview.html	Title 37 of the *Code of Federal Regulations,* providing regulations pertaining to the Copyright Office and registration procedures
www.law.cornell.edu/treaties/ berne/	Full text of the Berne Convention
www.law.emory.edu/fedcircuit	Emory University School of Law's site providing the full text of opinions of the Federal Circuit since 1995
www.fplc.edu	Home page of the Franklin Pierce Law Center "Intellectual Property Mall," arguably one of the best IP sites in existence, and offering access to hundreds of articles relating to IP, online copies of PTO patent exams, tools and strategies for IP professionals, basic IP info, and a comprehensive listing of other web sites and resources available on the Internet
http://fairuse.stanford.edu/articles	Stanford University's Copyright & Fair Use site, offering links to hundreds of articles and numerous journals relating to intellectual property law, with a special emphasis on copyright law
www.law.vill.edu/~rgruner/ patport.htm	This web site, entitled "The Patent Portal" and maintained by Professor of Law Richard S. Gruner, is an entry point to numerous patent resources on the Internet, including recent patent news, tips on

patent searching, frequently asked questions about patents, and other services and resources related to patents

Commercial Sites

www.bender.com/bender/open/ Webdriver?Mival=chan_main& channelID=intell	Publisher Matthew Bender offers basic information relating to IP, sample jury instructions, sample noncompetition clauses, computer contracts, and other IP information
www.ascap.com and www.bmi.com	Home pages of the performing rights societies ASCAP and BMI, offering general information about copyright licensing and summaries of new and pending legislation
www.ibm.com.patents	The IBM Patent Server, IBM's free, fully searchable database covering U.S. issued patents since 1971 with searching conducted by key word, Boolean connectors, patent numbers, or inventor name
www.thomson-thomson.com	Thomson & Thomson, the internationally known trademark and copyright search firm, offers a web site called SAEGIS for preliminary trademark searches
www.ipmag.com	Home page of *Intellectual Property Magazine,* offering general news and information, case digests, articles related to IP, and IP links
www.techlawjournal.com	Home page of *Tech Law Journal,* offering news, records, and analysis of legislation, litigation, and regulations affecting the computer and Internet industries
www.findlaw.com	A general purpose legal search engine that is an excellent starting place for intellectual property research; click on "Intellectual Property" for a wealth of IP-related information
www.legalnews.findlaw.com	Subscribe to this twice-weekly newsletter offering general information relating to a variety of legal topics, including intellectual property law and cyberspace law; updates are sent via e-mail and are easy to read and topical
www.ljx.com	Home page of *Law Journal EXTRA!,* offering electronic newsletters, one of which (*Intellectual Property Express*) is devoted strictly to IP issues; issues are sent via e-mail and are devoted to current IP developments
www.lectlaw.com	The 'Lectric Law Library, offering general legal information, including IP-related forms such as forms for assignments of IP
www.benedict.com	The Copyright Website, providing practical information relating to copyrights, including an overview of basic issues, late-breaking news, a copyright discussion group, and audio and visual examples of famous copyright infringements
www.lawworks-iptoday.com	*Intellectual Property Today,* a publication focused on issues in intellectual property
www.copyright.com	Home page of the Copyright Clearance Center, offering guidelines for creating policies for copyright compliance

www.nolo.com	Home page of Nolo Press, providing self-help information about a variety of legal topics, including trademarks, copyrights, patents, and trade secrets
www.bestdomains.com	Web site offering information on valuation of domain names
www.markwatch.com	Home page of MarkWatch, a company that monitors the Internet for potential trademark infringers
www.patents.com	A site offering contact information for more than twenty foreign patent offices.

Law Firm Sites

www.patents.com	Web site for Oppedahl & Larson of Colorado, providing general information on intellectual property law as well as great information on domain names and court decisions with links to other useful sites
www.kuesterlaw.com	Web site by Georgia intellectual property law firm, offering basic IP information, with a special emphasis on patent law and providing direct links to IP statutes, regulations, and cases
www.ipcounselors.com	Home page of Bazerman & Drangel, P.C., of New York City, offering general IP information as well as a free subscription to the firm's e-mail newsletter on IP topics and cases
www.piperpat.co.nz	Home page of Pipers patent firm in New Zealand, providing a directory of more than one hundred foreign patent offices with direct links to the home pages for the foreign patent offices.
www.oblon.com	Home page of Oblon Spivak McClelland Maier & Neustadt, P.C., of Arlington, Virginia, providing links to recent PTO decisions, IP news, and IP sources
www.execpc.com/~mhallign/	The Trade Secrets Home Page, provided by attorney R. Mark Halligan of Chicago, offering a wealth of information on trade secrets law
www.iwaynet.net/~jkwak/	The Patent Outline, offered by attorney Jim Kwak, detailing patent law and prosecution

GOVERNMENT AGENCIES

U.S. Patent and Trademark Office Commissioner of Patents and Trademarks Washington, DC 20231 TRAM line: (703) 305-8747	Register of Copyrights Copyright Office, Library of Congress 101 Independence Avenue, SE Washington, DC 20559-6000 Telephone: (202) 707-3000

STATE RESOURCES

Most states now have Internet home pages. In many instances, access can be gained by typing "www," adding the state's initials (for example, "ca" for California or "ny" for New York), and then adding ".gov."

Alternatively, access the site "www.llgu.edu" and select "state law." You will be presented with a map of the fifty states. By pointing the cursor to the appropriate state, you will be immediately connected to that state's web page. Use general search terms such as *trademarks* or *unfair competition* to locate pertinent information.

ORGANIZATIONS

World Intellectual Property Organization
P.O. Box 18
1211 Geneva 20, Switzerland
Telephone: (41-22) 338 91 11
www.wipo.org

European Patent Organization
Schottenfeldgasse 29
A-1072 Vienna, Austria
Telephone: (43 - 1) 521 26 0
www.epo.co.at/epo/

International Trademark Association
1133 Avenue of the Americas
New York, NY 10036-6710
Telephone: (212) 768-9887
www.inta.org

THE LAW LIBRARY

There are innumerable texts and treatises relating to intellectual property law. Locate the section of your law library that includes the IP materials (they will all be brought together in the same section or stacks). Browse the shelves and examine the materials. You will find a wide range of texts, from the academic to the thoroughly practical, with many books offering forms, practice tips, and suggestions.

APPENDIX
D
Forms Appendix

Form 1   Trademark Application
Form 2   Statement of Use
Form 3   Request for Extension of Time to File Statement of Use
Form 4   Combined Affidavit Under Sections 8 and 15 of the Lanham Act
Form 5   Application for Renewal of Trademark Registration
Form 6   Request for Extension of Time to File Notice of Opposition
Form 7   Opposition to Registration of Trademark
Form 8   Consent to Use and Register Agreement
Form 9   Petition to Cancel Trademark Registration
Form 10   Complaint for Trademark Infringement
Form 11   Trademark Settlement Agreement
Form 12   Work for Hire Provisions
Form 13   Employee Nondisclosure and Noncompetition Agreement
Form 14   Evaluation Agreement
Form 15   Confidentiality Agreement

Form 1

TRADEMARK APPLICATION

TRADEMARK/SERVICE MARK APPLICATION, PRINCIPAL REGISTER, WITH DECLARATION	MARK (Word(s) and/or Design)	CLASS NO. (If known)

TO THE ASSISTANT COMMISSIONER FOR TRADEMARKS:

APPLICANT'S NAME:

APPLICANT'S MAILING ADDRESS:

(Display address exactly as it should appear on registration)

APPLICANT'S ENTITY TYPE: (Check one and supply requested information)

Individual - Citizen of (Country):

Partnership - State where organized (Country, if appropriate): _____
Names and Citizenship (Country) of General Partners: _____

Corporation - State (Country, if appropriate) of Incorporation:

Other (Specify Nature of Entity and Domicile):

GOODS AND/OR SERVICES:

Applicant requests registration of the trademark/service mark shown in the accompanying drawing in the United States Patent and Trademark Office on the Principal Register established by the Act of July 5, 1946 (15 U.S.C. 1051 et. seq., as amended) for the following goods/services (SPECIFIC GOODS AND/OR SERVICES MUST BE INSERTED HERE):

BASIS FOR APPLICATION: (Check boxes which apply, but never both the first AND second boxes, and supply requested information related to each box checked.)

[ ] Applicant is using the mark in commerce on or in connection with the above identified goods/services. (15 U.S.C. 1051(a), as amended.) Three specimens showing the mark as used in commerce are submitted with this application.
- Date of first use of the mark in commerce which the U.S. Congress may regulate (for example, interstate or between the U.S. and a foreign country): _____
- Specify the type of commerce: _____
  (for example, interstate or between the U.S. and a specified foreign country)
- Date of first use anywhere (the same as or before use in commerce date): _____
- Specify manner or mode of use of mark on or in connection with the goods/services: _____

(for example, trademark is applied to labels, service mark is used in advertisements)

[ ] Applicant has a bona fide intention to use the mark in commerce on or in connection with the above identified goods/services. (15 U.S.C. 1051(b), as amended.)
- Specify intended manner or mode of use of mark on or in connection with the goods/services: _____

(for example, trademark will be applied to labels, service mark will be used in advertisements)

[ ] Applicant has a bona fide intention to use the mark in commerce on or in connection with the above identified goods/services, and asserts a claim of priority based upon a foreign application in accordance with 15 U.S.C. 1126(d), as amended.
- Country of foreign filing: _____   • Date of foreign filing: _____

[ ] Applicant has a bona fide intention to use the mark in commerce on or in connection with the above identified goods/services and, accompanying this application, submits a certification or certified copy of a foreign registration in accordance with 15 U.S.C 1126(e), as amended.
- Country of registration: _____   • Registration number: _____

NOTE: Declaration, on Reverse Side, MUST be Signed

Form 1 (continued)

DECLARATION

The undersigned being hereby warned that willful false statements and the like so made are punishable by fine or imprisonment, or both, under 18 U.S.C. 1001, and that such willful false statements may jeopardize the validity of the application or any resulting registration, declares that he/she is properly authorized to execute this application on behalf of the applicant; he/she believes the applicant to be the owner of the trademark/service mark sought to be registered, or if the application is being filed under 15 U.S.C. 1051(b), he/she believes the applicant to be entitled to use such mark in commerce; to the best of his/her knowledge and belief no other person, firm, corporation, or association has the right to use the above identified mark in commerce, either in the identical form thereof or in such near resemblance thereto as to be likely, when used on or in connection with the goods/services of such other person, to cause confusion, or to cause mistake, or to deceive; and that all statements made of his/her own knowledge are true and that all statements made on information and belief are believed to be true.

_____   _____
DATE   SIGNATURE

_____   _____
TELEPHONE NUMBER   PRINT OR TYPE NAME AND POSITION

INSTRUCTIONS AND INFORMATION FOR APPLICANT

TO RECEIVE A FILING DATE, THE APPLICATION <u>MUST</u> BE COMPLETED AND SIGNED BY THE APPLICANT AND SUBMITTED ALONG WITH:

1. The prescribed **FEE ($245.00)** for each class of goods/services listed in the application;
2. **A DRAWING PAGE** displaying the mark in conformance with 37 CFR 2.52;
3. If the application is based on use of the mark in commerce, **THREE (3) SPECIMENS** (evidence) of the mark as used in commerce for each class of goods/services listed in the application. All three specimens may be the same. Examples of good specimens include: (a) labels showing the mark which are placed on the goods; (b) photographs of the mark as it appears on the goods, (c) brochures or advertisements showing the mark as used in connection with the services.
4. An **APPLICATION WITH DECLARATION** (this form) - The application must be signed in order for the application to receive a filing date. Only the following persons may sign the declaration, depending on the applicant's legal entity: (a) the individual applicant; (b) an officer of the corporate applicant; (c) one general partner of a partnership applicant; (d) all joint applicants.

SEND APPLICATION FORM, DRAWING PAGE, FEE, AND SPECIMENS (IF APPROPRIATE) TO:

Assistant Commissioner for Trademarks
Box New App/Fee
2900 Crystal Drive
Arlington, VA 22202-3513

Additional information concerning the requirements for filing an application is available in a booklet entitled **Basic Facts About Registering a Trademark,** which may be obtained by writing to the above address or by calling: (703) 308-HELP.

This form is estimated to take an average of 1 hour to complete, including time required for reading and understanding instructions, gathering necessary information, recordkeeping, and actually providing the information. Any comments on this form, including the amount of time required to complete this form, should be sent to the Office of Management and Organization, U.S. Patent and Trademark Office, U.S. Department of Commerce, Washington, D.C. 20231. Do NOT send completed forms to this address.

Form 2

STATEMENT OF USE

<table>
<tr><td>STATEMENT OF USE
UNDER 37 CFR 2.88, WITH
DECLARATION</td><td>MARK (Identify the mark)</td></tr>
<tr><td></td><td>SERIAL NO.</td></tr>
</table>

TO THE ASSISTANT SECRETARY AND COMMISSIONER OF PATENTS AND TRADEMARKS:

APPLICANT NAME:

NOTICE OF ALLOWANCE ISSUE DATE:

Applicant requests registration of the above-identified trademarks/service mark in the United States Patent and Trademark Office on the Principal Register established by the Act of July 5, 1946 (15 U.S.C. 1051 et. seq., as amended). Three specimens per class showing the mark as used in commerce are submitted with this statement.

☐ Check here if a Request to Divide under 37 C.F.R. 2.87 is being submitted with this statement.

Applicant is using the mark in commerce on or in connection with the following goods/services: (Check One)

☐ Those goods/services identified in the Notice of Allowance in this application.

☐ Those goods/services identified in the Notice of Allowance in this application except: (Identify goods/services to be deleted from application) _____

_____

_____

Date of first use of mark in commerce which the U.S. Congress may regulate: _____

Specify type of commerce: (e.g., interstate, between the U.S. and a specified foreign country)_____

_____

Date of first use anywhere: _____
(the same as or before use-in-commerce date)

Specify manner or mode of use of mark on or in connection with the goods/services: (e.g., trademark is applied to labels, service mark is used in advertisements) _____

_____

The undersigned being hereby warned that willful false statements and the like so made are punishable by fine or imprisonment, or both, under 18 U.S.C. 1001, and that such willful false statements may jeopardize the validity of the application or any resulting registration, declares that he/she is properly authorized to execute this Statement of Use on behalf of the applicant; he/she believes the applicant to be the owner of the trademark/service mark sought to be registered; the trademark/service mark is now in use in commerce; and all statements made of his/her own knowledge are true and all statements made on information and belief are believed to be true.

Date _____

Signature _____

Telephone Number _____

Print or Type Name and Position _____

PTO Form 1580 (REV. 6-96)
OMB No. 0651-0009
Exp. (06/30/98)   There is no requirement to respond to this collection of information unless a currently valid OMB Number is displayed.

U.S. Department of Commerce/Patent and Trademark Office

Form 3

REQUEST FOR EXTENSION OF TIME TO FILE STATEMENT OF USE

REQUEST FOR EXTENSION OF TIME TO FILE A STATEMENT OF USE, WITH DECLARATION	MARK (Identify the mark)
	SERIAL NO.

TO THE ASSISTANT SECRETARY AND COMMISSIONER OF PATENTS AND TRADEMARKS:

APPLICANT NAME:

NOTICE OF ALLOWANCE MAILING DATE:

Applicant requests a six-month extension of time to file the Statement of Use under 37 CFR 2.89 in this application.

Applicant has a continued bona fide intention to use the mark in commerce on or in connection with the following goods/services: (Check One below)

  ☐ Those goods/services identified in the Notice of Allowance.

  ☐ Those goods/services identified in the Notice of Allowance except: (Identify goods/services to be **deleted** from application)

_____

_____

_____

This is the_____ request for an Extension of Time following mailing of the Notice of Allowance.
  (Specify: First - Fifth)

If this is not the first request for an Extension of Time, check one box below. If the first box is checked explain the circumstance(s) of the non-use in the space provided:

☐ Applicant has not used the mark in commerce yet on all goods/services specified in the Notice of Allowance; however, applicant has made the following ongoing efforts to use the mark in commerce on or in connection with each of the goods/services specified above:

_____

If additional space is needed, please attach a separate sheet to this form

☐ Applicant believes that it has made valid use of the mark in commerce, as evidenced by the Statement of Use submitted with this request; however, if the Statement of Use does not meet minimum requirements under 37 CFR 2.88(e), applicant will need additional time in which to file a new statement.

The undersigned being hereby warned that willful false statements and the like so made are punishable by fine or imprisonment, or both, under 18 U.S.C. 1001, and that such willful false statements may jeopardize the validity of the application or any resulting registration, declares that he/she is properly authorized to execute this Request for an Extension of Time to File a Statement of Use on behalf of the applicant; and that all statements made of his/her own knowledge are true and all statements made on information and belief are believed to be true.

_____   _____
Date   Signature

                _____
_____   Type or Print Name and Position
Telephone Number

   Check here if Request to Divide is being submitted with this statement (if Applicant wishes to proceed to publication or registration with certain goods/services on or in connection with which it has used the mark in commerce and retain an active application for any remaining goods/services, a divisional application and fee are required. 37 C.F.R. §2.87)

PTO Form 1581 (REV. 6-96)   U.S. Department of Commerce/Patent and Trademark Office
OMB No. 0651-0009
Exp. (06/30/98) There is no requirement to respond to this collection of information unless a currently valid OMB Number is displayed.

Form 4

COMBINED AFFIDAVIT UNDER SECTIONS 8 AND 15 OF THE LANHAM ACT

In the United States Patent and Trademark Office

Registrant:	Reynolds & Sherman Co.
International Class:	16
Registration No.:	1,986,675
Registration Date:	October 1, 1992
Trademark:	DURAFIT

Box POST REG
FEE
Assistant Commissioner for Trademarks
2900 Crystal Drive
Arlington, VA 22202-3513

Combined Affidavit
Under Sections 8 and 15 of the Lanham Act

Dear Sir:

Pursuant to Sections 8 and 15 of the Lanham Act (15 U.S.C. §§ 1058a and 1065), Gerald Sherman, of Reynolds & Sherman Co., being duly sworn, deposes and says that Reynolds & Sherman Co., located at 855 16th Street, Seattle, WA 22041, is the owner of Registration No. 1,986,675, dated October 1, 1992, as shown by records in the U.S. Patent and Trademark Office; that said mark has been in continuous use for five consecutive years subsequent to the date of registration, in interstate commerce for all of the goods recited in the registration; that the mark is still in use in said commerce as evidenced by the accompanying current specimen; that there has been no final decision adverse to Registrant's claim of ownership of such mark to such goods, or to Registrant's right to register the same or to keep the same on the register; and that there is no proceeding involving said rights pending in the U.S. Patent and Trademark Office or in a court and not finally disposed of.

Declaration

The undersigned, being hereby warned that willful false statements and the like so made are punishable by fine or imprisonment or both, under Section 1001 of Title 18 of the United States Code, and that such willful false statements may jeopardize the validity of the application, or any resulting registration, declares: that he/she is properly authorized to execute this document on behalf of the Registrant; he/she believes the Registrant to be the owner of the above-identified registration; the trademark is in use in commerce; and that all statements made of his/her own knowledge are true and all statements made on information and belief are believed to be true.

Power of Attorney

Applicant hereby appoints Timothy J. Lyden and Harris & Harris, all members of the Bar of California, and all having an address at 8300 Greensboro Drive, San Diego, CA 92110, to file this Affidavit, with full power of substitution and revocation and to transact all business in the Patent and Trademark Office in connection therewith.

Reynolds & Sherman Co.
By: _____
Name: _____
Title: _____
Date: _____

Form 5

APPLICATION FOR RENEWAL OF TRADEMARK REGISTRATION

APPLICATION FOR RENEWAL OF REGISTRATION OF A MARK UNDER SECTION 9 OF THE TRADEMARK ACT OF 1946, AS AMENDED	MARK (Identify the mark)	
	REGISTRATION NO.	DATE OF REGISTRATION:

TO THE ASSISTANT SECRETARY AND COMMISSIONER OF PATENTS AND TRADEMARKS:

REGISTRANT'S NAME:[1]

REGISTRANT'S CURRENT MAILING ADDRESS: _____

_____

_____

GOODS AND/OR SERVICES AND USE IN COMMERCE STATEMENT:

The mark shown in Registration No. _____ owned by the above-identified registrant is still in use in

_____ commerce on or in connection with all of the goods and/or services identified in the

(type of)[2]

registration, (*except* for the following)[3] _____

_____

as evidenced by the attached specimen(s)[4] showing the mark as currently used.

DECLARATION

The undersigned being hereby warned that willful false statements and the like so made are punishable by fine or imprisonment, or both, under 18 U.S.C. 1001, and that such willful false statements may jeopardize the validity of this document, declares that he/she is properly authorized to execute this document on behalf of the registrant; he/she believes the registrant to be the owner of the above identified registration; the trademark/service mark is in use in commerce; and all statements made of his/her own knowledge are true and all statements made on information and belief are believed to be true.

_____
Date

_____
Signature

_____
Telephone Number

_____
Print or Type Name and Position
[if applicable][5]

Form 5 (continued)

FOOTNOTES

1. The present owner of the registration must file this form within 6 months prior to the expiration of the registration term. The form may also be filed within a 3 month grace period following the expiration of the registration term upon payment of the late fee. If ownership of the registration has changed since the registration date, provide supporting documentation if available or a verified explanation. The present owner should refer to itself as the registrant.

2. "Type of Commerce" must be specified as "interstate," "territorial," "foreign," or such other commerce as may lawfully be regulated by Congress. Foreign registrants must specify commerce which Congress may regulate, using wording such as "foreign commerce between the U.S. and a foreign country."

3. List only those goods and/or services for which registrant is no longer using the mark. You should fill in this blank only if you are no longer using the mark on all the goods or services in the registration.

4. A specimen showing current use of the registered mark for at least one product or service in each class of the registration must be submitted with this form. Examples of specimens are tags or labels for goods, and advertisements for services. The registration number should be printed directly on the specimen.

5. If the present owner is an individual, the individual should sign the declaration.

6. If the present owner is a partnership, the declaration should be signed by a General Partner.

7. If the present owner is a corporation or similar juristic entity, the declaration should be signed by an officer of the corporation/entity. Please print or type the officer title of the person signing the declaration.

NOTE: If the registration is owned by more than one party, as joint owners, each owner must sign this declaration.

PTO Notification

You should receive written notification from the PTO of either the acceptance or rejection of this post registration document. If you do not receive written notification from the PTO within six months after filing, you may wish to telephone the Trademark Status Line at (703) 305-8747 or the Post Registration Division at (703) 308-9500.

FEES

For each renewal application under Section 9, the required fee is $300.00 per class. Please be aware that our fees may change. Changes, if any, are normally effective October 1 of each year. If filed during the three month grace period a late fee of $100.00 per class must also be submitted. If this renewal application is intended to cover less than the total number of classes in the registration, please specify the classes for which the renewal application is submitted. The renewal application, with appropriate fee(s), should be sent to:

BOX POST REG
FEE
Assistant Commissioner for Trademarks
2900 Crystal Drive
Arlington, Virginia 22202-3513

MAILING INSTRUCTION BOX

You can ensure timely filing of this form by following the procedure described in 37 CFR 1.10 as follows: (1) on or before the due date for filing this form, deposit the completed form with the U.S. Post Office using the "Express Mail Post Office to Addressee" Service; (2) include a certificate of "Express Mail" under 37 CFR 1.10. Papers properly mailed under 37 CFR 1.10 are considered received by the PTO on the date that they are deposited with the Post Office.

When placing the certificate directly on the correspondence, use the following language:

Certificate of Express Mail Under 37 CFR 1.10

"Express Mail" mailing label number: _____
Date of Deposit: _____
I hereby certify that this paper and fee is being deposited with the United States Postal Service "Express Mail Post Office to Addressee" service under 37 CFR 1.10 on the date indicated above and is addressed to the Assistant Commissioner for Trademarks, 2900 Crystal Drive, Arlington, Virginia 22202-3513.

_____   _____
(Typed or printed name of person mailing paper & fee)   (Signature of person mailing paper & fee)

This form is estimated to take 15 minutes to complete. Time will vary depending upon the needs of the individual case. Any comments on the amount of time you require to complete this form should be sent to the Office of Management and Organization, U.S. Patent and Trademark Office, U.S. Department of Commerce, Washington, D.C. 20231, and to the Office of Information and Regulatory Affairs, Office of Management and Budget, Washington, D.C. 20503. **DO NOT SEND FORMS TO EITHER OF THESE ADDRESSES.**

Form 6

REQUEST FOR EXTENSION OF TIME TO FILE NOTICE OF OPPOSITION

In the United States Patent and Trademark Office
Before the Trademark Trial and Appeal Board

In the Matter of)
Miller & Hays, Inc.,)   Application Serial No. 75/045,120
        Opposer)   Filed: July 17, 1997
v.)   Published: May 28, 1998
Southern Flextel Co.,)
        Applicant)

REQUEST FOR EXTENSION OF TIME TO FILE A NOTICE OF OPPOSITION

Miller & Hays, Inc., located at 2814 Bradford Drive, Wilmington, DE 24576, through its undersigned attorneys, respectfully requests that it be granted a thirty (30) day extension of time to and including July 27, 1998, within which to file a Notice of Opposition to registration of the mark FLEXTEL, U.S. Application No. 75/045,120, filed July 17, 1997, owned by Southern Flextel Co., and published for opposition in the *Official Gazette* of May 28, 1998. The period for the filing of a Notice of Opposition is presently set to expire June 27, 1998.

Opposer believes that it may be damaged by the registration of the mark, and the additional time is required to afford Opposer the opportunity to complete its investigation and to further consult with its attorneys.

Respectfully submitted,

Bailey & Bailey, L.L.P.

By: _____

Theodore F. Bailey

4890 Terrace Plaza

Wilmington, DE 56902

(302) 789-5486

Date: _____

Form 7

OPPOSITION TO REGISTRATION OF TRADEMARK

OPPOSITION TO THE REGISTRATION OF A MARK, WITH DECLARATION	IN THE UNITED STATES PATENT AND TRADEMARK OFFICE BEFORE THE TRADEMARK TRIAL AND APPEAL BOARD

In the matter of trademark application Serial No. _____

Filed _____

For the mark _____

Published in the Official Gazette on _____

(Date)

_____

(Name of opposer)

v.

_____

(Name of applicant)

Opposition No. _____
(To be inserted by Patent & Trademark Office)

NOTICE OF OPPOSITION

State opposer's name, address, and entity information (1)
Name of individual as opposer, and business trade name, if any
Business address
Name of partnership as opposer
Name of partners
Business address of partnership
Name of corporation as opposer
State or country of incorporation
Business address of corporation

The above-identified opposer believes that it/he/she will be damaged by registration of the mark shown in the above-identified application, and hereby opposes the same. (2)

The grounds for opposition are as follows: (3)

By _____   _____

(Signature)(4)   (Identification of person signing)(5)

FOOTNOTES

(1) If opposer is an individual, state the opposer's name, business trade name, if any, and business address. If opposer is a partnership, state the name of the partnership, the names of the partners, and the business address of the partnership. If opposer is a corporation, state the name of the corporation, the state (or country, if opposer is a foreign corporation) of incorporation, and the business address of the corporation. If opposer is an association or other similar type of juristic entity, state the information required for a corporation changing the term "corporation" throughout to an appropriate designation.

(2) The required fee must be submitted for each party joined as opposer for each class opposed, and if fewer than the total number of classes in the application are opposed, the classes opposed should be specified.

(3) Set forth a short and plain statement here showing why the opposer believes it/he/she would be damaged by the registration of the opposed mark, and the state of grounds for opposing.

(4) The opposition need not be verified and may be signed by the opposer or by the opposer's attorney or other authorized representative. If an opposer signing for itself is a partnership, the signature must be made by a partner; if an opposer signing for itself is a corporation or similar juristic entity, the signature must be made by an officer of the corporation or other juristic entity who has authority to sign for the entity and whose title is given.

(5) State the capacity in which the signing individual signs, e.g., attorney for opposer, opposer (if opposer is an individual), partner of opposer (if opposer is a partnership), officer of opposer identified by title (if opposer is a corporation), etc.

REPRESENTATION INFORMATION

If the opposer is not domiciled in the United States, and is not represented by attorney or authorized representative located in the United States, a domestic representative must be designated.

If the opposer wishes to furnish a power of attorney, it may do so, but an attorney at law is not required to furnish a power.

This form is estimated to take an average of 1 hour to complete, including time required for reading and understanding instructions, gathering necessary information, recordkeeping, and actually providing the information. Any comments on this form, including the amount of time required to complete this form, should be sent to the Office of Management and Organization, U.S. Patent and Trademark Office, U.S. Department of Commerce, Washington, D.C. 20231. Do NOT send completed forms to this address.

PTO Form 4-17a   U.S. Department of Commerce/Patent and Trademark Office
OMB No. 0651-0009   (Exp. 06/30/98)   There is no requirement to respond to this collection of information unless a currently valid OMB Number is displayed.

Form 8

CONSENT TO USE AND REGISTER AGREEMENT

This Agreement is effective as of the last day of execution.

WHEREAS, Miller & Hays, Inc. ("Miller"), 2814 Bradford Drive, Wilmington, DE 24576, is the owner of U.S. Trademark Registration No. 1,256,871 in International Class 9 for the mark FLEXTONE;

WHEREAS, Southern Flextel Co. ("Southern"), 2450 Central Drive, Los Angeles, CA 93014, has filed U.S. Application No. 75/045,120 for the trademark FLEXTEL in International Class 38 for satellite-based communication systems;

WHEREAS, Miller is primarily active in the field of computer hardware and related peripherals;

WHEREAS, Southern is primarily active in the field of satellite-based communication services and related wire-based and other telecommunications services, including cable television;

WHEREAS, the parties are desirous of avoiding confusion of the public as to the source of the goods and services offered under the marks of the respective parties;

WHEREAS, the goods and services offered or provided, and the marketing channels, channels of trade, and types of customers for the parties' respective goods and services are different and distinct;

WHEREAS, the parties believe that provided the terms of this Agreement are followed by each party there is no likelihood of confusion as to the use of their respective marks in connection with their respective goods or services;

WHEREAS, the parties are unaware of any instances of actual confusion between use of their respective marks; and

WHEREAS, the parties now seek to resolve this matter;

NOW, THEREFORE, the parties agree as follows:

1. Miller agrees it will not use the mark FLEXTONE or any marks confusingly similar to those of Southern on or in connection with any product or service confusingly similar to those provided by Southern and will limit its use of FLEXTONE to computer hardware and related peripherals.

2. Southern agrees it will not use the mark FLEXTEL or any marks confusingly similar to those of Miller on or in connection with any product or service confusingly similar to those provided by Miller and will limits its use of FLEXTEL to satellite-based communications and related wire-based and other telecommunications services and cable television.

3. Miller hereby consents to use and registration of the mark FLEXTEL as stated in U.S. Application No. 75/045,120 and will not oppose or petition to cancel any registration resulting therefrom so long as Southern is in compliance with the terms of this Agreement.

4. Southern hereby consents to use and continued registration of the mark FLEXTONE as stated in U.S. Reg. No. 1,256,871 and agrees it will not petition to cancel the registration thereof so long as Miller is in compliance with the terms of this Agreement.

5. Neither of the parties will object to or interfere with the other party's rights of registration, renewal, or use of their trademarks as limited above.

6. Neither party will attempt to associate itself with the other party or its goods or services.

7. This Agreement is binding upon the parties and their successors and assigns.

8. No alteration or variation of any of the terms or provisions of this Agreement shall be valid unless made in writing and signed by both parties hereto.

9. This instrument contains the entire Agreement between the parties with respect to the subject matter expressed herein. It supersedes and cancels any prior oral or written understandings, agreements, or negotiations concerning the subject matter hereof.

Form 8 (continued)

10. In the event any confusion between use of the parties' respective marks arises, the parties will cooperate and find ways to eliminate or minimize any confusion.

11. The parties intend to be bound by the terms of this Agreement and agree it is in their commercial interest to do so.

MILLER & HAYS, INC.

By: _____

SOUTHERN FLEXTEL CO.

By: _____

Form 9

PETITION TO CANCEL TRADEMARK REGISTRATION

In the United States Patent and Trademark Office
before the Trademark Trial and Appeal Board

In the Matter of)
Registration No. 1,784,047)
)
Triumph International, Inc.,)   Cancellation No. 46783
         Petitioner)
v.)
Martha M. Powell,)
         Registrant)

PETITION FOR CANCELLATION

Petitioner Triumph International, Inc., a corporation organized under the laws of the State of Michigan, and having a principal place of business at 6890 Orchard Hill Place, Detroit, MI 06040, believes that it is being damaged by Registration No. 1,784,047 and hereby petitions to cancel the same.

The grounds for the petition are as follows:

1. Petitioner has adopted and continuously used the mark ANGEL TOTS in connection with sale of jewelry in interstate commerce since at least as early as June 1992, well before December 18, 1994, the date of first use alleged by Registrant Martha M. Powell ("Powell") in Registration No. 1,784,047.

2. As a result of Petitioner's extensive and continuous use of ANGEL TOTS in interstate commerce in the United States, the purchasing public has come to recognize ANGEL TOTS as indicating that the jewelry promoted in connection with the mark originates with Petitioner.

3. Petitioner filed an application for registration of the mark ANGEL TOTS on the Principal Register on September 13, 1996, which application was assigned Serial No. 75/109,987. Registration of Petitioner's application was refused by the Trademark Office on the grounds of likelihood of confusion with Powell's SPIRIT TOTS mark in Registration No. 1,784,047.

4. Powell has obtained registration of the mark SPIRIT TOTS in connection with the sale of jewelry on the Principal Register. Powell's mark was registered July 27, 1995, as Registration No. 1,784,047.

5. Powells's first date of use in interstate commerce is June 1993, eighteen months after Petitioner's date of first use.

6. The goods offered in connection with Powell's mark are jewelry in International Class 14, the same class of goods offered by Petitioner under its mark.

7. Because Petitioner's date of first use of the mark ANGEL TOTS precedes Powell's date of first use of the mark SPIRIT TOTS, Petitioner has superior rights in and to the mark.

8. Petitioner further believes Registration No. 1,784,047 is likely to cause confusion and mistake in the mind of the public as to the origin of Registrant's goods.

9. Based on the foregoing, Registration No. 1,784,047 has caused injury and damage to Petitioner in that the Registration is an obstacle to Petitioner's right to the registration of its ANGEL TOTS mark.

Form 9 (continued)

WHEREFORE, Petitioner prays that Registration No. 1,784,047 be canceled and that this cancellation be sustained.

Petitioner hereby appoints Claire S. Hubbard and Moffatt & Hubbard, all having an address at 555 28th Street NW, Portland, OR 49078, to act as attorneys in the matter of the above cancellation, to prosecute said cancellation, to transact all business with the Patent and Trademark Office and the United States courts connected with this cancellation proceeding, and to sign its name to all papers that may hereafter be filed in connection with this Petition for Cancellation and to receive the official communications in connection with the same.

Respectfully submitted,

Claire S. Hubbard

Moffatt & Hubbard

555 28th Street, NW

Portland, OR 49078

(607) 895-8990

FORM 10

COMPLAINT FOR TRADEMARK INFRINGEMENT

In the United States District Court for the District of Massachusetts

Hanson Industries, Ltd.,)
        Plaintiff)
v.)
Brady Designs Co.,)
        Defendant)

Civil Action No. 95047

COMPLAINT FOR FEDERAL TRADEMARK INFRINGEMENT

COMES NOW Plaintiff, Hanson Industries, Ltd. ("Plaintiff"), by and through its attorneys, and files its Complaint against Defendant Brady Designs Co. ("Defendant") and alleges as follows:

Jurisdiction

1. This is an action arising under the trademark laws of the United States. The jurisdiction of this Court is based upon 15 U.S.C. § 1121 relating to the Lanham Act and 28 U.S.C. § 1332(a), the Plaintiff being a corporation organized under the laws of Florida and the Defendant being a corporation organized under the laws of Massachusetts and the amount in controversy, exclusive of interests and costs, exceeding the sum of $75,000.

Parties

2. Plaintiff, Hanson Industries, Ltd., is a Florida corporation having a principal place of business at 6810 Bay Front Drive, Ft. Myers Beach, FL 34901.
3. Defendant, Brady Designs Co., is a Massachusetts corporation having a principal place of business at 210 12th Street, Boston, MA 98721.

FIRST CAUSE OF ACTION (TRADEMARK INFRINGEMENT)

4. Plaintiff is the owner of U.S. Trademark Registration No. 1,687,245 for TRADITIONS for women's clothing in International Class 25. A copy of the Certificate of Registration is attached hereto as Exhibit A. Under the Trademark Act of July 5, 1946, Plaintiff has the exclusive rights to said mark and the use thereof.
5. Plaintiff is now and continuously has been engaged in the design, manufacture, and sales of women's clothing in interstate commerce under the TRADITIONS mark since at least as early as December 1, 1990 and has used its TRADITIONS mark to identify and distinguish its goods and services from those of others.

Form 10 (continued)

6. Plaintiff is informed and believes and thereon alleges that Defendant is engaged in the design, manufacture, marketing, and sale of women's and men's clothing in interstate commerce under the mark CLASSIC TRADITIONS.

7. Plaintiff is informed and believes and thereon alleges that the goods of Defendant are substantially similar to those of Plaintiff, and are sold to the same customers and through the same trade channels as the goods of Plaintiff.

8. On June 1, 1995, Plaintiff registered the trademark TRADITIONS with the U.S. Patent and Trademark Office, under the Trademark Act of July 5, 1946, Registration No. 1,687,245, for women's clothing and said trademark registration is now in full force and effect. The TRADITIONS mark has been continuously used in interstate commerce and applied by Plaintiff to the goods described herein.

9. Since long prior to any use by the Defendant of the mark complained of, Plaintiff has expended a great amount of money, time, and effort in promoting and advertising its goods offered under its TRADITIONS mark. By virtue of such efforts, said mark has become associated in the minds of customers and in the mind of the general public and trade with the Plaintiff alone, and valuable goodwill has been built up in the TRADITIONS mark for women's clothing.

10. On information and belief, long after Plaintiff first used its mark, Defendant began infringing and continues to infringe upon the rights of Plaintiff by offering women's and men's clothing under the designation CLASSIC TRADITIONS.

11. Defendant's use of CLASSIC TRADITIONS is likely to cause and has caused confusion and mistake and is likely to deceive and has deceived the public into the belief that Defendant's goods are the goods of the Plaintiff or emanate from the Plaintiff or are associated with or sponsored or endorsed by the Plaintiff, to the damage and injury of Plaintiff.

12. Defendant's conduct constitutes a violation of the U.S. Trademark Act of 1946, 15 U.S.C. § 1114.

13. Upon information and belief, Defendant's use of CLASSIC TRADITIONS has impaired, damaged, and diminished the Plaintiff's mark and the value thereof, and has caused and is likely to cause confusion with respect to the source and origin of Plaintiff's goods and has caused mistake and deception by causing the public to believe that Defendant's goods are those of the Plaintiff, all of which has damaged and will continue to cause damage to Plaintiff unless enjoined.

14. Since on or about June 1, 1995, Plaintiff has given notice that its mark is registered in the U.S. Patent and Trademark Office by displaying the federal registration symbol ® with the mark.

15. Although Plaintiff has demanded that Defendant cease and desist from further infringement of Plaintiff's mark, Defendant has refused to comply with Plaintiff's demand and continues to use the infringing mark, all to Plaintiff's damage.

WHEREFORE, Plaintiff demands judgment against the Defendant as follows:

1. That the Defendant and any of its agents or representatives be enjoined during the pendency of this action and permanently thereafter from: infringing U.S. Trademark Registration No. 1,687,245; using any name or mark confusingly similar to Plaintiff's TRADITIONS mark in connection with the advertising, offering, or sale of Defendant's goods or any other goods that are likely to cause confusion or mistake, or to deceive purchasers with respect to the origin or source of such goods.

2. That the Defendant be required to account and pay over to Plaintiff all profits and gains derived by Defendant by its infringement of Plaintiff's mark.

3. That the Defendant be required to pay to Plaintiff damages for the injury Plaintiff has sustained arising out of Defendant's infringement.

4. That Defendant be required to deliver up for impounding during the pendency of this action and for destruction upon final judgment, all documents, products, or other materials bearing any trademark confusingly similar to Plaintiff's trademark.

Form 10 (continued)

5. That the Court award punitive and exemplary damages against the Defendant and in favor of the Plaintiff by reason of Defendant's willful and intentional infringement.

6. That because of the willful and wanton nature of Defendant's infringement, that judgment be entered for treble the amount of the aforesaid damages.

7. That Defendant be required to pay the Plaintiff the costs of this action and reasonable attorneys' fees.

8. That the Court order such other and further relief as the Court deems just and proper.

Respectfully submitted,

Scott T. Hudson

Hudson & Adler

11 Dupont Circle NW

Washington, DC 20005

Attorneys for Plaintiff Hanson Industries, Ltd.

Form 11

TRADEMARK SETTLEMENT AGREEMENT

This Trademark Settlement Agreement ("Agreement") is entered into by and between Hanson Industries, Ltd. ("Hanson"), a Florida corporation, located at 6810 Bay Front Drive, Ft. Myers Beach, FL 34901, and Brady Designs Co. ("Brady"), a Massachusetts corporation, located at 210 12th Street, Boston, MA 98721.

WHEREAS, Hanson is the owner of the mark TRADITIONS registered on June 1, 1995, with the U.S. Patent and Trademark Office as U.S. Reg. No. 1,687,245 for women's clothing in International Class 25 (the "Mark");

WHEREAS, Brady is the owner of the mark CLASSIC TRADITIONS registered on July 1, 1997, with the U.S. Patent and Trademark Office as U.S. Reg. No. 1,982,542 for women's and men's clothing in International Class 25 (the "Brady Mark");

WHEREAS Hanson has filed a complaint alleging trademark infringement in the United States District Court for the District of Massachusetts; and

WHEREAS, the parties wish to settle this matter and all controversies between them;

NOW, THEREFORE, in consideration of the mutual covenants set forth in this Agreement, the parties agree as follows:

1. Brady agrees that any use or display of the Brady Mark shall be accompanied by the design shown in Exhibit A hereto and that Brady shall not use the Brady Mark alone in connection with any of its advertising, promotion, services, products, or packaging.

2. Brady will be solely responsible for filing a trademark application for the Brady Mark (& Design) with the U.S. Patent and Trademark Office and pay any fees in connection therewith, and Brady shall use its best efforts to prosecute said application.

3. Brady acknowledges Hanson's sole and exclusive right, title, and interest in and to the Mark and expressly agrees it has no interest whatsoever in the Mark and that nothing in this Agreement gives Brady any right to use the Mark.

4. Brady represents and expressly agrees it will not at any time or anywhere throughout the world use or attempt to register the Mark or any mark confusingly similar to the Mark or take any action to challenge, contest, petition to cancel, or oppose any use whatsoever or registration by Hanson of the Mark, and Brady will not use the Mark or any other mark or name in any manner that would cause confusion with Hanson, its Mark, or products.

5. Brady acknowledges that the existence of any registration that results from any application for the Brady Mark (& Design) will not grant Brady any superior rights as against Hanson or its Mark.

6. Hanson agrees to provide any needed consent, and to execute any necessary documents, for Brady to register the Brady Mark (& Design) in connection with men's and women's clothing.

7. Subject to the faithful compliance by Brady with the terms of this Agreement, Hanson agrees not to contest or challenge the use or application to register the Brady Mark (& Design) in connection with men's and women's clothing.

8. The parties agree that irreparable harm will result in the event of breach of any provision hereof. Should any party default in the performance of any of its obligations under the terms of this Agreement, and such default not be cured within thirty (30) days of notice of the breach, in addition to any other legal or equitable relief, damages, and remedies that may be available, any other party shall be entitled to an injunction to restrain the violation hereof.

9. The parties agree to execute any further agreements, consents, or other documents that may be necessary to carry out the intent of this Agreement.

10. Upon execution of this Agreement, Hanson shall cause to be filed a dismissal with prejudice of that action for trademark infringement filed against Brady and known as Civil Action No. 95047.

Form 11 (continued)

11. Upon execution of this Agreement, Hanson and Brady mutually release and discharge each other from any claims either arising out of or connected with Civil Action No. 95047 or that could have been alleged therein.

12. The parties hereto agree that this Agreement and the circumstances giving rise to it are confidential and shall not be disclosed to any person without obtaining the other party's prior written consent, which shall not be unreasonably withheld or delayed.

13. This Agreement comprises the entire understanding of the parties with respect to the subject matter hereof, all prior oral and written communications or understanding being merged herein, and shall be binding upon and inure to the benefit of the parties, as well as any related parties, subsidiaries, affiliates, successors, or assigns.

14. This Agreement shall be governed by the laws of Florida.

WHEREOF, the parties have caused this Agreement to be duly executed.

Hanson Industries, Ltd.   Brady Designs Co.

By: _____   By: _____

Title: _____   Title: _____

Form 12

WORK FOR HIRE PROVISIONS

Note: The following provisions may be added to agreements to ensure that works prepared by employees or specially commissioned works are works "made for hire" under the Copyright Act.

Provision for Use in Employment Agreement

Employee confirms that the relationship between him and ABC Consulting, Inc. ("ABC") is that of employee-employer. Employee agrees that all inventions, developments, discoveries, processes, software programs, data, or any other "works," as defined by the U.S. Copyright Act (collectively, the "Works"), created by him, whether alone or with others, while employed by ABC and that relate to work assigned to him by ABC or any business of ABC are the sole and exclusive property of ABC.

Employee further agrees that said Works shall be "works made for hire" as that term is defined in the U.S. Copyright Act, and Employee agrees to disclose promptly all works to ABC and to assist ABC in any way and perform all acts and execute all documents necessary or desirable to protect ABC's rights in and title to any such Works.

In the event any of the Works are determined not to be "works made for hire," as that term is defined in the U.S. Copyright Act, Employee hereby immediately and irrevocably assigns to ABC all right, title, and interest in and to any such Works.

Employee will not contest or challenge ABC's ownership, rights, or title in or to the Works.

Provision for Use in Agreement with Independent Contractor

Contractor and XYZ Management, Inc. ("XYZ") expressly agree that the work which Contractor has been commissioned by XYZ to create is a part of a motion picture (the "Work") and that their intent is that XYZ shall own all right, title, and interest in and to the Work with no rights of ownership or use in Contractor.

The parties agree that the Work is a "work made for hire" as defined by the U.S. Copyright Act and that by virtue of this Agreement it shall be owned solely, completely, and exclusively by XYZ, free and clear from all claims of any nature relating to Contractor's contributions and other efforts, and XYZ shall have the right to copyright the Work in its name as the author and proprietor thereof.

Contractor agrees that in the event the Work is determined by a court of competent jurisdiction not to be a work made for hire under the U.S. Copyright Act, this Agreement shall operate as an immediate and irrevocable assignment by Contractor to XYZ of all right, title, and interest in and to the Work.

Under this irrevocable assignment, Contractor hereby assigns to XYZ the sole and exclusive right, title, and interest in and to the Work, without further consideration, and agrees to assist XYZ in registering and from time to time enforcing all copyrights and other rights and protections relating to the Work.

It is Contractor's specific intent to assign all right, title, and interest whatsoever in the Work, in any media, in all countries, and for any purpose, to XYZ. Therefore, Contractor agrees to execute and deliver any reasonably necessary documents requested by XYZ in connection therewith and appoints XYZ as its agent and attorney-in-fact to act for and in its behalf and stead to execute, register, and file any documents or other applications and to do all other lawfully permitted acts to further the registration, protection, or issuance of copyrights with the same legal force and effect as if executed by Contractor.

Contractor agrees that it shall not at any time dispute or contest XYZ's exclusive right, title, and interest in and to the Work.

Form 13

EMPLOYEE NONDISCLOSURE AND NONCOMPETITION AGREEMENT

This Nondisclosure and Noncompetition Agreement is entered into this _____ day of _____, 20_____, by and between Donoghue Communications, Inc. (the "Company"), a New York corporation with its principal address at _____, and Robert Lawrence ("Employee"), an individual with an address at _____.

WHEREAS, the Company desires to employ the Employee as a senior computer consultant and developer; and

WHEREAS, the Employee is willing to accept such employment with the Company and to enter into this Agreement.

NOW, THEREFORE, in consideration of the foregoing, and for other good and valuable consideration, the receipt and sufficiency of which are hereby acknowledged by the Employee, it is agreed by the Employee as follows:

1. **Acknowledgments.** The Employee acknowledges that (i) the Company is engaged and in the future will be engaged in the business of providing computer software consulting services (the foregoing, together with any other businesses that the Company engages in during the Restricted Period (as defined below), being hereinafter referred to as the "Company Business"); (ii) his position has and will allow him access to trade secrets of and confidential information concerning the Company and its operations; (iii) the Company Business is national and international in scope; (iv) the Company would not have employed Employee but for the agreements and covenants contained in this Agreement; and (v) the agreements and covenants contained in this Agreement are essential to protect the business and goodwill of the Company during the Restricted Period.

2. **Covenant Not to Compete.** During the Restricted Period, Employee shall not within a one hundred (100) mile radius of any Company office or location, either directly or indirectly:
   a. engage in any business or activity that competes with Company Business; or
   b. solicit business or perform work for any past or present client of the Company for the benefit of anyone other than the Company or participate or assist in any way in the solicitation of business from or performance of work for any such client as an independent contractor or consultant to any other entity; or
   c. except for employment by the Company, enter into the employ of any person or entity engaged in any business that competes with the Company Business; or
   d. hire any past or present employee of the Company or solicit or encourage any employee to leave the employment of the Company; or
   e. have an interest in any entity engaged in any business that competes with the Company Business, directly or indirectly, in any capacity, including, without limitation, as a member, partner, shareholder, officer, director, principal, agent, or trustee or any other relationship or capacity; provided, however, Employee may own, solely as an investment, securities of any entity which are publicly traded if Employee is not a controlling person of, or a member of a group that controls, such entity or does not, directly or indirectly, own five percent (5%) or more of any class of securities of such entity; or
   f. Interfere with business relationships (whether formed heretofore or hereafter) between the Company and clients of the Company.

3. **Confidential Information.** During the Restricted Period, Employee shall keep secret and retain in strictest confidence, and shall not use for the benefit of himself or others except in connection with the business and affairs of the Company, all confidential information relating to the Company Business, including, without limitation, know-how, trade secrets, client lists, details of contracts, pricing policies,

Form 13 (continued)

marketing plans or strategies, financial information, business development techniques or plans, business acquisition plans, personnel information, processes, designs and design projects, inventions and research projects, and other business affairs relating to the Company Business (collectively, "Confidential Information"), learned by Employee heretofore or hereafter, and shall not disclose them to anyone outside of the Company except with the Company's express prior written consent. Notwithstanding the foregoing, the obligations of Employee under this Section shall not apply to Confidential Information:

a. which at the date hereof or thereafter becomes a matter of public knowledge without breach by Employee of this Agreement; or

b. which is obtained by Employee from a person or entity (other than the Company) under circumstances permitting its disclosure to others.

4. **Ownership of Work Product.** Unless otherwise specified in writing, all programs, software, documentation, modifications to software or documentation, specifications, work of authorship, inventions, techniques, concepts, and ideas developed or provided under this Agreement ("Work Product"), whether or not copyrightable or patentable, are the proprietary property of Company, and all right, title, and interest therein is vested in the Company and shall belong exclusively to the Company free and clear of any lien or claim of any kind by Employee. Such Work Product shall be "work made for hire" as that term is defined in the United States Copyright Act, and consequently, the Company shall be the author for copyright purposes of such Work Product and shall own the copyright to all of such Work Product. To the extent that any of such Work Product may not be work made for hire, Employee agrees to and hereby does immediately and irrevocably assign to Company the ownership of all copyrights, patents, trademarks, and any other proprietary rights throughout the world in such Work Product. To the extent that any of the foregoing waivers and assignments are not valid and enforceable under applicable laws, Employee hereby grants Company a perpetual, irrevocable, royalty-free, exclusive, assignable right and license throughout the world, to use, modify, market, and create derivative works based upon the Work Product without attribution to Employee. Employee further agrees to assist and cooperate with Company and take any action reasonably necessary for Company to perfect its rights in the Work Product, including signing and prosecuting applications for trademark, copyright, and patent, and any other action necessary to fulfill the intent of this Agreement.

5. **Restricted Period.** For purposes of this Agreement, the term "Restricted Period" shall mean the period commencing on the date of this Agreement and continuing for one year after the termination of Employee's employment with the Company for any reason.

6. **Restrictive Covenants.** For purposes of this Agreement, the term "Restrictive Covenants" shall mean the provisions of Sections 2 and 3 of this Agreement.

7. **Absence of Conflict.** Employee represents that his performance of all of the terms of this Agreement does not and will not breach any agreement entered into by Employee.

8. **Specific Performance.** Notwithstanding anything to the contrary herein contained, if Employee breaches or threatens to commit a breach of any of the Restrictive Covenants, the Company shall have the right to have the Restrictive Covenants specifically enforced by any court having equity jurisdiction, it being acknowledged and agreed that any such breach or threatened breach will cause irreparable injury to the Company and that money damages will not provide an adequate remedy to the Company.

9. **Severability.** Employee acknowledges and agrees that the Restrictive Covenants are reasonable in nature and in geographic and temporal scope and in all other respects. If any court or arbitrator determines that any of the Restrictive Covenants, or any part thereof, is invalid or unenforceable, the

Form 13 (continued)

remainder of the Restrictive Covenants shall not thereby be affected and shall be given full effect, without regard to the invalid portions.

10. **Blue-Penciling.** If any court or arbitrator determines that any of the Restrictive Covenants, or any part thereof, is unenforceable because of the nature, duration, or geographic scope of such provision, such court or arbitrator shall have the power to reduce the nature, duration, or scope of such provision, as the case may be, and, in its reduced form, such provision shall then be enforceable and shall be enforced.

11. **Entire Agreement and Amendment.** This Agreement contains the entire understanding and agreement of the parties relating to the subject matter thereof and supersedes all prior oral or written agreements between the parties with respect to such matters. This Agreement may be amended only by a writing signed by both parties hereto.

12. **Remedies Cumulative.** The remedies provided herein shall be cumulative, and shall not preclude any party from asserting any other rights or seeking any other remedies against the other party or such other party's successors or permitted assigns, pursuant to this Agreement and as provided by applicable law.

13. **Assignment; Binding Effect.** This Agreement may not be assigned by either party without the prior written consent of the other party. This Agreement shall be binding upon and inure to the benefit of the parties hereto and their respective successors and permitted assigns.

14. **Governing Law; Severability.** This Agreement shall be governed by and construed in accordance with the laws of the State of _____ regardless of the laws that might otherwise govern under applicable principles of conflicts of laws thereof. In the event that any provision of this Agreement shall be held invalid or unenforceable, such holding shall not invalidate or render unenforceable any other provision hereof.

15. **Counterparts.** This Agreement may be executed in one or more counterparts, each of which shall be deemed to be an original, but all of which together shall constitute one and the same instrument.

IN WITNESS WHEREOF, each of the parties has executed this Agreement or caused this Agreement to be duly executed on its behalf by a party duly authorized, as of the date provided hereinabove.

DONOGHUE COMMUNICATIONS, INC.

By: _____

Name: _____

Title: _____

ROBERT LAWRENCE

_____

Form 14

EVALUATION AGREEMENT

This Evaluation Agreement is entered into this _____ day of _____, 20_____, by and between Paul Gibson ("Gibson") and American Data Systems, Inc. ("ADS").

WHEREAS, Gibson and ADS intend to engage in discussions and negotiations for the purpose of developing a mutually beneficial relationship; and

WHEREAS, Gibson will furnish to ADS certain confidential information relating to a product invented, developed, and owned by Gibson (the "Product") and ADS will review and evaluate the Product for the purpose of determining whether ADS will manufacture, market, and sell the Product.

NOW, THEREFORE, for good and valuable consideration, the receipt and sufficiency of which are hereby acknowledged, the parties agree as follows:

1. Gibson will make available the Product to ADS, which will review and evaluate the Product solely for the purposes expressed herein.
2. ADS agrees to hold in strict trust and confidence the Product and any materials related thereto disclosed by Gibson to ADS.
3. Neither ADS nor its agents, representatives, or employees will use the Product or any materials related thereto for any purpose other than as stated herein and shall not copy, reproduce, sell, reverse engineer, reveal, or otherwise disclose the Product and any materials related thereto to any person.
4. No copies may be made or retained by ADS of the Product or any materials related thereto without Gibson's prior written consent.
5. In the event Gibson and ADS shall not enter into a business arrangement or other written agreement, ADS shall return to Gibson the Product and all materials related thereto upon Gibson's written demand therefor and will destroy any notes, copies, photographs, or other materials relating to the Product.
6. ADS shall not circumvent or otherwise try to avoid, directly or indirectly, any term or provision or intent or purpose expressed herein.
7. The obligations of this Agreement shall remain in force for a period of five (5) years after termination of any discussions between the parties with respect to the subject matter hereof.

_____

Paul Gibson

American Data Systems, Inc.

By: _____

Its: _____

Date: _____

Date: _____

Form 15

CONFIDENTIALITY AGREEMENT

Harris & Marston, Inc. ("HMI"), a corporation with its principal place of business at 123 Elm Street, Kansas City, MO, is interested in entering into discussions with GMA TechLab Co. (the "Company"), with its principal place of business at 4365 Canyon Avenue, Phoenix, AZ, to evaluate a possible business relationship between HMI and the Company (the "Transaction"). In the course of discussing the Transaction, HMI expects to disclose to the Company certain confidential trade and business information and HMI wishes to ensure that the confidentiality of such information will be protected in accordance with the terms and conditions of this Agreement. Therefore, the parties agree as follows:

1. Except as may be required by relevant law, the Company agrees that it will maintain in strict confidence all records, drawings, designs, inventions, marketing plans, customer lists, and other information ("Information") received from HMI or its representatives during the course of their discussions. The Company further agrees that any Information obtained from HMI or its representatives will not be revealed or otherwise disclosed to any third party, except to each party's authorized representatives who need to know such Information for the purpose of evaluating any such possible Transaction. The Company agrees to maintain at least the same procedures regarding the Information that it maintains with respect to its own confidential information. In the event either party terminates the discussions, the Company will promptly return to HMI upon demand all Information, books, records, and other documents acquired from HMI during the course of discussions and will not retain any copies of such materials.

2. The parties agree that they will not make or indirectly cause any third party to make any communications, whether oral or written, to the public or to any third party concerning the existence or status of these discussions, except that communications can be made to duly authorized representatives of the parties.

3. The Company represents that it will use Information obtained from HMI for the sole and exclusive purpose of evaluating a possible business arrangement between them and for no other purpose whatsoever.

4. The Company shall not be subject to the restrictions imposed herein with respect to any information if the information:
   a. was known to the Company or had been independently developed by it at the time of receipt without breach of this Agreement or any other agreement;
   b. becomes generally available to the public other than as a result of disclosure by the Company; or
   c. was lawfully obtained by the Company from another source without any breach of confidentiality.

5. The Company will not circumvent or otherwise try to avoid, directly or indirectly, any terms or provisions or the intent hereof.

6. The obligations of this Confidentiality Agreement shall remain in force for a period of two years after the termination of the discussions.

7. Information shall not be disclosed to any employee of or consultant to either party, or to any third party, unless they agree to execute and be bound by the terms of this Agreement.

8. If the Company breaches or threatens to commit a breach of this Agreement, HMI shall have the right to have this Agreement specifically enforced by any court of competent jurisdiction, it being acknowledged and agreed that any such breach or threatened breach will cause irreparable injury to HMI and that money damages will not provide an adequate remedy to HMI. Such rights and remedies shall be in addition to, and not in lieu of, any other rights and remedies available to HMI.

Form 15 (continued)

9. This Agreement contains the entire understanding and agreement of the parties relating to the subject matter hereof and supersedes all prior oral or written agreements between the parties and may be amended only by a writing signed by both parties hereto.

HARRIS & MARSTON, INC.

By: _____

Its: _____

Date: _____

GMA TECHLAB CO.

By: _____

Its: _____

Date: _____

APPENDIX
E
Selected Statutes

Trademarks
Copyrights
Patents

§ 1051 Registration; application; payment of fees; designation of resident for service of process and notice [Section 1]

Section 1. (a)(1) The owner of a trademark used in commerce may request registration of its trademark on the principal register hereby established by paying the prescribed fee and filing in the Patent and Trademark Office an application and a verified statement, in such form as may be prescribed by the Commissioner, and such number of specimens or facsimiles of the mark as used as may be required by the Commissioner.

(2) The application shall include specification of the applicant's domicile and citizenship, the date of the applicant's first use of the mark, the date of the applicant's first use of the mark in commerce, the goods in connection with which the mark is used, and a drawing of the mark.

(3) The statement shall be verified by the applicant and specify that—

A) the person making the verification believes that he or she, or the juristic person in whose behalf he or she makes the verification, to be the owner of the mark sought to be registered;

B) to the best of the verifier's knowledge and belief, the facts recited in the application are accurate;

C) the mark is in use in commerce; and

D) to the best of the verifier's knowledge and belief, no other person has the right to use such mark in commerce either in the identical form thereof or in such near resemblance thereto as to be likely, when used on or in connection with the goods of such other person, to cause confusion, or to cause mistake, or to deceive, except that, in the case of every application claiming concurrent use, the applicant shall—

(i) state exceptions to the claim for exclusive use; and

(ii) shall specify, to the extent of the verifier's knowledge—

(I) any concurrent use by others;

(II) the goods on or in connection with which and the areas in which each concurrent use exists;

(III) the periods of each use; and

(IV) the goods and area for which the applicant desires registration.

(4) The applicant shall comply with such rules or regulations as may be prescribed by the Commissioner. The Commissioner shall promulgate rules prescribing the requirements for the application and for obtaining a filing date herein.

(b)(1) A person who has a bona fide intention, under circumstances showing the good faith of such person, to use a trademark in commerce may request registration of its trademark on the principal register hereby established by paying the prescribed fee and filing in the Patent and Trademark office an application and a verified statement, in such form as may be prescribed by the Commissioner.

(2) The application shall include specification of the applicant's domicile and citizenship, the goods in connection with which the applicant has a bona fide intention to use the mark, and a drawing of the mark.

(3) The statement shall be verified by the applicant and specify—

(A) that the person making the verification believes that he or she, or the juristic person in whose behalf he or she makes the verification, to be entitled to use the mark in commerce;

(B) the applicant's bona fide intention to use the mark in commerce;

(C) that, to the best of the verifier's knowledge and belief, the facts recited in the application are accurate; and

(D) that, to the best of the verifier's knowledge and belief, no other person has the right to use such mark in commerce either in the identical form thereof or in such near resemblance thereto as to be likely, when used on or in connection with the goods of such other person, to cause confusion, or to cause mistake, or to deceive.

Except for applications filed pursuant to section 44, no mark shall be registered until the applicant has met the requirements of subsections (c) and (d) of this section.

(4) The applicant shall comply with such rules or regulations as may be prescribed by the Commissioner. The Commissioner shall promulgate rules prescribing the requirements for the application and for obtaining a filing date herein.

(c) At any time during examination of an application filed under subsection (b), an applicant who has made use of the mark in commerce may claim the benefits of such use for purposes of this Act, by amending his or her application to bring it into conformity with the requirements of subsection (a).

(d) (1) Within six months after the date on which the notice of allowance with respect to a mark is issued under section 13(b)(2) [§ 1063(b)(2)] to an applicant under subsection (b) of this section, the applicant shall file in the Patent and Trademark Office, together with such number of specimens or facsimiles of the mark as used in commerce as may be required by the Commissioner and payment of the prescribed fee, a verified statement that the mark is in use in commerce and specifying the date of the applicant's first use of the mark in commerce, and those goods or services specified in the notice of allowance on or in connection with which the mark is used in commerce. Subject to examination and acceptance of the statement of use, the mark shall be registered in the Patent and Trademark Office, a certificate of registration shall be issued for those goods or services recited in the statement of use for which the mark is entitled to registration, and notice of registration shall be published in the Official Gazette of the Patent and Trademark Office. Such examination may include an examination of the factors set forth in subsections (a) through (e) of section 2 [§ 1052]. The notice of registration shall specify the goods or services for which the mark is registered.

(2) The Commissioner shall extend, for one additional 6-month period, the time for filing the statement of use under paragraph (1), upon written request of the applicant before the expiration of the 6-month period provided in paragraph (1). In addition to an extension under the preceding sentence, the Commissioner may, upon a showing of good cause by the applicant, further extend the time for filing the statement

of use under paragraph (1) for periods aggregating not more than 24 months, pursuant to written request of the applicant made before the expiration of the last extension granted under this paragraph. Any request for an extension under this paragraph shall be accompanied by a verified statement that the applicant has a continued bona fide intention to use the mark in commerce and specifying those goods or services identified in the notice of allowance on or in connection with which the applicant has a continued bona fide intention to use the mark in commerce. Any request for an extension under this paragraph shall be accompanied by payment of the prescribed fee. The Commissioner shall issue regulations setting forth guidelines for determining what constitutes good cause for purposes of this paragraph.

(3) The Commissioner shall notify any applicant who files a statement of use of the acceptance or refusal thereof and, if the statement of use is refused, the reasons for the refusal. An applicant may amend the statement of use.

(4) The failure to timely file a verified statement of use under paragraph (1) or an extension request under paragraph (2) shall result in abandonment of the application, unless it can be shown to the satisfaction of the Commissioner that the delay in responding was unintentional, in which case the time for filing may be extended, but for a period not to exceed the period specified in paragraphs (1) and (2) for filing a statement of use.

§ 1052 Trademark registrable on principal register; concurrent registration [Section 2]

No trademark by which the goods of the applicant may be distinguished from the goods of others shall be refused registration on the principal register on account of its nature unless it—

(a) Consists of or comprises immoral, deceptive, or scandalous matter; or matter which may disparage or falsely suggest a connection with persons, living or dead, institutions, beliefs, or national symbols, or bring them into contempt, or disrepute; or a geographical indication which, when used on or in connection with wines or spirits, identifies a place other than the origin of the goods and is first used on or in connection with wines or spirits by the applicant on or after one year after the dat on which the WTO Agreement (as defined in section 2(9) of the Uruguay Round Agreements Act) enters into force with respect to the United States.

(b) Consists of or comprises the flag or coat of arms or other insignia of the United States, or of any State or municipality, or of any foreign nation, or any simulation thereof.

(c) Consists of or comprises a name, portrait, or signature identifying a particular living individual except by his written consent, or the name, signature, or portrait of a deceased President of the United States during the life of his widow, if any, except by the written consent of the widow.

(d) Consists of or comprises a mark which so resembles a mark registered in the Patent and Trademark Office, or a mark or trade name previously used in the Untied States by another and not abandoned, as to be likely, when used on or in connection with the goods of the applicant, to cause confusion, or to cause mistake, or to deceive: *Provided,* That if the Commissioner determines that confusion, mistake, or deception is not likely to result from the continued use by more than one person of the same or similar marks under conditions and limitations as to the mode or place of use of the marks or the goods on or in connection with which such marks are used, concurrent registrations may be issued to such persons when they have become entitled to use such marks as a result of their concurrent lawful use in commerce prior to (1) the earliest of the filing dates of the applications pending or of any registration issued under this Act; (2) July 5, 1947, in the case of registrations previously issued under the Act of March 3, 1881, or February 20, 1905, and continuing in full force and effect on that date; or (3) July 5, 1947, in the case of applications filed under the Act of February 20, 1905, and registered after July 5, 1947. Use prior to the filing date of any pending application or a registration shall not be required when the owner of such application or registration consents to the grant of a concurrent registration to the applicant. Concurrent registrations may also be issued by the Commissioner when a court of competent jurisdiction has finally determined that more than one person is entitled to use the same or similar marks in commerce. In issuing concurrent registrations, the Commissioner shall prescribe conditions and limitations as to the mode or place of use of the mark or the good son or in connection with which such mark is registered to the respective persons.

(e) Consists of a mark which (1) when used on or in connection with the goods of the applicant is merely descriptive or deceptively misdescriptive of them, (2) when used on or in connection with the goods of the applicant is primarily geographically descriptive of them, except as indications of regional origin may be registrable under section 4, (3) when used on or in connection with the goods of the applicant is primarily geographically deceptively misdescriptive of them, (4) is primarily merely a surname, or (5) comprises any matter that, as a whole, is functional.

(f) Except as expressly excluded in subsections (a), (b), (c), (d), (e)(3), and (e)(5) of this section, nothing herein shall prevent the registration of a mark used by the applicant which has become distinctive of the applicant's goods in commerce. The Commissioner may accept as prima facie evidence that the mark has become distinctive, as used on or in connection with the applicant's goods in commerce, proof of substantially exclusive and continuous use thereof as a mark by the applicant in commerce for the five years before the date on which the claim of distinctiveness is made. Nothing in this section shall prevent the registration of a mark which, when used on or in connection with the goods of the applicant, is primarily geographically deceptively misdescriptive of them, and which became distinctive of the applicant's goods in commerce before the date of the enactment of the North American Free Trade Agreement Implementation Act.

A mark which when used would cause dilution under section 43(c) may be refused registration only pursuant to a proceeding brought under section 13. A registration for a mark which when used would cause dilution under section 43(c) may be canceled pursuant to a proceeding brought under either section 14 or 24.

§ 1053 Service marks registrable [Section 3]

Subject to the provisions relating to the registration of trademarks, so far as they are applicable, service marks shall be registrable, in the same manner and with the same effect as are trademarks, and when registered they shall be entitled to the protection provided herein in the case of trademarks. Applications and procedure under this section shall conform as nearly as practicable to those prescribed for the registration of trademarks.

§ 1054 Collective marks and certification marks registrable [Section 4]

Subject to the provisions relating to the registration of trademarks, so far as they are applicable, collective and certification marks, including indications of regional origin, shall be registrable under this act, in the same manner and with the same effect as are trademarks, by persons, and nations, States, municipalities, and the like, exercising legitimate control over the use of the marks sought to be registered, even though not possessing an industrial or commercial establishment, and when registered they shall be entitled to the protection provided herein in the case of trademarks, except in the case of certification marks when used so as to represent falsely that the owner or a user thereof makes or sells the goods or performs the services on or in connection with which such mark is used. Applications and procedure under this section shall conform as nearly as practicable to those prescribed for the registration of trademarks.

§ 1057 Certificates of registration [Section 7]

(a) *Issuance and form.*—Certificates of registration of marks registered upon the principal register shall be issued in the name of the United States of America, under the seal of the Patent and Trademark Office, and shall be signed by the Commissioner or have his signature placed thereon, and a record thereof shall be kept in the Patent and Trademark Office. The registration shall reproduce the mark, and state that the mark is registered on the principal register under this Act, the date of the first use of the mark, the date of the first use of the mark in commerce, the particular goods or services for which it is registered, the number and date of the registration, the term thereof, the date on which the application for registration was received in the Patent and Trademark Office, and any conditions and limitations that may be imposed in the registration.

(b) *Certificate as prima facie evidence.*—A certificate of registration of a mark upon the principal register provided by this Act shall be prima facie evidence of the validity of the registered mark and of the registration of the mark, of the registrant's ownership of the mark, and of the registrant's exclusive right to use the registered mark in commerce on or in connection with the goods or services specified in the certificate, subject to any conditions or limitations stated in the certificate.

(c) *Constructive use.*—Contingent on the registration of a mark on the principal register provided by this Act, the filing of the application to register such mark shall constitute constructive use of the mark, conferring a right of priority, nationwide in effect, on or in connection with the goods or services specified in the registration against any other person except for a person whose mark has not been abandoned and who, prior to such filing—

(1) has used the mark;

(2) has filed an application to register the mark which is pending or has resulted in registration of the mark; or

(3) has filed a foreign application to register the mark on the basis of which he or she has acquired a right of priority, and timely files an application under section 44(d) [§ 1126(d)] to register the mark which is pending or has resulted in registration of the mark.

§ 1058 Duration of registration; cancellation; affidavit of continued use; notice of Commissioner's action [Section 8]

(a) Each registration shall remain in force for 10 years, except that the registration of any mark shall be canceled by the Commissioner for failure to comply with the provisions of subsection (b) of this section, upon the expiration of the following time periods, as applicable:

(1) For registrations issued pursuant to the provisions of this Act, at the end of 6 years following the date of registration.

(2) For registrations published under the provisions of section 12(c), at the end of 6 years following the date of publication under such section.

(3) For all registrations, at the end of each successive 10-year period following the date of registration.

(b) During the 1-year period immediately preceding the end of the applicable time period set forth in subsection (a), the owner of the registration shall pay the prescribed fee and file in the Patent and Trademark Office—

(1) an affidavit setting forth those goods or services recited in the registration on or in connection with which the mark is in use in commerce and such number of specimens or facsimiles showing current use of the mark as may be required by the Commissioner; or

(2) an affidavit setting forth those goods or services recited in the registration on or in connection with which the mark is not in use in commerce and showing that any such nonuse is due to special circumstances which excuse such nonuse and is not due to any intention to abandon the mark.

(c)(1) The owner of the registration may make the submissions required under this section within a grace period of 6 months after the end of the applicable time period set forth in subsection (a). Such submission is required to be accompanied by a surcharge prescribed by the Commissioner.

(2) If any submission filed under this section is deficient, the deficiency may be corrected after the statutory time period and within the time prescribed after notification of the deficiency. Such submission is required to be accompanied by a surcharge prescribed by the Commissioner.

(d) Special notice of the requirement for affidavits under this section shall be attached to each certificate of registration and notice of publication under section 12(c).

(e) The Commissioner shall notify any owner who files 1 of the affidavits required by this section of the Commissioner's acceptance or refusal thereof and, in the case of a refusal, the reasons therefor.

(f) If the registrant is not domiciled in the United States, the registrant shall designate by a written document filed in the Patent and Trademark Office the name and address of some person resident in the United States on whom may be served notices or process in proceedings affecting the mark. Such notices or process may be served upon the person so designated by leaving with that person or mailing to that person a copy thereof at the address specified in the last designation so filed. If the person so designated cannot be found at the address given in the last designation, such notice or process may be served upon the Commissioner.

§ 1059   Renewal of registration [Section 9]

(a) Subject to the provisions of section 8, each registration may be renewed for periods of 10 years at the end of each successive 10-year period following the date of registration upon payment of the prescribed fee and the filing of a written application, in such form as may be prescribed by the Commissioner. Such application may be made at any time within 1 year before the end of each successive 10-year period for which the registration was issued or renewed, or it may be made within a grace period of 6 months after the end of each successive 10-year period, upon payment of a fee and surcharge prescribed therefor. If any application filed under this section is deficient, the deficiency may be corrected within the time prescribed after notification of the deficiency, upon payment of a surcharge prescribed therefor.

(b) If the Commissioner refuses to renew the registration, the Commissioner shall notify the registrant of the Commissioner's refusal and the reasons therefor.

(c) If the registrant is not domiciled in the United States, the registrant shall designate by a written document filed in the Patent and Trademark Office the name and address of some person resident in the United States on whom may be served notices or process in proceedings affecting the mark. Such notices or process may be served upon the person so designated by leaving with that person or mailing to that person a copy thereof at the address specified in the last designation so filed. If the person so designated cannot be found at the address given in the last designation, such notice or process may be served upon the Commissioner.

§ 1060   Assignment of mark; execution; recording; purchaser without notice [Section 10]

(a) A registered mark or a mark for which an application to register has been filed shall be assignable with the good will of the business in which the mark is used, or with that part of the good will of the business connected with the use of and symbolized by the mark. Notwithstanding the preceding sentence, no application to register a mark under section 1(b) shall be assignable prior to the filing of an amendment under section 1(c) to bring the application into conformity with section 1(a) or the filing of the verified statement of use under section 1(d), except for an assignment to a successor to the business of the applicant, or portion thereof, to which the mark pertains, if that business is ongoing and existing. In any assignment authorized by this section, it shall not be necessary to include the good will of the business connected with the use of and symbolized by any other mark used in the business or by the name or style under which the business is conducted. Assignments shall be by instruments in writing duly executed. Acknowledgment shall be prima facie evidence of the execution of an assignment, and when the prescribed information reporting the assignment is recorded in the Patent and Trademark Office, the record shall be prima facie evidence of execution. An assignment shall be void against any subsequent purchaser for valuable consideration without notice, unless the prescribed information reporting the assignment is recorded in the Patent and Trademark Office within 3 months after the date of the assignment or prior to the subsequent purchase. The Patent and Trademark Office shall maintain a record of information on assignments, in such form as may be prescribed by the Commissioner.

§ 1063   Opposition to registration [Section 13]

(a) Any person who believes that he would be damaged by the registration of a mark upon the principal register, including as a result of dilution under section 43(c) may, upon payment of the prescribed fee, file an opposition in the Patent and Trademark Office, stating the grounds therefor, within thirty days after the publication under subsection (a) of section 12 [§ 1062] of this Act of the mark sought to be registered. Upon written request prior to the expiration of the thirty-day period, the time for filing opposition shall be extended for an additional thirty days, and further extensions of time for filing opposition may be granted by the Commissioner for good cause when requested prior to the expiration of an extension. The Commissioner shall notify the applicant of each extension of the time for filing opposition. An opposition may be amended under such conditions as may be prescribed by the Commissioner.

(b) Unless registration is successfully opposed—

(1) a mark entitled to registration on the principal register based on an application filed under section 1(a) [§ 1051(a)] or pursuant to section 44 [§ 1126] shall be registered in the Patent and Trademark Office, a certificate of registration shall be issued, and notice of the registration shall be published in the Official Gazette of the Patent and Trademark Office; or

(2) a notice of allowance shall be issued to the applicant if the applicant applied for registration under section 1(b) [§ 1051(b)].

§ 1064   Cancellation of registration [Section 4]

A petition to cancel a registration of a mark, stating the grounds relied upon, may, upon payment of the prescribed fee, be filed as follows by any person who believes that he is or will be damaged, including as a result of dilution under section 43(c) by the registration of a mark on the principal register established by this Act, or under the Act of March 3, 1881, or the Act of February 20, 1905:

(1) Within five years from the date of the registration of the mark under this Act.

(2) Within five years from the date of publication under section 12(c) hereof [§ 1062(c)] of a mark registered under the Act of March 3, 1881, or the Act of February 20, 1905.

(3) At any time if the registered mark becomes the generic name for the goods or services, or a portion thereof, for which it is registered, or is functional, or has been abandoned, or its registration was obtained fraudulently or contrary to

the provisions of section 4 [§ 1054] or of subsection (a), (b), or (c) of section 2 [§ 1052] for a registration under this Act, or contrary to similar prohibitory provisions of such prior Acts for a registration under such Acts, or if the registrant so as to misrepresent the source of the goods or services on or in connection with which the mark is used. If the registered mark becomes the generic name for less than all of the goods or services for which it is registered, a petition to cancel the registration for only those goods or services may be filed. A registered mark shall not be deemed to be the generic name of goods or services solely because such mark is also used as a name of or to identify a unique product or service. The primary significance of the registered mark to the relevant public rather than purchaser motivation shall be the test for determining whether the registered mark has become the generic name of goods or services on or in connection with which it has been used.

§ 1065   Incontestability of right to use mark under certain conditions [Section 15]

Except on a ground for which application to cancel may be filed at any time under paragraphs (3) and (5) of section 14 [§ 1064] of this Act, and except to the extent, if any, to which the use of a mark registered on the principal register infringes a valid right acquired under the law of any State or Territory by use of a mark or trade name continuing from a date prior to the date of registration under this Act of such registered mark, the right of the registrant to use such registered mark in commerce for the goods or services on or in connection with which such registered mark has been in continuous use for five consecutive years subsequent to the date of such registration and is still in use in commerce, shall be incontestable: *Provided,* That—

(1) there has been no final decision adverse to registrant's claim of ownership of such mark for such goods or services, or to registrant's right to register the same or to keep the same on the register; and

(2) there is no proceeding involving said rights pending in the Patent and Trademark Office or in a court and not finally disposed of; and

(3) an affidavit is filed with the Commissioner within one year after the expiration of any such five-year period setting forth those goods or services stated in the registration on or in connection with which such mark has been in continuous use for such five consecutive years and is still in use in commerce, and the other matters specified in paragraphs (1) and (2) of this section; and

(4) no incontestable right shall be acquired in a mark which is the generic name for the goods or services or a portion thereof, for which it is registered.

Subject to the conditions above specified in this section, the incontestable right with reference to a mark registered under this Act shall apply to a mark registered under the Act of March 3, 1881, of the Act of February 29, 1905, upon the filing of the required affidavit with the Commissioner within one year after the expiration of any period of five consecutive years after the date of publication of a mark under the provisions of subsection (c) of section 12 [§ 1062] of this Act.

The Commissioner shall notify any registrant who files the above-prescribed affidavit of the filing thereof.

§ 1091 Marks registrable on supplemental register; application and proceedings for registration; nature of mark; mark used in foreign commerce [Section 23]

(a) In addition to the principal register, the Commissioner shall keep a continuation of the register provided in paragraph (b) of section 1 of the Act of March 19, 1920, entitled "An Act to give effect to certain provisions of the convention for the protection of trademarks and commercial names, made and signed in the city of Buenos Aires, in the Argentine Republic, August 20, 1910, and for other purposes," to be called the supplemental register. All marks capable of distinguishing applicant's goods or services and not registrable on the principal register herein provided, except those declared to be unregistrable under subsections (a), (b), (c), and (d) and (e)(3) of section 2 [§ 1052] of this Act, which are in lawful use in commerce by the owner

thereof, on or in connection with any goods or services may be registered on the supplemental register upon the payment of the prescribed fee and compliance with the provisions of subsections (a) and (e) of section 1 [§ 1051] so far as they are applicable. Nothing in this section shall prevent the registration on the supplemental register of a mark, capable of distinguishing the applicant's goods or services and not registrable on the principal register under this Act, that is declared to be unregistrable under section 2(e)(3), if such mark has been in lawful use in commerce by the owner thereof, on or in connection with any goods or services, since before the date of the enactment of the North American Free Trade Agreement Implementation Act.

(b) Upon the filing of an application for registration on the supplemental register and payment of the prescribed fee the Commissioner shall refer the application to the examiner in charge of the registration of marks, who shall cause an examination to be made and if on such examination it shall appear that the applicant is entitled to registration, the registration shall be granted. If the applicant is found not entitled to registration the provisions of subsection (b) of section 12 [§ 1062] of this Act shall apply.

(c) For the purposes of registration on the supplemental register, a mark may consist of any trademark, symbol, label, package, configuration of goods, name, word, slogan, phrase, surname, geographical name, numeral, device, any matter that as a whole is not functional, or any combination of any of the foregoing, but such mark must be capable of distinguishing the applicant's goods or services.

§ 1111 Notice of registration; display with mark; recovery of profits and damages in infringement suit [Section 29]

Notwithstanding the provisions of section 22 [§ 1072] hereof, a registrant of a mark registered in the Patent and Trademark Office may give notice that his mark is registered by displaying with the mark the words "Registered in U.S. Patent and Trademark Office" or "Reg. U.S. Pat. & Tm. Off." or the letter R enclosed within a circle, thus ®; and in any suit for infringement under this Act by such a registrant failing to give such notice of registration, no profits and no damages shall be recovered under the provisions of this Act unless the defendant had actual notice of the registration.

§ 1115 Registration on principal register as evidence of exclusive right to use mark; defenses [Section 33]

(a) Any registration issued under the Act of March 3, 1881, or the Act of February 20, 1905, or of a mark registered on the principal register provided by this Act and owned by a party to an action shall be admissible in evidence and shall be prima facie evidence of the validity of the registered mark and of the registration of the mark, of the registrant's ownership of the mark, and of the registrant's exclusive right to use the registered mark in commerce on or in connection with the goods or services specified in the registration subject to any conditions or limitations stated therein, but shall not preclude another person from proving any legal or equitable defense or defect, including those set forth in subsection (b), which might have been asserted if such mark had not been registered.

(b) To the extent that the right to use the registered mark has become incontestable under section 15 [§ 1065], the registration shall be conclusive evidence of the validity of the registered mark and of the registration of the mark, of the registrant's ownership of the mark, and of the registrant's exclusive right to use the registered mark in commerce. Such conclusive evidence shall relate to the exclusive right to use the mark on or in connection with the goods or services specified in the affidavit filed under the provisions of section 15 [§ 1065], or in the renewal application filed under the provisions of section 9 [§ 1059] if the goods or services specified in the renewal are fewer in number, subject to any conditions or limitations in the registration or in such affidavit or renewal application. Such conclusive evidence of the right to use the registered mark shall be subject to proof of infringement as defined in section 32 [§ 1114], and shall be subject to the following defenses or defects:

(1) That the registration or the incontestable right to use the mark was obtained fraudulently; or

(2) That the mark has been abandoned by the registrant; or

(3) That the registered mark is being used, by or with the permission of the registrant or a person in privity with the registrant, so as to misrepresent the source of the goods or services on or in connection with which the mark is used; or

(4) That the use of the name, term, or device charged to be an infringement is a use, otherwise than as a mark, of the party's individual name in his own business, or of the individual name of anyone in privity with such party, or of a term or device which is descriptive of and used fairly and in good faith only to describe the goods or services of such party, or their geographic origin; or

(5) That the mark whose use by a party is charged as an infringement was adopted without knowledge of the registrant's prior use and has been continuously used by such party or those in privity with him from a date prior to (A) the date of constructive use of the mark established pursuant to section 7(c) [§ 1057(c)], (B) the registration of the mark under this Act if the applicant for registration is filed before the effective date of the trademark Law Revision Act of 1988, or (C) publication of the registered mark under subsection (c) of section 12 [§1062] of this Act: *Provided, however,* That this defense of defect shall apply only for the area in which such continuous prior use is proved; or

(6) That the mark whose use is charged as an infringement was registered and used prior to the registration under this Act or publication under subsection (c) of section 12 [§1062] of this Act of the registered mark of the registrant, and not abandoned: *Provided, however,* That this defense or defect shall apply only for the area in which the mark was used prior to such registration or such publication of the registrant's mark; or

(7) That the mark has been or is being used to violate the antitrust laws of the United States; or

(8) That the mark is functional; or

(9) That equitable principles, including laches, estoppel, and acquiescence are applicable.

§ 1125   False designations of origin, false descriptions, and dilution [Section 43]

(a) (1) Any person who, on or in connection with any goods or services, or any container for goods, uses in commerce any word, term, name, symbol, or device, or any combination thereof, or any false designation of origin, false or misleading description of fact, or false or misleading representation of fact, which—

>   (A) is likely to cause confusion, or to cause mistake, or to deceive as to the affiliation, connection, or association of such person with another person, or as to the origin, sponsorship, or approval of his or her goods, services, or commercial activities by another person, or

>   (B) in commercial advertising or promotion, misrepresents the nature, characteristics, qualities, or geographic origin of his or her or another person's goods, services, or commercial activities,

shall be liable in a civil action by any person who believes that he or she is or is likely to be damaged by such act.

(2) As used in this subsection, the term "any person" includes any State, instrumentality of a State or employee of a State or instrumentality of a State acting in his or her official capacity. Any State, and any such instrumentality, officer, or employee, shall be subject to the provisions of this Act in the same manner and to the same extent as any nongovernmental entity.

(3) In a civil action for trade dress infringement under this Act for trade dress not registered on the principal register, the person who asserts trade dress protection has the burden of proving that the matter sought to be protected is not functional.

(b) Any goods marked or labeled in contravention of the provisions of this section shall not be imported into the United States or admitted to entry at any customhouse of the United States. The owner, importer, or consignee of goods refused entry at any customhouse under this section may have recourse by protest or appeal that is given under the customs revenue laws or may have the remedy given by this Act in cases involving goods refused entry or seized.

(c) (1) The owner of a famous mark shall be entitled, subject to the principles of equity and upon such terms as the court deems reasonable, to any injunction against another person's commercial use in commerce of a mark or trade name, if such use begins after the mark has become famous and causes dilution of the distinctive quality of the famous mark, and to obtain such other relief as is provided in this subsection. In determining whether a mark is distinctive and famous, a court may consider factors such as, but not limited to—

>   (A) the degree of inherent or acquired distinctiveness of the mark;

>   (B) the duration and extent of use of the mark in connection with the goods or services with which the mark is used;

>   (C) the duration and extent of advertising and publicity of the mark;

>   (D) the geographical extent of the trading area in which the mark is used;

>   (E) the channels of trade for the goods or services with which the mark is used;

>   (F) the degree of recognition of the mark in the trading areas and channels of trade of the mark's owner and the person against whom the injunction is sought;

>   (G) the nature and extent of use of the same or similar marks by third parties; and

>   (H) whether the mark was registered under the Act of March 3, 1881, or the Act of February 20, 1905, or on the principal register.

(2) In an action brought under this subsection, the owner of a famous mark shall be entitled only to injunctive relief as set forth in section 34 unless the person against whom the injunction is sought willfully intended to trade on the owner's reputation or to cause dilution of the famous mark. If such willful intent is proven, the owner of a famous mark shall also be entitled to the remedies set forth in sections 35(a)

and 36, subject to the discretion of the court and the principles of equity.

(3) The ownership by a person of a valid registration under the Act of March 3, 1881, or the Act of February 20, 1905, or on the principal register shall be a complete bar to an action against that person, with respect to that mark, that is brought by another person under the common law or statute of a State and that seeks to prevent dilution of the distinctiveness of a mark, label, or form of advertisement.

(4) The following shall not be actionable under this section:

(A) Fair use of a famous mark by another person in comparative commercial advertising or promotion to identify the competing goods or services of the owner of the famous mark.

(B) Noncommercial use of a mark.

(C) All forms of news reporting and news commentary.

§ 1127   Construction and definitions; intent of chapter [Section 45]

In the construction of this Act, unless the contrary is plainly apparent from the context—

The United States includes and embraces all territory which is under its jurisdiction and control.

The word "commerce" means all commerce which may lawfully be regulated by Congress.

The term "principal register" refers to the register provided for by sections 1 through 22 hereof [§§ 1051–1072], and the term "supplemental register" refers to the register provided for by sections 23 through 28 thereof [§§ 1091–1096].

The term "person" and any other word or term used to designate the applicant or other entitled to a benefit or privilege or rendered liable under the provisions of this Act includes a juristic person as well as a natural person. The term "juristic person" includes a firm, corporation, union, association, or other organization capable of suing and being sued in a court of law.

The term "person" also includes the United States, any agency or instrumentality thereof, or any individual, firm, or corporation acting for the United States and with the authorization and consent of the United States. The United States, any agency or instrumentality thereof, and any individual, firm, or corporation acting for the United States and with the authoriztion and consent of the United States, shall be subject to the provisions of this Act in the same manner and to the same extent as any nongovernmental entity.

The term "person" also includes any State, any instrumentality of a State, and any officer or employee of a State or instrumentality of a State acting in his or her official capacity. Any State, and any such instrumentality, officer, or employee, shall be subject to the provisions of this Act in the same manner and to the same extent as any nongovernmental entity.

The terms "applicant" and "registrant" embrace the legal representatives, predecessors, successors and assigns of such applicant or registrant.

The term "Commissioner" means the Commissioner of Patents and Trademarks.

The term "related company" means any person whose use of a mark is controlled by the owner of the mark with respect to the nature and quality of the goods or services on or in connection with which the mark is used.

The terms "trade name" and "commercial name" mean any name used by a person to identify his or her business or vocation.

The term "trademark" includes any word, name, symbol, or device, or any combination thereof—

(1) used by a person, or

(2) which a person has a bona fide intention to use in commerce and applies to register on the principal register established by this Act,

to identify and distinguish his or her goods, including a major product, from those manufactured or sold by others and to indicate the source of the goods, even if that source is unknown.

The term "service mark" means any word, name, symbol, or device, or any combination thereof—

(1) used by a person, or

(2) which a person has a bona fide intention to use in commerce and applies to register on the principal register established by this Act,

to identify and distinguish the services of one person, including a unique service, from the services of others and to indicate the source of the services, even if that source is unknown. Titles, character names, and other distinctive features of radio or television programs may be registered as service marks notwithstanding that they, or the programs, may advertise the goods of the sponsor.

The term "certification mark" means any word, name, symbol, or device, or any combination thereof—

(1) used by a person other than its owner, or

(2) which its owner has a bona fide intention to permit a person other than the owner to use in commerce and files an application to register on the principal register established by this Act,

to certify regional or other origin, material, mode of manufacture, quality, accuracy, or other characteristics of such person's goods or services or that the work or labor on the goods or services was performed by members of a union or other organization.

The term "collective mark" means a trademark or service mark—

(1) used by the members of a cooperative, an association, or other collective group or organization, or

(2) which such cooperative, association, or other collective group or organization has a bona fide intention to use in commerce and applies to register on the principal register established by this Act,

and includes marks indicating membership in a union, an association, or other organization.

The term "mark" includes any trademark, service mark, collective mark, or certification mark.

The term "use in commerce" means the bona fide use of a mark in the ordinary course of trade, and not made merely to reserve a right in a mark. For purposes of this Act, a mark shall be deemed to be in use in commerce—

(1) on goods when—

(A) it is placed in any manner on the goods or their containers or the displays associated therewith or on the tags or labels affixed thereto, or if the nature of the goods makes such placement impracticable, then on documents associated with the goods or their sale, and

(B) the goods are sold or transported in commerce, and

(2) on services when it is used or displayed in the sale or advertising of services and the services are rendered in commerce, or the services are rendered in more than one State or in the United States and a foreign country and the person rendering the services is engaged in commerce in connection with the services.

A mark shall be deemed to be "abandoned" when either of the following occurs:

(1) When its use has been discontinued with intent not to resume such use. Intent not to resume may be inferred from circumstances. Nonuse for 3 consecutive years shall be prima facie evidence of abandonment. "Use" of a mark means the bona fide use of that mark made in the ordinary course of trade, and not made merely to reserve a right in a mark.

(2) When any course of conduct of the owner, including acts of omission as well as commission, causes the mark to become the generic name for the goods or services on or in connection with which it is used or otherwise to lose its significance as a mark. Purchaser motivation shall not be a test for determining abandonment under this paragraph.

The term "dilution" means the lessening of the capacity of a famous mark to identify and distinguish goods or services, regardless of the presence or absence of—

(1) competition between the owner of the famous mark and other parties, or

(2) likelihood of confusion, mistake, or deception.

The term "colorable imitation" includes any mark which so resembles a registered mark as to be likely to cause confusion or mistake or to deceive.

The term "registered mark" means a mark registered in the United States Patent and Trademark Office under this Act or under the Act of March 3, 1881, or the Act of February 20, 1905, or the Act of March 19, 1920. The phrase "marks registered in the Patent and Trademark Office" means registered marks.

The term "Act of March 3, 1881," "Act of February 20, 1905," or "Act of March 19, 1920," means the respective Act as amended.

A "counterfeit" is a spurious mark which is identical with, or substantially indistinguishable from, a registered mark.

Words used in the singular include the plural and vice versa.

The intent of this Act is to regulate commerce within the control of Congress by making actionable the deceptive and misleading use of marks in such commerce; to protect registered marks used in such commerce from interference by State, or territorial legislation; to protect persons engaged in such commerce against unfair competition; to prevent fraud and deception in such commerce by the use of reproductions, copies, counterfeits, or colorable imitations of registered marks; and to provide rights and remedies stipulated by treaties and conventions respecting trademarks, trade names, and unfair competition entered into between the United States and foreign nations.

COPYRIGHTS:
TITLE 17 *UNITED STATES CODE*

§ 101 Definitions

As used in this title, the following terms and their variant forms mean the following:

An "anonymous work" is a work on the copies or phonorecords of which no natural person is identified as author.

An "architectural work" is the design of a building as embodied in any tangible medium of expression, including a building, architectural plans, or drawings. The work includes the overall form as well as the arrangement and composition of spaces and elements in the design, but does not include individual standard features.

"Audiovisual works" are works that consist of a series of related images which are intrinsically intended to be shown by the use of machines or devices such as projectors, viewers, or electronic equipment, together with accompanying sounds, if any, regardless of the nature of the material objects, such as films or tapes, in which the works are embodied.

The "Berne Convention" is the Convention for the Protection of Literary and Artistic Works, signed at Berne, Switzerland, on September 9, 1886, and all acts, protocols, and revisions thereto.

The "best edition" of a work is the edition, published in the United States at any time before the date of deposit, that the Library of Congress determines to be most suitable for its purposes.

A person's "children" are that person's immediate offspring, whether legitimate or not, and any children legally adopted by that person.

A "collective work" is a work, such as a periodical issue, anthology, or encyclopedia, in which a number of contributions, constituting separate and independent works in themselves, are assembled into a collective whole.

A "compilation" is a work formed by the collection and assembling of preexisting materials or of data that are selected, coordinated, or arranged in such a way that the resulting work as a whole constitutes an original work of authorship. The term "compilation" includes collective works.

A "computer program" is a set of statements or instructions to be used directly or indirectly in a computer in order to bring about a certain result.

"Copies" are material objects, other than phonorecords, in which a work is fixed by any method now known or later developed, and from which the work can be perceived, reproduced, or otherwise communicated, either directly or with the aid of a machine or device. The term "copies" includes the material object, other than a phonorecord, in which the work is first fixed.

"Copyright owner", with respect to any one of the exclusive rights comprised in a copyright, refers to the owner of that particular right.

For purposes of section 411, a work is a "United States work" only if—

(1) in the case of a published work, the work is first published—

(A) in the United States;

(B) simultaneously in the United States and another treaty party or parties, whose law grants a term of copyright protection that is the same as or longer than the term provided in the United States;

(C) simultaneously in the United States and a foreign nation that is not a treaty party; or

(D) in a foreign nation that is not a treaty party, and all of the authors of the work are nationals, domiciliaries, or habitual residents of, or in the case of an audiovisual work legal entities with headquarters in, the United States;

(2) in the case of an unpublished work, all the authors of the work are nationals, domiciliaries, or habitual residents of the United States, or, in the case of an unpublished audiovisual work, all the authors are legal entities with headquarters in the United States; or

(3) in the case of a pictorial, graphic, or sculptural work incorporated in a building or structure, the building or structure is located in the United States.

A work is "created" when it is fixed in a copy or phonorecord for the first time; where a work is prepared over a period of time, the portion of it that has been fixed at any particular time constitutes the work as of that time, and where the work has been prepared in different versions, each version constitutes a separate work.

A "derivative work" is a work based upon one or more preexisting works, such as a translation, musical arrangement, dramatization, fictionalization, motion picture version, sound recording, art reproduction, abridgment, condensation, or any other form in which a work may be recast, transformed, or adapted. A work consisting of editorial revisions, annotations, elaborations, or other modifications which, as a whole, represent an original work of authorship, is a "derivative work".

A "device", "machine", or "process" is one now known or later developed.

A "digital transmission" is a transmission in whole or in part in a digital or other non-analog format.

To "display" a work means to show a copy of it, either directly or by means of a film, slide, television image, or any other device or process or, in the case of a motion picture or other audiovisual work, to show individual images nonsequentially.

An "establishment" is a store, shop, or any similar place of business open to the general public for the primary purpose of selling goods or services in which the majority of the gross square feet of space that is nonresidential is used for that purpose, and in which nondramatic musical works are performed publicly.

A "food service or drinking establishment" is a restaurant, inn, bar, tavern, or any other similar place of business in which the public or patrons assemble for the primary purpose of being served food or drink, in which the majority of the gross square feet of space that is nonresidential is used for that purpose, and in which nondramatic musical works are performed publicly.

The term "financial gain" includes receipt, or expectation of receipt, of anything of value, including the receipt of other copyrighted works.

A work is "fixed" in a tangible medium of expression when its embodiment in a copy or phonorecord,
by or under the authority of the author, is sufficiently permanent or stable to permit it to be perceived, reproduced, or otherwise communicated for a period of more than transitory duration. A work consisting of sounds, images, or both, that are being transmitted, is "fixed" for purposes of this title if a fixation of the work is being made simultaneously with its transmission.

The "Geneva Phonograms Convention" is the Convention for the Protection of producers of Phonograms Against Unauthorized Duplication of Their Phonograms, concluded at Geneva, Switzerland, on October 29, 1971.

The "gross square feet of space" of an establishment means the entire interior space of that establishment, and any adjoining outdoor space used to serve patrons, whether on a seasonal basis or otherwise.

The terms "including" and "such as" are illustrative and not limitative.

An "international agreement" is—

(1) the Universal Copyright Convention;

(2) the Geneva Phonograms Convention;

(3) the Berne Convention;

(4) the WTO Agreement;

(5) the WIPO Copyright Treaty;

(6) The WIPO Performances and Phonograms Treaty; and

(7) any other copyright treaty to which the United States is a party.

A "joint work" is a work prepared by two or more authors with the intention that their contributions be merged into inseparable or interdependent parts of a unitary whole.

"Literary works" are works, other than audiovisual works, expressed in words, numbers, or other verbal or numerical symbols or indicia, regardless of the nature of the material objects, such as books, periodicals, manuscripts, phonorecords, film, tapes, disks, or cards in which they are embodied.

"Motion pictures" are audiovisual works consisting of a series of related images which, when shown in succession, impart an impression of motion, together with accompanying sounds, if any.

To "perform" a work means to recite, render, play, dance, or act it, either directly of by means of any device or process or, in the case of a motion picture or other audiovisual work, to show its images in any sequence or to make the sounds accompanying it audible.

A "performing rights society" is an association, corporation, or other entity that licenses the public performance of nondramatic musical works on behalf of copyright owners of such works, such as the American Society of Composers, Authors and Publishers (ASCAP), Broadcast Music, Inc. (BMI), and SESAC, Inc.

"Phonorecords" are material objects in which sounds, other than those accompanying a motion picture or other audiovisual work, are fixed by any method now known or later developed, and from which the sounds can be perceived, reproduced, or otherwise communicated, either directly or with the aid of a machine or device. The term "phonorecords" includes the material object in which the sounds are first fixed.

"Pictorial, graphic, and sculptural works" include two-dimensional and three-dimensional works of fine, graphic, and applied art, photographs, prints and art reproductions, maps, globes, charts, diagrams, models, and technical drawings, including architectural plans. Such works shall include works of artistic craftsmanship insofar as their form but not their mechanical or utilitarian aspects are concerned; the design of a useful article, as defined in this section, shall be considered a pictorial, graphic, or sculptural work only if, and only to the extent that, such design incorporates pictorial, graphic, or sculptural features that can be identified separately from, and are capable of existing independently of, the utilitarian aspects of the article.

A "proprietor" is an individual, corporation, partnership, or other entity, as the case may be, that owns an establishment or a food service or drinking establishment, except that no owner or operator of a radio or television station licensed by the Federal Communications Commission, cable system or satellite carrier, cable or satellite carrier service or programmer, provider of online services or network access or the operator of facilities therefor, telecommunications company, or any other such audio or audiovisual service or programmer now known or as may be developed in the future, commercial subscription music service, or owner or operator of any other transmission service, shall under any circumstances be deemed to be a proprietor.

A "pseudonymous work" is a work on the copies or phonorecords of which the author is identified under a fictitious name.

"Publication" is the distribution of copies or phonorecords of a work to the public by sale or other transfer of ownership, or by rental, lease, or lending. The offering to distribute copies or phonorecords to a group of persons for purposes of further distribution, public performance, or public display, constitutes publication. A public performance or display of a work does not of itself constitute publication.

To perform or display a work "publicly" means—

(1) to perform or display it at a place open to the public or at any place where a substantial number of persons outside of a normal circle of a family and its social acquaintances is gathered; or

(2) to transmit or otherwise communicate a performance or display of the work to a place specified by clause (1) or to the public, by means of any device or process, whether the members of the public capable of receiving the performance or display receive it in the same place or in separate places and at the same time or at different times.

"Registration", for purposes of sections 205(c)(2), 405, 406, 410(d), 411, 412, and 506(e), means a registration of a claim in the original or renewed and extended term of copyright.

"Sound recordings" are works that result from the fixation of a series of musical, spoken, or other sounds, but not including the sounds accompanying a motion picture or other audiovisual work, regardless of the nature of the material objects, such as disks, tapes, or other phonorecords, in which they are embodied.

"State" includes the District of Columbia and the Commonwealth of Puerto Rico, and any territories to which this title is made applicable by an Act of Congress.

A "transfer of copyright ownership" is an assignment, mortgage, exclusive license, or any other conveyance, alienation, or hypothecation of a copyright or of any of the exclusive rights comprised in a copyright, whether or not it is limited in time or place of effect, but not including a nonexclusive license.

A "transmission program" is a body of material that, as an aggregate, has been produced for the sole purpose of transmission to the public in sequence and as a unit.

To "transmit" a performance or display is to communicate it by any device or process whereby images or sounds are received beyond the place from which they are sent.

A "treaty party" is a country or intergovernmental organization other than the United States that is a party to an international agreement.

The "United States", when used in a geographical sense, comprises the several States, the District of Columbia and the Commonwealth of Puerto Rico, and the organized territories under the jurisdiction of the United States Government.

A "useful article" is an article having an intrinsic utilitarian function that is not merely to portray the appearance of the article or to convey information. An article that is normally a part of a useful article is considered a "useful article".

The author's "widow" or "widower" is the author's surviving spouse under the law of the author's domicile at the time of his or her death, whether or not the spouse has later remarried.

The "WIPO Copyright Treaty" is the WIPO Copyright Treaty concluded at Geneva, Switzerland, on December 20, 1996.

The "WIPO Performances and Phonograms Treaty" is the WIPO Performances and Phonograms Treaty concluded at Geneva, Switzerland, on December 20, 1996.

A "work of visual art" is—

(1) a painting, drawing, print, or sculpture, existing in a single copy, in a limited edition of 200 copies or fewer that are signed and consecutively numbered by the author, or, in the case of a sculpture, in multiple case, carved, or fabricated sculptures of 200 or fewer that are consec-

utively numbered by the author and bear the signature or other identifying mark of the author; or

(2) a still photographic image produced for exhibition purposes only, existing in a single copy that is signed by the author, or in a limited edition of 200 copies or fewer that are signed and consecutively numbered by the author.

A work of visual art does not include—

(A) (i) any poster, map, chart, technical drawing, diagram, model, applied art, motion picture or other audiovisual work, book, magazine, newspaper, periodical, data base, electronic information service, electronic publication, or similar publication;

(ii) any merchandising item or advertising, promotional, descriptive, covering, or packaging material or container;

(iii) any portion or part of any item described in clause (i) or (ii);

(B) any work made for hire; or

(C) any work not subject to copyright protection under this title.

A "work of the United States Government" is a work prepared by an officer or employee of the United States Government as part of that person's official duties.

A "work made for hire" is—

(1) a work prepared by an employee within the scope of his or her employment; or

(2) a work specially ordered or commissioned for use as a contribution to a collective work, as a part of a motion picture or other audiovisual work, as a translation, as a supplementary work, as a compilation, as an instructional text, as a test, as answer material for a test, or as an atlas, if the parties expressly agree in a written instrument signed by them that the work shall be considered a work made for hire. For the purpose of the foregoing sentence, a "supplementary work" is a work prepared for publication as a secondary adjunct to a work by another author for the purpose of introducing, concluding, illustrating, explaining, revising,

commenting upon, or assisting in the use of the other work, such as forewords, afterwords, pictorial illustrations, maps, charts, tables, editorial notes, musical arrangements, answer material for tests, bibliographies, appendixes, and indexes, and an "instructional text" is a literary, pictorial, or graphic work prepared for publication and with the purpose of use in systematic instructional activities.

The terms "WTO Agreement" and "WTO member country" have the meanings given those terms in paragraphs (9) and (10), respectively, of section 2 of the Uruguay Round Agreements Act.

§ 102 Subject matter of copyright: In general

(a) Copyright protection subsists, in accordance with this title, in original works of authorship fixed in any tangible medium of expression, now known or later developed, from which they can be perceived, reproduced, or otherwise communicated, either directly or with the aid of a machine or device. Works of authorship include the following categories:

(1) literary works;

(2) musical works, including any accompanying words;

(3) dramatic works, including any accompanying music;

(4) pantomimes and choreographic works;

(5) pictorial, graphic, and sculptural works;

(6) motion pictures and other audiovisual works;

(7) sound recordings; and

(8) architectural works.

(b) In no case does copyright protection for an original work of authorship extend to any idea, procedure, process, system, method of operation, concept, principle, or discovery, regardless of the form in which it is described, explained, illustrated, or embodied in such work.

§ 103 Subject matter of copyright: Compilations and derivative works

(a) The subject matter of copyright as specified by section 102 includes compilations and derivative works, but protection for a work employing preexisting material in which copyright subsists does not extend to any part of the work in which such material has been used unlawfully.

(b) The copyright in a compilation or derivative work extends only to the material contributed by the author of such work, as distinguished from the preexisting material employed in the work, and does not imply any exclusive right in the preexisting material. The copyright in such work is independent of, and does not affect or enlarge the scope, duration, ownership, or subsistence of, any copyright protection in the preexisting material.

§ 106 Exclusive rights in copyrighted works

Subject to sections 107 through 120, the owner of copyright under this title has the exclusive rights to do and to authorize any of the following:

(1) to reproduce the copyrighted work in copies or phonorecords;

(2) to prepare derivative works based upon the copyrighted work;

(3) to distribute copies or phonorecords of the copyrighted work to the public by sale or other transfer of ownership, or by rental, lease, or lending;

(4) in the case of literary, musical, dramatic, and choreographic works, pantomimes, and motion pictures and other audiovisual works, to perform the copyrighted work publicly;

(5) in the case of literary, musical, dramatic, and choreographic works, pantomimes, and pictorial, graphic, or sculptural works, including the individual images of a motion picture or other audiovisual work, to display the copyrighted work publicly; and

(6) in the case of sound recordings, to perform the copyrighted work publicly by means of a digital audio transmission.

§ 106A Rights of certain authors to attribution and integrity

(a) *Rights of attribution and integrity.*—Subject to section 107 and independent of the exclusive rights provided in section 106, the author of a work of visual art—

(1) shall have the right—

(A) to claim authorship of that work, and

(B) to prevent the use of his or her name as the author of any work of visual art which he or she did not create;

(2) shall have the right to prevent the use of his or her name as the author of the work of visual art in the event of a distortion, mutilation, or other modification of the work which would be prejudicial to his or her honor or reputation; and

(3) subject to the limitations set forth in section 113(d), shall have the right—

(A) to prevent any intentional distortion, mutilation, or other modification of that work which would be prejudicial to his or her honor or reputation, and any intentional distortion, mutilation, or modification of that work is a violation of that right, and

(B) to prevent any destruction of a work of recognized stature, and any intentional or grossly negligent destruction of that work is a violation of that right.

§ 107 Limitations on exclusive rights: Fair use

Notwithstanding the provisions of sections 106 and 106A, the fair use of a copyrighted work, including such use by reproduction in copies or phonorecords or by any other means specified by that section, for purposes such as criticism, comment, news reporting, teaching (including multiple copies for classroom use), scholarship, or research, is not an infringement of copyright. In determining whether the use made of a work in any particular case is a fair used the factors to be considered shall include—

(1) the purpose and character of the use, including whether such use is of a commercial nature or is for nonprofit educational purposes;

(2) the nature of the copyrighted work;

(3) the amount and substantiality of the portion used in relation to the copyrighted work as a whole; and

(4) the effect of the use upon the potential market for or value of the copyrighted work.

The fact that a work is unpublished shall not itself bar a finding of fair use if such finding is made upon consideration of all the above factors.

§ 110 Limitations on exclusive rights: Exemption of certain performances and displays

Notwithstanding the provisions of section 106, the following are not infringements of copyright:

(1) performance or display of a work by instructors or pupils in the course of face-to-face teaching activities of a nonprofit educational institution, in a classroom or similar place devoted to instruction, unless, in the case of a motion picture or other audiovisual work, the performance, ro the display of individual images, is given by means of a copy that was not lawfully made under this title, and that the person responsible for the performance knew or had reason to believe was not lawfully made;

(2) performance of a nondramatic literary or musical work or display of a work, by or in the course of a transmission, if—

(A) the performance or display is a regular part of the systematic instructional activities of a governmental body or a nonprofit educational institution; and

(B) the performance or display is directly related and of material assistance to the teaching content of the transmission; and

(C) the transmission is made primarily for—

(i) reception in classrooms or similar places normally devoted to instruction, or

(ii) reception by persons to whom the transmission is directed because their disabilities or other special circumstances prevent their attendance in classrooms or similar places normally devoted to instruction, or

(iii) reception by officers or employees of governmental bodies as a part of their official duties or employment;

(3) performance of a nondramatic literary or musical work or of a dramatico-musical work of a religious nature, or display of a work, in the course of services at a place of worship or other religious assembly;

(4) performance of a nondramatic literary or musical work otherwise than in a transmission to the public, without any purpose of direct or indirect commercial advantage and without payment of any fee or other compensation for the performance to any of its performers, promoters, or organizers, if—

(A) there is no direct or indirect admission charge; or

(B) the proceeds, after deducting the reasonable costs of producing the performance, are used exclusively for educational, religious, or charitable purposes and not for private financial gain, except where the copyright owner has served notice of objection to the performance under the following conditions;

(i) the notice shall be in writing and signed by the copyright owner or such owner's duly authorized agent; and

(ii) the notice shall be served on the person responsible for the performance at least seven days before the date of the performance, and shall state the reasons for the objection; and

(iii) the notice shall comply, in form, content, and manner of service, with requirements that the Register of Copyrights shall prescribe by regulation;

(5) (A) except as provided in subparagraph (B), communication of a transmission embody-

ing a performance or display of a work by the public reception of the transmission on a single receiving apparatus of a kind commonly used in private homes, unless—

(A) a direct charge is made to see or hear the transmission; or

(B) the transmission thus received is further transmitted to the public;

(B) communication by an establishment of a transmission or retransmission embodying a performance or display of a nondramatic musical work intended to be received by the general public, originated by a radio or television broadcast station licensed as such by the Federal Communications Commission, or, if an audiovisual transmission, by a cable system or satellite carrier, if—

(i) in the case of an establishment other than a food service or drinking establishment, either the establishment in which the communication occurs has less than 2,000 gross square feet of space (excluding space used for customer parking and for no other purpose), or the establishment in which the communication occurs has 2,000 or more gross square feet of space (excluding space used for customer parking and for no other purpose) and—

(I) if the performance is by audio means only, the performance is communicated by means of a total of not more than 6 loudspeakers, of which not more than 4 loudspeakers are located in any 1 room or adjoining outdoor space; or

(II) if the performance or display is by audiovisual means, any visual portion of the performance or display is communicated by means of a total of not more than 4 audiovisual devices, of which not more than 1 audiovisual device is located in any 1 room, and no such audiovisual device has a diagonal screen size greater than 55 inches, and any audio portion of the performance or display is communicated by means of a total of not more than 6 loudspeakers, of which not more than 4 loudspeakers are located in any 1 room or adjoining outdoor space;

(ii) in the case of a food service or drinking establishment, either the establishment in which the communication occurs has less than 3,750 gross square feet of space (excluding space used for customer parking and for no other purpose), or the establishment in which the communication occurs has 3,750 gross square feet of space or more (excluding space used for customer parking and for no other purpose) and—

(I) if the performance is by audio means only, the performance is communicated by means of a total of not more than 6 loudspeakers, of which not more than 4 loudspeakers are located in any 1 room or adjoining outdoor space; or

(II) if the performance or display is by audiovisual means, any visual portion of the performance or display is communicated by means of a total of not more than 4 audiovisual devices, of which not more than one audiovisual device is located in any 1 room, and no such audiovisual device has a diagonal screen size greater than 55 inches, and any audio portion of the performance or display is communicated by means of a total of not more than 6 loudspeakers, of which not more than 4 loudspeakers are located in any 1 room or adjoining outdoor space;

(iii) no direct charge is made to see or hear the transmission or retransmission;

(iv) the transmission or retransmission is not further transmitted beyond the establishment where it is received; and

(v) the transmission or retransmission is licensed by the copyright owner of the work so publicly performed or displayed;

(6) performance of a nondramatic musical work by a governmental body or a nonprofit agricultural or horticultural organization, in the course of an annual agricultural or horticultural fair or exhibition conducted by such body or organization; the exemption provided by this clause shall extend to any liability for copyright infringement that would otherwise be imposed on such body or organization, under doctrines of vicarious liability or related infringement, for a performance by a concessionnaire, business establishment, or other person at such fair or exhibition, but shall not excuse any such person from liability for the performance;

(7) performance of a nondramatic musical work by a vending establishment open to the public at large without any direct or indirect admission charge, where the sole purpose of the performance is to promote the retail sale of copies or phonorecords of the work, or of the audiovisual or other devices utilized in such performance, and the performance is not transmitted beyond the place where the establishment is located and is within the immediate area where the sale is occurring;

(8) performance of a nondramatic literary work, by or in the course of a transmission specifically designed for and primarily directed to blind or other handicapped persons who are unable to read normal printed material as a result of their handicap, or deaf or other handicapped persons who are unable to hear the aural signals accompanying a transmission of visual signals, if the performance is made without any purpose of direct or indirect commercial advantage and its transmission is made through the facilities of: (i) a governmental body; or (ii) a noncommercial educational broadcast station (as defined in section 397 of title 47); or (iii) a radio subcarrier authorization (as defined in 47 CFR 73.293–73.295 and 73.593–73.595); or (iv) a cable system (as defined in section 111(f)).

(9) performance on a single occasion of a dramatic literary work published at least ten years before the date of the performance, by or in the course of a transmission specifically designed for and primarily directed to blind or other handicapped persons who are unable to read normal printed material as a result of their handicap, if the performance is made without any purpose of direct or indirect commercial advantage and its transmission is made through the facilities of a radio subcarrier authorization

referred to in clause (8)(iii), *Provided,* That the provisions of this clause shall not be applicable to more than one performance of the same work by the same performers oi under the auspices of the same organization; and

(10) notwithstanding paragraph (4), the following is not an infringement of copyright: performance of a nondramatic literary or musical work in the course of a social function which is organized and promoted by a nonprofit veterans' organization or a nonprofit fraternal organization to which the general public is not invited, but not including the invitees of the organization to which the general public is not invited, but not including the invitees of the organizations, if the proceeds from the performance, after deducting the reasonable costs of producing the performance, are used exclusively for charitable purposes and not for financial gain. For purposes of this section the social functions of any college or university fraternity or sorority shall not be included unless the social function is held solely to raise funds for a specific charitable purpose.

The exemptions provided under paragraph (5) shall not be taken into account in any administrative, judicial, or other governmental proceeding to set or adjust the royalties payable to copyright owners for the public performance or display of their works. Royalties payable to copyright owners for any public performance or display of their works other than such performances or displays as are exempted under paragraph (5) shall not be diminished in any respect as a result of such exemption.

§ 117 Limitations on exclusive rights: Computer programs

(a) Making of additional copy or adaptation by owner of copy—. Notwithstanding the provisions of section 106, it is not an infringement for the owner of a copy of a computer program to make or authorize the making of another copy or adaptation of that computer program provided:

(1) that such a new copy or adaptation is created as an essential step in the utilization of the computer program in conjunction with a machine and that it is used in no other manner, or

(2) that such new copy or adaptation is for archival purposes only and that all archival copies are destroyed in the event that continued possession of the computer program should cease to be rightful.

§ 201 Ownership of copyright

(a) *Initial ownership.*—Copyright in a work protected under this title vests initially in the author or authors of the work. The authors of a joint work are coowners of copyright in the work.

(b) *Works made for hire.*—In the case of a work made for hire, the employer or other person for whom the work was prepared is considered the author for purposes of this title, and, unless the parties have expressly agreed otherwise in a written instrument signed by them, owns all of the rights comprised in the copyright.

(c) *Contributions to collective works.*—Copyright in each separate contribution to a collective work is distinct from copyright in the collective work as a whole, and vests initially in the author of the contribution. In the absence of an express transfer of the copyright or of any rights under it, the owner of copyright in the collective work is presumed to have acquired only the privilege of reproducing and distributing the contribution as part of that particular collective work, any revision of that collective work, and any later collective work in the same series.

(d) *Transfer of ownership.*—

(1) The ownership of a copyright may be transferred in whole or in part by any means of conveyance or by operation of law, and may be bequeathed by will or pass as personal property by the applicable laws of intestate succession.

(2) Any of the exclusive rights comprised in a copyright, including any subdivision of any of the rights specified by section 106, may be transferred as provided by clause (1) and owned separately. The owner of any particular exclusive right is entitled, to the extent of that right, to all of the protection and remedies accorded to the copyright owner by this title.

§ 202   Ownership of copyright as distinct from ownership of material object

Ownership of a copyright, or of any of the exclusive rights under a copyright, is distinct from ownership of any material object in which the work is embodied. Transfer of ownership of any material object, including the copy or phonorecord in which the work is first fixed, does not of itself convey any rights in the copyrighted work embodied in the object; nor, in the absence of an agreement, does transfer of ownership of a copyright or of any exclusive rights under a copyright convey property rights in any material object.

§ 204   Execution of transfers of copyright ownership

(a) A transfer of copyright ownership, other than by operation of law, is not valid unless an instrument of conveyance, or a note or memorandum of the transfer, is in writing and signed by the owner of the rights conveyed or such owner's duly authorized agent.

§ 302   Duration of copyright: Works created on or after January 1, 1978

(a) *In general.*—Copyright in a work created on or after January 1, 1978, subsists from its creation and, except as provided by the following subsections, endures for a term consisting of the life of the author and 70 years after the author's death.

(b) *Joint works.*—In the case of a joint work prepared by two or more authors who did not work for hire, the copyright endures for a term consisting of the life of the last surviving author and 70 years after such last surviving author's death.

(c) *Anonymous works, pseudonymous works, and works made for hire.*—In the case of an anonymous work, a pseudonymous work, or a work made for hire, the copyright endures for a term of 95 years from the year of its first publication, or a term of 120 years from the year of its creation, whichever expires first. If, before the end of such term, the identity of one or more of the authors of an anonymous or pseudonymous work is revealed in the records of a registration made for that work under subsections (a) or (d) of section 408, or in the records provided by this subsection, the copyright in the work endures for the term specified by subsection (a) or (b), based on the life of the author or authors whose identity has been revealed. Any person having an interest in the copyright in an anonymous or pseudonymous work may at any time record, in records to be maintained by the Copyright Office for that purpose, a statement identifying one or more authors of the work; the statement shall also identify the person filing it, the nature of that person's interest, the source of the information recorded, and the particular work affected, and shall comply in form and content with requirements that the Register of Copyrights shall prescribe by regulation.

(d) *Records relating to death of authors.*—Any person having an interest in a copyright may at any time record in the Copyright Office a statement of the date of death of the author of the copyrighted work, or a statement that the author is still living on a particular date. The statement shall identify the person filing it, the nature of that person's interest, and the source of the information recorded, and shall comply in form and content with requirements that the Register of Copyrights shall prescribe by regulation. The Register shall maintain current records of information relating to the death of authors of copyrighted works, based on such recorded statements and, to the extent the Register considers practicable, on data contained in any of the records of the Copyright Office or in other reference sources.

(e) *Presumption as to author's death.*—After a period of 95 years from the year of first publication of a work, or a period of 120 years from the year of its creation, whichever expires first, any person who obtains from the Copyright Office a certified report that the records provided by subsection (d) disclose nothing to indicate that the author of the work is living, or died less than 70 years before, is entitled to the benefits of a presumption that the author has been dead for at least 70 years. Reliance in good faith upon this presumption shall be a complete defense to any action for infringement under this title.

§ 304   Duration of copyright: Subsisting copyrights

(a) *Copyrights in their first term on January 1, 1978.*—

(1) (A) Any copyright, the first term of which is subsisting on January 1, 1978, shall endure for 28 years from the date it was originally secured.

(B) In the case of—

(i) any posthumous work or of any periodical, cyclopedic, or other composite work upon which the copyright was originally secured by the proprietor thereof, or

(ii) any work copyrighted by a corporate body (otherwise than as assignee or licensee of the individual author) or by an employer for whom such work is made for hire,

the proprietor of such copyright shall be entitled to a renewal and extension of the copyright in such work for the further term of 67 years.

(C) In the case of any other copyrighted work, including a contribution by an individual author to a periodical or to a cyclopedic or other composite work—

(i) the author of such work, if the author is still living,

(ii) the widow, widower, or children of the author, if the author is not living,

(iii) the author's executors, if such author, widow, widower, or children are not living, or

(iv) the author's next of kin, in the absence of a will of the author,

shall be entitled to a renewal and extension of the copyright in such work for a further term of 67 years.

(2) (A) At the expiration of the original term of copyright in a work specified in paragraph (1)(B) of this subsection, the copyright shall endure for a renewed and extended further term of 67 years, which—

(i) if an application to register a claim to such further term has been made to the Copyright Office within 1 year before the expiration of the original term of copyright, and the claim is registered, shall vest, upon the beginning of such further term, in the proprietor of the copyright who is entitled to claim the renewal of copyright at the time the application is made; or

(ii) if no such application is made or the claim pursuant to such application is not registered, shall vest, upon the beginning of such further term, in the person or entity that was the proprietor of the copyright as of the last day of the original term of copyright.

(B) At the expiration of the original term of copyright in a work specified in paragraph (1)(C) of this subsection, the copyright shall endure for a renewed and extended further term of 67 years, which—

(i) if an application to register a claim to such further term has been made to the Copyright Office within 1 year before the expiration of the original term of copyright, and the claim is registered, shall vest, upon the beginning of such further term, in any person who is entitled under paragraph (1)(C) to the renewal and extension of the copyright at the time the application is made; or

(ii) if no such application is made or the claim pursuant to such application is not registered, shall vest, upon the beginning of such further term, in any person entitled under paragraph (1)(C), as of the last day of the original term of copyright, to the renewal and extension of the copyright.

(3) (A) An application to register a claim to the renewed and extended term of copyright in a work may be made to the Copyright Office—

(i) within 1 year before the expiration of the original term of copyright by any person entitled under paragraph (1) (B) or (C) to such further term of 67 years; and

(ii) at any time during the renewed and extended berm by any person in whom such further term vested, under paragraph (2) (A) or (B), or by any successor or assign of such person, if the application is made in the name of such person.

(B) Such an application is not a condition of the renewal and extension of the copyright in a work for a further term of 67 years.

(4) (A) If an application to register a claim to the renewed and extended term of copyright in a work is not made within 1 year before the expiration of the original term of copyright in a work, or if the claim pursuant to such application is not registered, then a derivative work prepared under authority of a grant of a transfer or license of the copyright that is made before the expiration of the original term of copyright may continue to be used under the terms of the grant during the renewed and extended term of copyright without infringing the copyright, except that such use does not extend to the preparation during such renewed and extended term of other derivative works based upon the copyrighted work covered by such grant.

(B) If an application to register a claim to the renewed and extended term of copyright in a work is made within 1 year before its expiration, and the claim is registered, the certificate of such registration shall constitute prima facie evidence as to the validity of the copyright during its renewed and extended term and of the facts stated in the certificate. The evidentiary weight to be accorded the certificates of a registration of a renewed and extended berm of copyright made after the end of that 1-year period shall be within the discretion of the court.

(b) *Copyrights in their renewal term at the time of the effective date of the Sonny Bono Copyright Term Extension Act.*—Any copyright still in its renewal term at the time that the Sonny Bono Copyright Term Extension Act becomes effective shall have a copyright term of 95 years from the date copyright was originally secured.

(c) *Termination of transfers and licenses covering extended renewal term.*—In the case of any copyright subsisting in either its first or renewal term on January 1, 1978, other than a copyright in a work made for hire, the exclusive or nonexclusive grant of a transfer or license of the renewal copyright or any right under it, executed before January 1, 1978, by any of the persons designated by subsection (a)(1)(C) of this section, otherwise than by will, is subject to termination under the following conditions:

(1) In the case of a grant executed by a person or persons other than the author, termination of the grant may be effected by the surviving person or persons who executed it. In the case of a grant executed by one or more of the authors of the work, termination of the grant may be effected, to the extent of a particular author's share in the ownership of the renewal copyright, by the author who executed it or, if such author is dead, by the person or persons who, under clause (2) of this subsection, own and are entitled to exercise a total of more than one-half of that author's termination interest.

(2) Where an author is dead, his or her termination interest is owned, and may be exercised, as follows:

(A) the widow or widower owns the author's entire termination interest unless there are any surviving children or grandchildren of the author, in which case the widow or widower owns one-half of the author's interest;

(B) the author's surviving children, and the surviving children of any dead child of the author, own the author's entire termination interest unless there is a widow or widower, in which case the ownership of one-half of the author's interest is divided among them;

(C) the rights of the author's children and grandchildren are in all cases divided among them and exercised on a per stirpes basis according to the number of such author's children represented; the share of the children of a dead child in a termination interest can be exercised only by the action of a majority of them.

(D) in the event that the author's widow or widower, children, and grandchildren are not living, the author's executor, administrator, personal representative, or trustee shall own the author's entire termination interest.

(3) Termination of the grant may be effected at any time during a period of five years beginning at the end of fifty-six years from the date copyright was originally secured, or beginning on January 1, 1978, whichever is later.

(4) The termination shall be effected by serving an advance notice in writing upon the grantee or the grantee's successor in title. In the case of a grant executed by a person or persons other than the author, the notice shall be signed by all of those entitled to terminate the grant under clause (1) of this subsection, or by their duly authorized agents. In the case of a grant executed by one or more of the authors of the work, the notice as to any one author's share shall be signed by that author or his or her duly authorized agent or, if that author is dead, by the number and proportion of the owners of his or her termination interest required under clauses (1) and (2) of this subsection, or by their duly authorized agents.

(A) The notice shall state the effective date of the termination, which shall fall within the five-year period specified by clause (3) of this subsection, or, in the case of a termination under subsection (d), within the five-year period specified by subsection (d)(2), and the notice shall be served not less than two or more than ten years before that date. A copy of the notice shall be recorded in the Copyright Office before the effective date of termination, as a condition to its taking effect.

(B) The notice shall comply, in form, content, and manner of service, with requirements that the Register of Copyrights shall prescribe by regulation.

(5) Termination of the grant may be effected notwithstanding any agreement to the contrary, including an agreement to make a will or to make any future grant.

(6) In the case of a grant executed by a person or persons other than the author, all rights under

this title that were covered by the terminated grant revert, upon the effective date of termination, to an of those entitled, to terminate the grant under clause (1) of this subsection. In the case of a grant executed by one or more of the authors of the work, all of a particular author's rights under this title that were covered by the terminated grant revert, upon the effective date of termination, to that author or, if that author is dead, to the persons owning his or her termination interest under clause (2) of this subsection, including those owners who did not join in signing the notice of termination under clause (4) of this subsection. In all cases the reversion of rights is subject to the following limitations:

(A) A derivative work prepared under authority of the grant before its termination may continue to be utilized under the terms of the grant after its termination, but this privilege does not extend to the preparation after the termination of other derivative works based upon the copyrighted work covered by the terminated grant.

(B) The future rights that will revert upon termination of the grant become vested on the date the notice of termination has been served as provided by clause (4) of this subsection.

(C) Where the author's rights revert to two or more persons under clause (2) of this subsection, they shall vest in those persons in the proportionate shares provided by that clause. In such a case, and subject to the provisions of subclause (D) of this clause, a further grant, or agreement to make a further grant, of a particular author's share with respect to any right covered by a terminated grant is valid only if it is signed by the same number and proportion of the owners, in whom the right has vested under this clause, as are required to terminate the grant under clause (2) of this subsection. Such further grant or agreement is effective with respect to all of the persons in whom the right it covers has vested under this subclause, including those who did not join in signing it. If any person dies after rights under a terminated grant have vested in him or her, that person's legal representatives, legatees, or heirs at law represent him or her for purposes of this subclause.

(D) A further grant, or agreement to make a further grant, of any right covered by a terminated grant is valid only if it is made after the effective date of the termination. As an exception, however, an agreement for such a further grant may be made between the author or any of the persons provided by the first sentence of clause (6) of this subsection, or between the persons provided by subclause (C) of this clause, and the original grantee or such grantee's successor in title, after the notice of termination has been served as provided by clause (4) of this subsection.

(E) Termination of a grant under this subsection affects only those rights covered by the grant that arise under this title, and in no way affects rights arising under any other Federal, State, or foreign laws.

(F) Unless and until termination is effected under this subsection, the grant, if it does not provide otherwise, continues in effect for the remainder of the extended renewal term.

(d) *Termination rights provided in subsection (c) which have expired on or before the effective date of the Sonny Bono Copyright Term Extension Act.*—In the case of any copyright other than a work made for hire, subsisting in its renewal term on the effective date of the Sonny Bono Copyright Term Extension Act for which the termination right provided in subsection (c) has expired by such date, where the author or owner of the termination right has not previously exercised such termination right the exclusive or nonexclusive grant of a transfer or license of the renewal copyright or any right under it, executed before January 1, 1978, by any of the persons designated in subsection (a)(1)(C) of this section, other than by will, is subject to termination under the following conditions:

(1) The conditions specified in subsections (c) (1), (2), (4), (5), and (6) of this section apply to terminations of the last 20 years of copyright term as provided by the amendments made by the Sonny Bono Copyright Term Extension Act.

(2) Termination of the grant may be effected at any time during a period of 5 years beginning at the end of 75 years from the date copyright was originally secured.

§ 401 Notice of copyright: Visually perceptible copies

(a) *General provisions.*—Whenever a work protected under this title is published in the United States or elsewhere by authority of the copyright owner, a notice of copyright as provided by this section may be placed on publicly distributed copies from which the work can be visually perceived, either directly or with the aid of a machine or device.

(b) *Form of notice.*—If a notice appears on the copies, it shall consist of the following three elements:

(1) the symbol © (the letter C in a circle), or the word "Copyright", or the abbreviation "Copr."; and

(2) the year of first publication of the work; in the case of compilations, or derivative works incorporating previously published material, the year date of first publication of the compilation or derivative work is sufficient. The year date may be omitted where a pictorial, graphic, or sculptural work, with accompanying text matter, if any, is reproduced in or on greeting cards, postcards, stationery, jewelry, dolls, toys, or any useful articles; and

(3) the name of the owner of copyright in the work, or an abbreviation by which the name can be recognized, or a generally known alternative designation of the owner.

(c) *Position of notice.*—The notice shall be affixed to the copies in such manner and location as to give reasonable notice of the claim of copyright. The Register of Copyrights shall prescribe by regulation, as examples, specific methods of affixation and positions of the notice on various types of works that will satisfy this requirement, but these specifications shall not be considered exhaustive.

(d) *Evidentiary weight of notice.*—If a notice of copyright in the form and position specified by this section appears on the published copy or copies to which a defendant in a copyright infringement suit had access, then no weight shall be given to such a defendant's interposition of a defense based on innocent infringement in mitigation of actual or statutory damages, except as provided in the last sentence of section 504(c)(2).

§ 408 Copyright registration in general

(a) *Registration permissive.*—At any time during the subsistence of the first term of copyright in any published or unpublished work in which the copyright was secured before January 1, 1978, and during the subsistence of any copyright secured on or after that date, the owner of copyright or of any exclusive right in the work may obtain registration of the copyright claim by delivering to the Copyright Office the deposit specified by this section, together with the application and fee specified by sections 409 and 708. Such registration is not a condition of copyright protection.

(b) *Deposit for copyright registration.*—Except as provided by subsection (c), the material deposited for registration shall include—

(1) in the case of an unpublished work, one complete copy or phonorecord;

(2) in the case of a published work, two complete copies or phonorecords of the best edition;

(3) in the case of a work first published outside the United States, one complete copy or phonorecord as so published.

§ 409 Application for copyright registration

The application for copyright registration shall be made on a form prescribed by the Register of Copyrights and shall include—

(1) the name and address of the copyright claimant;

(2) in the case of a work other than an anonymous or pseudonymous work, the name and nationality or domicile of the author or authors, and, if one or more of the authors is dead, the dates of their deaths;

(3) if the work is anonymous or pseudonymous, the nationality or domicile of the author or authors;

(4) in the case of a work made for hire, a statement to this effect;

(5) if the copyright claimant is not the author, a brief statement of how the claimant obtained ownership of the copyright;

(6) the title of the work, together with any previous or alternative titles under which the work can be identified;

(7) the year in which creation of the work was completed;

(8) if the work has been published, the date and nation of its first publication;

(9) in the case of a compilation or derivative work, an identification of any preexisting work or works that it is based on or incorporated, and a brief, general statement of the additional material covered by the copyright claim being registered;

(10) in the case of a published work containing material of which copies are required by section 601 to be manufactured in the United States, the names of the persons or organizations who performed the processes specified by subsection (c) of section 601 with respect to that material, and the places where those processes were performed; and

(11) any other information regarded by the Register of Copyrights as bearing upon the preparation or identification of the work or the existence, ownership, or duration of the copyright.

If an application is submitted for the renewed and extended term provided for in section 304(a)(3)(A) and an original term registration has not been made, the Register may request information with respect to the existence, ownership, or duration of the copyright for the original term.

§ 410 Registration of claim and issuance of certificate

(a) When, after examination, the Register of Copyrights determines that, in accordance with the provisions of this title, the material deposited constitutes copyrightable subject matter and that the other legal and formal requirements of this title have been met, the Register shall register the claim and issue to the applicant a certificate of registration under the seal of the Copyright Office. The certificate shall contain the information given in the application, together with the number and effective date of the registration.

(b) In any case in which the Register of Copyrights determines that, in accordance with the provisions of this title, the material deposited does not constitute copyrightable subject matter or that the claim is invalid for any other reason, the Register shall refuse registration and shall notify the applicant in writing of the reasons for such refusal.

(c) In any judicial proceedings the certificate of a registration made before or within five years after first publication of the work shall constitute prima facie evidence of the validity of the copyright and of the facts stated in the certificate. The evidentiary weight to be accorded the certificate of a registration made thereafter shall be within the discretion of the court.

(d) The effective date of a copyright registration is the day on which an application, deposit, and fee, which are later determined by the Register of Copyrights or by a court of competent jurisdiction to be acceptable for registration, have all been received in the Copyright Office.

§ 411 Registration and infringement actions

(a) Except for an action brought for a violation of the rights of the author under section 106A(a), and subject to the provisions of subsection (b), no action for infringement of the copyright in any United States work shall be instituted until registration of the copyright claim has been made in accordance with this title. In any case, however, where the deposit, application, and fee required for registration have been delivered to the Copyright Office in proper form and registration has been refused, the applicant is entitled to institute an action for infringement if notice thereof, with a copy of the complaint, is served on the Register of Copyrights. The Register may, at his or her option, become a party to the action with respect to the issue of registrability of the copyright claim by entering an appearance within sixty days after such service, but the Register's failure to become a party shall not

deprive the court of jurisdiction to determine that issue.

(b) In the case of a work consisting of sounds, images, or both, the first fixation of which is made simultaneously with its transmission, the copyright owner may, either before or after such fixation takes place, institute an action for infringement under section 501, fully subject to the remedies provided by sections 502 through 506 and sections 509 and 510, if, in accordance with requirements that the Register of Copyrights shall prescribe by regulation, the copyright owner—

(1) serves notice upon the infringer, not less than 48 hours before such fixation, identifying the work and the specific time and source of its first transmission, and declaring an intention to secure copyright in the work; and

(2) makes registration for the work, if required by subsection (a), within three months after its first transmission.

§ 412 Registration as prerequisite to certain remedies for infringement

In any action under this title, other than an action brought for a violation of the rights of the author under section 106A(a) or an action instituted under section 411(b), no award of statutory damages or of attorney's fees, as provided by sections 504 and 505, shall be made for—

(1) any infringement of copyright in an unpublished work commenced before the effective date of its registration; or

(2) any infringement of copyright commenced after first publication of the work and before the effective date of its registration, unless such registration is made within three months after the first publication of the work.

§ 501 Infringement of copyright

(a) Anyone who violates any of the exclusive rights of the copyright owner as provided by sections 106 through 118, or of the author as provided in section 106A(a), or who imports copies or phonorecords into the United States in violation of section 602, is an infringer of the copyright or right of the author, as the case may be. For purposes of this chapter (other than Section 506), any reference to copyright shall be deemed to include the rights conferred by Section 106A(a). As used in, this subsection, the term "anyone" includes any State, any instrumentality of a State, and any officer or employee of a State or instrumentality of a State acting in his or her official capacity. Any State, and any such instrumentality, officer, or employee, shall be subject to the provisions of this title in the same manner and to the same extent as any nongovernmental entity.

(b) The legal or beneficial owner of an exclusive right under a copyright is entitled, subject to the requirements of section 411, to institute an action for any infringement of that particular right committed while he or she is the owner of it. The court may require such owner to serve written notice of the action with a copy of the complaint upon any person shown, by the records of the Copyright Office or otherwise, to have or claim an interest in the copyright, and shall require that such notice be served upon any person whose interest is likely to be affected by a decision in the case. The court may require the joinder, and shall permit the intervention, of any person having or claiming an interest in the copyright.

§ 512   Limitations on liability relating to material online

(c) Information residing on systems or networks at director of users—

(1) In general—A service provider shall not be liable for monetary relief, or, except as provided in subsection (j), for injunctive or other equitable relief, for infringement of copyright by reason of the storage at the direction of a user of material that resides on a system or network controlled or operated by or for the service provider, if the service provider—

(A) (i) does not have actual knowledge that the material or an activity using the material on the system or network is infringing;

(ii) in the absence of such actual knowledge, is not aware of facts or circumstances from which infringing activity is apparent; or

(iii) upon obtaining such knowledge or awareness, acts expeditiously to remove, or disable access to, the material;

(B) does not receive a financial benefit directly attributable to the infringing activity, in a case in which the service provider has the right and ability to control such activity; and

(C) upon notification of claimed infringement as described in paragraph (3), responds expeditiously to remove, or disable access to, the material that is claimed to be infringing or to be the subject of infringing activity.

(2) Designated agent—The limitations on liability established in this subsection apply to a service provider only if the service provider has designated an agent to receive notifications of claimed infringement described in paragraph (3), by making available through its service, including on its website in a location accessible to the public, and by providing to the Copyright Office, substantially the following information:

(A) the name, address, phone number, and electronic mail address of the agent.

(B) other contact information which the Register of Copyrights may deem appropriate.

The Register of Copyrights shall maintain a current directory of agents available to the public for inspection, including through the Internet, in both electronic and hard copy formats, and may require payment of a fee by service providers to cover the costs of maintaining the directory.

(3) Elements of notification—

(A) To be effective under this subsection, a notification of claimed infringement must be a written communication provided to the designated agent of a service provider that includes substantially the following:

(i) A physical or electronic signature of a person authorized to act on behalf of the owner of an exclusive right that is allegedly infringed.

(ii) Identification of the copyrighted work claimed to have been infringed, or, if multiple copyrighted works at a single online site are covered by a single notification, a representative list of such works at that site.

(iii) Identification of the material that is claimed to be infringing or to be the subject of infringing activity and that is to be removed or access to which is to be disabled, and information reasonably sufficient to permit the service provider to locate the material.

(iv) Information reasonably sufficient to permit the service provider to contact the complaining party, such as an address, telephone number, and, if available, an electronic mail address at which the complaining party may be contacted.

(v) A statement that the complaining party has a good faith belief that use of the material in the manner complained of is not authorized by the copyright owner, its agent, or the law.

(vi) A statement that the information in the notification is accurate, and under penalty of perjury, that the complaining

party is authorized to act on behalf of the owner of an exclusive right that is allegedly infringed.

(B) (i) Subject to clause (ii), a notification from a copyright owner or from a person authorized to act on behalf of the copyright owner that fails to comply substantially with the provisions of subparagraph (A) shall not be considered under paragraph (1)(A) in determining whether a service provider has actual knowledge or is aware of facts or circumstances from which infringing activity is apparent.

(ii) In a case in which the notification that is provided to the service provider's designated agent fails to comply substantially with all the provisions of subparagraph (A) but substantially complies with clauses (ii), (iii), and (iv) of subparagraph (A), clause (i) of this subparagraph applies only if the service provider promptly attempts to contact the person making the notification or takes other reasonable steps to assist in the receipt of notification that substantially complies with all the provisions of subparagraph (A).

PATENTS:
TITLE 35 *UNITED STATES CODE*

§ 100 Definitions

When used in this title unless the context otherwise indicates–

(a) The term "invention" means invention or discovery.

(b) The term "process" means process, art or method, and includes a new use of a known process, machine, manufacture, composition of matter, or material.

(c) The terms "United States" and "this country" mean the United States of America, its territories and possessions.

(d) The word "patentee" includes not only the patentee to whom the patent was issued but also the successors in title to the patentee.

§ 101 Inventions patentable

Whoever invents or discovers any new and useful process, machine, manufacture, or composition of matter, or any new and useful improvement thereof, may obtain a patent therefor, subject to the conditions and requirements of this title.

§ 102 Conditions for patentability; novelty and loss of right to patent

A person shall be entitled to a patent unless–

(a) the invention was known or used by others in this country, or patented or described in a printed publication in this or a foreign country, before the invention thereof by the applicant for patent, or

(b) the invention was patented or described in a printed publication in this or a foreign country or in public use or on sale in this country, more than one year prior to the date of the application for patent in the United States, or

(c) he has abandoned the invention, or

(d) the invention was first patented or caused to be patented, or was the subject of an inventor's certificate, by the applicant or his legal representatives or assigns in a foreign country prior to the date of the application for patent in this country on an application for patent or inventor's certificate filed more than twelve months before the filing of the application in the United States, or

(e) the invention was described in a patent granted on an application for patent by another filed in the United States before the invention thereof by the applicant for patent, or on an international application by another who has fulfilled the requirements of paragraphs (1), (2), and (4) of section 371(c) of this title before the invention thereof by the applicant for patent, or

(f) he did not himself invent the subject matter sought to be patented, or

(g) before the applicant's invention thereof the invention was made in this country by another who had not abandoned, suppressed, or concealed it. In determining priority of invention there shall be considered not only the respective dates of conception and reduction to practice of the invention, but also the reasonable diligence of one who was first to conceive and last to reduce to practice, from a time prior to conception by the other.

§ 103 Conditions for patentability; nonobvious subject matter

(a) A patent may not be obtained though the invention is not identically disclosed or described as set forth in section 102 of this title, if the differences between the subject matter sought to be patented and the prior art are such that the subject matter as a whole would have been obvious at the time the invention was made to a person having ordinary skill in the art to which said subject matter pertains. Patentability shall not be negatived by the manner in which the invention was made.

§ 111 Application

(a) *In General.*—

(1) *Written application.*—An application for patent shall be made, or authorized to be made, by the inventor, except as otherwise provided in this title, in writing to the Commissioner.

(2) *Contents.*—Such application shall include—

(A) a specification as prescribed by section 112 of this title;

(B) a drawing as prescribed by section 113 of this title; and

(C) an oath by the applicant as prescribed by section 115 of this title.

(3) *Fee and oath.*—The application must be accompanied by the fee required by law. The fee and oath may be submitted after the specification and any required drawing are submitted, within such period and under such conditions, including the payment of a surcharge, as may be prescribed by the Commissioner.

(4) *Failure to submit.*—Upon failure to submit the fee and oath within such prescribed period, the application shall be regarded as abandoned, unless it is shown to the satisfaction of the Commissioner that the delay in submitting the fee and oath was unavoidable or unintentional. The filing date of an application shall be the date on which the specification and any required drawing are received in the Patent and Trademark Office.

(b) *Provisional Application.*—

(1) Authorization.—A provisional application for patent shall be made or authorized to be made by the inventor, except as otherwise provided in this title, in writing to the Commissioner. Such application shall include—

(A) a specification as prescribed by the first paragraph of section 112 of this title; and

(B) a drawing as prescribed by section 113 of this title.

(2) *Claim.*—A claim, as required by the second through fifth paragraphs of section 112, shall not be required in a provisional application.

(3) *Fee.*—

(A) The application must be accompanied by the fee required by law.

(B) The fee may be submitted after the specification and any required drawing are submitted, within such period and under such conditions, including the payment of a surcharge, as may be prescribed by the Commissioner.

(C) Upon failure to submit the fee within such prescribed period, the application shall

be regarded as abandoned, unless it is shown to the satisfaction of the Commissioner that the delay in submitting the fee was unavoidable or unintentional.

(4) *Filing date.*—The filing date of a provisional application shall be the date on which the specification and any required drawing are received in the Patent and Trademark Office.

(5) *Abandonment.*—The provisional application shall be regarded as abandoned 12 months after the filing date of such application and shall not be subject to revival thereafter.

(6) *Other basis for provisional application.*—Subject to all the conditions in this subsection and section 119(e) of this title, and as prescribed by the Commissioner, an application for patent filed under subsection (a) may be treated as a provisional application for patent.

(7) *No right of priority or benefit of earliest filing date.*—A provisional application shall not be entitled to the right of priority of any other application under section 119 or 365(a) of this title or to the benefit of an earlier filing date in the United States under section 120, 121, or 365(c) of this title.

(8) *Applicable provisions.*—The provisions of this title relating to applications for patent shall apply to provisional applications for patent, except as otherwise provided, and except that provisional applications for patent shall not be subject to sections 115, 131, 135, and 157 of this title.

§ 119   Benefit of earlier filing date; right of priority

(a) An application for patent for an invention filed in this country by any person who has, or whose legal representatives or assigns have, previously regularly filed an application for a patent for the same invention in a foreign country which affords similar privileges in the case of applications filed in the United States or to citizens of the United States, shall have the same effect as the same application would have if filed in this country on the date on which the application for patent for the same invention was first filed in such foreign country, if the application in this country is filed within twelve months from the earliest date on which such foreign application was filed; but no patent shall be granted on any application for patent for an invention which had been patented or described in a printed publication in any country more than one year before the date of the actual filing of the application in this country, or which had been in public use or on sale in this country more than one year prior to such filing.

§ 122 Confidential status of applications

Applications for patents shall be kept in confidence by the Patent and Trademark Office and no information concerning the same given without authority of the applicant or owner unless necessary to carry out the provisions of any Act of Congress or in such special circumstances as may be determined by the Commissioner.

§ 131 Examination of application

The Commissioner shall cause an examination to be made of the application and the alleged new invention; and if on such examination it appears that the applicant is entitled to a patent under the law, the Commissioner shall issue a patent therefor.

§ 151 Issue of patent

If it appears that applicant is entitled to a patent under law, a written notice of allowance of the application shall be given or mailed to the applicant. The notice shall specify a sum, constituting the issue fee or a portion thereof, which shall be paid within three months thereafter.

Upon payment of this sum the patent shall issue, but if payment is not timely made, the application shall be regarded as abandoned.

Any remaining balance of the issue fee shall be paid within three months from the sending of a notice thereof and, if not paid, the patent shall lapse at the termination of this three-month period. In calculating the amount of a remaining balance, charges for a page or less may be disregarded.

If any payment required by this section is not timely made, but is submitted with the fee for delayed payment and the delay in payment is shown to have been unavoidable, it may be accepted by the Commissioner as though no abandonment or lapse had ever occurred.

§ 154 Contents and term of patent

(a) *In General.*—

(1) *Contents.*—Every patent shall contain a short title of the invention and a grant to the patentee, his heirs or assigns, of the right to include others from making, using, offering for sale, or selling the invention throughout the United States or importing the invention into the United States, and, if the invention is a process, of the right to exclude others from using, offering for sale or selling throughout the United States, or importing into the United States, products made by that process, referring to the specification for the particulars thereof.

(2) *Terms.*—Subject to the payment of fees under this title, such grant shall be for a term beginning on the date on which the patent issues and ending 20 years from the date on which the application for patent was filed in the United States, or, if the application contains a specific reference to an earlier filed application or applications under section 120, 121, or 365(c) of this title, from the date on which the earliest such application was filed.

(3) *Priority.*—Priority under section 119, 365(a), or 365(b) of this title shall not be taken into account in determining the term of a patent.

(4) *Specification and drawing.*—A copy of the specification and drawing shall be annexed to the patent and be a part of such patent.

§ 161 Patents for plants

Whoever invents or discovers and asexually reproduces any distinct and new variety of plant, including cultivated spores, mutants, hybrids, and newly found seedlings, other than a tuber propagated plant or a plant found in an uncultivated state, may obtain a patent therefore, subject to the conditions and requirements of this title.

The provisions of this title relating to patents for inventions shall apply to patents for plants, except as otherwise provided.

§ 171 Patents for designs

Whoever invents any new, original and ornamental design for an article of manufacture may obtain a patent therefore, subject to the conditions and requirements of this title.

The provisions of this title relating to patents for inventions shall apply to patents for designs, except as otherwise provided.

§ 173   Term of design patent

Patents for designs shall be granted for the term of fourteen years from the date of grant.

§ 261   Ownership; assignment

Subject to the provisions of this title, patents shall have the attributes of personal property.

Applications for patent, patents, or any interest therein, shall be assignable in law by an instrument in writing. The applicant, patentee, or his assigns or legal representatives may in like manner grant and convey an exclusive right under his application for patent, or patents, to the whole or any specified part of the United States.

A certificate of acknowledgment under the hand and official seal of a person authorized to administer oaths within the United States, or, in a foreign country, of a diplomatic or consular officer of the United States or an officer authorized to administer oaths whose authority is proved by a certificate of a diplomatic or consular officer of the United States, or apostille of an official designated by a foreign country which, by treaty or convention, accords like effect to apostilles of designated officials in the United States, shall be prima facie evidence of the execution of an assignment, grant or conveyance of a patent or application for patent.

An assignment, grant or conveyance shall be void as against any subsequent purchaser or mortgagee for a valuable consideration, without notice, unless it is recorded in the Patent and Trademark Office within three months from its date or prior to the date of such subsequent purchase or mortgage.

§ 271   Infringement of patent

(a) Except as otherwise provided in this title, whoever without authority makes, uses, offers to sell or sells any patented invention, within the United States or imports into the United States any patented invention during the term of the patent therefor, infringes the patent.

(b) Whoever actively induces infringement of a patent shall be liable as an infringer.

(c) Whoever offers to sell or sells within the United States or imports into the United States a component of a patented machine, manufacture, combination or composition, or a material or apparatus for use in practicing a patented process, constituting a material part of the invention, knowing the same to be especially made or especially adapted for use in an infringement of such patent, and not a staple article or commodity of commerce suitable for substantial noninfringing use, shall be liable as a contributory infringer.

§ 292   False marking

(a) Whoever, without the consent of the patentee, marks upon, or affixes to, or uses in advertising in connection with anything made, used, offered for sale, or sold by such person within the United States, or imported by the person into the United States, the name or any imitation of the name of the patentee, the patent number, or the words "patent," "patentee," or the like, with the intent of counterfeiting or imitating the mark of the patentee, or of deceiving the public and inducing them to believe that the thing was made, offered for sale, sold, or imported into the United States by or with the consent of the patentee; or

Whoever marks upon, or affixes to, or uses in advertising in connection with any unpatented article, the word "patent" or any word of number importing that the same is patented, for the purpose of deceiving the public; or

Whoever marks upon, or affixes to, or uses in advertising in connection with any article, the words "patent applied for," "patent pending," or any word importing that an application for patent has been made, when no application for patent has been made, or if made, is not pending, for the purpose of deceiving the public—

Shall be fined not more than $500 for every such offense.

Glossary

A

abandonment: Loss of trademark rights through nonuse coupled with an intent not to resume use; loss of patent rights through express intention to relinquish rights

abstract: A concise statement of an invention

access: Availability of a copyrighted work to a defendant so that the defendant had a reasonable opportunity to copy it

acquired distinctiveness: See *secondary meaning*

actual reduction to practice: Construction of an invention in physical form, making or testing an invention or its prototype

actual use application: A trademark application based on an applicant's use in interstate commerce of a trademark

Affidavit of Incontestability: Document filed by the owner of a mark registered on the Principal Register after five years of continuous use that reduces the challenges that may be made to a mark; also called *Section 15 Affidavit*

Affidavit of Use: Document filed by a trademark registrant between fifth and sixth years and every ten years after registration verifying the mark is still in use; also called *Declaration of Use* or *Section 8 Affidavit*

Amendment to Allege Use: Document filed during prosecution of an intent-to-use trademark application, alleging that use of the mark has begun

anonymous work: A copyrighted work in which the author is not identified

anticipation, doctrine of: See *doctrine of anticipation*

arbitrary mark: A mark using a common dictionary word for an unrelated product, such as APPLE for computers

architectural work: The design of a building as embodied in any tangible medium of expression

article of manufacture: See *manufacture*

asexual reproduction: Growing something other than from a seed, often by grafting or placing cuttings in soil

assignment: Transfer of all rights in a trademark, copyright, patent, or other property to another

assignment in gross: A purported transfer of a trademark without the business goodwill that the mark symbolizes; it is insufficient to transfer trademark rights

associates: Attorneys in foreign law firms who work with attorneys in U.S. firms regarding intellectual property matters

attribution: The right of an author to be known as the author of a work

audiovisual work: A work consisting of a series of related images intended to be shown by the use of a machine such as a projector together with its accompanying sounds

author: For copyright purposes, a person who creates a work or, if the work is one made for hire, the employer or commissioning party

automated database: A body of facts, data, or other information assembled into an organized format suitable for use in a computer and comprising one or more files

B

background: The portion of a specification in a patent application that discusses how the invention differs from the prior art

Berne Convention: An international convention adhered to by more than one hundred and thirty-five nations that requires its members to treat nationals of other countries as their own nationals for purposes of copyright

best edition: The deposit edition of a copyrighted work most suitable for purposes of the Library of Congress; generally, clean, legible, and superior deposit materials

blackout period: The period after approval of an application for publication in the *Official Gazette* within which an amendment to allege use of a mark cannot be filed

blue penciling: The revision of a noncompetition clause by a court to make it enforceable, generally because it is unreasonable in regard to scope, territory, or duration

blurring: A form of trademark dilution that whittles away the value of a famous trademark through its unauthorized use on a dissimilar product or with a dissimilar service

C

cancellation: A proceeding initiated after registration of a trademark seeking to cancel registration of a mark registered on the Principal or Supplemental Register

cease and desist letter: Correspondence sent to a party demanding that it cease and desist from certain action (in the intellectual property context, from further use of a trademark, copyright, patent, or trade secret)

Certificate of Registration: Document issued by the PTO confirming registration of a trademark

certification mark: A word, name, symbol, or device used by one person to certify that the goods or services of others have certain features in regard to quality, material, or some other characteristics

chain of title: Documentation of continuity of ownership or title to a trademark, copyright, patent, or other property right

Chapter I: The first phase of a patent application filed under the Patent Cooperation Treaty, consisting of a search of the application and generally lasting for 20 months

Chapter II: The second phase of a patent application filed under the Patent Cooperation Treaty during which an International Preliminary Examination is conducted of the application, generally lasting ten months

choreographic work: The composition and arrangement of dance movements and patterns

claim: The portion of a specification in a patent application that defines the scope of the invention

click-wrap license: A license of software that comes into existence by the clicking of a computer keystroke, by which act the licensee agrees to terms governing use of the software

coined mark: See *fanciful mark*

collateral use: Acceptable use of another's trademark, such as in comparative advertising

collective mark: A mark used by a collective membership organization (such as a union or fraternity) to identify that the person displaying the mark is a member of the organization

collective work: A work such as a periodical issue or anthology in which a number of contributions, constituting separate and independent works, are assembled into a collective whole

combination patents: New inventions consisting of a combination of older, known elements

common law trademark: A mark used by a party without any governmental registration

Community Trademark (CTM) System: A trademark system allowing trademark owners to file one single trademark application that covers all fifteen members of the European Union

companion application: Related trademark applications by the same applicant

comparative advertising: Advertising that compares one product or service with another or that states that one product works with or is compatible with another

compensatory damages: Damages awarded to a plaintiff to compensate it for injury suffered

compilation: A work formed by the collection of preexisting material arranged in such a way that the resulting work is original; includes *collective works*

composite mark: A mark consisting of words and a design element

composition of matter: In patent law, a combination of two or more chemical or other materials into a product

comprehensive search: A search of trademarks registered or applied for at the PTO, state trademark registrations, and common law sources such as periodicals, directories, and the Internet

compulsory license: The imposition of a statutorily set fee for use of a copyrighted work

computer program: A set of instructions used directly or indirectly in a computer to produce a certain result

conception of an invention: The completion of the devising of the means for accomplishing an invention's result

concurrent use proceeding: A proceeding initiated at the Trademark Trial and Appeal Board to determine specific geographic areas in which parties with confusingly similar marks can each use the mark

confidentiality agreement: See *nondisclosure agreement*

conflicting application: Trademark applications filed by different parties for conflicting or confusingly similar marks

consent agreement: Private agreement entered into between two trademark owners whereby each consents to the use of the other's mark, generally with some limitations or restrictions; also called *consent to use agreement*

constructive reduction to practice: The filing of a patent application that fully discloses an invention

constructive use: Use of trademark other than actual use; for intent-to-use trademark applications, the application filing date constitutes constructive use of the mark (assuming the mark achieves registration)

continuation application: A patent application that claims priority from a previously filed application and contains no new information

continuation-in-part application: A patent application that adds new matter to a previous patent application

contributory infringement: In the intellectual property context, causing, inducing, or assisting in infringement of another's trademark, copyright, or patent

copy: In copyright law, a material object (other than a phonorecord) from which a work can be perceived, reproduced, or communicated, either by human perception or with the help of a machine

copyhoarding: Retaining all rights in a work and refusing to allow others to use it

copylefting: Licensing users of software to use it for any purpose

copyright: Right protecting original works of authorship, including literary, musical, dramatic, artistic, and other works, from unauthorized reproduction, sale, performance, distribution, or display

counterfeiting: A form of trademark infringement in which a trademark is affixed to goods or services that do not originate with the trademark owner

creation: In copyright law, the fixation of a work in a copy or phonorecord for the first time

cybersquatting: A practice in which a person, without permission, registers another's name as a domain name and then attempts to sell the domain name to its true owner

D

deadwood: Unused marks that the PTO desires to clear from its records

declaration: A statement by an applicant for a trademark registration acknowledging that statements in the application are true

Declaration of Use: See *Affidavit of Use*

deep linking: The process by which an Internet user can proceed directly to certain information at another's web site, bypassing the home page at the second site

deposit: The best edition of a work provided to the Copyright Office in support of an application to register a copyright for the work

deposit account: Prepaid accounts established with the PTO, against which application and other fees are drawn by applicants

derivative work: A work based on one or more pre-existing works, such as a translation, fictionalization, revision, or abridgment; also called a *new version*

descriptive mark: A mark that describes some characteristic of the goods or services offered under it and is unregistrable unless secondary meaning is shown

design application: An application for a design patent

design patent: A patent covering new, original, and ornamental designs for useful articles

dilution: Unauthorized acts that tend to blur the distinctiveness of a famous mark or to tarnish it

direct infringement: In patent law, making, using, or selling another's patented invention

disclaimer: In trademark law, an acknowledgment by an applicant that exclusive rights in certain wording in a mark, usually descriptive or generic wording, are not claimed; a notice placed on trademarked goods that the owner of the goods is not affiliated with another; in patent law, the cancellation of invalid claims in an issued patent

distinctiveness: See *secondary meaning*

divisional application: A patent application separated from another application when the original or parent application covers more than one invention

Doctrine of Anticipation: Theory that an invention was known or used by others such that its invention was anticipated

doctrine of equivalents: Principle that if an accused invention is equivalent to a patented invention in its purpose and achieves the same result, it infringes the patent even if a claim in the patent is not literally copied

domain name: Internet address used by a company or individual

domestic representative: A person or law firm in the United States designated by a foreign applicant to receive documents and notices affecting a trademark application

double patenting: In patent law, a principle prohibiting the issuance of more than one patent for the same invention

downstream infringement: Infringement by users who obtain copyrighted items from legitimate users

dramatic work: A theatrical performance or play performed for stage, movies, television, or radio

drawing: The display of the mark applied for in a trademark application; may be a *typed form* (typewritten display) or *special form* (a design mark or a design mark with words)

droit de suite: A doctrine in foreign countries that allows the authors of fine works to share in the appreciation of those works, even after they have parted with ownership of those works

due diligence: A type of audit of intellectual property, usually conducted when a company is sold, when it borrows money, or when it acquires another company

duty of candor: Requirement that patent applicants disclose to the PTO any information that is material to the patentability of a claimed invention

E

equivalents, doctrine of: See *doctrine of equivalents*

estoppel: A defense often raised in infringement actions, alleging the plaintiff is precluded from making certain assertions due to the plaintiff's conduct or acquiescence in the infringement

European Patent Organization: An organization with twenty-four member nations founded in 1973 to provide a uniform patent system in Europe

European Union (EU): An association of fifteen European nations

Examiner's Amendment: A written communication from the PTO setting forth an agreed-upon clarification or correction to a trademark application

exclusive license: A grant of rights to one party with no other party having any rights

exhaustion theory: In trademark and patent law, the extinguishment or exhaustion of a trademark or patent owner's rights once a lawful first sale has been made of trademarked goods or a patented invention; in copyright law, the extinguishment of a copyright owner's right to distribute a copyrighted work once a lawful first sale has been made; also see *first sale doctrine*

F

fair use: A defense asserted in trademark or copyright infringement actions; a noninfringing use of copyrighted work such as a parody or for criticism, scholarly research, or educational purposes

false advertising: False or deceptive representations about one's own goods or services

fanciful mark: A wholly invented mark; also called *coined mark*

Federal Trade Commission (FTC): The federal regulatory agency charged with protecting consumers from unfair or deceptive acts and practices

file wrapper: The official PTO file containing all papers relating to a trademark or patent application

file wrapper estoppel: See *prosecution history estoppel*

filing receipt: Document mailed by the PTO to an applicant to confirm filing and details of an application

final action: Action by the PTO refusing a trademark or patent application; also called final refusal

first sale doctrine: In copyright and patent law, the principle that once the owner of copyrighted material or a patented item sells it, the buyer can treat the object as his or her own and freely sell, lease, or lend the work to another; also see *exhaustion theory*

fixation: The embodiment of a work in a sufficiently permanent or stable form to permit it to be perceived, reproduced, or communicated for more than a transitory period

foreign filing license: The grant by the PTO of permission to an inventor to file a patent application in another country for an invention made in the United States, required before a foreign application may be filed

freeware: Software that is allowed to be used for free but in which certain rights are maintained to ensure the work is not reverse engineered

G

General Agreement on Tariffs and Trade (GATT): Agreement adhered to by most industrialized nations aimed at increasing international trade and that resulted in some changes to U.S. trademark and patent law, notably relating to the duration of patent protection

genericide: Loss of rights in a trademark occurring when consumers begin calling a product or service offered under a mark by the mark itself

generic mark: An unprotectable common name for a product or service

generic top-level domain: The portion of a domain name to the right of a period, such as ".com" or ".gov"

goodwill: The value inherent in achieving consumer loyalty to a particular product or service through maintenance of consistent quality of the products or services offered under a mark

grace period: A period within which late documents are accepted by the PTO; in patent law, the one-year period within which a patent application must be filed after the invention is in public use, on sale, or described in the inventor's printed publication

gray market goods: Unauthorized importation of goods into the United States for resale after the goods are distributed in foreign markets

H

hyperlink: A symbol designating another's web page

I

idea-expression dichotomy: Doctrine that ideas are not protectable by copyright although the expression of those ideas is copyrightable

idea submission: The submission of an idea for an invention, process, game, or entertainment show in the hope it will be developed and marketed by the recipient

impoundment: Seizure, generally of infringing goods

incontestable: A trademark registered on the Principal Register that is protected from certain challenges after its registrant files a section 15 affidavit alleging continuous use for five years

inducement of infringement: In patent law, actively and intentionally encouraging another to infringe a patent

industrial property: The term used in some foreign countries to refer to intellectual property

Information Disclosure Statement (IDS): A document filed by an inventor with the PTO identifying information material to patentability of an invention

infringement: A violation of some right; in the intellectual property context, a violation of a party's rights in a trademark, copyright, or patent

injunction: A court order prohibiting or compelling some act

innocent infringement: Infringement of another's intellectual property rights without any intent to infringe; not a valid defense in copyright or patent infringement actions

integrity: See *right of integrity*

intellectual property: The result or product of human creativity, including trademarks, copyrights, and inventions; generally *intellectual property* comprises the field of trademarks, copyrights, patents, and trade secrets

intellectual property audit: A review of the trademarks, copyrights, patents, and trade secrets owned by a person or company

Intent-to-use application: A trademark application for which no actual use of a mark has been made but rather alleging the applicant's bona fide intent to use the mark in the future

interference: A proceeding before the Trademark Trial and Appeal Board when marks in two pending trademark applications are confusingly similar or when a mark in a pending application may be confusingly similar to a registered mark that is not yet incontestable; a proceeding initiated by the PTO to determine which of two or more patents has priority

International Classes: The categorization of goods and services into forty-two separate topics for trademark purposes; class(es) of goods or services must be identified in a trademark application

international patent: A patent filed under the Patent Cooperation Treaty

International Trademark Association (INTA): A not for profit international association devoted to promoting trademarks

inter partes proceedings: Literally, "between parties"; proceedings handled by the Trademark Trial and Appeal Board; may be oppositions, cancellations, interferences, or concurrent use proceedings

interstate commerce: Commerce between or among states

intrastate commerce: Commerce conducted within the borders of one state

invention developer: One who assists an inventor in bringing a discovery to market or negotiates with others for assignment or licensing of an inventor's rights; also called an *invention promoter*

Invention Disclosure Document: A document filed with the PTO that describes an invention and is intended to provide evidence of the date of conception and reduction to practice of an invention

invention promoter: See *invention developer*

issue fee: A fee required by the PTO for a patent to be granted

J

Jepson claim: A type of claim in a patent specification used for improvements to existing inventions that identifies what is new to the invention

joint application: An application for a trademark, copyright, or patent registration made by more than one person

joint inventors: Two or more people who contribute to an invention

joint work: A copyrightable work created by two or more authors with the intent that their contributions be merged into a unitary whole

K

knockout search: A preliminary search of PTO records designed to disclose identical or nearly identical marks; often followed by a *comprehensive search*

L

laboratory notebooks: Books and notes kept by inventors as work progresses on an invention, often used in determining conception of invention and reduction to practice of an invention

laches: An unreasonable delay in asserting one's rights that causes prejudice or harm to another; a common defense asserted in intellectual property infringement actions

Lanham Act: The federal statute found at 15 U.S.C. § 1051 *et seq.* governing the law of trademarks; also called the *United States Trademark Act*

Library of Congress: The agency charged with examining copyright applications, issuing registrations, and maintaining copyright deposits

license: A limited transfer of rights, such as permission to another to use a trademark, copyright, patent, or trade secret subject to some conditions, rather than an outright transfer of all rights

literal copying: Identical duplication or copying of another's copyrighted work

literal infringement: An accused invention that falls within the language used in a claim in an issued patent

literary work: A work expressed in words, numbers, or other verbal or numerical symbols, such as a book or computer program

little FTC acts: State statutes that prohibit deceptive and unfair trade practices

logo: A design used as a trademark

M

machine: In patent law, a device that accomplishes a result

Madrid Protocol: An agreement adhered to by nearly thirty countries and the E.U. (but not the United States) that provides an "international trademark registration" that would be valid in all member nations

maintenance fees: Fees due at 3½, 7½, and 11½ years after issuance of a utility patent required to keep it in force

Manual of Patent Examining Procedure (MPEP): A PTO publication containing rules and regulations relating to examination and issuance of patents

manufacture: In patent law, anything made by humans

mark: A trademark or service mark

mask works: Stencils used to etch or encode an electronic circuit on a semiconductor chip

merger doctrine: The principle that if there are few alternative ways of expressing something, only literal copying will infringe because the expression merges with the idea and ideas are uncopyrightable

mime: See *pantomime*

misappropriation: The taking or using of property created or secured at great effort by another

misuse: A defense often asserted in infringement actions alleging that the owner of an intellectual property right has so misused its rights as to be precluded from recovery

moral rights: Personal rights retained by authors in their works (often works of fine arts) to protect their honor and reputation even after they no longer own the copyright in the work

motion picture: Audiovisual work consisting of a series of related images that, when shown in succession, impart an impression of motion, together with accompanying sounds

musical work: Original musical compositions or arrangements, including lyrics

N

naked license: Granting permission to another to use a trademark and retaining no control over the nature or quality of the goods or services offered under the mark; a naked license results in a loss of the licensor's rights in a mark

national phase: The final phase of a patent application filed under the Patent Cooperation Treaty consisting of prosecution of the patent in countries designated in the application

national treatment: Principle that member countries adhering to a treaty guarantee to the citizens of other member adherents the same rights in intellectual property matters that they provide to their own citizens

new version: See *derivative work*

noncompetition agreement: An agreement prohibiting an employee from competing against the employer during and after the term of employment; also called *restrictive covenant*

nondisclosure agreement: An agreement requiring a party to maintain information in confidence; also called *confidentiality agreement*

nonenabling specification: A specification in a patent application rejected by the PTO on the basis that it is not sufficient to teach or enable another to make or use the invention

nonexclusive license: A grant of rights to more than one party

nonobviousness: In patent law, the requirement that subject matter sought to be patented be sufficiently different from what has been used or described before such that it may be said to be nonobvious to a person having ordinary skill in the area of technology related to the invention

North American Free Trade Agreement (NAFTA): A trade agreement entered into in 1991 by the United States, Canada, and Mexico

Notice of Allowance: Document issued by the PTO informing a trademark applicant that an intent-to-use application has been allowed and granting the applicant a specified time period within which to begin use of the mark in order to secure registration for it; document issued by the PTO informing a patent applicant that a patent application has been allowed and granting the applicant a specified time period within which to pay an issue fee so a patent will be issued

notice of copyright: A mark informing the public that a work is protected by copyright and identifying its owner and year of publication

Notice of Opposition: The document that initiates an opposition proceeding and that sets forth a short and plain statement of the reasons why the opposer believes he or she will be damaged by registration of a mark

novelty: In patent law, a new invention; one not known or used by another

novelty search: A search of prior art to determine if an invention is new and nonobvious

O

object code: A computer language consisting of zeroes and ones that is machine-readable

Office Action: Written communication from the PTO refusing registration of a trademark or patent and specifying reasons for the refusal

Official Filing Receipt: A document issued by the PTO confirming the filing of a trademark application

Official Gazette: The weekly publication of the PTO that publishes trademarks for purposes of opposition and publishes information about issued patents and patents available for sale or license

on sale bar: The doctrine precluding granting of a patent unless a patent application is filed less than one year from the time the invention is in public use, on sale in the United States, or described in the inventor's printed publication anywhere

opposition: A proceeding initiated at the Trademark Trial and Appeal Board by one who believes he or she may be damaged by registration of a trademark

originality: In copyright law, a work that is independently created (not copied) and that exhibits a minimal amount of creativity

orphan drug: A drug needed to treat a disease affecting fewer than two hundred thousand people

P

palming off: See *passing off*

pantomime: A performance using gestures as expression to communicate with no accompanying sound

parallel imports: See *gray market goods*

parent application: An original trademark or patent application that is the source or parent of a later separate application

Paris Convention: An agreement adhered to by more than one hundred and thirty-five member nations providing that foreign trademark and patent owners may obtain in a member country the same protection for their trademarks and patents as can citizens of the member country

passing off: Attempting to sell one's goods or services as those of another; also called *palming off*

patent: A grant from the U.S. government permitting its owner to exclude others from making, selling, or using an invention for a limited period of time

patent agent: A nonattorney engineer or scientist who passes a PTO exam testing patent knowledge and may engage in patent prosecution but may not give legal advice or appear in court

Patent and Trademark Depository Libraries: Public libraries throughout the United States that maintain selected trademark and patent records

patent attorney: A licensed attorney who passes a PTO exam testing patent knowledge and who may engage in patent prosecution, give legal advice, and appear in court

Patent Cooperation Treaty (PCT): A 1978 treaty adhered to by approximately one hundred countries that provides a centralized way of filing, searching, and examining patent applications in several countries simultaneously

patentee: The owner of a patent issued by the PTO

patent misuse: See *misuse*

PCT application: A patent application that has applicability and effect in designated member nations adhering to the Patent Cooperation Treaty

performing rights society: An organization of copyright owners (such as ASCAP or BMI) that licenses the rights to use copyrighted music to third parties, collects fees therefor, and remits those fees to its members, the authors of the works

Petition to Cancel: The document initiating a trademark cancellation proceeding that sets forth a short and plain statement of the reasons a petitioner would be damaged by continued registration of a mark

phonorecord: A material object in which sounds (other than those accompanying a motion picture or other audiovisual work) are fixed and from which the sounds can be perceived, reproduced, or communicated by human perception or with the help of a machine

pioneer patent: A patent representing an important advance or significant breakthrough

plant application: An application for a patent for a plant

plant patent: A patent covering asexually reproduced and distinct plant varieties

Plant Variety Protection Act: Federal law allowing quasipatent protection for certain sexually reproduced plants

posting of ports: Monitoring of ports of entry into the United States by the Customs Department for the purpose of seizing unauthorized goods bearing a party's registered trademark

Principal Register: The most preferred roll or register for registration of trademarks conferring wide protection for a mark and indicating that the mark distinguishes the registrant's goods and services from those of others

prior art: In patent law, the generally available public knowledge relating to an invention at the time of its creation

process: A patentable method of doing something to produce a given result

product disparagement: Making false representations about another's goods or services; also called *trade libel*

prosecution: The process of moving a trademark or patent application through the PTO

prosecution history estoppel: The principle that an inventor or patentee is bound by acts taken and statements made during the prosecution of a patent and cannot later take an inconsistent position; also called *file wrapper estoppel*

provisional patent application: A patent application that is less formal than a utility patent application; within twelve months of its filing, it must be following by a standard utility patent application at the PTO

pseudonymous work: A copyrighted work in which the author is identified under a fictitious name, such as the name "Mark Twain" used by Samuel Clemens

publication: The distribution of copies of a work to the public for sale or other transfer of ownership by rental, lease, or lending

public domain: A work or invention that is free for all members of the public to use

puffing: An exaggerated and highly subjective statement upon which no reasonable person would rely; generally, nonactionable opinion

punitive damages: Damages intended to punish a defendant rather than to compensate a plaintiff

R

receiving office: A patent office in which a patent application prepared in accordance with the Patent Cooperation Treaty is filed

recordation: Filing of certain documents with the PTO, Library of Congress, or other official body to provide public notice of the contents of a document or a transaction, such as an assignment or transfer of intellectual property, a grant of a security interest in intellectual property, or a change in the chain of title of intellectual property

reduction to practice: Construction of an invention in physical form (called *actual reduction to practice*) or filing a patent application for an invention (called *constructive reduction to practice*)

reexamination of patent: Proceeding initiated at the PTO to review or reexamine a claim in an issued patent to determine its validity

registered user agreement: Agreement by which an owner of a registered mark allows or licenses another to use its mark and is required to be filed by many foreign trademark offices for the grant to be effective

registrant: The owner of a trademark registration issued by the PTO

reissue patent: A proceeding to correct defects in an issued patent or to enlarge the claims of an issued patent

renewal: Document filed with the PTO or Library of Congress to maintain a trademark or copyright registration for an additional term

restriction requirement: Requirement by the PTO that a patent applicant limit a patent application to one invention when two or more distinct inventions are claimed in one application

restrictive covenant: *See* noncompetition agreement

reverse doctrine of equivalents: In patent law, the principle that even if there is literal infringement of claims, if the accused resulting device differs from the patented device, there is no infringement

reverse engineering: Disassembling an object, usually a computer program, to understand its functional elements

right of integrity: A personal right of a copyright author to ensure that his or her work not be distorted, mutilated, or used in a way that would injure the author's reputation

right of publicity: Protection of a person's identity, voice, likeness, or persona against unauthorized commercial exploitation

royalties: Periodic payments paid by one who uses or licenses property owned or created by another, usually based on sales or licenses of the property

rule of doubt: Policy followed by the Copyright Office to resolve doubts about copyrightability in favor of a copyright applicant

S

scenes a faire: Literally, "scenes which must be done"; stock characters and devices in a work that are uncopyrightable

secondary considerations: In patent law, nontechnical and objective factors considered in determining whether an invention is nonobvious, namely, its commercial success, the long-felt need for the invention, commercial acquiescence to it by others, and copying of it by others

secondary level domain: The part of a domain name to the left of a period, such as "ibm" in "ibm.com"

secondary meaning: An association by a consumer who has learned to link a mark with its source; also called *acquired distinctiveness*

secrecy order: An order issued by the PTO requiring that an invention be kept secret and prohibiting publication of it or patent applications for it in another country, generally for national security reasons

Section 8 Affidavit: See *Affidavit of Use*

Section 15 Affidavit: See *Affidavit of Incontestability*

Section 44(d) Application: Trademark application filed with the PTO by a non-U.S. citizen based upon an application filed in a foreign country

Section 44(e) Application: Trademark application filed with the PTO by a non-U.S. citizen based upon a registration secured in a foreign country

security agreement: In intellectual property law, an agreement by which one party grants an interest to another in its intellectual property, usually in order to obtain or secure a loan; if the owner defaults on the loan, the lender usually obtains ownership of the intellectual property

semiconductor chip: A product having two or more layers of metallic, insulating, or semiconductor material placed on or removed from semiconductor material and intended to perform electronic circuitry functions

service mark: A word, name, symbol, or device used to indicate the origin, quality, and ownership of a service

shareware: Copyrighted software that has been released under the condition that if the user likes it, the user will pay a license fee therefor

shrink-wrap license: A license of software that comes into existence by the opening of the plastic wrapping on the software and by which act the licensee agrees to terms governing use of the software

shop right: An employer's nonexclusive royalty-free license to use an invention or trade secret when the employer and employee do not agree in advance about who will own the invention or trade secret conceived by the employee while on company time

small entity: A business with fewer than five hundred employees, an individual inventor, a university, or a not-for-profit organization entitled to a 50 percent reduction in standard patent fees

softlifting: The act of software piracy by which one makes unauthorized copies of computer software

sound recording: A work that results from the fixation of a series of musical, spoken, or other sounds

source code: An alphanumeric computer language that is human-readable

special handling: Expedited processing of copyright applications and other documents for specified reasons upon payment of a fee

specification: The part of a patent application that describes an invention and the manner and process of making and using it

specimens: Samples of tags, labels, packaging, or advertising materials showing how a trademark or service mark is used in commerce

Statement of Use: Document filed by an intent-to-use trademark applicant verifying that the mark is in actual use in interstate commerce; required to receive a trademark registration

statutory damages: Damages awarded by a court in an infringement action as specified by statute, generally elected when a plaintiff will have difficulty proving actual damages

suggestive mark: A mark that suggests something about the goods or services offered under it; a suggestive mark is registrable without proof of secondary meaning

Supplemental Register: The roll or register for marks not qualifying for registration on the PTO Principal Register; registration on the Supplemental Register is an indication that the mark does not yet distinguish the registrant's goods or services from those of others

supplementary copyright registration: An application to correct an error or amplify information in a copyright registration

T

tarnishment: A form of dilution in which a famous trademark is portrayed in an unsavory or embarrassing manner

terminal disclaimer: An agreement by an inventor that the term of protection for a second patented invention will terminate upon expiration of the term for the first patented invention

trade dress: The overall image of a product or service

trade libel: See *product disparagement*

trademark: A word, logo, phrase, or device used to indicate the origin, quality, and ownership of a product or service; technically, *trademark* refers to a mark that identifies a product, while *service mark* refers to a mark that identifies services

trademark compliance policy: A guide to use of a trademark to ensure a mark is not misused or does not become generic or abandoned

Trademark Manual of Examining Procedure: A PTO publication containing rules and regulations related to the prosecution and registration of trademarks

Trademark Trial and Appeal Board (TTAB): Department of the PTO that resolves inter partes proceedings and other matters affecting trademarks

trade name: A name used to identify a business or company

Trade-Related Aspects of Intellectual Property Rights (TRIPS): Agreement promulgated in accordance with the 1994 General Agreement on Tariffs and Trade providing intellectual property protection for GATT members

trade secret: Any valuable commercial information that, if known by a competitor, would provide some benefit or advantage to the competitor

TRAM line: The Trademark Reporting and Monitoring system maintained by the PTO allowing individuals to check the status of a trademark application or registration (703/305-8747)

traverse: Arguments made in response to objections by the PTO to a trademark or patent application

U

unclean hands: A defense often raised in infringement actions; an assertion that the plaintiff's own wrongful conduct precludes it from obtaining relief

unfair competition: A branch of law protecting against deceptive and improper conduct in the marketplace

United States Patent and Trademark Office (PTO): The agency within the Department of Commerce charged with registering trademarks and granting patents

United States Trademark Act: See *Lanham Act*

Universal Copyright Convention (UCC): An international convention relating to copyright requiring that works originating in a member nation must be given the same protection in all member nations as is granted by the country of origin of the work

Uruguay Round Agreements Act: A 1994 act that implemented GATT and amended U.S. copyright law to provide remedies for pirated sound recordings of live performances and to provide automatic restoration of copyright in certain foreign works

useful article: An article having an intrinsic utilitarian value

usefulness: In patent law, a process or invention that is of some present value to humanity

utility application: A patent application for a new, useful, and nonobvious process, machine, article of manufacture, composition of matter, or some improvement thereof

utility patent: A patent for a useful article, invention, or discovery

V

vicarious infringement: Liability imposed for copyright infringement on a party due to its special relationship (such as employer-employee) with another infringer

W

watch service: Service provided by a private company, usually a trademark search firm, to review the *Official Gazette* and PTO records for potentially conflicting marks

work made for hire: A work that is presumed to be authored by an employer because it was created by an employee on company time or authored by a commissioning party when the parties have agreed the commissioning party will own the copyright and the work falls into one of nine statutorily enumerated categories

World Intellectual Property Organization (WIPO): A specialized agency of the United Nations with more than one hundred and sixty member nations that promotes intellectual property throughout the world and administers various multilateral treaties dealing with intellectual property, including the Berne Convention

World Trade Organization (WTO): An international organization established in 1995 with more than one hundred and thirty member countries, created by the Uruguay Round negotiations to handle trade disputes and monitor national trade policies

Index

A

Abandonment, 75
Abstract, 280
Access, 209
ACLU v. Miller, 114
Actual reduction to practice, 304
Actual use application, 65
Affidavit of Incontestability, 73–74
Affidavit of Use, 72–73
Ali v. Playgirl, Inc., 364
Allen v. National Video, Inc., 364
Amendment to Allege Use, 65
American Geophysical Union v. Texaco, Inc., 215
Anonymous work, 188
Arbitrary mark, 24
Architectural work, 145
ASCAP, 161–62, 166
Asexual reproduction, 268
Assignment, 79
Assignment in gross, 79
Associates, 39
Attribution, 164–65
Audiovisual work, 144
Author, 170
Automated databases, 230–31

B

Background, 280
Baker v. Selden, 145–46
Bally Total Fitness Holding Corp. v. Faber, 115
Basic Books, Inc. v. Kinko's Graphics Corp., 214–15
Berne Convention, 10, 162, 246–48
Best edition, 194
Blackout period, 66
Blue penciling, 347
Blurring, 104
BMI, 161–62, 166
Bonito Boats, Inc. v. Thunder Craft Boats, Inc., 319
Brights Tunes Music Corp. v. Harrisongs Music, Ltd., 209

C

Campbell v. Acuff-Rose Music, Inc., 216

Cancellation, 94
Carson v. Here's Johnny Portable Toilets, 363–4
Cease and desist letter, 101–2
Certificate of Registration, 66
Certification mark, 19
Chain of title, 72
Chapter I (patents), 329
Chapter II (patents), 330
Choreographic work, 143
Claim, 280
Click-wrap license, 229
Cochrane v. Deener, 259
Collateral use, 79
Collective mark, 19
Collective work, 150, 171–72
Columbia Pictures Indus., Inc. v. Professional Real Estate Investors, Inc., 159
Combination patents, 264
Common law trademark, 21
Community for Creative Non-Violence v. Reid, 172–74
Community Trademark System, 119, 126–27
Companion application, 58
Comparative advertising, 368
Compensatory damages, 219, 317
Compilation, 149–50
Composite mark, 61
Composition of matter, 260
Comprehensive search, 38
Compulsory license, 166
Computer Associates International, Inc. v. Altai, Inc., 227
Computer programs
    deposit requirements, 225–26
    infringement of, 227–28
    licensing of, 228–29
    notice of copyright, 226
    protectable elements, 224–25
    revisions and modifications, 226–27
    software piracy, 229–30
    video games, 226
Conception of an invention, 304
Concurrent use proceeding, 95
Conflicting application, 58
Consent agreement, 93
Constructive reduction to practice, 304
Constructive use, 56
Consumers Union of United States, Inc. v. General Signal Corp., 215

Continuation application, 278
Continuation in-part application, 278
Contributory infringement, 103, 211, 312–13
Copy, 140
Copyhoarding, 238
Copying, 209–11
Copylefting, 238–39
Copyright Act (1909), 180, 203
Copyright Act (1976), 136–38, 155, 180–81, 203, 232
Copyrights, 3, 6, 133–34. *See also* International copyright law
    for automated databases, 230–31
    compilations, collections, derivative works, 149–51
    for computer programs, 224–30
    duration of, 169, 179–82
    in electronic age, 231–35
        legal trends, 235–38
        terminology, 238–39
    exclusions from protection, 145–49
    infringement, 207
        actions, 218–19
        contributory and vicarious, 211–12
        defenses to, 212–18
        elements of, 208–11
        remedies for, 219–21
    notice of, 200–203
    ownership, 169–75
    registration of, 6
        application, 186–91, 195–98
        deposit materials, 191–95
        obtaining records and deposit materials, 199–200
        searching Copyright Office records, 198–99
    rights under, 134–36, 155–66
    subject matter of, 139–45
    transfer of, 169, 175–79
    U.S. Copyright Office, 136–37, 185
CORDS, 196
Counterfeiting, 105
Creation, 135
Cybersquatting, 112–13

D

Data East USA, Inc. v. Epyx, Inc., 210
Deadwood, 68

Declaration, 54–55
Deep linking, 114
Deposit, 193
Deposit account, 56
Derivative work, 150, 156–57, 171–72
Descriptive mark, 23
Design application, 278
Design patent, 266–67
Detective Comics Inc. v. Bruns Publications, Inc., 148
Diamond v. Chakrabarty, 265
Diamond v. Diehr, 265
Dickinson v. Zurko, 62, 95, 288
Dilution, 103, 370–71
Direct infringement, 311–12
Disclaimer, 60
Divisional application, 279
Doctrine of anticipation, 261
Doctrine of equivalents, 313–14
Domain name, 110
Domestic representative, 121
Double patenting, 269, 290
Downstream infringement, 239
Dr. Seuss Enterprises, L.P. v. Penguin Books USA, Inc., 216
Dramatic work, 142
Drawing, 53
Droit de suite doctrine, 158–59
Due diligence, 198
Due diligence review, 376
Duty of candor, 283–85

E

Eastern Europe, 127–28
Economic Espionage Act, 354
E.I. duPont de Nemours & Co. v. Christopher, 96, 345
Electronic Design & Sales Inc. v. Electronic Data Systems Corp., 98
Elvis Presley Ent. Inc. v. Capece, 359
Ely-Morris Safe Co. v. Mosler Safe Co., 367
Employer-employee relationships, 345–47
Estoppel, 100, 217
European Patent Organization, 331–32
European Union, 126
Evans Products Co. v. Boise Cascade Corp., 28
Examiner's Amendment, 59

Exclusive license, 84
Exhaustion theory, 105

F

Fair use, 100, 212–16
False advertising, 367–69
Fanciful mark, 24
Federal Trade Commission, 369
Federal Trademark Dilution Act, 89, 91, 103, 112, 370
Feist Publications, Inc. v. Rural Telephone Service Co., 140, 148, 150, 217, 248
Feltner v. Columbia Pictures Television, Inc., 220
File wrapper estoppel, 57–58, 315
Filing receipt, 285
Final action, 288
First Amendment, 113–14, 365
First sale doctrine, 157–58, 313
Fixation, 140–41
Fleet v. CBS, 366
Foreign filing license, 332–33
Foresight Resources Corp. v. Pfortmiller, 227
Freeware, 239

G

Gates Rubber Co. v. Bando Chem. Indus., Ltd., 211, 228
GATT (General Agreement on Tariffs and Trade), 11, 128, 248, 333, 355
Gay Toys, Inc. v. Buddy L. Corp., 143
G.D. Searle & Co. v. Charles Pfizer & Co., 97
Genericide, 75
Generic mark, 23
Generic top-level domain, 110
Goodwill, 18
Gorham Mfg. v. White, 266
Grace period, 262
Graham v. John Deere Co., 263–64, 268
Graver Tank & Mfg. Co. v. Linde Air Products Co., 314
Gray market goods, 105, 250
Greyhound Corp. v. Both Worlds, Inc., 28

H

Harper & Row Publishers, Inc. v. Nation Enterprises, 214
Hasbro Inc. v. Internet Entertainment Group Ltd., 104, 112, 371
Hirsch v. S.C. Johnson & Sons, Inc., 364
Horgan v. MacMillan, Inc., 143
Hunter Publishing Co. v. Caulfield Publishing Ltd., 23
Hyperlinking, 113

I

Idea-expression dichotomy, 146
Idea submission, 348
Impoundment, 219
Incontestable, 73
Independent creation, 349–50
Inducement of infringement, 312
Industrial property, 4
Information Disclosure Statement (IDS), 285
Infringement
  of computer programs, 227–28
  of copyrights, 207–22
  of patents, 311–20
  of trade dress, 371–72
  of trademarks, 96–103
Injection Research Specialists, Inc. v. Polaris Indus., L.P., 352
Injunction, 101, 316
Innocent infringement, 209
In re American Safety Razor Co., 97
In re Bed & Breakfast Registry, 23
In re Brana, 260
In re Clarke, 26
In re Cotter & Co., 28
In re E. I. DuPont DeNemours & Co., 61
In re Four Seasons Hotels Ltd., 93
In re Hutchinson Technology, Inc., 29
In re Jeep Corp., 98
In re Lamson Oil Co., 97
In re Martin's Pastry Shoppe, Inc., 61
In re Mogen David Wine Corp., 267
In re Mucky Duck Mustard Co., 99
In re Nantucket, Inc., 29
In re Opryland USA, Inc., 29

In re Optica Int'l, 26
In re Owens-Corning Fiberglas Corp., 26
In re Shapely, Inc., 28
Intellectual property. *See also* Copyrights; Patents; Trademarks; Trade secrets; Unfair competition
   defined, 3–4
   importance of protecting rights, 11–13
   organizations, agencies, treaties, 10–11
   rationale for protection of, 4
   types of, 4–8
Intellectual property audit
   conducting, 377–80
   defined, 375–76
   postaudit activity, 380–81
   practical aspects of, 376–77
Intent-to-use application, 20
Interference, 95, 290–91
Intermatic v. Toeppen, 112
International Classes, 47–52
International copyright law, 245–46
   Berne Convention, 246–47
      treaties supplementing, 247–48
   gray market goods, 250
   Universal Copyright Convention, 249
   Uruguay Round Agreements Act, 248–49
International News Service v. Associated Press, 362
International patent, 326
International patent law, 325–26
   Agreement on Trade-Related Aspects of Intellectual Property Rights, 333
   European Patent Organization, 331–32
   foreign applications for U.S. patents, 333–34
   foreign filing licenses, 332–33
   Paris Convention, 326–27
   Patent Cooperation Treaty, 328–31
International Star Class Yacht Racing Ass'n v. Tommy Hilfiger U.S.A., Inc., 36
International Trademark Association (INTA), 10, 128
International trademark law, 119
   international associations, 128–29
   NAFTA and GATT, 128

   protection in foreign countries, 123–28
International trade secret law, 354–55
Internet, 109–16
Inter partes proceedings
   cancellations, 94–95
   concurrent use proceedings, 95–96
   defined, 91
   interferences, 95
   oppositions, 92–93
Interstate commerce, 20
Intrastate commerce, 22
Invention developer, 308
Invention Disclosure Document, 305
Issue fee, 276

J

Jepson claim, 280
J & J Snack Foods Corp. v. McDonald's Corp., 97–98
Joint application, 282
Joint inventors, 304
Joint work, 170–71

K

Kendall-Jackson Winery, Ltd. v. E & J Gallo Winery, 23
Knockout search, 38

L

Laboratory notebooks, 305
Laches, 100, 218, 350
Lack of secrecy, 349
LaMacchia Loophole, 220
Lanham Act, 22, 71, 88, 91, 105–6, 120, 361–62, 367, 373
Lawful copy, 162
Lewis Galoob Toys, Inc. v. Nintendo of America, Inc., 227
Library of Congress, 9–10
License, 81
Literal copying, 210
Literal infringement, 313–14
Literary work, 142
Little FTC acts, 369

Lockhead Martin Corp. v. Network Solutions, Inc., 111
Logo, 35
Lotus Development Corp. v. Borland International, Inc., 225, 324

M

Machine, 259
Madrid Protocol, 10, 127
Maintenance fees, 299
Manual of Patent Examining Procedure, 257
Manufacture, 259–60
Mark, 19
Markman v. Westview Instruments, Inc., 319
Marobie-FL v. National Ass'n of Fire Equipment Distributors, 232
Mask works, 239
Merger doctrine, 146
Midler v. Ford Motor Co., 364
Misappropriation, 343–45, 362
   defenses to, 349–50
   remedies for, 350–51
Misuse, 218
Moral rights, 164–65
Morrissey v. Procter & Gamble Co., 146
Motion picture, 144
MP3, 238
Murray v. NBC, 348
Musical work, 142

N

NAFTA (North American Free Trade Agreement), 11, 128, 353
Naked license, 81–84
National Information Infrastructure, 232–33
National Lead Co. v. Wolfe, 29
National phase, 328
National Stolen Property Act, 354
National treatment, 246
Nichols v. Universal Pictures Corp., 210
No Electronic Theft Act, 220–21
Noncompetition agreement, 346
Nondisclosure agreement, 8
Nonenabling specification, 279
Nonexclusive license, 84

Nonobviousness, 263–65
Norris Indus. v. International Tel. & Tel. Corp., 143
Norwich Pharmacal Co. v. Sterling Drug, Inc., 26
Notice of Allowance, 65
Notice of copyright, 200
Notice of Opposition, 92–93
Novelty, 260–63
Novelty search, 273

O

Object code, 225
Office Action, 58
Official Filing Receipt, 58
Official Gazette, 53, 63–65, 69, 123, 291, 295
Olson v. NBC, 149
On sale bar, 262
Opposition, 92
Orange Crush Co. v. California Crushed Fruit Co., 24
Oreck Corp. v. U.S. Floor Systems, Inc., 99–100
Originality, 140
Orphan drug, 270
Orphan Drug Act, 270

P

Panavision Int'l, L.P. v. Toeppen, 112
Pantomime, 142
Parallel imports, 105
Parent application, 289
Paris Convention, 11, 120, 123, 326–27, 372–73
Parody, 216
Passing off, 361–62
Patent agent, 277
Patent and Trademark Depository Libraries, 38
Patent attorney, 276
Patent Cooperation Treaty (PCT), 278, 323, 328–31
Patentee, 291
Patents, 3, 6–7, 255–56. *See also* International patent law
application
overview, 275–77
preparing, 279–85
prosecuting, 285–92

types of, 277–79
assignment of rights, 306
design patent, 266–67
disputes over inventorship, 304–5
double patenting, 269
infringement
claims interpretation, 313–15
contributory, 312–13
defenses to, 315–16
direct, 311–12
dispute resolution, 318
inducement of, 312
litigation, 318–19
remedies for, 316–18
invention developers and promoters, 308
inventions by employees and independent contractors, 305–6
licensing of rights, 308
maintenance of, 299
new legal developments, 324–25
Orphan Drug Act, 270
ownership rights, 303–4
plant patent, 267–69
postissuance actions, 292–99
registration of, 7
rights under federal law, 256–57
searches, 273–75
sole and joint inventors, 304
subject matter of, 259–66
term of, 299
U.S. Patent and Trademark Office, 257–59
PCT application, 278–9
Performing rights society, 161–2
Petition to Cancel, 94
Pfaff v. Wells Electronics, Inc., 262
Philadelphia Spelling Book (Barry), 134
Phonorecord, 141
Photocopies, 216–17
Pioneer patent, 314
Plant application, 278
Plant patent, 267–69
Plant Variety Protection Act, 268–69
Playboy Enterprises v. Frena, 236
Posting of ports, 106–7
Principal Register, 55
Prior art, 263
Privilege, 350
ProCD, Inc. v. Zeidenberg, 229
Process, 259
Product disparagement, 369–70
Prosecution, 45

Prosecution history estoppel, 315
Provisional patent application, 277–78
Pseudonymous work, 188
Publication, 135
Public domain, 147
Puffing, 368
Punitive damages, 317

Q

Qualitex Co. v. Jacobson Products Co., 26
Quality King Distributors, Inc. v. L'anza Research International, 158, 250

R

Receiving office, 328
Recordation, 80
Reduction to practice, 305
Reexamination of patent, 297–98
Registered user agreement, 126
Registrant, 66
Registration
copyrights, 6
patents, 7
trademarks, 5, 21–22, 45–68
Reissue patent, 293–95
Renewal, 74
Restriction requirement, 289
Reverse doctrine of equivalents, 314
Reverse engineering, 228
Richard v. Du Bon, 260
Right of integrity, 165
Right of publicity, 362–66
Rights
copyrights
to prepare derivative works, 156–57
to display the work publicly, 162–63
of distribution and first sale doctrine, 157–59
limitations on exclusive rights, 163–64
moral rights, 164–65
to perform copyrighted sound recordings, 163
to perform the work publicly, 159–62

of reproduction, 156
patents, 256–57
  assignment of, 306
  licensing of, 308
  trademarks, 20–21
Royalties, 84
Rule of doubt, 196

S

Sailor Music v. Gap Stores, Inc.,
  161–62
Samara Bros. Inc. v. Wal-Mart
  Stores, Inc., 372
Scenes a faire, 149
Scott Pater Co. v. Scott's Liquid
  Gold, 99
Secondary considerations, 264
Secondary level domain, 110
Secondary meaning, 23
Secrecy order, 299
Section 44(d) Application, 120–23
Section 44(e) Application, 120–23
Securacomm Consulting Inc. v.
  Securacom Inc., 36
Security agreement, 84
Sega Enterprises Ltd. v. Accolade,
  Inc., 228
Sega v. Maphia, 236
Semiconductor chip, 239
Semiconductor Chip Protection Act,
  223–24, 239–42
Service mark, 4–5, 19
Shareware, 238
Shop right, 305
Shrink-wrap license, 229
Silverman v. CBS Inc., 76
Small entity, 283–84
Softlifting, 238
Solventol Chemical Prods. v.
  Langfield, 97
Sony Corp. of America v. Universal
  City Studios Inc., 211, 214
Sound recording, 144, 159–60, 163,
  201
Source code, 225
Special handling, 197
Specification, 279
Specimens, 54
Statement of Use, 65
State Street Bank & Trust Co. v.
  Signature Financial Group Inc.,
  324–25

Statute of limitations, copyrights,
  218
Statutory damages, 219–20
Suggestive mark, 24
Supplemental Register, 55
Supplementary copyright
  registration, 197

T

Tarnishment, 104
Tasini v. New York Times Co., 237
Technological developments, 223–42
Terminal disclaimer, 269
Tiffany & Co. v. Boston Club, Inc.,
  103, 370
T.J. Hooker v. Columbia Pictures
  Industries, Inc., 365
Toys "R" Us, Inc. v. Akkaouli, 104,
  371
Trade dress, 26
Trademark Act, 5
Trademark compliance policy, 76
Trademark license agreement, 85–87
Trademark Manual of Examining
  Procedure, 46
Trademarks, 3–5. *See also*
  International trademark law
  Affidavit of Incontestability, 73–74
  Affidavit of Use, 72–73
  dilution of, 103–4
  docketing requirements, 74–75
  foreign applications and
    registrations, 120–23
  infringement, 96–103
    related claims, 105–7
  and Internet, 109–16
  inter partes proceedings, 91–96
  loss of rights, 75–76
  mark categories, 23–24
  mark types, 18–19
  matter excluded from protection,
    28–30
  policing and maintenance, 78
  purpose and function of, 17–18
  registration, 5, 21–22, 66–68
    docketing critical dates, 57
    examination process, 58–63
    filing application, 56–57
    initial role of PTO, 57–58
    postexamination procedure,
      63–66
    preparing application, 45–56

  PTO TRAM line, 59, 68–9
  related claims, 105–7
  renewal of registrations, 74
  rights acquisition, 20–21
  selecting and evaluating, 35–36
  subject matter of, 25–27
  trademark search, 36–42
  transfer of ownership or rights in,
    79–87
  use and compliance policies, 76–78
  use of third party marks, 79
Trademark Trial and Appeal Board
  (TTAB), 9, 89, 91–95
Trade name, 25
Trade secrets, 3, 7–8, 339–40. *See*
  also International trade secret law
  employer-employee relationships,
    345–47
  interplay with copyright and
    patent law, 341–42
  law governing, 340–41
  litigation, 351–52
  misappropriation of, 343–45
    defenses to, 349–50
    remedies for, 350–51
  new legal developments, 354–56
  protection for submissions, 347–49
  protection programs, 352–54
  status determination, 342–43
TRAM line (PTO), 59, 67
Traverse, 289
TRIPS (Trade-Related Aspects of
  Intellectual Property Rights), 22,
  248, 323, 333
Two Pesos, Inc. v. Taco Cabana, Inc.,
  26, 372

U

Umbro Int'l, Inc. v. 3263851
  Canada, Inc., 111
Unclean hands, 100, 217–18, 350
Unfair competition, 106, 359–61
  dilution, 370–71
  false advertising, 367–69
  infringement of trade dress,
    371–72
  international protection against,
    372–73
  misappropriation, 362
  passing off, 361–62
  product disparagement, 369–70
  right of publicity, 362–66

Uniform Trade Secrets Act (UTSA), 340–41

Universal Copyright Convention (UCC), 249

Uruguay Round Agreements Act (GATT), 22, 248–49, 323, 333

U.S. Constitution, 256–57, 260

U.S. Copyright Office, 6, 136, 138, 185–86, 198–200

U.S. Patent and Trademark Office (PTO), 5, 8–9, 30–31, 255, 257–59, 282–99

Useful article, 143

Usefulness, 260

Utility application, 278

Utility patent, 259

V

Vicarious infringement, 212

Visual Artists Rights Act, 164

Visually perceptible copies, 200–1

W

Warner Jenkinson Co. v. Hilton Davis Chem. Co., 314

Watch service, 65

Watercare Corp. v. Midwesco Enterprise Inc., 97

Wawa Inc. v. Haaf, 371

White-Smith Music Publishing Co. v. Apollo Co., 141

White v. Samsung Electronics America, Inc., 364

WIPO Copyright Treaty, 247–48

WIPO Performances and Phonograms Treaty, 247–48

WIPO (World Intellectual Property Organization), 10, 129, 246, 329

Works made for hire, 172–75

World Trade Organization (WTO), 249

Written agreements, 346–47